THE FLOATING WORLD

Issues in International Trade Theory

World Scientific Studies in International Economics

(ISSN: 1793-3641)

Vol. 30 The Role of Central Banks in Financial Stability: How Has It Changed?
edited by Douglas D Evanoff (Federal Reserve Bank of Chicago, USA), Cornelia Holthausen (European Central Bank, Germany), George G Kaufman (Loyola University Chicago, USA) & Manfred Kremer (European Central Bank, Germany)

Vol. 31 Exchange Rates and Global Financial Policies
by Paul De Grauwe (London School of Economics, UK)

Vol. 32 Asian Free Trade Agreements and WTO Compatibility: Goods, Services, Trade Facilitation and Economic Cooperation
by Shintaro Hamanaka (Asian Development Bank, Philippines)

Vol. 33 Economics and Politics of Trade Policy
by Douglas R Nelson (Tulane University, USA)

Vol. 34 Applied Trade Policy Modeling in 16 Countries: Insights and Impacts from World Bank CGE Based Projects
by David G Tarr (Consultant and Former Lead Economist, The World Bank, USA)

Vol. 35 The Floating World: Issues in International Trade Theory
by Wilfred J Ethier (University of Pennsylvania, USA)

Vol. 36 Trade Policy in Asia: Higher Education and Media Services
edited by Christopher Findlay (University of Adelaide, Australia), Hildegunn Kyvik Nordas (Organisation for Economic Co-operation and Development, France) & Gloria Pasadilla (APEC Secretariat, Singapore)

Vol. 37 The Path of World Trade Law in the 21st Century
by Steve Charnovitz (The George Washington University, USA)

The complete list of the published volumes in the series can be found at
http://www.worldscientific.com/series/wssie

35 World Scientific Studies in International Economics

THE FLOATING WORLD

Issues in International Trade Theory

Wilfred J Ethier
University of Pennsylvania, USA

World Scientific
NEW JERSEY · LONDON · SINGAPORE · BEIJING · SHANGHAI · HONG KONG · TAIPEI · CHENNAI

Published by

World Scientific Publishing Co. Pte. Ltd.
5 Toh Tuck Link, Singapore 596224
USA office: 27 Warren Street, Suite 401-402, Hackensack, NJ 07601
UK office: 57 Shelton Street, Covent Garden, London WC2H 9HE

Library of Congress Cataloging-in-Publication Data
Ethier, Wilfred J.
The floating world : issues in international trade theory / Wilfred J. Ethier, University of Pennsylvania, USA.
pages cm. -- (World scientific studies in international economics ; v. 35)
Includes bibliographical references and index.
ISBN-13: 978-9814590310 (hardcover : alk. paper)
ISBN-10: 9814590312 (hardcover : alk. paper)
1. International trade. I. Title.
HF1379.E934 2014
382.01--dc23

2014000074

British Library Cataloguing-in-Publication Data
A catalogue record for this book is available from the British Library.

In-house Editor: Philly Lim

Typeset by Stallion Press
Email: enquiries@stallionpress.com

Printed in Singapore

Acknowledgements

For:

Being wonderful children .... CHRISTINE AND JOHN ETHIER
My late parents .... ALFRED AND AGNES ETHIER
Guidance at a formative time .... HIROSHI ATSUMI
Demonstrating how trade theory should be done..... RONALD W. JONES
The Last Chronicle of Barset .... ANTHONY TROLLOPE
Example of a true economic theorist .... LIONEL MCKENZIE
Encouragement when it mattered .... HERBERT GRUBEL
Sybaritic pleasure .... LOBSTER THERMIDOR
Suggesting this volume .... ROBERT STERN
Initiating this volume .... ZVI RUDER
Ably planning this volume .... MONICA LESMANA
Wonderful editorial assistance with this volume .... PHILLY LIM
Hair stylist .... MAXAMILLION
Profound influence both plus and minus .... HIROFUMI UZAWA
Exceptional nagging .... EDDY BERRY
Influence at Pennsylvania .... IRVING KRAVIS
Support at Pennsylvania .... ARTHUR BLOOMFIELD

Table of Contents

Introduction

In this volume, I have collected together some of my published papers. It is what you do when you get old. This collection is a combination of (sort of) well-known papers and more obscure ones, for which I have a fondness. A fondness often shared, I suspect, with no one else.

The papers are grouped according to major concerns and research programs about trade theory that have preoccupied me during my career. For each I supply comments, beyond those in the papers themselves, about why I thought the program important, about how the included papers contributed to it, as well as some trivia. But I also sometimes cite additional papers (not included in this volume), that were part of the respective research program, and explain how they fitted in.

I warn you that much of this will be self-indulgent. Perhaps you will bear with me.

I am a "pure" trade theorist, in the sense that I have done no formal empirical work, and the papers in this volume reflect this. But I have always been motivated strongly by real-world problems and by what I have thought could properly be inferred from good empirical work. Perhaps the papers also reflect this. The quality of empirical work in international trade has improved enormously over the course of my career (not that I have had anything to do with that).

There is, in some quarters, a recent attitude that any valid paper on trade should include an empirical component. For trade economists to disdain, in their own work, the principle of comparative advantage is indeed a most delicious irony. I love it!

For over half a century, the more important developments in trade theory have been driven by a tension between that theory and the apparent implications of empirical work. This has been true, above all, in two areas: (i) the (actual) challenge to the factor-endowments theory posed by the Leontief Paradox, and (ii) the (apparent) challenge to comparative-advantage theory posed by the empirical realization of the practical importance of trade in similar goods between similar (industrial) countries.

Certainly much of my own work has been thus motivated, and I have more to say about this below. This empirical literature, however, is not directly relevant to my major concerns during the more recent decade or so: trade policy and its underlying political-economy basis. But here also, I have been centrally motivated by a concern about what really drives policy makers and also about what I perceive as a tendency for really-good empirical work to be interpreted really badly. But again, more about this below.

Let me bore you a bit with something of my background. When I arrived, as a new undergraduate freshman, at the University of Rochester in 1961 I had no idea at all of what economics was about, and I also had a vague intention to become an electrical engineer. But in my dormitory I met two first-year economics graduate students also residing there: Hiroshi Atsumi and Vikas Chitre. They influenced me enormously. Atsumi, in particular, was in effect my mentor.

Also of critical importance was the state then of Rochester's economics department. Some years earlier, Lionel McKenzie had been brought in to rejuvenate that department, which he had done spectacularly. One of his accomplishments was to identify and hire a collection of very able young economists. This collection included the trade theorist Ronald Jones. The courses I took from Jones and McKenzie were critical to my development, and the papers in this collection vividly display Jones's influence.

PART I:
Factor-Endowments Theory

Factor-Endowments Theory: *Commentary*

The factor-endowments theory (aka the Heckscher-Ohlin theory) is a central component of trade theory. Indeed, until fairly recently it was also commonly referred to as the "modern" theory of international trade. But it reflects a very pronounced research philosophy.

This philosophy is to take for granted that trade is due to comparative advantage — as opposed to economies of scale or imperfect competition. And that comparative advantage is determined by differences in relative factor endowments — as opposed to differences in technology, tastes, or government policies. And its basic results are derived in the $2 \times 2 \times 2$ Heckscher-Ohlin-Samuelson (HOS) model. The pay-off to this courageous but limiting stance is a set of very strong predictions about, in addition to the pattern of comparative advantage itself (the Heckscher-Ohlin theorem), the relation between trade and the domestic distribution of income (Stolper-Samuelson), the relation between economic growth and trade (Rybczynski), and the respective roles of international markets in goods and in factors (Factor-Price Equalization).

This is an approach just made for a confrontation with reality. That was not long in happening: the Leontief Paradox. The resulting empirical literature, after more than half a century, has yet to reach a generally accepted conclusion.

My concern, though, was not with the empirical literature itself. Though that certainly has influenced me greatly. Rather, I was anxious to address the issue of theoretical robustness. Accepting a focus on comparative-advantage trade (that is, ignoring trade due to economies of scale or to imperfect competition), I wondered whether the four basic results reflected the nature of factor-endowments based trade or simply the extreme simplicity of the HOS model.

That the answer was the latter seemed to be the conclusion that trade theory had reached by the 1970s, at least by implication. Many papers had striven to show that the four basic results did not hold literally outside the $2 \times 2 \times 2$ HOS model, or that they could be made to hold only with additional restrictions that in effect required that a more general framework had to behave like the $2 \times 2 \times 2$ HOS model. By contrast, Ron Jones did eloquently argue the practical usefulness of a low-dimension approach.

In my paper, "Some of the Theorems of International Trade with Many Goods and Factors," included in this volume, I tried to reformulate the four basic results for a higher-dimensional context than HOS and to ask whether they held more generally. My conclusion was that, yes, the four basic results, properly interpreted, reflected the basic nature of factor-endowments trade, not the dimensionality of HOS. (I regard this as among my very best papers. But I've always been embarrassed by how badly written this paper is. So over the years I've tried to convince myself that the bad writing was really due to the insistence of a constipated editor: But in the end my own name is on the paper.)

Alan Deardorff, Avinash Dixit and Victor Norman had meanwhile given higher-dimensional interpretations of comparative advantage (and of the Heckscher-Ohlin theorem) as properties holding "on average," or in terms of correlations. My paper, "The General Role of Factor Intensity in the Theorems of International Trade," included in this volume, used their perspective to examine the four basic results. This furnished another avenue of support for the basic generality of those results.

These two papers were but part of my research program into the theoretical robustness of the four basic results of the HOS model. The survey [1] summarized, explained, pontificated, and further developed the argument that the basic economic core of these results is independent of the dimensionality of the HOS model.

Other papers comprising the program addressed limitations of the model other than dimensionality. The addition of a non-traded good to HOS, the subject of [2], also changes the model's dimensionality. This paper reported the results of my very first efforts in economic research. So it predated the conception of the research program.

The HOS model assumes a production function for each good that produces only that good, i.e., it excludes joint production. This is relied upon by the proofs of the Stolper-Samuelson and Rybczynski theorems. In [3] and [4] Murray Kemp, Winston Chang and I asked how dependent upon this assumption the basic messages of the four results really are. Our conclusion, surprising to us, was that this dependence is actually limited. This is dramatically true when, as in [4], the rest of the panoply of the HOS structure is maintained. (Of course, you should remember that the basic purpose of this research program was to determine what would still be true without much of that panoply).

A prominent part of the trade-theory literature in the 1970s concerned time-phased production. This amounted to replacing the abstract notion of "capital" with an explicit modeling of goods being produced today but used tomorrow. This aspect of trade theory was an offshoot of the "Cambridge controversies" of the day. If you do not know what those were, good for you. This literature argued strongly that traditional trade theory in general, and HOS in particular, delivered conclusions that were deeply suspect and misleading, because of its neglect of the time-phased nature of production.

I was intrigued by this. Were these people actually on to something, or were they just using a different language for obfuscation? Answering this required a common language. So, in [5] and [6], I adopted the time-phased models, defined "capital" as the value of the goods produced today but used tomorrow, and restated the conclusions of the time-phased literature in these terms. This made it clear that literature was simply restating well-understood results in its own language. (There were some distinct results, but they were minor and peripheral). That is, the time-phased literature really was just using a different language for obfuscation. This literature fortunately disappeared into obscurity in the 1980s. I deny any culpability.

The HOS model excludes international markets in the factors of production, although the factor-price equalization theorem addressed the consequences of that limitation. In [6] Lars Svensson and I investigated directly the consequences of that exclusion for the general validity of the HOS results. Our basic conclusion was that the HOS messages, adjusted in a natural way for the new environment, continue to hold.

The basic message from this research program was that, in contrast to the predominant attitude in the 1970s, the basic HOS results reflect fundamental properties of comparative-advantage trade due to relative factor-endowment differences, and *not* the special HOS assumptions. At least, I drew that conclusion.

The Other Articles

[1] Ethier, WJ (1984). Higher Dimensional Issues in Trade Theory. In: PB Kenen and RW Jones (eds.), *Handbook of International Economics*, pp. 131–84. Amsterdam: North Holland.

[2] Ethier, WJ (1972). Nontraded Goods and the Heckscher-Ohlin Model. *International Economics Review* 13 (1), pp. 132–47.

[3] Ethier, WJ and MC Kemp (1976). A Note on Joint Production and the Theory of International Trade. In: MC Kemp, *Three Topics in the Theory of International Trade,* pp. 81–4. Amsterdam: North Holland.
[4] Chang, WW, WJ Ethier and MC Kemp (1980). The Theorems of International Trade with Joint Production. *Journal of International Economics* 10 (3), pp. 377–94.
[5] Ethier, WJ (1979). The Theorems of International Trade in Time-Phased Economies. *Journal of International Economics* (2), pp. 225–38.
[6] Ethier, WJ (1981). A Reply to Professors Metcalfe and Steedman (1981). *Journal of International Economics* 11 (2), pp. 273–7.
[7] Ethier, WJ and LEO Svensson (1986). The Theorems of International Trade with Factor Mobility. *Journal of International Economics* 20 (1/2), pp. 21–42.

Journal of International Economics 4 (1974) 199–206. © North-Holland Publishing Company

SOME OF THE THEOREMS OF INTERNATIONAL TRADE WITH MANY GOODS AND FACTORS

Wilfred ETHIER*

University of Pennsylvania, Philadelphia, Penn. 19174, U.S.A.

The Heckscher–Ohlin model yields three important results beyond the Heckscher–Ohlin theorem itself: the Rybczynski, Stolper–Samuelson, and factor price equalization theorems. Recent years have witnessed many investigations of whether these results generalize to the case of n goods and n factors. This literature has succeeded both in clarifying our understanding of the neoclassical production model and in obtaining difficult and frequently elegant results. However, most of these results imply that the n by n generalizations of the simple and powerful 2 by 2 properties are true only subject to conditions on the relevant determinants that are at once stringent, complicated, and, frequently, economically arcane. A reader might not unnaturally conclude that the most significant implication is that the interesting 2 by 2 properties can not in practice be expected to hold in any essential way in the more general n by n environment and therefore reflect nothing more than the simplification to a world of two goods and two factors.[1] This I think would be a mistake. It is the primary intent of this note to argue that to a significant degree the powerful 2 by 2 results reflect essential properties of the neoclassical general equilibrium of production (as opposed to properties of a 2 by 2 model) and that therefore a central economic core of these results generalizes in a straightforward way to the n by n case.[2] These generalizations depend on no complicated matrix properties and indeed follow immediately from the most elementary properties of the model.

Secondarily, I shall argue that economic considerations suggest a somewhat different route for the n by n generalizations of the strongest properties than has thus far been taken, and I shall make some efforts in that direction.

*This paper owes much to the comments, criticisms, and suggestions of John Chipman and Murray Kemp; thanks are also due to David Humphrey and Ronald Jones.

[1]This impression would be reinforced by the fact that the conditions for many of the n by n results to hold can be interpreted as requiring that the $n \times n$ case reduce in some sense to the 2×2 case. See in particular Kemp and Wegge (1969), Uekawa (1971), and Uekawa, Kemp and Wegge (1973).

[2]For the contrary point of view see, for example, Pearce (1970).

Let me first present my notation by briefly setting out the basic model. All n goods are produced by means of the n factors according to strictly quasi-concave, linear homogeneous production functions: $1 = f_j(\theta_{1j}, \ldots, \theta_{nj})$, where $j = 1, \ldots, n$. θ_{ij} denotes the number of units of factor i being employed in the production of one unit of good j and depends upon factor prices: $\theta_{ij} = \theta_{ij}(w) \equiv \theta_{ij}(w_1, \ldots, w_n)$ for $i, j = 1, \ldots, n$, where w_j denotes the price of the jth factor. Assume always positive marginal products so that all resources are fully employed in equilibrium. Then if X, K, P, and w denote the (strictly positive) vectors of outputs, factor endowments, and commodity and factor prices respectively, and if all goods are produced,

$$K = \theta(w)X, \tag{1}$$

$$P = w\theta(w), \tag{2}$$

where $\theta(w)$ denotes the matrix of $\theta_{ij}(w)$'s. It can be shown [see, e.g., Samuelson (1953)] that

$$\left[\frac{\partial K_i}{\partial X_j}\right] = \theta(w), \tag{3}$$

$$\left[\frac{\partial P_j}{w_i}\right] = \theta(w), \tag{4}$$

or, in elasticity terms:

$$\left[\frac{X_j}{K_i}\frac{\partial K_i}{\partial X_j}\right] = \hat{K}^{-1}\left[\frac{\partial K_i}{\partial X_j}\right]\hat{X} = \hat{K}^{-1}\theta(w)\hat{X} \equiv [a_{ij}] \equiv A, \tag{5}$$

$$\left[\frac{w_i}{P_j}\frac{\partial P_j}{\partial w_i}\right] = \hat{w}\left[\frac{\partial P_j}{\partial w_i}\right]\hat{P}^{-1} = \hat{w}\theta(w)\hat{P}^{-1} \equiv [b_{ij}] \equiv B, \tag{6}$$

where $\hat{X}$ etc. denote the diagonal matrices formed from the vectors X etc. (i.e, $\hat{X}_{ii} = X_i, \hat{X}_{ij} = 0$ if $i \neq j$). It is easily seen that a_{ij} equals the proportion of the total supply of factor i devoted to industry j so that eq. (1) implies that $\Sigma_j a_{ij} = 1$ and so A is row stochastic. Similarly b_{ij} equals the distributive share of factor i in industry j so that as a consequence of Euler's theorem on homogeneous functions B is column stochastic. I shall assume that θ, A, and B have all strictly positive elements; the implications of zeroes are easily deduced.

In the 2 by 2 case[3] the Stolper–Samuelson and Rybczynski theorems are easily derived directly from eqs. (5) and (6). Since A and B are stochastic matrices A^{-1} and B^{-1} must each have one negative term and one term exceeding

[3]See, for example, Jones (1965) for an analysis of the 2 by 2 model. Also Ethier (1972) has a discussion of how these theorems are affected by nontraded goods.

unity in each row and each column. Thus it is possible to assign the goods and factors to each other in such a way that an increase in one commodity price increases by a greater proportion the corresponding factor reward while reducing absolutely the reward to the other factor, etc. The only condition is that A^{-1} and B^{-1} exist, i.e., that $\theta(w)$ be non-singular.

In the n by n case it is likewise desirable to know whether associations of factors and goods exist which lead to similar conclusions. But many different criteria are possible. Chipman (1969) has suggested two. The first, dubbed by Chipman the weak Stolper–Samuelson property, requires that for some numbering of goods and factors B^{-1} have diagonal elements that all exceed unity. Thus an increase in any commodity price would induce a change in the corresponding factor reward independent of index number considerations. Alternatively the strong Stolper–Samuelson property, as defined by Chipman, requires that for some numbering of goods and factors B^{-1} have elements exceeding unity along the diagonal and have all other elements negative, i.e., an increase in any commodity price must increase by a greater proportion the reward of the associated factor while reducing absolutely the rewards of all other factors. Inada (1971) has pointed out that an alternative non-equivalent strong property would be for B^{-1} to have negative elements along the diagonal and all other elements positive.

Considerable effort has been devoted to deriving necessary and sufficient conditions for these criteria.[4] However, it will be useful to first look more closely at the fundamental economic issues involved.

The basic problem is to establish the existence of one or more associations of *each* factor with *some* good and of one or more associations of *each* good with *some* factor that possess certain comparative statics properties of economic interest. I shall use S to refer to an association of each good (price) with some factor (price) and R to refer to an association of each factor (quantity) with some good (quantity). Also an association will be termed intensive if the changes in associated goods and factors are in the same direction, non-intensive if they are in opposite directions.

Taking the 2 by 2 case as an analogy, there seem to be two distinct economic properties that are of interest. First an association should be *unambiguous*. I call an S association, for example, unambiguous if an increase in any commodity price causes a change in the associated factor price that is independent of index number considerations, i.e., if the appropriate element of B^{-1} does not lie between zero and unity.

The second property of interest is *duality*. I say that an S intensive association, for example, is dual if an increase in any commodity price induces an unambiguous increase in the associated factor price *and* if, at constant prices, an increase in the supply of that factor induces an unambiguous rise in the output

[4]See in particular Chipman (1969), Kemp and Wegge (1969), Kemp (1969), Uekawa (1971), Wegge and Kemp (1969), Inada (1971), and Uekawa, Kemp and Wegge (1973).

of that commodity, i.e., the corresponding elements of A^{-1} and of B^{-1} both exceed unity.[5]

Chipman's weak criterion is concerned only with the first of these two properties and implies nothing about duality. The economic essence of this criterion seems to be that some unambiguous S association exist. Now, whereas the weak criterion in the specific matrix form originally stated by Chipman is not implied simply by the non-singularity of θ as in the 2 by 2 case, but instead requires strict additional conditions on B, it is true that a property actually stronger than the above general reformulation of the weak criterion does hold and that this property follows directly from eqs. (5) and (6) in as simple a fashion as in the 2 by 2 case.[6]

Theorem 1. *Let $\theta(w)$ be non-singular. Then there exist:*

(a) unambiguous, dual R-non-intensive and S-non-intensive associations,

(b) unambiguous, R-intensive and unambiguous, S-intensive associations.

Proof. Since θ is non-singular $AA^{-1} = I$, where I denotes the indentity matrix. Since A is row stochastic some positive weighted average of each column of A^{-1} equals zero; thus each such column must contain a negative element. Also some positive weighted average of each column equals unity; this together with a negative element in each column implies an element exceeding unity in each column. In like manner B^{-1} has a negative element and an element exceeding unity in each row. Finally, since $\hat{K}^{-1}$, $\hat{X}$, $\hat{w}$, and $\hat{P}^{-1}$ have strictly positive diagonals, θ^{-1}, A^{-1}, and B^{-1} have the same sign pattern.

Theorem 1 appears to me to be the strongest result obtainable without additional restrictions.[7] Immediate implications are that A has a dual R-intensive association if for some S-intensive association the total reward to each factor is at least as great as the output of its S-intensive good, and that B has a dual S-intensive association if for some R-intensive association the value of the total output of each good is at least as great as the total reward to its R-intensive factor.

Whereas I have thus far discussed 'weak' questions concerned with whether each good can be associated with some factor, etc., one can also follow the

[5]Duality and unambiguity represent the two general ideas that seem to be of interest although one could of course instead consider somewhat stronger or weaker alternative specific definitions. A stronger version of duality, for example, would be to require an S-intensive association to be the inverse of an R-intensive; a weaker version would be to require each factor to be S-intensive in some good.

[6]Murray Kemp has informed me that much of Theorem 1 was deduced by James Meade in private correspondence in 1968.

[7]Murray Kemp has shown that much of the theorem can be extended to the case of unequal numbers of goods and factors; see Kemp (1973). Also for a further discussion of duality see Kemp and Ethier (1973).

spirit of Chipman's discussion and investigate 'strong' questions concerned with whether each good can be associated with each factor, etc. Accordingly I say that a technology is strongly R-unambiguous if A^{-1} has no elements between zero and unity, strongly S-unambiguous if B^{-1} has no elements between zero and unity, and strongly dual if in addition all associations are dual. Note that a technology can be strongly R-unambiguous but neither strongly S-unambiguous nor strongly dual. However, since A^{-1} and B^{-1} must always have the same sign pattern, strong duality is equivalent to a technology being both strongly R-unambiguous and strongly S-unambiguous.

Now Chipman's strong criterion applied to B^{-1} is of course a particular example of a strongly S-unambiguous technology. But it also implies that the technology is strongly R-unambiguous and thus dual as well. This follows from the facts that A^{-1} must have the same sign pattern as B^{-1} and that the inverse of a row stochastic matrix also has unit row sums ($Au = u$ implies $u = A^{-1}\, u$, where u denotes the vector of ones) so that the positive diagonal elements of A^{-1} must also exceed unity. Thus Chipman's strong property is quite strong indeed.

It should be emphasized that the situation regarding Inada's alternative is, surprisingly enough, radically different from an economic point of view, despite a symmetry of mathematical results [for the latter see Inada (1971), and Uekawa, Kemp and Wegge (1973)]. For if B^{-1} has negative diagonal elements and positive off-diagonal elements the positive elements need not exceed unity (if n is greater than two) and thus B^{-1} need not be strongly S-unambiguous. And even if the positive elements are assumed to be greater than unity it does not follow that the technology is dual or strongly R-unambiguous. Thus despite the severe mathematical conditions necessary to establish Inada's criterion it is basically a 'weak' rather than a 'strong' result and indeed gives economic information of about the same value as that which Theorem 1 yields in 'almost all' cases.[8]

'Strong' properties need not hold 'almost always' and so additional necessary and sufficient conditions must be considered. Such conditions tend to be complicated and need not be of any interest because if they require one to perform tests involving an entire matrix one might just as well simply calculate the inverse in the first place. Attention thus focuses on conditions which can be given some intuitive interpretation, such as that the economy reduce to a 2 by 2 economy in some sense. Following Uekawa (1971), such a condition will be presented for the technology to be strongly unambiguous. In the 2 by 2 case good one is said to be intensive in factor one if $\theta_{11}/\theta_{21} > \theta_{12}/\theta_{22}$. An alternative statement of this condition would be to require that for each factor (say the first) there exists some good (in this case the first) and some positive proportional increases y_1 and y_2 in the present output levels X_1 and X_2 such that $\theta_{21}X_1y_1 = \theta_{22}X_2y_2$, $\theta_{11}X_1y_1 > \theta_{12}X_2y_2$ and $\theta_{11}X_1(y_1-\delta) < \theta_{12}X_2(y_2+\delta)$ for some positive $\delta \leqq y_1$.

[8] Inada's criterion is weaker than Theorem 1 in that it says nothing about intensive associations, stronger in that the nonintensive is unique and one to one.

It is in the context of this formulation of the factor intensity condition that the n by n economy will be required in a sense to reduce to a 2 by 2 economy. The following result is obtained easily enough.

Theorem 2. A non-singular positive $\theta(w)$ is strongly R-unambiguous if and only if for each factor k there exists some decomposition of the n goods into two groups J and $\bar{J}$ and some positive vector y such that if each industry output X_j is increased in the proportion y_j, then

(*a*) *the goods in J will together require exactly as much additional input of each factor other than k as will the goods in $\bar{J}$ together,*

(*b*) *the goods in J will together increase their use of factor k more than will the goods in $\bar{J}$ together,*

(c) *for some uniform reduction in the y_j of the J goods and increase in the y_j of the $\bar{J}$ goods, the latter will together require more additional units of k than will the former.*

Proof. The condition means that for some decomposition $J, \bar{J}$ of $\{1, \ldots, n\}$ and some positive y

$$\sum_{j\in J} a_{ij}y_j = \sum_{j\in \bar{J}} a_{ij}y_j, \qquad i \neq k, \tag{7}$$

$$\sum_{j\in J} a_{kj}y_j > \sum_{j\in \bar{J}} a_{kj}y_j, \tag{8}$$

$$\sum_{\in J} a_{kj}(y_j-\delta) < \sum_{j\in \bar{J}} a_{kj}(y_j+\delta), \quad \text{where } y_j-\delta \geqq 0, j\in J. \tag{9}$$

Since A is row stochastic, eq. (9) can be rewritten as

$$\delta > \sum_{j\in J} a_{kj}y_j - \sum_{j\in \bar{J}} a_{kj}y_j,$$

or

$$1 > \sum_{j\in J} a_{kj}\left(\frac{y_j}{\delta}\right) - \sum_{j\in \bar{J}} a_{kj}\left(\frac{y_j}{\delta}\right) \equiv m,$$

or

$$1 = \sum_{j\in J} a_{kj}z_j - \sum_{j\in \bar{J}} a_{kj}z_j, \quad \text{where} \quad z_j = y_j/\delta m. \tag{9'}$$

Now eq. (8) implies that $1 > m > 0$, which together with $y_j-\delta \geqq 0$ for $j\in J$ implies that $z_j > 1$ for $j\in J$. Let x be the vector such that $x_j = z_j$ for $j\in J$ and $x_j = -z_j$ for $j\in\bar{J}$. Thus eqs. (7) and (9′) are equivalent to $Ax = e_k$, where e_k denotes the vector with the kth component equal to unity and all others zero. Then $A^{-1}e_k = x$, where x has no component between zero and unity. As the argument applies to each k this proves that the condition of the theorem is equivalent to A^{-1} having no element between zero and unity.[9]

[9]The method of Theorem 2 can also be applied to obtain an analogous condition for θ to be strongly S-unambiguous. Strong duality requires that the two conditions hold simultaneously.

In order to give some idea of how these 'strong' properties compare with Chipman's formulation of the strong criterion, it is desirable to have conditions for the latter based on that concept of factor intensity which motivated Theorem 2. The proof of this theorem immediately implies that A^{-1} has an element exceeding unity in each row and column and all other elements negative if and only if the set J in Theorem 2 has precisely one good. Also A^{-1} has a negative element in each row and column and all other elements greater than unity (i.e., the strengthened form of Inada's criterion) if and only if the set $\bar{J}$ in Theorem 2 has precisely one good.[10] Finally, it can easily be shown that a technology possesses Chipman's strong property if and only if for any set J of factors there exists a corresponding equal-sized set of goods and a positive vector y of proportional changes in outputs for which the goods in J will together use exactly as much additional input of each factor in $\bar{J}$ and uniformly more additional input of each factor in J than will the goods in $\bar{J}$ together.

I now turn briefly to the factor price equalization property. Most n by n treatments have been concerned[11] with the global univalence of the cost function (2). This problem is of interest in its own right and is central to whether complete diversification implies factor price equalization. But it is not relevant to what seems to me to be the essential message of factor price equalization: if trading countries have 'sufficiently similar' factor endowments commodity trade will completely substitute for factor movements whereas if the endowments are not 'sufficiently similar' factor prices can not possibly be equalized by trade regardless of the actual pattern of specialization. This result does not depend upon the global properties of the cost function and can easily be shown to generalize in full strength to the n by n case:

(a) For any P such that eq. (2) holds for some w there exists some closed cone $H(P)$ such that all countries with non-zero endowments in $H(P)$ will have equal factor prices if engaged in free trade at world prices P.
(b) For any K there exists a closed cone $G(K)$ such that for any positive $K' \in G(K)$ there exists a closed cone $M(K, K')$ such that countries with positive endowments K and K' will have equal factor prices if engaged in free trade at any world prices $P \in M(K, K')$.
(c) The cones $H(P)$ and $G(K)$ can be made exhaustive in the sense that $K \in H(P)$ and $K' \notin H(P)$ imply that countries with endowments K and K' can not have equal factor prices when trading at commodity prices P and that $K' \notin G(K)$ implies that countries with endowments K and K' can never have equal factor prices.[12]

[10]Note that if J contains but one good then part (c) of Theorem 2 must be trivially satisfied, i.e., it becomes a restriction only when J contains at least two goods.

[11]See, for example, Samuelson (1953, 1967), McKenzie (1955, 1960, 1967), Gale and Nikaido (1965), Pearce (1967), and Chipman (1969). For a notable exception see McKenzie (1955) and cf. also Pearce (1970, chs. 12 and 16).

[12]Proposition (a) is essentially McKenzie's (1955) Theorem 1 and propositions (b) and (c) can be proved in roughly similar fashion.

I have argued that the 2 by 2 Heckscher–Ohlin model is quite robust in the specific sense that an essential core of basic results generalizes in a straightforward way to the n by n case. Indeed it is the Heckscher–Ohlin theorem itself which is apparently the least robust (and recall that this is quite fragile in the 2 by 2 case; see Jones' classic paper (1956–57) for example). Of course it must be a matter of opinion as to what is called the 'essential core'. But, once it is known that the strongest possible interpretations do not generalize without additional restrictions, there is reason to point out what does.

References

Chipman, S., 1969, Factor price equalization and the Stolper–Samuelson theorem, International Economic Review 10, 399–406.

Ethier, W., 1972, Non-traded goods and the Heckscher–Ohlin model, International Economic Review 13, 132–147.

Gale, D. and H. Nikaido, 1965, The Jacobian matrix and global univalence of mappings, Mathematische Annalen 159, 81–93.

Inada, Ken-Ichi, 1971, The production coefficient matrix and the Stolper–Samuelson condition, Econometrica 39, 219–240.

Jones, R.W., 1956–57, Factor proportions and the Heckscher–Ohlin theorem, Review of Economic Studies 24, 1–10.

Jones, R.W., 1965, The structure of simple general equilibrium models, Journal of Political Economy 73, 557–572.

Kemp, M.C., 1969, The pure theory of international trade and investment (Prentice-Hall, Englewood Cliffs).

Kemp, M.C., 1973, Relatively simple generalizations of the Stolper–Samuelson and Samuelson–Rybczynski theorems, unpublished.

Kemp, M. C. and W. Ethier, 1973, A note on joint production and the theory of international trade, Department of Economics Discussion Paper no. 265 (University of Pennsylvania, Philadelphia).

Kemp, M.C. and L.L. Wegge, 1969, On the relation between commodity prices and factor rewards, International Economic Review 10, 407–413.

McKenzie, L.W., 1955, Equality of factor prices in world trade, Econometrica 23, 239–257.

McKenzie, L.W., 1960, Matrices with dominant diagonals and economic theory, in: Arrow, Karlin and Suppes, eds., Mathematical methods in the social sciences, 1959 (Stanford University Press, Stanford) 47–62.

McKenzie, L.W., 1967, The inversion of cost functions: A counter-example, International Economic Review 8, 271–278.

Pearce, I., 1967, More about factor price equalization, International Economic Review 8, 255–270.

Pearce, I., 1970, International trade (Norton, New York).

Samuelson, P.A., 1953, Prices of factors and goods in general equilibrium, Review of Economic Studies 21, 1–20.

Samuelson, P.A., 1967, Summary on factor price equalization, International Economic Review 8, 286–295.

Uekawa, Y., 1971, Generalization of the Stolper–Samuelson theorem, Econometrica 39, 197–218.

Uekawa, Y., M.C. Kemp and L.L. Wegge, 1973, *P*- and *PN*-matrices, Minkowski- and Metzler-matrices, and generalization of the Stolper–Samuelson and Samuelson–Rybczynski theorems, Journal of International Economics 3, 53–76.

Wegge, L.L. and M.C. Kemp, 1969, Generalizations of the Stolper–Samuelson and Samuelson–Rybczynski theorems in terms of conditional input–output coefficients, International Economic Review 10, 414–425.

Economics Letters 10 (1982) 337–342 North-Holland Publishing Company

THE GENERAL ROLE OF FACTOR INTENSITY IN THE THEOREMS OF INTERNATIONAL TRADE *

Wilfred J. ETHIER

University of Stockholm, S-106 91 Stockholm, Sweden

Received 1 April 1982

The pattern of factor intensities often allows predictions of directions of change in 2×2 trade theory, but the most general higher dimensional extensions have said little about analogous predictions. This paper obtains general results in an elementary way.

1. Introduction

The Stolper–Samuelson theorem (as does its Rybczynski analog) contains two assertions: that relative commodity price changes produce unambiguous changes in real factor rewards, and that the direction of the latter can be predicted from relative factor intensities. The Heckscher–Ohlin theorem likewise predicts trade flows on the basis of such intensities.

Higher dimensional generalization has followed two paths. That concerned with stronger results [1] has touched on both aspects of the theorems, with the existence of desired relations between goods and factors shown to be equivalent to the satisfaction of stringent factor intensity conditions. But the second, more general, path [2] has focused on the first aspect and ignored whether relative factor intensities allow a prediction

* Research for this paper was supported by the National Science Foundation. Lars Svensson and Avinash Dixit contributed valuable suggestions.

[1] See Uekawa (1971), and Kemp (1976, ch. 3).

[2] See Ethier (1974), Kemp (1976, chs. 4, 7), Jones and Scheinkman (1977) and Ethier (1983, app. One).

of the direction of factor-reward responses or of trade flows. [3] This paper obtains general results in an elementary way.

2. Stolper–Samuelson type and Rybczynski type results

Allow any number of goods and factors. Consider a change in commodity prices, and denote by p^0 and p' the respective vectors of prices of those goods actually produced *both* before and after the change. Let $c(w) = wA(w)$ denote the cost functions of those goods, where w denotes the vector of factor rewards and $A(w)$ the matrix of least-cost techniques.

Thus $p^0 = c(w^0)$ and $p' = c(w')$. Define $b(w) = c(w)(p' - p^0)$. By the mean value theorem there exists some vector $\bar{w}$ of factor rewards such that

$$b(w') = b(w^0) + (w' - w^0)\,\mathrm{d}b(\bar{w}), \qquad (1)$$

where $\mathrm{d}b(\bar{w})$, the Hessian matrix of b, equals $[A(\bar{w}) + \bar{w}\mathrm{d}A(\bar{w})](p' - p^0)$. Now $\bar{w}\mathrm{d}A(\bar{w}) = 0$ as a condition of cost minimization. Thus (1) can be written

$$\left[c(w') - c(w^0)\right](p' - p^0) = (w' - w^0)A(\bar{w})(p' - p^0). \qquad (2)$$

Noting that $c(w') - c(w^0) = p' - p^0$, (2) implies

$$(w' - w^0)A(\bar{w})(p' - p^0) \geqslant 0. \qquad (3)$$

This is the basic result: $(w' - w^0)$ is positively *correlated* with $A(\bar{w})(p' - p^0)$, or $(p' - p^0)$ is positively correlated with $(w' - w^0)A(\bar{w})$. Large values of $(w_i' - w_i^0)$ tend to accompany large values of a_{ij} and of $(p_j' - p_j^0)$; commodity price changes on average raise the most the rewards of the factors used most intensively by the goods whose prices increase the most, etc. In the two-by-two case (3) gives the usual rigid link, but when dimensionality increases the relation says nothing about the direction of change of individual factor rewards and merely describes *average* changes.

[3] Exceptions are Uekawa (1979), unrelated to the present paper, Deardorff (1981), and Dixit and Norman (1980), discussed below.

Note the great generality of (3). It follows directly from cost minimization without any special restriction on dimensionality, technology, or endowments.[4] The present proposition relates the direction of factor reward changes to the direction of changes in the prices of goods that continue to be produced. Goods not produced in either or both states contribute no information, although they would of course be relevant to the magnitude of changes in *real* rewards.

For sufficiently small changes, $\bar{w} = w^0$ will work in (3), but large changes could demand a $\bar{w}$ close to neither w^0 nor w', so that $A(\bar{w})$ could be quite distinct from observed techniques. But this is *not* a penalty of higher dimensions: the point can be grasped in a two-by-two world. Suppose that, because of a factor-intensity reversal, $p^0 = c(w^0) = c(w^{00})$, and $p' = c(w') = c(w'')$, with $w_2''/w_1'' > w_2^0/w_1^0 > w_2^{00}/w_1^{00} > w_2'/w_1'$. Then the movement from w^0 to w' involves the opposite direction of change of relative factor rewards to the movement from w^{00} to w''. $A\bar{w}$ satisfying (3) need imply the appropriate pattern of factor intensities in the former case, but the latter case requires a quite different $\bar{w}$ with the opposite intensity pattern. The ability to choose $\bar{w}$ appropriately is the reason I have a global Stolper–Samuelson-type result without ruling out factor intensity reversals or their higher dimensional analogs.

A similar Rybczynski type result is easily obtained. Let v^0 and v' be two endowment vectors and x^0 and x' the corresponding vectors of outputs of those goods actually produced in *both* states. Then, *if* $w^0 = w'$,

$$v' - v^0 = A(w^0)(x' - x^0) \tag{4}$$

and multiplying both sides by the vector $(v' - v^0)$

$$(v' - v^0)A(w^0)(x' - x^0) \geqslant 0. \tag{5}$$

This is a general Rybczynski-type result: on average, endowment changes cause the largest increases in the outputs of the goods which most intensively use the factors that have increased relatively the most in supply, etc. The requirement that $w^0 = w'$ limits applicability. The change $v' - v^0$ must not be large enough to depart from the relevant diversifica-

[4] Of course the mean value theorem must be applicable, so $b(w)$ should be continuously differentiable over some path of non-negative factor prices connecting w^0 and w'. But no restrictions are placed on production patterns over that path, endowments can change in any way between equilibria, and A need not even be non-singular. But constant returns to scale and no joint production are assumed.

tion cone. If $n \geqslant m$, where n and m denote the numbers of produced goods and factors, the factor-price-equalization theorem can be appealed to for $w^0 = w'$, and my result is again a direct consequence of cost minimization. But if $m > n$, the elements of $v' - v^0$ cannot be chosen at will: n of them may be specified arbitrarily, with the remaining $m - n$ then set to equilibrate factor markets at prices w_0 (as would be the case if $m - n$ factors were freely traded at world prices). This limits the result in a way not necessary with its Stolper–Samuelson analog. But such asymmetry should come as no surprise. [5]

3. Heckscher–Ohlin type theorems

Let w' and w^0 denote home and foreign autarky prices. Then define $d(w) = c(w)M$, where M denotes the vector of home free-trade imports. The same logic which produced (3) implies, for some $\overline{w}$,

$$(p' - p^0)M = (w' - w^0)A(\overline{w})M.$$

Now $(p' - p^0)M \geqslant 0$ by the general law of comparative advantage, [6] so

$$(w' - w^0)A(\overline{w})M > 0. \tag{6}$$

This correlation is a generalized price version of the Heckscher–Ohlin theorem: on average countries tend to import the goods most intensive in the use of the factors most abundant in a price sense, etc. [7] This is a very general result, depending only on cost minimization and requiring no restrictions on demand or on technology – including no exclusion of higher-dimensional analogs of factor intensity reversals.

Turning to the quantity version, let v' and v^0 denote home and foreign endowments and suppose at least as many produced goods as factors. With endowments given, commodity prices uniquely relate to factor

[5] See, for example, Kemp (1976, ch. 4) or Jones and Scheinkman (1977).

[6] See Deardorff (1980), Dixit and Norman (1980, pp. 94–96) or Ethier (1983, app. One).

[7] Deardorff (1981) obtains in a different way a similar result with $A(\overline{w})$ replaced by a matrix A^0, which can be obtained by using in each column the technique actually employed in free trade in the country of export of the respective goods. Thus $A(\overline{w})$ has the advantage of consistent comparison across industries since its techniques would actually be chosen under some common factor rewards, and A^0 the advantage of being constructed from observed (post-trade) techniques. See also Ethier (1983, app. One).

prices [see McKenzie (1955)], so I can write $w = f(p, v)$. Define $h(p, v) = f(p, v)(v' - v^0)$ and proceed as above to obtain, for some $\bar{w} = f(\bar{p}, \bar{v})$,

$$g(p', v') - g(p^0, v^0) = (p' - p^0) f_p(\bar{p}, \bar{v})(v' - v^0) + (v' - v^0) f_v(\bar{p}, \bar{v})(v' - v^0),$$

where f_p and f_v denote the appropriate matrices of partial derivatives. Now $f_v(\bar{p}, \bar{v}) = 0$ by the factor price equalization theorem and $f_p(\bar{p}, \bar{v}) = A^{-1}(\bar{w})$, where $A(\bar{w})$ is made square, if necessary, by arbitrarily deleting enough goods. Also it is known [8] that $(w' - w^0)(v' - v^0) \leqslant 0$, with identical homothetic tastes. So

$$(p' - p^0) A^{-1}(\bar{w})(v' - v^0) \leqslant 0. \tag{7}$$

This correlation is a generalized quantity version: countries tend on average to have a comparative advantage in those goods that most intensively employ the most relatively abundant factors. [9] Note the relation between the concepts of relative factor intensity in my price and quantity generalizations: the former interprets factor intensity as a matter of the relative magnitude of the elements of A whereas the latter looks at the elements of A^{-1}, and the two are likely evaluated at different factor prices. These two concepts become distinct when the numbers of goods and factors exceed two.

Next, assume that all countries have identical homothetic tastes and that in free trade factor-price equalization holds. Then it is well-known that the *factor content* of trade will reflect relative factor abundance in a quantity sense, [10] but there are no results on commodity composition. To obtain one, define, in (5), $x^0 = (1 - g)x^H$, $x' = gx^F$, $v^0 = (1 - g)v^H$, $v' = gv^F$, where v^H and v^F denote the home and foreign endowment vectors, x^H and x^F home and foreign free trade outputs, and g a scalar:

$$\left[gv^F - (1 - g)v^H \right] A(\bar{w}) \left[gx^F - (1 - g)x^H \right] \geqslant 0. \tag{8}$$

Now if g is set equal to free trade home income as a fraction of world

[8] See Dixit and Norman (1980, p. 99) or Ethier (1983, app. One).

[9] Dixit and Norman (1980, p. 100) obtain a result like (7) on the strong assumption that $c(w)$ is globally invertible. The present approach demonstrates that such an assumption is unnecessary, and the discussion following (3) explains why.

[10] See, for example, Vanek (1968).

income, identical homothetic tastes imply that $M = g(x^H + x^F) - x^H = gx^F - (1-g)x^H$. Thus

$$\left[g(v^F + v^H) - v^H \right] A(\overline{w}) M \geqslant 0. \tag{9}$$

This correlation says that on average a country tends to import those goods which make most intensive use of the country's relatively scarce factors, where factor scarcity is measured in a quantity sense by comparing the national endowment to the world endowment scaled down by the aggregate value of national factor service supplies as a fraction of the aggregate value of world supplies.

References

Deardorff, A.V., 1980, The general validity of the law of comparative advantage, Journal of Political Economy 88, 941–957.

Deardorff, A.V., 1981, The general validity of the Heckscher-Ohlin theorem, processed.

Dixit, A.K. and V. Norman, 1980, Theory of international trade (Nisbet, Cambridge, London).

Ethier, W., 1974, Some of the theorems of international trade with many goods and factors, Journal of International Economics 4, 194–206.

Ethier, W., 1983, Modern international economics (Norton, New York).

Jones, R.W. and J. Scheinkman, 1977, The relevance of the two-sector production model in trade theory, Journal of Political Economy 85, 909–935.

Kemp, M.C., 1976, Three topics in the theory of international trade (North-Holland, Amsterdam).

McKenzie, L.W., 1955, Equality of factor prices in world trade, Econometrica 23, 239–257.

Uekawa, Y., 1971, Generalization of the Stolper-Samuelson theorem, Econometrica 39, 197–218.

Uekawa, Y., 1979, On the concepts of factor intensities and the relation between commodity prices and factor rewards, in: J.R. Green and J.A. Scheinkman, eds., General equilibrium, growth, and trade (Academic, New York).

Vanek, J., 1968, The factor proportions theory: The n-factor case, Kyklos 21, 749–755.

PART II:
Economies of Scale

Economies of Scale: *Commentary*

As mentioned in the Introduction, much work in the 1970s and 1980s was motivated by a dawning realization that a dominant share of world trade involved the exchange of relatively similar, manufactured goods (intra-industry trade) between relatively similar (industrial) countries.

This realization was significantly due to the work of Grubel and Lloyd (Though there had been important earlier contributions, notably Balassa's empirical work and the unjustly ignored contribution by Gray). Herb Grubel was sometimes dismissed as a lightweight, but the fact is that, during the 1960s and 1970s, he was consistently ahead of the curve on the important issues. And I confess to a soft spot for him: Herb was the first established economist to say that he thought I had done something useful and interesting.

Comparative-advantage trade, of course, is trade to exploit international *differences*. So there was a wide belief that this actual trade could not be comparative-advantage trade. It was this wide belief that stimulated a huge amount of work into economies of scale and imperfect competition as alternative reasons for trade.

I recall Herb mentioning that Harry Johnson had told him that intra-industry trade was no big deal: just a matter of getting into the comparative-advantage details. For those too young to know, Johnson was a dominant influence in trade (and macroeconomics and development economics) from the 1950s through the 1970s. This dominance was based largely on personality: Johnson was a bully. Of course such dominance also required a supporting intellect, certainly not lacking in Johnson's case.

Although Johnson was wrong about much, I think he was basically right here. But he died in 1977, and the literature on scale economies and imperfect competition then proceeded at a heady pace (If your influence depends upon intimidation, your influence disappears when you do).

To put it succinctly, the comparative-advantage assertion that: "trade is due to international differences" simply does *not* imply "the greater the differences, the greater the trade." Countries are similar, in the relevant economic sense, if, in the absence of trade, they would have autarky relative prices that do not differ greatly. This means, in a comparative-advantage world, that trade cannot cause large changes in relative prices within countries. But if the similar countries are trading similar goods, price elasticities should be quite high. So modest price changes can indeed be expected to produce large trade volumes.

Consider this in the context of the HOS model addressed in the previous section of this book. If the home country and the rest of the world have only modest differences in factor endowments, the factor content of trade will indeed be small. But if they trade similar goods, i.e., goods whose relative factor intensities do not differ greatly, a large volume of commodity trade will be required to affect even a modest volume of factor-content trade. I recall John Chipman arguing years ago (at a conference I do not otherwise recall) that a large volume of trade in similar goods between similar countries was quite consistent with comparative advantage. At the time I berated him for saying what I thought was obvious. But he was right and I was wrong: Most of the profession did indeed have the quite different, erroneous, view that John was critical of.

So the "new" trade theory's emphasis on scale economies and imperfect competition was based on false pretenses. Like the US invasion of Iraq to deal with weapons of mass destruction. But that does not imply that it was not constructive ("new trade theory," I mean, not the invasion). It stimulated much interesting work. Indeed, it was very helpful to me. I was at the time much interested in scale economies, and so the desire for a "new trade theory" helped give me an audience.

There was, at the time, a small but old literature on trade and increasing returns. The main concern of this literature was how increasing returns could alter established, comparative-advantage, results. The concern of my research project was the idea that, in a globalized economy (but we were then not yet saying "globalization"), Adam Smith's classic notion of the division of labor constrained by the size of the market amounted to scale economies determined by the size of the world market.

My first preliminary step in, "Decreasing Costs in International Trade and Frank Graham's Argument for Protection," was to reformulate the existing theory in a way more useful for my purpose. Though this was the first of the three papers in this research program to be written, it was the last to be published, because of contemporary chaos at *Econometrica*.

The second paper, "Internationally Decreasing Costs and World Trade," tried to set out my basic views on the subject. I have always regarded this paper both as one of my very best papers and as the center-piece of this project that contained its basic contribution. The other two papers, however, have each received much more attention.

This paper was published in the *Journal of International Economics* at the start of 1979. Other central contributions to intra-industry trade by Paul Krugman, Kelvin Lancaster, and Elhanan Helpman, were also submitted there in due course. As my paper had been the first to arrive, the editor, Jagdish Bhagwati, sent me each of the other papers to referee as it was submitted.

In each case I submitted a report and enthusiastically recommended acceptance. For example, my letter of 21 November 1978 to Jagdish Bhagwati concerning Krugman's paper stated that the paper, "is skillfully and elegantly executed, and yields interesting and original insights about trade.... [my] suggestions do not address the substance of the paper, and, even if Krugman should be completely recalcitrant, you should not hesitate to publish the paper." I was proud to have assisted in the publication of these excellent papers.

Years later *The Journal of Economic Perspectives* published an article by Joshua S. Gans and George B. Shepherd that quoted Jagdish Bhagwati as saying, about Krugman's paper, "I published it myself *despite* two adverse referee reports by very distinguished experts on the theory of increasing returns! It did take some courage and also a strong sense of the importance of the paper for me to do so." So much for my pride about being helpful.

"National and International Returns to Scale in the Modern Theory of International Trade," the third paper, exploited the second paper, linking it with the literature on trade and monopolistic competition as well as with the factor-endowments theory. A useful exercise, I thought, but derivative of the earlier papers. Still, it has probably been the most cited of my papers.

Econometrica, Vol. 50, No. 5 (September, 1982)

DECREASING COSTS IN INTERNATIONAL TRADE AND FRANK GRAHAM'S ARGUMENT FOR PROTECTION

BY WILFRED J. ETHIER[1]

Over half a century ago Frank Graham argued that decreasing costs could justify protection. Although this contention stimulated a huge literature, a correct analysis has never been made. The present paper attempts to fill this gap. It is shown that Graham's case applies to trade between approximately equally-sized economies and that a greater degree of increasing returns actually reduces its likelihood. Furthermore, increasing returns yield a positive analysis nearly completely symmetric to that of Ricardian constant costs. A new analytical tool, the allocation curve, is introduced, with which Marshallian stability is fully analogous to Walrasian instability with offer curves.

OVER HALF A CENTURY AGO Frank Graham [**7**] argued that increasing returns to scale could justify protection. This contention stimulated a huge literature, to which contributions continue to be made. While much discussion centered on the empirical relevance of external economies, a tangential issue, the balance of the literature concerned itself with the logical consistency of Graham's argument, which was in the form of arithmetic examples. The discussion reached a climax in the analysis of Tinbergen [**18**, Appendix I], which has since served as the basic reference. But, as Murray Kemp [**9**, p. 111] has pointed out, "Tinbergen's treatment is wrong in essentials." A correct and thorough analysis of Graham's argument has never been made, and it remains an open question half a century after it was raised.[2] The present paper attempts to fill this gap.

Although the central body of modern international trade theory is based upon the assumption of constant returns to scale, the belief is widespread that increasing returns are important in reality, and there is in fact a large body of literature specifically addressed to the theoretical issues which emerge.[3] The conclusions of this literature are characterized by multiple equilibria with extensive specialization.[4] Thus the standard comparative-statics results become quite arbitrary, and much attention focuses on the dynamics of adjustment to equilibrium. The approach followed in almost all of this literature is to simply graft increasing returns onto a general neoclassical model. Thus surprisingly little has been said about the implications of increasing returns to scale in and of themselves; the basic conclusions reflect a complex interaction of these returns with the various neoclassical elements.

This paper has three objectives beyond an analysis of Graham's argument. (i) I

[1] I am grateful to Murray Kemp for helpful comments and suggestions on an earlier draft. This research was supported in part by the National Science Foundation.

[2] Indeed the basic argument considerably antedates Graham. See Viner [**19**, pp. 473–475] for references and a discussion.

[3] The central modern references are the seminal paper of Matthews [**13**] and the excellent discussions by Meade [**14**] and Kemp [**8**].

[4] An exception is Ethier [**6**] which incorporates increasing returns into international trade theory in a basically different manner. That manner will play no role in the present paper.

shall first examine the consequences of increasing returns when the two trading countries are alike in all respects save possibly for scale. Thus I shall attempt to isolate the implications of increasing returns themselves.[5] (ii) Increasing returns supply a strong tendency for specialization, yet they have generally been incorporated into neoclassical models where increasing opportunity costs would otherwise allow incomplete specialization. Thus I should think valuable perspective can be gained by the analysis of a simple Ricardian model where specialization would be expected even if trade were due to differences in technology rather than scale economies.[6] I shall argue that, in sharp contrast to the neoclassical context, increasing returns in a Ricardian world give a positive analysis nearly identical to that implied by international differences in constant cost technology. (iii) Virtually all authors in this area analyze international equilibrium by means of offer curves. This is convenient for drawing a contrast with the constant-returns literature, where such curves are widely used, and is also an excellent means of showing multiple equilibria, which follow easily from the "re-entrant" shape increasing returns can impart. But the offer-curve technique is quite clumsy in other respects, notably for the dynamic stability analysis that becomes prominent when increasing returns are discussed. This suggests that an alternative technique could be useful, particularly at this stage of development of the subject. An objective of this paper is to develop and employ a new tool, which I call the allocation curve, especially useful in those respects where the offer curve becomes most cumbersome.[7]

The central conclusions of this paper are embodied in three of the following propositions. The symmetry theorem (Proposition 7) establishes that increasing returns yield a positive analysis almost perfectly symmetric to that of the familiar Ricardian model. The stability theorem (Proposition 6) gives allocation curves a rôle in Marshallian adjustment that is just opposite to the role of offer curves in Walrasian adjustment. Finally, Proposition 10 elucidates Graham's argument. The paper closes with a discussion of various complications and international assymetries.

1. INCREASING RETURNS TO SCALE IN THE SIMPLE RICARDIAN MODEL

I assume that in each of two countries a single productive factor, or factor-composite, which I call labor, is used to produce two commodities, called wheat and manufactures. Wheat is produced subject to constant returns to scale and

[5] To my knowledge this question has not been addressed at all in the literature, with the single exception of Melvin [**15**]. But Melvin was not concerned with the other goals of this paper, and gave much attention to factor mobility, which I ignore. Thus there is very little overlap between the two papers.

[6] The excellent discussion of increasing returns in Chacholiades [**4**] also adopts this perspective and so anticipates a few of the conclusions in the early part of this paper. But his approach is otherwise different and the overlap is accordingly very limited.

[7] I have also used the allocation curve in Ethier [**6**], which is, however, concerned with a fundamentally different problem.

manufactures subject to increasing returns. Define a unit of labor to be that quantity required to produce each unit of wheat, and a unit of manufactures to be that quantity which could be produced by a single unit of labor. I assume that the economies of scale in manufacturing can be realized at a constant rate, denoted $\alpha > 1$, so that the production side of the home economy can be written

$$(1) \qquad M = (L_M)^\alpha,$$

$$(2) \qquad W = L_W,$$

$$(3) \qquad L_M + L_W = L,$$

where M and W denote the outputs of manufactures and wheat, L_M and L_W the labor employed in the respective sectors, and L total labor.

Define a unit of foreign labor to be that quantity required in the rest of the world to produce the first full unit of manufactures. I assume for now that technology is internationally identical, so that α applies to the rest of the world and a single unit of foreign labor is required to produce each unit of foreign wheat. The two economies need not be of equal size, so L need not equal L^* (throughout this paper I use asterisks to refer to the rest of the world).

In each country the wheat industry is competitive, so that the supply price of wheat equals the wage rate. I assume that average-cost pricing prevails in the manufacturing sector. This will be the case either if the increasing returns are due to economies external to the firm, or if the economies are internal to the firm but entry to the industry is free, so that competitive equilibrium will require a single firm earning zero profit.[8]

With these assumptions, the relative supply price P_S of manufactures in terms of wheat is given by

$$(4) \qquad P_S = \frac{wL_M}{M} / w = L_M / M = M^{1/\alpha - 1}.$$

The production possibility frontier implied by (1), (2), and (3) is illustrated in Figure 1. The distance OB indicates the size L of the labor force, and OA equals L^α. The slope of the frontier at any point is given by $dW/dM = -L_M/\alpha M$, so that, from (4), $P_S = -\alpha dW/dM = (L - W)/M$. Thus the relative supply price corresponding to any point on the frontier, such as C in Figure 1, is reflected in the slope of a budget line connecting that point with B. The supply curve S in Figure 2 below records for each level of manufacturing output that value of the relative supply price which will bring forth that output in equilibrium. It is clear from the discussion of Figure 1 that the supply curve must have a negative slope; differentiation of (4) confirms that the curve declines at a decreasing rate.

[8]That is, with free entry, perfect competition is consistent with an equilibrium in which a single firm offers the price-output combination specified by the general equilibrium described below. This was pointed out by Kemp [9, p. 155]. Though truly competitive, such a firm would not be a "price-taker."

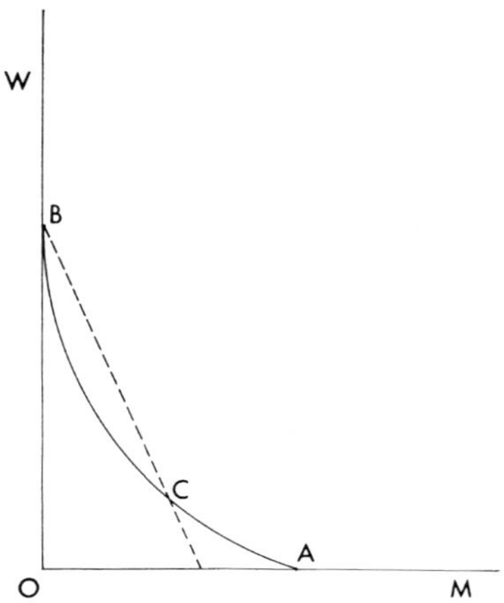

FIGURE 1.

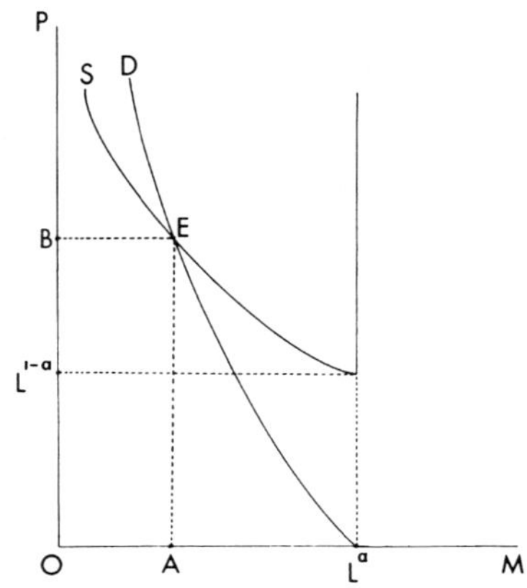

FIGURE 2.

2. EFFICIENT PATTERNS OF WORLD OUTPUT

The above analysis applies equally well to both countries, which differ only in size. It is now a simple matter to deduce those patterns of specialization in the two countries consistent with global production efficiency. Obviously complete specialization by both countries will always be efficient, and diversification by both countries will always be inefficient. If world output of manufactures is no larger than the manufacturing capacity of the smaller country, the relative sizes of the two countries will not matter and so, since they differ in no other respect, any pattern of specialization will be efficient as long as at least one country specializes completely. But once world manufacturing output exceeds the capacity of the small country, efficiency requires that as much of total world manufacturing activity as possible be concentrated in the larger economy so as to reap the advantages of scale economies. That is, the small country should never produce any manufactures if the large economy produces some wheat (and the large economy should never produce any wheat if the small economy produces some manufactures). Note that this is precisely the prescription that emerges in the standard constant-returns, dissimilar-technology case when the large country has a comparative advantage in manufactures according to the usual comparison of relative labor productivities. In view of this analogy, I shall say that the large country has a comparative advantage in that good subject to increasing returns and the small country a comparative advantage in the other. Then the above argument can be summarized.

PROPOSITION 1: *If the world output of manufactures is large enough for the pattern of specialization to matter (i.e., larger than the capacity of the smaller country), then the efficient patterns are precisely those dictated by comparative advantage as in the usual Ricardian model.*

3. AUTARKIC EQUILIBRIA

I assume at this point that tastes in the two countries are identical, and can be represented by a demand function for $M : \phi(P, W + PM)$. The demand price P_D is that relative price which, for any specified value of M, will cause the economy to demand that quantity; that is, P_D is the solution to

$$(5) \qquad M = \phi(P_D, L - M^{1/\alpha} + P_D M).$$

The demand curve D, showing the value of P_D corresponding to each level of M, is depicted in Figure 2. The intersection of the two curves, where demand price coincides with supply price, is autarkic equilibrium. This is depicted at point E in Figure 2. The two curves need not have an interior intersection, so that autarkic equilibrium could involve specialization in either good.[9]

Suppose that an interior equilibrium such as E exists. Then from (4) and (5), at such an equilibrium

$$(6) \qquad \frac{M}{P}\left(\frac{dP_S}{dM} - \frac{dP_D}{dM}\right) = \frac{\alpha - 1}{\alpha} \frac{\eta - \dfrac{\alpha}{\alpha - 1}}{\gamma - \eta}$$

where $\eta = -(P/M)\phi_1$, the elasticity of demand for manufactures, and $\gamma = P\phi_2$, the marginal propensity to consume manufactures. I assume that aggregate demand is sufficiently regular to satisfy the properties that demand theory implies for an individual's demand curves. This would be true if ϕ were generated by a system of "well-behaved" community indifference curves, as is almost universally assumed in this area. Then $\eta - \gamma$ must be positive.[10] Thus (6) says that the demand curve is steeper than the supply curve if and only if

$$(7) \qquad \frac{\alpha}{\alpha - 1} > \eta.$$

That inequality (7) hold for all intersections of the D and S curves is the condition for the existence of a unique autarkic equilibrium. If the curves intersect, as in Figure 2, then (7) implies that there is no other intersection and no specialization equilibrium; if the curves do not intersect there is a single specialization equilibrium determined by the relative positions of the D and S curves. If (7) is always violated, there can likewise be no more than one interior equilibrium, but there will also in this case be two specialization equilibria.

I shall adopt the common Marshallian adjustment process: the output M of manufactures is rising if the corresponding demand price exceeds the correspond-

[9] If ϕ is thought of as generated by a system of community indifference curves, an interior equilibrium requires that the curves be "sufficiently convex," a point that has been widely noted (see Tinbergen [**18**, Appendix I], Matthews [**13**], Meade [**14**], and Chipman [**5**]). Chacholiades [**4**, p. 189] wrongly asserts that this is erroneous; with "insufficient convexity" his PCC curve in his Figure 7.2 need not intersect the interior of his production possibility frontier.

[10] For an individual, $\eta - \gamma$ would equal the pure substitution elasticity, by the Slutsky equation.

ing supply price and falling if supply price exceeds demand price. Evidently that (7) hold at any intersection ensures that the unique equilibrium is stable.[11]

In the limiting case of constant returns to scale ($\alpha = 1$), (7) necessarily holds as the left-hand side becomes infinite. Also (7) must hold, regardless of the degree of increasing returns, if the demand for manufactures is inelastic. But with elastic demand (7) will be violated if increasing returns to scale are sufficiently rapid; this is easy to understand, because higher values of α give the production possibility frontier more convexity, the usual source of trouble. We may summarize with the following proposition.

PROPOSITION 2: *If condition* (7) *holds, autarkic equilibrium is unique and stable.*

The analysis thus far applies to both countries. As they differ only in size, their autarkic equilibria will be completely described by the relation between L and the equilibrium P. This relation is determinate at an interior equilibrium. In such a case, $\phi(P, L) = P^{\alpha/(1-\alpha)}$. Differentiation of this expression yields

$$\frac{dP}{dL} = \frac{\gamma/M}{\eta - \frac{\alpha}{\alpha - 1}}.$$

Thus the now-familiar condition (7) is also equivalent to the proposition that an increase in the labor force reduces the relative autarkic price of manufactures. Thus we have the following proposition:

PROPOSITION 3: *If both countries produce both goods in autarky and if* (7) *holds, the larger country will have the lower autarkic relative price of the good subject to increasing returns.*

The subsequent discussion will be simplified by assuming that aggregate demand is of the familiar Mill-Graham type: a constant fraction γ of income is spent on manufactures.[12] In this case $\eta = 1$ so that (7) must hold. Also it is easy to see that the autarkic equilibrium must be as pictured in Figure 2, with $OA = (\gamma L)^{\alpha}$ and $OB = (\gamma L)^{1-\alpha}$. Thus the ratio of autarkic relative prices is

$$\frac{P}{P^*} = \left(\frac{L^*}{L}\right)^{\alpha - 1},$$

a simple example of Proposition 3.

[11]Note that this Marshallian process is the familiar one of the *Principles*, and not that of Marshall's foreign trade analysis [**12**, Appendix J]. The process is simple and appealing in the presence of increasing returns, but of course alternative assumptions are possible. Note that the Walrasian process would be troublesome since in Figure 2 each value of P close to OB corresponds to three different levels of output.

[12]Little will be lost by this simplification as I have carried the more general analysis far enough to indicate what qualifications to the Mill-Graham case it mandates.

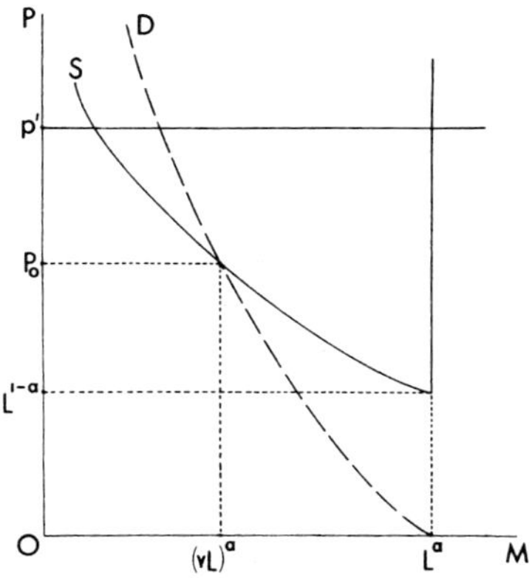

FIGURE 3.

4. A SMALL OPEN ECONOMY

Suppose now that the small country is truly small, in the sense that it can trade at an international relative price p' which it cannot influence. Figure 3 illustrates a typical case. Suppose that such an economy, with autarkic relative price equal to P_0, enters into international trade at the fixed international price p'. If $p' > P_0$, as in Figure 3, the economy will be driven to specialize in manufactures. If $p' < P_0$, free trade will analogously cause the economy to specialize in wheat.

Two notable features emerge from this analysis. First, the small country must gain from free trade in both cases. This is illustrated in Figure 4, where the consumption-possibility frontier under free trade dominates that under autarky for both of the possible configurations of relative prices. This is in notable contrast to some of the existing literature, which implies that a country forced by free trade to contract the size of the increasing returns industry must lose.

Second, these conclusions are precisely the same as those that follow in the standard Ricardian model.

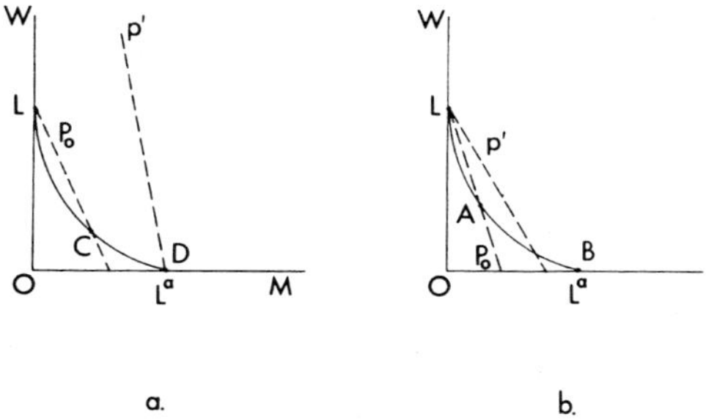

FIGURE 4.

PROPOSITION 4: *A small country entering into international trade will be driven to specialize (under the Marshallian adjustment process) in that commodity with the lower autarkic relative price. Regardless of which commodity that is, the small country will gain from free trade relative to autarky.*

If $p' = P_0$ the small country will produce and consume the same under free trade as under autarky and so will neither gain nor lose. The sole difference with the standard Ricardian model lies in the fact that such an equilibrium is unstable.

5. THE ALLOCATION CURVE

It is time to drop the small country assumption and examine full international equilibrium. To do this I shall first describe a new tool, the allocation curve.

In free trade the supply price in each country will be determined as described above, but there will now be a single world demand price determined by outputs in both countries. This relative demand price, p_D, is the solution to

$$M + M^* = \phi(p_D, L - M^{1/\alpha} + p_D M) + \phi^*(p_D, L^* - M^{*1/\alpha} + p_D M^*). \tag{8}$$

With internationally identical Mill-Graham demand functions, the solution of (8) is

$$p_D = \frac{\gamma}{1-\gamma} \frac{(L + L^*) - (L_M + L_M^*)}{L_M^\alpha + L_M^{*\alpha}}. \tag{9}$$

Now each value of L_M determines the home supply price P_S, as indicated in (4). Then there is some value of L_M^* which will equate the world demand price in (9) to the home supply price. This relation between L_M and L_M^* I call the *home allocation curve*: the collection of L_M and L_M^* for which the home economy is in equilibrium in the international market. Setting $p_D = P_S$ in (4) and (9) gives the implicit formula for the home allocation curve:

$$L_M^{1-\alpha} = \frac{\gamma}{1-\gamma} \frac{(L + L^*) - (L_M + L_M^*)}{L_M^\alpha + L_M^{*\alpha}}. \tag{10}$$

Similarly the foreign allocation curve shows the collection of L_M and L_M^* for which the rest of the world is in equilibrium in the international market: for each value of L_M^* that value of L_M which equates p_D to P_S^*. Substituting (9) into the foreign version of (4):

$$L_M^{*1-\alpha} = \frac{\gamma}{1-\gamma} \frac{(L + L^*) - (L_M + L_M^*)}{L_M^\alpha + L_M^{*\alpha}}. \tag{11}$$

Equations (10) and (11) require demand price to equal supply price in the two countries. But equilibrium is consistent with $p_D > P_S$ if the home economy

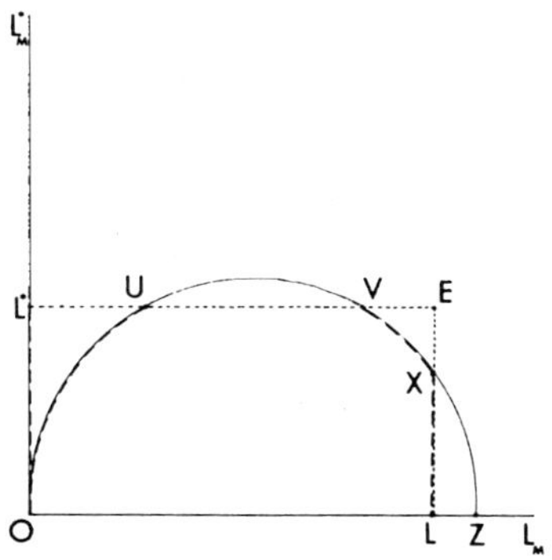

FIGURE 5.

specializes to M and with $p_D < P_S$ if it specializes to W, so the allocation curve must also take this into account. The home allocation curve is illustrated in Figure 5. The curved line through O, U, V, X and Z is the graph of (10). It is easy to verify that demand price exceeds home supply price below this curve and falls short above, and that the distance OZ equals $\gamma(L + L^*)$. Suppose that the total labor forces in the two countries are as indicated by point E. Then those parts of the curve outside the box $OLEL^*$ are irrelevant. The segment OL^*, where the home economy specializes to wheat and $p_D < P_S$, and the segment XL, where it specializes to manufactures and $p_D > P_S$, are consistent with equilibrium. Thus the full home allocation curve consists of L^*OU plus VXL.

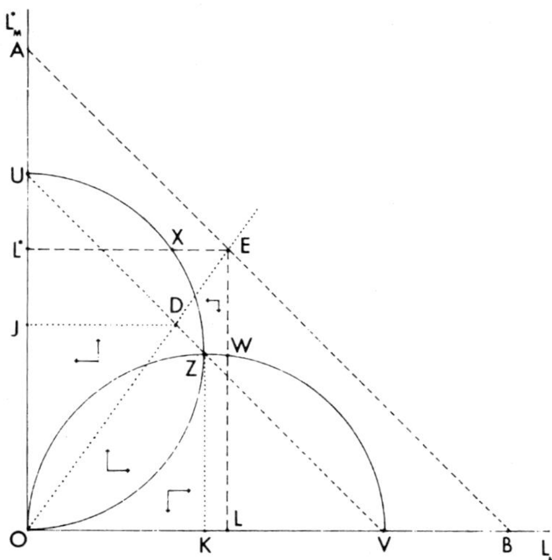

FIGURE 6.

In Figure 6 both allocation curves are drawn. Because the two countries are identical except for size, the home curve $OZWV$ and the foreign curve $OZXU$ are symmetric about the 45° line, on which they intersect at Z. The distance OK is $\gamma(L + L^*)/2$, or half the distance $OV(= OU)$; the world labor force $L + L^*$ is measured by $OA(= OB)$. If the labor in the two countries are as indicated by E in the figure, the full home allocation curve is L^*OZWL and the foreign curve is $LOZXL^*$. These curves intersect in three places—at L^*, Z, and L. At such intersections the supply price in each country is equal to a common world demand price, so the world is in free trade equilibrium.

PROPOSITION 5: *The international equilibria are given by the intersections of the two allocation curves.*

Note that, in Figure 6, the equilibria L and L^* both involve complete specialization by both countries and so imply, by the discussion of Section 2, efficient world output, whereas Z implies diversification by both countries and therefore inefficient world output.[13]

Figure 6 also shows the pre-trade situation. The conclusions reached in Section 3 imply that if both countries are in autarkic equilibrium the world will be at D, the intersection of OE and UV. The distance OJ equals γL^*; since $L^* > L$ at E, the home relative autarkic price P exceeds the foreign price P^* at D.

The allocation curve technique is simply an alternative way to accomplish what is usually done with offer curves. Which method is more convenient depends upon circumstances. Each country's allocation curve depends upon data from the other country. Thus many comparative-statics exercises which can be depicted as shifts of one offer curve and movements along the other would involve shifts of both allocation curves, so that the former method is likely to be more convenient. But this is no longer the case if the exercises are not of this type or if the offer curves are not independent of each other.[14] Note that the curves in Figure 6 resemble in shape normal "well-behaved" offer curves. The offer curves corresponding to this situation, on the other hand, are of the cumbersome "re-entrant" type.[15] For my present purposes allocation curves are in fact much more convenient, for two distinct reasons. The first is that they simplify the dynamic stability analysis, to which I now turn.

[13]The curves must be drawn as in Figure 6 if tastes in the two countries can be represented by identical sets of strictly convex community indifference curves, regardless of whether they also satisfy the Mill-Graham assumption.

[14]This is why I found allocation curves to be more convenient in Ethier **[6]**. Since I have drawn the curves in the $L - L^*$ plane, they may appear to depend upon the assumption of a single factor of production. However the present technique can in fact be used whenever the allocation of resources in a country can be represented by a single variable, as it can in any model with two goods related by a monotonic transformation curve. See Ethier **[6]** for an example. Thus the technique can be applied to the same models as can offer curves.

[15]See Chacholiades **[4]** for a derivation of the offer curves.

6. STABILITY

When a country is on its allocation curve, demand price and supply price are equal so there is no tendency for a reallocation of resources. Below the curve, the relative demand price of manufactures exceeds the relative supply price so that, by the Marshallian process, the manufacturing sector will be expanding. Similarly wheat output will be rising when above the allocation curve. Thus the two curves divide the box $OLEL^*$ in Figure 6 into four regions, where the directions of movement are shown by arrows. The equilibrium at Z is unstable (actually a saddle point) while those at L and L^* are stable. If the world enters into free trade from autarky, so that D is the initial state, the actual free trade equilibrium will be at L^*, where each country specializes in the good with the lower relative autarkic price.

Some notation is useful at this point. Denote the world demand price by

$$p_D = H(L_M, L_M^*)$$

and assume that $H_1, H_2 < 0$. The discussion in this section will not use the assumptions of identical technology or identical Mill-Graham demands, so that H need not be restricted to the form implied by (8) and (9). Similarly I denote the relative supply prices

$$p_S = G(L_M),$$

$$p_S^* = G^*(L_M^*).$$

The home allocation curve is the solution to $H(L_M, L_M^*) - G(L_M) = 0$, which I denote $L_M^* = f(L_M)$. Similarly the foreign allocation curve, denoted $L_M = f^*(L_M^*)$, is the solution to $H(L_M, L_M^*) - G^*(L_M^*) = 0$.

The Marshallian adjustment process can be represented by:

$$\hat{L}_M = \frac{H(L_M, L_M^*)}{G(L_M)} - 1,$$

$$\hat{L}_M^* = \frac{H(L_M, L_M^*)}{G^*(L_M^*)} - 1,$$

where $\hat{L}_M = (1|L_M)dL_M|dt$, etc., or as a linear approximation about an equilibrium $L_{M_0}, L_{M_0}^*$:

$$\hat{L}_M = a_1[L_M - L_{M_0}] + a_2[L_M^* - L_{M_0}^*], \tag{12}$$

$$\hat{L}_M^* = a_2^*[L_M - L_{M_0}] + a_1^*[L_M^* - L_{M_0}^*], \tag{13}$$

where $a_1 = (H_1 - G')/G$, $a_2 = H_2/G$, $a_2^* = H_1/G^*$, and $a_1^* = (H_2 - G^{*\prime})/G^*$, all evaluated at equilibrium.

Since the allocation curves in Figure 6 bear a close resemblance to conventional offer curves, it is tempting to derive stability conditions in terms of elasticities analogous to the usual import price elasticities. This I define

$$e \equiv -\frac{(L_M^*/L_M)}{L_M}\frac{dL_M}{d(L_M^*/L_M)} = \frac{1}{1-\dfrac{L_M}{L_M^*}f'} = \frac{L_M^* a_2}{L_M^* a_2 + L_M a_1}$$

and analogously

$$e^* \equiv \frac{L_M a_2^*}{L_M a_2^* + L_M^* a_1^*}\,.$$

Also define $e = -\infty$ if $L_M = 0$ and $L_M^* > 0$, and $e = 0$ if $L_M = L$, and analogously for e^*. I have defined e and e^* so that the usual geometric techniques involving import elasticities and offer curves can be applied straightforwardly to e and e^* and the allocation curves. A little experimentation with Figure 6 quickly suggests the following.[16]

PROPOSITION 6 (Stability Theorem): *The dynamic system* (12) *and* (13) *is unstable if either* e *or* e^* *is negative for a country that is producing both goods. Otherwise stability is equivalent to* $e + e^* < 1$, *the violation of the "Marshall-Lerner" condition.*

In Figure 6 for example, $e + e^* > 1$ at point Z, which is unstable. At point $L^*, e = -\infty, e^* = 0$ and both countries specialize, whereas at point $L, e = 0, e^* = -\infty$ and again both countries specialize; both equilibria are stable.

To prove the proposition, consider first equilibria where both countries produce both goods. Then the stability conditions for (12) and (13) are

(14) $\quad a_1 + a_1^* < 0,$

(15) $\quad a_1 a_1^* - a_2 a_2^* > 0.$

Now substitution gives

$$e + e^* - 1 = \frac{ee^*}{a_2 a_2^*}(a_2 a_2^* - a_1 a_1^*).$$

We have $a_2, a_2^* < 0$, so that $e < 0$ requires $a_1 > 0$ and $e^* < 0$ requires $a_1^* > 0$. Thus if both e and e^* are negative, (14) must be violated. Suppose that the elasticities are of opposite signs, say $e > 0$ and $e^* < 0$. Then $e + e^* < 1$ implies that (15) is violated; $e + e^* > 1$ requires $e > 1$ which in turn requires $a_1 > 0$, so that (14) is violated. Suppose next that both elasticities are positive. Then $e + e^* > 1$ implies that (15) is violated. Suppose $e + e^* < 1$. Then (15) is satisfied; also it must be that $e < 1$ and $e^* < 1$, which require $a_1 < 0$ and $a_1^* < 0$, thus

[16] A similar theorem for a quite different model is proved in Ethier [**6**].

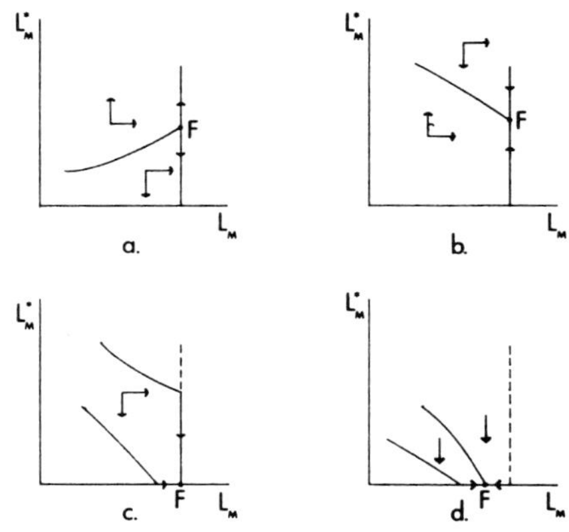

FIGURE 7.

satisfying (5). This proves the proposition for interior equilibria. On the boundary four cases are possible (plus four more by reversing the roles of the countries); these are illustrated in Figure 7. Each panel illustrates the neighborhood of an equilibrium, denoted F; the home allocation curve is drawn with long dashes and the foreign with small dashes. The arrows depict directions of movement. The proposition is demonstrated, case (a) being unstable and the others stable.

7. ALTERNATIVE POSSIBILITIES

The second present advantage of the allocation curve technique is that it allows a simple comprehensive treatment of all possibilities. This is due to the fact that the (interior) allocation curves are independent of L and L^* individually, and depend only on the total world labor force $L + L^*$; this is evident from (10) and (11). Thus by allowing L^*/L to vary while keeping $L + L^*$ constant, one can depict all possible cases without the need for any cumbersome shifting of curves.

Thus in Figure 6 imagine that E is shifted down the line AB from A to the 45° line (continuing to B would simply duplicate the cases by reversing the roles of the two countries). As this is done, autarkic equilibrium moves along the line UV from U to Z, and the box OL^*EL shifts in response to the movement of E. In all cases there are multiple equilibria. It is always the case that one of these (point L in Figure 6) has the small country specialized to manufactures and the large country to wheat. Another (point L^* in Figure 6) will always have the small country specialized to wheat while the large country either specializes to manufactures (if point L^* in Figure 6 is below U, that is, if $L^*/L < \gamma/(1 - \gamma)$) or produces both goods (if $\gamma/(1 - \gamma) < L^*/L$). This latter condition is easy to understand: if the large country is to specialize in the good subject to increasing

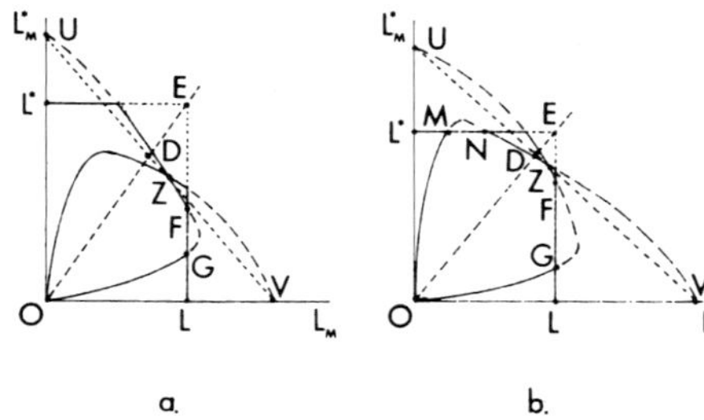

FIGURE 8.

returns, the world must have a sufficient liking for that good to allow a competitive equilibrium with the resultant large output to be possible.

There are also one or more additional equilibria. If, as in Figure 6, e exceeds unity at Z, there will in fact be one more. This additional equilibrium will be at Z, where both countries produce both goods and world manufacturing output is equally divided, if the small country is large enough,[17] i.e., if L lies to the right of K. Otherwise this equilibria will occur where the segment OZ of the foreign allocation curve intersects the line EL, and will thus feature specialization of the smaller economy to manufactures and diversification in the larger economy. Note that, in view of Proposition 1, the "middle" equilibrium will always feature an inefficient pattern of specialization, while the specialization in the other two equilibria will necessarily be efficient.

If the curves are inelastic at Z, there could be more than three equilibria. Figure 8 illustrates the two additional, qualitatively distinct, possibilities. The equilibria Z, F, and G in both panels all involve inefficient patterns of specialization, whereas M and N in Figure 8(b) are efficient.

Why do low elasticities allow additional equilibria? If $e < 1$ at Z, that is, if the home allocation curve has a negative slope there, a shift of domestic labor from wheat to manufactures will cause an excess supply of manufactures, driving the demand price below the home supply price. (This is indicated by the fact that a foreign reallocation from manufactures to wheat would be required to restore the home economy to equilibrium). Whether this will happen depends upon whether the supply price declines gently enough, that is, upon whether the degree of increasing returns is not too great. Manipulation of (10) confirms this by revealing that $e < 1$ at Z if and only if

(16) $$\alpha - 1 < 1/(1 - \gamma).$$

Thus, although the existence of increasing returns imply multiple equilibria, moderation in those returns renders a large number of equilibria *more* likely.

[17]The relevance of this condition should also be clear; for both economies to diversify the total output of manufactures must be equally divided because technology is internationally identical. Then the relative size of the smaller country is the crucial consideration for whether it is possible, at any price, to produce enough manufactures to satisfy world demand.

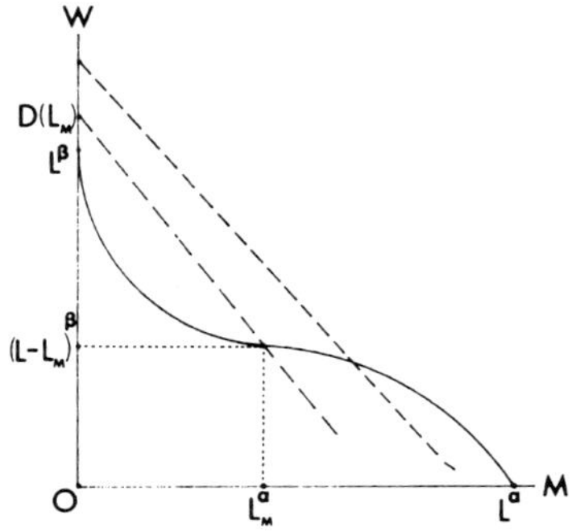

a.

FIGURE 9a.

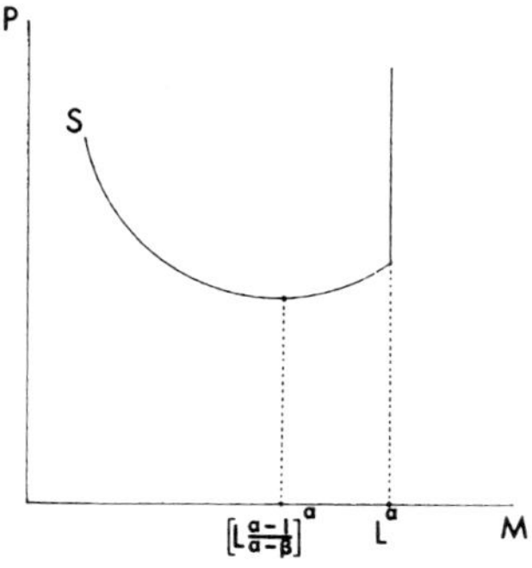

b.

FIGURE 9b.

Note that, with the Marshallian adjustment process, the equilibria are in all cases alternatively stable and unstable. What other general conclusions emerge? Note first that, if the world moves from autarky, at D, to free trade, the actual equilibrium that is attained will be point N in Figure 8(b), and the equilibrium located on the L_M^* axis in every other case; thus the small country will in fact export wheat and the large country will export manufactures. Second, the actual free trade equilibrium in each of these cases involves, as a consequence of Proposition 1, an efficient pattern of international specialization. Third, as a consequence of Proposition 3, relative autarkic prices in the two countries correctly predict what the pattern of trade would be in the equilibrium that would emerge as a result of the commencement of free trade.[18]

These conclusions, together with Propositions 1, 3, and 4, reveal a nearly perfect symmetry, with regard to positive conclusions, between the familiar simple Ricardian model and the present case where trade is due solely to increasing returns to scale. This result can be summarized, recalling that I say the large country has a comparative advantage in manufactures:

PROPOSITION 7 (Symmetry Theorem): *Suppose that the Marshallian adjustment process applies and that condition* (7) *holds. Then each country has a lower relative autarkic price in the good in which it has an advantage; if the two countries commence free trade from autarky they will reach an equilibrium in which each exports the good in which it has a comparative advantage and in which at least one country, and possibly both, specializes completely. The pattern of specialization will be efficient.*

[18] Indeed, since $P^* < P$ above the 45° line and $P^* > P$ below, the comparative autarkic prices corresponding to *any* point in OL^*EL always predict the pattern of trade characterizing the free-trade equilibrium that would emerge if the Marshallian adjustment process were commenced from that point. The sole exception is that, if the point L in Figure 6 were to the left of K, there would be a "perverse" zone between the 45° line and the interior portion of the home allocation curve. But, with identical homothetic tastes, autarkic equilibrium can never occur in this zone.

The only positive conclusion of the usual Ricardian model that does not carry over is the proposition that the terms of trade will lie between the two relative autarkic prices; the scale economies realized by specialization can clearly allow the free-trade relative price of manufactures to be smaller than both autarkic prices. On the other hand, the increasing-returns model is simpler than the usual Ricardian in the sense that the larger country will consume the same under free trade as under autarky only in the limiting case where L^*/L goes to infinity; in the usual Ricardian model this situation emerges for L^*/L sufficiently large, but finite.

The symmetry theorem is remarkable in light of the great differences that increasing returns make when added to neoclassical models. The theorem implies, for example, that a trading equilibrium due to differences in constant costs would be indistinguishable from one due to size differences and increasing returns, so that the empirical evidence that is generally interpreted to support the former[19] also supports the latter just as well. Indeed it is a corollary of the symmetry theorem that the pattern of actual average productivities in an increasing-returns equilibrium will be identical to the pattern of constant productivities that would generate such an equilibrium in a Ricardian model.

The most important condition required for Proposition 7 is the Marshallian adjustment process. This is because with increasing returns there must always exist multiple equilibria with different patterns of trade. Thus I cannot dismiss the possibility that there exists a plausible dynamic hypothesis which would invalidate the symmetry theorem.

8. THE NORMATIVE IMPLICATIONS OF FREE TRADE

The symmetry theorem establishes a strong result with respect to positive conclusions and production efficiency. It should be evident that no similarly strong proposition can hold for other normative questions. Average-cost pricing introduces a widely-understood distortion. Autarkic equilibrium is not Pareto optimal in either country, and any full-trade equilibrium in which one of the countries produces both goods must be inefficient in the sense that a reallocation of resources, in the diversified country, towards manufacturing could potentially make some better off while harming none.[20]

Even if both countries specialize and the world equilibrium is Pareto optimal in a local sense, it need not be so globally, because of the convexity of the production possibility frontiers. For example, if the taste for manufactures or the degree of increasing returns are sufficiently modest, the equilibrium at L in

[19] See MacDougall [**11**], Stern [**17**], and Balassa [**2**].

[20] Except in the singular case $L^*/L = (1 - \gamma)/\gamma$, this is also true of the equilibrium at L where the small country specializes to manufactures and the large to wheat. Although this involves complete specialization it produces the same world outputs as would specialization of the small economy to wheat and appropriate diversification of the large economy. Thus point L does not correspond to a kink on the world production possibility frontier.

Figure 6 could be preferable to that at L^*. A simple way to illustrate this is afforded by the assumption, consistent with identical Mill-Graham demand functions, that world welfare can be measured by $(M + M^*)^{\gamma}(W + W^*)^{1-\gamma}$. It is easily seen that world welfare is higher at point L^* in Figure 6 than at L if and only if $L^{*\alpha\gamma}L^{1-\gamma} > L^{\alpha\gamma}L^{*1-\gamma}$. Thus point L must be preferred to L^* if L^*/L is sufficiently close to unity, provided that $\alpha\gamma > 1 - \gamma$.

Nevertheless, it is possible to derive unambiguous normative conclusions under certain circumstances. Suppose free-trade equilibrium is point L^* in Figure 6, so the large country specializes to manufactures and the small to wheat. Denote the terms of trade by P^F. Now, using Figure 4, it is easy to see that, if $L/L^{\alpha} > P^F > L^*/L^{*\alpha}$, the world budget line lies outside the world production possibility frontier. Also each country must gain from trade in this case. With identical Mill-Graham demand functions, $P^F = \gamma L/(1 - \gamma)L^{*\alpha}$ when the large country specializes to manufactures and the small to wheat. A little manipulation confirms that this situation corresponds to $L^*/L < \gamma/(1 - \gamma) < (L^*/L)^{\alpha}$. This must hold for some range of L^*/L greater than unity if $\gamma > 1/\alpha$, and is impossible otherwise. We may summarize as follows:

PROPOSITION 8: *Suppose that the Marshallian adjustment process applies, that condition* (7) *holds, and that* $\gamma > 1/\alpha$. *Then there exists a range of values of* L^*/L *for which free trade is Pareto optimal and confers gains on both countries.*

This proposition is far weaker than the symmetry theorem and than the constant-returns-to-scale situation; if $\alpha < 1/\gamma$ the proposition is empty. Note one interesting fact: the existence of increasing returns causes problems, but, once this is conceded, greater degrees of increasing returns, and greater demand for manufactures, *increase* the range of relative country sizes for which the conventional results continue to hold. Note the similarity to the question of the existence of multiple equilibria.

9. GRAHAM'S ARGUMENT FOR PROTECTION

The fact that Proposition 8 is considerably weaker than Proposition 7 should come as no surprise: the welfare effects of relative-price distortions have received extensive attention for a quarter of a century. Of more interest is the question of whether individual countries will gain from trade, the subject of the seminal paper by Graham [7]. I now turn to this issue.[21]

Consider, first, the larger country. By the symmetry theorem, this country will be driven by free trade to increase its production of manufactures, perhaps specializing completely. If the large country does not specialize, it will be driven by trade to shift production as indicated in Figure 4(b), for example, from A to B; then the free trade budget line LB lies outside the autarky point A, and the

[21] Graham's argument has also received a recent and lucid discussion in Panagariya [**16**], who nevertheless does not treat the points raised below.

country necessarily gains from trade. If free trade induces complete specialization, the abandonment of autarky can be illustrated by the movement from C to D in Figure 4(a), so that the country must gain if the terms of trade P^F are sufficiently great so that the free-trade budget line through D is steeper than the line connecting C and D, and therefore lies above C. This will be true when

$$P^F > -(1-\gamma)L^*/\left[(\gamma L^*)^\alpha - L^{*\alpha}\right] = L^{*1-\alpha}(1-\gamma)/(1-\gamma^\alpha),$$

the slope of the line connecting D and C. If the small country produces both goods this necessarily holds, since P^F must exceed the small country autarkic price, which must in turn exceed the slope of the line through D and C. If both countries specialize, $P^F = \gamma L/(1-\gamma)L^{*\alpha}$. For both countries to specialize, Figure 6 reveals that $(1-\gamma)L^* < \gamma L$ is necessary. Thus

$$P^F > \frac{(1-\gamma)L^*}{(1-\gamma)L^{*\alpha}} = L^{*1-\alpha} > L^{*1-\alpha}\frac{1-\gamma}{1-\gamma^\alpha}.$$

Thus the large country gains from trade in this case also. We may summarize as follows:[22]

PROPOSITION 9: *The large country must be better off, relative to autarky, in the equilibrium that is attained as a result of a movement from autarky to free trade.*

This Proposition, like Propositions 7 and 8, confirms the classical theory.[23] But Graham's argument applied to the country with the comparative advantage in wheat; in view of Proposition 3 this is the smaller country.

The smaller country exports wheat and in fact specializes in it, except for the case illustrated in Figure 8(b). In this case the movement from autarky to free trade can be represented by the shift in production from B to A in Figure 4(b). The free-trade budget line is inside the autarkic budget line, so that the small country loses. Thus this is Graham's case; when will it occur? An equilibrium such as N in Figure 8(b) will exist if the allocation curve is inelastic at Z, and if the endowment point E is not as high as the maximum of the interior home allocation curve. Now it is clear from the geometry that the latter condition implies the former, and that the latter is more likely to be possible, for E close enough to the 45° line, the more inelastic is the allocation curve at Z, and the closer is point Z to the line AB in Figure 8(b). The latter means the larger is γ, that is, the greater is the taste for manufactures, whereas low elasticities require, as discussed earlier, low values of γ and high values of α. Algebraic manipulation indeed reveals that an equilibrium like N in Figure 8(b) must exist for L

[22] Proposition 9 could have alternatively been deduced from Proposition 7 by applying Theorem 1 of Negishi and Kemp [**9**, Ch. 9].

[23] Proposition 9 is, however, at odds with part of the literature. The classic paper by Matthews concluded [**13**, pp. 155–156] that the large country, and not the small, was the possible loser.

sufficiently close to L^* provided that

$$(17) \qquad (\alpha - 1)(1 - \gamma) < [\gamma(\alpha - 1)/\alpha]^{\alpha}.$$

Since the right-hand side of (17) is less than unity, this condition is a stronger version of (16).

Consider next the free trade outcomes in which the small country specializes to wheat. This involves a movement from B to L in Figure 4(b). Evidently the small country will gain relative to autarky if and only if the free-trade price P^F is less than the autarkic price $P = (\gamma L)^{1-\alpha}$. If the large country is incompletely specialized, then $P^F < P^* < P$, so that the small country must gain. Consider then an equilibrium in which both countries specialize. Then $P^F = \gamma L/(1 - \gamma)L^{*\alpha}$. It is then easy to verify that the small country will lose if and only if[24]

$$\left(\frac{L^*}{L}\right)^{\alpha} < \frac{\gamma^{\alpha}}{1-\gamma}.$$

Clearly the small country will not lose if it is sufficiently small, so that L^*/L is sufficiently large, nor can it possibly lose if the right hand side is less than unity. If

$$(18) \qquad \gamma^{\alpha} > 1 - \gamma,$$

then the small country will lose if L is sufficiently close to L^*. Note that, since $[(\alpha - 1)/\alpha]^{\alpha} < \alpha - 1$, condition (17) implies (18). Thus (18) is the condition for the existence of Graham's case, and (17) merely determines whether the small country diversifies or not. Thus we have the following Proposition:

PROPOSITION 10 (Graham): *Suppose condition* (18) *holds. Then if L is sufficiently close to L* the small country will lose from a move from autarky to free-trade, and the large country will gain. If condition* (18) *fails, or if L is sufficiently small relative to L*, both countries must gain.*

Three features of the Graham case deserve emphasis. First, greater tastes for wheat, i.e., lower values of γ, render the Graham case less likely. Indeed (18) is impossible if $1 - \gamma$ exceeds one-half. That a sufficient relative importance of wheat should reduce the likelihood of a country losing by abandoning the production of manufactures seems reasonable enough, although the fact that $1 - \gamma > \frac{1}{2}$ implies gains regardless of the size of α is perhaps surprising.

Second, the fact that (18) is less likely the *greater* the degree of increasing returns is definitely surprising, and quite at odds with the impression conveyed by Graham's paper and the subsequent discussion. But the explanation is simple: high values of α imply that the dominant consideration is the large cost reduction

[24] Note that this condition implies $L^*/L < \gamma/(1 - \gamma)$, so that the large country does in fact specialize.

from concentrating manufacturing output in the country. This is the same "knife-edge" phenomenon that has appeared several times thus far: the existence of increasing returns introduces the possibility of distinct features, but they are less likely the greater the degree of increasing returns.

Thirdly, and again surprisingly in view of the literature, the smaller the small country is, relative to the larger country, the greater the likelihood that it will gain. The reason is simply that a sufficiently large size disparity renders the switch of manufacturing activity to the larger country the dominant consideration. The Graham case is not therefore a matter of the large exploiting the small. Rather, it is a case of two approximately-equally-matched countries confronting each other in a situation where one must gain and one must lose.[25] Thus Graham's argument would seem to have little present relevance to individual LDCs.

What are the implications of Graham's case for commercial policy? The small country will benefit from a tariff on manufactures; the less trade the better. Note that this is not an infant-industry argument: the small country would never, as a result of the tariff, export manufactures, and the protection must be permanent, as Graham insisted.

The existence of multiple equilibria raises the possibility of using commercial policy to attain an equilibrium other than the one that would follow a movement from autarky to free trade. Now condition (18) implies that any equilibrium with the small country specialized to wheat entails losses, and the small country always loses if nonspecialized and exporting wheat. Thus only equilibria which reverse the pattern of trade are candidates (in Figure 8(b), L^*, M, and N all leave the small country worse off than autarky). Using the above methods, it is easy to verify that, if the Graham case holds so that the small country loses from free trade, then it must be true that at point L in Figures 6, 8(a), and 8(b) the small country would gain from trade and the large country would lose. This would also be true at points Z, F, and G when they are equilibria. Thus the small country has an incentive, whether starting from autarky or free trade, to subsidize the export of manufactures until the world moves below the 45° line in the figures. From there it will converge to an equilibrium in which the small country will gain and the large lose; the commercial policy can be abandoned because this latter equilibrium will now be reachable and sustainable by free trade. This is essentially the infant industry argument, and one ignored by Graham and his followers. But note that tariff protection is not enough—manufactured exports must be actually subsidized, at least for a while.

In order to keep close to the discussion of commercial policy in the post-Graham literature I have assumed that the large country remains passive. But the present analysis renders such an assumption dubious. For the Graham case arises

[25] It is interesting to note that a reader would *not* have received a contrary impression from Graham [7], where the discussion was in terms of a two-country numerical example, and where solely large-country applications were discussed. Only more recently have expositions centered on a single country facing a given world price, and thereby obscured a central feature.

when two countries are of nearly equal size, and then the collection of free-trade equilibria can be divided into those where one country gains and the other loses and those where the reverse is true. This is a recipe for bilateral conflict.

The characteristics of Graham's case exposed above have been completely ignored in the extensive literature.[26] The latter preoccupied itself with issues (e.g., the existence of external economies, the irreversibility of returns to scale, the association of scale economies with industry generally or with specific products) which were not really relevant to Graham's basic point, and then typically concluded that "the basis for the kind of protection defended by Graham is all but completely destroyed" (Anderson [**1**, p. 167]). Such conclusions now appear, at least to this reader, to have been mainly wishful thinking.[27]

10. INCREASING COSTS IN WHEAT PRODUCTION

Graham's examples differed from the above analysis by featuring increasing costs in the wheat sector. I now investigate what difference this makes. The most direct line of attack is to retain the production model used thus far, except to replace (2) by (2a):

$$W = (L_W)^{\beta} \tag{2a}$$

where $1 > \beta > 0$. In this case, the production possibility frontier, drawn in Figure 9(a), is convex near the W-axis, concave near the M-axis, and has a single inflection point (see Panagariya [**16**] for a detailed description of this technology).

I assume marginal-cost pricing in wheat (the decreasing returns to labor are assumed due to a second factor—land—in inelastic supply and specific to wheat). Then the relative supply price is

$$P_s = \beta \frac{W}{L_W} \frac{L_M}{M} = \beta (L - L_M)^{\beta - 1} L_M^{1-\alpha}. \tag{4a}$$

The supply price is related to the production possibility frontier as before, $P_s = -\alpha(dW/dM)$. The supply curve is accordingly shaped as in Figure 9(b).

The demand price is defined as in Section 3, and it is easily seen that, at autarkic equilibrium,

$$\frac{M}{P}\left(\frac{dP_S}{dM} - \frac{dP_D}{dM}\right) = \frac{L_M}{L_W}\frac{1-\beta}{\alpha} + \frac{\alpha - 1}{\alpha}\frac{\eta - (\alpha/\alpha - 1)}{\gamma - \eta}. \tag{6a}$$

Thus condition (7) remains sufficient for the supply curve to cut the demand curve from below, and Proposition 2 continues to hold. The relative autarkic

[26] See Caves [**3**, pp. 169–174] for references.

[27] I have argued elsewhere (Ethier [**6**]) the case that modern conditions mandate a reformulation of the theory of international trade and increasing returns in a direction which would, incidentally, invalidate Graham's argument for protection. But Graham himself had said that his argument was mainly of historical interest.

equilibrium price is

$$P = \frac{\gamma}{1-\gamma} \frac{\left[\beta(1-\gamma)\right]^{\beta}}{\gamma^{\alpha}} \left[\gamma + \beta(1-\gamma)\right]^{\alpha-\beta} L^{\beta-\alpha}$$

so that $P/P^* = (L^*/L)^{\alpha-\beta}$; the smaller country has the higher relative autarkic price of manufacture in terms of wheat.

Turning to international equilibrium, the home allocation curve is now

$$\text{(10a)} \qquad \gamma\left[(L-L_M)^{\beta} + (L^* - L_M^*)^{\beta}\right]$$
$$-(1-\gamma)\beta(L-L_M)^{\beta-1} L_M^{1-\alpha}\left[L_M^{\alpha} + L_M^{*\alpha}\right] = 0.$$

As before, the home supply price exceeds the world demand price above this curve, and indeed all the earlier qualitative properties are preserved, with one important exception: L and L^* now influence the shape of the curve independently, so that a change in relative country sizes which preserves $L + L^*$ no longer leaves the allocation curves unaltered. Now (4a) and its foreign analog imply that, where the home allocation curve intersects the 45° line, $P_s^* < P_s = P_D$ if and only if $L^* > L$. It then follows that the two allocation curves intersect below the 45° line when $L^* > L$ and above it when $L > L^*$.

PROPOSITION 11: *If the endowments in the two countries permit a free-trade equilibrium in which neither country specializes, the smaller country produces more manufactures in that equilibrium than does the larger.*

The positive analysis in Sections 6 and 7 can now proceed as before. In particular, the stability and symmetry theorems continue to hold. Consider next the normative analysis and Graham's argument.

$D(L_M)$ in Figure 9(a) indicates, for any value of L_M, the intersection with the W-axis of the budget line determined by that L_M and corresponding supply price. Thus

$$D(L_M) = (L - L_M)^{\beta}\left[1 + \beta\frac{L_M}{L - L_M}\right].$$

Then $D(0) = L^{\beta}$ and $dD/dL_M > 0$. It follows that the movement from autarky to free trade must benefit the large country, which exports manufactures in a stable equilibrium, and must harm the small country in any stable equilibrium in which the latter does not specialize. The remaining analysis of Graham's argument proceeds as in the previous section. In particular, if the home country specializes to wheat and the foreign country to manufactures, then $P^F > P$ if and only if

$$(L^*/L)^\alpha < \left[\frac{\gamma + \beta(1-\gamma)}{\beta(1-\gamma)}\right]^\beta \left[\frac{\gamma}{\gamma + \beta(1-\gamma)}\right]^\alpha.$$

This condition is satisfied for L^* sufficiently close to L provided that

$$\text{(18a)} \qquad \gamma^\alpha > (1-\gamma)^\beta \beta^\beta [\alpha + \beta(1-\gamma)]^{\alpha-\beta}.$$

Proposition 10 and the previous section's qualitative discussion of Graham's case is unaltered.[28] In addition the role of β can be isolated. Note that (18a) reduces to (18) when $\beta = 1$. With γ and α unchanged, a small reduction in β below 1 reduces the right-hand side of (18a). *Thus a greater degree of increasing costs in wheat production enlarges the range of parameter values giving Graham's case.* This is true for any reduction in β which does not drop the latter below one-half. But if $\gamma > (1-\gamma)(\alpha+1)$, a fall in β could raise the right-hand side, and thereby reverse the above conclusion, if β is initially small enough.

In sum, the addition of neoclassical features, in the form of decreasing returns in wheat, by itself leaves the central conclusions of this paper unaltered.

11. INTERNATIONAL DIFFERENCES

It is time to relax the assumption that the two countries are alike in all respects except size. Consider differences in technology, and again set $\beta = 1$. I shall continue to assume that the degree α of increasing returns is the same in both countries, but I shall now allow differences in labor efficiency. Denote by b the quantity of wheat that can be produced by each unit of domestic labor, so that (2) becomes

$$\text{(2b)} \qquad W = bL_W.$$

Equations (1) and (3), and the foreign counterparts of (1), (2), and (3), all remain unchanged.

The 45° line is replaced by the line $L^*/L = (1/b)^{1/(\alpha-1)}$ as the dividing line. Proceeding as before, the home allocation curve (10) becomes

$$\text{(10b)} \qquad L_M^{1-\alpha} = \frac{\gamma}{1-\gamma}\,\frac{(bL + L^*) - (bL_M + L_M^*)}{L_M^\alpha + L_M^{*\alpha}}$$

and similarly for the foreign curve. Note that (10a) will be impervious to changes in L^*/L as long as the total $bL + L^*$ is unchanged. Thus the analysis of international equilibrium is essentially unchanged; Figures 6, 8(a) and 8(b) can

[28] For example, one can derive a condition for the existence of an equilibrium in which the small country diversifies (and loses from trade):

$$\text{(17a)} \qquad \left(\frac{a}{\alpha}\right)^{\alpha/(\alpha-1)} + 1 < \left[\left(\frac{a}{\alpha}\right)^{1/(\alpha-1)} - 1\right]a.$$

still be used as before. All the earlier conclusions, including the analysis of Graham's case, continue to hold except for occasional straightforward modifications. Only one of the latter is deserving of mention.

Assume without loss of generality that $b < 1$. Then if $L^* < L$ it is inefficient to produce any wheat at home if some manufactures are being produced abroad; the two determinants of comparative advantage (L^*/L and b) reinforce each other. If $L^* > L$ they conflict. When L^*/L is small, the size of b is the dominant consideration for the efficient pattern of specialization. But as L^*/L increases there will come a point, for a given structure of demand, at which scale economies dominate, and the efficient pattern of specialization will reverse itself. I call such a point an "advantage reversal." Such a reversal point will be compatible with *either* home specialization in wheat and foreign diversification *or* home specialization in manufactures and a different pattern of foreign diversification.[29] Foreign production anywhere between these two diversification patterns is never efficient. For such an advantage reversal to exist, L^*/L must be large enough.[30] In such a case, a move from autarky to free trade could result in an inefficient pattern of specialization, so the symmetry theorem requires this slight qualification.

The second respect in which technology could differ between countries is if the degree α of increasing returns at home differs from that abroad, denoted α^*. Assume for simplicity that $b = 1$ once again. It is simple to deduce that the comparative relative autarkic prices are $P/P^* = \gamma^{\alpha^* - \alpha} L^{1-\alpha}/L^{*1-\alpha^*}$, so that the role played by the 45° line in the earlier analysis is now assumed by the curve

$$(19) \qquad L^* = \gamma^{(\alpha - \alpha^*)/(\alpha^* - 1)} L^{(\alpha - 1)/(\alpha^* - 1)}$$

and we can say that the foreign country is the "larger" or not according as L^* exceeds the right-hand side of (19) or not.

Proceeding as before, the earlier analysis continues to hold with only straightforward alteration.

Again, only one modification deserves mention. Suppose without loss of generality that $\alpha^* > \alpha$. If $L^* > L$ it is clearly inefficient for the large country to produce any wheat if the small country produces some manufactures; the two determinants of comparative advantage (L^*/L and $\alpha^* - \alpha$) reinforce each other. But if $L > L^*$, the two determinants conflict. If the home economy is sufficiently large, an "advantage reversal" will take place, as in the previous section. Analogous conclusions apply.

Note the similarity of the present situation to that implied by the symmetry theorem. The latter established that increasing returns led to the same positive conclusions as the classical theory. In perfect analogy, differences in increasing returns lead to the same sort of conclusions as differences in constant costs.

[29] Such a situation is illustrated in Figure 5 of Lerner [**10**, p. 353]. See also his accompanying discussion.

[30] This will happen if L^*/L is at least as large as μ, the positive solution to: $(\mu + b)^\alpha - \mu^\alpha - 1 = 0$.

The final way in which the two countries might differ is in tastes. I continue to assume Mill-Graham demand functions, but allow the proportion γ of home income spent on manufactures to differ from the foreign proportion γ^*. For simplicity I again assume identical technologies.

Let g denote the ratio γ/γ^*. Then the line $L^*/L = g$ replaces the 45° line in the earlier analysis. The home allocation curve is

$$(10c) \qquad L_M^{1-\alpha} = \frac{K}{1-K} \frac{(L+L^*) - (L_M + L_M^*)}{L_M^\alpha + L^{*\alpha}_M}$$

where $K = (\gamma L + \gamma^* L^*)/([1-\gamma]L + (1-\gamma^*]L^*)$. Note that (10c) is identical to (10) except that K replaces γ. The analysis now proceeds just as before, except that, when considering all possible cases, as E shifts along the line AB in Figure 6 (that is, as L and L^* change so as to hold $L + L^*$ constant), γ and γ^* should also be changed so as to hold K and g constant. The earlier treatment can be duplicated in detail, with one minor change. Autarkic equilibrium will not be given by point D in Figures 6, 8(a), and 8(b). Rather it will be given by the intersection of the line UV with the ray through the origin whose slope equals $(1/g)$ times the slope of the ray OE. Note that, as a consequence, if the endowment point is between the 45° line and the ray $L^*/L = g$, then the larger country will have a comparative advantage in wheat (and export it in free trade) and the smaller country in manufactures. I call such a case a "demand reversal" because it is a precise analog to the situation of that name in the Heckscher-Ohlin model. If a demand reversal is present the pattern of specialization in free-trade could be inefficient, so this slight qualification to the symmetry theorem is again called for.

University of Pennsylvania

Manuscript received May, 1979; revision received December, 1981.

REFERENCES

[1] ANDERSON, K.: "Tariff Protection and Increasing Returns," in *Explorations in Economics: Notes and Essays Contributed in Honor of F. W. Taussig*. New York: McGraw-Hill, 1936.
[2] BALASSA, B.: "An Empirical Demonstration of Classical Comparative Cost Theory," *Review of Economics and Statistics*, 45(1963), 231–238.
[3] CAVES, R.: *Trade and Economic Structure*. Cambridge, Mass: Harvard University Press, 1960.
[4] CHACHOLIADES, M.: *International Trade Theory and Policy*. New York: McGraw-Hill, 1978.
[5] CHIPMAN, J.: "A Survey of the Theory of International Trade: Part 2, The Neoclassical Theory," *Econometrica*, 33(1965), 685–760.
[6] ETHIER, W.: "Internationally Decreasing Costs and World Trade," *Journal of International Economics*, 9(1979), 1–24.
[7] GRAHAM, F.: "Some Aspects of Protection Further Considered," *Quarterly Journal of Economics*, 37(1923), 199–227.
[8] KEMP, M. C.: *The Pure Theory of International Trade and Investment*. Englewood Cliffs, New Jersey: Prentice-Hall, 1969.
[9] ———: *Three Topics in the Theory of International Trade*. Amsterdam: North-Holland, 1976.

[10] Lerner, A.: "The Diagrammatic Representation of Cost Conditions in International Trade," *Economica*, 34(1932), 346–356.
[11] MacDougall, G. D. A.: "British and American Exports: A Study Suggested by the Theory of Comparative Costs," *Economic Journal*, 61(1951), 487–521.
[12] Marshall, A.: *Money, Credit and Commerce*. New York: Augustus Kelley, 1960.
[13] Matthews, R. C. O.: "Reciprocal Demand and Increasing Returns," *Review of Economic Studies*, 17(1950), 149–158.
[14] Meade, J.: *A Geometry of International Trade*. London: George Allen and Unwin, 1952.
[15] Melvin, J.: "Increasing Returns to Scale as a Determinant of Trade," *Canadian Journal of Economics*, 2(1969), 389–402.
[16] Panagariya, A.: "Variable Returns to Scale in Production and Patterns of Specialization," *American Economic Review*, 71(1981), 221–230.
[17] Stern, R.: "British and American Productivity and Comparative Costs in International Trade," *Oxford Economic Papers*, 14(1962), 275–296.
[18] Tinbergen, J.: *International Economic Cooperation*. Amsterdam: Elsevier, 1945.
[19] Viner, J.: *Studies in the Theory of International Trade*. New York: Harper, 1937.

Journal of International Economics 9 (1979) 1–24. © North-Holland Publishing Company

INTERNATIONALLY DECREASING COSTS AND WORLD TRADE

Wilfred ETHIER*

University of Pennsylvania, Philadelphia, PA 19104, U.S.A.

Received September 1977, revised version received September 1978

This paper seeks to reformulate the existing theory of international trade and increasing returns by arguing that such returns depend upon the size of the world market rather than national output. The result is the disappearance of the tendency towards interindustry specialization and multiple equilibrium and the emergence of a theory of trade in intermediate goods. A new analytical tool – the allocation curve – is developed for this context.

1. Introduction

Increasing returns in production have long been recognized as determinants of international trade. Nonetheless they have never played a central theoretical role. In his survey John Chipman (1965, p. 737) noted, 'It is probably correct to say that economies of scale tend to be ignored in theoretical models not so much on empirical grounds as for the simple reason that the theoretical difficulties are considerable.... That this is a poor reason for excluding them is evident, especially if it is true that they constitute one of the principal sources of international trade.' Another reason is probably the conclusion to which decreasing costs have led. To quote Chipman (1965, p. 749) once again, 'the most important conclusion...was...that the presence of economies of large scale production leads to multiple equilibrium, and therefore introduces an intrinsic arbitrariness into the determination of the international pattern of specialization and trade.' Such arbitrariness[1] leaves the customary comparative-statics exercises unattractive. Furthermore the relevance of a theory yielding such conclusions

*I take pleasure in acknowledging the helpful comments of Bela Balassa, Herbert Grubel, Murray Kemp, Arvind Panagariya, Asaaf Razin, and the participants of seminars at the University of Pennsylvania and Johns Hopkins University.

[1]This characteristic, basically due to what Edgeworth (1894) termed 're-entrant' offer curves, is clear in the central modern treatments of the subject: Matthews (1949/50), Meade (1952), and Kemp (1969). For a slightly different point of view see Ethier (1978), and also see the interesting recent paper by Panagariya (1978).

to a world in which the lion's share of trade involves the exchange of manufactures and intermediate goods between similar economies is questionable at best, despite the fact that scale economies have repeatedly been shown to have empirical significance in such trade.

The purpose of this paper is to reformulate the traditional theory of international trade and increasing returns in a fundamental way. I shall argue that the result is the disappearance of the tendency towards specialization and 'arbitrariness,' and the emergence of a theory of trade in intermediate goods. My central theme is the interdependence of world industrial activity, and I shall fashion a new tool – the allocation curve – expressly for such a context.

2. Internationally decreasing costs

The central element in this reformulation is the idea of internationally decreasing costs – that average cost depends, with free trade, on the size of the international market rather than national output.

Consider the traditional example of the Swiss watch industry – frequently used to illustrate decreasing costs which are also external to the firm. An increase in watch output (presumably a large increase, with a long time allowed for adjustment) would allow the development of additional specialized crafts and so generate economics of scale. World production is thus most efficient when world output of watches is concentrated in one country.[2] This is the usual argument – basically Adam Smith's pin-factory parable writ large.

But note that international specialization is not really central to this argument, if free trade in intermediate goods is possible. Economies could be realized just as well by having Swiss craftsmen concentrate on one part of the watch and German craftsmen on another as by having two groups of Swiss concentrate on the two parts. That is, international specialization could be entirely confined to the detailed operations comprising watch production and need not extend at all to the industry level. This view of scale economies as largely, or at least substantially, a matter of the division of labor is central to Adam Smith and subsequent extensions, such as Young (1928), and is also prominent in contemporary investigations.[3] The key is the division of the production process into a large number of distinct operations and not the concentration of the overall industry to a single place. The distinct operations can just as profitably be dispersed over the globe.

[2]But note that the argument does not indicate why Switzerland should be that country. This is a facet of the 'arbitrariness' referred to above.

[3]See Balassa (1961, 1967), Daly, Key, and Spence (1968), and also the many references cited in these works.

The neoclassical writers would not have subscribed to this view. For they envisioned the realization of economies of scale as an organic process[4] involving learning-by-doing and extensive communication between industry participants. Thus geographical concentration was taken as a matter of course.

Though such a presumption may have been quite natural in the nineteenth century, it is surely not so today. Advances in communications and transport have nearly fused the major industrial countries into a singular integrated economy within which former boundaries retain only residual significance as determinants of channels of technological communication. The dominant form of industrial organization is now the multinational corporation, arranging the stages of production on a global scale and internalizing relevant information flows. These firms rely on international pools of bankers and managers (not infrequently members of international trade organizations) and operate in a milieu significantly influenced by international bureaucracies and international academic communities. To a large (and increasing) degree trade consists of exchanges of intermediate industrial goods, significantly classifiable as intraindustry trade even on a fairly disaggregated basis. I doubt that an observer unfamiliar with the existing literature on increasing returns and international trade would ever spontaneously advance that literature's central and universal premise: that decreasing costs depend upon national output and not international output.

Let me not push the case too strongly. As long as communication is not perfect mere propinquity must go for something. Add to this historical cultural barriers. Nevertheless, the assumption in what follows that (with free trade) decreasing costs are a function solely of world output need not rest entirely on the efficiency of a direct focus on the central concern of this paper.

Some economies do require by their very nature that industry production be concentrated at a single place. Balassa (1967, ch. 5) refers to these as "economies of scale in the traditional sense" in contrast to 'horizontal specialization' and 'vertical specialization,' which he regards as more important and which correspond to the economies I have discussed above as due to the division of labor. I shall not treat such 'traditional' economies in what follows. These economies are specific to particular, narrowly-defined products whereas my analysis will be in terms of the usual two-sector, general-equilibrium approach. The very existence of these narrowly-defined products can itself be thought of as a consequence of economies of scale. Recall that, while discussing his pin factory, Smith noted that pin-making itself had been rendered a distinct trade by the division of labor. Furthermore, I do not think that explicit consideration of these economies would much influence

[4]See, for example, Taussig (1927, pp. 84–86).

what follows. The analysis can proceed on the assumption that all such economies are always fully exploited. This is because this paper will not depend upon a distinction between internal and external economies.

Since Marshall, writers have assumed that economies of scale are external to the firm. Occasional deviants were severely taken to task, and much of the literature involved whether such economies exist, either logically[5] or empirically. The reasons were the beliefs that the conclusions of the theory required perfect competition and that the latter was inconsistent with increasing returns internal to the firm.

International economies and free entry do indeed imply that in equilibrium industry output will be concentrated in one firm. But costless entry will constrain that firm to choose efficient techniques and to sell at average cost – precisely how the industry would behave if the economies were external.[6] There may be only one firm in existence, but potential competitors are what count, and costless entry means there are always plenty of these. However, in a two-sector economy with one sector a single firm, free entry appears far more stringent than in a world of many small competitors.[7] At any rate I assume that the industry possessing increasing returns is characterized by average-cost pricing, regardless of the number of firms.

3. Production

Consider a world of two goods, manufactures (M) and wheat (W). Manufactures are subject to increasing returns. The domestic scale m of manufacturing operations is related to domestic wheat output by a concave production-possibility frontier $m=T(W)$ of the usual neoclassical sort. An analogous curve $m^*=S(W^*)$ applies to the rest of the world (I employ asterisks to refer to the foreign country). The extent k of scale economies in manufacturing is defined by $k\equiv M/m$, where M denotes the output of manufactures.[8] Similarly $k^*\equiv M^*/m^*$.

The key point of departure of the present paper is the argument that k and k^* depend upon world manufacturing activity. I suppose accordingly that a percentage increase in $m+m^*$ increases $M+M^*$ by α percent, assuming for simplicity that α is constant (and greater than unity). Thus[9] with free trade

$$k=k^*=(m+m^*)^{\alpha-1}. \tag{1}$$

[5]See Chipman (1970) for a recent contribution.

[6]To my knowledge this has been recognized only by Murray Kemp (1969, 1976), and he appears to go to the opposite extreme of treating free entry as no more restrictive than usual.

[7]Thus one must not assume that Graham would have silenced Knight with such an argument.

[8]Note the assumption, common in the literature, that the production function for M is separable into m and k.

[9]The existing theory assumes by contrast that k depends on m alone and k^* on m^* alone. Note that I have simplified by assuming that k and k^* are identical functions of $m+m^*$.

The two countries are distinguished by the shapes of their production-possibility frontiers. Assume that $T' < S'$ whenever 'average outputs' are equal, $m/W = m^*/W^*$. This would be the case if the production-possibility frontiers were generated by a Heckscher–Ohlin production structure (without a separating factor-intensity reversal), and the home country was relatively abundant in the factor relatively intensive in the production of manufactures.

This assumption would ensure, with constant returns to scale ($k = 1 = k^*$), that the home country has a comparative advantage in manufactures, assuming away a 'demand reversal.' As the latter is of no concern, I suppose that the two countries possess identical Mill–Graham demand functions: everyone in the world always spends a constant proportion (γ) of his income on manufactures.

4. Efficient world output

Which allocations of production are efficient, in the sense that world outputs are on the world production-possibility frontier? Suppose that world wheat output $W + W^*$ is constrained to equal some feasible level. Then the problem is to find allocations of resources in the two countries which maximize the world output $M + M^*$ of manufactures subject to this constraint. But $M + M^* = (m + m^*)^\alpha$, so that maximizing $M + M^*$ is equivalent to maximizing $m + m^*$, regardless of the magnitude of α. In particular this is so if $\alpha = 1$; thus the efficient allocations with internationally decreasing costs are identical to those with constant returns to scale.

Proposition 1. Internationally increasing returns to scale have no effect upon the efficient patterns of production.

The efficient allocations are determined solely by the shapes of $T(W)$ and $S(W^*)$, and not at all by α. Therefore the home country has a comparative advantage in manufactures and the foreign country in wheat, if the term 'comparative advantage' is used in a purely normative sense.

From a technical point of view proposition 1 is trivial, once it has been formulated. Nonetheless it is fundamental, for it completely undercuts the standard model's pervasive tendency towards specialization and 'arbitrariness.'

Proposition 1 is basic, but I must be clear about what it does *not* say. (i) It does not mean that equilibrium output patterns, trade flows, and prices are independent of internationally increasing returns; the latter contribute to general equilibrium. (ii) Proposition 1 does not say anything about what will happen, only about what should happen for production efficiency. (iii) The proposition addresses only the allocation between manufactures and wheat, and not allocations within the manufacturing sector. As will subsequently become clear, intraindustry trade will in fact play an important role. (iv) 'Efficiency' refers, here and elsewhere, only to production efficiency. With average-cost pricing in manufactures, equilibrium will not in general be Pareto Optimal. This problem is familiar and I shall not subsequently allude to it. (But note that there are some interesting questions of national economic policy here, particularly if the increasing returns are due to economies external to the firm but internal to the *international* market.)

Formal illustrations[10]

In view of the importance of proposition 1 I briefly digress to illustrate it formally. The home production-possibility curve between manufactures and wheat is given by

$$M = kT(W) = [T(W) + m^*]^{\alpha-1} T(W). \tag{2}$$

If the rest of the world produces only wheat, or if the home economy is in autarky, in the sense that it derives no scale economies from foreign manufacturing, this becomes $M = T(W)^\alpha$. This is a curve with negative slope and a second derivative given by

$$\frac{d^2M}{dW^2} = \alpha m^{\alpha-1}\left[T'' + (\alpha-1)\frac{(T')^2}{T}\right]. \tag{3}$$

With 'Ricardian' constant costs ($T''=0$) the curve is convex to the origin; with constant returns to scale ($\alpha=1$) it is concave; in general it may be either convex or concave or some combination, depending upon the size of α and shape of T. Eq. (3) simply illustrates the well-known expression in Tinbergen (1945, eq. (6)).

But all this changes in an open economy if the rest of the world produces some manufactures. No longer is it meaningful to speak of *the* production-possibility frontier, because, as is clear from (2), its very shape depends upon the foreign pattern of production, and vice-versa. But proposition 1 in effect refers to the world production-possibility frontier, which is still meaningful.

Let W_0 and W_0^* denote the maximum possible outputs of wheat at home and abroad, so that $T(W_0) = 0 = S(W_0^*)$, and let W_1 be the level of domestic wheat production for which $T'(W_1) = S'(W_0^*)$, with W_1 set equal to zero if T is everywhere steeper than all points on S. The world production possibility frontier is illustrated by the curve $ABCD$ in fig. 1. Along AB the foreign country specializes to wheat and the home economy produces both goods, between B and C both countries produce both goods, and between C and D

[10]Subsections (with *italic* headings) can be skipped without loss of continuity.

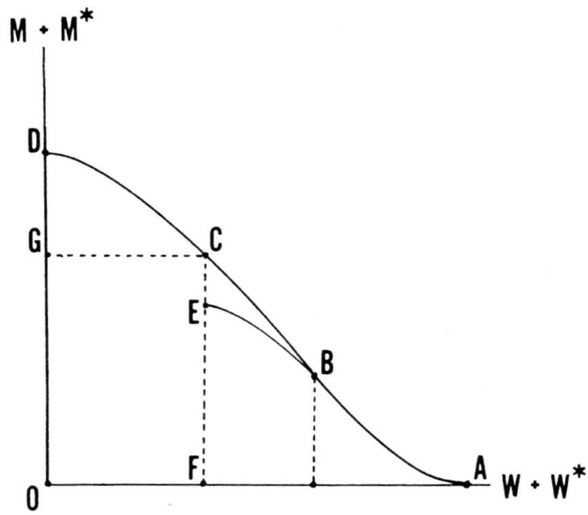

Fig. 1

the home country specializes to manufactures while the rest of the world diversifies. The domestic production bloc in autarky is $FABE$. This coincides with ABC on the world PPF when the foreign economy produces only wheat. The segment BC lies outside BE for two reasons: because the foreign economy is producing some manufactures (and less wheat), and also because foreign manufacturing shifts the domestic PPF upwards.

If T is everywhere steeper than all points of S (as in the Heckscher–Ohlin case if the two countries have sufficiently dissimilar relative factor endowments) points B and C coincide, so that one country always specializes, and FAB represents the domestic autarkic production block. However GCD does not represent the foreign block, because a movement from C towards D will increase the domestic output of manufactures. At $B(=C)$ the world PPF will now have a cusp, at which the ratio of the right-hand derivative to the left-hand derivative equals

$$\alpha T(0)^{\alpha-1}T'(0)/\alpha[T(0)+S(W_0^*)]^{\alpha-1}S'(W_0^*)=T'(0)/S'(W_0^*),$$

which is the size of the kink which the world PPF would have with constant returns to scale.

5. Autarkic equilibrium

In autarky international increasing returns must be indistinguishable from national increasing returns. Fig. 2 illustrates domestic autarkic equilibrium.

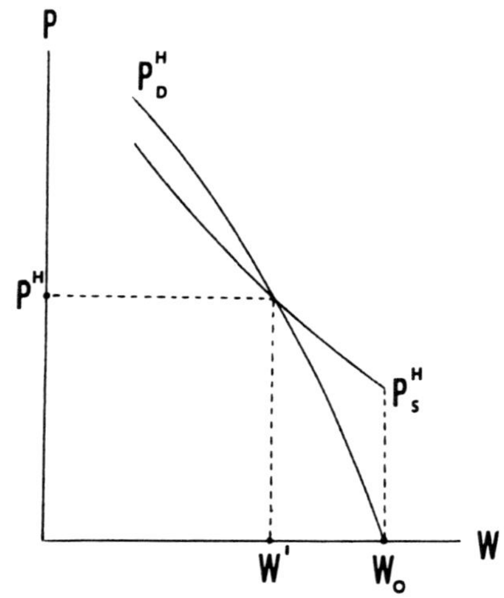

Fig. 2

P^H_D denotes the home relative demand price of wheat in terms of manufactures: the price that will equate demand to supply for any specific level of W and corresponding M. Thus $P^H_D=(1-\gamma)T(W)^{\alpha}/\gamma W$. Similarly P^H_S, the home relative supply price, denotes the price at which firms would willingly produce any specific level of W and corresponding M. Thus, with average-cost pricing in the manufacturing sector, $P^H_S=-kT'$ or $-T(W)^{\alpha-1}T'(W)$ in autarky. Intersection of the two curves determines equilibrium, so that the domestic relative autarkic price P^H is given by

$$P^H=-T(W')^{\bar{\alpha}-1}T'(W'), \tag{4}$$

where W' is the solution to $-T'(W)=(1-\gamma)T(W)/\gamma W$.

The P^H_D curve has a negative slope and is cut from below by the P^H_S curve. Thus W' is unique and stable with respect to the 'Marshallian' adjustment process: output increases whenever demand price exceeds supply price.

Note from (4) that P^H depends positively upon the scale variable $T(W')$: thus a larger country is likely to have a higher relative autarkic price of wheat than a small country. This is familiar from the existing literature on national increasing returns.

It is now apparent that there are two contrasting influences at work. If comparative advantage is defined with respect to production efficiency, proposition 1 says it is determined in the same way as with constant returns to scale. But if comparative advantage is defined in terms of relative autarkic prices it is determined in the same way as with national increasing returns. To see how these two tendencies interact, and what determines comparative advantage in the sense of a predictor of trade patterns, requires an analysis of international equilibrium.

6. International equilibrium: Allocation curves

International equilibrium is commonly analyzed with offer curves, which are also used by Marshall, Matthews, Meade, and Kemp for their discussions of increasing returns. I could do the same now, but the resulting analysis would be exceedingly cumbersome: international increasing returns imply that a movement along one country's offer curve results in a shift of the other. Therefore I shall develop a new analytical technique, that of allocation curves, which allows a cleaner and more direct treatment.

Each point in the planes of fig. 3 corresponds to a particular allocation of resources in both countries: the coordinates indicate wheat outputs, and the manufacturing scales follow from $m=T(W)$ and $m^*=S(W^*)$. An allocation curve can be drawn for each country. The domestic allocation curve AB indicates for each level W of home wheat output that foreign allocation (or allocations) of resources W^* which will cause the domestic economy to be in equilibrium in world markets. That is, W and W^* are on the home allocation curve if the world demand price P_D, which clears world markets when wheat output is $W+W^*$ and manufacturing output is $[T(W)+S(W^*)]^\alpha$, is equal to the home supply price P_S^H, for which domestic firms willingly supply the quantity W of wheat and $kT(W)$ of manufactures. Such a curve is illustrated by AB in each panel of fig. 3.

On the allocation curve $P_D=P_S^H$. A rise of W^* above the curve must reduce the world demand price as it increases world wheat output and lowers manufacturing output, both directly through reducing m^* and indirectly through reducing k. The supply price also falls because of the reduction in k. But the reduction in P_S^H must be less than that in P_D because the former is not affected directly by the fact that fewer manufactures are

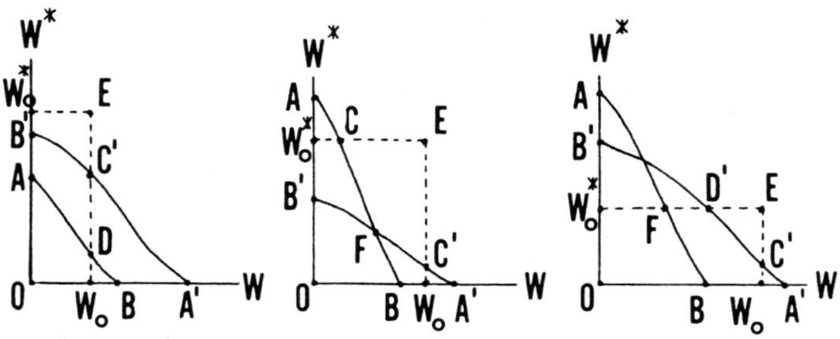

(a) (b) (c)

Fig. 3

being produced abroad. Thus $P_D < P_S^H$ above the allocation curve, and similarly $P_D > P_S^H$ below. Also the fall in demand price below supply price caused by a rise in W^* can be rectified for analogous reasons by a fall in W: the allocation curve must have a negative slope.

Point E in each panel of fig. 3 shows what wheat outputs in the two countries would be if both produce only wheat. Thus, with the given resources, only the rectangles $OW_0EW_0^*$ matter, and the portions of the curves lying outside these rectangles, such as the segment DB in fig. 3(a), are irrelevant. Also, if the domestic economy is specialized to wheat, domestic equilibrium is consistent with $P_D > P_S^H$, as there are no further resources to respond to the price differential by flowing from manufacturing to wheat. Similarly $P_D < P_S^H$ is consistent with domestic equilibrium if $W=0$. Thus the complete domestic allocation curve, taking into account existing resources, is given by $W_0^*ADW_0$ in fig. 3(a), by CB in fig. 3(b), and by FB in fig. 3(c).

A foreign allocation curve relating W to W^* can be described in analogous fashion. International equilibrium requires an allocation W and W^* which enables each country to be in equilibrium in the world economy:

Proposition 2. International equilibrium is given by the intersection of the two allocation curves.

This is illustrated in fig. 3. The three panels depict the three qualitatively distinct cases, with equilibrium denoted by F in each panel. The home country is specialized in manufacturing in panel (a), the foreign economy to wheat in panel (c), and both countries diversify in panel (b). Each country's supply price is relatively more sensitive to its own level of wheat output than to foreign, and I have assumed internationally identical demand conditions. Thus the home allocation curve is steeper than the foreign, and equilibrium is unique.

The two curves need not have an interior intersection, as required for (b). If they do, then $P_S^H = P_S^F$ in equilibrium (P_S^F denotes the foreign relative supply price), so that $-kT' = -kS'$ or $T' = S'$. Thus if T is everywhere steeper than all points on S such an intersection does not take place.[11] This is depicted in panel (a).

International equilibrium involves a pattern of production consistent with efficient world output, regardless of relative autarkic prices. The latter are thus poor indicators of comparative advantage, to which Proposition 1 emerges as centrally relevant.

[11]If T and S are generated by a Heckscher–Ohlin technology without a separating factor-intensity reversal, fig. 3(b) illustrates a case implying factor-price equalization. This is precluded by sufficiently dissimilar relative factor endowments.

Proposition 3. With free trade international equilibrium necessarily involves an efficient pattern of world production.

If the foreign country is relatively large it might indeed have a higher autarkic relative price of wheat than the home country, but this will not influence the equilibrium pattern of international trade.

6.1. *International equilibrium further considered*

The argument of the previous section, culminating in propositions 2 and 3, requires formal justification.

If W and W^* are the respective wheat outputs, the world demand price, with free trade, is given by $P_D = (1-\gamma)[T(W)+S(W^*)]^{\alpha}/\gamma[W+W^*]$. The home allocation curve is the collection of W and W^* for which $P_S^H = P_D$ and the foreign allocation curve the collection for which $P_S^F = P_D$. Substitution yields the following expressions for the interior parts of the home and foreign curves respectively:

$$(1-\gamma)[T(W)+S(W^*)]+\gamma T'(W)[W+W^*]=0, \tag{5}$$

$$(1-\gamma)[T(W)+S(W^*)]+\gamma S'(W^*)[W+W^*]=0. \tag{6}$$

Differentiation confirms that supply price exceeds demand price above a country's allocation curve and falls short below.

Let E denote the point in the W–W^* plane where the world specializes to wheat: $W = W_0$ and $W^* = W_0^*$. Consider the limiting value of P_D/P_S^H as point E is approached, with W converging to W_0 from below and W^* to W_0^* from below:

$$\lim \frac{P_D}{P_S^H} = \lim \frac{1-\gamma}{\gamma} \frac{T(W)+S(W^*)}{T'(W)[W+W^*]} = 0.$$

Similarly P_D/P_S^F converges to zero as E is approached from below. Thus, with $\gamma < 1$, the world demand price must exceed both supply prices near point E. This means that E lies above the interior parts of both allocation curves, so that the latter must pass through the rectangles $OW_0EW_0^*$ in fig. 3.

Implicit differentiation of (5) and (6) yields

$$\left.\frac{dW^*}{dW}\right|_{HA} = -\frac{T'+\gamma(W+W^*)T''}{\gamma T'+(1-\gamma)S'}, \tag{7}$$

$$\left.\frac{dW^*}{dW}\right|_{FA} = -\frac{\gamma S'+(1-\gamma)T'}{S'+\gamma(W+W^*)S''}, \tag{8}$$

which imply that both curves have negative slopes. Either the two curves intersect within $OW_0EW_0^*$ or not. Suppose they do. Then $P_S^H = P_S^F$ at the intersection, whence $T' = S'$. Then (7) and (8) imply that the home curve must be steeper at the intersection than the foreign. This means the intersection must be unique. It also means that the home allocation curve intersects the boundary OW_0^*E above and/or to the right of the foreign curve. This precludes an equilibrium on that boundary. Similarly the home allocation curve intersects the boundary OW_0E below and/or to the left of the foreign curve, ruling out an equilibrium on that boundary. The interior equilibrium is therefore unique; both countries diversify.

Suppose alternatively that the two allocation curves do not intersect in the interior of $OW_0EW_0^*$. Then one of the curves must lie outside the other everywhere inside the rectangle. Consider the point where the (interior) home allocation curve strikes the boundary OW_0E. There are two possibilities. (i) The intersection is on W_0E. Then at this point $W = W_0$ and W^* is the solution to $(1-\gamma)S(W^*) = -\gamma T'(W_0)[W_0 + W^*]$. Thus

$$P_D - P_S^F = S(W^*)^{\alpha-1}[(1-\gamma)S(W^*) + \gamma S'(W^*)(W_0 + W^*)]$$

$$= (1-\gamma)S(W^*)^{\alpha}\left[1 - \frac{S'(W^*)}{T'(W_0)}\right].$$

(ii) The intersection is on OW_0. Then $W^* = 0$ and W is the solution to $(1-\gamma)[T(W) + S(0)] = -\gamma T'(W)W$. Thus

$$P_D - P_S^F = [T(W) + S(0)]^{\alpha-1}[S'(0) - T'(W)].$$

In both cases the assumption I have made about the relative shapes of T and S implies that $P_D > P_S^F$. This means that the (interior) home allocation curve lies inside the foreign near OW_0E, and therefore throughout the rectangle as well. Accordingly there can be no equilibrium on OW_0E and there must be a unique equilibrium on OW_0^*E; in this equilibrium either the home country specializes to manufactures or the foreign country to wheat, or both.

6.2. *The Ricardian case*

The case where T' and S' are constant yields further insight and facilitates a more detailed analysis. Choose units so that $T' = -1$ and denote $-S'$ by s, which is less than unity. Then (7) and (8) reveal that the allocation curves are straight lines whose relative slopes reflect the pattern of 'comparative costs' s. The interior parts of the home and foreign curves are illustrated by the lines AB and $B'A'$ in fig. 4. The allocation curve technique allows all

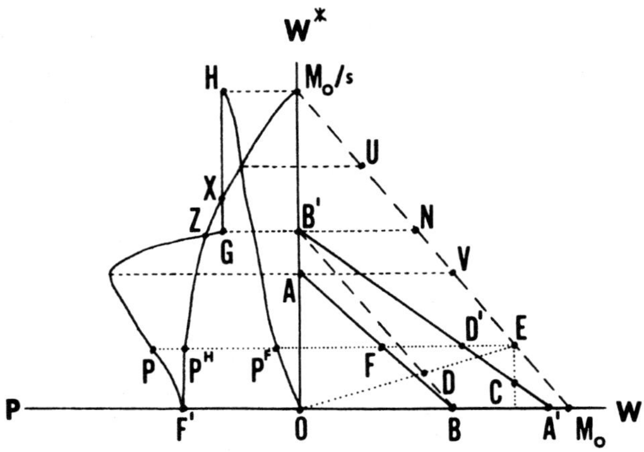

Fig. 4

relative country sizes W_0^*/W_0 to be considered without shifting the (interior) allocation curves. This is because, as (5) and (6) confirm, those curves are invariant as long as W_0 and W_0^* are constrained by a constant world capacity of manufacturing scale $M_0 = W_0 + sW_0^*$. This is depicted by the dashed line $(M_0/s)M_0$ in fig. 4. Specifying any endowment, such as E, determines the relevant rectangle $(OW_0^*EW_0)$ and completes the allocation curves (FB for the home country and $W_0^*D'C'$ for the foreign). Free-trade equilibrium is thus at F. Accordingly VM indicates the range of relative endowments for which the foreign country specializes to wheat and the home country diversifies, NV the range for which foreigners specialize to wheat and the home economy to manufactures, and $(M_0/s)N$ the range for which the foreign economy diversifies while domestic production is concentrated in manufacturing.

The dashed line $B'B$ – parallel to $(M_0/s)M_0$ but only the fraction $(1-\gamma)$ as far from the origin – indicates autarkic equilibria. Thus with endowment E the allocations in autarky are indicated by point D.

The three curves in the left-hand quadrant of fig. 4 depict the free trade and respective autarkic relative prices of wheat corresponding to each possible endowment E on $(M_0/s)M_0$. The curve $F'PGH$ indicates the free trade price, $F'P^{H}(M_0/s)$ the home autarkic price, and $OP^{F}H$ the foreign autarkic price. Thus with endowment E, points P, P^{H}, and P^{F} denote the respective relative prices. The segment $U(M_0/s)$ depicts the range of endowments where comparative autarkic prices incorrectly predict comparative advantage.

Sliding E along $(M_0/s)M_0$ thus allows all possible free-trade and autarkic equilibria for both countries to be completely illustrated. A few of the resulting observations warrant explicit mention.

Note first that, in contrast to the case of constant returns to scale, free trade prices always differ from autarkic prices, with the possible exception of the two singular cases corresponding to points X and Z (and of course the cases where the world consists of only one country). Furthermore the country (foreign) with the comparative advantage in wheat must always experience an increase in the relative price of wheat as a result of trade. This implies that that country must gain from trade, no matter how large her relative size. Thus an international character to increasing returns invalidates an old argument against free trade.

The home country autarkic price curve may or may not cut the terms of trade curve and pass outside point G as illustrated (it will do so if and only if $s>\gamma^{\alpha-1}$). If it does, there will exist a range of relative endowments, contained in the interval UV, yielding the conventional result that the terms of trade falls between the relative autarkic prices. Otherwise the relative price of wheat must rise in both countries as a result of trade (and this always happens in the intervals $(M_0/s)U$ and VM_0). This reflects the fact that merely opening the countries up to trade increases manufacturing productivity, even without reallocations of resources between the two sectors in either country.

7. Stability

The allocation curve simplifies the treatment of the Marshallian dynamic adjustment process, according to which an industry is expanding if demand price exceeds supply price. This is because the curves subdivide the plane on the basis of the relation between world demand price and supply price in each country. Thus it is easy to see that the equilibria in fig. 3 are in fact stable, with a noncyclical approach to equilibrium in each case.

A more complex and interesting situation is depicted in fig. 5 (where I have temporarily abandoned the assumption of identical Mill–Graham demand functions). The home allocation curve is $W_0^*ADW_0$ and the foreign $W_0A'B'$. Equilibria are depicted at B', F', F, F'', and W_0; arrows depict the directions of movement. Clearly the equilibria are alternatively stable and unstable, with stable equilibria at B', F, and W_0, and unstable at F' and F''.

Fig. 5 suggests an interesting result. Imagine the allocation curves to be offer curves, with home and foreign wheat production playing the role of 'imports' and 'exports' respectively. Define ε as the domestic offer-curve elasticity in the usual way (percentage fall in W/percentage rise in (W^*/W)), with ε equal to minus infinity along W_0^*A where an improvement in the 'terms of trade' is accompanied by a finite fall in 'exports.' Similarly ε^* denotes the elasticity of the foreign 'offer curve.' Then fig. 5 illustrates the following result, easily confirmed by experimenting with other hypothetical cases.

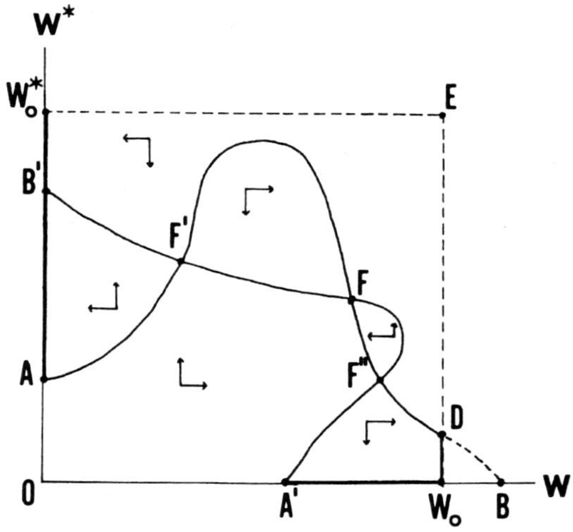

Fig. 5

Proposition 4. If an equilibrium has a negative elasticity for a country producing both goods it is unstable. Otherwise stability is equivalent to the violation *of the familiar Marshall–Lerner condition.*

Point F', where $\varepsilon < 0$ and $\varepsilon^* < 1$, illustrates the first sentence of proposition 4. The Marshall–Lerner condition is met at F'' and violated at B', F, and W_0.

Proof of proposition 4

Write $P_D = \phi(W, W^*)$, $P_S^H = \psi(W, W^*)$ and $P_S^F = \psi^*(W, W^*)$. I assume[12] that an increase in either country's wheat output reduces the demand price both absolutely and relatively to that country's supply price, and lowers the other country's supply price:

$$\phi_W, \phi_{W^*}, \phi_W - \psi^*_{W^*}, \phi_{W^*} - \psi^*_{W^*}, \psi_{W^*}, \psi^*_{W^*} < 0 \tag{9}$$

The (interior) home and foreign allocation curves $W^* = A(W)$ and $W = A^*(W^*)$ are the respective solutions to $\phi = \psi$ and $\phi = \psi^*$. The dynamic adjustment process can be represented by:

$$\hat{W} = [\phi(W, W^*)/\psi(W, W^*)] - 1,$$

$$\hat{W} = [\phi(W, W^*)/\psi^*(W, W^*)] - 1,$$

[12]These assumptions are implied by, but much weaker than, the model of section 3.

where $\hat{W}$ denotes $(1/W)(\mathrm{d}W/\mathrm{d}t)$, etc. The local stability conditions of this system reduce to

$$a_{11}+a_{22}<0, \tag{10}$$

$$a_{12}a_{21}-a_{11}a_{22}<0, \tag{11}$$

where $a_{11}=W(\phi_{\mathrm{W}}-\psi_{\mathrm{W}})/\phi$, $a_{22}=W^*(\phi_{\mathrm{W}*}-\psi^*_{\mathrm{W}*})/\phi$, $a_{12}=W(\phi_{\mathrm{W}*}-\psi_{\mathrm{W}*})/\phi$, and $a_{21}=W^*(\phi_{\mathrm{W}}-\psi^*_{\mathrm{W}})/\phi$.

The 'offer-curve elasticity' is defined by

$$\varepsilon\equiv\frac{-(W^*/W)}{W}\ \frac{\mathrm{d}W}{\mathrm{d}(W^*/W)}$$
$$=W^*/(W^*-WA')=W^*a_{12}/(W^*a_{12}+Wa_{11}).$$

Similarly $\varepsilon^*=Wa_{21}/(Wa_{21}+Wa_{22})$. Substitution yields the following expression for the 'Marshall–Lerner' term:

$$\varepsilon+\varepsilon^*-1=\frac{\varepsilon\varepsilon^*}{a_{21}a_{22}}(a_{12}a_{21}-a_{11}a_{22}). \tag{12}$$

Assumption (9) implies that $a_{12}<0$ and $a_{21}<0$. The following possibilities exist. (i) $\varepsilon,\varepsilon^*<0$. Then a_{11} and a_{22} are necessarily positive and the system is unstable. (ii) $\varepsilon>0$, $\varepsilon^*<0$. If $\varepsilon+\varepsilon^*<1$, then (12) implies that (11) is violated. If $\varepsilon+\varepsilon^*>1$, then necessarily $\varepsilon>1$ and $\varepsilon^*<0$, implying $a_{11}>0$ and $a_{22}>0$ so that (10) is violated. (iii) $\varepsilon<1$, $\varepsilon^*>0$. This is completely analogous to (ii). (iv) ε, $\varepsilon^*>0$. Then (12) implies that $\varepsilon+\varepsilon^*>1$ is equivalent to the violation of (11). If $\varepsilon+\varepsilon^*<1$, (11) is met and furthermore $\varepsilon<1$, $\varepsilon^*<1$ which implies that $a_{11}<0$, $a_{22}<0$ so that (10) is met as well. This completes the proof of proposition 4 for an internal equilibrium. The boundary cases, which are tedious but straightforward, are left to the reader.[13]

The above dynamic process (not to be confused with that used by Marshall in his foreign-trade discussions (1930, 1960)) is straightforward enough. But note that it abstracts from both an irreversibility of increasing returns and any dynamic aspect to the realization of scale economies-notions prominent in the neoclassical literature.

8. Trade in intermediate goods

Thus far I have been concerned solely with the exchange of wheat for

[13]See Ethier (1978) for a complete proof (including boundary cases) of the special case of proposition 4 for which $\psi_{\mathrm{W}*}=0=\psi^*_{\mathrm{W}}$ (which excludes internationally decreasing costs).

manufactures. But, since the source of internationally decreasing costs is world-wide specialization *within* the manufacturing sector, trade in intermediate manufactures must also be prominent. Indeed the principal argument of this paper is that in the modern world economy decreasing costs imply (intraindustry) trade in intermediate manufactures rather than 'arbitrary' patterns of industry specialization.

A complete description of such intermediate-goods trade requires details of the manufacturing sector beyond the scope of this paper. But some general conclusions can be drawn even with the present description of manufactures as a single, aggregate good produced by an integrated world-wide industry. If the foreign country specializes to wheat there is no trade in intermediates. Otherwise the volume of such trade must be at least as large as I_m, the smaller of the two national outputs of manufactures.

Proposition 5. The minimum possible volume of trade in intermediate goods is equal to the smaller of km and km.*

The line $E'E$ in fig. 6 below depicts the combinations of wheat outputs for which $T(W) = S(W^*)$. Thus domestic output of manufactures exceeds foreign output above $E'E$ and vice-versa below. The line HKN in panel (a) depicts

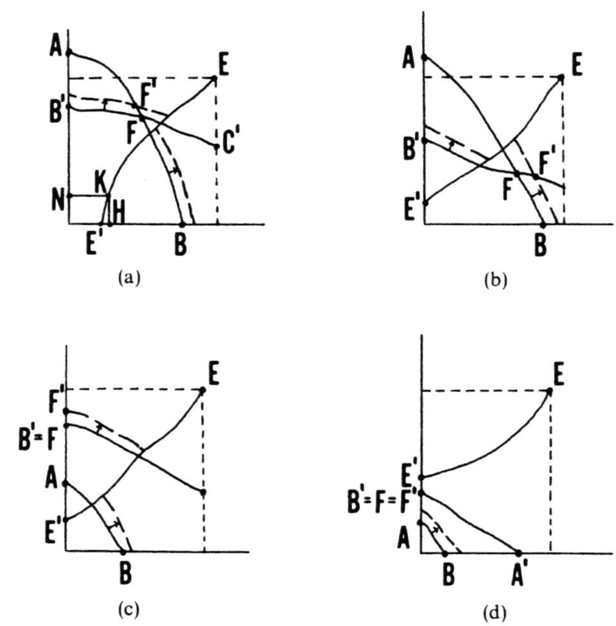

Fig. 6

an I_m contour: allocations of W and W^* yielding identical values of I_m. Movements away from the origin pass through contours corresponding to successively lower values of I_m, with K moving along $E'E$.

Two examples usefully illustrate the argument. Suppose first that the world manufacturing sector consists of the independent production of separate components which can be costlessly assembled into the single final manufactured good. The scale economies are associated with the number of components, with the two countries specializing, in free trade, in the production of distinct components. Then the volume of trade in intermediate goods must equal $M[M_c^*/(M+M^*)]+M^*[M_c/(M+M^*)]$, where M_c and M_c^* denote domestic and foreign consumption of (finished) manufactures. Since $M_c+M_c^*=M+M^*$, this volume equals I_m if $M=M^*$ and exceeds it otherwise. There need be no trade involving final manufactures, so that intermediates are exchanged for wheat as well as each other. Unless enough additional structure is put into the model to mandate the assignment of specific components to the two countries, the volume of intraindustry trade corresponding to any specific disaggregation of manufactures must be indeterminate.

For the second example suppose the world manufacturing sector has a vertical structure in which output passes through successive 'stages' to emerge as finished manufactures. The volume of trade in intermediates will be minimized (and equal to I_m) if the country with the smaller manufacturing sector performs the earlier stages and exports its output to the other country. International trade will then involve the exchange of wheat, finished manufactures, and a specific type of unfinished manufactured good. But without additional structure the volume of trade in intermediate goods, as well as of intraindustry trade (for any specified disaggregation), must be indeterminate, because the stages can be distributed between the two countries in any way: manufactures might pass back and forth between the two countries many times in the course of the international production process. The volume of trade in intermediates, as well as the variety of goods entering into such trade, is limited above only by the number of stages. But if this trade is measured only with respect to value-added, so that essentially entrepôt trade is netted out, the volume cannot exceed the world output of manufactures. Thus it is bounded by I_m and $M+M^*$.

These examples should make clear that proposition 5 is about as far as it is possible to go without a more specific model. Clearly there is much work to be done in the way of formulating and exploring such models. Such work would also address the relation between nationally increasing returns and internationally increasing returns.

One further point deserves mention. The more alike the two economies are, the more evenly will they share the world production of manufactures. While this limits the scope for the interindustry exchange of wheat and manufactures emphasized by the conventional theory, it enlarges that for intraindustry exchanges of intermediate manufactured goods.

Proposition 6. Internationally decreasing costs imply a presumption that a greater similarity of $T(W)$ and $S(W^*)$ results in a larger volume of trade in intermediate manufactured goods, both absolutely and relatively to the volume of interindustry trade.

If T and S are sufficiently different so that the foreign country specializes to wheat, international trade will consist entirely of the exchange of wheat for finished manufactures. At the other extreme, there is no basis at all for interindustry trade if T and S are identical, and international trade would consist of the exchange of intermediate (and perhaps finished) manufactures.

This can be looked at from a different point of view. Suppose T and S are generated by a Heckscher–Ohlin model, and that some capital is moved from the capital-abundant country to the other. This will substitute for international trade in wheat and manufactures, so that the volume of such trade will probably fall, as is well known. But, since this will probably also tend to equalize the sizes of the manufacturing sectors in the two countries, it will stimulate intraindustry trade in intermediates; if k is large such trade could be greatly stimulated.[14]

9. Tariffs on trade in intermediate goods

Assume that the world manufacturing sector is similar to that discussed in the second example of section 8. That is, manufactures are produced by a (timeless) integrated global process in which output passes through (a continuum of) successive stages before emerging as finished goods. An expansion of world activity raises k by allowing the employment of additional stages.

How is international equilibrium influenced by commercial policy? Many types of policy could be considered, but I shall focus on just one: a uniform tariff levied by both countries on all intermediate manufactures, with trade in wheat and finished manufactures remaining free, and with tariff revenues spent like other income. I consider this policy both because it applies to the distinct assumptions of this paper, and also because it is natural to wonder whether the results summarized in propositions 1–6 are in fact crucially dependent upon free trade in intermediates.

Suppose then that the two countries impose such a tariff on all imports of

[14] I leave to the reader the task of formalizing this by proving the present model's version of the Rybczynski Theorem. Clearly the magnitude of k and the sizes of the two manufacturing sectors will figure prominently in such a theorem.

intermediate goods.[15] World production of manufactures will then arrange itself[16] so that the country with the smaller manufacturing sector produces the earlier stages. Trade in intermediates will therefore equal I_m, and tariffs will actually be collected only by the country with the larger manufacturing sector. The tariff of the other country will appear redundant, but it will not in fact be so.

The world demand price P_D will still equal $(1-\gamma)(M+M^*)/\gamma(W+W^*)$, since the tariff does not apply to finished manufactures. Suppose first that the home country has the larger manufacturing sector: $T(W)>S(W^*)$. Then, with a tariff, output will consist of finished manufactures and perhaps wheat, both free of tax. Thus home supply price is still $P_S^H=-kT'$, so that the home allocation curve is not affected by the tariff. If, on the other hand, $T(W)<S(W^*)$, the home manufacturing sector produces intermediates which are subject to the foreign tariff. The home supply price is accordingly equal to $P_S^H=-kT'/(1+t)$, which implies that the allocation curve shifts out. Similar considerations apply to the foreign country.

Proposition 7. The imposition by both countries of a common tariff on intermediate manufactured goods shifts the home allocation curve out where $T<S$ and leaves it unchanged where $T>S$. The foreign allocation curve shifts out where $T>S$ and is unchanged where $S>T$. Also home manufacturing concentrates on earlier stages and foreign manufacturing on later stages when $T<S$, and vice versa where $T>S$.

The results are illustrated in fig. 6. The separate panels depict the four possible initial states of interest; if the foreign country initially specializes to wheat, intermediate goods do not enter trade and so the tariff has no effects.

If the home country specializes to manufactures but is small enough so that its manufacturing sector is nonetheless smaller than the foreign, as in panel (d), a small tariff has no effects beyond the international rearrangement of the stages of production. Supply price initially exceeds the world price, so the reduction in the former produced by the tariff does not matter. In all other cases a (small) tariff involves a shift of one allocation curve and movement along the other. Algebraic manipulation confirms that world wheat output increases while manufacturing production falls. If the home economy produces no wheat, as in panel (a), this is brought about entirely via a reallocation of resources in the foreign country, although domestic output also falls because of the reduction in k.

[15]It is easy to see that, if only one country levies the tariff, this country will produce the earlier stages and the other country the later stages, no tariffs will actually be collected, and the preceding analysis will be unchanged.

[16]It might be conjectured that the scale economies are due to some type of externalities that removes all incentives for the manufacturing sector to minimize its exposure to the tariff. I will not further consider this possibility.

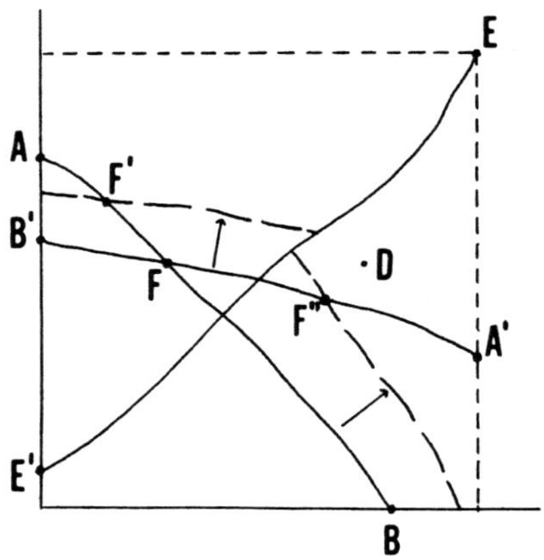

Fig. 7

If neither country specializes, the common tariff will also induce an international reallocation of manufacturing activity from the country with the smaller manufacturing sector to that with the larger. This produces the striking result that manufacturing production becomes more concentrated, not less, as a result of protection. This is clear in panels (a) and (b) of fig. 6. Note that the reallocation may run counter to the pattern of comparative advantage or not.

A large tariff can generate multiple equilibria, as illustrated in fig. 7. The two tariff-ridden equilibria differ with respect to which country has the larger manufacturing sector. Thus they imply opposite arrangements of the stages of production, and opposite directions for the reallocation of manufacturing activity.

If proposition 4 is applied to fig. 7, both F' and F'' are stable. But if F is the initial position, the economy will in fact converge to F' so that F'' is irrelevant and the above small-tariff discussion applies, with fig. 7 equivalent to fig. 6(a).

But there are two reasons to be sceptical about such a dynamic argument. First, if the economy is initially in autarkic equilibrium at D a movement from autarky to limited trade would establish equilibrium at F''.

Second, the dynamic adjustment process discussed in section 7 does not specifically involve the rearrangement of the stages of production implied by a tariff. In free trade the arrangement is indeterminate; suppose that in fact the home country produces the earlier stages and the foreign country the latter. As this is the same arrangement as at F'', and opposite that at F', one can easily imagine that a dynamic process incorporating this consideration would move the economy from F to F''. Apparently there is scope for considerable work involving adjustment in a tariff-ridden context.

One might conjecture that a barrier to intermediate-goods trade could in fact cause an overlapping of stages in the two countries, or the (partial or complete) development of independent nationally-integrated industries in addition to the effects discussed in this section. Such a conjecture is false. Space precludes a detailed discussion.

10. Concluding remarks

This paper has advanced and investigated the idea that increasing returns depend upon the scale of the world market rather than that of the national market. This consideration removes from the theory its emphasis upon multiple equilibrium and provides instead a basis for a theory of trade in intermediate goods between similar economies. A secondary purpose has been to illustrate the allocation-curve technique. Specific conclusions are summarized in the seven propositions and need not be repeated now; in general they clearly bring the theory into much closer resemblance to the facts of modern trade.[17]

In some ways this paper must be regarded as a preliminary treatment of the subject it raises. I have indicated several places above where further formal development appears warranted, and other instances should be apparent. Also those ideas should be further investigated in conjunction with those topics to which they have a natural affinity, such as international capital movements, the multinational firm, and the theory of time-phased systems.

The virtually complete concentration for so many years of the increasing-returns-and-trade literature upon the case of nationally increasing returns is a puzzle, in view of the great difference that assumption makes. One reason, as mentioned earlier, is that the ease of communication, the predominance of the international firm, and the integrated world economy have to a significant degree only recently appeared. But this can hardly be a complete explanation. The preoccupation of much of the earlier literature on the use of increasing returns as a justification for protection may also be part of the reason. But more important, I think, is the nature of the internal development of the theory of international trade.

The idea of internationally decreasing costs is at bottom an application to the world arena of Adam Smith's notion of the gains from the division of labor, independently of its geographical location. International trade theory has by contrast followed Ricardo in examining the international allocation of specified production processes. Cairnes (1874, pp. 297–302) clearly distinguished the two possible sources of gains from trade. But he argued that the former had little to do with international trade and indeed went so far as

[17] I have struggled manfully against the temptation to continually call attention to this fact.

to say that this was one of the principle factors distinguishing domestic trade from foreign trade. In this he was clearly influenced by his view of the world of his day. More recently, Grubel and Lloyd (1975) and Balassa (1975) have noted the tendency for trade liberalization to stimulate intraindustry trade rather than interindustry specialization, and have speculated that significant economies result. But the implication for the pure theory of international trade was not pursued. Harberler (1936, pp. 130–131) repeated Cairnes' argument and also linked it to the familiar examples of increasing returns and trade, but only on a national level.

The sole explicit reference to internationally decreasing costs which I have found in the literature is a single paragraph in Viner (1965, p. 480). As it is quite short I shall quote it in full (so that the present paper will contain the total existing literature on its subject):

> In the first place, if the external economies are a function of the size of the world industry, and not of the national portion of it, as may well be the case, they will still be retained by a national industry which shrinks in size if this shrinkage is offset by a corresponding expansion of the foreign industry. Suppose that as the watch industry as a whole expands and increases its purchases of watchmaking machinery, such machinery can consequently be obtained at lower unit prices. If there is free trade in machinery, this economy in machinery costs will not be lost to the watch industry in a particular country merely because it is shrinking in size, if there is no shrinkage in the size of the watch industry as a whole.

Viner is here advancing internationally decreasing costs as a reason to reject Frank Graham's argument for protection. Section 6.1 demonstrated that they can fulfill this role.

References

Balassa, B., ed., 1975, European economic integration (North-Holland, Amsterdam).

Balassa, B., 1961, The theory of economic integration (Irwin, Homewood).

Balassa, B., 1967, Trade liberalization among industrial countries (McGraw-Hill, New York).

Cairnes, J.E., 1874, Some leading principles of political economy newly expounded (Macmillan, London).

Chipman, J., 1970, External economies of scale and competitive equilibrium, Quarterly Journal of Economics 84, 347–385.

Chipman, J., 1965, A survey of the theory of international trade: Part 2, The neoclassical theory, Econometrica 33, 685–760.

Daly, D.J., B.A. Keys and E.J. Spence, 1968, Scale and specialization in Canadian manufacturing, Staff study no. 21, Economic Council of Canada.

Edgeworth, F.Y., 1874, The theory of international values, II, Economic Journal 4, 424–443.

Ethier, W., 1978, Increasing returns to scale and international trade, mimeo.

Grubel, H.G. and P.J. Lloyd, 1975, Intra-industry trade: The theory and measurement of international trade in differentiated products (Macmillan, London).

Haberler, G., 1936, The theory of international trade, with its applications to commercial policy (W. Hodge, London).

Kemp, M., 1976, Three topics in the theory of international trade: Distribution, welfare and uncertainty (North-Holland, Amsterdam).
Kemp, M., 1969, The pure theory of international trade and investment (Prentice-Hall, Englewood Cliffs).
Marshall, A., 1960, Money, credit, and commerce (Augustus Kelley, New York)..
Marshall, A., 1930, The pure theory of foreign trade and the pure theory of domestic values (London School of Economics and Political Science, London).
Matthews, R.C.O., 1949/50, Reciprocal demand and increasing returns, Review of Economic Studies 17, 149–158.
Meade, J.E., 1952, A geometry of international trade (George Allen and Unwin, London).
Panagariya, A., 1978, Variable returns to scale in production and patterns of specialization, mimeo.
Taussig, F.W., 1927, International trade (Macmillan, New York).
Tinbergen, J., 1945, International economic cooperation (Elsevier, Amsterdam).
Viner, J., 1965, Studies in the theory of international trade (Augustus Kelley, New York).
Young, A., 1928, Increasing returns and economic progress, Economic Journal 38, 527–542.

National and International Returns to Scale in the Modern Theory of International Trade

By WILFRED J. ETHIER*

For over a quarter century, the Heckscher-Ohlin-Samuelson (H-O-S) trade model has thoroughly dominated work in the pure theory of international trade. Indeed this model is often identified as "the" modern theory of trade. But this dominance has always been rendered uneasy by a widespread suspicion that the salient facts of modern commerce are inconsistent with the theoretical structure. Two broad areas of suspicion may be identified.

The first, concerned with whether actual trade patterns and factor endowments are related as predicted by the theory, consists of the Leontief Paradox and the huge volume of work it stimulated. My interpretation of this literature is that the factor-endowments theory of trade fares reasonably well, but that its two-factor, two-commodity version is essentially an inadequate description of reality. I have on other occasions investigated the consequences of many goods and factors, and do not wish to do so now. This paper will accordingly confine itself to a factor-endowments model with two primary factors and two final goods.

The second (by no means unrelated) area of suspicion centers on the stylized fact that the largest and fastest growing component of world trade since World War II has been the exchange of manufactures between the industrialized economies. By contrast, the H-O-S model, and neoclassical theory generally, sees little basis for trade between similar economies. Two manifestations of this point may be found in the empirical literature. The first, of relevance to international monetary problems, concerns departures from purchasing-power parity among the industrial countries even for fairly disaggregated indices of traded goods (see Irving Kravis and Richard Lipsey). The second, a central concern of this paper, involves intraindustry trade.

Although two-way trade had long been observed, it first became of major concern when economists investigated the consequences of economic integration in Europe (see, for example, P. J. Verdoorn; Bela Balassa, 1966) and noted a tendency, not towards increased specialization, but rather for all countries to simultaneously increase exports of most categories of manufactures. Indeed in some cases specialization actually declined. Subsequent work divorced the phenomenon of intraindustry trade from economic integration, and exposed the pervasive expansion of such trade between all industrial countries and across most manufacturing sectors, irrespective of tariff barriers or their changes (Helmut Hesse; Herbert Grubel and Peter Lloyd, 1975; Emilio Pagoulatos and Robert Sorenson; and Richard Caves), furthermore this expansion does not appear to be a matter of transition between equilibria[1] (Caves).

The most natural explanations of intraindustry trade, advanced by Gottfried Haberler (p. 34) long ago, are product heterogeneity within aggregates and border trade (and its seasonal analog). But accumulated empirical work (for example, Hesse; Grubel and Lloyd, 1975; and Caves) strongly suggests that these explanations are inadequate.[2] Attention has

*Professor of economics, University of Pennsylvania. The research for this paper was supported by the National Science Foundation under grant no. SES-7925614. I have benefitted from seminars at the universities of Pennsylvania, Western Ontario, and Wisconsin, and Northwestern University. Richard Caves also supplied useful comments and suggestions.

[1] See Gary Hufbauer and John Chilas for a contrasting argument that intra-industry trade is due to the GATT method of tariff reduction and to transitory responses with quasi-fixed factors of production. Joseph M. Finger also offers some contrasting evidence.

[2] Grubel and Lloyd (1975), for example, found significant Australian intraindustry trade even at the seven-digit level. I do not mean to suggest that such trade indicates a violation of commodity arbitrage and

accordingly shifted to product differentiation and economies of scale (in theory the two go together, as scale economies supply the limitation to the degree of differentiation).[3]

International trade theory does contain a sizable literature on increasing returns to scale (see, for example, R. C. O. Matthews; James Meade; and Murray Kemp, 1969), but this literature would not appear to offer much that is relevant to the phenomenon at issue. Indeed it has not on balance had great influence on trade theory generally. This is no doubt largely because increasing returns establish a strong presumption for complete specialization, multiple equilibria, and indeterminancy, conclusions that both vitiate the standard comparative statics methodology of trade theory and that also bear questionable relevance to the facts of contemporary trade. Furthermore, this theory has generally assumed that the economies of scale were external to the firm and appropriate at an aggregate level, assumptions that preclude much relevance to intraindustry trade. Empirical work has likewise encountered difficulty in coming to grips with scale economies, although many researchers have argued their importance (for example, Balassa, 1961, 1967; Donald J. Daly et al., Nicholas Owen, and Caves), and some have found relevance to intraindustry trade.

Recently I pointed out (1979a) that scale economies resulting from an increased division of labor rather than from, say, an increased plant size, depended at an aggregate level upon the size of the world market rather than upon geographical concentration of the industry, as supposed in the traditional theory. Such "international" returns to scale were shown to be free of the presumption of indeterminancy and multiple equilibria[4] characteristic of "national" returns to scale, to imply a theory of intraindustry trade in intermediate goods, and generally to lead to conclusions much more in accord with the stylized facts of modern trade.

The purpose of this paper is to argue that, in the context of international returns, the factor-endowments theory is consistent with, and indeed helps to explain, the stylized facts discussed above. In order to do this I shall construct a simple but detailed model yielding international returns to scale, and employ this model to systematically explore the relations between such international returns, the traditional national returns to scale, and the modern (or factor endowments) theory of international trade. I have four broad messages. 1) International returns depend in an essential way on an interaction between the two types of scale economies, which is also an interaction of internal and external (to the firm) economies. 2) The basic theorems of the factor-endowments theory are essentially robust in the presence of such scale economies, in contrast to the conclusions of the traditional literature.[5] Nevertheless there are some important modifications. 3) Intraindustry trade, like interindustry trade, has a factor-endowments basis. However, such trade is basically *complementary* to international factor mobility. 4) Although the existence of internal-scale economies and product differentiation are essential to the theory, the degree of such phenomena need not be an essential determinant of the degree of intraindustry trade.

Recently Paul Krugman (1979, 1981); Avinash Dixit and Viktor Norman; Elhanen Helpman; and Colin Lawrence and Pablo Spiller have extended to an international context the Avinash Dixit-Joseph Stiglitz formalization of Chamberlinian monopolistic

could not be made to disappear completely in the face of relentless disaggregation. Indeed the theory to follow will make use of product differentiation. Rather the point is that intraindustry trade appears significant even with sufficient disaggregation to remove relative cost differences between sectors as a likely determinant of such trade, so that the traditional theory, while not necessarily contradicted, fails to offer an explanation.

[3]Theoretical discussions of intraindustry trade can be found in Grubel; H. Peter Gray; Grubel and Lloyd (1975); and Robert Davies.

[4]International scale economies actually "bury" these problems rather than eliminate them, as will become clear below.

[5]In this respect the present paper complements recent work establishing the general validity of the basic H-O-S propositions. See Kemp (1976); Ronald Jones and José Scheinkman; my 1974, 1979b articles; Winston Chang, et al.

competition; and Kelvin Lancaster has also applied to international trade his product-characteristics approach to consumption theory. These authors are concerned with the same stylized facts that my earlier paper (1979a) had been, and they reach some broadly analogous conclusions, although from entirely different theoretical starting points. The present paper is not concerned with the differentiated consumer goods that are their subject. However I do hope to treat the differentiated producer goods central to my own theory in such a way as to bring out the parallels between the approaches of these other authors and my earlier work on intra-industry trade (I cannot resist the temptation to point out that producers' goods are in fact much more prominent in trade than are consumers' goods).

I. National and International Scale Economies

A. *Production*

Capital and labor combine to produce wheat (W) and manufactures (M). Wheat is produced subject to constant returns to scale via a smooth production function of the familiar sort. Manufactures, on the other hand, are potentially subject to increasing returns to scale, and I suppose that the production function for M is separable in the sense that I can write $M = km$, where k is an index of scale economies and m an index of the scale of operations; m can be thought of as produced via a familiar smooth production function. Thus the endowment of capital and labor determines a transformation curve:

$$W = T(m). \tag{1}$$

The possibility of returns to scale in manufacturing arises, first, from exploitation of the division of labor, as in the hoary examples of Adam Smith's pin factory and the Swiss watch industry. Finished manufactures are costlessly assembled from intermediate manufactured components.[6] The number n of components that are actually produced will be endogenously determined, and, I assume, only a fraction of a large number of potentially producible intermediate goods.[7] I am not interested in issues which depend upon distinctions between potential intermediate goods, so I assume that they are all producible from capital and labor via identical production functions, and that all produced components contribute in totally symmetric fashion to the finished manufactures. Under these assumptions, all components which are actually produced will be produced in equal amounts, and I denote the output of each such component by x, so that the total number of produced components of all types is nx. Assume that the output of finished manufactures is given by

$$M = n^{\alpha-1}(nx) \tag{2}$$

for some parameter $\alpha > 1$. It will be convenient to adopt the following specific form of the production function (2), where x_i denotes the quantity of the ith component and β is a parameter, $1 > \beta > 0$.

$$M = n^{\alpha}\left[\sum_{i=1}^{n}\left(x_i^{\beta}/n\right)\right]^{1/\beta}. \tag{2'}$$

With all the x_i equal to a common x, as will be the case in equilibrium, (2′) reduces to (2). A higher value of β indicates that components can be more easily substituted for each other in the assembly of finished manufactures. Thus lower values of β correspond to greater "product differentiation" within the manufacturing sector. (Note the analogy to the ways in which Dixit-Stiglitz; Krugman, 1979, 1981; Dixit-Norman; and Helpman measure the utility obtained from a bundle of differentiated consumer goods.)

The gains from an increased division of labor would mandate the production of an infinitesimal amount of an infinite number of separate components if that were possible.

[6]One could instead interpret the intermediate goods as successive stages, Austrian fashion, or alternatively, allow some of the components to be assembly services, so that assembly is not costless. Either interpretation would leave the balance of this paper unscathed.

[7]I ignore the difficulty of interpreting nonintegral values of n.

I assume that indivisibilities in the production of components prevents this[8] (the division of labor is limited by the extent of the market). If the scale variable m is interpreted as an index of the number of bundles of factors devoted to manufacturing production, suppose that the number of such bundles required to produce x units of any component is $ax + b$, for some $a, b > 0$. Then

$$m = n(ax + b). \tag{3}$$

The technology of the model is formally summarized by equations (1), (2) (or (2′)), and (3), with the usual H-O-S model behind the transformation curve $T(m)$.

Note that there are two distinct sources of increasing returns to scale. The individual component production functions, $ax + b$, display what Balassa (1967, ch. 5) refers to as "economies of scale in the traditional sense," and which I term "national" returns. These involve considerations of minimal plant size and the like, and they require total production x to be geographically concentrated. I assume that these economies are internalized by firms, and I shall examine equilibria in which the total output of each produced component is provided by a single firm in a single location. (I shall sometimes refer casually to b in equation (3) as "fixed costs," but I will not assume that b is variable in the long run.)

The finished-manufactures production function (2), or (2′), displays constant returns to scale for a given value of n. But an expansion of the manufacturing sector arising from an increased number of components (a rise in n with constant x) displays increasing returns, since M rises in greater proportion than nx. These economies reflect not an increased plant size but rather a greater division of labor; they are what Balassa (1967, ch. 5) refers to as "horizontal specialization" or "vertical specialization," and were the subject of my earlier paper (1979a), where they were called "international" returns to scale. Economies of this sort depend upon the size of the market for finished manufactures, and they do not require that all manufacturing output be concentrated at a single place. I assume that these economies are external to the individual firm. Components are assembled into finished manufactures by many competitive firms, each of which takes n as a parameter and consequently views itself as subject to constant returns to scale.

[8]This assumption was implicit in my earlier paper (1979a) and explicit in Dixit-Stiglitz and in Krugman (1979).

B. *Autarkic Equilibrium*

Consider a closed economy with the above technology. An individual producer of finished manufactures uses components, subject to (2′), with n as a parameter. If q_0 and q denote the prices, in terms of wheat, of some pair of produced components with outputs x_0 and x, then cost minimization by producers of M, subject to (2′), requires

$$x_0 = x(q/q_0)^{1/1-\beta}. \tag{4}$$

If n is sufficiently large so that the producer of each component acts as though his behavior does not influence that of other component producers, condition (4) is the demand curve faced by the producer of x_0, for given q and x. This curve has an elasticity of $1/(1-\beta)$. The component-producer purchases the services of primary factors in competitive markets and therefore has a cost function given by $-T'(m)[ax_0 + b]$, where $T'(m)$ is exogenous to the individual firm. This firm will therefore equate marginal revenue and marginal cost, and maximize its profit, by charging the price

$$q_0 = -T'(m)a/\beta. \tag{5}$$

Because of the symmetry assumption, q_0 is the price of each component that is actually produced. The profit of each component-producing firm is $q_0x_0 + T'(m)[ax_0 + b]$. These profits will be driven to zero in equilibrium by the entry and exit of firms, that is, by variations in n, as each component is produced by only one firm. Thus, from equation (5),

$$x_0 = b\beta/a(1-\beta). \tag{6}$$

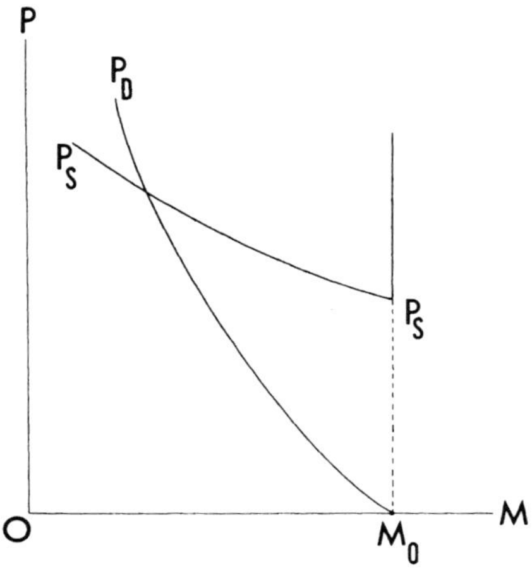

FIGURE 1

Finally, the number n of components is given by equation (3), for any given m and for $x = x_0$.

(7) $$n = (1-\beta)m/b.$$

Equations (5), (6), and (7) now imply the value of k for $M = km$:

(8) $$k = \left([(1-\beta)/b]^{\alpha-1}\beta/\alpha\right)m^{\alpha-1}.$$

The relative supply price P_S of M in terms of wheat is given by $P_S M = q_0 nx$, or $P_S n^\alpha x = q_0 nx$, or $P_S = n^{1-\alpha}q_0$. Thus substitution yields the supply curve of M:

(9) $$P_S = -T'(m)/k.$$

The supply curve is illustrated in Figure 1. The term M_0 denotes the value of M when $T = 0$, and the curve P_S shows for each value of M the minimum price at which that quantity would be supplied (i.e., expression (9)). Note from (6) that x is independent of m. Thus a reallocation of resources from W to M involves an expansion of M production by an increase in n. The manufacturing sector thus displays increasing returns to scale, allowing a negatively sloped supply curve, as illustrated.

The picture of autarkic equilibrium is completed by a description of the demand for final goods. I assume that a constant fraction γ of income is always spent on manufactures. Each output combination M and W determines a demand price P_D that will clear commodity markets: $P_D M = \gamma[W + P_D M]$. Thus the demand curve can be written as

(10) $$P_D = [\gamma/(1-\gamma)]T(m)/km.$$

The demand curve has a negative slope, as illustrated in Figure 1, and it is easy to show that equations (9) and (10) imply that the demand curve intersects the supply curve from above. Thus in autarky the economy possesses a unique equilibrium which features production of both final goods.

C. *International Equilibrium*

Consider next free international trade between two economies—of the sort just described—identical in all respects other than factor endowments. Let m and m^* denote the scale of manufacturing operations at home and abroad (variables pertaining to the foreign country will be distinguished by an asterisk). In free-trade equilibrium the total output of each component will be concentrated in a single country. Thus, if m and m^* are both positive, the two countries produce distinct collections of components. Equation (4) continues to represent the demand curve faced by each component producer (in either country), and the same argument as before establishes that (6) gives the output of each component actually produced somewhere. Then, if n_H and n_F denote the number of components produced at home and abroad, respectively, it follows as before that $n_H = (1-\beta)m/b$ and $n_F = (1-\beta)m^*/b$ so that $n = n_H + n_F$ is given by

(11) $$n = (1-\beta)(m+m^*)/b,$$

and so, from (2), the world output of finished manufactures is

(12) $$M + M^* = (\beta/\alpha) \times [(1-\beta)/b]^{\alpha-1}(m+m^*)^\alpha.$$

What determines m, m^* and the relative prices? To answer this question I use the allocation-curve technique[9] developed in my 1979a and forthcoming articles. For any m and m^*, the world demand price of finished manufactures in terms of wheat is given by

$$(13)\quad P_D = \frac{\gamma}{1-\gamma}\frac{T(m)+S(m^*)}{M+M^*}$$
$$= \frac{\gamma}{1-\gamma}\frac{a}{\beta}\left(\frac{b}{1-\beta}\right)^{\alpha-1}\frac{T(m)+S(m^*)}{(m+m^*)^{\alpha}}$$

where $S(m^*) = W^*$ denotes the foreign transformation curve. The home supply price P_S^H must be given by

$$(14)\quad P_S^H = -[(1-\beta)(m + m^*)/b]^{1-\alpha}T'(m)a/\beta.$$

Home-country equilibrium requires $P_D = P_S^H$, or, from equations (13) and (14),

$$(15)\quad \gamma[T(m)+S(m^*)] + (1-\gamma)(m+m^*)T'(m) = 0.$$

Equation (15) defines the "home allocation curve": the collection of m and m^* for which the home country is in equilibrium in the international economy. This relation is depicted as the HH' curve in each panel of Figure 2. It is easily shown that the curve has a negative slope, that $P_D < P_S^H$ above the curve, and that $P_D > P_S^H$ below. In Figure 2, m_0 and m_0^* denote the manufacturing scales if the home and foreign economies, respectively, specialize to manufactures, so the world is confined to the rectangle $0m_0Em_0^*$ in each panel, and that part of the graph of (15) lying outside this rectangle is irrelevant (it is easy to see that the graph of (15) cannot be completely excluded from the rectangle). If the home economy specializes, equilibrium is consistent with an excess of the relative demand price of the produced good over its relative supply price. Thus the home allocation curve also contains any part of $0m_0^*$ that lies above the intersection of $H'H$ with the vertical axis, and also any part of m_0E below its intersection with $H'H$.

Similarly, the foreign allocation curve, showing the m and m^* for which $P_D = P_S^H$, the foreign relative supply price, is given by

$$(16)\quad \gamma[T(m)+S(m^*)] + (1-\gamma)(m+m^*)S'(m^*) = 0.$$

The graph of (16) is shown as FF' in each panel of Figure (2). As illustrated, FF' must decline less steeply than $H'H$, reflecting the fact that each country's supply price is relatively more sensitive than the world demand price to that country's allocation of resources compared to the foreign allocation. Any part of m_0^*E lying below FF' and any part of $0m_0$ above FF' also constitute part of the foreign allocation curve.

International equilibrium requires each country to be individually in equilibrium in the world economy and is therefore determined by the intersection of the two allocation curves. Figure 2 depicts the five qualitatively distinct possibilities; equilibrium is shown by points F, H', D, H, and F' in panels (a)–(e), respectively (in addition there are the two boundary cases, featuring complete specialization in both countries, between cases (a) and (b) and between (d) and (e)). Evidently each case yields a unique international equilibrium.

The equilibrium values of m and m^* determine the relative price of finished manufactures in terms of wheat from equation (13) (or (14)). Then n is given by (11) and x by (6). The price of each component is as indicated by (5), or, if the home economy specializes to wheat, by the foreign analog.

Note that equation (12) can also be written $M + M^* = k(m+m^*)$ where $k = (\beta/a)\cdot[(1-\beta)/b]^{\alpha-1}(m+m^*)^{\alpha-1}$, thereby emphasizing that the extent of external scale economies depends on the size of the world market alone. If M and M^* denote the quantities of finished manufactures to which the respective countries obtain effective title as a result of their manfacturing activity (i.e., the

[9] The remainder of this section is rather terse as it closely follows my 1979a article, to which the reader is referred for more detail.

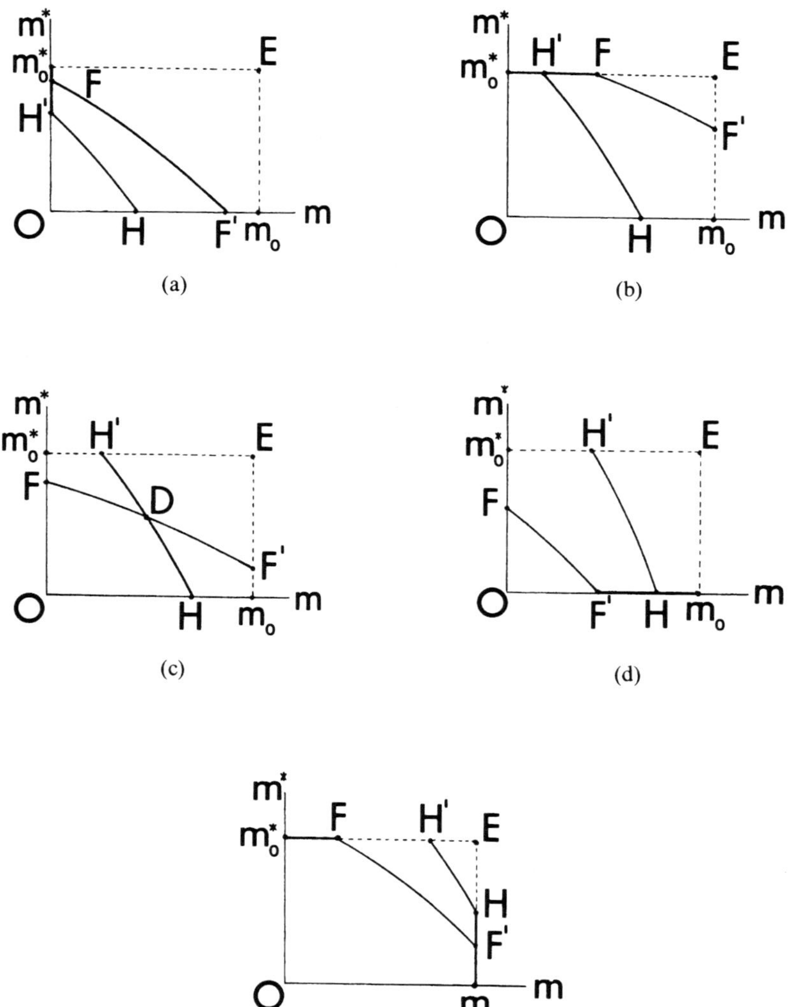

(a) (b) (c) (d) (e)

FIGURE 2

most finished manufactures each country could consume without offering any wheat in exchange), then,

$$(17) \qquad M = km;\ M^* = km^*.$$

Note that M and M^* need not equal the quantities of finished manufactures actually assembled in each country. With assembly costless it can be divided in any way between the two countries. (If one of the components were an assembly process, $M + M^*$ would be all assembled in the country where that process happened to be located.)

II. The Modern Theory

Armed with a complete description of international equilibrium, this section inquires into the fate of the four central propositions supplied by the H-O-S model.[10] Henceforth manufacturing is assumed relatively capital intensive and wheat relatively labor intensive. Since inherent properties of the two factors do not figure in this paper, this pattern of factor intensities is in a formal sense only a definition. But the definition is not arbitrary: one intuitively associates a greater division of labor with significant use of capital. This could be introduced by letting manufacturing production explicitly take time, adding a positive interest rate, and allowing components to be producers' goods generally. It is straightforward to extend the main results of this paper to such a context by using the techniques in my article (1979b), provided attention is restricted to steady states.

A. *Factor-Price Equalization*

Suppose that both countries operate both sectors, so that equilibrium is as in Figure 2(c). Then equations (15) and (16) hold, implying that $T'(m) = S'(m^*)$. Likewise, T' and S' are necessarily unequal if one or both countries specializes completely.[11] Now, with the assumption of identical technology, equality of T' and S' implies that domestically produced components sell at the same price as all foreign-produced components, from (14) and its foreign counterpart. Since T and S are generated by conventional H-O-S technologies, the standard factor-price equalization argument can now be employed to yield

PROPOSITION 1: *Factor-Price Equalization. If both countries operate both sectors, and are not separated by a factor-intensity reversal, free trade implies factor-price equalization. A separating reversal, or (nonincipient) specialization in either country, precludes such equalization.*

B. *The Rybczynski Theorem*

Note, first, that if domestic factor endowments are altered and $T'(m)$ is kept unchanged, the standard Rybczynski argument applies exactly: an increase in capital will cause a more than proportionate rise in m and a fall in W.

The next step is to relate the change in m to the production of individual components and finished manufactures. Expression (5) implies that constancy of $T'(m)$ is equivalent to constancy of the relative prices of components in terms of wheat. Then (6) implies that endowment changes cause *no* changes in the outputs of those components that are produced both before and after, while (7) reveals that the *number* of produced components varies in proportion to m. Thus:

PROPOSITION 2: *Rybczynski. At constant relative component prices, an increase in the capital stock will absolutely reduce the production of wheat, have no effect on the outputs of all components initially produced, and increase the number of produced components in greater proportion than the rise in the capital stock itself.*

Several features of this Rybczynski theorem deserve emphasis. First, despite the pervasive presence of economies of scale, the standard results are completely preserved at the interindustry level: changes in endow-

[10] For a discussion of the basic H-O-S propositions see, for example, Caves and Ronald Jones.

[11] Except, of course, for the borderline case of "incipient diversification" in one country.

ments produce magnified changes in the outputs of wheat and aggregate manufactures. Because all produced components sell at the same price and have equal outputs, aggregate component production can be measured by nx which changes proportionally to n since the adjustment of manufacturing output occurs through variations in the *number* of components rather than in the *outputs* of individual components.

Second, at a disaggregated level, endowment changes produce magnified changes in the outputs of wheat and of those components which change status (and thereby experience infinite proportional output changes). The (zero) proportional output changes of the other components will be weighted averages of proportional endowment changes if and only if the latter are in opposite directions.

Note, third, that the present version of the Rybczynski theorem places no restrictions on the relative price of finished manufactures. Nor does it make any claims about the effective output M of these final goods. This is because international economies of scale influence the production of final manufactures independently of the internal, national, economies associated with the production of individual components. The extent of the former depends upon patterns of production in both countries. Thus, in order to describe the effects of endowment changes in one country on that country's (effective) output of finished manufactures, the behavior of the rest of the world must be considered.

With relative component prices held fixed, m^* will be unchanged. Now equation (17) implies that the proportional change in M equals that in m plus that in k. With m^* constant, the proportional change in k equals that in m multiplied by $[(\alpha-1)m/(m+m^*)]$. This is straightforward: an increase in m takes the form of an increased number of components and thereby raises M both directly and indirectly through the scale economies made possible by the increased division of labor. The latter *scale effect* depends upon the rate $\alpha-1$ at which scale economies are realized, plus the extent to which an increase in m constitutes an increase in world manufacturing $m+m^*$. In any event, M changes in the same direction as m and in even greater proportion, so that the effect of economies of scale is to simply accentuate the standard results.

With constant component prices, changes in the scale of manufacturing activity must change the relative price of finished manufactures. Equation (14) reveals that this price falls in the proportion $(\alpha-1)[m/(m+m^*)]\hat{m}$, where I use a circumflex to denote proportional change. This is the same scale effect as above, entering in for the same reason. The relative price of finished manufactures falls in the proportion that k rises; thus the *value* of finished manufactures, in terms of either wheat or components, rises in the same proportion as aggregate component output. This is a reflection of the external character of the relevant scale economies.

PROPOSITION 3: *At constant relative component prices, an increase in capital increases the output of finished manufactures relative to that of components (and therefore to the capital stock), and also reduces the price of finished manufactures, so that the value of the output of finished manufactures rises in the same proportion as that of aggregate components.*

It is natural to wonder how the Rybczynski theorem is affected when the relative price of finished manufactures in terms of wheat is held constant. The exercise is not in fact very interesting because of the international interdependence. For example, equation (14) reveals that any increase in m brought about by endowment changes must be accompanied by an increase in T' sufficient to leave $(m+m^*)^{1-\alpha}T'$ unchanged. Thus the relative price of components in terms of wheat rises, and the factor prices and techniques must change as well. Furthermore, if the rest of the world is not specialized to wheat, the equilibrium condition of equal component prices requires foreign changes in factor prices and techniques.

C. *The Stolper-Samuelson Theorem*

Expression (5) implies that the wheat price of components is linked to factor prices in essentially the same way as are commodity prices in the standard H-O-S model. Then the usual argument establishes the following:

(18) $$\hat{P}_C = \theta_{km}\hat{r} + \theta_{Lm}\hat{w};$$

(19) $$\hat{P}_W = \theta_{kW}\hat{r} + \theta_{LW}\hat{w}.$$

In these equations P_C, P_W, r, and w denote the nominal prices of industrial components, wheat, capital and labor, respectively (so that $q = P_C/P_W$). The θ_{kW} and θ_{LW} denote capital's and labor's distributive shares in the wheat industry and analogously for θ_{km} and θ_{Lm} in the components industry. The following is immediate from (18) and (19).

PROPOSITION 4: *An increase in the price of wheat relative to the price of all components will raise the wage relative to the prices of both wheat and components and will reduce the rent relative to the prices of both wheat and components.*

Industrial components are intermediate goods, and only wheat and finished manufactures are consumed. Thus Proposition 4 says nothing about real factor rewards and so fails to come to grips with the essence of the Stolper-Samuelson Theorem. The price P_M of finished manufactures is related to that of components by $P_M = n^{1-\alpha}P_C$, so that

(20) $$\hat{P}_M = \hat{P}_C - (\alpha - 1)\hat{n}.$$

Now $\hat{n} = \hat{m}[m/(m+m^*)]$, and $\hat{m}$ can be related to $\hat{P}_M - \hat{P}_W$ by differentiation of (14) to obtain

(21)
$$(\hat{P}_m - \hat{P}_W) = \left[m\frac{T''}{T'} - (\alpha - 1)\frac{m}{m+m^*}\right]\hat{m}.$$

Substitution into (20) gives

(22) $$(\hat{P}_M - \hat{P}_C) = Z(\hat{P}_M - \hat{P}_W)$$

where the elasticity of the *intraindustry* price structure P_M/P_C with respect to the *interindustry* price structure P_M/P_W is $Z = 1/(1 - [mT''/T']/[(\alpha-1)m/(m+m^*)])$.

Note first that, although Z may be of either sign, it can never fall between zero and unity. Thus variations in the intra-industry price structure are never damped versions of variations in the interindustry structure. This reflects the role of scale economies. A change in relative prices involves a reallocation of resources. If resources move into manufacturing, that is, if $\hat{m} > 0$, this will be associated with an increase in P_C/P_W to a degree dependent upon the curvature of the transformation curve. Since the cost of components contributes towards the cost of manufactures, this will also tend to be associated with a rise in P_M/P_W. This effect is simply the familiar H-O-S phenomenon, and I accordingly call it the *intersectoral price effect* of $\hat{m}$; it is reflected in the first term in the brackets in (21).

The variation in m will involve a variation in n rather than x, so individual firms will not experience internal scale economies. But the expansion of world manufacturing will induce external scale economies, and this *scale effect* will tend to reduce the cost of finished manufactures and will therefore work against the intersectoral effect. This scale effect, reflected in the second term in brackets in (21), is the same elasticity of k with respect to m encountered above. If the intersectoral effect dominates, P_M/P_W will therefore change in the same direction as, but to a lessor extent than, P_C/P_W, whereas a dominant scale effect[12] means that a rise in P_C/P_W actually reduces P_M/P_W.

PROPOSITION 5: *If the scale effect dominates the intersectoral effect* ($Z > 0$), *changes in the intrasectoral price structure* P_M/P_C *are magnifications of changes in the intersectoral structure* P_M/P_W. *If the intersectoral effect dominates the scale effect* ($Z < 0$), *the two relative prices always change in opposite directions.*

We are now in a position to relate factor rewards to final-goods prices. Substituting equation (22) into (18) and (19) gives

(23) $$\hat{P}_M = \theta_{kW}\left[\frac{(\theta_{km}/\theta_{kW}) - Z}{1 - Z}\right]\hat{r} + \theta_{LW}\left[\frac{(\theta_{Lm}/\theta_{LW}) - Z}{1 - Z}\right]\hat{w}$$

[12] These conclusions can perhaps be made clearer by rewriting equation (22) as $(\hat{P}_C - \hat{P}_W) = (1 - Z)(\hat{P}_M - \hat{P}_W)$ and noting that Z cannot fall between zero and unity.

$$(19) \qquad \hat{P}_W = \theta_{kW}\hat{r} + \theta_{LW}\hat{w}.$$

Note first that (19) is not affected, so that the proportional change in the price of wheat is still a weighted average of those in the two factor rewards. Second, the coefficients of $\hat{w}$ and $\hat{r}$ in (23) sum to unity, as in (18). With labor designated intensive to wheat, $\theta_{Lm} < \theta_{LW}$, so that the exclusion of Z from between zero and unity renders the coefficients of $\hat{w}$ in (23) positive. Thus that of $\hat{r}$ is less than unity. This is all that can be said without restrictions on technology.

If $Z<0$, the coefficient of $\hat{r}$ in (23) is positive, so that $\hat{P}_M$ is a weighted average of $\hat{r}$ and $\hat{w}$. Furthermore, the coefficient of $\hat{r}$ in (23) exceeds that of $\hat{r}$ in (19), and the usual Stolper-Samuelson argument follows. If, on the other hand, $Z>0$, then in fact $Z>1$, so the coefficient of $\hat{r}$ in (23) is less than that in (19) and the standard results can not possibly hold.

PROPOSITION 6: *Stolper-Samuelson. An increase in the price of manufactures relative to wheat raises the rent and lowers the wage relative to both final-goods prices, if and only if the intersectoral effect dominates the scale effect.*

The reason for this result is straightforward. A dominant intersectoral effect ensures that a change in P_M/P_W produces a larger change, in the same direction, in P_C/P_W, to which Proposition 4 can be applied to yield the standard result. A dominant scale effect precludes this result by causing P_C/P_W to change in the opposite direction. Note that Propositions 5 and 6 together give a very simple test for the validity of the Stolper-Samuelson theorem: The intrasectoral price structure P_M/P_C and the intersectoral structure P_M/P_W should always change in opposite directions.

If Z exceeds unity it may or may not also exceed θ_{km}/θ_{kW}. If the scale effect is sufficiently dominant so that Z does exceed this latter term, the coefficient of $\hat{r}$ in equation (23) is again positive and $\hat{P}_M$ is a weighted average of $\hat{w}$ and $\hat{r}$. But the coefficient of $\hat{r}$ in (23) is less than that of $\hat{r}$ in (19). Thus the standard Stolper-Samuelson argument applies, but with the role of the factor-intensity pattern reversed, so that an "anti-Stolper-Samuelson" result follows.

PROPOSITION 7: *An increase in the price of manufactures relative to wheat raises the wage and reduces the rent relative to both final-good prices, if and only if the scale effect dominates the intersectoral effect sufficiently so that* $Z > \theta_{km}/\theta_{kW}$.

Finally, if Z lies between unity and θ_{km}/θ_{kW}, the coefficient of $\hat{r}$ in (23) is negative, and that of $\hat{w}$ in (23) exceeds that of $\hat{w}$ in (19). Thus any change in P_M/P_W causes w to rise relative to one final-good price and fall relative to the other, but the rental still behaves as above.

PROPOSITION 8: *The relative price of manufactures and the real income of capital vary in the same or opposite directions according as the intersectoral and intrasectoral price structures vary in identical or opposite directions.*

Note that a large scale effect tends to destroy the duality between the Stolper-Samuelson and Rybczynski theorems, since it works to reverse the former while leaving the latter unscathed.[13]

D. *The Heckscher-Ohlin Theorem*

Suppose that both countries produce both goods in international equilibrium, as in Figure 2(c). Then $T'(m) = S'(m^*)$, and Proposition 3 implies that the output ratio M/W is higher in the country endowed with the higher capital-labor ratio. Since the two countries consume the two final goods in equal proportions, each country is a net exporter of the sector intensive to its relatively abundant factor.

Next suppose that at least one country specializes completely. As illustrated in Figure 2, the home allocation curve is steeper than the foreign and, in this case, must lie

[13]See Krugman (1981) for an interesting alternative treatment of income distribution in a model featuring relative factor-endowment differences and intraindustry trade in differentiated consumer goods.

either wholly outside or wholly inside the foreign. In the former case (Figure 2, panels (d) and (e)) the home country is a wheat importer and in the latter case (Figure 2, panels (a) and (b)) a wheat exporter. What distinguishes the two cases?

At point F', m and m^* satisfy equation (16). In the home country, from equations (13) and (14),

$$P_D - P_S^H = \frac{a}{\beta}\left(\frac{b}{1-\beta}\right)^{\alpha-1}(m+m^*)^{1-\alpha} \times\left[\frac{\gamma}{1-\gamma}\frac{T+S}{m+m^*}+T'\right].$$

Substitution of (16) into this expression reveals that, at F', $P_D - P_S^H$ has the same sign as $[T'(m)-S'(m^*)]$. Now, if F' falls in the interval $0m_0$, $m^*=0$ and $0<m\leqslant m_0$, whereas $0\leqslant m^*<m_0^*$ and $m=m_0$ if F' lies in the interval m_0E. In either case, $T'-S'$ is necessarily negative if the foreign country is relatively capital abundant, provided that the two countries are not separated by a factor-intensity reversal. Then $P_D<P_S^H$ at F, which implies that F' lies above the home allocation curve. A similar argument applied to F reveals that the home allocation curve necessarily lies above the foreign when the home country is relatively capital abundant. Panels (a) and (b) of Figure accordingly illustrate home relative labor abundance, and panels (d) and (e) illustrate home capital abundance.

PROPOSITION 9: *Heckscher-Ohlin. In international equilibrium, each country necessarily exports the good intensive in its relatively abundant factor, if the two countries are not separated by a factor-intensity reversal.*

The quantity version of the Heckscher-Ohlin theorem remains intact. Clearly the price version cannot similarly escape unscathed: the scale effect can alter the relation between commodity and factor prices. Also, Section I showed that relative autarkic commodity prices depend upon national size as well as relative endowments. Since only the latter determine trade patterns, these patterns need not reflect autarkic price differences.

But in spite of all this, the price version does have a role to play, a role that depends on a distinction between intraindustry trade and interindustry trade. Basically, the pattern of free *interindustry* trade (the net exchange of manufactures for wheat) will correspond to what the pattern of relative factor prices in the two countries would be in the absence of such trade but with free *intraindustry* trade (the exchange of components). The latter in effect isolates the influence of internationally decreasing costs.

To see this, consider a *quasi-autarkic equilibrium* in which the two countries freely exchange industrial components, but in which there is no trade in wheat. That is, the home economy consumes $W=T(m)$ and $M=km$, where $k=\beta[(m+m^*)(1-\beta)/b]^{\alpha-1}/a$, and analogously abroad. Such an equilibrium is as described in Section I.B. for each country, except that the two economies are linked by a common value of k dependent upon $m+m^*$. The equilibrium values of m and m^* are the solution to

$$\gamma T(m)-(1-\gamma)T'(m)(m+m^*)=0$$

$$\gamma S(m^*)+(1-\gamma)S'(m^*)(m+m^*)=0.$$

In such an equilibrium, the home relative demand and supply prices are given by equations (10) and (9), and analogously abroad. If relative demand prices happen to be equal in the two countries, (10) implies $T(m)/m=S(m^*)/m^*$, since in quasi-autarkic equilibrium the countries share common values of k and n. Thus $T'(m)/m$ exceeds or falls short of $S'(m^*)/m^*$ according as the home country is relatively capital or labor abundant (in a physical sense). Or, in view of (9), the home relative supply price is less or greater than the foreign according as the home economy is relatively capital abundant or not. For demand price to equal supply price in each country, it is consequently necessary that the quasi-autarkic equilibrium relative price of manufactures be less in the relatively capital-abundant country. Proposition 9 then implies that the free-trade exchange of wheat for manufactures is accurately predicted by comparative quasi-autarkic relative commodity prices.

Since in quasi autarky the two countries have distinct relative prices but common values of n and k, the logic of Proposition 6 can be employed to compare the two national equilibria in the absence of a scale effect. This gives the present form of the price version of the Heckscher-Ohlin Theorem.

PROPOSITION 10: *Quasi-Autarky Theorem. In the absence of a separating factor-intensity reversal, each country in free trade is a net exporter of the sector relatively intensive in that factor with the lower relative quasi-autarkic price in that country.*

Note that the quasi-autarky theorem applies to a world such as that envisioned by Gary Hufbauer and John Chilas, who stress that trade between industrial countries is largely intraindustry and involves much less interindustry specialization than does interregional trade within the United States. They see this as due in large part to the pattern of tariff reductions made since the war.

III. The Factor-Endowments Basis of Intraindustry Trade

The previous sections have established the continued relevance to *interindustry* trade of the basic Heckscher-Ohlin idea that trade is a substitute for international factor mobility. The present environment, for example, does no violence to the factor-price-equalization theorem.

The purpose of this section is to establish that *intraindustry* trade likewise has a factor-endowments basis, but that such trade is *complementary* to international factor mobility. Thus a similarity of factor endowments between nations tends to promote such trade as it limits the scope for interindustrial exchange. This property is emerging as a central feature of models with intraindustry trade. The result was first deduced in my article (1979a) and subsequently appeared in the quite distinct work based on differentiated consumer goods.

A. *The Complementarity Theorem*

Recall the assumption that finished manufactures are costlessly assembled from bundles of all components. The above analysis established that if both countries produce manufactures, they specialize to distinct collections of components.

It will prove convenient, and consistent with both the balance of this paper and most empirical work, to measure intraindustry trade as what it would be if finished manufactures were assumed to be costlessly assembled where consumed, and if no component entered trade more than once, so that international trade in manufactures therefore consisted entirely of the shipment of components from their country of manufacture to where they are combined with other components and consumed. Then the home country's import M_C and export X_C of manufactures (components) must be

$$M_C = n_F x g, \quad X_C = n_H x(1-g);$$

where g equals domestic national income as a fraction of world income (i.e., $(PM+W)/[P(M+M^*)+W+W^*]$). I shall use the relative index[14] employed by Hesse, Grubel and Lloyd, Caves and others: $\rho = 1 - |X_C - M_C|/(X_C+M_C)$. Then substitution yields

(24)

$$\rho = 2gn_F/[(1-g)n_H + gn_F] \quad \text{if } n_H \geqslant gn,$$
$$2(1-g)n_H/[(1-g)n_H + gn_F] \quad \text{if } n_H \leqslant gn.$$

Higher values of ρ indicate relatively more intraindustry trade; $\rho = 1$ if all manufacturing trade is intraindustry and $\rho = 0$ if it is all interindustry.

The complementarity between intraindustry trade and factor movements should now be apparent. Let h and h^* denote the capital-labor endowment ratios at home and abroad, and designate the home country as the capital abundant one, so that $h > h^*$. Suppose that the two countries freely trade, with neither country specialized and with

[14]Alternative measures are discussed in Grubel and Lloyd (1971).

factor prices equalized. Suppose now that the factors are slightly "traded" between the two countries so as to reduce $h - h^*$ while leaving each country's income unchanged at the unchanged factor prices and commodity prices. Then n_H falls, n_F rises by the same amount, and g is unchanged. Now, since the home economy is relatively capital abundant, its share of the world output of components (n_H/n) must exceed its share of world income, g. Thus ρ equals the top expression in (24), which directly reveals that a relative-endowment-equalizing trade of factors must raise ρ.

PROPOSITION 11: *Complementarity Theorem. If both countries initially produce both goods, and if there are no separating factor-intensity reversals, a small relative-endowment-equalizing trade of primary factors will increase* ρ.

The basic complementarity property becomes most apparent upon the comparison of extreme cases. If the two countries' endowments differ sufficiently so that one country specializes to wheat there is no intraindustry trade and all trade is interindustrial. If, on the other hand, $K = K^*$ and $L = L^*$, there is no basis at all for interindustry trade (each country will be self-sufficient in wheat), but intraindustry trade will be maximized since the two countries will produce distinct collections of an equal number of components.

B. *Technological Structure and Intraindustry Trade*

While the Complementarity Theorem establishes that intraindustry trade is sensitive to factor endowments, it is nonetheless clear that the existence of such trade is due to the assumptions about the technology of manufacturing production. Attention thus naturally focuses on the sensitivity of my measure of intraindustry trade to the technological parameters: a, b, and β.

Note, first, that these parameters do not influence the basic allocation of resources which, by Proposition 9, is determined as described by the modern theory of international trade. The intersection of the allocation curves determines m and m^*, and these curves are invariant with respect to all three parameters. Attention therefore focuses on equations (6) and (7).

Consider the relative measure ρ. Changes in the technological parameters will not change g, because they produce offsetting changes on the volume and the relative price of finished manufactures, from (12) and (14). Substitution of (7) into the top line of (24) gives $\rho = 2gm^*/[(1-g)m + gm^*]$. This immediately yields

PROPOSITION 12: *The relative index of intraindustry trade is invariant with respect to the degree of product differentiation and the levels of fixed and marginal costs.*

An increase in marginal costs, by reducing x with n_H and n_F constant, lowers both types of trade in proportion. An increase in product differention also reduces interindustry trade *pari-passu* with intraindustry trade. This is surprising: with the existence of intraindustry trade dependent upon product differentiation, one might expect more differentation to increase such trade. But the explanation is simple. From (7) the number of components does rise, but (6) reveals that the output of each falls in even greater proportion, because of fixed costs.

In sum, the technological parameters play a knife-edge role: their existence is crucial for the present theory, but changes in their values have few effects, or sometimes counterintuitive effects, upon intraindustry trade. Empirical investigations have so far produced mixed results (see Pagoulatos and Sorenson; Caves; and references cited therein).

C. *Multilateral Trade*

A brief consideration of this paper's implications for multilateral trade further illustrates the above discussion and also brings out some features that can not arise at all in the two-country framework, but that reflect the stylized facts of modern trade.

The model used thus far is retained, except that many countries of the sort described

TABLE 1—POSSIBILITIES IN MULTILATERAL TRADE

Case	Endowment	Production	Intraindustry Trade	Interindustry Trade
I	$h \geqslant h_m$	specialized to m	with all other I, II, III, IV countries	imports W from IV and V
II	$h_m > h \geqslant h'$	diversified	with all other I, II, III, IV countries	imports some W from IV and V
III	$h = h'$	diversified	with all other I, II, III, IV countries	none
IV	$h' > h > h_W$	diversified	with all other I, II, III, IV countries	exports some W to I and II
V	$h_W \geqslant h$	specialized to W	none	exports W to I and II

above are allowed. Suppose that no factor-intensity reversal is displayed by the common technology. Let h_m and h_W denote the capital-labor ratios in the two sectors in countries which diversify production at the existing prices. Denote by h' the capital labor ratio having the property that any country with an endowment $h > h'$ necessarily imports wheat, and any country with an endowment $h < h'$ necessarily exports wheat.[15] Assume $h_m > h' > h_W$. The various possibilities an individual country could experience are indicated in Table 1.

The concerns of the Complementarity Theorem are best brought out in Cases II, III, and IV where similarities of endowments (to each other and to the world as a whole) foster intraindustry trade while limiting interindustry trade. Cases I and V, on the other hand, illustrate behavior that can not arise in a two-country context. Countries in Case I engage in extensive intraindustry trade with the rest of the world (including other Case I countries), by virtue of their specialization to manufacturing, despite the fact that their endowments are quite different from that of the rest of the world as a whole. Countries in Case V, because they specialize to wheat, engage in no intraindustry trade at all with each other (or with anyone else), no matter how closely the factor endowments of these countries resemble each other. The relevance of all this to the stylized facts of contemporary trade should be clear.

[15] If all countries diversify in production, h' equals the world capital-labor ratio.

IV. Conclusion

This paper has developed a simple model of the interaction of national scale economies —internal to individual firms—with international returns to scale—external to firms—and with the modern, factor-endowments, theory of international trade. The result furnishes a detailed microeconomic backdrop to my earlier paper (1979a). In addition two conclusions emerge.

First, as formalized in the Complementarity Theorem, intraindustry trade in manufactures is complementary to international factor movements. Although the existence of such trade depends upon product differentiation and scale economies, these features play a knife-edge role and thereby leave the determination of the level of intraindustry trade largely to relative factor endowments. Second, the basic propositions of the modern theory of international trade remain, on the whole, essentially valid in the presence of scale economies, although some significant modifications do arise.

The second conclusion contrasts rather strongly with the traditional increasing-returns literature—thoroughly preoccupied with national returns to scale. The present treatment also gives national returns a prominent place. The indeterminancy and multiple equilibria characteristic of the standard analysis are still present (because national returns are still present), in terms of the location of production of individual components. But the sharp difference in my conclusions follows from the fact that, when national and international economies are allowed to interact, disturbances to equilibrium typically take the form of changes in the number of production units rather than in their size, so that the concerns of the traditional theory do not arise. Of course it is possible to chip away at this conclusion by relaxing some of my assumptions, especially those that components are symmetric and that internal scale economies arise solely from fixed costs. These assumptions reflect in simple form my views of what is relatively important, but they cannot be literally accurate.

My earlier paper (1979a) argued that international increasing returns to scale are significant in the modern world economy. The present paper suggests that the conclusions of the earlier need not be altered even if national scale economies are also widespread and important. The resulting theory appears empirically relevant, with respect to both the stylized facts cited at the beginning of this article and also to recent studies—see Caves, and Rudolf Loertscher and Frank Wolter.

REFERENCES

Balassa, Bela, *The Theory of Economic Integration*, Homewood: Irwin, 1961.

______, "Tariff Reduction and Trade in Manufactures among the Industrial Countries," *American Economic Review*, June 1966, *56*, 466–73.

______, *Trade Liberalization among Industrial Countries*, New York: McGraw-Hill, 1967.

Caves, Richard, "Intra-Industry Trade and Market Structure in the Industrial Countries," *Oxford Economic Papers*, March 1981, *33*, 203–33.

______ **and Jones, Ronald W.,** *World Trade and Payments*, 2nd ed., Boston: Little Brown, 1977.

Chang, Winston, Ethier, Wilfred J., and Kemp, Murray C., "The Theorems of International Trade with Joint Production," *Journal of International Economics*, August 1980, *10*, 377–94.

Daly, Donald J., Key, B. A., and Spence, E. J., *Scale and Specialization in Canadian Manufacturing*, Staff Study No. 21, Economic Council of Canada, 1968.

Davies, Robert, "Two-Way International Trade: A Comment," *Weltwirtschaftliches Archiv*, 1977, No. 1, *113*, 179–81.

Dixit, Avinash, K. and Norman, Viktor, *Theory of International Trade*, Cambridge: Cambridge University Press, 1980.

______ **and Stiglitz, Joseph,** "Monopolistic Competition and Optimum Product Diversity," *American Economic Review*, June 1977, *67*, 297–308.

Ethier, Wilfred J., "Some of the Theorems of International Trade With Many Goods and Factors," *Journal of International Economics*, May 1974, *4*, 199–206.

______, (1979a) "Internationally Decreasing Costs and World Trade," *Journal of International Economics*, February 1979, *9*, 1–24.

______, (1979b) "The Theorems of International Trade in Time-Phased Economies," *Journal of International Economics*, May 1979, *9*, 225–38.

______, "Decreasing Costs in International Trade and Frank Graham's Argument for Protection," *Econometrica*, forthcoming.

Finger, Joseph M., "Trade Overlap and Intra-Industry Trade," *Economic Inquiry*, December 1975, *13*, 581–89.

Gray, H. Peter, "Two-Way International Trade in Manufactures: A Theoretical Underpinning," *Weltwirtschaftliches Archiv*, 1973, No. 1, *109*, 19–29.

Grubel, Herbert G., "The Theory of Intra-Industry Trade," in I. A. McDougall and R. H. Snape, eds., *Studies in International Economics*, Amsterdam: North-Holland, 1970.

______ **and Lloyd, Peter J.,** "The Empirical Measurement of Intra-Industry Trade," *Economic Record*, December 1971, *47*, 494–517.

______ **and** ______, *Intra-Industry Trade: The Theory and Measurement of International Trade in Differentiated Products*, London: Macmillan, 1975.

Haberler, Gottfried, *The Theory of International Trade, with its Applications to Commercial Policy*, London: W. Hodge, 1936.

Helpman, Elhanen, "International Trade in the Presence of Product Differentiation, Economies of Scale and Monopolistic Competition," *Journal of International Economics*,

August 1981, *11*, 305–40.

Hesse, Helmut, "Hypotheses for the Explanation of Trade Between Industrial Countries, 1953–1970," in H. Giersch ed., *The International Division of Labour: Problems and Perspectives*, Tubingen: J. C. B. Mohr, 1974.

Hufbauer, Gary C. and Chilas, John C., "Specialization by Industrial Countries: Extent and Consequences," in H. Giersch, ed., *The International Division of Labour: Problems and Perspectives*, Tubingen: J. C. B. Mohr, 1974.

Jones, Ronald and Scheinkman, José A., "The Relevance of the Two-Sector Production Model in Trade Theory," *Journal of Political Economy*, October 1977, *85*, 909–36.

Kemp, Murray C., *The Pure Theory of International Trade and Investment*, Englewood Cliffs: Prentice-Hall, 1969.

______, *Three Topics in the Theory of International Trade*, Amsterdam: North-Holland, 1976.

Kravis, Irving B. and Lipsey, Richard E., "Price Behavior in the Light of Balance of Payments Theories," *Journal of International Economics*, May 1978, *8*, 193–246.

Krugman, Paul, "Increasing Returns, Monopolistic Competition, and International Trade," *Journal of International Economics*, November 1979, *9*, 469–80.

______, "Intraindustry Specialization and the Gains from Trade," *Journal of Political Economy*, October 1981, *89*, 959–73.

Lancaster, Kelvin, "Intra-Industry Trade under Perfect Monopolistic Competition," *Journal of International Economies*, May 1980, *10*, 151–76.

Lawrence, Colin and Spiller, Pablo, "Product Diversity, Economies of Scale and International Trade," mimeo., 1980.

Loertscher, Rudolf and Wolter, Frank, "Determinants of Intra-Industry Trade," *Weltwirtschaftliches Archiv*, 1980, *116*, 280–93.

Matthews, R. C. O., "Reciprocal Demand and Increasing Returns," *Review of Economic Studies*, 1950, No. 2, *17*, 149–58.

Meade, James E., *A Geometry of International Trade*, London: George Allen and Unwin, 1952.

Owen, Nicholas, "Scale Economies in the EEC," *European Economic Review*, February 1976, *7*, 143–63.

Pagoulatos, Emilio and Sorenson, Robert, "Two-Way International Trade: An Econometric Analysis," *Weltwirtschaftliches Archiv*, 1975, No. 3, *111*, 454–65.

Verdoorn, P. J., "The Intra-Block Trade of Benelux," in E. A. G. Robinson, ed., *Economic Consequences of the Size of Nations*, London: Macmillan, 1960.

PART III:
International Factor Markets

International Factor Markets: *Commentary*

My interest in international factor transactions involved both factor trade in general and the mobility of particular factors. Regarding the latter, I have been concerned, to some degree, with both capital and labor. But not land.

Regarding factor movements in general, my work with Lars Svensson [2] established the general relevance of the HOS results in a context where goods trade and factor trade were clearly substitutes. In a key paper, Jim Markusen established that, if trade were not driven by factor-endowment differences, as in the HOS world, goods trade and factor trade would much more likely be complementary.

This intrigued me. It seemed obvious that in virtually all public debate where the relation between goods trade and factor trade mattered (e.g., debates about immigration policy, trade agreements, etc.), all sides to the debate accepted without question that the two were substitutes, not complements. But I found Markusen's arguments persuasive. My explanation, in [3], was that the relation between goods trade and factor trade really matters for the welfare of most people only when there are dramatic differences in factor endowments. And this is just when the two are most likely to be substitutes.

My interest in labor migration was sparked by the realization that very much of it was temporary, at least in original intent, as opposed to the "across the wide ocean" story of permanent mass movements. So my attention was naturally drawn to the likely expected contractual (or non-contractual) relation between migrant and employer. I addressed this in "International Trade and Labor Migration," which I think of as my basic contribution to labor migration.

Of course, I could not resist the usual temptation to spin off. "Illegal Immigration: The Host Country Problem" looked at the issues faced by host countries that declare much migration illegal and then try to control it. In [1] I tried to relate labor migration to the traditional theory of factor movements.

My interest in international capital movements centered on direct investment. The dominant theoretical paradigm of direct investment views it as the result of three considerations. (i) *Ownership* (the investing firm has some attribute it can exploit abroad); (ii) *Locational* (it pays to exploit the attribute by producing abroad rather than by exporting); and, (iii) *Internalization* (there is a reason to have control over the foreign production rather than completely delegating it to another firm). There was a well-developed theoretical literature, with empirical support, based on (i) and (ii). Much less had been done regarding internalization aspects. This was my concern in "The Multinational Firm," my basic contribution to the literature on direct investment, and another paper that I regard as among my best.

My basic approach was that contracts between firms are necessarily incomplete, in an uncertain world, and that internalization basically amounted to retaining *ex post* control. Thus internalization concerns should mandate direct investment, rather than arms-length contracts, where such control was likely to be important. In the industrial-organization literature, Grossman and Hart were at the same time grappling with similar concerns. But I was unaware of their efforts, and so did not profit from them. Too bad: Could have saved me some time.

A basic result was that *ex post* control was likely to be most important when source and host countries were similar. In that case unexpected shocks were most likely to dominate the division of activities between the two countries rendering *ex post* control crucial. If the countries are very different, the division of activities between them is much less likely to be subject to unexpected shocks. This offered an explanation of why direct investment is much greater between countries with similar factor endowments than between those with dissimilar endowments.

The Other Articles

[1] Ethier, WJ (1986). International Trade Theory and International Migration. In: O Stark (ed.), *Migration Theory, Human Capital and Development*, pp. 27–74. Greenwich: JAI Press.

[2] Ethier, WJ and LEO Svensson (1986). The Theorems of International Trade with Factor Mobility. *Journal of International Economics* 20 (1/2), pp. 21–42.

[3] Ethier, WJ (1996). Theories about Trade Liberalization and Migration: Substitutes or Complements?" In: PJ Lloyd and L Williams (eds.), *International Trade and Migration in the Asia Pacific Region*, pp. 50–68. Oxford: Oxford University Press.

International Trade and Labor Migration

By WILFRED J. ETHIER*

Footloose labor is prominent in the contemporary international economy. Migrant workers have accounted for up to a quarter of the Swiss labor force, and 10 per cent of that of northern Europe generally. A number of American industries now depend heavily upon migrant labor (both legal and illegal) from Mexico and the Caribbean. South Asia supplies a large part of the labor for oil-financed Middle Eastern economic development. Pakistan, for example, now earns almost three-quarters as much foreign exchange from the remittances of temporary migrants abroad as from conventional exports; China has begun formally to contract the export of labor services.[1]

For years, a number of European countries have administered formal guest-worker systems, and it has become commonplace to argue that such arrangements have helped insulate native populations from the rigors of industrial fluctuations and have also allowed the preservation of import-competing industries that would have succumbed completely to foreign competition without a supply of cheap migrant labor. But note the possibility of a latent contradiction between these two alleged benefits: preserving jobs for native workers in the face of an economic downturn by sending migrants home requires the two types of labor to be *substitutes*, but preserving domestic jobs by hiring cheap migrant workers requires *complementarity*. It is evident, then, that formal analysis is necessary to understand these host-country issues.

Although migrant labor has generated a large descriptive literature, formal economic treatment is scanty, especially in comparison with that accorded international capital movements. Two basic approaches may be noted. The first is concerned with the brain drain. The characteristic feature here is the coincidence of labor movements with that of human capital. Since the present paper is by contrast motivated by the large-scale movements of temporary migrants with few skills, I shall not allude further to this literature.

The second approach has been simply to introduce international labor mobility into standard factor-endowment models of international trade.[2] This results, for the most part, in treating migration symmetrically with international capital mobility. There can be no doubt that this approach is valuable. Useful insights have emerged, and the standard trade models have done all that can reasonably be asked of them. But, at the same time, certain central characteristics of contemporary experience are fundamentally alien to this approach.

At the risk of some oversimplification, one might isolate the following stylized facts as characteristic[3] of a preponderant share of modern migration.

*Professor of Economics, University of Pennsylvania, 3718 Locust Walk/CR, Philadelphia, PA 19104. This paper has benefited from seminar discussions at the universities of Pennsylvania and Rochester, the Institute for International Economic Studies in Stockholm, the Stockholm School of Economics, the Bijeenkomst Vakgroepen International Economies at Erasmus University on May 21, 1982, the 1982 NBER Summer Institute, and Columbia, Tel Aviv, and Yale universities. Helpful comments were also contributed by Eitan Berglas, Rob Feenstra, Gene Grossman, Lars Svensson, Chuck Wilson, and several anonymous referees.

[1]An excellent general treatment of labor migration may be found in Michael Piore (1979). See U. Hiemenz and K. W. Schatz (1979) for details about foreign workers in Germany, Ariadne Marshall (1973) for the Netherlands, C. Kennedy-Brenner (1979) for France, A. F. Corwin (1978) for Mexican migrants in the United States, J. S. Birks and C. A. Sinclair (1980) for the Middle East, and K. C. Zachariah and J. Conde (1981) for West Africa.

[2]See Bertil Ohlin (1967, ch. XVI), W. Max Corden (1955), Harry Johnson (1965, ch. III, part III), Murray Kemp (1969, ch. 9), James Markusen and James Melvin (1979), Avinash Dixit and Victor Norman (1980, pp. 146–49), Jagdish Bhagwati and Richard Brecher (1980), Brecher and Bhagwati (1981), and Bhagwati (1979).

[3]See the books mentioned in fn. 1, plus further references cited in those works.

(*i*) *Migration is regarded as temporary.* Migrants typically intend to work abroad only long enough to accumulate nest eggs to establish themselves back home, and host countries typically issue temporary work permits. Although both sometimes discover that "you can't go home again," the common view of migration as temporary is a distinctive characteristic of its role in the host-country economy. The employment arrangements of native labor are by contrast generally regarded as much more permanent.

(*ii*) *Migrant labor and native labor are imperfect substitutes in production.* It is often said that migrants hold jobs which native workers would not accept, and this seems to be crucial to the political acceptance of immigration in host countries. But, as noted above, complete complementarity would preclude attempts to use migrants to shield native workers from the business cycle.

(*iii*) *Migrants accept unpredictable variations in employment conditions more readily than do native workers.* The latter typically possess a degree of job security not accorded migrants.

(*iv*) *Migrant labor seems to be in practically unlimited supply at exogenously determined (but sometimes changing) terms.* Once they have established connections with source-country labor pools, host countries generally experience little difficulty in recruiting all the migrants they are willing to accept. When changing conditions close off one source of supply, other sources are quickly found.

(*v*) *Host countries typically experience much international capital mobility as well as labor mobility.* Both direct investment and portfolio investment transactions tend to be large. But general conclusions are not obvious about either the directions or net amounts of physical capital movements.

Although some of these characteristics can indeed be embodied into traditional trade models in quite straightforward fashion, others clearly cannot, and the stylized facts (*i*)–(*v*) on the whole describe a quite different world. Thus a new theoretical approach is needed. The present paper attempts to develop a theory that embodies the five characteristics and yet remains consistent with standard factor-endowments theory in the sense that the latter emerges as a special case. I then use the new theory to analyze the role of migration in host countries, addressing, for example, the questionable relation between the two frequently alleged benefits referred to above.

I. International Equilibrium

A. *Migrant Labor and Traded Goods*

A small country, call it Switzerland, produces a traded good, say chocolate. Chocolate is only a minor component of the Swiss consumption bundle: assume for simplicity that all chocolate is exported. These exports pay for imports of a composite traded good, which is consumed, and for the services of migrant labor.

Chocolate is produced by native labor and migrant labor, which are imperfect substitutes for each other. I assume that chocolate output is given by $Nf(m)$, where N denotes the employment of native labor, m the ratio of migrant to native labor employed, and f is a neoclassical production function (so that $f' > 0$ and $f'' < 0$).

Switzerland is too small to influence the relative prices of her imports, which can accordingly be treated as a single good, but the country is a sizable source of supply in the market for chocolate. Thus the price of chocolate (in terms of imports, i.e., Switzerland's commodity terms of trade) depends upon Swiss supply. It also depends upon the state of nature; for simplicity I assume there are only two possible states, each with probability one-half of occurrence. Thus equilibrium in each state is described by

$$X_A D(P_A) = eNf(m_A), \tag{1}$$

$$X_B D(P_B) = Nf(m_B). \tag{2}$$

A subscript refers to the state of nature, $D(P_i)$ denotes the state-invariant component of world demand for Swiss chocolate, X_i is the random variable, and P_i denotes the price of Swiss chocolate in terms of the numeraire: imports. N is the employment of native labor in state B, and e denotes the ratio of state A employment of natives to N. I label as A the state resulting in lower native employment, so $e \leq 1$. Migrant labor is in perfectly elastic supply at an exogenous (but possibly state-dependent) wage, and firms can decide their employment of migrants after the state of nature is realized. Firms maximize expected profit and so in each state hire migrants to ensure

$$f'(m_A) = v_A/P_A \tag{3}$$

$$f'(m_B) = v_B/P_B, \tag{4}$$

where v_i denotes the exogenous migrant wage in state i.

Equations (2) and (4) jointly determine the state B terms of trade P_B and production technique m_B, provided that N is given exogenously. Equations (1) and (3) yield a relation between P_A, e, and m_A. Solving out m_A yields

$$(P_A/e)(d_e/dP_A) = -\rho_A/(1-\theta_{MA}).$$

In this expression $\rho_A = \theta_{MA}\sigma_A + (1-\theta_{MA})\eta_A$, where σ_i, η_i, and θ_{Mi}, respectively, denote state i elasticity of substitution between native and migrant labor $(-f'(m_i)[1-(m_i f'(m_i)/f(m_i))]/m_i f''(m_i))$, elasticity of demand for Swiss chocolate $(-P_i D'(P_i)/D(P_i))$, and migrant labor's distributive share $(m_i f'(m_i)/f(m_i))$. Next, denote by a_i the value of the marginal product of native labor in chocolate production in state i:

$$a_i = P_i[f(m_i) - m_i f'(m_i)].$$

Note that a_B will be determined by (2) and (4), given N, but that a_A depends upon the actual combination of e and P_A. The latter cannot be specified independently of the native labor market, about which I have as yet said nothing.

Relations (1), (3), and the definition of a_A imply

$$\hat{e} = -\rho_A \hat{a}_A, \tag{5}$$

where a circumflex denotes proportional change. Since e denotes the ratio of state A employment of natives in the chocolate industry to state B employment, it can be interpreted as a measure of employment volatility: lower values of e indicate more native employment volatility. Similarly, with a_B set by equations (2) and (4), lower values of a_A indicate more volatility across states of the marginal productivity of native workers in the chocolate industry (and thus, in a sense, of the degree of Switzerland's comparative advantage in chocolate production). Equation (5) then says that the international markets in which Switzerland deals present that country with a basic tradeoff: by accepting more volatility in the degree of comparative advantage, chocolate employment can be rendered less volatile. This tradeoff is depicted by the International Markets schedule, labeled IM in Figure 1. This curve, which from (5) has an elasticity of ρ_A, shows for each value of a_A that level of e consistent with equilibrium in the two international markets (chocolate and migrant labor) in which Swiss firms deal.

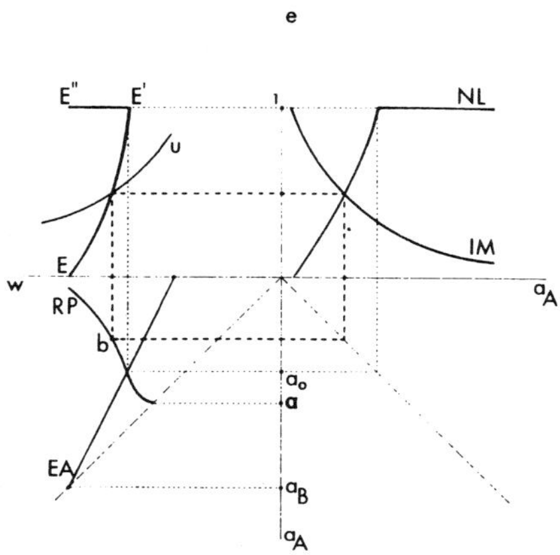

FIGURE 1

B. *The Substitution of Migrants for Native Workers*

The terms of the tradeoff along the International Markets schedule are measured by the basic substitution elasticity ρ_A: the greater the degree of substitutability, the greater the reduction in employment volatility that can be "purchased" by an increase in comparative advantage volatility. Note that ρ_A is made larger by larger values of both the elasticity of production and the elasticity of demand for chocolate, and that a rise in the relative importance of migrants in production, as measured by θ_{MA}, will raise or lower ρ_A as the elasticity of substitution is greater than or less than the elasticity of demand.

These elasticities are also crucial in determining how the *location* of the International Markets schedule relates to the stochastic process confronting Switzerland. This process is summarized by the values of (v_A, X_A) and (v_B, X_B). Consider how changes in v_A and X_A shift the *IM* schedule, with (v_B, X_B) held fixed as a point of reference.

Suppose, first, that X_A rises. Equations (1) and (3) reveal that if $\hat{e} = \hat{X}_A$ (a circumflex denotes proportional change), this will be consistent with unchanged P_A, m_A, and, therefore, a_A. Thus the International Markets schedule shifts up in the proportion $\hat{X}_A$. Given the degree of comparative advantage in state A, a rise in world chocolate demand allows an equiproportional rise in native employment, and in migrant employment as well. The ability to hire migrants allows the productivity of native workers to be maintained, free of the penalty of diminishing returns, regardless of the degree of substitutability between the two types of labor.

Suppose, next, that v_A increases instead. Equation (3) reveals that, if m_A remains unchanged, $\hat{P}_A = \hat{v}_A$. Thus from the definition of a_A, $\hat{a}_A = \hat{P}_A = \hat{v}_A$ as well. Also, equation (1) requires that $\hat{e} = -\eta_A \hat{P}_A = -\eta_A \hat{v}_A$. Thus the effect of an increase $\hat{v}_A$ in state A migrant wages can be depicted as a rightward shift of the *IM* schedule in the amount $\hat{v}_A$ accompanied by a downward shift of $\eta_A \hat{v}_A$. Now we can see from (5) that, for a movement *along* the *IM* schedule, a rightward movement of $\hat{v}_A$ must be accompanied by a downward movement of $\rho_A \hat{v}_A$. Thus the net effect of the rise in v_A must be to shift up the International Markets schedule if and only if $\rho_A \hat{v}_A > \eta_A \hat{v}_A$, which is equivalent to $\sigma_A > \eta_A$. This reflects that fact that a rise in the state A cost of migrant labor influences native employment in two ways. On the one hand, natives are substituted for the now-more-expensive migrants; high values of σ_A obviously facilitate this substitution. But the rise in v_A also raises the cost of chocolate production, and thus the price that Swiss firms must charge. This will reduce world demand for Swiss chocolate and thereby tend to depress native employment; high values of η_A obviously magnify this effect. Thus it is not surprising that, given a_A, higher migrant wages v_A correspond to higher native employment levels e if and only if $\sigma_A > \eta_A$.

The present model in a very simple way gives the degree of substitutability between native labor and migrants very definite roles to play: setting the terms of the tradeoff between employment volatility and terms of trade volatility, and helping to position the International Markets schedule. To see where the economy actually operates on this tradeoff requires consideration of the native labor market, to which I now turn.

C. *The Native Labor Market*

This paper distinguishes migrants from native workers in two crucial ways. The previous subsection focused on the assumption that the two types of labor are imperfect substitutes in production. Now I focus on the second difference: the way each type relates to chocolate firms. Migrants can be hired freely by domestic firms at prevailing wages once the state of the world becomes known, but firms and native workers have a more long-term relationship. In particular, they establish a (possibly implicit) contractual relationship before the state of nature becomes known.[4]

In light of stylized fact (v) noted in the introductory remarks, I assume that Switzerland is integrated into the world capital market in the sense that chocolate firms are owned by capitalists with globally diversified portfolios. Further, I suppose that this capital market affords complete opportunities to

[4] This subsection draws upon the early implicit contract literature. See for example, Costas Azariadis (1975).

hedge Swiss risks, so that the integration is manifested by risk neutrality on the part of chocolate firms.

The contractural arrangements between firms and native workers potentially can take alternative forms. Two cases seem worthy of mention. In what I term the *European mode*, the contract fully specifies the transaction that will take place irrespective of the state of nature that actually materializes: a firm that takes on a worker commits itself to employ him at a predetermined wage, come hell or high water. Thus *ex post* discretion for the firm is limited to the migrant employment decision. This contract form is intended to model situations where legal restrictions, trade unions, etc., in effect leave firms with little ability to lay off workers.

Native employment is therefore invariant across states, in the European mode, and equals the exogenously determined native labor force, when markets clear in equilibrium. Thus $e = 1$ and N equals the supply of native workers.

I assume that chocolate firms are rational in the sense that, although they do not know in advance what the state of nature will be, they do understand sufficiently well the world in which they operate to know what would happen in each state. In particular, they know P_A and P_B and anticipate hiring migrants as described in Section I, Part A. Thus a_A and a_B are known to the firms.

Risk-neutral firms maximize expected profit, and this expected profit is driven to zero in equilibrium by the entry and exit of firms. This implies, in view of (3) and (4), that the equilibrium (state invariant) native wage equals the expected value of the marginal product of native labor: $(a_A + a_B)/2$.

In the alternative schema, which I call the *American mode*, firms and workers negotiate a state-dependent contract. This contract specifies the wage to be paid in each state to employed workers, and the conditional probability for each state that a worker under contract would not be laid off, should that state materialize. I assume for simplicity that the identities of laid-off workers are determined by a random draw from all contracted workers once the state of nature is known. Thus the probability of not being laid off should state i materialize equals state i employment as a fraction of total contracts.

Risk-averse workers prefer higher wages and higher probabilities of not being laid off —I assume that, unlike capitalists, workers cannot diversify risks away in the international capital market. Since chocolate firms compete with each other in the labor market, no firm would contract more native labor than it planned to employ in the more favorable state, B, since to do so would only make its contracts less attractive to workers. Thus the conditional probability of a contracted worker retaining a job is unity in state B and e in state A. Workers who are laid off from the chocolate industry are employed in a secondary sector which produces the composite traded good, using only native labor, at constant marginal productivity α.

Let $h(w)$ denote the strictly concave utility function of each native worker. If w_i denotes the native wage in state i, the contract (w_A, w_B, e) will yield a worker the expected utility

$$(6)\quad u(w_A, w_B, e) = \tfrac{1}{2}h(w_B) + \tfrac{1}{2}\left[eh(w_A) + (1-e)h(\alpha)\right].$$

In what follows I analyze in detail only the American mode. Modifications implied by the European mode are easily noted.

D. *Equilibrium in the Native Labor Market (American Mode)*

Each chocolate firm is competitive in the market for native workers, so the contract it offers must yield utility $u(w_A, w_B, e)$ equal to the market determined level u. Thus the decision problem faced by each chocolate firm is to choose (w_A, w_B, e) to maximize expected profit per contract:

$$\tfrac{1}{2}(a_A - w_A)e + \tfrac{1}{2}(a_B - w_B),$$

subject to $\quad u(w_A, w_B, e) = u; \quad e \le 1.$

Because of constant returns to scale, the number of contracts offered by an individual chocolate firm is indeterminate but immaterial.

The first-order conditions for this problem[5] imply a state-invariant wage, a basic result of ("first generation") implicit contract theory: $w_A = w_B \equiv w$. In market equilibrium, the expected profit of chocolate firms is driven to zero by entry and exit, and u also adjusts so as to clear the market for native labor. Thus N in (1)–(4) will equal the (assumed exogenous) supply of native laborers. The zero-profit condition plus the first-order conditions reduce to the following:

$$e(a_A - w) + (a_B - w) = 0 \tag{7}$$

$$a_A - w + \phi(w) \geq 0 \tag{8}$$

$$(1-e)[a_A - w + \phi(w)] = 0 \tag{9}$$

where $\phi(w) \equiv [h(w) - h(\alpha)]/h'(w)$, so that $\phi' > 1$ if $w > \alpha$. In addition, the utility of each native worker is given by (6).

E. *Full Equilibrium*

Consider in more detail the native labor market described by (6)–(9). If the economy remains completely specialized to chocolate in both states, that is, if $e = 1$, (9) will be met and (7) determines the wage

$$w = (a_A + a_B)/2. \tag{10}$$

Native labor is paid the expected value of its marginal product, as in the European mode. This will indeed be an equilibrium if the wage specified in (10) is consistent with (8).

Let the function $\omega(a_A)$ be the solution to $a_A - \omega + \phi(\omega) = 0$. The graph of this function is called the Risk Premium curve and is labeled *RP* in the third quadrant of Figure 1. The Risk Premium curve shows for each value of a_A what wage w is necessary to pay workers the premium $\phi(w)$ above the value of their marginal product, as compensation for the risk of unemployment they assume if e falls below 1. Note that $\omega' < 0$ and $\omega = \alpha$ if $a_A = \alpha$. Points on or below this curve satisfy (8).

The line labeled *EA* in Figure 1 graphs (10) and so shows, for each value of a_A, the wage that equals the expected value of the marginal product of native labor, given the state *B* equilibrium. This line intersects the w axis at $w = a_B/2$ and the 45° line at $w = a_B = a_A$. Points on this line below the *RP* curve satisfy (8) and so are consistent with equilibrium. Thus for any value of a_A at least as great as a_0 in Figure 1, the corresponding point on *EA* indicates the equilibrium wage, and $e = 1$.

If a_A is strictly less than a_0, it is not possible to have $e = 1$: the economy will not completely specialize in chocolate production in state *A*. In this case (9) will require $w = \omega(a_A)$ and (7) will then determine e:

$$e = [a_B - \omega]/[a_A - \omega]. \tag{11}$$

The Equilibrium Employment curve, labeled *EE′* in the second quadrant of Figure 1, records all combinations of w and e consistent with (11). Together with the linear segment *E′E″*, corresponding to full employment in both states, it displays all combinations of those two variables consistent with equilibrium in the native labor market.

It is now possible to determine, for each value of a_A, that level of e consistent with equilibrium in the market for native labor. This is done in Figure 1 and the result recorded in the first quadrant as the Native Labor schedule, labeled *NL*. Full equilibrium is determined by the intersection of the International Market and Native Labor schedules.

Figure 1 depicts an equilibrium in which Switzerland is incompletely specialized in state *A*. The values of a_A, w, and e can be read off the diagram, and the (*ex ante*) utility of native residents is then given by (6). The curve labeled u in the second quadrant is the indifference curve corresponding to the equilibrium utility level. Indifference curves must cut the *EE′* curve from above, as drawn.[6]

[5] See the Appendix for further details.

[6] In the European mode, the Native Labor schedule is a horizontal line with $e = 1$, point E' is directly above $w = a_B/2$, and the Equilibrium Employment and Risk Premium curves become irrelevant.

II. Characteristics of Equilibrium

The degree of the Swiss (marginal) comparative advantage in chocolate in state i can be thought of as measured by $a_i - \alpha$. By assumption there is such an advantage in state B. If the equilibrium $a_A > \alpha$ as well, Switzerland always has a comparative advantage in chocolate and always specializes completely in the product. In this case, the sole significance of the quasi-permanent relations between firms and native workers is stabilization of the native wage: if instead natives, like migrants, were hired in spot markets after realization of the state of nature, the wage would equal a_i but Switzerland would still specialize completely in chocolate production in both states.

When $a_A < \alpha$, Switzerland has a (marginal) comparative disadvantage in chocolate in state A, and the native contractual arrangements influence the pattern of specialization. For example, if $a_0 \leq a_A < \alpha$, the Swiss still specialize completely in chocolate production, whereas spot markets would cause them to diversify.

The Swiss populace is exposed to uncertainty through both of the international markets in which it deals. Risk-neutral firms provide partial insulation from this uncertainty. The insulation they can provide is in turn related in two ways to their own activity on world markets. By hiring foreign workers in good times and discharging them in bad times, firms help insulate Swiss workers. The second method has to do with the pricing of chocolate. Equation (3) says that in state A firms pay migrants the value of their marginal product, and (8) implies that Swiss workers are paid more than the value of their marginal product. Thus Switzerland exports chocolate at a price less than its cost of production, that is, Swiss products are dumped[7] in world markets in state A. Note that this dumping would appear aggressive to foreign competitors, since Swiss firms employ no fixed factors at all but dump in order to avoid laying off workers. Chocolate is sold above cost in state B, so that firms expect to break even in the long run.[8]

The expulsion of foreign workers and the dumping of commodities has each received great attention throughout the previous decade, but the relation between the two has been largely ignored. The present paper offers a framework for the investigation of this relationship.

The Swiss economy is exposed to uncertainty through the two international markets in which it deals. The stochastic process relating to labor migration—reflected in the magnitudes of v_A and v_B—would in practice be quite sensitive to national immigration policy. For example, a guest worker system might be operated in a relatively closed fashion, allowing only a modest volume of immigration and adjusting that in response to disturbances so as to stabilize the migrant wage faced by individual domestic firms. Alternatively, the authorities might be more willing to allow the domestic economy to exploit the opportunity to obtain cheap migrant labor services and so operate a more open guest worker system, insisting that all migrants have jobs but not trying to shield chocolate firms from external fluctuations in

[7]See my 1982 article for a fuller, two-country theory of dumping.

[8]At this point, consider briefly Switzerland's international payments. In state A the excess of the value of Swiss chocolate exports over imports and remittances of migrant wages equals

$$eN[P_A f(m_A) - w - v_A m_A] = eN(a_A - w).$$

(Note that this is independent of how migrants divide their wages between remittances and local expenditures.) Let π_A denote total state A profits of the chocolate industry, γ the share of that industry owned by Swiss capitalists, and π_A^F total profits received by Swiss capitalists from ownership of industries in the rest of the world. Thus the state A Swiss current account surplus equals

$$eN[a_A - w] + \pi_A^F - (1-\gamma)\pi_A.$$

But $eN(a_A - w) = \pi_A$, so the current account surplus equals $\pi_A^F + \gamma\pi_A$, or total state A profits received by Switzerland. In like manner, the current account surplus (identically equal to net Swiss capital accumulation) in state B equals total profit in that state. Assuming that Swiss capitalists have been able to diversify away all risk by means of the international exchange of securities, the current account is state invariant.

migrant wages. The authorities might also vary their administration of a guest worker system in response to fluctuations in the world demand for chocolate. This diversity of possibilities demands an investigation of how economic performance varies in response to changes in the stochastic process facing Switzerland. I turn next to this problem.

III. Alternative Stochastic Processes

Consider now how the equilibrium described in Section I is influenced by changes in the stochastic process confronting Switzerland. Note that this comparative statics exercise is to be distinguished from the simpler question—whose answer is immediate from the foregoing analysis—of how state A behavior differs from state B behavior for a given stochastic structure. There are two reasons for addressing the present question. The first is the possibility, raised above, that the stochastic structure is sensitive to immigration policy. The second is that my assumption of just two states of nature, made solely for expositional purposes, is too limiting in the presence of two random variables. For example, one might wish to ask how Swiss behavior depends upon whether v and X are positively correlated or negatively correlated. Thus a full understanding of the model requires consideration of alternative stochastic processes.

Changes in X_B and v_B produce changes in a_B. The effects, easily traced through Figure 1, imply shifts of the Native Labor schedule and consequent movements along the International Markets schedule. Changes in X_A and v_A by contrast shift IM and thereby causes movements along NL. The degree of volatility confronting Switzerland is determined by the differences $X_B - X_A$ and $v_B - v_A$. To have a frame of reference, I shall take X_B and v_B as immutable (so that equilibrium values of P_B, m_B, and a_B do not change) and consider alternative values of X_A and v_A. Each pair of values of X_A, v_A determines, from Section I, equilibrium levels of e, P_A, m_A, a_A, and w. I shall examine in turn the effects of variations in X_A and v_A upon equilibrium.

A. *World Demand for Chocolate*

Consider, first, a rise in X_A in the proportion $\hat{X}_A$. With unchanged X_B, this constitutes an increase in expected world demand for chocolate. I have labeled the states so that $a_A < a_B$, so there is a presumption (but not a certainty) that $X_A < X_B$. If so, the rise in X_A constitutes also a reduction in the volatility of world chocolate demand. As discussed in Section II, Part B above, the International Markets schedule in Figure 1 shifts upward in the proportion $\hat{X}_A$. Thus equilibrium moves to the right along the Native Labor schedule. If initially $e = 1$, this produces a rise in w and consequent rise in utility u. If $e < 1$ initially, w *falls* but e rises, and on balance the increase in job security outweighs the reduction in the wage rate in the sense that u still rises. Note the contrast in *ex post* consequences in the two cases. With complete specialization ($e = 1$) the *ex ante* and *ex post* utility of each Swiss resident is $h(w)$ and clearly rises as a consequence of the rise in expected world demand for chocolate. If $e < 1$, the *ex ante* utility u of each Swiss likewise increases. But should state B materialize, the *ex post* utility $h(w)$ of each resident will be *lower* than what it would have been with the lower X_A. Should state A materialize, the *ex post* utility of laid-off workers, $h(\alpha)$, is of course unchanged, and the *ex post* utility of chocolate workers who would have been employed there even if X_A had not risen (workers' identities are of course unknown) is strictly lower. The only *ex post* utility that is increased[9] is that of chocolate workers in state A who would have been laid off with the lower X_A.

B. *Migrant Wages*

Now consider the effects of a reduction in state A migrant wages in the proportion $\hat{v}_A < 0$. As discussed in Section II, Part B above, the International Markets schedule shifts up or down, according as σ_A is less than η_A or not, and equilibrium moves in a corresponding fashion along the Native Labor schedule.

[9] Note the analogy with the Stolper-Samuelson theorem in factor-endowments models.

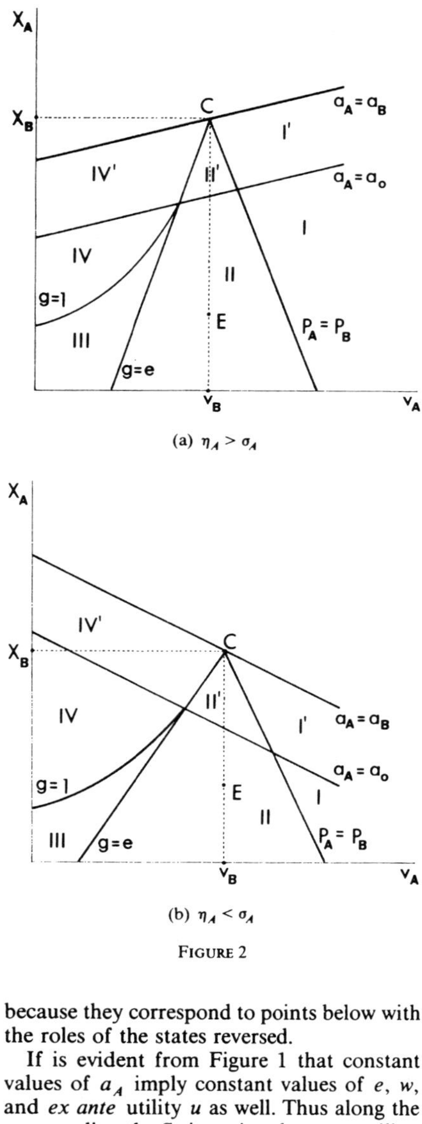

(a) $\eta_A > \sigma_A$

(b) $\eta_A < \sigma_A$

FIGURE 2

Note, incidentally, that we can easily see, with the aid of Figure 1, that a reduction in v_A brings about the paradoxical result that native utility falls, as long as $\sigma_A > \eta_A$. (It can easily be shown that a fall in both v_A and v_B, so that migrant wages fall with certainty, can also reduce u.) But the reason is simple: lower migrant wages can induce chocolate firms to increase production by enough so that the resulting deterioration in the terms of trade produces a welfare loss.[10] Such possibilities disappear if Switzerland becomes small in the world chocolate market (so that η_A becomes very large), or if the country levies an optimal export tax on chocolate.

C. *The Array of Possibilities*

It is time to examine all possible equilibria corresponding to different stochastic processes. With X_B and v_B immutable, each pair of values of X_A and v_A determines a particular equilibrium. Each point in each panel of Figure 2 corresponds to a distinct hypothetical stochastic process confronting Switzerland. At point C, $X_A = X_B$ and $v_A = v_B$, so that the future is certain. Thus both states have identical, complete-specialization equilibria: $a_A = a_B$ and $e = 1$. Employment of migrants also does not vary across states, so that $g = 1$, where g denotes the ratio of state A employment of migrants to state B employment, and thus $g = em_A/m_B$. At C the present model in effect reduces to the standard factor-endowments model with complete specialization in the production of exportables.

Consider first combinations of X_A and v_A that leave a_A unchanged. It follows from Parts A and B above that, in order that a_A not change, increases in X_A must be accompanied by increases in v_A if $\eta_A > \sigma_A$ and by decreases in v_A if $\eta_A < \sigma_A$. Each case is allotted its panel in Figure 2, and in each panel two a_A contours are drawn. Downward movements bring one to contours corresponding to lower values of a_A. The $a_A = a_B$ contour must pass through the certainty point C; points above this line will be ignored because they correspond to points below with the roles of the states reversed.

If is evident from Figure 1 that constant values of a_A imply constant values of e, w, and *ex ante* utility u as well. Thus along the $a_A = a_B$ line the Swiss enjoy the same utility, both *ex ante* and *ex post*, as in the certainty case. The $a_A = a_0$ line corresponds to the lowest value of a_A for which $e = 1$, and to the lowest wage w. Moving from $a_A = a_B$ to

[10]See Bhagwati (1968 and 1973) for the appropriate analogous treatment of immiserizing growth.

TABLE 1—POSSIBLE EQUILIBRIA

Zone	Employment	Terms of Trade
I	$1 > e > g$	$P_A > P_B$
I′	$1 = e > g$	$P_A > P_B$
II	$1 > e > g$	$P_A < P_B$
II′	$1 = e > g$	$P_A < P_B$
III	$1 > g > e$	$P_A < P_B$
IV	$g > 1 > e$	$P_A < P_B$
IV′	$g > 1 = e$	$P_A < P_B$

$a_A = a_0$ reduces a_A and w, keeps Switzerland completely specialized in both states ($e = 1$), and reduces utility (*ex ante* = *ex post*). Continuing downwards brings one to equilibria with lower values of e and a_A, higher values of w, and lower *ex ante* utility (but higher *ex post* utility for chocolate workers).

The line labeled $P_A = P_B$ shows the assumptions that result in sticky terms of trade across states. It slopes downwards because P_B is constant and P_A is increased by rises in both X_A and v_A. $P_A > P_B$ above this line and $P_A < P_B$ below.

Swiss employment in chocolate varies across states in the same proportion as migrant employment on the $g = e$ line. This happens when $m_A = m_B$, which, in view of the constancy of m_B, requires a constant m_A. Equation (3) implies that m_A will be unaltered if increases in v_A are accompanied by large enough increases in X_A to raise P_A in the same proportion (thereby raising a_A as well). Thus the $g = e$ line has a positive slope and cuts a_A contours from below. Above this line $g > e$ and below it $g < e$.

Finally, migrant employment is stable across states along the $g = 1$ schedule. This line is found by solving the system of equilibrium conditions, (1), (3), (7), and (8)—with equality—for X_A as a function of v_A, subject to the restriction that $em_A = m_B$. Points above this line imply $g > 1$ and points below it imply $g < 1$. The various lines divide each panel of Figure 2 into several zones, whose properties are summarized in Table 1.

With the European mode, the analysis is basically the same except that only the full-employment states (*I′*, *II′*, and *IV′*) are relevant (so of course there can be no case where migrant employment is less volatile than native). Sufficiently low values of X_A (and/or of X_B) cause the economy to instead specialize completely in the production of the composite traded consumption good in both states.

D. *Dumping Goods and Dumping Migrants*

Suppose initially that $v_A = v_B$, as at points E in Figure 2. Then Switzerland is exposed to uncertainty solely through the chocolate market. As is clear from the figure, this necessarily results in an equilibrium in zone *II* or *II′*. Suppose the former—whenever the unfavorable state A materializes, Swiss workers are laid off ($e < 1$). But Swiss firms moderate this in two ways: they reduce prices ($P_A < P_B$) and dump chocolate abroad, and they also lay off migrant workers in greater proportion than Swiss workers ($g < e$). Thus both chocolate and migrants are dumped abroad when foreign demand for Swiss goods falls. Zone *II* equilibria would characterize guest worker systems administered in a "closed" way as discussed in Section II above.

Now let v_A fall; that is, consider leftward movements in Figure 2. This consists of cases where low values of X_i are accompanied by low values of v_i: unfavorable commodity-market conditions are correlated with favorable labor-market conditions. This would be the case if Swiss chocolate, and its close substitutes, were to a large degree sold in the same countries from which migrant labor comes: both conditions would be sensitive to aggregate demand in those countries. Such movements depart further from the $P_A = P_B$ line in Figure 2, implying larger state A price reductions in chocolate to stimulate demand. This is made possible by the cost-reducing effect of lower values of v_A. The latter also furnishes a motive to reduce fluctuations in the employment of migrants, and g indeed rises with leftward movements in Figure 2. Thus domestic employment is tugged in two directions by the tendency, on the one hand, to *substitute* foreign workers for domestic workers in state A—made easier by higher values of σ_A—and by the tendency, on the other, to increase state A production—made easier by higher values of η_A—which affects foreign and migrant employment in a *complementary* way. If Switzerland is basically a small country in the world chocolate market (very large η_A) the complementarity aspect necessarily dominates, but with less than infinite elasticity of demand the opportunity to expand chocolate sales is limited. In general, the complementarity or the substitutability aspect will dominate according as $\eta_A > \sigma_A$ or the reverse, since Figure 2 shows that this is the condition deciding whether a leftward movement increases or decreases a_A, e (if initially less than unity), and *ex ante* utility u.

If v_A falls enough the economy finds itself in zone *III* where migrant employment is more stable than domestic employment. But migrants are still being used to stabilize Swiss employment conditions: since migrant wages fall when the demand for chocolate falls, retaining more foreign workers on the payroll in state A reduces costs and may still allow more Swiss workers to be retained also, if $\eta_A > \sigma_A$. The problem is that maintaining employment through maintaining production in state A causes the terms of trade to deteriorate: prices fall as well as costs. If migrants and natives are not sufficiently complementary and/or if chocolate demand is not sufficiently elastic, $\sigma_A > \eta_A$ and *ex ante* utility falls.

If chocolate conditions and foreign labor conditions are sufficiently negatively correlated, the economy will be in zone *IV*, so that employment of migrants actually rises in state A. Chocolate dumping and migrant dumping cease to be complementary and become substitutes: chocolate is dumped in state A and migrants in state B. It could also become unclear whether the migrant labor market is being exploited to shield Switzerland from shocks in the chocolate market, or whether the reverse is the case. For example, if $\eta_A < \sigma_A$ zone *IV* (or *IV'*) contains cases where $X_A > X_B$ and $v_A < v_B$: in state A domestic unemployment due to the substitution of cheap migrant labor is ameliorated by an increased foreign demand for chocolate. In any event the dumping of chocolate that takes place in state A would seem very aggressive indeed to Switzerland's foreign competitors: the Swiss *increase* their employment of migrants to be able to dump chocolate abroad!

Positions to the right of point E in Figure 2 correspond to cases where favorable commodity conditions are positively correlated with favorable (for the Swiss) migrant labor conditions. This could be the case if chocolate is sold in a part of the world with economic conditions negatively correlated with those in the part of the world from which the migrants come. Since labor costs rise in state A, the Swiss are less able to reduce prices, though they still dump chocolate. Instead they are more inclined to lay off migrants and substitute domestic labor: $e > g$ to the right of E. If $\sigma_A > \eta_A$, this substitution effect will outweigh the complementarity effect resulting from the depressing influence of higher costs, and the increase in v_A will move the Swiss closer to the $e = 1$ region. With high enough positive correlation between chocolate and migrant labor conditions. Switzerland will be in zone *I*, characterized by the apparent paradox that the Swiss increase the price of chocolate when they dump it ($P_A > P_B$). The reason is simply that they raise prices to cover part, but not all, of their increased labor costs.

Public discussion of labor migration emphasizes two, basically inconsistent, alleged benefits to host countries: isolation of native workers from the business cycle by varying the employment of migrants (which requires a substitutability of domestic and foreign labor in production), and preservation of domestic jobs in domestic industries by reliance on cheap migrant labor (which emphasizes complementarity). The present analysis provides a framework for the study of these two alleged benefits and shows how they relate to the nature of the stochastic process facing the host country, as well as to basic parameters such as elasticities of demand and of substitution (which determine the shape and position of the curves in Figure 2). The dividing line between the two cases is the $g = e$ curve, the locus of possibilities for which production techniques are unchanged across states. In zones *I* and *II*, the Swiss respond to a recession by substituting domestic workers for migrants and sending the latter home: the recession is (partly) passed on to foreign workers. In zones *III* and *IV*, a recession by contrast causes migrants to be substituted for domestic labor, and it is the resulting cost reduction that allows larger chocolate production—and native employment—than would otherwise be possible. This latter possibility requires, but is not assured by, a negative correlation between conditions in the two markets. A higher elasticity of chocolate demand increases the ability of a price reduction—and thus cost reduction—to maintain chocolate output. Thus larger values of η_A cause the $g = e$ line to become steeper (this is confirmed in the Appendix) and so expand zones *III* and *IV* at the expense of *I* and *II*. But, unless η_A is infinite, zone *II* necessarily contains cases where $v_A < v_B$.

The parameter σ_A measures the extent to which domestic and migrant labor are similar and thus highly substitutable for each other. As σ_A increases, zone *IV* expands at the expense of the other three zones.

IV. The Effect of Migration and Migration Policy

The preceding discussion of alternative stochastic processes was intended to expose the role of temporary migration in the host economy. I turn now to its significance: in what ways is the behavior of the host country different from what it would be if there were no temporary migration?

A. *Captive Migrants*

Suppose, first, that the economy possesses a fixed supply M of unskilled labor that does not vary in response to the state of nature. The supply M might consist of native unskilled workers or permanent immigrants. Unskilled labor is hired in spot markets after the state of nature is known. Thus, in equations (1)–(4), $m_B = M/N$, $m_A = M/eN$, and v_A and v_B are now endogenously determined. In other respects the model is unchanged. A distinct equilibrium is now determined for each set of values of X_A, X_B, and M rather than, as before, for each set of values of X_A, X_B, v_A, and v_B.

Each combination of X_A, X_B, and M will give an equilibrium corresponding to some point on the $g = 1$ line of the relevant version of Figure 2. Thus, in terms of the classification in Table 1, equilibrium will be on the boundary of zones *II′* and *IV′* or on that of *III* and *IV*. Equilibria with the characteristics of all other zones are thus essentially dependent upon labor mobility. For example, there will no longer be cases where, in state *A*, chocolate firms simultaneously raise prices and dump their product abroad.

Next, I wish to compare an equilibrium with labor mobility to a "naturally corresponding" one without. But what set of values of X_A, X_B, and M corresponds naturally to a particular choice of X_A, X_B, v_A, and v_B? One would wish, I should think, to keep X_A and X_B the same as with labor mobility, but in the choice of M one cannot avoid being arbitrary. Purely for the sake of illustration, then, I will arbitrarily choose that value of M that causes v_B to have the same value in the no-mobility case as in the comparison equilibrium with labor mobility.

Suppose, then, that initially $X_A = X_B$ and $v_A = v_B$ with migration possible. If migration is now ruled out, X_A and X_B are kept unchanged, and M is set to generate the same value of v_B as before, equilibrium will not in fact change: both cases correspond to point C in each panel of Figure 2. Now consider how equilibrium (migration and no-migration) responds to a comparative statics reduction in X_A. The change in the migration equilibrium corresponds to a downward vertical movement in each panel of Figure 2, from point C toward E (and perhaps beyond). The related no-migration equilibrium shifts down by the same vertical amount, but along the $g = 1$ curve instead.

Three conclusions are immediately apparent from Figure 2. First, both P_A and v_A are lower in the no-migration case: migration reduces the variability of prices across states. Second, the comparative welfare of native workers depends critically upon the relative magnitudes of η_A and σ_A. In panel (a), where $\eta_A > \sigma_A$, the presence of migration results in an equilibrium with a higher value of a_A. Thus, as a result of migration, native labor has a lower level of (*ex ante*) utility, in some situations migration leads to state A unemployment when the absence of migration would preserve full employment in both states, and, if $e < 1$ in both equilibria, it is lower with migration. Panel (b) shows that these conclusions are exactly reversed if $\eta_A < \sigma_A$. The reason for this discrepancy should be clear from the discussion in preceding sections. If migrants are not sent packing when the world demand for chocolate falls, production will be higher than it would otherwise be. If world demand for chocolate is sufficiently inelastic, the resulting deterioration in the terms of trade will be the dominant consideration. But if the elasticity of substitution is sufficiently low, the resulting reduction in the spot wage of unskilled workers will prove decisive.

The third observation is that v_A is always less without migration. Since v_B is the same in both cases, unskilled workers are a "captive" labor force in the sense that they unambiguously suffer because of the lack of the option to emigrate. Of course, a judgment about host-country welfare should be sensitive to that of unskilled workers as well as the skilled, once emigration is ruled out. On this basis, the absence of labor mobility harms both skilled workers and the unskilled if $\sigma_A > \eta_A$, but benefits the former at the expense of the latter when $\eta_A > \sigma_A$.

B. *Immigration Quotas*

I pointed out above that the choice of which size of M to compare to any v_A, v_B pair was inherently arbitrary. My choice involved a larger unskilled labor force in one state than migration would produce. We could of course consider other choices, in particular some that involve less unskilled labor in both states than would migration. I leave to the reader the straightforward investigation of alternative choices and I instead approach the question somewhat differently. Consider now the effects on the initial equilibrium of a quota on immigration.

Suppose a (state-invariant) quota Q. If Q is initially greater than the immigration that would originally occur in either state, it would of course have no effect, so suppose that Q is reduced until it just becomes binding in one state. If the initial equilibrium is in zone *IV* or *IV'* in Figure 2, this will be state B; otherwise it will be state A. Assume for now the latter.

Such a quota will not impinge upon equations (1) and (3), so the International Markets schedule in Figure 1 is unchanged.

The quota will reduce m_B in equation (2), causing P_B to rise in an amount inversely proportional to η_B. Thus a_B can either rise or fall. Not surprisingly, this depends upon whether η_B exceeds σ_B or not. Suppose it does, so that the effect of the quota is to lower a_B. (Equation (4) shows the effect of the quota on the state B migrant wage, which is accordingly driven above v_B. I suppose that these rents go to those migrants who happen to be fortunate enough to get in.)

It is immediate from the discussion of the full equilibrium in Section II, Part E, that the reduction in a_B shifts the Equilibrium Employment curve EE' in Figure 1 down, leaves the Risk Premium curve RP unchanged, and shifts the EA line to the left. These imply that that Native Labor schedule NL, in the first quadrant, shifts to the right.

If the initial equilibrium in the first quadrant of Figure 1 is characterized by $e = 1$, a small shift of the NL schedule will not alter that fact. But the right-hand shift of the EA line implies that w falls. The prospect of a binding immigrant quota should state B materialize results in a lower wage for (fully employed) native workers in both states: firms will pay less for native workers because the prospect of a constraint on migrant employment in one state reduces the expected value of the marginal product of native labor. Native workers are unambiguously worse off, *ex ante* and *ex post*.

If instead the initial equilibrium features $e < 1$, imposition of a quota causes that equilibrium to shift down and to the right along the International Markets schedule. Thus e falls and a_A rises, and the fixity of the RP curve implies that w again falls. The prospect of a binding quota in state B again reduces the *ex ante* value of native employment. This is reflected again by a reduction of w (in both states), but also now by a reduction in e as well. Because of the prospect of a quota on migrants, firms are less willing to commit themselves to natives, and so plan to rely relatively *more* on migrants should the nonbinding state A arise. It is conceivable that the imposition of a quota could actually increase *ex post* immigration! In any event, native workers are unambiguously worse off, both *ex ante* and *ex post*.

If $\sigma_B > \eta_B$, the imposition of a quota causes a_B to rise and all the above conclusions are reversed. The reasons for this should be clear by now.

If the initial equilibrium is in zone IV or IV', so that a small quota is initially binding in state A rather than B, the effects are quite different. Now equations (2) and (4) are unaffected, so that a_B does not change. Instead it follows from (1), and the definition of a_A, that a small quota will shift the International Markets schedule to the left or the right, according as η_A exceeds σ_A or not. Suppose the former. It is immediate from Figure 1 that, if the initial equilibrium features full employment $e = 1$, the effect of the quota is to lower w in both states, just as in the preceding case. If initially $e < 1$, the leftward shift of the International Markets schedule produces a downward movement along the Native Labor schedule and a corresponding downward movement along the EE' curve. The quota lowers e but raises w. As the economy moves to a lower indifference curve, the *ex ante* utility of native workers necessarily declines. But should state B actually materialize, the fact that a quota would have been binding in state A makes native workers better off *ex post*! If instead state A comes about, there is an *ex post* distributional effect. Native workers who retain their jobs are better off while those who lose their jobs, as a result of the quota, are worse off. If $\sigma_A > \eta_A$, all these conclusions are reversed.

To summarize, the effects of an immigration quota depend upon three considerations: whether $\eta_A > \sigma_A$ or not; whether there is initially full employment in both states; and whether migrant dumping is a complement to or a substitute for commodity dumping. If $e = 1$ initially, a quota necessarily lowers the native wage in both states if $\eta_A > \sigma_A$ and raises it if $\eta_A < \sigma_A$. If initially $e < 1$, the quota lowers e and *ex ante* welfare if $\eta_A > \sigma_A$ (and raises them in the opposite case), but other *ex post* consequences depend critically upon whether or not migrant dumping substitutes for commodity dumping. More stringent quotas can be analyzed in similar fashion. When the quota becomes binding in both states, so that there is a state-invariant unskilled labor force $M = Q$, the International Markets and Native Labor schedules shift simultaneously.

V. Concluding Remarks

This paper has developed a theory of international trade and labor mobility built squarely upon the five stylized facts pointed to at the outset, but which reduces to a standard factor-endowments model under special circumstances (certainty). The dominant theme is that of the smoothing out of native labor employment fluctuations by means of a combination of commodity dumping and migrant dumping. It is the link between these two that in fact clarifies the seemingly inconsistent claims that the substitution of domestic labor for migrants allows unemployment to be exported and that the complementarity of the two types of labor permits cost reductions that sustain domestic employment. Three features emerged as key determinants of behavior: the elasticity of substitution between migrant workers and natives in production; the world elasticity of demand for home exports; and the correlation between conditions in the export market and in the migrant labor market. The role of these determinants, the relations between production, labor markets and international trade, and the implications for host-country welfare were investigated in detail.

The present paper leans heavily on simplifying assumptions, because my prime concern has been to sketch out the essentials of a theory radically different from the standard one derived from factor-endowment trade models.[11] The need for further development

[11] The present theory is actually closer in spirit to the dual economy models employed in development economics. See Corden (1974, ch. 6). Of the references cited

should be obvious. Potential developments of greatest interest, in my judgement, include consideration of the effects of uncertainty of domestic origin and also of the relation between migration and internal resource allocation and income distribution. It is often claimed that the ability to hire migrants reduces the need to reallocate native labor between sectors or between regions in response to changing circumstances. Analysis along these lines would entail the development of a multisectoral version of the present model. It is often noted that migrant workers are much more intensively employed in some sectors than in others. The relation of this observation to the reallocation argument is unclear and could certainly benefit from formal analysis.[12]

The present analysis was solely from a host-country perspective. Analysis of source countries is necessary to obtain a full treatment of international equilibrium and to investigate the welfare of migrants and of those they leave behind. Also of considerable interest would be the investigation of the consequences of asymmetric access to information by domestic firms, native workers, and migrant laborers.

Appendix

The firm's problem is to choose w_A, w_B, e to maximize

$$\text{(A1)} \quad \tfrac{1}{2}(a_A - w_A)e + \tfrac{1}{2}(a_B - w_B),$$

subject to

$$\text{(A2)} \quad \tfrac{1}{2}h(w_B) + \tfrac{1}{2}[eh(w_A) + (1-e)h(\alpha)] = u$$

$$\text{(A3)} \quad e \leq 1.$$

The first-order conditions for this problem are

$$\text{(A4)} \quad \frac{e}{2}[\lambda h'(w_A) - 1] = 0$$

$$\text{(A5)} \quad \tfrac{1}{2}[\lambda h'(w_B) - 1] = 0$$

$$\text{(A6)} \quad \tfrac{1}{2}[a_A - w_A + \lambda h(w_A) - \lambda h(\alpha)] - \mu = 0$$

$$\text{(A7)} \quad \mu(1-e) = 0$$

$$\text{(A8)} \quad \mu \geq 0,$$

where λ and μ are the dual variables. Conditions (A4) and (A5) imply that $w_A = w_B \equiv w$, and $\lambda = 1/h'(w)$. Substituting this value of λ into (A6) and noting (A8) yields equation (8) in the text. Multiplying (A6) by $(1-e)$ and noting (A7) yields equation (9). In equilibrium, u will adjust to clear the native labor market, and firms will enter and exit to drive expression (A1) to zero. This latter condition is equation (7), and now (A2) merely measures the equilibrium value of u.

Differentiation of the definitions of a_A and a_B and of equations (1)–(4), (7) and (8) (with equality) yield the following (for $e < 1$):

$$\text{(A9)} \quad \sigma_A(\hat{a}_A - \hat{P}_A) = \theta_{MA}\hat{m}_A$$

$$\text{(A10)} \quad \sigma_B(\hat{a}_B - \hat{P}_B) = \theta_{MB}\hat{m}_B$$

$$\text{(A11)} \quad \hat{X}_A - \eta_A\hat{P}_A = \hat{e} + \hat{N} + \theta_{MA}\hat{m}_A$$

$$\text{(A12)} \quad \hat{X}_B - \eta_B\hat{P}_B = \hat{N} + \theta_{MB}\hat{m}_B$$

$$\text{(A13)} \quad \theta_{DA}\hat{m}_A = \sigma_A(\hat{P}_A - \hat{v}_A)$$

$$\text{(A14)} \quad \theta_{DB}\hat{m}_B = \sigma_B(\hat{P}_B - \hat{v}_B)$$

$$\text{(A15)} \quad \frac{\theta_{DA}\theta_{MA}}{\sigma_A}\hat{m}_A = \gamma_A\hat{w} - \theta_{DA}\hat{P}_A$$

$$\text{(A16)} \quad \frac{\theta_{DB}\theta_{MB}}{\sigma_B}\hat{m}_B = \gamma_B\hat{w} - \theta_{DB}\hat{P}_B + (\theta_{DB} - \mu_{DB})\hat{e}.$$

In these equations, $\theta_{Di} \equiv 1 - \theta_{Mi}$, $\mu_{Di} \equiv w/P_i f(m_i)$, $\lambda \equiv w\phi'(w)/\phi(w)$, and $\gamma_i \equiv \lambda\theta_{Di} + (1-\lambda)\mu_{Di}$ for $i = A, B$.

in ft. 2, Ohlin actually comes closest to the concerns of the present paper.

[12] Such a multisectoral model would also allow more extensive formal utilization of the ideas in the naturally related area of segmented labor markets. See Peter Doeringer and Piore (1971) and David Gordon, Richard Edwards, and Michael Reich (1982).

To derive the properties of the various curves in Figure 2, set $\hat{X}_B = \hat{v}_B = \hat{N} = 0$. Then

$$(a_A = a_0;\ \hat{a}_A = 0)\ \hat{X}_A = (\eta_A - \sigma_A)\theta_{MA}\hat{v}_A,$$

$$(P_A = P_B;\ \hat{P}_A = 0)\ \hat{X}_A = -\theta_{MA}\left[\frac{\sigma_A}{\theta_{DA}} - \frac{\gamma_B}{\gamma_A}\frac{1}{\theta_{DB} - \mu_{DB}}\right]\hat{v}_A,$$

$$(g = e;\ \hat{m}_A = 0)\ \hat{X}_A = \left[n_A - \frac{\gamma_B}{\gamma_A}\frac{\theta_{DA}}{\theta_{DB} - \mu_{DB}}\right]\hat{v}_A,$$

$$(g = 1;\ \hat{e} + \hat{m}_A = 0)\ \hat{X}_A = \left[\eta_A - \frac{\gamma_B}{\gamma_A}\frac{\sigma_A - \eta_A}{\dfrac{\sigma_A}{\theta_{DA}} - \dfrac{\gamma_B}{\gamma_A}\dfrac{1}{\theta_{DB} - \mu_{DB}}}\right]\hat{v}_A.$$

Thus the slope of the $e = 1$ line depends upon the sign of the term $\eta_A - \sigma_A$, the $P_A = P_B$ line has negative slope, and the $g = e$ and $g = 1$ lines both have positive slopes, with the latter the steeper. In the special case $\eta_A = \sigma_A$, the a_A lines are flat and the elasticity of $g = 1$ is the elasticity of demand.

As a second comparative statics exercise, consider a general rise in migrant wages: $\hat{v}_A = \hat{v}_B = \hat{v}$. Let $\hat{X}_A = \hat{X}_B = \hat{N} = 0$ in (A9)–(A16) and solve for the endogenous variables. This gives the following

$$\text{(A17)}\quad \hat{P}_A = \frac{\theta_{DA}\gamma_A}{Z}\left[(\theta_{DB} - \mu_{DB})\theta_{MA}(\sigma_A - \eta_A) - \frac{\theta_{DB}\vartheta_{MB}}{\rho_A}(\sigma_B - \eta_B) + \frac{Z}{\theta_{DA}\gamma_A}\right]\hat{v}$$

$$\text{(A18)}\quad \hat{P}_B = (\theta_{MB}\sigma_B/\rho_B)\hat{v}$$

$$\text{(A19)}\quad \hat{M} = -(\eta_B\sigma_B/\rho_B)\hat{v}$$

$$\text{(A20)}\quad \hat{e} = (1/Z\rho_B)[\theta_{MB}\theta_{DB}\gamma_A\rho_A(\sigma_B - \nu_B) - \theta_{MA}\theta_{DA}\gamma_B\rho_B(\sigma_A - \eta_A)]\hat{v}$$

$$\text{(A21)}\quad \hat{w} = (1/Z\rho_B)[\theta_{DA}\theta_{MA}(\theta_{DB} - \mu_{DB})\rho_B(\sigma_A - \eta_A) - \theta_{DB}\theta_{MB}\theta_{DA}(\sigma_B - \eta_B)]\hat{v}$$

$$\text{(A22)}\quad \hat{g} - \hat{e} = (1/Z\rho_B) \times [\theta_{MA}(\theta_{DB} - \mu_{DB})\gamma_A\sigma_A\rho_B(\sigma_A - \eta_A) - \theta_{DB}\theta_{MB}\gamma_A\sigma_A(\sigma_B - \eta_B) + Z(\eta_B\sigma_B - \rho_B\sigma_A)]\hat{v}$$

where M denotes the employment of migrants in state B, and $Z = \rho_A(\theta_{DB} - \mu_{DB})\gamma_A - \theta_{DA}\gamma_B < 0$. If $\hat{v} > 0$, then P_B increases and M falls. The direction of change of all other terms is ambiguous, with e rising or falling as σ_A exceeds or falls short of η_A; the other terms are all sensitive to the sizes of these elasticities as well as to various shares. In the special case $\eta_A = \sigma_A = \sigma_B = \eta_B$, these equations give

$$\hat{M} < 0; \quad \hat{P}_A - \hat{v} > \theta_{MB}\hat{v} = \hat{P}_B > 0;$$
$$\hat{e} = \hat{g} = \hat{w} = 0.$$

REFERENCES

Azariadis, Costas, "Implicit Contracts and Underemployment Equilibria," *Journal of Political Economy*, December 1975, *83*, 1183–202.

Bhagwati, Jagdish N., "Distortions and Immiserizing Growth: A Generalization," *Review of Economic Studies*, October 1968, *35*, 481–85.

______, "The Theory of Immiserizing Growth: Further Applications," in Michael B. Connelly and Alexander D. Swoboda, eds., *International Trade and Money*, Toronto: University of Toronto Press, 1973.

______, "International Factor Movements and National Advantage," 9th V. K. Ramaswami Memorial Lecture, Delhi, 1979.

______ **and Brecher, Richard A.,** "National Welfare in an Open Economy in the Presence of Foreign-Owned Factors of Production," *Journal of International Economics*, February 1980, *10*, 103–16.

Birks, J. S. and Sinclair, C. A., *International Migration and Development in the Arab Region*, Geneva: International Labor Organization, 1980.

Brecher, Richard A. and Bhagwati, Jagdish N., "Foreign Ownership and the Theory of Trade and Welfare," *Journal of Political Economy*, June 1981, *89*, 497–511.

Corden, W. Max, "The Economic Limits to Population Increase," *Economic Record*, September 1955, *31*, 242–60.

______, *Trade Policy and Economic Welfare*, Oxford: Oxford University Press, 1974.

Corwin, A. F., *Immigrants — and Immigrants: Perspectives on Mexican Labor Migration to the United States*, Westport: Greenwood Press, 1978.

Dixit, Avinash and Norman, Victor, *Theory of International Trade*, London: Cambridge University Press, 1980.

Doeringer, Peter and Piore, Michael J., *Internal Labor Markets and Manpower Analysis*, Lexington: D.C. Heath, 1971.

Ethier, Wilfred J., "Dumping," *Journal of Political Economy*, June 1982, *90*, 487–506.

Gordon, David, Edwards, Richard and Reich, Michael, *Segmented Work, Divided Workers*, London: Cambridge University Press, 1982.

Hiemenz, U. and Schatz, K. W., *Trade in Place of Migration: An Employment-Oriented Study with Special Reference to the Federal Republic of Germany, Spain and Turkey*, Geneva: International Labor Organization, 1979.

Johnson, Harry G., *International Trade and Economic Growth*, Cambridge: Harvard University Press, 1965.

Kemp, Murray C., *The Pure Theory of International Trade and Investment*, Englewood Cliffs: Prentice-Hall, 1969.

Kennedy-Brenner, C., *Foreign Workers and Immigration Policy — The Case of France*, Paris: Organization for Economic Cooperation and Development, 1979.

Markusen, James R. and Melvin, James R., "Tariffs, Capital Mobility, and Foreign Ownership," *Journal of International Economics*, August 1979, *9*, 395–409.

Marshall, Ariadne, *The Import of Labor*, Rotterdam: Rotterdam University Press, 1973.

Ohlin, Bertil, *Interregional and International Trade*, rev. ed., Cambridge: Harvard University Press, 1967.

Piore, Michael J., *Birds of Passage: Migrant Labor and Industrial Societies*, London: Cambridge University Press, 1979.

Zachariah, K. C. and Conde, J., *Migration in West Africa: Demographic Aspects*, New York: Oxford University Press, 1981.

Illegal Immigration: The Host-Country Problem

By WILFRED J. ETHIER*

What can the pure theory of international trade tell us about international migration? I have long found it curious that, although migration is a central feature of the international economy and has been for a long time, and although regional economists have devoted considerable attention to the phenomenon, it has never received from the pure theory of international trade more than a small fraction of the attention lavished on the theory of international capital movements. No doubt part of the reason for this is the widely appreciated fact that much of the latter is in effect a theory of factor movements, if for no better reason than that nothing which might distinguish one factor from another is allowed to play a significant role. Thus, one might argue, we do in fact have a significant literature on migration: all that is necessary is that the word "capital" be replaced by "labor" in much of the theory of international capital movements. Indeed, a good part of what trade theorists have written about migration has in effect done just that, with labor distinguished in no essential way from other factors. This approach to migration is all to the good, as far as it goes. It does, after all, give us a useful theory, and it gives us that theory on the cheap. But we are quite noticeably without a theory addressed in any substantive way to those aspects of migration that are distinctive to it.[1]

A notable exception is the recognition that labor movements involve migration of the owner of a factor service as well as of the service itself. This has both positive and normative implications, each addressed in the literature. On the positive side, an export of labor does not generate in exchange a flow of payments, unless wages are repatriated. The analysis to follow in this paper is not sensitive to such an assumption, so I shall not further allude to the issue. The normative implication is that one must decide whether to treat the welfare of migrants as of policy concern to the country from which they have come, to that to which they have gone, or to neither.[2] The host-country perspective of this paper precludes adoption of the first alternative and the illegal status of migration limits the relevance of the second, though it will occasionally become pertinent to what follows.

There are, I believe, three key parameters that in fact distinguish incidents of migration from each other and with which any serious theory of migration must come to grips.[3] The first parameter involves whether the migration is intended to be temporary or permanent. This consideration is central to the role of migrants in both the source and host economies. Although temporary migration seems to be significantly more common in

*Department of Economics, University of Pennsylvania, Philadelphia, PA 19104. This paper has benefited from discussions during seminars at Indiana University, the Institute for International Economic Studies in Stockholm, the International Economics Study Group in London, and Pennsylvania State University, and also from both an International Trade Workshop held at the University of Western Ontario in March of 1984 and a Migration Workshop conducted in March 1985 by the Royal Institute of International Affairs and the Centre for Economic Policy Research in London.

[1] In simple factor-endowments models, international capital mobility is a perfect substitute for international labor mobility; this could limit interest in the explicit consideration of the latter. But, as a referee has pointed out, there are in fact many industries which have no feasible substitute for labor migration: some, like agriculture, use a factor that is not internationally mobile, and others, such as services, produce nontraded outputs.

[2] See, for example, Jagdish Bhagwati (1979).

[3] For a more detailed discussion of the implications of conventional trade theory for migration and of the distinguishing characteristics of the latter, see my paper (1984). The three parameters discussed below are not necessarily of significance *only* for labor mobility. As a referee has noted, the temporary or permanent nature of a flow is often important for the implications of capital movements.

the contemporary world, both types are clearly important in practice.

The second key consideration is whether migration involves skilled or unskilled labor. The former is in effect a simultaneous movement of labor and human capital. The migration of unskilled labor seems more common at present, but, again, both types are important.

The third central parameter is the legality of the migration. Though restrictions might in principle be imposed by both source and host countries, it is the (potential) hosts which in fact do so.[4] An appraisal of the relative quantitative importance of illegal immigration is, by its very nature, hard to get a handle on, but for some countries—notably the United States—it seems to be at least as large as legal migration.

The various permutations of these characteristics are not, of course, of equal importance. Some can be ignored altogether: the illegal migration of skilled workers, both temporary and permanent, is of little interest simply because most countries are quite willing to admit such migrants. The permanent legal migration of unskilled labor is the natural area of application of our existing theories (those, that is, which ignore all distinctive features of labor), although this particular type seems to be of relatively modest practical importance. The migration of skilled labor has spawned its own distinctive literature (that devoted to the "brain drain"). The temporary migration of unskilled labor, both legal and illegal, constitutes the larger part of actual migration. I have elsewhere (1985) investigated the temporary aspect of this. This paper accordingly addresses the notable outstanding gap: the illegal migration of unskilled labor.[5] As the paper ventures into untrodden terrain it will be preoccupied with the formulation of theory. I shall have to make many arbitrary decisions about what to include and what to exclude. One decision is reflected in my title: this paper will confine itself to a host-country perspective.[6]

This focus is primarily a division of labor, not a judgement of what is significant and what is not. As will become apparent, my development of the topic has been strongly influenced by policy issues in the United States. But I submit that this is increasingly convenient from a broader Atlantic perspective as well: the important European problems in this area now look (compared to the 1950's and 1960's, at any rate) more and more like the outstanding American problems, and policy reforms under discussion in the United States sound more and more like European practice.

I. Border Enforcement

The subject of illegal immigration is presumably defined by partially successful attempts to prevent that migration. The modeling of these enforcement efforts should accordingly occupy center stage in the theory to be developed.[7] This section seeks to present, in as simple a context as possible, the salient aspects of border enforcement policy.

A. *A Simple Model of Border Enforcement*

Suppose that skilled workers (S) and unskilled workers (U) can be used to pro-

[4]Communist countries constitute exceptions to this, but very few of our theories have been formulated with regard to their ability to accommodate these states.

[5]Although we do not have a theory of illegal immigration, there is a substantial amount of work on smuggling and illegal trade. See Bhagwati and Bent Hansen (1973), Mark Pitt (1981), and other references cited in the useful overview by Bhagwati (1981). This paper differs from that literature in important ways, beyond the obvious one that I examine factor movements rather than commodity trade. The smuggling literature is concerned with the efforts of importers (sometimes involving the expenditure of real resources) to expand trade by evading tariffs; the enforcement effort (and its real cost) is typically taken as given. I am concerned with the efforts of the host country (involving the expenditure of real resources) to limit the inflow of migrants, and I accordingly treat the degrees of various types of enforcement as central instrumental variables. Perhaps each literature could profit by exploiting the insights of the other, but that is not the purpose of this paper.

[6]For a look at international interdependence, see Slobodan Djajic (1985).

[7]My efforts will be very much in the spirit of the economic theory of crime pioneered by Gary Becker (1968). See also Isaac Ehrlich (1974).

duce output (Q) via a neoclassical production function:

$$Q = Sf(u)$$

where u denotes employment of unskilled workers per skilled worker. Skilled workers are all natives. Unskilled labor consists of two parts, $U = L + I$, with L denoting the supply of native unskilled workers plus legal immigrants, and I the number of illegal immigrants present in the host country.

Of those (M) who illegally attempt to immigrate, a certain number (C) are caught and denied entry,[8] so that $I = M - C$. The authorities' success in preventing illegal entry presumably depends upon the resources devoted to border enforcement.[9] Denote by E the quantity, in terms of output, of such resources. An increase in E would increase the authorities' apprehension ratio, C/M, although probably at a decreasing rate. I accordingly assume that

$$C/M = g(E)$$

where $g(0) = 0$, $g' > 0$, $g'' < 0$, $g < 1$.

Although I have announced my intention to stick to a host-country perspective, it is crucial that the decision to migrate be explicitly modeled in some way. I assume that foreign workers in the source country have the choice of remaining there and earning the wage (or wage equivalent) w^*, which I take to be exogenous, or of attempting to migrate. If successful they earn the expected wage $\tilde{w}$, received by host-country unskilled workers, because either legal or illegal migrants are indistinguishable to firms or else the distinction is of no consequence to them.[10] If unsuccessful, the would-be migrants earn $w^* - k$, where k is the (wage equivalent of) the penalty suffered by those who are caught. The probability of a typical potential migrant getting caught is C/M, or $g(E)$. Assuming that foreign workers are risk neutral, attempted migration adjusts so as to equate the expected reward from migration to the local wage:

$$(w^* - k)g + \tilde{w}(1 - g) = w^*.$$

Thus we have

$$(1) \quad \tilde{w} = w^* + k[g(E)/(1 - g(E))] = w(E)$$

It follows then that the expected wage of unskilled labor is directly determined by the effort put into border enforcement. The submarkets in which illegal migrants are important are usually characterized by relatively high unemployment rates. I suppose therefore that the unskilled labor market has a rigid wage, w, presumably at a level above the market-clearing one. Suppose that this market operates in a familiar Harris-Todaro fashion:[11] firms employ unskilled labor to the point at which the rigid wage just equals the value of the worker's marginal product, and the consequently scarce jobs are allocated among workers by means of a random draw, so the expected wage $\tilde{w}$ confronted *ex ante* by unskilled workers is ew, where $e(I + L)$ denotes the total employment of unskilled labor. Then

$$(2) \quad w = f'(u),$$

$$(3) \quad ew = w(E),$$

where $u = e(I + L)/S$ and $w(E)$ is as in (1). The market for skilled workers, by con-

[8] The variable M actually denotes the total number of attempts to migrate, not the number of individuals making such attempts. Some of those who at first do not succeed will presumably try again.

[9] I have in mind illegal entry, rather than illegal "overstaying." While the former is the main focus of interest in the United States, the latter is relatively more important in some European countries. Much of my analysis does in fact apply to overstaying as well, but I will not explicitly address that form of illegal immigration.

[10] This point will be investigated in great detail later in the paper.

[11] See John Harris and Michael Todaro (1970). A similar assumption has been made when unemployment has been considered in the brain drain literature: see Bhagwati and Koichi Hamada (1974) and Carlos Rodriguez (1975). See also Djajic.

trast, is assumed to clear, and they are paid a wage v reflecting the value of their marginal product:

$$v = f(u) - uf'(u). \tag{4}$$

I assume that E is financed by a tax on the wages of skilled workers only:

$$E = tvS. \tag{5}$$

Now E determines e from (1) and (3), w determines u from (2), (4) gives v, and (5) determines the tax rate t. Then each value of E yields a unique equilibrium, and an increase in E will raise e, reduce I, require a larger t, and leave u and v unchanged. Such a policy change consequently harms skilled workers and benefits employed unskilled workers, both those in the country legally and those there illegally. The improvement takes the form of better job prospects, in view of the assumed rigid wage. Potential migrants are neither better off nor worse off in an *ex ante* sense, although the smaller number who actually succeed in entering the country do then have improved prospects.

Note that equations (1), (2), and (3) imply that

$$\tilde{w} - w^* = [uwS/(I + L)] - w^*.$$

Thus increases in the wage gap, $\tilde{w} - w^*$, will be associated with *decreases* in the actual volume I of illegal immigration. A large part of the substantial empirical literature on migration proceeds, by contrast, from the presumption that actual migration ought to be positively correlated with the wage gap.

B. *Objectives of Enforcement*

Why should a nation have an interdiction policy? The international capital movements literature, with its emphasis on the optimal rate of taxation of foreign earnings, suggests one answer: to exploit market power with respect to mobile labor; that is, to maximize national income. A second policy objective could be the internal distribution of income between skilled and unskilled workers. A final objective consistent with the present model is I itself; the authorities might wish to control the number of immigrants in the country for social reasons.

What policy instruments are available to the authorities to help achieve these three targets? There is, of course, border interdiction, E. The tax rate t is clearly not a distinct policy tool. However, L, the number of legal unskilled workers, is, because it is determined by the authorities' decision about how many migrants to admit legally. Thus, in the context of the present model, there are apparently three potential policy targets and two potential instruments.

The actual situation, however, differs in several ways from the potential one. Consider the first target, the maximization of national income. One would expect border enforcement to be inferior to a tax on migrant wages, since the former uses up revenues instead of generating them.[12] But a migrant wage tax may not be feasible—much is infeasible in this area of inquiry. How then, would an increase in the border interdiction effort E affect host-country national income? To see this, measure home real income as

$$Y = weL + vS - E. \tag{6}$$

Note that I include the wages of native unskilled workers and legal migrants, but exclude wages paid to illegal immigrants. Now an increase in E will have no effect on w, L, v, or S, but will raise e (benefiting unskilled workers) and E (harming skilled workers). National income will obviously rise if and only if

$$[weL/E]\, \hat{e} > \hat{E},$$

where a circumflex denotes proportional change (for example, $\hat{e} = de/e$). Differentiation of (1) and (3) reveals that

$$\hat{e} = [(ew - w^*)/ew]\, \varepsilon_B / [1 - g(E)]\, \hat{E},$$

where ε_B denotes the elasticity of the border

[12]A fee for temporary migration has been advocated by Edwin Harwood, in Nathan Glazer (1985).

enforcement schedule (Eg'/g). Thus an increase in the interdiction effort E will succeed in raising host-country national income only if an increase in E is sufficiently effective so that

$$(7) \qquad \varepsilon_B > [1-g]E/[we - w^*]L.$$

If immigration policy does in fact raise national income, it will not do so by exploiting monopoly power in the international labor market: I have assumed away such power, and migrant workers, like native unskilled workers, are paid the rigid wage w in any event. Instead, the possibility of an increase in national income reflects the assumed distortion in the host unskilled labor market; if migrants are successfully excluded, there are more jobs available at an unchanging wage for legal workers. Indeed the possession of monopoly power in the world market for unskilled workers could easily make it *more* difficult for an increase in E to raise national income! For suppose that a rise in E, by making attempts at migration less tempting to foreign workers and therefore inducing more to remain in the source country labor market, lowers w^*. This in turn makes staying at home less attractive: the rise in E is less effective in reducing the temptation to migrate when w^* can fall than when it is unresponsive. Thus fewer jobs could be freed for legal residents,[13] and the condition for host-country national income to rise would accordingly become stricter than (7).

This analysis should leave us, I believe, with considerable skepticism about the ability of interdiction policy to influence national income. With any effect on the international market for unskilled workers likely to be counterproductive, the full burden falls on ε_B. But skepticism about the ability of marginal changes in E to have significant effect is widespread in practice. Furthermore, in this model national income can be raised only by redistributing income from skilled to unskilled workers. With this distribution itself a policy target there is no freedom to influence national income even if it is feasible to do so. Finally, it is the presence of a distorted home labor market that makes it possible to use E to raise Y. One would expect, therefore, that this possibility would disappear if instead w were to adjust to clear the market for unskilled labor.[14]

With immigration policy ineffective in the exploitation of market power in the migrant labor market, we would appear to be left with two targets and two instruments. But this is not so. Although L can be varied directly, it is not, in fact, a meaningful instrument. As we have seen, the rigid wage w directly determines the technique of production, $u = e[L + I]/S$, with e determined by E. It follows, therefore, that any change in L will simply cause an offsetting change in I, and thus in C and M also. Reducing the number of legal immigrants will increase by a greater amount those who attempt illegal entry, and by an equal amount those who succeed. We have, therefore, only one policy instrument.

We still have two potential targets, e (or the internal *ex ante* distribution of income) and I. But note that equation (2) inextricably binds these two targets together: with u set by the rigid wage, e directly determines I. There is no way to unbundle these two targets. Unless the authorities just happen to desire a consistent combination of e and I, they will have to trade off one goal for the other, even before considering what tools might be available.

This, then, is the policy environment implied by my simple model. I close this part of the paper by discussing in turn the roles of two central assumptions of the model: that there is a rigid wage for unskilled labor and that all taxes are borne by skilled workers. Each assumption is closely related to a real-life issue of considerable importance.

[13] The paradoxical possibility arises because the policy under consideration is the interdiction effort E and would disappear in the presence of an optimal tax on migrant earnings.

[14] This modification to the model is considered below.

C. *Flexible Wages*

To see the significance of a rigid wage for unskilled labor, consider now the opposite case where w is flexible. Then, in equations (2) and (3), $e = 1$ and w becomes a variable. The subsequent analysis is unchanged except that w takes the role previously performed by e. In particular, the policy environment implied by the model is basically the same. The largest change has to do with the effect of a rise in E on national income, so let us take a look at that.

Differentiation of (6), now that $e = 1$ and both w and v are variables, gives $(dY/dE) = L(dw/dE) + S(dv/dE) - 1$. Taking note of (2) and (3), this reduces to

$$(8) \qquad dY/dE = -I(dw/dE) - 1.$$

That is, the welfare cost of an increased interdiction effort is the sum of the direct cost of the effort itself plus the increase in the wages paid to the initial body of illegal immigrants. This will indeed almost surely be a welfare *cost*, because there is little chance that dw/dE will be negative. Because workers are paid their marginal product, a fall in w would have to be accompanied by a *rise* in actual immigration I. But with w^* exogenous, the fall in w and rise in E would deter immigration rather than encourage it. If the host country possesses power in the international labor market, it is conceivable that w^* might fall enough to encourage more immigration. But if a fall in w^* requires a larger labor supply in source-country markets, there is little chance that this will be consistent with *both* a larger volume of successful emigration and a larger host-country apprehension ratio (due to the larger E).

The earlier skepticism about the ability of interdiction policy to raise national income is thus even stronger in the presence of a flexible wage. I leave it to the reader appropriately to rephrase the other previous results. In the rest of this paper I continue to allow a flexible wage. This makes it easier to relate my discussion to the standard theory of international trade, my point of departure. It is also (marginally) more convenient analytically. But the parallel between a flexible wage and a rigid wage is so strong that detailed separate consideration of the latter would be redundant.

D. *The Fiscal Issue*

Since border enforcement requires real resources, it must be financed. I have assumed that this is done by a tax on the earnings of skilled workers so that illegal immigrants, in particular, pay no taxes. This confronts my theory with an outstanding real-life issue: the net effect of illegal immigrants on the budget of the host-country government. It is a matter of considerable controversy, at least in the United States, whether such aliens pay taxes greater than the additional expenses that they cause. What difference does it make? To find the answer (in the world of my model at any rate), consider the alternative case in which illegal immigrants do form part of the tax base of the home country. (Since the only role of the government in my model is its enforcement activity, this amounts to specifying who pays for that enforcement). Suppose a proportional tax on production (or on value-added or on incomes) at the rate $t = E/Q$. Thus firms pass on the tax to their workers and the (post-tax) wages w and v of unskilled and skilled workers are now

$$(2') \qquad w = (1-t)f'(u)$$

$$(4') \qquad v = (1-t)[f(u) - uf'(u)].$$

Illegal immigrants will automatically be part of the tax base. Equation (5) now becomes

$$(5') \qquad E = tSf(u).$$

As before, E directly determines w so as to equilibrate the international labor flow. Then (2′) and (5′) jointly determine t and u, which in turn imply v, from (4′), and I. But (2′) and (5′) each defines a negative relation between t and u—for any given level of E—and (2′) has no particular curvature. Thus multiple solutions are possible, and if there are multiple solutions, some of them will necessarily respond in perverse fashion to changes in E.

We are accordingly driven to the conclusion that border enforcement policy—in the form of a choice of E—is an effective means of influencing the wage paid to those native unskilled workers and legal migrants that compete directly with illegal immigrants, but that it could well be an unpredictable and unstable influence upon both the number of illegal immigrants who actually enter the country and upon the wages of native skilled workers who compete only indirectly with the migrants. By contrast, if the tax base is restricted to skilled labor, equilibrium is unique and responds in an intuitive way to changes in E.[15]

E. *Overview of Border Enforcement*

To sum up, the present model has directed attention to three issues. The *fiscal issue*, whether the migrants on balance contribute to or detract from the host-government surplus, is relevant to the ability of the authorities to use interdiction policy to control actual migration. The *income issue* concerns the effect of enforcement on the national income of the host country. This is likely negative, so that such policy is costly and so confronts the country with the problem of minimizing the cost of an enforcement policy pursued for some other reason. Finally the authorities are confronted with the *bundling problem*: how to attain simultaneously independent goals regarding the volume of immigration and the domestic distribution of income.

II. Internal Enforcement Policy

The discussion thus far furnishes two good reasons to hunt for an additional policy tool to supplement interdiction. First, border enforcement is quite probably costly. This raises the possibility of trying to find an assortment of policies to produce the same result at lower cost. Public debate in the United States has for years been dominated by the belief that a border enforcement policy consistent with national goals would in fact prove far too costly.

The second reason is that the authorities are likely to have independent goals regarding both internal income distribution and the volume of immigration. Thus there is need for an instrument capable of unbundling these two targets.

The rest of this paper concerns the second instrument. Enforcement has thus far been assumed confined to the border so that, once inside, illegal immigrants are indistinguishable from other unskilled workers. I now consider domestic enforcement policies intended to make it relatively more difficult for illegal immigrants in the domestic marketplace. Such policies seem very promising in regard to the two reasons just discussed for looking at additional tools. First, as is suggested by the frequent public suggestions that illegal entry attempts will abate once the employment prospects of immigrants are reduced, such domestic enforcement promises to exert an effect independent from that of border enforcement. Thus a combination of such policies could potentially reduce costs. Second, if the employment of illegal immigrants is prohibited, and if this prohibition is backed up by some degree of enforcement, firms will no longer see the two types of workers as identical. Thus such a policy fosters the hope of unbundling the two goals of internal income distribution and the volume of immigration.

[15] The model is simple enough to render these conclusions reasonably transparent. An intensification of border enforcement E must raise the domestic wage received by unskilled workers. There are two ways this can come about. One is to reduce the number of unskilled workers per skilled worker, so that the marginal product of the former rises. This requires a reduction in immigration. A low elasticity of substitution between the two types of labor obviously makes it easier to produce a change in real wages in this way. The second method is to increase national product enough so that the after-tax wage received by unskilled workers rises, even if their marginal product falls. Such an increase in output can come about only if more migrants are employed. This method is facilitated by a high elasticity of substitution between the two types of workers (which limits the decline in the migrants' marginal product when more of them are employed) and by a large share of unskilled labor in national income (which limits the proportional rise in I necessary to expand output significantly). The corresponding algebra is straightforward.

There are also practical reasons for considering domestic enforcement. Policy debate in the United States has for several years focused upon the advisability and consequences of the adoption of such policies. Also they are important in many northern European countries, where only modest efforts are devoted to border enforcement.

A. *Domestic Enforcement*

Suppose that domestic enforcement takes the form of random inspections of firms. Let J denote the number of illegal immigrants discovered at work by such inspections, and let D denote the total resources, in terms of domestic output, devoted to the inspection effort. I assume that

$$J/I = h(D)$$

where $h' > 0,\ h'' < 0,\ h(0) = 0,\ h < 1$. Suppose for simplicity that illegal immigrants who are caught working are paid anyway, so that only employers are subjected to direct penalties. (Thus the direct punishment from border enforcement falls exclusively upon migrants and that from domestic enforcement exclusively upon firms.) Suppose that this penalty can be expressed as an incremental cost of k^* per discovered illegal immigrant.[16] Continue to denote by w the wage received by illegal immigrants and by e the employment rate of unskilled workers. My earlier argument continues to apply, so w is still determined by border enforcement E—again, I take w^* as exogenous. Now let w_L denote the wage received by domestic unskilled workers and by legal migrants. A crucial consideration is whether domestic firms are able to distinguish these workers from illegal immigrants. If they cannot, $w = w_L$ and the effect of domestic enforcement will be to disadvantage unskilled workers relative to native skilled workers. For the firm that hires one of the former takes the risk that the new employee is an illegal immigrant and that the authorities will discover this fact, thereby increasing the expected cost to the firm of employing this worker by $k^*h(D)I/U$. But if firms can distinguish illegal immigrants, domestic enforcement will disadvantage these laborers relative to native unskilled workers and legal migrants. Thus the effect of the policy upon the welfare of this latter group is essentially sensitive to the ability of firms to distinguish between the two types of potential employees. I consider first the case where a firm can distinguish.

B. *Complete Discernment*

If firms can tell whether a prospective unskilled employee is an illegal immigrant or not, (2) will apply only to native unskilled workers and legal migrants and so is replaced by

$$w_L = f'(u). \tag{2''}$$

Risk-neutral firms will ensure that w_L equals the expected labor cost of hiring an illegal immigrant:

$$w_L = w + h(D)k^*. \tag{9}$$

Finally, taxes must now finance both enforcement policies:

$$D + E = tvS. \tag{10}$$

Thus E determines w in (1), this then gives w_L from (9), which then determines u from (2″), v from (4), and t from (10). Each policy pair (D, E) generates a unique equilibrium.[17]

[16] This paper treats as exogenous the two penalties, k and k^*. This is quite compelling as regards k, since the penalty born by aliens who fail to gain entry consists to a large degree of the opportunity cost of the time lost in being sent back. But the penalty k^* levied on employers presumably would correspond in substantial part to fines and/or prison sentences, so there is a good case for treating both D and k^* as policy variables. But to make k^* endogenous in a satisfactory way would require addressing the relation between that variable and the performance of enforcement officials, with regard to zeal, corruption, and so on. All this does not seem to me a natural and essential part of the topic of this paper, so I sidestep it by simply taking k^* as exogenous.

[17] The above argument assumes that k^* is a social cost. If it is not, in whole or in part (for example, if k^*

I wish to expose the considerations relevant to the choice of policy mix between D and E. The authorities might be using policy to try to control the level of illegal immigration I for fundamentally social reasons, or to try to influence domestic income distribution by affecting w_L. An immediate conclusion is that the mix of policy tools is irrelevant to any tradeoff between these possible targets; that is, the addition of border enforcement does not solve the unbundling problem. This is because w_L is directly related to u—and therefore to I as well—by equation (2″), regardless of the relative reliance of the authorities on border enforcement or on internal enforcement.

Consider, then, whether combining domestic enforcement with border enforcement might allow a reduction in the cost of whatever policy goal is chosen. Suppose that the authorities have as a policy target a particular level of w_L, either for its own sake or because of its associated level of I. Then substitution of this target value and of equation (1) into (9) yields

$$(11) \quad w_L = w^* + kg(E) / [1 - g(E)] + h(D)k^*.$$

Equation (11) determines all combinations of the policy variables D and E that will achieve the stipulated target. These combinations are graphed as the AA' schedule in Figure 1. As drawn, the schedule has a negative slope and is strictly convex to the origin.

At point A, the wage received by illegal immigrants $w = w^*$. Moving down the schedule, with border enforcement substituted for domestic enforcement so as to keep the actual level I of illegal immigration unchanged, the wage given the latter, w, steadily rises, until at point A' it equals w_L, the (constant) wage received by native unskilled workers and legal migrants. It is also clear that such a substitution, by raising E, must increase the

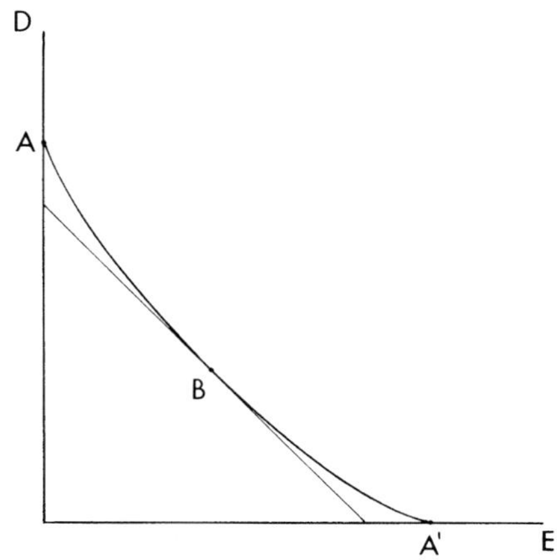

FIGURE 1

ratio C/M. With I unchanged and D falling, J must fall as well.

What determines which (D, E) combination the authorities should choose? This depends, of course, upon their objectives. To minimize the total cost $D + E$ of immigration policy, the authorities need to choose that combination of D and E for which the AA' schedule has a slope of minus unity, illustrated by point B in Figure 1.

By moving from A to B, the host country can *both* reduce its net costs *and* improve the welfare (*ex post*) of migrants illegally residing within its borders, while continuing to attain the w_L target. But beyond B, native welfare must be sacrificed in order to raise migrant welfare further. Moving toward A' will clearly raise w. The level of I will be unchanged, as will the incomes of S and L. The rise in wI must just equal, from (9), the fall in k^*J: penalties on employers are substituted by the wages of illegal immigrants.[18]

In order to find the socially optimal point on AA', it is necessary to be more specific

reflects a fine collected by the government), then the appropriate amount should be deducted from the right-hand side of (10). This does not affect the argument that each (D, E) generates a unique equilibrium.

[18]Since $D + E$ is increased by any departure from B, the after-tax incomes of skilled workers necessarily fall, with v remaining constant.

about the employer penalties k^*J. These penalties might constitute a real social cost in the form of lost output—as I have implicitly assumed thus far—or they might simply be fines which accrue to the government—in which case they should be deducted from the left-hand side of expression (10). Suppose the former. Then national income, net of immigration policy, is equal to: $Sf(u) - wI - E - D - k^*J = Sf(u) - w_L I + h(D)k^*I - E - D - k^*J = Sf(u) - w_L I - E - D$. Now $Sf(u) - w_L I$ is determined by the presumed social policy. Thus national income is maximized by minimizing $E + D$, the cost of enforcement. If, on the other hand, the employer penalties are not real costs but instead fines collected by the government, the term $-k^*J$ should not be included in the maximand. In this case maximizing national income is the same as minimizing $E + D - k^*J$. But now this latter term measures the cost of enforcement. Thus in either case this cost should be minimized in order to maximize national income.

When employer penalties constitute a real social cost, this will of course be at point B in Figure 1. If instead the penalties levied on firms take the form of fines, it will evidently be in the national interest to depart from point B in a northwest direction along AA'.

Finally, it should be pointed out that, given the policy variables D and E, changes in legal migration L would again be exactly offset by equal changes in I (and so also in J, M and C), leaving w_L and U unaltered. But, if $D > 0$, $w_L > w$ so that it is better (from the native point of view) to keep any migration illegal, that is, $L = 0$ is now optimal policy.

This analysis has, of course, proceeded on the assumption that the markets in which the illegal immigrants find themselves do in fact clear. Consider instead the unemployment model discussed earlier. Suppose that the unskilled labor wage w_L is again exogenously determined. Then the spending on internal enforcement, D, will directly determine the wage w received by employed illegal immigrants, from equation (9), but this has no effect on host-country income distribution. Again we have $w(E) = ew$, so, once D is given, spending on interdiction E directly determines the employment rate e of illegal immigrants. This is in turn linked to the volume of immigration, since $e(L + I) = Su$. Thus it remains true that the volume of immigration is bundled with domestic unskilled labor market conditions (interpreted as the employment rate, in this case). Internal enforcement offers extra control only over the national cost of the chosen policy, since variations in D produce only variations in what must be spent for immigrant labor, w.[19]

In summary, supplementing interdiction at the border with domestic enforcement does allow the authorities to achieve their chosen policy target at a lower cost than would the use of border enforcement alone. However, the basic problem that the internal distribution of income and the level of immigration are rigidly linked together remains.

C. *No Discernment*

These conclusions are based on the assumption that domestic firms are indeed able to distinguish illegal immigrants from legal unskilled workers. To get a handle on the significance of this assumption, consider briefly the opposite case. That is, assume now that firms are unable to distinguish the two.[20] Then a firm will think that there is a probability equal to $I/[L + I]$ that any unskilled worker applying for a job is in fact an illegal immigrant. As before, the expected penalty for hiring an illegal alien is $h(D)k^*$. If workers are paid the expected value, to the firm, of their marginal product, then the wage received by both legal and illegal unskilled labor must satisfy

$$(9') \quad w = f'(u) - h(D)[1 - (L/uS)]k^*.$$

[19] Note that if w is pegged, instead of the legal wage, spending on internal enforcement D will directly influence the latter, so that the bundling problem will be solved. But this description of the labor market seems less intuitively appealing then the one in the text. In any case, discriminating between the two would require a detailed analysis quite beyond the scope of the present paper.

[20] Since this case is of interest only if the government can distinguish illegal aliens when it inspects firms, it is necessary that the government have access to some means of verification not available to private firms.

Since the immigrant wage must still be given by $w(E)$, this implies that (2) must now be replaced by

$$(2''') \qquad w(E) = f'(u) - h(D)[1-(L/uS)]k^*.$$

It is immediate from (2‴) that the addition of a second policy tool has now unbundled the internal distribution of income and the level of illegal immigration. Furthermore, the instruments should be assigned to the two targets in a very specific way. Border enforcement E will determine directly the unskilled labor wage, w, irrespective of domestic enforcement D. The latter can accordingly then be adjusted to cause u (and therefore I) to assume its desired value.[21]

Notice the peculiar position in which legal unskilled workers find themselves. On the one hand, the fact that firms cannot distinguish them from illegal aliens means they must share the latter's fate: both are disadvantaged relative to skilled workers. But it is just this which breaks the link between w and I, and so allows the authorities free rein to use interdiction policy to influence w, without concern for the affect of such policy on the volume of immigration.[22]

D. *Endogenous Discernment*

I've looked at the two extreme cases where firms either completely distinguish legal unskilled workers from illegal aliens, or completely fail to make such a distinction. Consider now the more realistic situation where limited discernment takes place. This will not merely constitute a mix of the two cases just considered, but will introduce distinctive features of its own, especially when account is taken of the fact that the degree of discernment will be at least partially endogenous.

If firms cannot distinguish between illegal immigrants and other unskilled workers, domestic enforcement will disadvantage unskilled workers (including native unskilled workers and legal immigrants) relative to skilled native workers. Thus legitimate unskilled workers have an incentive to adopt measures to distinguish themselves from their illegal rivals, and to support public policies designed to produce such distinctions.

It is not surprising, then, that the policies should be central to public debate on immigration enforcement in host countries. In an analysis of the issues they raise, two aspects seem crucial: the effort illegal immigrants devote to trying to pass themselves off as legal, and the effects on those legal residents who might be mistaken for illegal entrants.

Suppose that a proposed policy attempts to distinguish illegal migrants from legitimate unskilled workers. This presumably involves "doing something" to the latter, since the former would not cooperate with such an effort. The policy could be one of issuing identification cards to legal workers.

The unskilled labor force consists, as before, of illegal immigrants I plus legal unskilled workers L who would never be mistaken for illegal entrants, but now there is also a group N of legal unskilled workers who could be so mistaken. Thus the total unskilled labor force is $U = L + N + I$. Let p denote the probability that a member of I succeeds in passing himself off as a member of N. Presumably attaining any positive value of p requires the migrant to spend some amount μ on deceptive efforts (such as the purchase of counterfeit identification cards):

$$\mu = H(p)$$

where $H(0) = 0$, $0 < p < 1$, $H' > 0$, $H'' > 0$. For simplicity it is assumed that H is of constant elasticity $e_D = pH'/\mu$, the "elasticity of deception."

[21] Note that I am here interpreting the internal distribution target as concern about the wage of unskilled workers. The wage of skilled workers will still depend upon u, and the taxes they pay will depend upon $D + E$.

[22] The unemployment variation of this model is again qualitatively similar. Interdiction policy E directly determines the employment rate e of unskilled labor from the relation $w(E) = ew$, where w is the pegged wage. Equation (9′) shows how domestic enforcement policy D directly determines u. Since $L + I = Su/e$, D can be used to control the volume of immigration independently of the employment rate implemented by the choice of E.

As before, a potential migrant who attempts entry faces the probability g of failing, and thus earning $(w^* - k)$, and the probability $(1-g)$ of gaining entry. In the latter event, he spends μ on deception and faces the conditional probability p of successfully passing himself off as a member of N and thereby earning their wage w_N, and the conditional probability $(1-p)$ of being recognized as a member of I and thereby earning their wage, w. Assuming as before that attempted migration M adjusts to equate the expected reward of attempting entry to that of staying behind,

$$(12) \quad w^* = (w^* - k)g + [w_N p + w(1-p) - \mu](1-g).$$

Illegal entrants will choose μ so as to maximize their expected earnings, $w_N p + w(1-p) - \mu$. Setting the derivative of this expression equal to zero gives the condition

$$(13) \qquad w_N - w = \mu\varepsilon_D / p.$$

The second-order condition is $\varepsilon_D > 1$, which I henceforth assume. A boundary solution, with p equal to either 0 or 1, is also possible. If $p = 0$, illegal immigrants in fact make no attempts at deception, and members of N are treated just like members of L: my earlier analysis of discriminating firms remains relevant. If, on the other hand, $p = 1$, members of N find themselves treated just like members of I, with $w_N = w(E) + \mu$. Since these boundary cases are easily understood, I now assume an interior solution.

Workers recognized as illegal immigrants will, as before, be paid the value of their marginal product adjusted for the chance that they will be discovered and their employers penalized:

$$(14) \qquad w + h(D)k^* = f'(u).$$

Substituting (13) and (14) into (12) then gives

$$f'(u) - h(D)k^* = w(E) + (1-\varepsilon_D)\mu$$

where $w(E)$ is as defined previously in (1). Rearranging this term and recalling the

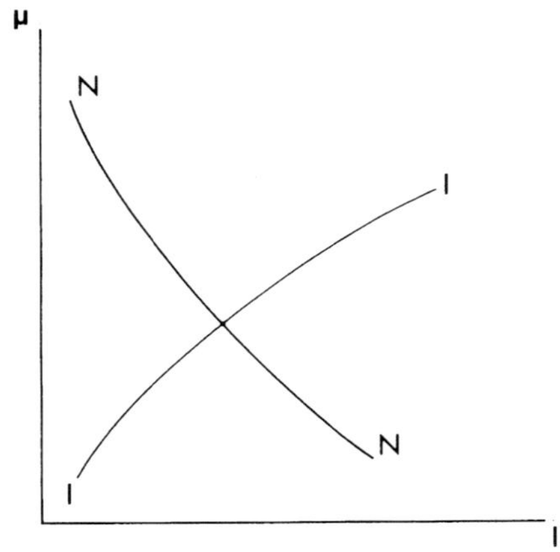

FIGURE 2

definition of u gives

$$(15) \quad f'([N + I + L]/S) - (1-\varepsilon_D)\mu = w(E) + h(D)k^*.$$

This expression is graphed as the II schedule in Figure 2. It depicts those combinations of illegal entrants I and deceptive efforts μ which cause the illegal labor market to clear. Everywhere along this schedule the numbers attempting to migrate are just such as to equilibrate the expected earnings from migration to the earnings from staying, successful entrants make the optimal deceptive effort, and those entrants recognized by employers for what they are receive the value of their marginal product less the expected employer penalty.

Clearly the II schedule will have a positive slope, as depicted in Figure 2, since the elasticity of deception exceeds unity. Note also that equation (15) can be written as $w = w(E) + (1-\varepsilon_D)\mu$. Recall that $w(E)$ is the wage that illegal immigrants would receive were there no possibility of deception, and w is the wage paid those perceived to be illegal. Thus migrants known to be illegal entrants are paid less than they would receive with the same border enforcement effort, were deception impossible. For those migrants this is a secondary burden, since they also pay μ for the deception attempt. For their employers it is a benefit, since they pay less for the illegal labor they hire.

Next consider the markets for legal unskilled workers. Those who are clearly legal (L) will receive a wage w_L equal to the value of their marginal product, as described in (2′). But a member of N could, from the viewpoint of a prospective employer, actually be an illegal immigrant whose employment would bring with it the possibility of a penalty. The chance that an apparent member of N is actually a member of I is $pI/(N+pI)$, and the expected penalty from employing an illegal alien is hk^*. Thus members of N earn the wage satisfying

$$(16) \quad w_N + [pI/(N+pI)]h(D)k^* = f'(u).$$

Subtracting (16) from (14) and using (13) gives

$$(17) \quad [(pI+N)/N]\mu/p = h(D)k^*/\varepsilon_D.$$

This relation, graphed as the NN schedule in Figure 2, shows all combinations of I and μ that clear the market for legal unskilled workers apparently of type N. Clearly the NN schedule must have a negative slope, as depicted in Figure 2, since $\varepsilon_D > 1$.

It is evident from (15) and (17) that an intensification of border enforcement E will shift the II schedule to the left while leaving the NN schedule untouched. Thus an increase in E will reduce the volume of illegal immigration I, but cause those entrants to devote more effort to deception. This means that the perceived volume of illegal immigration, $(1-p)I$, will fall by more than will I itself: the intensification of border enforcement will appear to be more successful than it really is (and than it would appear to be if there were no policy of internal enforcement).

An increase in domestic enforcement D will also shift the II schedule to the left, while in addition shifting NN to the right. Thus the rise in D has an ambiguous effect on illegal immigration but does significantly increase attempts at deception. Thus such a policy shift is likely to produce a large decline in perceived immigration, and thus appear to be quite successful, even if in fact it has little effect on I!

To proceed further, let us examine analytically the effects of policy changes. Differentiating the expressions for the II and NN schedules (equations (15) and (17)) with respect to E and solving yields

$$\hat{\mu} = -ew[w(E)/N\Delta]\hat{E}$$

and

$$\hat{I} = \varepsilon_w[w(E)/N\Delta] \times [(N(\varepsilon_D - 1) + pI\varepsilon_D)/pI\varepsilon_D]\hat{E}.$$

In these expressions, ε_w denotes the elasticity of $w(E)$, $[w'E/w(E)$, and

$$\Delta = -[\theta_S w_L/eU][(N(\varepsilon_D - 1) + pI\varepsilon_D)/pN\varepsilon_D] - (\varepsilon_D - 1)\mu/N < 0,$$

where θ_S denotes the distributive share of skilled labor. That is, Δ is the Jacobian determinant of the system (15),(17):

$$\Delta = \begin{bmatrix} [-\theta_S w_L]/eU & \varepsilon_D - 1 \\ \mu/N & [N(\varepsilon_D - 1) + pI\varepsilon_D]/pN\varepsilon_D \end{bmatrix}$$

These expressions confirm that an increase in border enforcement E will lower illegal immigration I and intensify attempted deception μ. The net effect on the volume of aliens successfully passing themselves off as legitimate unskilled workers, pI, is then given by

$$\hat{p} + \hat{I} = (\hat{\mu}/\varepsilon_D) + \hat{I} = \varepsilon_w[w(E)/N\Delta][(\varepsilon_D - 1)/\varepsilon_D] \times [(pI+N)/pI]\hat{E}.$$

Thus pI must fall as a result of the rise in border enforcement: the intensified deception effort does not make up for the reduction in illegal immigration.

We can now see how the increased border enforcement affects the various labor groups. The fall in I implies a fall in U and therefore in u as well; this implies, from (2′) and (14), that the wages of native unskilled workers of unambiguous identity, w_L, and those of illegal migrants recognized as such, w, both increase, and in identical amounts. Because of the fall in pI, the wages of members of N (and of those illegal migrants passing themselves off as legitimate) increases even more than w_L and w. (This conclusion is by no means obvious; it depends critically upon $\varepsilon_D > 1$—the second-order condition for optimal deception.) The losers are native skilled workers and those migrants who fail to gain entry as a result of the rise in E. The basic conclusion, then, is that it is the members of that group susceptible to being confused with illegal migrants that stands to gain the most from an intensification of border enforcement, in spite of the fact that one of the consequences of such an intensification will be to induce illegal entrants to redouble their efforts to pass themselves off as members of the susceptible group.

An intensification of internal enforcement in the percentage $\hat{D}$ produces the following results.

$$\hat{\mu} = -[(pI+N)/pN][\varepsilon_I/\Delta] \times [(\theta_S w_L/eU)+(\varepsilon_D \mu/N)]\hat{D}$$

$$\hat{I} = (hk^*\varepsilon_I/\Delta)([(1-p)/pI] \times [(\varepsilon_D - 1)/e_D] + (1/N))\hat{D}$$

where $\varepsilon_I = h'D/h$, the elasticity of the internal enforcement schedule.

It follows from these expressions that an intensification of internal enforcement increases the deception effort μ, as indicated by the geometry, but also unambiguously reduces the volume of illegal immigration I. Thus the wages of clearly legal unskilled workers (L) rise as a result of the increase in D. However the effect on pI is ambiguous, and therefore so also is the effect on the wage (w_N) of legal workers who might be mistaken for illegal immigrants. Indeed it could be the case that the welfare of members of N might actually be improved by an increase in internal enforcement efforts! Clearly illegal immigrants are also affected ambiguously; in (14) both the value of these worker's marginal product, $f'(u)$, and the unexpected penalty of employing them, $h(D)k^*$, rise. Obviously these workers are disadvantaged relative to the clearly legal, with $w_L - w$ rising in the proportion $eI\hat{D}$, from (14). They are also disadvantaged relative to the ambiguous group: it follows from (13) that $w_N - w$ rises in the proportion $[(\varepsilon_D - 1)/\varepsilon_D]\hat{\mu}$.

An intensification of either border enforcement or internal enforcement will raise the wages of those workers liable to be mistaken for illegal immigrants relative to those who clearly are illegal immigrants. But whereas more border enforcement definitely makes the former group better off both absolutely and relative to clearly legal unskilled workers, increased internal enforcement need not do so.

D. *Unemployment and Endogenous Discernment*

As before, there is a parallel analysis featuring rigid wages and unemployment. I will describe the model and its equilibrium, but leave to the reader the task of repeating the above exercises in the new context.

Suppose, again, that the wage w paid to workers recognized to be illegal immigrants is exogenously determined, that jobs are allocated among these workers on the basis of a random draw, and that e denotes the employed fraction of all workers known to be illegal (not of all workers actually illegal). The wages w_L and w_N continue to be flexible. Then ew replaces w in equations (12) and (13), which can be substituted into each other to yield

$$ew = w(E) - \mu(\varepsilon_D - 1). \tag{18}$$

This is the analog to the II schedule. For each level E of border enforcement, it gives a positive relation between the employment rate e in the illegal immigrant labor market and the degree μ of deceptive effort. Note that this relation is invariant with respect to D.

With w rigid, equation (14) gives u as a function of D. Equation (16) is unchanged. Actual employment of workers believed to be members of N equals $N + pI$, and the actual employment of workers known to be present illegally equals $e(1-p)I$, so

$$u = [L + N + pI + e(1-p)I]/S.$$

Thus we have $N/[N + pI] = [p + e(1-p)]/[p([uS - L]/N) + e(1-p)] = \Omega(p, e, u)$. Substituting (14), (16), and (13) into each other—and recalling that ew replaces w in the latter—gives

$$(19) \quad \mu\varepsilon_D/p + (e-1)w = h(D)k^*\Omega(p, e, u).$$

Since u is determined directly by D, equation (19) gives another relation between e and μ, for each value of D. This is the analog to the earlier NN schedule. Note that its position is independent of E, but its slope is not determinate from our assumptions.

Equilibrium is once again determined by the intersection of the II and NN schedules, that is, by the simultaneous solution of (18) and (19). The same comparative statics exercises as before can be performed in this analogous framework.

III. Conclusions

The more important implications of this paper appear to be the following.

Border enforcement policy is an effective means of controlling the unskilled labor employment rate, or, in the flexible wage version of the model, the wage of unskilled labor.

However, if illegal immigrants form part of the tax base, such interdiction could well be an unpredictable and unstable influence upon both the number of illegal immigrants who actually enter the country and upon the wages of native skilled workers who compete only indirectly with the migrants.

With a given interdiction policy, varying the number of immigrants admitted legally will have no effect on the number who actually enter.

Border enforcement policy will probably reduce national income, even if the country has power in the international labor market.

The wage of unskilled workers (or their employment rate) and the volume of illegal immigration are likely to be distinct policy targets, but they are linked together technologically and cannot be unbundled with border enforcement policy.

Domestic enforcement policies will disadvantage illegal aliens relative to legal workers if firms can distinguish the former, but if they cannot, such policies will harm all unskilled workers relative to skilled labor.

A country can reduce the cost of its immigration policy by employing a mixture of border and domestic measures rather than relying on just one type of enforcement.

Domestic enforcement cannot unbundle the unskilled labor wage and the volume of immigration if firms distinguish illegal aliens, but it can do so if they do not distinguish.

If illegal aliens can take measures to improve their chances of passing themselves off as legal residents, both border enforcement and, especially, domestic enforcement will appear to be more successful than they actually are.

An intensification of border enforcement will be especially attractive to those legal workers liable to be confused with illegal aliens. The use of domestic enforcement allows the authorities to unbundle the wage of this group from the volume of immigration.

REFERENCES

Becker, Gary S., "Crime and Punishment: An Economic Approach," *Journal of Political Economy*, March/April 1968, *76*, 169–217.

Bhagwati, Jagdish N., "Alternative Theories of Illegal Trade: Economic Consequences and Statistical Detection," *Weltwirtschaftliches Archiv*, 1981, *117*, 409–27.

______, "International Migration of the Highly Skilled: Economics, Ethics and Taxes," *Third World Quarterly*, July 1979, *1*, 17–30.

______ **and Hamada, Koichi**, "The Brain Drain,

International Integration of Markets for Professionals and Unemployment: A Theoretical Analysis," *Journal of Development Economics*, June 1974, *1*, 19–42.

______ **and Hansen, Bent,** "A Theoretical Analysis of Smuggling," *Quarterly Journal of Economics*, May 1973, *87*, 172–87.

Djajic, Slobodan, "Illegal Aliens, Unemployment and Immigration Policy," unpublished manuscript, 1985.

Ehrlich, Isaac, "Participation in Illegitimate Activities: An Economic Analysis," in G. S. Becker and W. M. Landes, eds., *Essays in the Economics of Crime and Punishment*, New York: Columbia University Press, 1974.

Ethier, Wilfred. J., "International Trade and Labor Migration," *American Economic Review*, September 1985, *75*, 691–707.

______, "International Trade Theory and International Migration," Discussion Paper No. 5, Migration and Development Program, Harvard University, January 1984.

Glazer, Nathan, *Clamor at the Gates: The New American Immigration*, San Francisco: Institute for Contemporary Studies, 1985

Harris, John R. and Todaro, Michael, "Migration, Unemployment and Development: A Two-Sector Analysis," *American Economic Review*, March 1970, *60*, 126–42.

Pitt, Mark M., "Smuggling and Price Disparity," *Journal of International Economics*, November 1981, *11*, 447–58.

Rodriguez, Carlos A., "Brain Drain and Economic Growth: A Dynamic Model," *Journal of Development Economics*, September 1975, *2*, 223–247.

THE MULTINATIONAL FIRM

WILFRED J. ETHIER

Direct investment is incorporated into a simple general equilibrium model of international trade. The analysis focuses on an attempt to endogenize the internalization decision. It is argued that a reasonable approach assumes that arm's length contracts must be "simple" so that "complex" arrangements require internalization. The model relates direct investment to the degree of underlying uncertainty and to fundamental trade determinants, such as relative factor endowments. The behavior of the model contrasts sharply with that of the Markusen-Helpman model, which takes internalization for granted.

A particular framework of thought about foreign direct investment is now dominant. This framework suggests why multinational firms should exist at all in the face of presumed penalties for operating across national and cultural boundaries. It has three constituents. First, the firm should possess some *ownership* advantage, such as a patent or the ability to manage or organize some specific endeavor. Second, *locational* considerations, such as tariffs or comparative advantage, should mandate that the firm not concentrate all operations in one country and export to others. Finally, the *internalization* of international transactions must be preferable to the arm's length use of markets. The firm, for example, should find it advantageous to conduct foreign manufacturing itself rather than to license a foreign firm to do it.

Internalization appears to be emerging as the Caesar of the OLI triumvirate. See, for example, McCulloch [1984, p. 5], Buckley and Casson [1976], Casson [1979], and Rugman [1980], who has gone so far as to assert [p. 370] that, "the existing theories of FDI are really subcases of the theory of internalization."

I claim that, quite independently of how one reacts to all this, internalization should be the focus of theories of direct investment. Internalization is the only one of the three key elements not already incorporated into trade theory. Locational consider-

*An early version of this paper was written at the Institute for International Economic Studies in Stockholm and presented to the 1984 Annual Conference of the International Economics Study Group, held at the University of Sussex Conference Centre, September 7–9, 1984. I am grateful to Lorraine Eden, Gene Grossman, Henrik Horn, and James Markusen for helpful suggestions. I have also received useful comments during seminars at the Universities of Maryland, Michigan, Pittsburgh, Southern California, and Virginia; at Queen's, Princeton, Howard, Harvard, Erasmus, and Duke Universities; the University of California at Berkeley and at the University of Western Ontario International Trade Conference of March 1985.

The Quarterly Journal of Economics, November 1986 CCC 0033-5533/86/040805-29$04.00

ations are basic to the pure theory of international trade, and ownership advantages figure prominently in our recent theories of trade and imperfect competition. Internalization, by contrast, is one of our critical "black boxes," always appealed to but never explained. The central task of any general equilibrium theory of the multinational corporation must be to elucidate the role of the internalization issue.

The OLI framework, or "eclectic theory," as John Dunning has dubbed it, has received an increasingly wide application.[1] Theoretical and empirical investigations of the multinational enterprise are very often conducted with reference to this framework,[2] and it is now standard stuff in undergraduate textbooks.[3] The literature on direct investment is truly gargantuan, and it has a commonly accepted framework for thought. Nevertheless, there has thus far been, with one notable exception, no attempt to supply a general equilibrium theory. The notable exception is the work of James Markusen and Elhanan Helpman on multinational enterprises generated by multiplant scale economies.[4] These economies (or possession of the factors of production that enable the economies to be generated) are the basis for ownership advantages, and locational considerations are determined by relative factor endowments and technological parameters. That the exploitation of multiplant economies should be internalized is taken as a matter of course. Thus, this work falls squarely within the OLI framework.[5]

A general equilibrium theory is essential if we are to connect systematically direct investment to its fundamental determinants and if we are to understand the relation between standard inter-

1. This approach to the theory of the firm derives from Coase [1937] and many followers. Important contributions with respect to the multinational corporation include Hymer [1960], Kindleberger [1969], Caves [1971, 1974], Buckley and Casson [1976], Dunning [1977, 1981], Casson [1979], and Rugman [1981], among others.

2. The literature on direct investment is vast and has been surveyed many times. (A survey article of the surveys would not be out of order.) Useful guides and collections include Kindleberger [1970], Dunning [1971, 1973, 1977], Stevens [1974], Hufbauer [1975], Vernon [1977], Lall and Streeten [1977], Hood and Young [1979], Agarwal [1980], Caves [1982], and Kindleberger and Audretsch [1983].

3. See, for example, Ethier [1983, Ch. 7].

4. See Markusen [1984], Horstmann and Markusen [1986a], Helpman [1983a, 1983b, 1984], and Helpman and Krugman [1985]. An interesting alternative is provided by Cherkes [1984], who analyzes how historically sunk fixed costs can generate multinational firm activity.

5. Markusen and Helpman are both primarily concerned, however, to link their treatments of direct investment to the theory of international trade, not to the OLI framework.

national trade theory and the multinational firm. Two central outstanding issues well illustrate the need for such an understanding.

The first is the relation of direct investment to the relative factor abundance of countries. Conventional trade theory teaches us that differences in factor endowments induce international factor flows, but the larger part of actual direct investment is between countries with relatively similar factor endowments. Furthermore, two-way direct investment within industries is becoming increasingly prominent. (One cannot help but be reminded of how the uneasy relation between conventional theories and the relatively large volume of intraindustry trade between similar economies stimulated recent developments in trade theory.) The usual response to this puzzle is that direct investment concerns ownership and need not coincide at all with physical capital movements. Indeed the OLI framework does not address real capital flows. But such an answer is no answer at all. My intuition would have been that the considerations emphasized by the OLI framework—like the potential for physical factor movements—become more significant with larger differences in factor endowments. The latter certainly cause locational considerations to become more pronounced, and by making countries less alike can be expected to increase disparities in ownership advantages.[6] This intuition may be incorrect (and I shall in fact argue below that it is), but the OLI framework, when divorced from a general equilibrium theory, can take us no farther.

The second issue is the effect of direct investment on the incomes of the factors—labor in particular—employed at home by the multinational firm. This is in fact the preeminent source-country policy issue. But we completely lack the equipment to approach this question in the same way that international trade theory allows us to analyze the effects of commercial policy issues.

The present paper, like those of Markusen and Helpman, is concerned with general equilibrium theories. But whereas Markusen and Helpman each took internalization for granted, I wish to endogenize it. In the process I hope to shed some light on the two issues alluded to above. My conclusions differ dramatically from the implications of the Markusen-Helpman model. This establishes the potential importance of modeling internalization, regardless of how satisfactory my way of doing so might be.

6. Indeed this is basically what happens in the Markusen-Helpman model.

I. Internalization and Information

Internalization is largely a matter of the international economics of information. That is, the critical consideration determining whether a particular international transaction should be internalized usually reduces to an analysis of the exchange of information between two agents. The argument is probably best advanced by explicit consideration of the more important examples.

Consider first the very large class of cases where the ownership advantage is itself the unique possession of some knowledge. The firm wishes to exploit this knowledge in a second, foreign, market, by selling goods embodying the knowledge in that market or by importing from that country goods to be marketed at home. In either case the transaction can be done at arm's length: by selling the knowledge to a foreign collection of factors (or "firm"); or via internalization—by itself employing the foreign factors. The basic consideration working against the arm's length alternative is the fact that in order to sell its information for its full value, the firm must convincingly indicate what it has to sell, thereby losing, at least in part, its monopoly advantage. Note that the critical feature of this class of examples is not the market imperfection represented by the monopoly position of the firm. Rather it is the problem of transacting in information.

As a second class of examples consider multiplant economies, as in the Markusen-Helpman model. Separate plants in different countries draw upon a "home office" utilizing a particular factor. In principle, the relation between the plants and the home office might be either arm's length or internalized. If the home office input is in effect knowledge (such as a research effort applicable to all the plants), this class of examples is a subset of the preceding one. So suppose that the input is something else, such as a coordinating function of some kind. This coordination could be done either at arm's length or internally: the home office and the plants would "do" the same thing in either case, with this behavior dictated alternatively by a contract or by centralized directives. But a contract that makes arm's length behavior identical to internalized behavior becomes infeasible when the home office and plants must exchange a large volume of diverse information. This does not mean that internalization dominates; with much information to be processed decentralized decision making is likely to be attractive. The point is rather that the arm's length and internalized industrial structures will no longer be identical but will confront the various agents with different sets of incentives.[7] Which structure is better will depend upon circumstances.

I do not claim that problems of information exchange are invariably central to direct investment, but only that this is sufficiently often the case to render it compelling that they occupy a central position in any general equilibrium theory. Further examples could be given, but those already cited include as special cases a good proportion of multinational activity and so suffice to make my point. What are the strategic implications for the construction of a general equilibrium theory of the multinational enterprise? The details of such a model must be colored, I should think, by the two aspects of information exchange that emerged in the above examples. That is, the public good nature of information, discussed with respect to the first class of examples[8] and the size and diversity of information flows, central to the second.

The rest of this paper is devoted to a rudimentary model of international trade motivated by the discussion thus far. The purpose is to illustrate how the above issues should be reflected in the crude details of simple model construction. In particular, I wish the model to have a pair of parameters that I can associate with the two critical aspects of information exchange I have just identified. This will enable me to isolate the role played by these basic considerations.

II. The Rudimentary Model

The model contains two countries, two factors, and two goods. Both factors are nontraded. One of the goods, called wheat (W), is produced by the two factors, land (T) and labor (L). Land is specific to wheat production, so the second good, manufactures (M), uses only labor. Wheat production in the home country can be represented by $W = F(L_W,T)$, where F is a neoclassical production function and L_W denotes the amount of labor employed in the wheat sector. Foreign country variables will be distinguished by asterisks.

Manufactures are a collection of n differentiated goods, with n determined endogenously. Manufacturing involves three stages:

7. This view of internalization is forcefully espoused by Grossman and Hart [1984].

8. Magee [1977a, 1977b] gives a very useful treatment of what is called "appropriability." See also Casson [1979].

research, upstream production, and downstream production. Upstream, each variant can be produced at a choice of quality levels, indexed by Q, $0 \leq Q \leq Q_1$. Labor is the only input into upstream production; the variable cost of production of one unit of a manufacture (of any variety) of quality Q is aQw, where a is a technological parameter and w denotes the wage rate in terms of wheat (so that $w = F_L(L_W,T)$). Q is the variable that will be used below to discuss the role of the size and diversity of information flows.[9]

The research activity helps determine the value of the parameter a. This latter can assume either of two values, $a_H > a_L$. The greater the volume R of resources devoted to research, the greater the probability $p(R)$ that $a = a_L$. I assume that $p' > 0$ and $p'' < 0$. Labor is the only input into research, so R is assumed measured in units of labor. The public good aspect of information will be associated with the variable R. Research furnishes the proprietary information that makes the firm's product unique (thereby providing the ownership advantage) and that helps to determine a (thereby linking this proprietary information to the uncertainty facing the firm).

The final stage is a downstream activity that is nontraded—the easiest way to model locational advantages. This also uses only labor as an input, with q units of labor required, in each country, for the downstream activity associated with one unit of a manufacture (of any variety or quality).

I assume that labor must be committed to research and to downstream production before the resolution of uncertainty about the value of a (that is, about the success of the research effort). Afterwards the quality of each variety can be chosen. Ex ante, all varieties are symmetric, although ex post they differ in the realized value of a and the chosen value of Q. In equilibrium the chosen research effort R will accordingly be the same for each chosen variety. If the number n of varieties is sufficiently large, the economy-wide average of a will be known ex ante to (approximately) equal $p(R)a_L + [1 - p(R)]a_H$, even if the value of a pertaining to any particular variety is not yet known. Thus, the equilibrium amount of labor devoted to research, manufacturing, and downstream production will be determined ex ante, for any value of n. This value must then be such as to clear factor markets.

9. In the terminology of Shaked and Sutton [1983, 1984], the manufacturing sector is characterized by both "horizontal" and "vertical" product differentiation.

Consumers in the two countries possess identical tastes. Furthermore, if a certain variety of manufactures is consumed at all, it is consumed in a fixed amount, independently of quality. Define units of measurement so that exactly one unit is consumed, worldwide, of each variety that is produced in equilibrium. Let μ denote the fraction of this unit consumed at home and $1 - \mu$ the fraction consumed abroad. Assume that μ is the same for each variety. Finally, I suppose that consumers regard a unit of any variety of manufactures of quality Q to be a perfect substitute for Q units of wheat. Thus, domestic consumers will consume μ units of a variety of quality Q if its price, in terms of wheat, is no greater than Q, and they will consume none otherwise. I make this assumption simply to divorce the present paper from issues involving the division of labor or the benefits of increased product differentiation. These issues have been treated in depth in the recent literature.[10]

Let me briefly summarize the rationale of my model. I have identified two key aspects of information exchange—its public good nature and the size and diversity of information flows—and have accordingly provided the model with two variables, R and Q, to serve as "pegs" on which, respectively, to hang these issues. In order for informational problems to be present at all, the model must have some intrinsic source of uncertainty (at least from the viewpoints of individual agents). This is provided here by what I call the "dispersion": $a_H - a_L$. In order to relate direct investment to standard trade theory, fundamental parameters of the latter must be included as well. This is represented here by relative factor endowments: $(L/T) - (L^*/T^*)$. The basic idea of the model, then, is that the fundamental determinants (the dispersion and relative factor endowments) should interact in the background while alternatives about industrial structure are related to the way the informational variables (R and Q) are treated.

I submit that this general structure is pretty much inevitable, given the goals of this paper, once my earlier arguments are accepted. In this sense my model is quite general. In two other ways it is not. The dimensionality is low, with each of the four basic elements represented by a single variable. But all our simple trade models have low dimensionality: this is what makes them

10. See, for example, Ethier [1979, 1982], Helpman [1981], Krugman [1979, 1981] and Lancaster [1980].

simple. Less common is the linearity I have imposed on some basic functional forms, relating both to technology and to tastes.[11]

III. THE INTEGRATED EQUILIBRIUM

It will prove convenient to establish a point of reference by analyzing the model's solution when all stages for each variety are integrated within a single international firm. A single manufacturing firm, identified with a particular variety,[12] thus conducts research, upstream production, and downstream activity in both countries.

The Behavior of the Individual Firm

In order to allow the role of factor endowments to stand out in clear relief, I assume that the efficiency of labor in research relative to upstream production and to downstream production is the same at home as abroad. But the absolute productivities of the two nations' workers need not be the same, so let w^* denote the wage of an efficiency unit of foreign labor, that is, of that quantity of foreign labor that can do the same research (or other activity) that one unit of domestic labor can. It follows that, if $w \neq w^*$, all production and research will be conducted in the country with the lower wage, with such activities taking place in both countries only in the boundary case of international wage equalization. Consider first the case $w < w^*$.

Suppose for now that all firms are risk neutral. Let Q_L and Q_H denote the quality of goods delivered to home and foreign markets when $a = a_L$ and when $a = a_H$, respectively. The firm cannot influence the wage w, which will turn out to be state independent. Thus, the optimization problem confronted by the domestic manufacturer is to choose a combination (R, Q_L, Q_H) that maximizes expected profit:

$$(1) \qquad p(R)Q_L(1 - a_L w) + [1 - p(R)]Q_H(1 - a_H w) - (wR + qw^0),$$

11. However, I do conjecture that relaxations of my assumptions about functional forms would either leave the main results of this paper unchanged or alter them in ways that are obvious (at least to readers of Markusen [1984] and Helpman [1984]). A more significant question—also beyond the scope of this paper—is the sensitivity of my conclusions to the assumption about industrial structure that will be made in Section IV below.

12. This is for expositional convenience. Nothing changes if each firm produces an assortment of varieties, as long as there are many firms and potential firms.

where $w^0 = \mu w + (1 - \mu)w^*$ and w^* denotes the foreign wage. The firm is here cognizant of the fact that Q is the highest price it will be able to charge for a unit of final output of quality Q.

The optimal strategy obviously depends upon the wages w and w^* faced by the firm. There are three distinct possibilities.

(i) $w > (1/a_L) > (1/a_H)$. In this case the firm must lose money if it operates, regardless of which state emerges. Consequently, it will not enter the market at all, that is, the solution to its problem is $R = Q_L = Q_H = 0$.

(ii) $(1/a_L) > (1/a_H) > w$. In this case the firm may or may not choose to enter, depending upon whether expected profit is nonnegative. If it does enter, it knows ex ante that it will pay to provide the highest feasible quality level, Q_1, regardless of which state is realized. The research effort R will be carried to the point where its marginal cost just equals the marginal expected cost reduction: $w = Q_1 p'(R)[(1 - a_L w) - (1 - a_H w)]$. Thus, if it enters, the solution to the firm's problem is $Q_L = Q_H = Q_1$ and $R = R_1$, where R_1 is the solution to

$$p'(R_1) = 1/Q_1(a_H - a_L). \tag{2}$$

Note that the wage rate has no influence on R_1. Since goods of the highest quality will be produced in both states, research affects only the chance of producing in the low cost state rather than the high cost one, and the difference in costs is strictly proportional to the wage, as is the cost of research.

(iii) $(1/a_L) > w > (1/a_H)$. Again, the firm may or may not enter. If it does, it knows that, should $a = a_H$, it will not in fact produce anything (or, rather, that it will produce goods of lowest quality 0 at variable cost 0); so that resources devoted to research and downstream production will be lost. If $a = a_L$, the firm will wish to provide the highest feasible quality Q_1. The research effort will be optimized when $w = Q_1 p'(R)(1 - a_L w)$. Thus, the optimal operation strategy is $Q_H = 0$, $Q_L = Q_1$, and $R = R_2(w)$, where $R_2(w)$ is the solution to

$$p'(R_2) = w/Q_1(1 - a_L w). \tag{3}$$

(Note that $R_2(1/a_L) = 0$, $R_2(1/a_H) = R_1$, and $R'_2 < 0$ when $w < 1/a_L$.) This strategy will be the chosen one if it yields nonnegative expected profit:

$$p(R_2)Q_1(1 - a_L w) - (wR_2 + w^0 q) \geqslant 0. \tag{4}$$

Otherwise the firm will not enter: $Q_L = Q_H = R = 0$. The reason that R_2 depends upon w, while R_1 does not, is that in this case the research effort determines the chance that the firm will choose to produce at all and thus increase its earnings by $1 - a_L w$, which is not proportional to the wage. This difference between cases (ii) and (iii) will turn out to be at the very center of the role of multinationals in this model.

In addition to the above three possibilities, there are two boundary cases. If $w = 1/a_L$, the firm has no chance to offset its fixed costs and so will not enter at all, just as in (i). If $w = 1/a_H$, the firm will be indifferent about what level of quality to provide whenever $a = a_H$. This is the only circumstance under which the firm could choose to do something other than provide the highest possible quality Q_1 or not produce at all.

Equilibrium in the Manufacturing Sector

There is free entry into manufacturing, and expected profits are driven to zero, or below if only wheat is produced in equilibrium. This means that, if $(1/a_L) > w > (1/a_H)$, expression (4) must hold with equality. When $w < (1/a_H)$, the zero profit condition is

$$(5) \quad Q_1[1 - w[p(R_1)a_L + (1 - p(R_1))a_H]] - [wR_1 + w^0 q] = 0.$$

Thus, (4) and (5) determine the w and w^* consistent with manufacturing equilibrium (recall that $w^0 = \mu w + (1 - \mu)w^*$). In Figure I the Manufacturing Equilibrium schedule, labeled *ME*, shows for each value of w^* the corresponding equilibrium home wage w. The *ME* schedule is a straight line when $w < (1/a_H)$—reflecting the fact that (5) is a linear relation between w and w^*—but becomes steeper[13] as w exceeds $1/a_H$, since R_2 is a decreasing function of w in (4). Note that the nonlinear part of *ME* disappears if $p(R)$ is so responsive to increases in the research effort that $(p(R_1)/p'R_1) < R_1 + \mu q$.

All this supposes that $w < w^*$, and so applies only to the part of Figure I below the 45° line. But the opposite case of $w > w^*$ is easy to handle; simply reverse the roles of the two countries. Figure II shows both the home and foreign curves, labeled *ME*

13. Implicit differentiation of (4)—with equality—confirms that it defines a relation between w and w^* that is strictly convex to the origin, when the optimality condition (3) is satisfied.

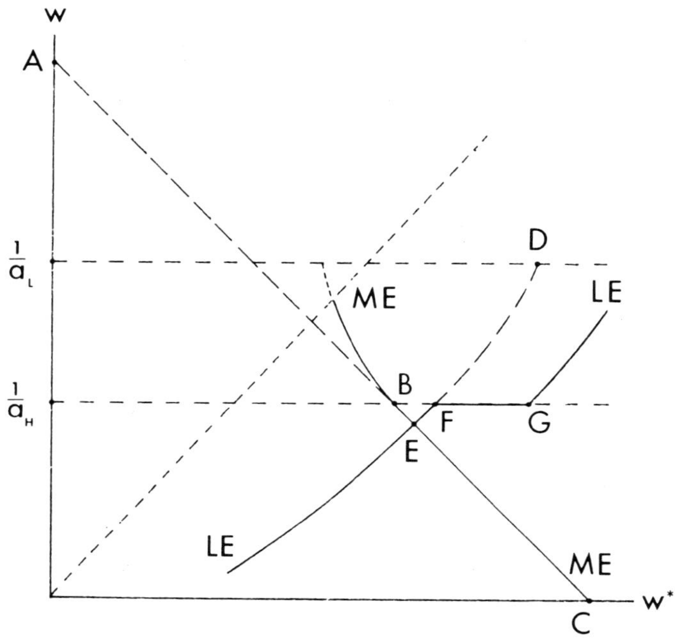

FIGURE I

and ME^*, respectively, in representative cases, where (a) the dispersion $a_H - a_L$ is small, and where (b) the dispersion is large. It is easily shown, from (4), (5), and their foreign analogs, that ME must intersect ME^* from below, so that multiple intersections are not possible. As Figure II makes clear, the single intersection will occur on the 45° line ($w = w^*$); this will be on the linear portions of ME and ME^* (that is, $w = w^* < 1/a_H$) if the dispersion is small and on the nonlinear portions ($w = w^* > 1/a_H$) if the dispersion is large.

Along a country's ME curve, profits in the manufacturing sector are zero; above, profits are negative, so research and production are not sustainable; below the curve, profits are positive and so not compatible with equilibrium. Thus, in Figure II international equilibrium must take place on the outer envelope of the ME and ME^* curves, that is, along ACE in panel (a) and along $ABCDE$ in panel (b). Below point C all research and production takes place in the home country; above C it all takes place abroad.

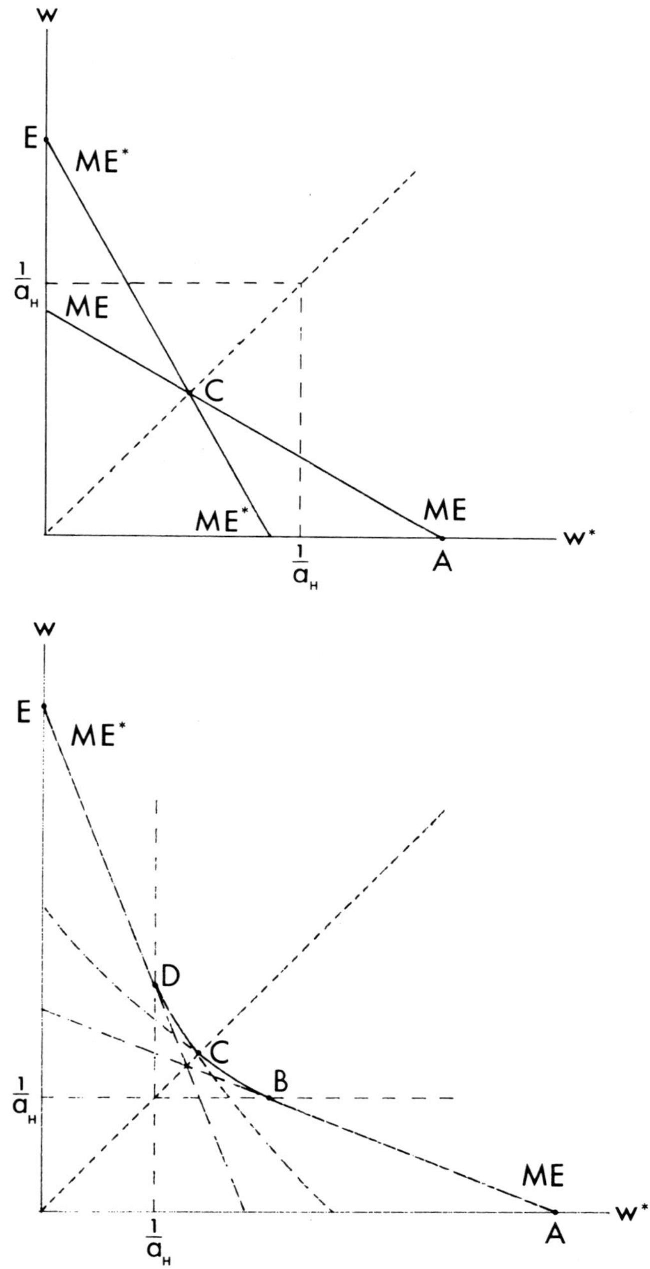

FIGURE II

General Equilibrium

In full equilibrium[14] labor in each country must be paid the value of its marginal product in wheat, a traded good. This establishes a second relation between w and w^* and so closes the system. Labor market equilibrium in the two countries is given, respectively, by

$$(6) \quad w = F_L(L_W,T) = F_L(L - n[a(w)Q_1 + R(w) + \mu q] - n^*\mu q, T)$$

and

$$(7) \quad \begin{aligned} w^* &= F_L^*(L_W^* T^*) \\ &= F_L^*(L^* - n(1-\mu)q - n^*[a(w^*)Q_1 + R(w^*) \\ &\quad - (1-\mu)q], T^*), \end{aligned}$$

where n denotes the number of firms with research and upstream production at home and n^* the number with such activities abroad. Here $a(w) = p(R_1)a_L + [1 - p(R_1)]a_H$ if $w < 1/a_H$ and $a(w) = p(R_2(w))a_L$ if $w > 1/a_H$. Also $R(w) = R_1$ if $w < 1/a_H$, and $R(w) = R_2(w)$ otherwise. Thus, $a(w)Q_1n$ denotes the total employment of labor in manufacturing production and is known ex ante, even though the employment of labor in the production of each variety is not known. In addition, $n = 0$ whenever $w > w^*$, and $n^* = 0$ whenever $w < w^*$.

Thus, when $w < w^*$, equations (6) and (7) give two relations in the three variables w, w^*, and n; when $w > w^*$, the variables are w, w^*, and n^*; and when $w = w^*$, they are n, n^*, and w. Eliminating n gives the Labor Equilibrium schedule relating w and w^*.

This schedule is depicted as the *LE* line in Figure I, which, you will recall, depicts only cases where $w < w^*$. (To limit clutter, Figure II does not also show the *LE* schedule.) This curve necessarily has a positive slope: a higher value of w^* requires a higher marginal product of labor in foreign wheat production and therefore less labor in that sector. This means that more labor is devoted to downstream production, which in turn means more manufactured goods, more domestic labor in the manufacturing sector, less labor in the wheat sector, and so a larger value of w. Note that the *LE* schedule is a step function, with a horizontal

14. I assume the existence of a unique equilibrium in which each country consumes all (produced) goods in positive amounts.

portion (depicted as FG in Figure I) when $w = 1/a_H$. This is because when $w = 1/a_H$, producers of manufactured goods for which $a = a_H$ are indifferent about which quality level to supply. Thus, a given manufacturing labor force can alternatively provide a larger number n of goods with less quality for those goods with $a = a_H$, or a smaller number of goods of greater quality. As we move from F to G in the figure, the quality level of those goods for which $a = a_H$ falls with n rising just enough so that L_W remains constant. But with downstream production costs independent of quality, the rise in n increases the size of the foreign downstream sector, thereby lowering L_W^* and so raising w^*.

Relations (6) and (7) determine a unique LE curve over all w and w^*. Suppose, for example, that for some value of w^* there is a corresponding $w > w^*$ that allows (6) and (7) to hold for $n = 0$ and for some $n^* > 0$. There cannot be another value of w, with $w < w^*$, that also satisfies (6) and (7) for some $n > 0$, $n^* = 0$, and the same w^*. For if (7) is to continue to hold for the same w^*, L_W^* must be unchanged so that the new value of n must be larger than the old value of n^*. But this will cause L_W to fall in equation (6), so that w will rise rather than fall; that is, $w < w^*$ is not possible. Similar arguments applied to the other possible cases establish that the LE curve is uniquely defined. Note that the curve will coincide with the 45° line for a range of values of $w = w^*$ allowing (6) and (7) to hold for nonnegative n and n^*.

International equilibrium is of course determined by the intersection of the Labor Equilibrium curve with the Manufacturing Equilibrium envelope. If that intersection is below the 45° line, all research and upstream production takes place at home; for intersections above the 45° line, they take place abroad. But the fact that the LE curve will in general coincide with the 45° line for part of its length implies that an intersection exactly on that line (that is, at point C in the panels of Figure II) cannot be dismissed as a fluke. Point E in Figure I depicts an equilibrium where $w < w^*$. The earlier analysis then shows how these wages determine n, R, Q_L, and Q_H. The fact that (2) holds with equality for each variety implies balanced trade, ex post as well as ex ante.

IV. Information and Industrial Structure

The previous section described equilibrium under a particular assumption about industrial structure. I now wish to examine how the informational considerations previously raised can be alternatively reflected in the structure of the model, and how these alternatives influence conclusions about the model's behavior and about the industrial structure to which it corresponds. The manufacturing sector contains four separate operations for each variety, so a substantial number of different types of integration could be considered. To limit the size of this paper, I consider only the possible integration of upstream production with both downstream activities, and leave to the reader consideration of other possibilities. In particular, I assume throughout that research and upstream production are integrated within a firm, and that no integration across varieties is considered. As foreign downstream production is the only activity not performed at home, the integration decisions that I consider include whether to become a multinational enterprise. They also involve both horizontal and vertical integration.[15]

Consider the behavior of the internationally integrated firm as described in the previous section. In principle, this behavior could be duplicated by an arm's length contract[16] between the home research and production firm and two independent downstream firms, with the contract calling for exactly the same behavior as described above. That is, the contract would commit the upstream firm to the same (R, Q_L, Q_H) as above and would call for the downstream firms to make some payment P per unit of output to the upstream firm. (Assuming free entry into the downstream activity in each country, P would simply equal that value which causes expected downstream profit to equal zero.) When is such a contract feasible?

The Public Good Nature of Information

The first point to notice is that the contract is conditional upon the results of the research undertaken by the home firm. But these results are proprietary to that firm, which presumably has an interest in keeping them secret. Thus, there is an inherent informational asymmetry. This need not render the contract infeasible: if the foreign distributor can be confident that the home

15. These three decisions (horizontal integration, vertical integration, and going multinational) could be disentangled by allowing q to differ across countries and to be sensitive to whether the downstream activity occurred in the same country as the research and manufacturing. I resist the temptation to perform the exercise.

16. In what follows, an "arm's length" arrangement can be interpreted as either simple exporting or licensing. For a recent treatment where the two are distinct, see Horstmann and Markusen [1986b].

firm will have no incentive to lie about the success, or the extent, of its research effort, then the two can agree that the home firm will declare, without outside verification, how successful its research has been.[17]

Since the home firm is risk neutral, it would not care if the state-invariant payment of P were replaced by a state-contingent payment schedule with the same expected value, that is, if the foreign distributor agreed to the price P_L when the home firm claimed $a = a_L$ and to the price P_H otherwise, where

$$P = p(R)P_L + [1 - p(R)]P_H. \tag{8}$$

It is possible to find an incentive-compatible arm's length contract that relieves the foreign firm from all risk. Consider the contract that calls for $Q_L = Q_1$ and $Q_H = 0$. If the foreign distributor is to bear no risk, P_H and P_L must be set so that $Q_1 - P_L - qw^* = 0 - P_H - qw^*$, or so that $Q_1 = P_L - P_H$. Substituting this into (8) reveals that $P_H = P - p(R)Q_1$ and $P_L = P + [1 - p(R)]Q_1$. This is incentive-compatible.[18] Verifying that the contracted amount of research is actually done is subject to the same informational problem. However, the contracted R will also be made incentive-compatible by the above state-contingent payment schedule. To see this, suppose that a contract (P_L,P_H,R,Q_L,Q_H) has been negotiated, and consider what level of R it is now in the firm's interest actually to undertake. Suppose that $w > 1/a_H$, so that $Q_L = Q_1$, $Q_H = 0$, and the contracted $R = R_2$ in equation (3). Then it will be in the home firm's interest actually to undertake the volume R of research that maximizes

$$p(R)[\mu Q_1 + (1 - \mu)P_L - a_L Q_1 w] + [1 - p(R)](1 - \mu)P_H - Rw - \mu qw.$$

Setting the derivative of this expression equal to zero yields the formula,

$$p'(R) = w/[Q_1(\mu - a_L w) + (1 - \mu)(P_L - P_H)].$$

The R that solves this expression will equal the contracted amount

17. The following argument applies ideas from the literature on contracting in the presence of asymmetric information. See D'Aspremont and Gerard-Varet [1979], for example.

18. Suppose, for example, that $a = a_L$. If the home firm tells the truth, it will earn $Q_1(1 - a_L w) + (1 - \mu)[P - p(R)Q_1] - [R + \mu q]w$. If instead the home firm claims that $a = a_H$, it will earn $(1 - \mu)[P - p(R)Q_1] - [R + \mu q]w$, which is less by the amount $Q_1(1 - a_L w)$.

R_2 (as given by equation (3)) if $P_L - P_H = Q_1$. This is just our state-contingent payment schedule.

This escape works because the home firm is risk neutral. How valid is this assumption? It is justified if the owners of the firms can diversify away risk, and in this model domestic capitalists can eliminate risk by buying shares of all home manufacturing firms. Note that purely national capital markets suffice. But the lack of such markets is sometimes associated with the formation of multinational firms.

If instead both firms are risk averse, it could well be that the requirement that an arm's length contract be incentive-compatible would prove costly, so that there would be a motive for integration. By introducing a countervailing cost to administering integrated units, this could serve in a straightforward way as the basis for a theory of the multinational firm. Analysis of this would bring us to the issues treated in depth by the literature on labor contracts with asymmetric information.[19] But this is not the route of the present paper. Instead I return now to the assumption of home risk neutrality.

To summarize, the public good nature of information produces an informational asymmetry between the home and foreign firms, preventing the latter from directly verifying either the actual research effort of the former or the results of that effort. It will nevertheless be possible for the two firms to design an optimal incentive-compatible contract *if* at least one of the firms is risk neutral and *if* it is feasible for the contract to call for the payment schedule of the foreign firm to vary across all conceivable states of nature. Both requirements are demanding, and in particular the latter would require in practice extremely detailed and complex contracts. This brings us to our second informational issue.

The Multivariate Nature of Quality

The contract calls for delivery of goods of a certain quality. The model assumes that quality can be indicated by a single number, but of course it is almost always much more than that. This suggests the difficulty of including quality specification in an enforceable contract.[20] This problem is minimized for simple standardized goods whose quality can be objectively measured.

19. See Hart [1983] for a recent survey.

20. Or, to put it another way, that we use the variable Q to represent relevant considerations, of whatever sort, that cannot be contracted.

The problem could be minimized also if the contract is simple enough. For example, if the required quality is state invariant, the partners to the contract might well allow the precise definition of quality to remain implicit and to rely on mutual goodwill to determine whether the goods in fact come up to snuff. (I would find it difficult to describe a McDonald's precisely, but I know one when I see it because they are always supposed to be the same.) This will be especially true if the model's equilibrium is interpreted as one that will be repeated over time. By contrast, the need for precision in defining quality becomes acute when the contract calls for quality to vary significantly across states. If there are countless aspects to quality, involving diverse facets of the good's preparation, design, delivery, and use, an enforceable contract involving state-dependent quality would necessarily be a very complex matter indeed. Perhaps so much so that its use would in truth constitute economic integration, de facto if not de jure.[21]

Modeling Internalization

These considerations strongly suggest how to distinguish between arm's length transactions and internalization. I assume that if the home and downstream firms are to implement a state-dependent contract, they must first become one firm, so that the transaction is internalized, and act so as to maximize joint profit. If the firms remain at arm's length, the contract they negotiate is constrained to call for state-invariant quality. This constraint responds to both of the informational problems raised in this section. A contract featuring state-invariant quality will necessarily be incentive-compatible, and as just pointed out, it will minimize the difficulties due to the multivariate nature of quality.[22]

The basic idea, then, is that it is infeasible to write contracts with a huge number of contingencies but feasible to do so if the number is more modest. In this model two is "too many," while one is "enough." There would of course be no problem if "quality" were always in fact an observable scaler, as modeled here, rather than an indefinite number of characteristics admitting of no ex ante summary measure. I shall not apologize for reducing the

21. For a more detailed discussion of related issues, see Williamson [1975].

22. Of course, this is just one of the conceivable ways of characterizing the motive for internalization, and it would be interesting to contrast its implications with those of some of the alternatives. But in order to limit the length of this paper, I consider only the case that I find most appealing.

complex reality to such a simple formal representation: this use of low dimensionality is basic to the simple trade models this paper attempts to emulate.

Equilibrium with National and Multinational Firms

Suppose first that $w < w^*$ and that the home upstream firm maintains an arm's length relation with the downstream firms so that their contracts are constrained to call for state-invariant quality. Recall from the preceding section that the home firm would actually prefer such a contract if $w < 1/a_H$, and that it would decline to enter if $w > 1/a_L$. Thus, the constraint will matter only when $1/a_L > w > 1/a_H$. In this case the home firm's optimization problem is to choose Q and R to maximize

$$Q[1 - a^0(R)w] - [wR + w^0q],$$

where $a^0(R) = p(R)a_L + [1 - p(R)]a_H$. Now in equilibrium w must be such as to make this profit zero, so that $1 > a^0(R)w$. But then the optimizing choice of Q is the largest one feasible: $Q = Q_1$. If the research effort is being carried to the point where an additional dollar offers a zero net benefit, it must be the case that $p'(R) = 1/Q_1(a_H - a_L)$. Thus, the firm behaves the same when $1/a_L > w > 1/a_H$ as when $1/a_H > w$. The Manufacturing Equilibrium schedule is thus now the graph of (5) for all values of w, and so, in Figure I, *ME* now becomes the straight line *ABC*.

It follows from this analysis that the Labor Equilibrium schedule in Figure I is the same as before for $w < 1/a_H$, but is depicted by *FD* when $w > 1/a_H$.

The arm's length equilibrium is now given by the intersection of the amended *ME* and *LE* schedules. The multinational equilibrium is of course just that analyzed earlier for the case of the internationally integrated firm.

The Emergence of Multinationals

If the amended *ME* and *LE* schedules in Figure I intersect sufficiently low so that the equilibrium $w < 1/a_H$, as is the case the way the figure is drawn, the arm's length equilibrium will be identical to the one with multinational firms. All firms will feel unconstrained by the need to deal in state-invariant contracts. Thus, there will be no reason for individual firms to form multinational enterprises, and no social consequences if they are not allowed to do so.

If the arm's length equilibrium calls for $w > 1/a_H$, the two equilibria will clearly differ. In this case, with an initial arm's length arrangement, firms would perceive it to be in their interest to form multinationals. If they are allowed to do so, it is therefore the equilibrium given by the original *ME* and *LE* schedules that is relevant.[23]

V. Patterns of Trade and Direct Investment

What is the influence of relative factor endowments? It should be apparent that they affect only the Labor Equilibrium schedule and are irrelevant to the Manufacturing Equilibrium envelope. For example, an increase in the stock of wheat-specific land must, at given L_W, increase the marginal productivity of labor in wheat production. It then follows from (6) and (7) that a rise in T^*, the foreign stock of land, or a fall in T will shift the *LE* schedule toward the right. A similar effect will be produced by a rise in L or reduction in L^*. Any combination of such changes will therefore raise w^* and lower w.

We have seen that since the *LE* schedule may coincide with the 45° line for a portion of its length, an equilibrium with $w = w^*$ is not necessarily unlikely. Consider the relation of such equilibria to factor endowments.

International Wage Equalization

As Figure II makes clear, point C will be the intersection of the linear parts of *ME* and *ME** if the dispersion is small enough and of the nonlinear parts for a sufficiently large dispersion. I discuss only the former case: the latter leads to similar conclusions. It follows from equation (5) that, at such a point C, the common value of w and w^* is given by

$$w_c = Q_1/[Q_1 a(w) + R_1 + q]. \tag{9}$$

23. The firms may or may not find it to their advantage to shift from an arm's length to a multinational arrangement, but they will never perceive it to be actually disadvantageous to do so. Much of the less formal literature has assumed or asserted that multinational operation is inherently costly. See also Ethier and Horn [1985]. The most natural way to introduce such considerations here would be to assume that the per unit downstream cost q is higher for an integrated firm. As the analysis is straightforward, it is omitted. The principal consequence would be to add a range of cases where a change from an arm's length arrangement to an integrated one would be costly. If, in addition, internalization raises foreign q more than it would raise home q (as it would if integration is more costly when it involves operating across national and cultural barriers), there will be a range of cases where it would be advantageous for the upstream manufacturer to integrate with the home downstream firm but not with the foreign one.

Setting the right-hand sides of (6) and (7) equal to this value enables one to solve those equations for n and n^* as functions of the factor endowments of the two countries. In order to study the role of these endowments, I shall hold fixed the world stocks of the two factors ($L_W = L + L^*$ and $T_W = T + T^*$) and see how international equilibrium responds to redistributions of these stocks between the two countries. Now equations (6) and (7) determine equilibrium wheat labor-land ratios in the two countries ($t = L_W/T$ and $t^* = L_W^*/T^*$):

$$w_c = F_L(t,1) = F_L^*(t^*,1).$$

Note that

$$L_M = L - tT \text{ and } L_M^* = L^* - t^*T^*. \tag{10}$$

The world endowment ratio L_W/T_W consequently must exceed at least one of t and t^* for both countries to undertake research and production. Otherwise at most one country will do so (endowments could be such that both countries produce only wheat in equilibrium). Figure III depicts the case where the world endowment

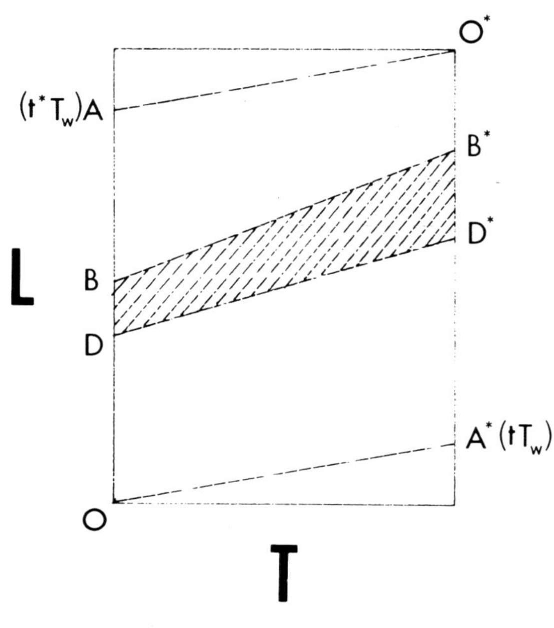

FIGURE III

ratio exceeds both t and t^*. The dimensions of the box equal L_W and T_W, respectively, with labor measured on the vertical axis and land on the horizontal, so that each point within the box represents one possible allocation of the world's factors. The home endowment is measured relative to the southwest corner of the box and the foreign endowment relative to the northeast corner. The slopes of the rays OA^* and O^*A, respectively, reflect t and t^*. Thus, the area between these two rays contains all allocations that are consistent with both $L_M > 0$ and $L_M^* > 0$. But this is only a necessary condition for n and n^* to be both positive, not a sufficient condition. The reason is that a country will provide downstream services even if it conducts no research or production. For both countries to do the latter, it is necessary for L_M and L_M^* to be such that equations (11) and (12) are solved for positive values of n and n^*:

$$(11) \qquad n[a(w)\,Q_1 + R_1 + \mu q] + n^*\mu q = L_M$$

and

$$(12) \qquad n(1 - \mu)q + n^*[a(w)Q_1 + R_1 + (1 - \mu)q] = L_M^*.$$

This will be the case when $b > (L_M/L_M^*) > d$, where

$$b = (a(w)\,Q_1 + R_1 + \mu q)/(1 - \mu)q$$

and

$$d = \mu q/[a(w)\,Q_1 + R_1 + (1 - \mu)q].$$

In Figure III the BB^* line shows endowment allocations for which $L_M/L_M^* = b$, and DD^* shows allocations where $L_M/L_M^* = d$. The "wage equalization region" is therefore DBB^*D^*. Allocations within this region result in an international equilibrium at point C in Figure II. Both countries have firms conducting research and production, and they have a common wage w_c.[24] Allocations above the region imply an international equilibrium in which all research and production takes place at home, and all such activity takes place abroad with an allocation below the region. This is superficially similar to factor price equalization in the familiar Heckscher-Ohlin-Samuelson model. It is worth pointing out, therefore, that wage equalization does not require identical pro-

24. More precisely, the international wage differential just equals the productivity differential of labor in the manufacturing sector (recall that foreign labor is measured in efficiency units).

duction functions across countries and does not imply equalization of the returns to land.

The Influence of Factor Endowments

It is now possible to indicate how relative factor endowments and the size of the dispersion interact to determine the industrial structure, the volume and type (interindustry, intraindustry, or intrafirm) of international trade, the volume and type of direct investment (unidirectional or two-way), and the international pattern of factor prices. In the following discussion I call the relatively labor-abundant country the home one.

Suppose first that relative factor endowments differ greatly between the two countries. Then international equilibrium will take place on the linear part of the Manufacturing Equilibrium envelope below point C in Figure II. Then home wages are less than foreign wages, all research and production takes place at home, there is no direct investment,[25] and all trade is interindustry (and interfirm), with the home country exporting unfinished manufactures in exchange for wheat. As relative factor endowments become more nearly equal, home wages rise (and home rents fall), foreign wages fall, and the volume of (interindustry) trade declines. If the dispersion is large enough so that $w_c > (1/a_H)$, sufficiently similar relative factor endowments will cause the home manufacturing firms to undertake direct investment. Trade and direct investment now appear to be substitutes, as the former contracts while the latter expands. But there is no causal relation between the two developments: they are both due to the assumed convergence of relative endowments across countries. International trade will consist of the interindustry exchange of wheat for unfinished manufactures, but the export of the latter will now be intrafirm trade.

If relative endowments become still more similar, equilibrium will take place at point C in panel (b) of Figure II. The foreign economy will now undertake some research and production, with these foreign activities conducted by multinational firms. Direct investment is now two-way, and international trade consists of both interindustry trade and intraindustry trade, with each country exporting unfinished manufactures. The latter constitutes two-way intrafirm trade. Wages will also be equalized

25. More precisely, there is no reason why any direct investment should take place.

across countries. If endowments become still more similar, factor prices will not change further, but intraindustry (and intrafirm) trade will continue to displace interindustry trade. Note that now direct investment and trade (intraindustry) appear to be complements. If the dispersion is instead small enough so that $w_c < (1/a_H)$, direct investment will never take place, and therefore, there will never be any intrafirm trade. But the above description of the effects of changes in relative factor endowments still applies to factor prices and to the respective roles of interindustry and intraindustry trade.

All this differs dramatically from the Markusen-Helpman model. There the formation of multinationals is associated with *differences* in relative factor endowments rather than similarities: multinationals cannot emerge at all if trade in goods would itself equalize factor prices (in that model both sectors use both factors and technology is identical across countries), though the presence of multinationals can produce factor price equalization in some cases where trade alone cannot do so. Furthermore, two-way direct investment cannot take place at all without impediments to international exchange.[26]

Degree of Technological Dispersion

Now consider the effect of changes in the degree of dispersion, $a_H - a_L$. (I shall examine only equilibria where $w < w^*$ and leave other possibilities to the reader.) Start with the case $a_H = a_L$, and ask what happens to the equilibria as a_H is gradually increased. Panels (a)–(d) of Figure IV illustrate the result with snapshots taken along the way. In each case the arm's length equilibrium is indicated by A and the multinational one by M. Small deviations of a_H above a_L of course give no benefit to integration. A range of larger dispersions results in $w = 1/a_H$; within this range,

26. All this is quite clear in Helpman [1984], but Markusen [1984] appears to have reached different conclusions. However, this disparity simply reflects the one significant respect in which Markusen's model differs from Helpman's: the former assumes that there is only one variety of manufacture, so that with a multinational equilibrium that sector contains but a single monopolistic firm. If the two countries have identical endowments, so that manufacturing activity occurs in both, that monopolist must ipso facto be a multinational. If, in addition, it pays to concentrate the public activity (analogous to my R) in one country, factor prices and resource allocation must differ in the two countries. But if there were instead many varieties, they could be divided among the two countries, allowing each variety to be produced entirely in one country and eliminating the need for multinationals. Thus, this model produces the same conclusions as Helpman's, once additional varieties are introduced, which is necessary to compare its implications with those of the present paper.

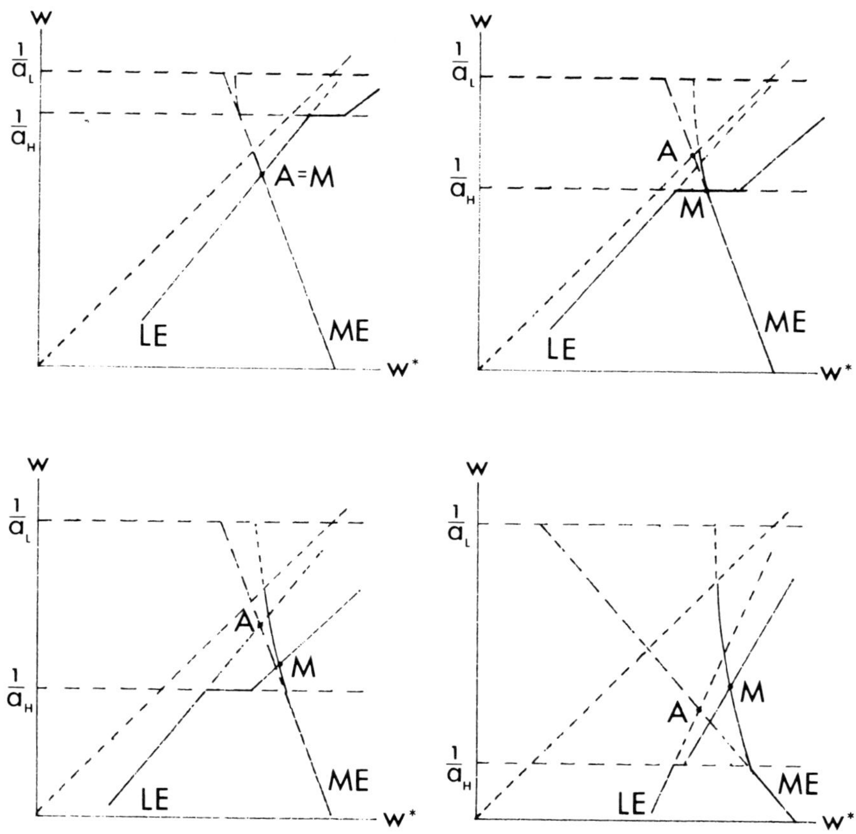

FIGURE IV

the larger the dispersion the larger is the number n of varieties, and the lower is the quality of those varieties for which $a = a_H$. Finally, very large dispersions introduce the possibility that the home wage is larger in an equilibrium with multinationals than in one with arm's length transactions.

In case (a), point A features $w < 1/a_H$, so $A = M$, and there is no incentive to form multinationals. In the other three cases $w > 1/a_H$ at A, so $A \neq M$. Because of the step-like shape of the amended LE schedule, it is not unlikely that $w = 1/a_H$ at point M, as shown in panel (b). In this case, with an integrated equilibrium, firms are indifferent about the quality of goods that they provide when $a = a_H$. Thus, they do not perceive that they derive any advantage from being multinational. However, if they were to respond by dismembering themselves, the now independent manufacturing firms would all have to offer Q_1 quality goods when $a = a_H$, which would cause w to rise. At the higher wage, the (now arm's length) firms wish to integrate.

In all cases where integration is beneficial, the multinational equilibrium features a higher foreign wage w^* than does the arm's length equilibrium. Therefore, land's rent is lower: the formation of multinationals redistributes income in the host country to the factor employed intensively in the multinational sector and away from the other factor. This is just the reverse of what happens in the Markusen-Helpman model. Panels (b) and (c) imply the opposite redistribution in the source country, but, as panel (d) demonstrates, it is possible for the establishment of multinationals to benefit labor worldwide at the expense of land. These possibilities also are at odds with the Markusen-Helpman model (and the latter case is quite different from the implications of international factor mobility in a factor-endowments trade model). Also, from (7) multinationalization increases n: there is a greater variety of goods with multinationals than without. When $a = a_L$, goods are produced at quality Q_1 with either form of industrial organization, the difference being the greater potential variety offered by multinationals. When $a = a_H$, arm's length firms would still offer goods of quality Q_1, but multinationals would not produce, except possibly in the case of panel (b). Thus, in equilibrium the number of goods actually offered for sale by the multinationals, $[1 - p(R)]n$, may be either greater or less than in an arm's length equilibrium.

Since the domestic wage may be either lower or higher with the multinational structure than with the arm's length one, it follows from (3)—and also from the description of the properties of $R_2(w)$ immediately following (3)—that research may be either greater or less. Thus, $p(R)$, which, socially, equals the fraction of varieties for which $a = a_L$, may be either greater or less.

VI. Concluding Remarks

This paper has developed a simple general equilibrium model of international trade offering an explanation for the emergence of multinational enterprises, within the general spirit of what Dunning calls the "eclectic theory," or the OLI framework. The paper first argues that the question critical for understanding direct investment in the context of trade theory is the nature of internalization, and that the essential aspect of the latter usually involves the exchange of information between agents. The central informational issues are the public good nature of information and the size and diversity of the information flows with which agents must contend.

A model was constructed to examine and reflect these concerns. The model contained two variables, research effort and product quality, respectively, associated with the two central informational issues. The basic parameters of the model were relative factor endowments and the dispersion (or degree of intrinsic uncertainty facing agents).

The roles of multinational activity was discussed and related to the basic parameters. The presence of multinational firms is positively related to the size of the dispersion. Also, similarity in relative factor endowments makes direct investment more likely, and also provides a basis for intraindustry trade and causes wages to be more nearly equal internationally. Sufficient endowment similarity (and the presence of a large enough dispersion) cause international wage equalization and two-way direct investment, making intraindustry trade and intrafirm trade large relative to interindustry trade.

These implications are dramatically different from those of the Markusen-Helpman model, which took internalization for granted. It would be premature, I believe, to interpret this difference in results as a picture of the significance of internalization, since it is unclear how robust either set of results is. What has been established is the inherent importance of explicitly modeling the internalization decision.

UNIVERSITY OF PENNSYLVANIA

REFERENCES

Agarwal, J. P., "Determinants of Foreign Direct Investment: A Survey," *Weltwirtschaftliches Archiv,* CXVI (1980), 739–73.

Buckley, P. J., and M. Casson, *The Future of the Multinational Enterprise* (London: Macmillan, 1976).

Casson, M., *Alternatives to the Multinational Enterprise* (London: Macmillan, 1979).

Caves, R. E., "International Corporations: The Industrial Economics of Foreign Investment," *Economica,* XXXVIII (1971), 1–27.

——, "International Trade, International Investment, and Imperfect Markets," *Special Papers in International Economics* No. 10 (Princeton: International Finance Section, Princeton University, 1974).

——, *Multinational Enterprise and Economic Analysis* (Cambridge: Cambridge University Press, 1982).
Cherkes, M., "The Theory of the Multinational Enterprise in Manufacturing Industries," University of Pennsylvania, Ph. D. thesis, 1984.
Coase, R. H., "The Theory of the Firm," *Economica,* IV (1937), 386–405.
D'Aspremont, C., and L. Gerard-Varet, "Incentives and Incomplete Information," *Journal of Public Economics,* XI (1979), 25–45.
Dunning, J. H., ed., *The Multinational Corporation* (London: George Allen and Unwin, 1971).
——, "The Determinants of International Production," *Oxford Economic Papers,* XXV (1973), 289–336.
——, "Trade, Location of Economic Activity and MNE: A Search for an Eclectic Approach," in B. Ohlin, P.-O. Hesselborn, and P. M. Wijkman, eds., *The International Allocation of Economic Activity* (London: Macmillan, 1977).
——, "Explaining the International Direct Investment Position of Countries; Towards a Dynamic or Developmental Approach," *Weltwirtschaftliches Archiv,* CXVII (1981), 30–64.
Ethier, W. J., "Internationally Decreasing Costs and World Trade," *Journal of International Economics,* IX (1979), 1–24.
——, "National and International Returns to Scale in the Modern Theory of International Trade," *American Economic Review,* LXXII (1982), 389–405.
——, *Modern International Economics* (New York: Norton, 1983).
——, and H. Horn, "Multinational Firms: the Cost Side," unpublished manuscript, 1985.
Grossman, S. J., and O. Hart, "The Costs and Benefits of Ownership: A Theory of Vertical Integration," unpublished manuscript, 1984.
Hart, O. D., "Optimal Labour Contracts under Asymmetric Information: An Introduction," *Review of Economic Studies,* L (1983), 3–35.
Helpman, E., "A Theory of Multinational Corporations and the Structure of Foreign Trade," unpublished manuscript, 1983a.
——, "A Theory of Multinational Corporations and the Structure of Foreign Trade—Part II: Vertical Integration," unpublished manuscript, 1983b.
——, "International Trade in the Presence of Product Differentiation, Economies of Scale and Monopolistic Competition," *Journal of International Economics,* XI (1981), 305–40.
——, "A Simple Theory of International Trade with Multinational Corporations," *Journal of Political Economy,* XCII (1984), 451–71.
——, and P. R. Krugman, *Market Structure and Foreign Trade* (Cambridge: MIT Press, 1985).
Hood, N., and S. Young, *The Economics of Multinational Enterprise* (London: Longman, 1979).
Horstmann, I., and J. Markusen, "Strategic Investments and the Development of Multinationals," *International Economic Review,* (1986a).
——, and ——, "Licensing versus Direct Investment: A Model of Internalization by the Multinational Enterprise," unpublished manuscript, (1986b).
Hufbauer, G. C., "The Multinational Corporation and Direct Investment," in P. B. Kenen, ed., *International Trade and Finance* (Cambridge: Cambridge University Press, 1975).
Hymer, S., "The International Operations of National Firms," Massachusetts Institute of Technology, Ph. D. thesis, 1960.
Kindleberger, C. P., *American Business Abroad: Six Lectures on Direct Investment* (New Haven: Yale University Press, 1969).
——, ed., *The International Corporation* (Cambridge: MIT Press, 1970).
——, and D. B. Audretsch, eds., *The Multinational Corporation in the 1980s* (Cambridge: MIT Press, 1983).
Krugman, P., "Increasing Returns, Monopolistic Competition, and International Trade," *Journal of International Economics,* IX (1979), 469–80.
——, Intraindustry Specialization and the Gains from Trade," *Journal of Political Economy,* LXXXIX (1981), 959–73.
Lall, S., and P. Streeten, *Foreign Investment, Transnationals and Developing Countries* (London: Macmillan, 1977).
Lancaster, K., "Intra-industry Trade under Perfect Monopolistic Competition," *Journal of International Economics,* X (1980), 151–76.

Magee, S. P., "Information and the Multinational Corporation: An Appropriability Theory of Direct Foreign Investment," in J. N. Bhagwati, ed., *The New International Economic Order: The North-South Debate* (Cambridge: MIT Press, 1977a).
——, "Multinational Corporations, the Industry Technology Cycle and Development," *Journal of World Trade Law* XI (1977b), 297–321.
Markusen, J. P., "Multinationals, Multi-Plant Economies, and the Gains from Trade," *Journal of International Economics,* XVI (1984), 205–26.
McCulloch, R., "U.S. Direct Foreign Investment and Trade: Theories, Trends, and Public Policy Issues," in: A. Erdilek, ed., *Multinationals as Mutual Invaders: Intraindustry Direct Foreign Investment* (Beckenham, England: Croom Helm, 1984).
Rugman, A. M., "Internalization as a General Theory of Foregn Direct Investment: A Re-Appraisal of the Literature," *Weltwirtschaftliches Archiv,* CXVI (1980), 365–79.
Shaked, A., and J. Sutton, "Natural Oligopolies," *Econometrica,* LI (1983), 1469–84.
——, and ——, "Natural Oligopolies and International Trade," in H. Kierzkowski, ed., *Monopolistic Competition and International Trade* (Oxford: Oxford University Press, 1984).
Stevens, G. V. G., "The Determinants of Investment," in J. H. Dunning, ed., *Economic Analysis and the Multinational Enterprise* (London: George Allen and Unwin, 1974).
Vernon, R., *Storm over the Multinationals: The Real Issues* (London: Macmillan, 1977).
Williamson, O. E., *Markets and Hierarchies: Analysis and Antitrust Implications: A Study in the Economics of Internal Organization* (New York: Free Press, 1975).

PART IV:
Regional Integration

Regional Integration: *Commentary*

Beginning in the late 1980s and early 1990s, the formation of regional trade agreements exploded, and they have now become virtually the sole arena for new international negotiations about trade policy. At essentially the same time, multilateralism became truly multilateral after the Uruguay Round, communism collapsed in most of the large part of the world that it had characterized, much of the less-developed world turned its back on decades of anti-trade policies, and direct investment also exploded and became much more multilateral. An extraordinary coincidence?

But my first foray into this area — at the time referred to as "customs-union theory" — was quite conventional. This was with Henrik Horn in, *A New Look at Economic Integration.* We were simply concerned with the implications of the then emerging theories of intra-industry trade for regional integration. Our results included the proposition that a limited regional arrangement, under certain weak conditions, would be Pareto improving, and that a limited retreat from a regional arrangement, again under weak conditions, would also be Pareto improving. These are much relevant to the current international situation, but we did not realize that at the time (at least, I did not realize it: probably Henrik did).

My interest in the "new regionalism" came later, as I began to ponder the "extraordinary coincidence" referred to above. A key moment for me was when I attended a seminar on the topic by John Whalley. I recall neither the occasion nor the title of the paper. John's argument was that the new regionalism was a way in which developing countries were trying to obtain insurance against a possible collapse of multilateralism into nationalistic trade wars. I did not buy that argument. But John's way of posing his question, and his setting of it in the context of the developing multilateral order, was a huge stimulus to my different approach to these issues. Thank you John.

My explanation of the new regionalism, and of the "extraordinary coincidence," came in the paper, *Regionalism in A Multilateral World* (This was expanded upon and clarified [I hope] in *The New Regionalism*). I regard this as among my very best papers. I do not mean most influential: The vast bulk of the academic literature in this area remains fixated on Vinerian concerns.

13
A New Look at Economic Integration*

Wilfred Ethier and Henrik Horn

The literature on customs unions theory is gargantuan. Nevertheless it strikes us as inadequate, both in the theoretical cases it addresses and in the actual circumstances of the world economy to which it is commonly thought relevant. This paper aims to spell out the details of this inadequacy and to indicate some lines along which the theory ought to be developed.

Section 1 very briefly describes basic ideas in contemporary customs union theory, and Section 2 then discusses at some length necessary extensions. Two general propositions are advanced in the next section, and proved in Section 4. Section 5 develops a specific model incorporating the new features, and Section 6 then exhibits aspects of this model via some special comparative-statics exercises.

1. BASICS OF CUSTOMS UNION THEORY

There is a huge literature in this area for three distinct reasons: (i) the *institutional* fact that there are many types of discriminatory trade besides customs unions proper (preferential trading arrangements, free trade areas, common markets, economic unions, and so on), (ii) the subject demands disaggregation beyond two-country, two-commodity models, and therefore gives rise to *many conceivable combinations* of characteristics of countries, commodities, and trade flows, and (iii) the subject requires comparisons of *distorted* equilibria which, in particular in conjunction with the second point, increases the mathematical complexity of the analysis. In practice the latter two factors have proved decisive, with analysis concentrated disproportionately upon the case of a customs union proper (free internal trade combined with a common external tariff).

Two basic ideas stand out from the wealth of specific analysis. The first, which might be called the *Vinerian Description*, is the notion that the net effect of a customers union is dependent on the balance of trade creation and trade diversion. This idea is in truth the very core of customs union theory.

(A) *Vinerian Description.* Formation of a customs union produces trade creation between the partners, in response to the mutual elimination of tariffs on one another's goods, and trade diversion from third countries to the partners, in response to the tariff discrimination produced by the union.

Trade creation is by presumption beneficial and trade diversion harmful. Union formation is thus seen as a second-best exercise, with one distortion replaced by another. This, together with the need for at least some disaggregation, accounts for the multitude of separate possibilities. Other aspects of union formation have of course also received attention. Notable examples, to which we shall return, include changes in the terms of trade – both within the union and *vis-à-vis* the outside world – and also economies of scale and the degree of competition.

Mention of the terms of trade relative to the rest of the world brings us to the second basic idea, due to Kemp, Vanek, Ohyama, and Wan. Setting the external tariffs at appropriate levels can cause the member countries, in the aggregate, to trade with the rest of the world exactly the same collection and quantities of goods that, in the aggregate, they traded prior to the union. Then the union will have no effect at all on the rest of the world, and the members must in the aggregate benefit, because the only effect they experience is the freeing of mutual trade. In essence, manipulation of the external tariff schedule allows any customs union to eliminate all trade diversion and so consist only of trade creation. By allowing a small deterioriation in its external terms of trade, the union can ensure that also non-members benefit.

(B) *Kemp–Vanek–Ohyama–Wan.* By an appropriate choice of common external tariffs and of lump-sum transfers among members, any customs union can assure that no countries in the world lose, and that some gain, as a result of the formation of the union.

This proposition applies irrespective of initial conditions, and so establishes a sense in which the countries of the world always have incentives to form additional unions until global free trade is achieved.

2. DESIRABLE DEPARTURES

Although the two ideas discussed above hardly begin to do justice to the vastness of customs union theory,[1] they do indicate the distinguishing features of the subject and are its most important conclusions. Thus we take the pair as a benchmark from which to enquire in what direction contemporary problems mandate that the subject be further developed. We indicate four directions. The four have by no means been completely ignored by the literature; and in some cases have received formal treatment, but they do depart substantially from the core of received customs unions theory.

(*i*) *Trade Modification*

The basic element of the conventional theory is tariff discrimination: the *same* good that can be imported free of duty from a partner faces a tariff when it comes from a non-partner country. But partners also trade among themselves some goods which they do not import at all (either before or after the union) from outside countries. For want of a better term, we describe as ***trade modification*** the change in trade with outside countries due to the elimination of tariffs on goods traded only within the union.[2] Thus trade modification differs from its familiar sister concept of trade diversion in that it can be produced by tariff changes consistent with the Most Favoured Nation clause and with the GATT, that is, by economic integration resulting from the non-discriminatory elimination by the partners of tariffs on goods they import only from each other.

Suppose, as an example, that France and Germany form a customs union, with France eliminating its tariff on German automotive supplies, also initially imported from America. This discriminatory tariff change would presumably induce trade diversion, with imports of German automotive supplies replacing some or all of the imports from America. Now suppose in contrast that France initially imports small cars from Germany and large cars from America, and that the integration takes the form of a French abolition of the tariff on small cars. Such a non-discriminatory tariff change is not usually considered as within the domain of customs union theory, even though it is likely to deflect French demand from American to German automotive products in about the same way as the previous case. Next, suppose instead that there is a unified world automobile industry, with France importing engines from Germany and bodies from America, and that France abolishes its tariff on engines. This again causes trade modification, but now French imports of American bodies will likely rise along with French imports of German engines.

Trade modification differs from trade diversion in that it is not the result of geographical tariff *discrimination* but rather of the replacement of one set of tariffs by another, with the property that the tariffs which are changed apply directly to trade flows between a strict subset of countries. As the example makes clear, degrees of substitutability and complementarity between goods become crucial.

Extending the scope of the theory to encompass trade modification might well therefore open the gates to another flood of special cases – hardly welcome in this field especially. And the bulk of empirical work in the area cannot be interpreted as distinguishing trade diversion from trade modification. But there are good reasons why the theory should include both. First, of course, is that both are in principle part of the problem. More significant is the large volume of empirical work, by Kravis and Lipsey (1971) and many others, that in the last decade has revealed extensive international price discrimination at even quite disaggregated levels. As a result economists now tend, much more than before, to think of international trade as the exchange of differentiated products, rather than of homogeneous goods. This shift in perception calls for a shift in emphasis from trade diversion towards trade modification.

But the most important consideration is the range of phenomena to which the theory of economic integration ought to apply. Although many attempts at customs unions and free trade areas have been made since the Second World War, the only actual, substantially successful, instance to which the theory reflected in the Vinerian Description literally applies is western European integration. An important instance, to be sure, but past history. Customs union theory thus appears seldom to be used as a framework for thought about contemporary problems. But issues to which a theory of economic integration *ought* to apply are legion. As a glaring example, consider the dominant post-war exercise in global commercial policy: the cumulative tariff reductions produced by successive GATT rounds. As often emphasized by economists and men of affairs alike, these reductions have concentrated on trade in manufactures among the developed countries and have been much less relevant to the trade of LDCs. Thus we have experienced on an historical scale (and continue to do so as the Tokyo Round cuts are implemented) the very sort of nationally biased tariff reductions that are the very essence of the theory of economic integration. But our theory has not been thought relevant because those cuts, implemented under the Most Favoured Nation clause, directly conflict with the Vinerian Description. The incorporation of trade modification in addition to (or instead of) trade diversion is essential to the practical relevance of customs union theory.

(*ii*) *Intra-Industry Trade and Product Differentiation*

Related to the distinction between trade diversion and trade modification is the observation that customs union theory assumes trade in homogeneous products whereas product differentiation and intra-industry trade are pervasive in actual commerce. Theoretical models of these latter phenomena have been developed in recent years, and extension of these models to the theory of economic integration is obviously called for. Recall that our present widespread appreciation of the large and growing significance of intra-industry trade in the industrial world actually dates from studies of the effects of economic integration in Europe.

(*iii*) *Imperfect Competition and Scale Economies*

These phenomena have been considered in the light of customs union theory in the past. What is clearly called for now is the application of recently developed general equilibrium approaches.

(*iv*) *'Small' Tariff Changes*

Customs union theory has generally considered only 'large' tariff changes between partners: the complete elimination of internal trade barriers. Exceptions[3] have usually been accompanied by apologetic explanations of the convenience of marginal analysis. Large changes have been considered an essential aspect of the problem because theorists have often had in the backs of their minds the example of European integration, with free internal trade an objective from the start, and because the GATT rules permitting customs unions and free trade areas require the abolition of internal tariffs: mere reciprocal tariff preferences are ruled out. But the latter consideration is eliminated by our interest in trade modification. Furthermore, a concern with contemporary problems should redirect attention towards small changes, rendering marginal analysis of interest in its own right. The successive GATT rounds have, at each stage, constituted an incremental change toward free trade among the developed countries. If translated into tariff equivalents, the numerous voluntary export restraints of the 'new protectionism' of recent years likewise constitute incremental changes, though in the direction of economic disintegration. Another potentially important example is furnised by the codes of conduct regarding non-tariff barriers formulated during the Tokyo Round. These codes are not automatically binding on the GATT nations, or limited to them, but are to be individually acceded to by individual states. Thus each code seems likely to develop a circle of participating countries applying *vis-à-vis* one another the provisions of the code as regards the respective non-tariff barrier, but applying more restrictive prior standards toward non-participating countries. Thus the codes might well produce non-tariff equivalents of preferential trading areas.

It is easier to undertake by stages the departures recommended here. Therefore, in the following two sections we ignore imperfect competition and scale economies, but allow trade modification and enquire into the consequences of a small preferential change in tariffs, in a conventional context. Two general propositions, analogous to results well known in the theory of trade and domestic distortions, follow easily once attention is directed towards small tariff changes; these proportions are stated in Section 3, and are formally proved in Section 4. In the rest of the paper we consider also the remaining two suggested departures from the standard treatment of economic integration: product differentiation, and imperfect competition and scale economies. To highlight the impact of these additions, we construct in Section 5 a special formal model that incorporates all four departures, but that abstracts from some features already studied. In Section 6 we analyse properties of this model by means of comparative-statics experiments. Finally, some brief concluding remarks are given in Section 7.

3. TWO ADDITIONAL GENERAL PROPERTIES

Consider first an initial state of non-discriminatory (but tariff-ridden) world trade. Suppose that some subset of countries then initiates a marginal mutual reduction of tariffs on trade with one another. (Since the role of the external terms of trade is understood, suppose for simplicity that no change takes place in the terms at which these countries deal with the rest of the world.) Since trade is initially non-discriminatory, an additional unit of imports or exports by any country has the same effect on the welfare of residents of that country regardless of with whom the additional trade takes place. Thus the trade diversion and/or trade modification generated by the marginal preferential tariff reduction must have a zero first-order effect on welfare. But since trade is tariff-ridden, an additional unit of imports will cost any country less than that unit's contribution to welfare: any trade creation must have a positive first-order effect.

(C) *Preferential Trade is Better than Free Trade.* If tariffs are positive but non-discriminatory, any sub-group of countries can raise its joint welfare by means of marginal preferential tariff reductions that increase the gross value of their total trade (in the specific sense that the new trade flows yield the partners more tariff revenue than the old flows, at the initial tariffs and prices), if the prices of goods exchanged between those countries and the rest of the world do not change.

This proposition differs from the result of Kemp and Wan (1978), Ohyama (1972), and Vanek (1965) in that it is limited to small tariff changes, whose relevance we have just advocated. What this limitation buys us is a dispensation from the need to adjust external tariffs so as to eliminate trade diversion and trade modification: their welfare effects will be swamped by those of trade creation.

Now consider the opposite initial situation: a group of countries, in a tariff-ridden world, have formed a customs union with free internal trade. Suppose these countries stage a 'marginal retreat' from the union by imposing a small tariff on imports from one another. Free initial internal trade implies that a marginal import by any member from a partner yields a welfare increase equal to the welfare loss due to the exports required in payment. Thus the 'trade destruction' caused by the marginal internal tariff will entail a zero first-order effect on welfare. But any increased trade with the rest of the world produces a positive first-order effect since the initial external tariffs imply that an additional import increases welfare by more than the sacrifice required to pay for it.

(D) *Preferential Trade is Better than a Customs Union.* If any group of countries has free mutual trade in a tariff-ridden world, their joint welfare will be increased by a marginal tariff on one another's goods that raises total trade with the rest of the world (in the specific sense that the new volume of trade yields the partners jointly more revenue than the old, at the original tariffs and prices), if the prices at which the partners trade with external countries do not change.

In essence, the net benefits from 'undoing' some trade diversion and trade modification necessarily swamp the losses entailed by 'trade destruction', for a small retreat from a customs union. This partially undercuts the consistent motives for union formation that seem to be supplied by idea (B). Also (C) and (D) together imply a motivation for tariff preferences that fall short of complete union. This is quite consistent with the prominent contemporary issues that the previous section argued ought to be addressable by the theory of economic integration.

4. A FORMAL TREATMENT

4.1. The model

This section supplies explicit proofs of propositions (C) and (D) and discusses them further. Assume three countries: two partners (A and B) and the rest of the world (distinguished by an asterisk). There is a total of n traded goods, divided into the twelve groups described in Table 13.1. Groups 1 to 5 contain goods imported by country A, exportables are collected in groups 6–10, whereas country A does not trade in groups 11 and 12.

For each group i, Q_i denotes the n-vector with a zero in each component corresponding to a good not in group i, and with the country A domestic price of the respective good in each component that does so correspond. Thus $Q = \Sigma_{i=1}^{12} Q_i$ is the vector of country A domestic prices. Vectors P_i apply analogously to the partner country, so $P = \Sigma_{i=1}^{12} P_i$ denotes the vector of country-B domestic prices.

In like fashion, P_i^* denotes the vector of prices actually paid to the rest of the world, or received from the rest of the world, for goods in group i (with zeros in components corresponding to other goods). Let $R^A = P_1 + P_2^* + P_3^* + P_4^* + P_5^* + Q_6 + Q_7 + P_8^* + P_9^* + P_{10}^*$. Then R_A is the vector of prices at which country A actually transacts with foreigners, *except* possibly for those goods in group 5 that are imported from country B. In like manner, $R^B = P_1 + P_2^* + P_4^* + P_5 + Q_6 + P_7^* + P_9^* + P_{10}^* + P_{11}^* + P_{12}^*$ denotes B's actual international transaction prices, *except* possibly for goods in group 7 imported from A.

T_i^A, for $i = 1, \ldots, 4$, is the $n \times n$ diagonal matrix with *ad valorem* tariff rates of country A on goods in group i as the appropriate diagonal elements, and zeros elsewhere. T_{5B}^A and T_{5*}^A likewise denote tariff matrices of country A on goods in group 5 imported from B and from the rest of the world respectively. Country B tariff matrices T_4^B, T_6^B, T_{10}^B, T_{12}^B, T_{7A}^B, and T_{7*}^B are defined analogously. Let $T^A = T_1^A + T_2^A + T_3^A + T_4^A + T_{5*}^A$ and $T^B = T_4^B + T_6^B + T_{7*}^B + T_{10}^B + T_{12}^B$. Then

TABLE 13.1. *Description of the Commodity Groups*

Group	Commodity description
1	B exports only to A
2	B exports to A and to the rest of the world
3	the rest of the world exports only to A
4	the rest of the world exports to A and B
5	the rest of the world and B both export to A
6	A exports only to B
7	the rest of the world and A both export to B
8	A exports only to the rest of the world
9	A and B both export to the rest of the world
10	A exports to both B and the rest of the world
11	B exports only to the rest of the world
12	the rest of the world exports only to B

$$Q = (I + T^A) R^A,$$
$$P = (I + T^B) R^B.$$

Note also that $(I + T^A_{5B}) P_5 = (I + T^A_{5*}) P_5^*$ and $(I + T^B_{7A}) Q_7 = (I + T^B_{7*}) P_7^*$.

M_i^A is the n-vector of country A net imports of goods in group i (with zeros elsewhere), and $M^A = \Sigma_{i=1}^{10} M_i^A$. Also $M_5^A = M_{5B}^A + M_{5*}^A$ and $M_{10}^A = M_{10B}^A + M_{10*}^A$ where the two vectors on the right in each case record trade with country B and the rest of the world respectively. Analogously for M_i^B, for $M^B = M_1^B + M_2^B + M_4^B + M_5^B + M_6^B + M_7^B + M_9^B + M_{10}^B + M_{11}^B + M_{12}^B$, and for both $M_2^B = M_{2A}^B + M_{2*}^B$ and $M_7^B = M_{7A}^B + M_{7*}^B$. (Note that $M_1^A = -M_1^B, M_2^A = -M_{2A}^B, M_{5B}^A = -M_5^B, -M_6^A = M_6^B, -M_7^A = M_{7A}^B$ and $-M_{10B}^A = M_{10}^B$).

In country A, total expenditure – denoted by the national expenditure function $e^A(Q, u_A)$, where u_A denotes the vector of utilities of A residents – must equal income, composed of tariff revenue plus the value of national production, the latter given by the national product function $y^A(Q)$. Thus

$$e^A(Q, u_A) = y^A(Q) + T^A R^A [M^A - M_{5B}^A] + T_{5B}^A P_5^A M_{5B}^A. \tag{13.1}$$

Analogously for the partner country:

$$e^B(P, u_B) = y^B(P) + T^B R^B [M^B - M_{7A}^B] + T_{7A}^B Q_7 M_{7A}^B. \tag{13.2}$$

4.2. A basic expression

Differentiating (13.1), noting that $\partial e^A/\partial Q - \partial y^A/\partial Q = M^A$ and that $dQ = dR^A + d(T^A R^A)$ gives

$$\frac{\partial e^A}{\partial u_A} du_A = -M^A dR^A - M_{5B}^A [d(T^A R^A) - d(T_{5B}^A P_5)] + T^A R^A d\bar{M}^A + T_{5B}^A P_5 dM_{5B}^A, \tag{13.3}$$

where $\bar{M}^A \equiv M^A - M_{5B}^A$. In a like manner, we obtain for the partner country

$$\frac{\partial e^B}{\partial u_B} du_B = -M^B dR^B - M_{7A}^B [d(T^B R^B) - d(T_{7A}^B Q_7)] + T^B R^B d\bar{M}^B + T_{7A}^B Q_7 dM_{7A}^B. \tag{13.4}$$

Equations (13.3) and (13.4) supply measures of the welfare effects on the partners of changes in commercial policy. The sources of these effects, spelled out on the right-hand sides of the equations, are analogous to the sources of welfare effects commonly discussed in conventional tariff theory.[4]

We measure the change in the joint welfare of the partner countries by $dW = (\partial e^A/\partial u_A) du_A + (\partial e^B/\partial u_B) du_B$. Remember that we suppose constancy in the prices at which A and B transact with the rest of the world, implying

$$M^A dR^A + M^B dR^B = -M_{5B}^A dP_5 - M_{7A}^B dQ_7.$$

With goods in group 5 (or group 7) being bought from the rest of the world at prices assumed to be unchanged, $d(T^A R^A)$ $(d(T^B R^B))$ will have zero elements corresponding to positive entries in M_{5B}^A (or M_{7A}^B), and therefore

$$\begin{aligned} dW = {} & M_{5B}^A [dP_5 + d(T_{5B}^A P_5)] + T_{5B}^A P_5(dM^A - d\bar{M}^A) + T^A R^A \, d\bar{M}^A \\ & + M_{7A}^B [dQ_7 + d(T_{7A}^B Q_7)] + T_{7A}^B Q_7(dM^B - d\bar{M}^B) + T^B R^B \, d\bar{M}^B, \end{aligned} \tag{13.5}$$

where $T_{5B}^A P_5(T_{7A}^B Q_7)$ has zeros corresponding to non-zero elements of $d\bar{M}^A$ $(d\bar{M}^B)$. Furthermore,

$$dP_5 + d(T_{5B}^A P_5) = d[(I + T_{5B}^A)P_5] = d[(I + T_{5*}^A)P_5^*] = P_5^* \, dT_{5*}^A,$$

$$dQ_7 + d(T_{7A}^B Q_7) = d[(I + T_{7A}^B)Q_7] = d[(I + T_{7*}^B)P_7^*] = P_7^* \, dT_{7*}^B.$$

Since also M_{5B}^A (M_{7A}^B) has zero elements corresponding to non-zero elements in $P_5^* \, dT_{5*}^A$ $(P_7^* \, dT_{7*}^B)$, our expression for the effect of tariff changes on the partners' joint welfare simplifies to

$$dW = (T_{5B}^A P_5) \, dM^A + (T_{7A}^B Q_7) \, dM^B + (T^A R^A) \, d\bar{M}^A + (T^B R^B) \, d\bar{M}^B. \tag{13.6}$$

This is our basic result. We now apply it to two special cases in order to derive propositions (C) and (D).

4.3. *The propositions*

Suppose first that all tariffs are initially non-discriminatory, so that $T_{5B}^A = T_{5*}^A$, $P_5 = P_5^*$, $T_{7A}^B = T_{7*}^B$, and $Q_7 = P_7^*$. Equation (13.6) then reduces to

$$dW = (T^A R^A) \, dM^A + (T^B R^B) \, dM^B. \tag{13.7}$$

Thus a small discriminatory tariff change (or any other small change) raises joint welfare if and only if the changes in trade volume would increase joint tariff revenues at the initial rates and prices, as was stated in proposition (C) above. Note in particular two aspects of this result.

First, the degree of trade diversion – reflected in the *composition* of dM_5^A between dM_{5B}^A and dM_{5*}^A and in the composition of dM_7^B between dM_{7A}^B and dM_{7*}^B – has no influence at all on dW. This is to be expected in the light of the previous section's informal discussion.

Second, trade modification – reflected in the magnitudes of dM_3^A, dM_4^A, dM_4^B, and dM_{12}^B – will add to or subtract from dW according as the goods involved are in this sense complementary to or substitutes for intra-union trade. This, again, is not surprising in view of the earlier discussion. Indeed, if the goods which countries A and B trade exclusively with the rest of the world are sufficiently strong substitutes for the goods they exchange with each other, they could have an incentive to form an 'anti-union', that is, to *add* a marginal discriminatory tariff on each others' goods. The two would have reason to seek separate preferential arrangements with the rest of the world, rather than with each other.

Suppose next that A and B initially have a full free trade area and impose marginal internal tariffs. Then $T_1^A = T_2^A = T_{5B}^A = T_6^B = T_{7A}^B = T_{10}^B = 0$ and (13.6) reduces to

$$dW = (T^A R^A)\, d\bar{M}^A + (T^B R^B)\, d\bar{M}^B. \tag{13.8}$$

Thus a marginal retreat from internal free trade will raise the partners' joint welfare if and only if it raises total tariff revenue collected on trade with the rest of the world, as stated above in proposition (D). It is instructive to decompose the right-hand side of (13.8) as follows:

$$dW = (T_{5*}^A P_5^* \, dM_{5*}^A + T_{7*}^B P_7^* \, dM_{7*}^B) + (T_3^A P_3^* \, dM_3^A + T_4^A P_4^* \, dM_4^A + T_4^B P_4^* \, dM_4^B + T_{12}^B P_{12}^* \, dM_{12}^B). \tag{13.9}$$

Note that an 'undoing' of trade diversion – indicated by positive terms within the first set of parentheses on the right-hand side of (13.9) – must increase W regardless of how great the accompanying reduction in intra-union trade in the same goods happens to be. This is a consequence of the initial free internal trade, as discussed in the previous section.

The influence of trade modification is summarized by the second parenthesized term on the right-hand side of (13.9). Joint partner welfare is thereby raised or lowered according as this term is positive or negative, that is, according as the goods traded exclusively with the rest of the world are in this sense on balance substitutes for or complementary to intra-partner trade.

Trade diversion and trade modification are central in both exercises. The presumptive role of trade diversion is clear: it should cause both a marginal reduction of a discriminatory tariff and a marginal retreat from a free trade area to raise joint partner welfare. But the role of trade modification depends crucially upon whether the goods traded exclusively with the rest of the world are on balance substitutes for or complements to intra-union trade, in the sense that discrimination in favour of the latter reduces or increases the volume of the former, with the change in this volume measured by the net changes in partner tariff revenue it would generate at initial prices and tariffs.

Neither non-discrimination nor a free trade area would constitute an optimal policy – for A and B jointly, given tariffs on goods from the rest of the world – without a very special balancing of the various influences discussed above. If exclusively external trade is on balance neither strongly substitutable for, nor complementary to, internal trade, optimal policy for the partners will presumably entail tariff preferences that fall short of a full free trade area, so that both non-discrimination and customs unions should be unstable.

Significant net *substitutability* both reduces the gain from initial preferences and increases the gain to a retreat from a full union. Thus one expects it to cause optimal policy to feature a lower degree of preference. Sufficient substitutability should make optimal an 'anti-union' with the members actually discriminating against one another. Significant net *complementarity*, finally, increasing the gain from initial preferences and reducing that from a retreat, presumably causes the optimal policy to approximate more closely free internal trade. Large enough complementarity could cause the optimal policy to be a 'super union' with internal trade actually stimulated by subsidies finance by tariffs on external trade. Note that the European Community's Common Agricultural Policy – which does not naturally come to mind in a discussion of optimality – does in fact possess some of the characteristics of such a case.

5. SCALE ECONOMIES AND PRODUCT DIFFERENTIATION: A SPECIAL MODEL

The previous sections focused on trade modification as well as trade diversion and considered small tariff changes rather than large ones. But we said nothing about induced change in the *number* of distinct commodities (that is, in the degree of product differentiation), and, more prominently yet, imperfect competition and scale economies are foreign to the optimality conditions central to the logic of the propositions. Thus we have set off on some but not all of those departures from standard theory that we have argued for.

We have no wish to construct the awesome structure that would simply add our further suggested innovations to what we have already done in the previous section. Instead we now consider a special model that incorporates our four desired departures in as sharp a fashion as possible: by abstracting from other features. For better or worse, this is also the strategy used in the recent literature on international trade and scale economies, imperfect competition, and product differentiation.

We continue to suppose three countries: the partners (A and B) and the rest of the world, denoted by an asterisk. A and B can be thought of as DCs, the rest of the world as an LDC. A and B produce goods in two common sectors: manufactures and food. There are n and m different variants of manufactures produced in A and B, respectively. They are all (equally) imperfect substitutes to each other from the consumer's point of view, although they are produced with the same homothetic technology, characterized by internal, increasing returns to scale. Food, on the other hand, is produced in all three countries, under constant returns to scale.

We consider the following special trade pattern. A and B export their respective manufactures to each other and to the rest of the world, and both countries import food from the latter. We assume furthermore that A and B have formed a customs union with their internal tariff τ set at zero, and with a common external tariff t. The rest of the world imposes no trade restrictions.

It is clear that, with such a trade pattern, this customs union does not cause any trade *diversion*, since the non-member country exports a different good from that exported by the union countries. But the union will give rise to trade *creation* and trade *modification*.

Following, e.g., Dixit and Stiglitz (1977), we assume the preferences of each country's representative consumer to be given by

$$U^k = \left(\sum_{i=1}^{n} (X_i^k)^\beta + \sum_{j=1}^{m} (Y_j^k)^\beta \right)^{\alpha/\beta} (Z^k)^{1-\alpha}; \quad k = A, B, * \qquad (13.10)$$

with $0<\alpha<1$, and $0<\beta<1$, and where X_i^k is the amount of the country A-produced manufacture i that is consumed in country k, Y_j^k is the amount of the country-B produced manufacture j that is consumed in k, and Z^k the consumed quantity of food in k.

Let us now turn to the production side. The production process for manufactures can be thought of as consisting of two stages: first primary factors are used to produce a (non-traded) intermediate input under constant returns to scale, in the amounts M^A and M^B in the two DCs. This input is transformed to final differentiated goods under increasing returns. Since the equilibrium under study is characterized by strong symmetry, in the sense that $X_i^k = X^k, \forall i$, and $Y_j^k = Y^k, \forall j$, each firm in the manufacturing sector in A employs M^A/n of the intermediate good, and correspondingly M^B/m in B. We assume that entry is free, so the condition for industry equilibrium is that profits are zero

$$PX = r^A \frac{M^A}{n}, \quad \text{and} \quad QY = r^B \frac{M^B}{m},$$

where P and Q are the prices received by producers of manufactured products in A and B, respectively, r is the price of the intermediate input, and where $X \equiv X^A + X^B + X^*$, and $Y \equiv Y^A + Y^B + Y^*$. The internal increasing returns to scale stem from a fixed cost a, coupled with a constant marginal cost b. We could therefore alternatively simply define

$$M^A \equiv n(a + bX), \quad \text{and} \quad M^B \equiv m(a + bY),$$

and consider r^A, and r^B, as the 'factor-price index' in the separable cost function.

The conditions for profit-maximization in the two manufacturing industries can be stated as

$$P\beta = r^A b, \quad \text{and} \quad Q\beta = r^B b. \qquad (13.12)$$

To express the conditions in this form we use the fact that each firm will adjust its quantities in the three markets in such a way that it receives the same price everywhere.

Now, from (13.11) and (13.12) we immediately get that the total output volume of a firm in the manufacturing sectors is fixed.

$$X = Y = \frac{a}{b} \frac{\beta}{1-\beta}.$$

This is in particular due to the homothetic technology. It then follows that

$$n = \frac{1-\beta}{\alpha} M^A, \quad \text{and} \quad m = \frac{1-\beta}{\alpha} M^B.$$

The union countries' respective output of food is given by the transformation functions $T(M^A)$ for A, and $S(M^B)$ for B. The domestic produce is sold at the same price as imported food: $P_F(1+t)$, where P_F denotes the price of food excluding the union's external tariff t. The price of the intermediate good must be the value of the alternative use of the resources devoted to the production of one unit of the good, or

$$\begin{aligned} r^A &= -P_F(1+t)\,T'(M^A), \\ r^B &= -P_F(1+t)\,S'(M^B). \end{aligned} \tag{13.13}$$

The rest of the world is assumed to use one factor only, with the reward r^*, and with the fixed supply L^*. It takes one unit of this factor to produce one unit of food, and the condition for profit maximization (and industry equilibrium) is therefore simply

$$P_F = r^*.$$

Two variables that will be of interest in the comparative-statics exercises are the internal and external terms-of-trade, $q \equiv Q/P$, and $p \equiv P_F/P$, respectively. With the aid of (13.11) and (13.13), and recalling the definitions of M^A and M^B, the two variables may be expressed as

$$q = \frac{S'(M^B)}{T'(M^A)} \tag{13.14}$$

$$p = \frac{-\beta}{bP_F(1+t)\,T'(M^A)}. \tag{13.15}$$

Let us finally, before proceeding to the comparative-statics exercises, give the clearing conditions for the goods markets (the respective demand functions are given in the Appendix)

$$X = \frac{\alpha}{P}\left[\frac{I^A}{n + my_A^{\beta}} + \frac{I^B/(1+\tau)}{n + my_B^{\beta}} + \frac{I^*}{n + my_*^{\beta}}\right] \tag{13.16}$$

$$Y = \frac{\alpha}{Q}\left[\frac{I^A/(1+\tau)}{ny_A^{-\beta} + m} + \frac{I^B}{ny_B^{-\beta} + m} + \frac{I^*}{ny_*^{-\beta} + m}\right] \tag{13.17}$$

$$L^* + T(M^A) + S(M^B) = \frac{(1-\alpha)}{P_F}\,[I^A/(1+t) + I^B/(1+t) + I^*], \tag{13.18}$$

where τ denotes the union's internal tariff.

Comparative-statics exercises will be conducted to expose the basic nature of our model. To have a recognizable point of departure and standard of comparison, we shall conduct an exercise similar to that of proposition (D) discussed in Sections 3 and 4. Thus we start with internal free trade ($\tau = 0$), and with a common positive external tariff ($t > 0$). We first increase the common external tariff and then increase the common internal tariff. To facilitate matters we make the following assumption: the partners have a transfer scheme such that the relative changes in their incomes I^A and I^B are identical and equal to $\hat{I}$. This reflects our concern with the partners' *joint* experience, but is not without practical relevance: the Common Market is an example of a union with an internal transfer scheme.

The rest of this section presents the comparative-statics results. Discussions of these results are postponed to Section 6.

Since we use P_F as the numeraire, we have from (13.18):

$$\frac{\hat{I}}{(1-\alpha)} = -\frac{PnX}{I^A + I^B}\hat{M}^A - \frac{QmY}{I^A + I^B}\hat{M}^B + \hat{t}, \tag{13.19}$$

where $\hat{t} \equiv dt/(1+t)$.

The numbers of firms in the manufacturing sectors are proportional to the outputs of the two intermediate goods

$$\hat{n} = \hat{M}^A,$$

$$\hat{m} = \hat{M}^B.$$

The terms-of-trade changes are directly obtained from (13.14) and (13.15)

$$\hat{q} = \sigma^B \hat{m} - \sigma^A \hat{n}, \tag{13.20}$$

$$\hat{p} = -\hat{t} - \sigma^A \hat{n}, \tag{13.21}$$

where

$$\sigma^A \equiv \frac{M^A T''(M^A)}{T'(M^A)}, \quad \text{and} \quad \sigma^B \equiv \frac{M^B T''(M^B)}{T'(M^B)}.$$

The changes in trade and consumption patterns are given by

$$\hat{y}_A = (\sigma^B \hat{m} - \sigma^A \hat{n} + \hat{\tau})/(\beta - 1), \tag{13.22}$$

$$\hat{y}_B = (\sigma^B \hat{m} - \sigma^A \hat{n} - \hat{\tau})/(\beta - 1), \tag{13.23}$$

$$\hat{y}_* = (\sigma^B \hat{m} - \sigma^A \hat{n})/(\beta - 1), \tag{13.24}$$

$$\hat{z}_A = \hat{n} + \frac{m}{n+m}\left(\frac{\beta}{1-\beta}\sigma^A - 1\right)(\hat{n} - \hat{m}) - \frac{m}{(n+m)}\frac{\beta}{(1-\beta)}\hat{\tau}, \tag{13.25}$$

$$\hat{z}_B = \hat{n} + \frac{m}{n+m}\left(\frac{\beta}{1-\beta}\sigma^A - 1\right)(\hat{n} - \hat{m}) + \left(1 + \frac{m}{n+m}\frac{\beta}{1-\beta}\right)\hat{\tau}, \tag{13.26}$$

$$\hat{z}_* = \hat{n} + \frac{m}{n+m}\left(\frac{\beta}{1-\beta}\sigma^A - 1\right)(\hat{n} - \hat{m}), \qquad (13.27)$$

where $\hat{\tau} \equiv d\tau/(1+\tau)$, and $z_k \equiv Z^k/X^k$ for $k = $ A, B, *.

The following two expressions are reduced forms of the market equilibrium conditions for X- and Y-goods, respectively, and they will be the starting point of the proceeding analysis:

$$-\theta^*\hat{t} - \left[\theta^B + (\theta^B - \theta^A)\frac{\beta}{(1-\beta)}\frac{m}{(n+m)}\right]\hat{\tau} = \left[\sigma^A + \frac{1}{1-\alpha}\right]\hat{n}$$
$$+ \frac{m}{n+m}\left[\frac{\beta}{1-\beta}\sigma^A - \frac{1}{1-\alpha}\right](\hat{n} - \hat{m})$$
$$+ \frac{m}{(n+m)}\frac{\beta}{(1-\beta)}(\sigma^A - \sigma^B)\hat{m}, \qquad (13.28)$$

$$-\theta^*\hat{t} - \left[\theta^A - (\theta^B - \theta^A)\frac{\beta}{(1-\beta)}\frac{n}{(n+m)}\right]\hat{\tau} = \left[\sigma^B + \frac{1}{1-\alpha}\right]\hat{m}$$
$$- \frac{n}{n+m}\left[\frac{\beta}{1-\beta}\sigma^B - \frac{1}{1-\alpha}\right](\hat{n} - \hat{m})$$
$$- \frac{n}{(n+m)}\frac{\beta}{(1-\beta)}(\sigma^A - \sigma^B)\hat{n}, \qquad (13.29)$$

where θ^k is the share of world income for country k.

We subsequently make the special assumption that $\sigma^A = \sigma^B \equiv \sigma$, i.e. that the elasticities of the slopes of the transformation curves are the same at the equilibrium point, in the two union countries. This has the merit, aside from increased analytical tractability, of highlighting aspects of particular interest: the importance of the degree of product differentiation and the importance of asymmetries between the member countries in the relative sizes of their manufacturing sectors and also in their relative incomes.

(13.28) and (13.20) give the following solution for relative changes in the number of variants in the member countries:

$$\hat{n} = -\frac{\theta^*}{\Delta}\hat{t} - \left[\theta^B + (\theta^B - \theta^A)\frac{1}{(1-\alpha)\sigma}\frac{m}{(n+m)}\right]\frac{1}{\Delta}\hat{\tau} \qquad (13.30)$$

$$\hat{m} = -\frac{\theta^*}{\Delta}\hat{t} - \left[\theta^A - (\theta^B - \theta^A)\frac{1}{(1-\alpha)\sigma}\frac{n}{(n+m)}\right]\frac{1}{\Delta}\hat{\tau} \qquad (13.31)$$

$$\hat{n} - \hat{m} = \frac{(\theta^A - \theta^B)}{\sigma}\hat{\tau} \qquad (13.32)$$

and

$$\hat{N} = -\frac{\theta^*}{\Delta}\hat{t} - \frac{\Gamma}{\Delta}\hat{\tau}, \tag{13.33}$$

where

$$N \equiv n + m,$$

$$\Delta \equiv \sigma + \frac{1}{1-\alpha} > 0$$

and

$$\Gamma \equiv \theta^A \frac{n}{n+m} + \theta^B \frac{m}{n+m} > 0.$$

The Appendix gives some intermediate steps in the derivation of the following two expressions for the relative changes in the indirect utilities V^A and V^*:

$$\hat{V}^A = \alpha\frac{\theta^*}{\Delta}\Lambda\hat{t} + \alpha\left(\frac{\Gamma}{\Delta}\Lambda - \frac{m}{n+m}\right)\hat{\tau} \tag{13.34}$$

$$\hat{V}^* = \alpha\left(\left(\sigma - \frac{1-\beta}{\beta}\right)\frac{\theta^*}{\Delta} - 1\right)\hat{t} + \alpha\left(\sigma - \frac{1-\beta}{\beta}\right)\frac{\Gamma}{\Delta}\hat{\tau}, \tag{13.35}$$

where

$$\Lambda \equiv \sigma - \frac{1-\beta}{\beta} + \frac{1}{\theta^A + \theta^B}\cdot\frac{1}{1-\alpha} \gtrless 0.$$

6. TARIFF CHANGES

Our comparative statics experiments incorporate the two types of changes in union commercial policy that are of interest: changes $\hat{t}$ in the common external tariff on imports of food, and the marginal imposition $\hat{\tau}$ of a mutual internal tariff on the exchange of differentiated manufactured goods. Consider each in turn.

6.1. *An Increase in the Common External Tariff*

Let us first examine the implication of an increase in the already positive common external tariff t. From (13.30) and (13.31):

$$\hat{n} = \hat{m} < 0.$$

The numbers of varieties of both types of differentiated goods fall as, in each partner country, resources are pulled from manufacturing into the now more highly protected agricultural sector. The contraction of manufacturing is entirely a reduction in the number of product varieties; each produced variety experiences no change in its level of production. With a common external tariff on food, (13.20) implies that $\hat{q} = \sigma(\hat{m} - \hat{n}) = 0$, so that no substitution between product varieties is induced.[5]

Our assumption about the third country ensures that it continues to export αL^* units of food. The shift of demand in A and B away from food turns the terms of trade in favour of the union. We have $\hat{p} = -\hat{t} - \sigma\hat{n}$, and substitution of (13.30) into this expression reveals that the relative price p of food in terms of manufactures does indeed fall, though by less than the tariff increase. The member countries hence have a terms-of-trade gain to set against the welfare loss from less product variety. But there is, of course, an additional source of gain: the increase in income. This source is partly reflected by the third term of Λ in (13.34). The direction of change in a member country's welfare is therefore ambiguous. We see that the total effect is more likely to be positive (i) the more sensitive the terms of trade are to given changes in product variety (higher σ), (ii) the less the evaluation of this variety (higher β), and (iii) the larger the share of the rest of the world in world income (smaller $\theta^A + \theta^B$).

The rest of the world has to face both a detrimental terms of trade effect and a reduction of product variety, and is therefore clearly worse off. Algebraically this is immediate from (13.35), noting that $(\sigma\theta^*/\Delta) - 1 < 0$.

6.2. *A Marginal Internal Barrier*

Now turn at last to the exercise treated by proposition (D) and suppose that $i = 0$ but $\hat{\tau} > 0$. As a starting point, assume that the partners have equal national incomes: $\theta^A = \theta^B$. Then again the numbers of varieties produced in the two member countries decline by a common amount, so that $\hat{q} = \sigma(\hat{m} - \hat{n}) = 0$.

Each partner attempts to protect manufacturing, but with resources shifting over to the agricultural sector the result is just the opposite! The reason is as follows. The tariff causes each union member to divert spending from the manufactures of its partner to its own manufactures, and the fact that $\hat{q} = 0$ means that the outside country has no reason to substitute between X goods and Y goods. Thus from (13.22)–(13.24) we see that $\hat{y}_A = -\hat{\tau}/(1-\beta) < 0$, $\hat{y}_B = \hat{\tau}/(1-\beta) > 0$, and $\hat{y}_* = 0$. As the partners are of equal size, these effects just cancel.

The higher price of the partner's manufactures reduces demand, so that with constant output volumes of individual firms there is downward pressure on the number of firms. This is reinforced by the fact that the proportion $(1-\alpha)$ of the tariff revenue raised in the manufacturing sector is channelled into the agricultural sector. Thus the net effect is to protect food, not manufacturing. From (13.22)–(13.26) we have that $\hat{y}_A - \hat{z}_A < 0$ and $\hat{y}_B - \hat{z}_B > 0$, that is, a 'reversal' of trade modification.

It is instructive to compare the discussion in Sections 3 and 4 of proposition (D) with behaviour in the altered context of the present model. First, recall that in the earlier context gains actually resulted when the reversal of trade modification caused the union to import more from the rest of the world. The structure of the present model allows us to concentrate on what is new by ensuring that such gains shrink to zero: our assumptions about the third country imply that it exports an unchanged quantity of food to the union. Exclusively external trade is neither a substitute for nor complement to internal trade, to use our earlier terminology, and there is also now no trade diversion to 'undo'. Second, the terms of external trade were assumed fixed in proposition (D), but now the shift of demand toward food turns the terms of trade in the outside world's favour. From (13.15), $\hat{p} = -\sigma\hat{n} > 0$. This could of course be neutralized by an appropriate increase $\hat{t}$ in the common external tariff. But the most significant difference follows from the role of imperfect competition, scale economies, and the endogenous number of product varieties. As in the conventional analysis, zero first-order welfare effects are caused by shifts in union expenditure between existing X goods and Y goods. But in our model the output levels of all product varieties which continue to be produced are unchanged, and instead the number of varieties of manufactures falls. This is deleterious. The total effect on the welfare of country A or B is ambiguous, as can be seen from (13.34). There is now one additional term, compared to the case with the external tariff, which influences the direction of change in welfare: the relative sizes of the manufacturing sectors. The larger the partner's share of total manufacturing output, the larger the share that will be hit by the tariff, and the more likely it is that the internal tariff will actually reduce welfare, and that a 'super-union' will be optimal.

The external country is affected in an ambiguous way. Its terms of trade improve, so that it consumes more manufactures than before along with the same quantity of food. But, on the other hand, those manufactures possess less product diversity than before. In summary, it is possible that all countries lose from the internal tariff, or that all gain, with $\theta^A = \theta^B$. It is also possible that the member countries gain and the rest of the world loses. But, if the member countries lose, then so must the external country, rendering a 'super-union' beneficial to all!

Thus far we have supposed that $\theta^A = \theta^B$. The role of size disparities between partners is now easily exposed. (13.30)–(13.33) show that the internal tariff will still cause a decline in total output of manufactures, but that the smaller country will have to adjust its manufacturing sector more than proportionally: $\hat{n} > \hat{m} < 0$. There is hence a *reallocation* of manufacturing from the smaller (in terms of national income) partner to the larger. Intuitively, small-country-located firms will have a larger share of production hit by the tariff, inducing more exit to keep profits at zero. Indeed, it might possibly be the case that the larger partner's manufacturing output actually rises, if the difference in national income is sufficiently large. This reallocation of production might be one reason why customs unions tend to be formed by similar economies.

6.3. *Intermediate goods*

There is an alternative interpretation of our model. Assume only two consumption goods, food and a final manufacture, but many differentiated intermediate goods, or components, used to assemble the final manufacture. This interpretation is entirely consistent with our formulation if we let the CES part of the utility function (13.10) be the assembly function for the final manufacture, X_i^k and Y_j^k represent the inputs of components i and j, and the parameter β reflect the degree of substitutability between different components. The technology is then such that each single producer of an intermediate good faces internal increasing returns to scale available when the production process is geographically concentrated: an example of 'national' economies of scale.[6] Assembly of the final manufacture is costless, and exhibits increasing returns to scale in the number of different components that are used. To see this, note that the CES assembly function gives an output of $n^{1/\beta}X$ in the symmetric version, and hence the output increases faster than the input nX. These economies of scale are 'international', since the size of the world market for the manufacture determines n, and they also reflect the benefits of an increased division of labour in the world economy; they are assumed to be external to individual assembly firms.

There is, in this interpretation, trade both in intermediate goods, and in the final good food. There is initially a tariff only on the latter good, which is exported by the external country. It is immaterial whether finished manufactures are assembled where consumed, or whether they are all assembled in one partner country and then exported. But in the latter case the interesting possibility of tariffs on final manufactures is not covered by our analysis, the components must be taxed the same whether imported directly or embodied in final manufactures, and exports of the latter must be allowed drawbacks of tariffs paid for imported components. The total impact on each country's welfare of tariff changes is, of course, the same irrespective of model interpretation. What differ are the sources of welfare changes. We saw above that an increase in either the internal or external tariff reduced both n and m unless the partners were too different in terms of their national incomes. Here this means that fewer components will be used in the production of manufactures, leading to a situation with less exploitation of international returns to scale. The main welfare-reducing effect of the tariffs is thus that they are detrimental to the division of labour by diminishing the world market for the final manufacture. But, there is no loss here stemming from reduced exploitation of the traditional, national returns to scale. The two developed countries are trying to protect their home industries, and manage in the sense that a higher proportion of inputs are locally made. But with both countries acting in a similar fashion no overall gain is ensured.

7. CONCLUDING REMARKS

We live in a multilateral world. Therefore any non-universal change in commercial policy – and they are all in fact non-universal – ought to fall within the domain of the theory of economic integration. But it has not been so.

since that theory usually has been too narrowly conceived. We have argued for four extensions: trade modification, consideration of small changes in policy, scale economies, and product differentiation under imperfect competition.

Adding the first two of these suggested extensions to the conventional framework we derived two basic propositions, suggested by familiar second-best theory, that are central to the characterization of the optimal policy for a subset of countries considering some degree of integration in a tariff-ridden world. We then developed a special, but illustrative, model incorporating all four of our suggested extensions and put it through its paces. Such an exercise is no more than an uncertain first step. But it is in the direction that must be followed, we maintain, if the theory of economic integration is to achieve the relevance to contemporary issues that it long since ought to have possessed.

APPENDIX

1. THE DEMAND FUNCTIONS

$$PX^A = \frac{\alpha I^A}{n + m y_A^{\beta}}, \quad \text{where } y_A \equiv \frac{Y^A}{X^A}$$

$$Q(1+\tau)Y^A = \frac{\alpha I^A}{n y_A^{-\beta} + m}$$

$$P_F(1+t)Z^A = (1-\alpha)I^A$$

$$P(1+\tau)X^B = \frac{\alpha I^B}{n + m y_B^{\beta}}, \quad \text{where } y_B \equiv \frac{Y^B}{X^B}$$

$$QY^B = \frac{\alpha I^B}{n y_B^{-\beta} + m}$$

$$P_F(1+t)Z^B = (1-\alpha)I^B$$

$$PX^* = \frac{\alpha I^*}{n + m y_*^{\beta}}, \quad \text{where } y_* \equiv \frac{Y^*}{X^*}$$

$$QY^* = \frac{\alpha I^*}{n y_*^{-\beta} + m}$$

$$P_F Z^* = (1-\alpha)I^*.$$

2. THE RELATIVE CHANGE IN THE INDIRECT UTILITIES

The indirect utility function for country A is

$$V^A = \gamma(R^A)^{-\alpha}(1+t)^{-(1-\alpha)}I^A,$$

where

$$R^A \equiv (nP^\rho + m(1+\tau)^\rho Q^\rho)^{1/\rho} = p^{-1}(n + m(1+\tau)^\rho q^\rho)^{1/\rho}$$

and

$$\rho \equiv \frac{\beta}{\beta - 1}$$

and for the third country

$$V^* = \gamma(R^*)^{-\alpha}I^*,$$

where

$$R^* = p^{-1}(n + mq^\rho)^{1/\rho}.$$

γ is a constant, and R^k is a price index defined over the differentiated goods. These expressions become, when differentiated logarithmically,

$$\hat{V}^A = -\alpha\hat{R}^A - (1-\alpha)\hat{t} + \hat{I}$$

and

$$\hat{V}^* = -\alpha\hat{R}^*,$$

where we use that $\hat{I}^A = \hat{I}^B \equiv \hat{I}$, and that $\hat{I}^* = 0$.

Concentrate for a moment on the change in the price index R^A. The relative change can be split up into two components:

$$\hat{R}^A = \left[\frac{m}{n+m}(\hat{q} + \hat{\tau}) - \hat{p}\right] - \frac{1-\beta}{\beta}\hat{N}. \qquad (13.\text{A}1)$$

The second term is the effect on the index of a change in the number of varieties available to the consumer, at given relative prices. This term is of course not present in the traditional analysis of customs unions, but will prove to be of considerable importance here.

Returning to the change in utility we get by substitution

$$\hat{V}^A = -\left[\hat{t} + \alpha\frac{m}{n+m}\hat{\tau} + \alpha\sigma\hat{N}\right] + \hat{I} + \alpha\frac{1-\beta}{\beta}\hat{N}. \qquad (13.\text{A}2)$$

By substituting (13.10) and (13.A1) into (13.A2) we arrive at expressions (13.34) and (13.35) in the text.

NOTES

* The authors received useful comments from Elhanan Helpman and from participants at a seminar at the Institute for International Economic Studies, University of Stockholm. Henrik Horn gratefully acknowledges financial support from Humanistisk-Samhällsvetenskapliga Forskningsrådet, Sweden.

1. For recent examples see Wonnacott and Wonnacott (1981) and Lloyd (1982).

2. See Meade (1955, 1956) and Ethier (1983, ch. 12).
3. The most notable exception is no doublt James Meade (1955, 1956), who was criticized in this regard. For example Lipsey (1968, p. 271) refers to this 'very serious, possibly crippling, limitation'. The subsequent literature has largely avoided marginal analysis. See, however, Berglas (1979), Reizman (1979), McMillan and McCann (1981), and Lloyd (1982).
4. For such a discussion, see section A.6 of Appendix I in Ethier (1983).
5. In the more general case $\sigma^A \neq \sigma^B$ we would have $\sigma^A \hat{n} = \sigma^B \hat{m}$ so that manufacturing contracts relatively more in the country with the greater ease of substitution of food for the non-traded manufacturing intermediate good; the structure of such economies remains irrelevant. Also we would still have $0 = \hat{q} = \sigma^B \hat{m} - \sigma^A \hat{n}$.
6. See Ethier (1979, 1982).

REFERENCES

Berglas, E. (1979), 'Preferential Trading Theory: The n Commodity Case', *Journal of Political Economy*, 87, 315–31.

Dixit, A. K. and Stiglitz, J. (1977), 'Monopolistic Competition and Optimum Product Diversity', *American Economic Review*, 67, 297–308.

Ethier, W. (1979), 'Internationally Decreasing Costs and World Trade', *Journal of International Economics*, 9, 1–24.

Ethier, W. J. (1982), National and International Returns to Scale in the Modern Theory of International Trade, *American Economic Review*, 72, 389–405.

Ethier, W. J. (1983), *Modern International Economics* (New York: W. W. Norton).

Kemp, M. C. (1964), *The Pure Theory of International Trade* (Englewood Cliffs: Prentice-Hall).

Kemp, M. C. and Wan, H. Y. (1976), 'An Elementary Proposition Concerning the Formation of Customs Unions', *Journal of International Economics*, 6, 95–8.

Kravis, I. B. and Lipsey, R. E. (1971), *Price Competitiveness in World Trade* (New York: National Bureau of Economic Research).

Kravis, I. B. and Lipsey, R. E. (1978), 'Price Behavior in the Light of Balance of Payments Theories', *Journal of International Economics*, 8, 193–246.

Lipsey, R. E. (1968), 'The Theory of Customs Unions: A General Survey', in R. E. Caves and H. G. Johnson (eds.), *Readings in International Economics* (Homewood: Richard D. Irwin).

Lloyd, P. (1982), '3 × 3 Theory of Customs Unions', *Journal of International Economics*, 12, 41–63.

McMillan, J. and McCann, E. (1981), 'Welfare Effects in Customs Unions', *Economic Journal*, 91, 697–703.

Meade, J. E. (1955), *Trade and Welfare* (London: Oxford University Press).

Meade, J. E. (1956), *The Theory of Customs Unions* (Amsterdam, North-Holland).

Ohyama, M. (1972), 'Trade and Welfare in General Equilibrium', *Keio Economic Studies*, 9, 37–73.

Reizman, R. (1979), 'A 3 × 3 Model of Customs Unions', *Journal of International Economics*, 9, 341–54.

Vanek, J. (1965), *General Equilibrium of International Discrimination* (Cambridge, Mass.: Harvard University Press).

Viner, J. (1950), *The Customs Union Issue* (New York: Carnegie Endowment for International Peace).

Wonnacot, P. and Wonnacot, R. (1981), 'Is Unilateral Tariff Reduction Preferable to a Customs Union? The Curious Case of the Missing Foreign Tariffs', *American Economic Review*, 71, 704–14.

Regionalism in a Multilateral World

Wilfred J. Ethier

University of Pennsylvania

Recent regional initiatives have been addressed from a Vinerian perspective of trade creation and trade diversion. This is true of both policy-oriented economists, who tend to be critical of the initiatives, and theorists, who have added dynamic and game-theoretic elements to the Vinerian structure. This paper describes the stylized facts of much recent regional integration and develops an alternative model. The analysis suggests that regional integration, far from threatening multilateral liberalism, may in fact be a direct consequence of the success of past multilateralism and an added guarantee for its survival.

I. Introduction

Regionalism rules. This was not true until recently: With the notable exception of Western Europe, the numerous regional initiatives of the 1950s and 1960s eventually amounted to virtually nothing. But the late 1980s attempt of the European Community to complete its internal market by the end of 1992 has induced (or preceded) a new global wave of regional integration: most notably (1) the U.S.-Canada Free Trade Agreement and the subsequent incorporation of Mexico into the North American Free Trade Agreement (NAFTA); (2) the entrance of Austria, Finland, and Sweden into the European Union; (3) the Europe Agreements between the Euro-

I thank L. Alan Winters and an anonymous referee for useful comments and suggestions. This paper was originally prepared during an enjoyable stay as Tinbergen Professor at the Tinbergen Institute, Rotterdam. It has profited from comments and suggestions received at seminars, workshops, and conferences—too numerous to mention—in all quarters of our shrinking world. I disclaim the usual disclaimer.

[*Journal of Political Economy*, 1998, vol. 106, no. 6]

pean Union and former communist states of central Europe; and (4) the Mercosur customs union between Brazil, Argentina, Paraguay, and Uruguay. These are prominent examples. But dozens of other initiatives—whether negotiation, sincere intention, or vague aspiration—have appeared in most parts of the world. More than 100 regional arrangements, accounting for well over half of world trade, now exist.

Trade theorists have not been slow to respond. Responses have centered on two questions: (i) Will the division of the world into regional trading blocs raise or lower welfare? So far, answers have been mixed (see Krugman 1991; Bhagwati and Panagariya 1996). (ii) Will regionalism help or hinder multilateral trade liberalization? Answers have basically been negative, though with some qualifications (see Bond and Syropoulos 1996; Bagwell and Staiger 1997*a*, 1997*b*). Common to these responses has been the treatment of regional integration as exogenous.[1] Also common has been a Vinerian perspective on regional integration as a combination of trade creation and trade diversion.[2]

By contrast, economists concerned with trade policy have been much less ambiguous. The dominant view is now strongly negative: The increase in regional arrangements reflects frustration with the process of multilateral liberalization (e.g., the prolonged pains of the Uruguay Round negotiations) and poses a serious threat to the continued existence of the present liberal trade order.[3]

The Vinerian perspective was a response to the "old regionalism" after World War II. But the international environment greeting the "new regionalism" that has emerged since the late 1980s differs from that experienced by the old regionalism in critical ways: (1) Multilateral liberalization (at least of trade in manufactures among the industrial countries) is much more complete now, and (2) scores of economically less advanced countries have abandoned basically autarkic, antimarket, policies and are now actively trying to join the multilateral trading system. So one can also make a *qualitative* distinction between the old regionalism and the new. For example, the Vinerian paradigm of trade creation versus trade diversion drove analysis of the former, but it is by no means clear that it should drive

[1] Some recent contributions do endogenize regional integration: See Yi (1996), Baldwin (1997), and Freund (1997) and, for surveys of some recent developments, Ethier (1998*a*, 1998*b*).

[2] For other developments in the Vinerian tradition, see Ethier and Horn (1984), Anderson and Blackhurst (1993), and de Melo and Panagariya (1993).

[3] I have the impression that, in North America at least, the general public believes professional economists to be much more in favor of regional arrangements than they in fact are. Perhaps the reason is that the highly visible debate over NAFTA degenerated into (or was elevated into) a debate over the merits of liberal trade.

analysis of the latter. Yet it *has*. This is central to the ambiguity noted above. This paper attempts to develop an idea of what the *qualitative* new regionalism should be.[4]

Section II describes the salient characteristics of the new regionalism and how they differ from those of the old regionalism motivating the Vinerian perspective. Section III then presents an elementary model of trade and trade policy incorporating these characteristics—or capable of doing so—and Section IV contributes a rudimentary theory of multilateralism. Section V then investigates the potential role of regional arrangements in such a framework.

The analysis suggests a radically different interpretation of regionalism: a theoretical structure far removed from the Vinerian perspective and a policy implication at odds with the common negative view. In particular, three possibilities emerge: (i) Regionalism is an endogenous response to the development of the multilateral trading system, and treating it as exogenous is misleading. (ii) The primary purpose of regionalism is to adapt to multilateral developments. Thus the paper suggests a presumption that regional integration facilitates multilateral liberalization.[5] (iii) Regionalism promotes the successful entry of reforming countries into the multilateral trading system in a way that multilateralism by itself cannot do.

II. What the New Regionalism Is

The following characteristics do not apply to all current regional initiatives, which are quite diverse, but do apply in varying degree to most of the more important ones.

1. Contemporary regionalism typically features one or more small countries linking up with a big country. In the examples above, Mexico and Canada are each small, economically, relative to the United States; the new members of the European Union are tiny compared to the European Union itself; so are the central European adherents to the Europe Agreements; and Brazil dominates Mercosur.

2. Very often the small countries have recently made, or are trying to make, significant unilateral reforms. This is most dramatically true of the central European countries (which had abandoned commu-

[4] One cannot expect the temporal and qualitative distinctions to correspond exactly to each other. Presumably some characteristics of the (qualitatively) new regionalism are relevant to earlier regional initiatives, and—more important, for present purposes—features of the (qualitatively) old regionalism remain relevant today. But I am interested in the nature of the new (qualitatively) regionalism.

[5] Chichilnisky (1994) also argues that, in the presence of economies of scale, regional integration may foster multilateral liberalization. But her argument is quite different from what follows.

nism), of Mercosur, and of Mexico. But it also characterizes, to a lesser degree, the small industrial country participants in the examples above. Canada had turned away from Trudeau-style economic nationalism, and the Scandinavian applicants to the European Union (except Norway, which significantly declined to join) had made notable reforms in some sectors (e.g., agriculture and banking). In Mercosur, in contrast to the other examples, the large country, Brazil, is also attempting unilateral reform.

3. Regional agreements seldom address only trade barriers: They usually involve what is known as "deep" integration. This is another reflection of the fact that the new regionalism is taking place in a context of wide economic reform.

4. A dramatic move to free trade between members is *not* what it is all about: The degree of liberalization is typically modest. Thus the Vinerian paradigm is not a natural starting point. The trade relations of Austria, Finland, and Sweden with the European Union are virtually identical to what they would have been had they decided not to join the Union! NAFTA provides only modest liberalization: U.S. tariffs were already low, and NAFTA hedges sensitive sectors. Canada and Mexico have done more, but the most significant measures (largely Mexican) were unilateral. The Europe Agreements provide for little in the way of concrete liberalization. Mercosur is admittedly more ambitious, but even here the liberalization is small relative to the members' unilateral liberalizations.

5. The liberalization that is achieved is due primarily to concessions by the small countries: The agreements are one-sided. The moderate liberalization in NAFTA is due much more to "concessions" by Mexico and Canada than by the United States (Ross Perot notwithstanding). In negotiations over enlargement, the European Union has been flexible on financial responsibilities and periods of adjustment but has always maintained a take-it-or-leave-it attitude regarding the nature and structure of the European Union itself. The Europe Agreements involve virtually no "concessions" by the European Union: Indeed the European Union instituted antidumping measures against some new partners even as the initial agreements were coming into effect! Mercosur does not display this asymmetry (perhaps because its big country is also a reformer?).

More typically the small countries get only small tariff advantages, often because the large countries have small tariffs to begin with. More important to the small countries is exemption from future acts of contingent protection—antidumping law, safeguards, and so forth. But usually they do not get much here either: The Europe Agreements were mentioned above; NAFTA does not give Canada and Mexico exemption from U.S.-administered protection; and as members of the European Area, Austria, Finland, and Sweden would not have been subject to E.U.-administered protection in any case.

In summary, *with regional integration, reform-minded small countries "purchase," with moderate trade concessions, deep links with large countries that confer relatively minor trade advantages*. So, why do the small countries do it?[6]

III. The Model

My first building block is a simple trade model in which to embed the stylized facts described above. I use a modified version of the familiar, many-country, specific-factors model.

Suppose, first, N (almost) identical industrial countries, each endowed with H units of human capital, L skilled labor, and U unskilled labor. Second, assume M (almost) identical less developed countries.

Developed Countries

Each developed country i can produce one output, x_i (which I call a *good*), using human capital and skilled labor, and another output, z_i (which I call a *commodity*), requiring skilled labor and unskilled labor. The respective goods are imperfect substitutes. Goods are tradable but commodities are nontraded.

Production

Production of each good is a two-stage process, with one stage, using only human capital, necessarily performed at home. The other stage, using only skilled labor, can be performed anywhere; that is, the home firm can employ labor located in any country (foreign direct investment) to perform this stage. If this is done abroad, the resulting unfinished goods must be exported from the foreign subsidiary. If a_i and b_i denote the levels of operations of the respective stages, final output is

$$x_i = f(a_i, b_i), \tag{1}$$

where f is a conventional neoclassical production function. Stage operations are

[6] Perroni and Whalley (1994) provide an answer very different from what follows to a related question.

$$a_i = H_i \tag{2}$$

and

$$b_i = kL_{bi}, \tag{3}$$

where H_i denotes the stock of human capital, L_{bi} the skilled labor allocated to stage b_i, and $k = k(\sum_{i=1}^{N} L_{bi})$, with $k' > 0$. Operation of each b_i stage thus entails increasing returns to scale that depend on the size of global second-stage activity for all N goods. I assume that these returns are external to the individual firm and that goods are produced in perfectly competitive markets. Furthermore, these scale economies are international in origin; that is, they depend on the *global* size of the labor employed in producing all b_i, not the labor employed in a single country. For international economies of scale, see Ethier (1979, 1982). As argued there, such economies will require trade in intermediate goods: trade in inputs to the various b_i themselves. But introducing this trade would complicate the model to no purpose, so I abstract from it.[7]

The nontraded commodity, z, is produced by competitive firms operating under constant returns to scale:

$$z = g(U, L_z). \tag{4}$$

Here g is also a standard neoclassical production function, U denotes the stock of unskilled labor, and L_z the amount of skilled labor allocated to commodity production. Thus

$$L = L_b + L_z. \tag{5}$$

Consumption

Each country behaves as though it has the utility function

$$u = N^{-\epsilon} \sum_{i=1}^{N} \frac{\epsilon}{\epsilon - 1} y_i^{(\epsilon-1)/\epsilon} + z, \tag{6}$$

where y_i denotes consumption of the good produced by country i and z consumption of the local commodity. This function will be used to measure the social welfare of developed countries. The implied demand for good i in each country is

$$y_i = \frac{1}{N} p_i^{-\epsilon}, \tag{7}$$

[7] Henceforth I dispense with the commodity/country subscript i whenever this generates no confusion.

where p_i denotes the relative price of y_i in terms of z. All other income is spent on z.

Free-Trade Equilibrium for the Developed Countries

To fix ideas, consider a symmetric free-trade equilibrium between the developed countries in which all goods are produced equally, sell for the same price, and are consumed equally by all countries. Each country performs b-stage production equal to the total production of precisely one good, and the allocation of b-stage activity among countries is indeterminate (so cross-penetration of direct investment may take place) but inconsequential. So assume that each x_i is produced by integrated firms located entirely in country i.

From (1), (2), and (3), the integrated production function for each country's good is

$$x = f(H, kL_b). \tag{8}$$

Designate z as numeraire, and let ω denote the wage of skilled labor. Since skilled labor is paid the value of its marginal product in each use,

$$\begin{aligned} \omega &= pf_L(H, kL_b)k, \\ \omega &= g_L(U, L_z), \end{aligned} \tag{9}$$

where subscripts denote partial differentiation.[8] Thus

$$pf_L(H, kL_b)k - g_L(U, L_z) = 0. \tag{10}$$

Equations (5), (8), and (10) determine the supply function for each good:

$$x = x(p, L; L_b(N-1)), \tag{11}$$

where $L_b(N-1)$ denotes the total labor allocated to b-stage production by the other $N-1$ countries. I make the following assumption.

ASSUMPTION 1. The response of the integrated production function to the second-stage input is sufficiently curved, relative to the degree of economies of scale in the b stage, that

$$\sigma_f > \frac{\sigma_k/N}{1 + (\sigma_k/N)},$$

[8] The term k is treated as a parameter by b producers since the economies of scale are external to the firm.

where

$$-\frac{kL_b f_{LL}}{f_L} \equiv \sigma_f, \quad \frac{NL_b k'}{k} \equiv \sigma_k.$$

This will ensure that $x_p > 0$.

International equilibrium is determined by the requirement that the world supply x of each good equal the world demand implied by (7):

$$y = p^{-\epsilon}. \tag{12}$$

Note that

$$\frac{L}{p}\frac{\partial p}{\partial L}\bigg|_x = -\frac{L}{p}\frac{x_L}{x_p} = -L\frac{g_{LL}}{-pf_L k} = -\frac{\sigma_g}{\lambda_z} < 0, \tag{13}$$

where

$$\sigma_g = -\frac{L_z g_{LL}}{g_L}, \quad \lambda_z = \frac{L_z}{L}.$$

Thus an increase in the available supply of skilled labor shifts the supply curve to the left, raising equilibrium x and lowering p. This change in output in one country will generate international spillovers, and consequent changes in foreign production will in turn generate repercussions in the original country.

Protection in the Industrial World

I assume that each developed country levies an ad valorem tariff, t, on the imports of each foreign good (and its own b-stage output, if that stage is performed abroad). I assume that all developed countries are identical, and I shall confine attention to symmetric equilibria, so t will be the same for all countries and all goods. The tariff revenue is distributed to the public in lump-sum fashion (and so is spent on z).

I assume that the commercial policy of each industrial country is the outcome of a political process in which unskilled labor attempts to secure rents. This will not be modeled explicitly. Instead I simply assume that the political process operates as though the country were maximizing a social welfare function that trades off labor's wage against aggregate welfare:

$$V = rw + (1 - r)u, \tag{14}$$

where $w = g_U(U, L_z)$. The parameter r thus reflects the influence unskilled labor has over the political process. Detail concerning the constraints under which V is maximized will be supplied below, when I consider explicit international commercial systems.

Less Developed Countries

Each less developed country implements a commercial policy that is the outcome of a political process in which special interests attempt to secure rents. As with the industrial countries, this process will not be modeled explicitly. I am concerned not with marginal changes in protection, but with the possibility of fundamental economic reform. For this reason, I assume that the government of each less developed country must choose one of just two possible policies: autarky or reform. With autarky, the special interests secure their rents. But if the social welfare benefit R of reform is expected to be sufficiently great, the government will attempt reform; let r^* denote the minimum the expected value of R must attain for the government to be tempted to forsake autarky for reform. The parameter r^* thus reflects the influence special interests have over the political process.

The only aspect of the less developed countries that I need to model explicitly for what follows is the potentially open sector, where R is generated. This potentially open sector contains an initial stock L_A^* of skilled labor, which, in autarky, can be used to produce, for local consumption, a rudimentary good:

$$x^* = k(L_A^*)L_A^*. \tag{15}$$

The function $k(\cdot)$ is the same as that pertinent to the developed countries but is evaluated as a function of local input alone, since the less developed country is in autarky and is not part of the multilateral trading system. Finally, local goods are rudimentary because their production is undertaken without benefit of the sophisticated a stage.

If the less developed country reforms successfully, firms from the developed countries will establish subsidiaries there that employ some quantity, F, of skilled labor for their own b-stage production. This production will then be exported for final assembly, and some portion of that will be paid to F as wages. Because final output has not been customized for the less developed countries, assume that they regard the finished goods of the various developed countries as perfect substitutes for each other; because their own rudimentary goods are indeed rudimentary, assume that they regard one unit of their own goods as a perfect substitute for α units of any developed-country good ($\alpha < 1$). The direct investment involves the transfer of global technology, so the subsidiaries' output will be $b^* = kF$, where k depends on the total amount of labor allocated to b-stage production by developed-country firms, including that of their subsidiaries in the less developed countries. In addition, with the less developed country now part of the multilateral trading system, global technology spills over to the production of rudimentary goods (valued in terms of finished goods): $y^* = \alpha(L^* - F)k$, with k given by its international value and L^* the stock of skilled labor in the open sector in the event of successful reform.

If ω^* denotes the wage, in terms of finished goods, paid by the foreign subsidiaries, the value R of successful reform, also in terms of finished goods, is $y^* + \omega^*F - \alpha x^*$. If the labor market is competitive, $\omega^* = \alpha k$, and suppose that L^* is a nondecreasing function of ω^*. Thus R is determined by

$$R(k) = \alpha[L^*(\alpha k)k - x^*]. \tag{16}$$

The less developed country will be tempted to undertake reform if and only if the global economy is sufficiently productive that $\rho R(k) \geq r^*$, where ρ equals the probability that reform will succeed (ρ will be endogenized in a subsequent section). Reform is successful if and only if the country succeeds in attracting foreign direct investment.

I assume that the less developed countries differ from each other in only one way: the propensity r^* to favor special interests. There are distinct classes of less developed countries, and I denote the value of r^* pertinent to class j by r_j^*, number the classes from zero to one, and rank them so that r_j^* rises as j rises. Let $M(j)$ denote the number of (identical) less developed countries in class j, that is, the number of countries for which $r^* = r_j^*$. I shall simplify the following analysis by assuming a continuum of classes: the more relevant case of a finite number of classes is straightforward but tedious.

Let $M_R^*(\rho, k)$ denote the number of less developed countries that, given ρ and k, would attempt reform. Then

$$M_R^*(\rho, k) = \int_0^i M(j), \tag{17}$$

where $r_i^* = \rho R(k)$. Clearly $M_R^*(\rho, k)$ is increasing in each of its arguments.

IV. Multilateralism

This section develops a simple theory of multilateralism, the second basic building block of this paper.

Unilateralism

First I describe an international equilibrium in which r and r^* are sufficiently large that $F = 0$ in each less developed country and in which each developed country sets some arbitrary (but equal) t. Then I proceed to the symmetric Nash equilibrium in which the choice of t is optimal, given that every other developed country chooses the same t and that the less developed countries all choose autarky. This characterizes unilateralism.

A Symmetric Protectionist Equilibrium

Suppose that each developed country levies a common ad valorem tariff t on imports of each of the $N-1$ foreign goods. Then equilibrium for each good is given by

$$\begin{aligned} f(H, k(NL_b)L_b) &= \frac{p^{-\epsilon}}{N} + \frac{N-1}{N}[p(1+t)]^{-\epsilon} \\ &= \frac{p^{-\epsilon}}{N}[1 + (N-1)(1+t)^{-\epsilon}]. \end{aligned} \tag{18}$$

An increase in t shifts the demand curve down, moving equilibrium along the supply curve, with x and p both falling. But the supply curve itself will also shift because of changes in b-stage production by the remaining $N-1$ countries. Differentiate (18) and (10) to obtain the final effects:

$$\begin{aligned} \hat{L}_b &= -\epsilon X \frac{\lambda_z}{\Delta} \frac{dt}{1+t}, \\ \hat{p} &= -\epsilon X \frac{\lambda_b \sigma_g + \lambda_z (1+\sigma_k)\{\sigma_f - [\sigma_k/(1+\sigma_k)]\}}{\Delta} \frac{dt}{1+t}, \end{aligned} \tag{19}$$

where

$$\Delta \equiv \epsilon \lambda_b \sigma_g + \lambda_z (1+\sigma_k)\left[\theta_{Lx} + \epsilon\left(\sigma_f - \frac{\sigma_k}{1+\sigma_k}\right)\right],$$

$$\theta_{Lx} \equiv \frac{wL_b}{px}, \quad X \equiv \frac{x - (p^{-\epsilon}/N)}{x}.$$

I make the following assumption.

ASSUMPTION 2. Suppose that the following condition is met: $\sigma_f > \sigma_k/(1+\sigma_k)$. Then an increase in the tariff does lower both p and L_b.

Note that assumption 1 does not imply assumption 2, so that, with assumption 1 alone, global protection could conceivably raise L_b and influence p in either direction. But, with assumption 2, which does imply assumption 1, p falls proportionately less than the tariff itself: The domestic price of imported goods rises. In a symmetric equilibrium there are no terms-of-trade effects, and the reduction in L_b worsens the distortion because of the presence of an externality, so the welfare of each country is reduced, relative to free trade.

A Nash Equilibrium in Policy: Unilateralism

Consider next the conduct of trade policy in a single developed country, given the policies of the remaining $N - 1$ countries. I assume that N is sufficiently large that the single country behaves as though its actions have no effect on the world prices of traded goods or on the global size of b-stage production.[9] Then the equilibrium of such a country corresponding to a choice of t is described by

$$\begin{aligned} f(H, kL_b) &= \frac{p^{-\epsilon}}{N} + \frac{P}{p}\frac{N-1}{N}[P(1+t)]^{-\epsilon}, \\ pf_L(H, kL_b)k - g_L(U, L - L_b) &= 0. \end{aligned} \tag{20}$$

Production of the national good equals domestic demand plus the exports required, at world prices, to pay for imports. The term P denotes the relative price, in terms of home commodities, of each of the $N - 1$ foreign goods. The small-country assumption is that the home government proceeds as though k and P/p are exogenous. Then (20) gives

$$\begin{aligned} \hat{L}_b &= \epsilon X \frac{\lambda_z}{\Delta'}\frac{dt}{1+t}, \\ \hat{P} = \hat{p} &= -\epsilon X \frac{\lambda_z\sigma_f + \lambda_b\sigma_g}{\Delta'}\frac{dt}{1+t}, \end{aligned} \tag{21}$$

where $\Delta' \equiv \lambda_z\theta_{Lx} + \epsilon(\lambda_z\sigma_f + \lambda_b\sigma_g)$. Thus an increase in t lowers both p and L_b. The reductions in p and P constitute a rise in the price of nontraded commodities relative to traded goods. Protection deflects

[9] Each country conducts trade policy by separately choosing $N - 1$ import constraints, symmetry assuring that the $N - 1$ choices are all the same; no deliberate export policy is chosen. This is important: While the small-country assumption can be appealed to as justification for each country's perceiving no influence in each of its import markets or on global economies of scale, the country is nonetheless the sole supplier of its own good.

spending from imported goods to commodities, raising their price and drawing skilled labor away from the production of goods. This in turn raises the reward of unskilled labor:

$$\hat{w} = \epsilon X \frac{\lambda_b \sigma_{gx}}{\Delta'} \frac{dt}{1 + t}, \tag{22}$$

where $\sigma_{gx} \equiv L_z(g_{UL}/g_L)$. With terms-of-trade effects and external scale effects both absent, the effect of a tariff change on utility, measured in terms of the numeraire, is simply the change in import volume multiplied by tp, the excess of the social value of a marginal import over its social cost:

$$\frac{du}{dt} = tp \frac{d\left\{\frac{N-1}{N}[(1+t)p]^{-\epsilon}\right\}}{dt}. \tag{23}$$

The effect on the government's objective is

$$\frac{dV}{dt} = r\frac{dw}{dt} + (1 - r)\frac{du}{dt}.$$

Note that $dV/dt > 0$ if $t = 0$: The government will always wish to institute some protection because, with t initially zero, protection will produce a first-order increase in the wage of unskilled labor with no first-order effect on utility. From (22) and (23), $dV/dt = 0$ when

$$t^2 + \Lambda t - \frac{r}{1 - r} \frac{x}{L_z} = 0, \tag{24}$$

with $\Lambda \equiv X\Delta' + \Delta' - X$. The positive solution to this quadratic equation defines the optimum (unilateral) tariff:

$$t^U = \frac{\left(\Lambda^2 + 4\frac{r}{1 - r}\frac{x}{L_z}\right)^{1/2} - \Lambda}{2}. \tag{25}$$

The symmetric noncooperative equilibrium is given by (10), (18), and (25), which simultaneously determine L_b, p, and t.

Multilateralism

I now consider the possibility of multilateral trade liberalization by the developed countries. In such a multilateral equilibrium, each developed country adopts the policy that is optimal, if all other developed countries adopt the *same* policy, given the policies adopted by the less developed countries. That is, the developed countries jointly choose a common t. The less developed countries do not participate in the multilateral process, and I continue to assume that each has chosen a policy of autarky.

Multilateral Equilibrium

Let t^M denote the optimal multilateral tariff, and let t° denote what this tariff would be if the developed countries ignored all terms-of-trade effects and scale effects of a tariff reduction, but otherwise took account of the fact that equations (19), rather than (21), indicate the effects on L_b and p when a tariff reduction is multilateral rather than unilateral. Because of the symmetry there will, in fact, be no terms-of-trade effects. If assumption 2 is met, however, a reduction in t will raise the common L_b, producing a positive scale effect. Since a small reduction of t below t° will have a zero first-order effect on each government's objective function other than the positive scale effect, it must be that $t^M < t^\circ$ as long as assumption 2 holds.

Next, t° is, by definition, given by formula (25), with Δ' replaced by Δ. Thus $t^\circ < t^U$ if $\Delta > \Delta'$, and, given assumption 2, a sufficient condition for this is the following assumption.

ASSUMPTION 3. $\theta_{Lx} > 1/(1 + \sigma_k)$.

Thus assumptions 2 and 3 provide sufficient (but by no means necessary) conditions that multilateralism produce a common tariff lower than that resulting from unilateral tariff setting.

Multilateralism: Summary

Proposition 1 summarizes the results of this section.

PROPOSITION 1. *Multilateralism.*—Suppose that assumptions 2 and 3 hold and that each less developed country chooses a policy of autarky. Then if a symmetric unilateral equilibrium among the developed countries is replaced by a symmetric multilateral equilibrium, (1) the common tariff falls; (2) b-stage production of each good rises, enhancing scale effects; and (3) the welfare of each developed country increases.

Remarks.—This section has developed, as a basic building block, a rudimentary theory of multilateralism. To be useful for the model, the theory must mimic, in a stylized and transparent way, the essentials of post–World War II experience. I now try to indicate the distinctive features of this theory.

First, in this model no country attempts to manipulate the terms of trade to its advantage. I ensure this by abstracting from export policy and by imposing a small-country assumption, but it really reflects a belief that such attempts have just not been important in practice.[10] For this reason I want to make it clear that I do not *require* terms-of-trade manipulation; introducing such manipulation would strengthen further the incentive for multilateral cooperation and so would complicate the model to no purpose.[11] The absence of terms-of-trade manipulation does imply a critical role for special interests: Countries would otherwise adopt free trade unilaterally.

Second, national concern for social welfare also plays a key role. Countries would have no incentive to enter into multilateral arrangements otherwise.

Third, the purpose of multilateralism in this model is to internalize an externality: The development of a multilateral trading system confers benefits of technological spillovers, external economies of scale, and so forth on all participants. Jointly setting their commercial policies allows countries collectively to address this. This model expresses these beneficial effects in terms of the single technology parameter k. Consequently, it is tempting to index the benefits as $B = k^M - k^U$, where k^U and k^M denote, respectively, the value of k in the unilateral equilibrium and in the multilateral equilibrium.

Fourth, the theory assumes, in contrast to much recent literature,[12] that individual countries can in fact credibly commit themselves to the multilateral policy even though, ex post, each government will not be doing the best it can—according to its own objective function—given the policies of the other governments. In practice, this has simply not been a significant problem with respect to the General Agreement on Tariffs and Trade (GATT)–sponsored rounds of multilateral tariff reductions by the industrial countries.[13] When these countries have retreated from liberal trade, they have done so not by repudiating in violation of the GATT the tariff bindings they have undertaken, but by utilizing other, internationally accepted tools (safeguards, antidumping duties, etc.) or by stepping outside the GATT structure (voluntary export constraints). Consideration of these latter possibilities is not needed for the purposes of this paper, and I want to keep the model of multilateralism as simple as possible.[14] Also, I would stray too far from my purpose were I to

[10] For an alternative view, see Bagwell and Staiger (1996).

[11] See Yi (1996) for a very different model in which endogenous integration is driven by the presence of terms-of-trade manipulation.

[12] For example, Bond and Syropoulos (1996) distinguish multilateralism from regionalism by assuming that, in the former, countries cannot precommit.

[13] It has sometimes been a problem in other contexts, such as China and the protection of intellectual property.

[14] An earlier version of this paper did in fact contain administered protection not determined multilaterally, but I deleted it because it had no fundamental effect on the theory of regionalism developed below. Instead, I address it in Ethier (1998*c*).

introduce features (e.g., trigger strategies in a repeated-game framework) to furnish explicit support for the multilateral equilibrium. So I simply assume that credible commitment to the multilateral policy is provided by something exogenous to the model. Presumably a higher value of the benefits index B would, other things equal, render such commitment easier, but consideration of such issues is beyond the scope of this paper.

V. Regionalism

The previous section assumed both that r_1^* was sufficiently large that $R(k) < r_1^*$ for the k determined in the unilateral equilibrium and that the less developed countries did not participate in the multilateral process. These assumptions in effect excluded the less developed countries from the model. Now I bring them back in. I assume the following sequence of moves. Initially, the developed countries are in a unilateral equilibrium and the less developed countries have each chosen autarky. Then the developed countries, without participation by the less developed countries, negotiate the multilateral equilibrium and implement it. Next, the less developed countries observe t^M and the multilateral equilibrium value of k and *individually* decide whether to reform or not, taking t^M and k as given. Finally, the reform efforts are made, they succeed or fail, and a new international equilibrium emerges, with t still fixed at t^M but k determined endogenously.

Multilateralism and the Less Developed Countries

Implications of Multilateralism for the Less Developed Countries

With assumptions 2 and 3, multilateralism will produce a lower tariff, and this could affect the less developed countries' unilateral choices of policy. From (19), the lower tariff will increase L_b, causing k to rise. The value of $R(k)$, increasing in k, also increases: Multilateralism increases the motivation for the less developed countries to reform. Interest centers on the case in which R rises enough so that some countries do indeed embark on reform. So I make the following assumption.

ASSUMPTION 4. $R(k^U) < r_1^* < R(k^M)$.

Assumption 4 ensures that all less developed countries choose autarky in the unilateral equilibrium and that some will attempt reform in the multilateral equilibrium if the probability of success ρ is sufficiently high.

An attempted reform in a less developed country will succeed if and only if some firms from the developed countries undertake direct investment there, so I turn to this question next. Direct investment will introduce trade in b-stage products, so developed-country barriers to such trade must now be considered. Suppose that imports of b into the developed countries are subject to protection at the (possibly negative) rate t_b. I postpone discussion of how t_b is determined.

If there is no direct investment, the cost, in terms of b, of obtaining a marginal unit of b by production in the home developed country is $\omega/pk = f_L(H, kL_b)$, and the cost of obtaining it by establishing a foreign subsidiary in some less developed country is $\omega^*(1 + t_b)/k = \alpha(1 + t_b)$. Thus direct investment will be undertaken—and a reform attempt by some less developed country will be successful—if, in the multilateral equilibrium with no direct investment, $f_L(H, kL_b) > \alpha(1 + t_b)$.

PROPOSITION 2. Suppose that assumptions 2, 3, and 4 hold. Then if the developed countries shift from a unilateral equilibrium to a multilateral equilibrium, some less developed countries will attempt reform if the probability of success is high enough. Such an attempt would be successful in some countries if, in the multilateral equilibrium, $f_L(H, kL_b) > \alpha(1 + t_b)$.

International Equilibrium

Next, consider a symmetric equilibrium in which the developed countries undertake direct investment in a set of reformed less developed countries. Let m denote the total employment of skilled labor by the foreign subsidiaries of each developed country. Assume an interior solution in which the developed countries transfer some, but not all, b-stage employment of skilled labor abroad, and not all of the skilled labor of the reformed less developed countries is employed by foreign subsidiaries. Equilibrium for each good is described as follows:

$$\begin{aligned} f(H, k(N(L_b + m))(L_b + m)) &= \frac{p^{-\epsilon}}{N}[1 + (N-1)(1+t)^{-\epsilon}] \\ &\quad + \alpha k(N(L_b + m))m, \\ f_L(H, k(N(L_b + m))(L_b + m)) &= \alpha(1 + t_b), \\ pf_L(H, k(N(L_b + m))(L_b + m)) &= g_L(U, L - L_b). \end{aligned} \tag{26}$$

The first equation of (26) requires that the supply of each good equal the total of demand at home, demand from other developed countries, and demand from less developed countries; the second that direct investment proceed until the cost of skilled labor to the firm is the same abroad as at home; and the third that the value of the marginal product of skilled labor be equated across alternative uses at home.

If, instead of an interior solution, each developed country shifts all b-stage production abroad, $L_b = 0$ and the third equation of (26) is dropped. If, on the other hand, all the skilled labor of each reformed less developed country is employed by foreign firms, $m = M_R L^* / N$, where M_R denotes the number of countries undertaking successful reform and L^* attains its maximal value, and the first equation of (26) is dropped.

Equations (26) determine p, m, and L_b, given N, t, t_b, and the endowment of each developed country. Note that (26) is independent of the number of less developed countries that undertake (M_R^*) or successfully implement (M_R) reform and that (26) does not determine how the total direct investment Nm is distributed among the reformers. A symmetric equilibrium would allocate Nm among all M_R^* in equal amounts $F = Nm/M_R^*$, thus ensuring that $M_R = M_R^*$. But there is no reason to expect this outcome because, from the viewpoint of the investing firms, all less developed countries are identical. So I assume that, when all potential hosts are equivalent, investing firms decide where to invest, among all potential hosts, by some random process.

If $Nm > (M_R^* - 1)L^*$, at least some investment must go to each potential host, so $\rho = 1$ and $M_R = M_R^*$. But otherwise distributions of Nm that leave some potential hosts without foreign subsidiaries do exist. With the location of direct investment determined at random,

$$\rho(M_R^*, m) = \phi\left[\frac{Nm}{(M_R^* - 1)L^*}\right], \tag{27}$$

where ϕ reflects the random process by which investment is allocated. Assume that $\phi = 0$ if $m = 0$, $\phi = 1$ if $Nm > (M_R^* - 1)L^*$, and $\phi' > 0$ otherwise. Clearly ρ is decreasing in M_R^* and increasing in m whenever its argument is less than unity.

Equations (26) determine k and m, and (17) and (27) then simultaneously determine ρ and M_R^*, and thus $M_R = \rho M_R^*$ as well. Since ρ and M_R^* are positively related in (17) and negatively related in (27), the solution is unique. Thus a switch from unilateralism to multilateralism induces some (M_R) less developed countries to reform successfully, some ($M_R - M_R^*$) to attempt reform and fail, and some ($\int_i^{i'} M(j)$, where $r_i^* = \rho R(k)$ and $r_{i'}^* = R(k)$) to wish to reform but to refrain from trying because of the fear of failure. The condition for this is the following assumption.

ASSUMPTION 5. With multilateralism and no investment, $f_L(H, kL_b) > \alpha(1 + t_b)$; with multilateralism and investment, $Nm < (M_R^* - 1)L^*$.

In summary, I present the following proposition.

PROPOSITION 3. *Unilateral reform.*—Suppose that assumptions 2–5 hold. Then if the developed countries shift from unilateralism to multilateralism, some less developed countries will attempt reform and succeed, some will attempt reform and fail, and some will wish to reform but not attempt it.

Implications of Reform for the Multilateral System

Successful reform by some less developed countries will influence the international equilibrium and thereby affect the developed countries. To investigate, suppose that $m = 0$ initially and ask what effect an introduction of direct investment (dm) will have on L_b. This can be deduced by differentiating the first and third equations of (26), solving, and evaluating at $m = 0$:

$$dL_b = -\frac{\lambda_z\theta_{Lx}[\sigma_k + 1 - (w^*/w)] + \epsilon\lambda_z[\sigma_f(1 - \sigma_k) - \sigma_k]}{\lambda_z\theta_{Lx}(\sigma_k + 1) + \epsilon\lambda_z[\sigma_f(1 - \sigma_k) - \sigma_k] + \epsilon\lambda_b\sigma_g}dm. \quad (28)$$

It thus follows from assumption 1 (or from assumption 2) that $dL_b < 0$ but $dL_b + dm > 0$. Reform causes the developed countries to lose second-stage jobs for skilled workers, but it creates such jobs worldwide. As a consequence, k rises, and, therefore, B does also.

PROPOSITION 4. Suppose that assumptions 2–5 hold. Then if the developed countries shift from unilateralism to multilateralism, the successful reforms by some less developed countries that follow will lower developed-country employment in b-stage production and increase world employment.

There are two important implications. *First,* reform raises the social welfare of the developed countries and the income of unskilled workers: Both components of the government's objective function rise. *Second,* the implied increase in k means that the benefit index B of being part of the multilateral system increases. Presumably this would enhance the strength of the commitment to that system.[15]

Thus far I have treated t_b as arbitrary, but in what follows it will prove convenient to know something of its magnitude. Also, the emergence of positive direct investment in this section suggests the possibility that the developed countries' objective function be modi-

[15] This statement is speculative since this paper does not model any commitment mechanism.

fied to reflect the fact that direct investment has long been a contentious policy issue.

The multilateral negotiations cannot have determined t_b since any nonnegative value is consistent with the multilateral equilibrium with all less developed countries in autarky. Also, setting $t_b = t^M$ is not satisfactory: As will be clear below, this will in general give each developed country an incentive unilaterally to reduce t_b. Instead I proceed as follows.

First, add to each developed-country government's objective function a third component, nonpositively related to m.[16] Second, suppose that t_b is at its symmetric Nash equilibrium value in the equilibrium described by (26). That is, t_b maximizes each developed country's objective function, in (26), given the multilateral solution $t = t^M$ and given that every other developed country has implemented the same t_b.[17]

Since reform affects the international equilibrium, it will induce the developed countries to renegotiate the multilateral tariff, and this would in turn induce a reconsideration in some less developed countries of whether to reform, and so on. One could analyze the outcome of such a sequence of events or, equivalently, analyze the multilateral process on the assumption that all countries correctly forecast the equilibrium response of the less developed countries and take this into account. The world negotiates the full equilibrium initially and directly implements it.

But this exercise is left to the reader: My interest is the direct implication of multilateral liberalization by the developed countries for policy reform in the less developed countries. There are two reasons. First, consideration of the full equilibrium promises to add nothing of interest. If the developed countries accurately forecast the equilibrium response of the less developed countries, they will negotiate a multilateral tariff, t^F, no higher than if they do not: $t^F \leq t^M$. The reason is that they anticipate (correctly) that a given reduction in t will produce a larger increase in k when less developed countries are induced to reform than when they are not. Propositions 1–4 (as well as propositions 5 and 6 to come) continue to hold, with t^F replacing t^M, so that the message of this paper would be unchanged. Working back to write down the equations determining t^F is a purely technical exercise. Second, the limited sequence described in this

[16] Note that this is consistent with a zero weight, i.e., with continuing to use (14).

[17] This does not require that $t_b > 0$. This can be assured by giving significant negative weight to m in the government's objective function or by adding other components to that function reflecting the welfare of human capital or of skilled labor. I do not assume this, however.

paper appears to parallel history better than an initial negotiation of the final outcome would.

Regionalism

I next introduce the possibility of regional arrangements between developed countries and less developed countries. Assume that such arrangements can be initiated after the developed countries switch from the unilateral equilibrium to the multilateral one, and while the less developed countries are considering whether to reform or not. I define such an arrangement as follows.

DEFINITION. *Regionalism.*—A regional arrangement is an agreement between one developed country and one less developed country in which (*a*) the less developed country agrees to attempt reform and to levy a tariff of t^L on imports of goods from all developed countries other than those of its partner, whose goods will not be subject to duty; and (*b*) the developed country agrees to make a marginal reduction, $dt_b < 0$, in the duty applicable to *b*-stage output imported from its partner country.

Note that this definition is motivated directly by the stylized facts described in Section II. Writing the reform attempt into the agreement reflects deep integration, making the developed-country tariff reduction marginal reflects asymmetric liberalization, and so forth.

A less developed country that attempts reform without entering into a regional initiative is assumed to set $t^L = 0$ without discrimination. Thus a less developed country is now allowed to choose either of two roads to reform: unilateral, nondiscriminatory free trade or bilateral preferential trade.[18] Assuming that $t^L > 0$ only with regionalism avoids stacking the deck in the latter's favor.

A Regional Initiative

The first task is to inquire whether any such regional arrangements will be negotiated. Suppose, then, that the developed countries have moved from a unilateral to a multilateral equilibrium and that assumptions 4 and 5 hold. Then some less developed countries will want to attempt reform, but $\rho < 1$. Consider how a regional arrangement would affect such a country.

[18] It is easy to see that a nondiscriminatory $t^L > 0$ will not in general be consistent with a Nash equilibrium for the less developed countries. Thus consideration of a nondiscriminatory protective policy would require that the model be given more structure.

The arrangement would commit the country to undertaking reform. This is a big commitment, but the country wants to do it anyway. The trade preference implies that all imports will come from the partner country, so that t^L will be prohibitive, regardless of its positive level. This might cause the country's trade pattern to differ greatly from what it would be without a regional arrangement, but, again, this is of no consequence since the less developed country regards all goods as perfect substitutes. But the preferential reduction in t_b, though only marginal, is much more significant. From the point of view of firms considering direct investment to produce b-stage output for the partner country's good, all less developed countries choosing reform are completely equivalent, except for this marginal preference. Thus it serves to attract all such investment.[19] This ensures that the reform effort will succeed: In effect ρ becomes equal to unity when the country signs the regional arrangement because of the "investment diversion" that the arrangement implies.

There will also be "investment creation." Distinguish variables pertaining to the developed country entering the regional arrangement by a degree symbol. Then equilibrium is described by

$$f(H, k((N-1)(L_b+m) + L_b^\circ + m^\circ)(L_b^\circ + m^\circ)) = \frac{(p^\circ)^{-\epsilon}}{N}[1 + (N-1)(1+t)^{-\epsilon}] + \alpha k((N-1)(L_b+m) + L_b^\circ + m^\circ)m^\circ, \quad (29)$$

$$f_L(H, k((N-1)(L_b+m) + L_b^\circ + m^\circ)(L_b^\circ + m^\circ)) = \alpha(1+t_b^\circ),$$

$$p^\circ f_L(H, k((N-1)(L_b+m) + L_b^\circ + m^\circ)(L_b^\circ + m^\circ)) = g_L(U, L - L_b^\circ)$$

and

$$f(H, k((N-1)(L_b+m) + L_b^\circ + m^\circ)(L_b+m)) = \frac{p^{-\epsilon}}{N}[1 + (N-1)(1+t)^{-\epsilon}] + \alpha k((N-1)(L_b+m) + L_b^\circ + m^\circ)m, \quad (30)$$

$$f_L(H, k((N-1)(L_b+m) + L_b^\circ + m^\circ)(L_b+m)) = \alpha(1+t_b),$$

$$pf_L(H, k((N-1)(L_b+m) + L_b^\circ + m^\circ)(L_b+m)) = g_L(U, L - L_b).$$

Equations (29) describe equilibrium for the developed country that is entering into a regional arrangement, and equations (30) describe the equilibrium of each of the remaining $N - 1$ developed

[19] Provided, of course, that L^* is large enough to accommodate all such investment. Boundary solutions will be left to the reader.

countries. To see the effect of a regional initiative, suppose that (29) and (30) are initially identical and differentiate them, with $dt_b^\circ < 0 = dt_b$. From the second equation of (29) and the second equation of (30),

$$\frac{d(L_b^\circ + m^\circ)}{L_b^\circ + m^\circ} = -\frac{N + (N-1)\sigma_k}{\sigma_f N(1+\sigma_k)} \frac{dt_b^\circ}{1+t_b} > 0,$$

$$\frac{d(L_b + m)}{L_b + m} = -\frac{\sigma_k}{\sigma_f N(1+\sigma_k)} \frac{dt_b^\circ}{1+t_b} < 0, \qquad (31)$$

$$\frac{N-1}{N}\frac{d(L_b + m)}{L_b + m} + \frac{1}{N}\frac{d(L_b^\circ + m^\circ)}{L_b^\circ + m^\circ} = -\frac{1}{\sigma_f N(1+\sigma_k)} \frac{dt_b^\circ}{1+t_b} > 0.$$

Thus the total labor allocated, worldwide, to production of the good of the partner developed country increases and the labor devoted to production of all other developed countries' goods falls; but the former effect dominates, so that k increases, with the international spillovers this implies. The first and third equations of (29) imply that this will come about via an increase in m° and a smaller fall in L_b°. These effects will not be large—I am talking about marginal changes here—but the direction is unambiguous.

Now consider the effect of a regional arrangement from the point of view of a potential developed-country partner. Such a country obtains a secure less-developed-country market for its good as a result of the preference it receives. But this may be of no real consequence: In equilibrium its export of goods to all less developed countries must equal the wage bill paid by its foreign subsidiaries, whether there is a regional arrangement or not. The developed country benefits from the agreement because of the investment creation it generates. This will produce a favorable effect on *social* welfare, but the marginal change in t_b will have a zero first-order effect on the *government's* objective function since t_b has been assumed to have been optimally set. The principal gain to the government is merely the assurance that it will not find itself facing a tariff of t^L—and thus higher production costs for its good—in the event that all reforming less developed countries conclude regional arrangements with other developed countries. Thus the government of a developed country may see little to gain from a regional arrangement. But it has nothing at all to lose, and its potential partner has much to gain. Thus it is reasonable to expect that, if necessary, a side payment by the potential partner would produce such an agreement. For this reason I assume that developed countries would agree to enter into regional arrangements. Furthermore, other developed countries should not

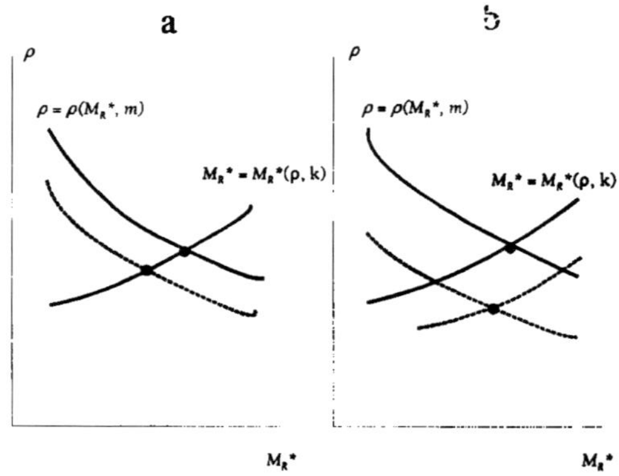

FIG. 1.—Reform destruction. *a*, No reform creation; *b*, reform creation

object to the regional arrangement because the only effect on them will be the favorable rise in k.

But the regional arrangement will not be uniformly benign. Other less developed countries wishing to reform will be harmed. Suppose that one less developed country enters into a regional arrangement, and suppose that this is a country that would undertake reform even in the absence of such an arrangement. Then the direct investment producing b-stage output for that country's partner will all be diverted there. Thus the numerator of the argument of ϕ in equation (27) falls by m; the denominator is unaffected since the less developed country with the regional arrangement still remains a potential host for other direct investment. Therefore, each value of M_R^* now corresponds to a lower value of ρ in equation (27) than before: The function shifts down (see fig. 1a). Equation (17) is unaffected. Accordingly, (17) and (27) now jointly determine lower values of both ρ and M_R^* than without the arrangement. Regionalism produces "reform destruction" by causing fewer countries to attempt reform and lowering the proportion of those that succeed.

Suppose now that the less developed country is one that, in the absence of the regional arrangement, would not have attempted reform at all. This can be termed "reform creation." Then the numerator of the argument of ϕ in equation (27) still falls by m, but the denominator now also rises by L^* since the number of potential hosts increases by one. Thus (27) shifts down even more than before, tending to reduce both ρ and M_R^* more than before. But, in addition, (17) now shifts to the right by one, again because the number of potential hosts increases by one. This tends to nullify the fall in M_R^* but further accentuate that in ρ (see fig. 1*b*). Thus the probability of success falls even more than before, but the number of countries attempting reform may either rise or fall, depending on the balance between reform creation and reform destruction.

PROPOSITION 5. *Regionalism.*—Suppose that assumptions 2–5 hold. Then if the developed countries shift from unilateralism to multilateralism, both the developed countries and the less developed countries would each wish to enter into regional arrangements. If one such arrangement takes place, (*a*) the less developed participant will successfully implement its reform by attracting all direct investment intended to supply *b*-stage output to its partner (investment diversion); (*b*) the opportunity to enter into the arrangement may induce a less developed country to reform that would otherwise not have attempted to do so (reform creation); (*c*) the arrangement will induce the developed-country partner to invest more abroad (investment creation); (*d*) equilibrium *k* will rise, conferring spillover benefits on all developed countries and on all less developed countries that successfully reform, and increasing the benefit *B* of multilateral liberalization; and (*e*) the number of less developed countries—other than the participant—that attempt reform will fall, as will their probability of success (reform destruction).

Regional Equilibrium

Proposition 5 describes the consequences of a single regional arrangement. But all developed countries would be willing to participate in such an arrangement, and all less developed countries that attempt reform will wish to do so. Furthermore, the reduction in ρ brought about by one initiative would, if anything, strengthen the resolve of the other less developed countries to do the same thing, and individual developed countries would also become more tempted as more less developed countries link up with other developed countries. So consider the international equilibrium that would emerge if all countries are allowed freely to enter into such arrangements. The fact that regional arrangements have become so widespread suggests that analysis of such a regional equilibrium is more important than that of a single arrangement.

I have defined a regional arrangement as one between a single developed country and a single less developed country. But I do not mean to exclude the possibility that one country might enter into several arrangements with different partners, thus, in effect, allowing larger groupings. Then, regardless of the relative number of developed and less developed countries, all can potentially participate in some arrangement. But there are some possible constraints.

The first is that, if many less developed countries enter into arrangements with a single developed country, these arrangements may not guarantee the success of their reform efforts. The reason is that, although the arrangements will divert investment from nonparticipants to participants, there is nothing to guarantee that it will be distributed among all participants. Suppose that M_{RR} less developed countries establish regional arrangements with one developed country. The condition $m > (M_{RR} - 1)L^*$ guarantees the success of each country's reform effort. A less developed country will never enter into a regional agreement that violates this condition if an agreement with some other developed country would not violate it. Thus regional groupings would emerge in such a way as to satisfy the requirement, if that is possible. The number of less developed countries that would wish to undertake reform if they could be certain of its success is $M_R^*(1, k)$. Then the condition that guarantees that it is possible to accommodate all less developed countries that wish with regional arrangements that guarantee the success of their reforms is the following.

Assumption 6. $N[(m/L^*) + 1] > M_R^*(1, k)$.

The second possible constraint concerns whether a country that has already entered into one regional arrangement would be willing to enter into another arrangement as well. Consider first the decision of a developed country. If its partner is not large enough to supply fully its need for *b*-stage goods from abroad, this country will have every reason to take on another partner. But with an interior solution, the developed country has nothing to gain from a second arrangement. It has nothing to lose either, and its potential partner has much to gain. Thus it is again reasonable to expect that a side payment by the potential partner would produce such an agreement, and I accordingly assume that developed countries would agree to enter into multiple arrangements.

Now consider whether a less developed country would be willing to undertake additional arrangements. They would attract more investment, but, with the success of its reform effort already guaranteed by one arrangement, there is no benefit to this. The less developed country has nothing to gain from additional arrangements, but nothing to lose either. The developed country, on the other hand, now has much to gain. With all less developed countries linked to developed countries through regional arrangements, the developed country without such a link will find its exports of goods required to pay for the labor employed in its foreign subsidiaries subject to the tariff of t^L, even though it must pay the same wage as everyone else. Since one party has much to gain and the other nothing to lose, I again assume that such an arrangement would be negotiated.

The nature of the regional equilibrium should now be apparent. With assumption 6, all developed countries, and all less developed countries that wish to reform if $\rho = 1$, will be involved in regional arrangements that guarantee the success of all the reform efforts. Reform destruction will not take place, but reform creation will.

PROPOSITION 6. *Regional equilibrium.*–Suppose that assumptions 2–5 hold. Then if the developed countries shift from unilateralism to multilateralism and assumption 6 also holds, and if regional arrangements are freely allowed, a regional equilibrium with the following characteristics will emerge: (*a*) The N developed countries will establish regional arrangements with $M_R^*(1, k)$ less developed countries. (*b*) Relative to the equilibrium without regionalism, more less developed countries undertake reform and more (i.e., all) of them succeed (reform creation). (*c*) Relative to the equilibrium without regionalism, more foreign direct investment takes place (investment creation), k is greater, and so is the benefit B of multilateral liberalization. (*d*) Relative to the equilibrium without regionalism, both social welfare and the value of each developed country's objective function are higher. (*e*) Exports of goods from the developed countries to the less developed countries are free of duty.

Remarks.—Several distinct features of this approach to regionalism should be noted. *First,* the major role of regionalism in this model is to facilitate reform in the less developed countries. A secondary role (because it is done marginally) is to stimulate investment.

Second, the relation between multilateralism and regionalism in this model is benign. Regionalism is the consequence of multilateral success, not failure, and it in turn strengthens rather than undermines the basis for a commitment to the multilateral order.

Third, I have used the terms "investment creation" and "investment diversion" to acknowledge one way in which the present theory does parallel the Vinerian paradigm. But in fact the analogy is much more apparent than real. For example, trade diversion is the major negative influence in the Vinerian world, but investment diversion is strongly positive here, as the force behind the major benefit of regionalism.

Fourth, in this model regional arrangements are ways in which reforming countries compete among themselves for direct investment. In reality they of course can compete in other ways as well, such as with subsidies, tax holidays, and the like. If these methods are used *in addition to* regionalism, the concerns of this paper remain relevant. Not so if they are used *instead.* There are two reasons to expect that this will not be so. Regionalism is a costless way to compete. But this could be only an artifact of my special assumptions, so the second reason is more important. Regardless of whether other incentives are present, direct investment will be sensitive to the credibility of the announced reform effort. Analysis of this would require additional modeling, but one suspects that such an analysis would complement and reinforce the present one. A regional arrangement establishes an external commitment to reform that (weakly, perhaps) binds future governments, thereby making the future preservation of reform (slightly, perhaps) more credible. This in turn makes the country more attractive for direct investment, relative to similar countries without such external commitments. The role of deep integration in this model is to write a commitment to reform into an arrangement with a big country that is a natural enforcer and, as a result of the investment induced by the arrangement, has an interest in enforcing it. Only regionalism has this property, so it can be expected to be employed even if other tools are used as well.

Fifth, in this model the global interest is served if reform is as widespread as possible, that is, if direct investment flows to all those countries that want to reform. But no agent has an interest in ensuring this: There is another externality here. The regional equilibrium serves as an invisible hand inducing competition among reforming countries in a form that effectively disperses direct investment.

Sixth, the discussion following proposition 4 pointed out that a full equilibrium had not been described, and suggested that multilateral liberalization could be stronger if it were performed by countries correctly anticipating the equilibrium responses of reformers who also correctly anticipated the nature of the final equilibrium. The same discussion applies now. Furthermore, the full equilibrium multilateral tariff when a regional equilibrium is correctly anticipated, t^{FR}, could well differ from the full equilibrium when it is correctly anticipated that regionalism will not be allowed, t^{F} again. The regional equilibrium maximizes the extent of successful reform. Then a given reduction in t can be expected to cause k to rise by no less if a regional equilibrium is correctly anticipated than it would if the world were constrained away from that equilibrium. Thus I expect $t^{FR} \leq t^{F} \leq t^{M}$. An equilibrium with a lower t is characterized by a larger k, a larger B, and a larger $M_R^*(1, k)$, yet another sense in which multilateralism and regionalism are mutually beneficial.

VI. Concluding Remarks

This paper described the stylized facts of the new regionalism and then constructed a simple formal model suggested by those facts. Analysis of that model generated a theory of regionalism, quite different from the standard Vinerian perspective, with strong conclusions about the nature and implications of regional integration.

The argument that is suggested consists of several components that give crucial roles to the success of postwar multilateralism, the role of direct investment, and policy reform in many countries. (1) The small-country participants in regional arrangements have embarked on programs of policy reform intended, at least in part, to enhance the role of international trade. (2) Direct investment has been surging since the late 1980s. (3) Reforming countries anxious to join the multilateral trading system as soon as possible see the attraction of foreign direct investment as a key step. (4) Attracting foreign direct investment requires making the country attractive relative to other, similar potential hosts, not relative to source countries.[20] (5) Regional arrangements can give a small country a marginal advantage—over other, similar, small countries—in attracting direct investment because they obtain marginally more favorable access to a large market than other nonparticipating small countries. (6) The regional arrangements, by in effect internalizing a critical externality, help spread the benefits of the multilateral trading system around the globe and enhance its value to all participants, thereby reinforcing, rather than undermining, support for multilateralism.

This paper developed a very special model and then imposed specific assumptions on its parameters, so I should offer some comments on robustness. *First,* assumptions 2–6 are sufficient conditions for my results, not necessary conditions. Furthermore, possible consequences of their failure can be examined in a straightforward way and do not threaten the validity of the basic approach of this paper.

Second, my results are obviously sensitive to the very special structure of my model. But that structure was chosen neither at random nor with a view to obtaining the present results. Instead it is intended to reflect—accurately but in sharp relief—just those features that I argued do in fact define the new regionalism. Indeed, relaxing some of the assumptions would likely strengthen the conclusions: Allowing countries to manipulate directly their terms of trade just increases the motivation for multilateralism; allowing other subsidiaries themselves to experience some of the externalities conferred on host countries by direct investment would cause that investment to cluster in fewer locations, thereby accentuating the basis for com-

[20] See Brainard and Riker (1997) and Riker and Brainard (1997) for relevant evidence that workers in foreign affiliates of multinational firms compete for jobs primarily with workers in other affiliates located in countries with similar characteristics, rather than with workers in dissimilar source countries.

petition between reforming countries for direct investment. But I want to emphasize two features of the model that I believe are of special importance for the relevance of the paper's conclusions. These are the assumptions that the less developed countries regard all goods as perfect substitutes and that the developed countries regard all the less developed countries as perfect substitutes for the location of *b*-stage production. The consequences of these assumptions are that harmful trade diversion does not emerge and that investment diversion is not harmful in the regional equilibrium. Harmful trade diversion is not absent from my model because countries, in Kemp-Wan (1976) fashion, choose to avoid it; it is absent because I do not let it in. So relaxation of these assumptions has the potential to introduce a downside to regionalism that is at present not in the model. My prime reason for making these assumptions is to abstract from Vinerian concerns and to focus sharply on what is new here. But a consequence of the dramatic change in the world trading environment between the 1950s and the 1990s is that trade diversion is much less important. There may be a huge volume of such diversion—indeed it may well be at an all-time high—but the welfare significance does not have the same order of magnitude as it would have 40 years ago.

Third, the formal model described the small-country participants as less developed and modeled them differently than the "large" industrial countries, but only some of the small countries in the examples that motivated this paper can be described as less developed. I suspect that the present analysis applies, in whole or in part, to the other cases as well. For example, the former communist countries of central Europe are eager to attract direct investment, the ultimate success of their reform efforts remains both in doubt and dependent on their ability to attract such investment, and the Europe Agreements have given them a small advantage over other, similar, countries: not by trade preferences, but by a higher implicit likelihood of future integration into the European Union. For small industrialized nations joining the European Union, the problem is not so much to attract new direct investment as to remain attractive sites, in an increasingly integrated world, for activities currently conducted there. The small advantage they obtain is not additional preference, but future participation in E.U. decision making.[21]

Fourth, the structure of the model I developed was motivated very strongly by the five stylized facts I described. So the relevance of the model is limited by the relevance of the stylizations. I think this relevance compelling, but I acknowledge that my list of stylized facts

[21] For more on this, see Baldwin and Flam (1994).

is neither universal nor exhaustive. There is a lot of diversity out there.

This paper suggests the following relation of regionalism to multilateralism. (1) The new regionalism is a direct result of the success of multilateral liberalization. (2) Regionalism is the means by which new countries enter the multilateral system and a means by which small countries already in it exploit its success. (3) Regionalism is creating new industrial groups with an interest in preserving the liberal trade order.

Of course, any changes—regional initiatives are no exceptions—offer protectionists new scope for their efforts. An argument that regional initiatives reflect causes much more benign than a desire to divide the globe into several highly protected blocs does not establish that this will not in fact be the ultimate result.

References

Anderson, Kym, and Blackhurst, Richard, eds. *Regional Integration and the Global Trading System*. New York: St. Martin's, 1993.

Bagwell, Kyle, and Staiger, Robert W. "Reciprocal Trade Liberalization." Working Paper no. 5488. Cambridge, Mass.: NBER, March 1996.

———. "Multilateral Tariff Cooperation during the Formation of Customs Unions." *J. Internat. Econ.* 42 (February 1997): 91–123. (*a*)

———. "Multilateral Tariff Cooperation during the Formation of Free Trade Areas." *Internat. Econ. Rev.* 38 (May 1997): 291–319. (*b*)

Baldwin, Richard E. "The Causes of Regionalism." *World Economy* 20 (November 1997): 865–88.

Baldwin, Richard E., and Flam, Harry. "Enlargement of the European Union: The Economic Consequences for the Scandinavian Countries." Occasional Paper no. 16. London: Centre Econ. Policy Res., September 1994.

Bhagwati, Jagdish N., and Panagariya, Arvind. "Preferential Trading Areas and Multilateralism: Strangers, Friends or Foes?" Working Paper no. 22. College Park: Univ. Maryland, Center Internat. Econ., 1996.

Bond, Eric W., and Syropoulos, Constantinos. "Trading Blocs and the Sustainability of Interregional Cooperation." In *The New Transatlantic Economy*, edited by Matthew B. Canzoneri, Wilfred J. Ethier, and Vittorio Grilli. Cambridge: Cambridge Univ. Press, 1996.

Brainard, S. Lael, and Riker, David A. "Are U.S. Multinationals Exporting U.S. Jobs?" Working Paper no. 5958. Cambridge, Mass.: NBER, March 1997.

Chichilnisky, Graciela. "Trading Blocks with Endogenous Technology and Increasing Returns." Manuscript. New York: Columbia Univ., 1994.

de Melo, Jaime, and Panagariya, Arvind, eds. *New Dimensions in Regional Integration*. Cambridge: Cambridge Univ. Press, 1993.

Ethier, Wilfred J. "Internationally Decreasing Costs and World Trade." *J. Internat. Econ.* 9 (February 1979): 1–24.

———. "National and International Returns to Scale in the Modern Theory of International Trade." *A.E.R.* 72 (June 1982): 389–405.

———. "Multilateral Roads to Regionalism." In *International Trade Policy and the Pacific Rim,* edited by John Piggott and A. Woodland. London: Macmillan, 1998 (in press). (*a*)

———. "The New Regionalism." *Econ. J.* 108 (July 1998). (*b*)

———. "Unilateralism in a Multilateral World." Manuscript. Philadelphia: Univ. Pennsylvania, Dept. Econ., 1998. (*c*)

Ethier, Wilfred J., and Horn, Henrik. "A New Look at Economic Integration." In *Monopolistic Competition and International Trade,* edited by Henryk Kierzkowski. Oxford: Oxford Univ. Press, 1984.

Freund, Carolyn. "Multilateralism and the Endogenous Formation of PTAs." Manuscript. Washington: Board Governors, Fed. Reserve System, 1997.

Kemp, Murray C., and Wan, Henry Y., Jr. "An Elementary Proposition Concerning the Formation of Customs Unions." *J. Internat. Econ.* 6 (February 1976): 95–97.

Krugman, Paul. "Is Bilateralism Bad?" In *International Trade and Trade Policy,* edited by Elhanan Helpman and Assaf Razin. Cambridge, Mass.: MIT Press, 1991.

Perroni, Carlo, and Whalley, John. "The New Regionalism: Trade Liberalization or Insurance?" Working Paper no. 4626. Cambridge, Mass.: NBER, January 1994.

Riker, David A., and Brainard, S. Lael. "U.S. Multinationals and Competition from Low Wage Countries." Working Paper no. 5959. Cambridge, Mass.: NBER, March 1997.

Yi, Sang-Seung. "Endogenous Formation of Customs Unions under Imperfect Competition: Open Regionalism Is Good." *J. Internat. Econ.* 41 (August 1996): 153–77.

The Economic Journal, **108** (*July*), 1149–1161. © Royal Economic Society 1998. Published by Blackwell Publishers, 108 Cowley Road, Oxford OX4 1JF, UK and 350 Main Street, Malden, MA 02148, USA.

THE NEW REGIONALISM

Wilfred J. Ethier

Once again, regionalism is afoot. Twin late-1980s announcements, by the United States and Canada of negotiations for a free-trade area, and by the EU of an attempt to complete its internal market, ignited a conflagration of regional integration. Well over a hundred regional arrangements, involving most nations, now exist. *Deja vu*: the 1950s and 1960s had likewise witnessed many 'old regionalism' initiatives. Except for Western Europe, these in the end amounted to little, however, and efforts for preferential trade became quiescent, until the dramatic advent of the 'new regionalism'.

1. Introduction

Trade theorists have responded to the new regionalism by investigating two questions. Will the formation of regional trading blocs raise or lower welfare? Will regionalism help or hinder multilateral trade liberalisation? Answers have been mixed.[1] These investigations have adopted a Vinerian perspective on regional integration as a combination of trade creation and trade diversion[2] (developed in response to the old regionalism) augmented, in many cases, with a significant use of game theory (reflecting developments in economic thought since the days of the old regionalism). Notable by its absence is investigation of the more fundamental question of *why* the new regionalism has emerged—it has simply been treated as exogenous.

Also absent has been appreciation of the fact that the international environment greeting the new regionalism differs from that experienced by the old regionalism in three dramatic, fundamental, and critical ways.

- The multilateral liberalisation of trade in manufactured goods among the industrial countries is much more complete now than it was then.

The GATT rounds of multilateral tariff reductions, still gathering steam in the days of the old regionalism, now constitute perhaps the most successful exercise of deliberate economic policy making in history. But the second distinguishing feature is even more important.

- Scores of economically less advanced countries have abandoned the basically-autarkic, anti-market, policies they followed during the days of the old regionalism and are now actively trying to join the multilateral trading system.

[1] See Bhagwati and Panagariya (1996), Krugman (1991), Bond and Syropoulos (1996) and Bagwell and Staiger (1996*a*, *b*, 1997).

[2] See Viner (1950), Lipsey (1960), Ethier and Horn (1984), and Panagariya (1996).

During the 1950s and 1960s the communist bloc was still communist and import substitution ruled the Third World, with most less developed countries highly suspicious of both trade and foreign direct investment. All this changed just as the new regionalism appeared. The third distinction involves the changing role of direct investment.

- Direct investment is much more prominent now than in the days of the old regionalism, and it has been surging since the advent of the new regionalism.

Formerly, direct investment was largely a matter of U.S. manufacturing firms expanding horizontally into other developed countries (aside from the traditional vertical integration by extractive firms). Since then, direct investment by the developed countries has become increasingly two-way, is growing faster than trade, and is increasingly likely to flow into developing and reforming countries.

Because of this radical change in environment one can make a *qualitative* distinction between the old regionalism and the new. To appreciate what this might be, it is necessary to investigate the causes of the new regionalism and not merely use the traditional tools to try to deduce its consequences. The old regionalism was, to a large extent, motivated by a desire to substitute for insufficient multilateral liberalisation and/or to facilitate holding aloof from what multilateral liberalisation there was. The Vinerian paradigm of trade creation versus trade diversion provided a natural frame of reference from which to analyse such an environment. Thus the Vinerian perspective was appropriately central to theoretical models motivated by the old regionalism. I argue that the new regionalism, by contrast, is largely motivated by a desire to facilitate entrance into a now much more developed multilateral trading system. The Vinerian perspective, though not irrelevant, should be secondary in theoretical models appropriate to an analysis of the new regionalism.

This paper concerns appropriate models of the new regionalism, models in which regionalism might emerge as a consequence of past multilateral success and extensive current reform attempts. But first I must set out what I believe to be the important characteristics of the new regionalism.

2. Characteristics of the New Regionalism

The following six characteristics are neither exhaustive nor universal (current regional initiatives are quite diverse), but do apply in varying degree to most of the more important regional arrangements.

(a) *The new regionalism typically involves one or more small countries linking up with a large country.*

In NAFTA, Mexico and Canada are each small, economically, relative to the United States; the new members of the EU (Austria, Finland and Sweden) are tiny relative to the EU itself; the same is true of the central

European adherents to the Europe Agreements with the EU; Brazil will likely dominate Mercosur, etc.

(b) *Typically, the small countries have recently made, or are making, significant unilateral reforms.*

This is dramatically true of the Europe Agreements' central European participants, who had abandoned communism, of the members of Mercosur, and of Mexico in NAFTA. But it also characterises, to a lesser degree, the small industrial country participants in regional initiatives. Canada had turned away from Trudeau-style economic nationalism before negotiating a free trade agreement with the United States, and the Scandinavian applicants to the EU (except Norway, which, significantly, declined to join) had made important reforms in some sectors (e.g. agriculture). Note that, in Mercosur, the large country, Brazil, is also a reformer.

(c) *Dramatic moves to free trade between members are not featured: The degree of liberalisation is typically modest. Thus the Vinerian paradigm is not a natural starting point.*

For example, NAFTA actually provides only modest liberalisation: United States tariffs were already low and NAFTA hedges sensitive sectors in all sorts of ways. Canada and Mexico have done somewhat more, but the most significant measures (largely Mexican) were unilateral and not part of NAFTA. The accession of new members to the EU is even more glaring: because of their membership in the EA, the trade relations of Austria, Finland and Sweden with the EU are virtually identical to what they would have been had they decided not to join! The Europe Agreements provide for little in the way of concrete liberalisation. Even with the admittedly more ambitious Mercosur the liberalisation involved is not large relative to the unilateral liberalisations of the members.

(d) *The liberalisation achieved is primarily by the small countries, not by the large country: The agreements are one-sided.*

The liberalisation in NAFTA is due much more to 'concessions' by Mexico and Canada than by the United States. In negotiations over enlargement, the EU has been flexible on financial responsibilities and periods of adjustment, but has always maintained a take-it-or-leave-it attitude regarding the nature and structure of the EU itself. The Europe Agreements involve virtually no 'concessions' by the EU: Indeed the EU instituted antidumping measures against some of its new partners even as the initial agreements were coming into effect! In a sense this asymmetry is a direct reflection of how the world has changed since the days of the old regionalism: one reason the small countries get only small tariff advantages is simply that the large countries have small tariffs to begin with. Mercusor is an exception: Brazil has made concessions at least as large as those of the smaller members. But recall that Brazil is also a reformer.

(e) *Regional arrangements often involve 'deep' integration: the partners seldom confine themselves to reducing or eliminating trade barriers, but also harmonise or adjust diverse assortments of other economic policies.*

The EU is a clear and dramatic example of this. The United States–Canada free-trade agreement and the subsequent NAFTA included a host of economic reform commitments by Canada and by Mexico. Sometimes partners in regional arrangements exempt each other from acts of administered protection (such as antidumping duties), but often they do not (e.g., NAFTA). Sometimes partners are in effect granted rights of appeal denied to nonpartners (NAFTA again). The three latest GATT rounds of multilateral negotiations tried, with significant success, to broaden the scope of multilateral arrangements. But a major attraction of the new regionalism is that negotiations with a small number of partners broadens the range of instruments over which negotiation is feasible.

(f) *Regional arrangements are regional geographically: The participants are neighbours.*

Unlike the other five stylised facts, this characteristic was probably just as true of the old regionalism as it is of the new.

In summary, regional integration now usually involves reform-minded small countries 'purchasing', with moderate trade concessions, links with a large, neighbouring country that involve 'deep' integration but that confer relatively minor trade advantages.

3. Regionalisation

Next, I advance several hypotheses inspired by the stylised facts of the new regionalism and by the differences in environment alluded to above, and I introduce theory to consider the hypotheses further. For exposition, I split this into three parts, introducing one by one the three ways in which the international environment has changed between the days of the old regionalism and today. This section exploits the fact that multilateral liberalisation is much more extensive now.

3.1. *Hypotheses*

The first set of hypotheses relate to regionalisation (an increase in the amount of trade with geographic neighbours relative to total trade) and its relation to liberalisation.

Hypothesis 1: *Liberalisation promotes regionalisation.* The familiar gravity equation—predicting that the volume of trade between two countries is positively related to their GDPs and negatively related to the economic distance between them—has repeatedly been shown to describe actual trade patterns well.[3]

[3] The gravity equation can be thought of as a reduced form consistent with many trade models, so that its empirical success reveals little about the underlying causes of trade. See Deardorff (1995).

Economic distance equals geographic distance (presumably proxying for transport costs and perhaps other things) plus trade barriers. A nondiscriminatory liberalisation, by making geographic distance more important relative to trade barriers, might be expected to cause a country's trade to become more regional. This is true both for multilateral liberalisation and for unilateral reform.

Hypothesis 2: *The fewer the number of participants in trade negotiations, the easier it is to reach agreement.* Fewer participants presumably mean fewer conflicts of interest and fewer areas of potential disagreement. Furthermore, a solution to a conflict between two participants is less likely to provoke a conflict with another participant the fewer the number of additional participants.

Hypothesis 3: *The fewer the number of participants in trade negotiations, the larger the number of issues on which it is possible to reach agreement.* That is, the deeper is the integration that can be negotiated.

3.2. *Theory*

I now discuss, in general terms,[4] theoretical considerations suggested by the above hypotheses. The discussion reflects the stylised facts (f), that regional arrangements are established by geographical neighbours, and (e), that they often involve 'deeper' integration. Consider the following model.

- Countries are identical, except that they are spatially separated. Assume, in particular, that countries are grouped into N continents of n countries each; the distance between any two countries in the same continent is less than the distance between any pair in different continents.
- The government of each country may negotiate a mutual reduction in trade barriers with other governments, but each government is constrained by negotiating costs. In subsequent periods there will be new rounds of negotiations, with the governments constrained by the same costs in negotiating further reductions in trade barriers.

At the outset of each negotiating round, each government decides whether to negotiate *regionally* (only with other countries in the same continent) or *multilaterally* (with all other countries); because of the symmetry, all governments make the same choice. The negotiating costs relate to the government's political support, not modelled explicitly. Hypotheses 2 and 3 suggest representing these costs as follows:

$$c = l + \gamma\pi \tag{1}$$

where c denotes the cost, l the degree of liberalisation that is achieved, and π the number of negotiating partners to whom that liberalisation applies. Thus π equals $n - 1$ if negotiations are regional and $nN - 1$ if they are multilateral. γ is a parameter reflecting the relative importance of the two determinants of

[4] See Garriga and Sanguinetti (1995, 1997); also see Ethier (1997).

c. I assume the total cost a government is willing to incur in a negotiating round is exogenously given.

- In its negotiations, each government strives to maximise, subject to the constraint on costs, an index of benefits. Benefits are greater the greater the reduction in trade barriers and the greater the number of partners to which those reductions apply.

Represent the benefits by:

$$b = l + \delta\pi \quad (2)$$

- The parameter δ is a decreasing function of the ratio of aggregate trade with negotiating partners to aggregate trade with nonpartners.

The government, for political reasons, wants to reduce the 'tax' on as much trade as possible, and existing trade matters more than trade that would exist if barriers were lower. Also, a higher partner-to-nonpartner trade ratio will likely imply a higher trade-creation-to-trade-diversion ratio.[5] Let δ_R denote the value δ would have if a country were initially to embark on regional negotiations, previous negotiations, if any, having all been multilateral. Hypothesis 1 suggests that the ratio of partner to nonpartner trade is a decreasing function of t, the existing trade barrier. So assume that δ_R is an increasing function of t, $\delta_R(t)$.

What will countries do? Maximising b subject to the constraint that c equal an exogenous value requires that π be minimised—that is, that negotiations be regional—if and only if $\gamma > \delta_R$. If initially $\gamma > \delta_R(t)$, countries will embark on regional negotiations which will reduce δ_R still more, so that multilateral negotiations can not even start until regionalism has gone to the limit. The world looks Vinerian. If, on the other hand, $\delta_R(t) > \gamma$ initially, negotiations will be multilateral. But the outcomes of these negotiations will drive $\delta_R(t)$ down toward γ. If the free-trade value, $\delta_R(0)$, exceeds γ, regionalism will never become appealing, and countries will continue on the multilateral path toward free trade. But if $\delta_R(0) < \gamma$, sufficiently successful multilateral negotiations will eventually be replaced by regional negotiations.

The latter possibility is the especially interesting one. Here the *success* of multilateral liberalisation *induces* a switch to regionalism, and this switch sustains the pace of liberalisation above what multilateral negotiations could deliver.

4. Commitment to Reform

The previous section exploited just one of the three basic changes in the international environment between the time of the old regionalism and that of the new: multilateral trade liberalisation. Now I add a second: efforts for fundamental reform by the former communist countries and throughout the third world.

[5] But see Bhagwati and Panagariya (1996) for a contrary view.

4.1. *Hypotheses*

Bringing the economy into the multilateral trading system is central to all contemporary reform programmes. Presumably the benefits that can be expected by being part of this system help determine how tempting reform is.

Hypothesis 4: *The greater the degree of multilateral integration, the greater the benefits to be expected from being part of the multilateral system.*

A major concern of most economic reformers is that their reforms not be undone in the future. That is, they want to *bind* future regimes to the reforms. This is desirable not only for its own sake, but also because a faith in the permanence of the reform effort is crucial to its success. One way—sometimes the only way—to bind future regimes to the reforms is to establish an external commitment.

Hypothesis 5: *The more likely that backsliding from an external commitment will induce retaliation, the more likely such a commitment is to sustain reform.* If future regimes can walk away without cost from an external commitment to reform, that commitment will not accomplish much.

Hypothesis 6: *The more that specific reform measures are embodied in an external commitment, the likelier that commitment is to sustain reform.* A vague commitment can be gutted in substance while fully adhered to in form.

4.2. *Theory*

Implications of the hypotheses are immediate. Successful multilateral liberalisation by the industrial countries makes participation in the international economy more rewarding, and thereby contributes to the decision to reform. Multilateral negotiations also offer reforming countries a potential external commitment binding future governments to the reform measures.

Multilateral negotiations are, however, of little practical use for this purpose. They provide no enforcement mechanism should a country backslide, and large industrial countries can hardly be expected to put the multilateral system at risk merely to punish a single deviant reformer. Even if they wanted to punish they are likely to have little formal justification for doing so, since multilateral agreements would not embody detailed reform measures by individual countries.

But regional arrangements can address both problems. The fact that the agreement is with a big country (often the dominant trading partner) adds a credible enforcement mechanism. Because such arrangements allow for deeper integration, they can contain obligations to undertake specific measures central to the reform effort. This is clearly illustrated by the free trade agreement between Canada and the United States and by the subsequent NAFTA.

Thus the stylised facts important here are (a), (b), and (e): reform-minded small countries linking up with a larger country in an arrangement featuring deeper integration.

5. Competition for Foreign Direct Investment

The previous sections have exploited two of the three basic changes in the international environment between the time of the old regionalism and that of the new. Now I bring in the third: foreign direct investment.

5.1. *Hypotheses*

This section,[6] like the previous, utilises the stylised facts that regionalism usually involves a big country linking up with one or more small ones making significant reforms. In addition, the stylised facts (c) and (d), that the degree of liberalisation is modest and asymmetrical, play a critical role. Thus all six stylised facts will have been brought in.

Hypothesis 7: *Reforming countries see the ability to attract foreign direct investment as the key to successful entry into the multilateral trading system.* Multinational firms are a prime means of technology transfer, and they can supply international contacts and modern commercial methods to countries which, because of their past policies, have precious little of either.[7]

Hypothesis 8: *Competition among reforming countries to attract foreign direct investment is likely to be keen.* Countries comprising a large part of the world are trying to reform at the same time, and most of them see direct investment as the key to success.

Hypothesis 9: *A small national advantage offers the hope of attracting a large amount of foreign direct investment.* There are three mutually reinforcing reasons to expect this. First, with similar countries competing, small advantages can prove decisive. Second, direct investment is lumpy: you have to put a factory in one place. Third, the basic advantages that reforming countries see in direct investment involve externalities, and these externalities render a site more attractive for additional direct investment.

5.2. *Theory*

Consider the following abstract framework. A large number of countries, hitherto aloof from the multilateral trading system, seek to undertake fundamental reform and become part of that system, at least in part because of the success of past multilateral liberalisation. These reforming countries do see direct investment as a key to successful reform (Hypothesis 7), and they will compete with each other to attract it (Hypothesis 8). Firms in the industrial countries are tempted to invest in the potential reformers, because of the latter's comparative advantages, but the former have substantial latitude in deciding where to invest, since there are many reformers with fairly similar economic characteristics.

A reform effort will presumably be more successful the more foreign direct

[6] For a full account see Ethier (1996).
[7] Not 'of ethier,' though that is true too.

investment the country can attract. To put this consideration into sharp relief, assume that a reform effort will succeed if and only if some direct investment is attracted. To focus on competition among reforming countries, assume that they are all alike so that, other things equal, industrial-country firms are indifferent about where to locate their foreign subsidiaries. But they will tend to locate together, because of the lumpy nature of direct investment and because of positive externalities between foreign subsidiaries.

The previous section's discussion of the relation between regional integration and the ability of a reforming government to bind the country to the reforms is also relevant here. In practice, the credibility of the commitment of the government to its announced reform can be crucial in attracting direct investment and, in that way, ensuring the success of the reform. Even a regional arrangement with only modest big-country preferences for the small country establishes an external commitment to reform that (weakly) binds future governments, thereby making the future preservation of reform (slightly) more credible. What matters here is what the small reforming country *gives*, in terms of trade concessions, not what it *gets*, because it is the former which influences the likelihood of retaliation by the partner in the event of backsliding. The external commitment in turn makes the country more attractive for direct investment, relative to similar countries without such external commitments. Thus, Hypothesis 9 suggests, the ability of a regional arrangement to bind the government to reform can be important for the success of that reform even when it confers only modest direct benefits.

But the credibility of a country's commitment to reform is but one consideration pertinent to a multinational firm's decision of where to invest. To focus on other considerations, assume now that the commitment of each reforming country to the reform is not in doubt. Suppose, further, that the industrial countries are all alike, except that their final products are differentiated—the basis for trade between them. These products are produced in multiple stages, with the more labour-intensive stages presumably candidates for transfer to subsidiaries in the reforming countries.

Under these circumstances, successful reform by an individual country will be uncertain, but more probable the greater the aggregate amount of direct investment from the industrial countries relative to the number of countries attempting reform, that is, relative to the number of potential targets of that investment. So its prospects will be improved if a reforming country can somehow distinguish itself from its rivals.

Consider the role of regional arrangements in this regard. Define a regional agreement to be the following.

An agreement between one industrial country and one reforming country in which:

The reforming country commits—

- *To the details of an attempted reform,*
- *To give the goods of its partner preferential treatment;*

The developed country commits—

◆ *To make a* small *reduction in the duty applicable to goods imported from its partner country.*

Note that this definition reflects the stylised facts that regional arrangements tend to involve one or more small reforming countries linking up with a large country in an arrangement characterised by asymmetrical concessions and deep integration.

Suppose for simplicity that each potential reformer regards the products of all industrial countries as perfect substitutes. Together with the assumptions already made, this will expunge from the analysis the possibility of negative welfare effects due to trade diversion. This oversimplification will emphasise that the changed world and the distinctive features of the new regionalism have made the old Vinerian concerns less important, and it will also highlight the new concerns.

Consider first the effects of such an arrangement on a potential reformer. The arrangement would establish an external commitment to reform, as discussed earlier. Also, the trade preference implies that all imports will come from the partner country, since the reforming country regards the goods of all industrial countries as perfect substitutes. But this trade diversion is of no consequence in this model, with the concern of the old regionalism assumed away to focus on the concerns of the new.

But the preference granted by the industrial-country partner, though only marginal, is much more significant. From the point of view of firms considering direct investment to provide intermediate–stage inputs for the industrial country partner's products, all reforming countries are equivalent, except for this marginal preference. Thus it attracts all such investment.[8] This ensures the reform will succeed because of the 'investment diversion' the regional arrangement implies.

This explains why reforming countries find regional arrangements attractive even though they typically receive only 'minor' concessions from their partners. The goal is to compete with other *similar* countries for direct investment, not to expand greatly exports to their partners or to attract from them direct investments that would otherwise not be made at all. Such 'investment creation' will be modest at best.

A regional arrangement will not be uniformly benign. Other countries desiring reform will suffer. Suppose one country that would undertake reform anyway enters into a regional arrangement. Then direct investment producing intermediate goods for that country's partner will all be diverted there, and the country still remains a potential host for other direct investment. Less direct investment remains for other reforming countries, reducing their prospects for success and perhaps deterring some of them from even embarking upon reform. Regionalism produces 'reform destruction', causing fewer countries to attempt reform and lowering the proportion of those who

[8] But if the externalities between foreign subsidiaries—which induce them to locate together—are strong enough, more than 'small' concessions may be required by the industrial partner.

succeed. On the other hand, the country with the regional arrangement may not itself have attempted reform in its absence: 'reform creation'. Thus the number of countries attempting reform may either rise or fall, depending on the balance between reform creation and reform destruction.

Thus far I have considered the effects of an isolated regional arrangement. But in fact they are becoming ubiquitous. So consider next the general equilibrium that will emerge if all countries are allowed freely to negotiate regional arrangements of the kind I have hypothesized, including the possibility of a single country entering multiple relationships.[9]

If several reforming countries establish regional arrangements with a single industrial country, the value of the arrangements to the former will be eroded because direct investment may well tend to cluster mainly in some subset of them all. For this reason, the reforming countries will tend to spread themselves out in their choices of partners. If there are at least as many industrial countries as potential reformers, each of the latter can find a partner that will guarantee the success of its reform effort. This may or may not be true if there are fewer industrial countries, depending upon the amount of direct investment that will be forthcoming. Nevertheless, the ability to enter freely into regional arrangements will maximise the extent and the probability of successful reform, and, by doing so, also maximise the number of countries that are induced to attempt reform.

In this framework, the global interest calls for successful reform to be as widespread as possible. This will maximise the extent of the multilateral trading system, accentuating both the benefits that it generates and the number of nations which receive those benefits. But this global externality will be ignored by multinational firms, who will be likely to cluster their foreign investments together. A single regional arrangement may be either good or bad in its results. But a *regional general equilibrium* as just described will in effect internalise the global externality and produce an outcome unambiguously superior to what can be achieved without regionalism.

The model of this and the preceding sections described the small-country participants as concerned with fundamental economic reform. But, although the small industrial countries entering into regional arrangements (e.g., Austria, Canada, Finland, Sweden) are also typically undertaking reforms, these reforms are hardly fundamental in the sense of what is happening in the third world or with the former communist countries.

For small industrialised nations, the model needs to be altered, but the basic analysis applies. For the small countries joining the EU, for example, the problem is not so much to attract new direct investment as to remain attractive sites, in an increasingly integrated world, for activities currently conducted there. The small advantages they obtain from regional arrangements are not additional preferences, but future participation in EU decision making.[10] Thus the basic story applies.

[9] These are sometimes called 'hub and spoke' arrangements. See Wonnacott (1996).

[10] For more on this, see Baldwin and Flam (1994).

6. Concluding Remarks

This paper has argued for a non-Vinerian analytical approach to regional integration, capable of explaining why the new regionalism has come about, and motivated by the stylised facts of the new regionalism and by the dramatic differences in international environment between the days of the old regionalism and today. The approach suggests the following relation of regionalism to multilateralism.

- The new regionalism is, in good part, a direct result of the success of multilateral liberalisation.
- Regionalism is the means by which new countries trying to enter the multilateral system (and small countries already in it) compete among themselves for the direct investment necessary for their successful participation in that system.
- Regionalism—by internalising an important externality—plays a key role in expanding and preserving the liberal trade order.

An individual regional arrangement may by itself do more harm than good. But widespread regionalism of the sort we are experiencing in effect internalises a critical global externality and produces an outcome superior to that obtainable by multilateralism alone.

My analytical framework has given a highly abstract picture of the world so that essentials stand out clearly. Additional detail of course adds ambiguity. Thus even someone who accepts with enthusiasm the basic arguments suggested above could well retain serious concerns about the new regionalism. I suggest four such grounds for concern.

- I have made assumptions that render trade diversion innocuous. In reality it remains a cause for concern, especially in some parts of the world.

Still, this just is not nearly as important now as it was thirty years ago. Under present conditions, a huge *volume* of trade diversion could well imply little effect on *welfare*.

- Even if regional arrangements have come into existence for the reasons indicated above, and even if they are in fact promoting successful reform, they still might ultimately lead to a break-up of the world economy into hostile blocs.

I see no signs that this is in fact about to happen, but things could change. The remaining two concerns, though, I regard as more significant than the first two.

- Protection-seeking, special-interest groups will always be with us, and the fact that regionalism is where the action is means that this is where the battles will be fought. Furthermore, the deeper integration characteristic of the new regionalism gives protectionists more avenues of attack.

This is a powerful reason to maintain a healthy level of vigilance and suspicion toward new regional initiatives.

- In the above theory regionalism plays a transitory, though critical, role in the reform process, but the regional arrangements themselves are permanent, so 'what happens next' matters.

But make no mistake: The bottom line of this paper is that the new regionalism reflects the success of multilateralism—not its failure.

University of Pennsylvania

References

Bagwell, K. and Staiger, R. W. (1996*a*), 'Multilateral tariff cooperation during the formation of customs unions.' *Journal of International Economics*. (forthcoming).

Bagwell, K. and Staiger, R. W. (1996*b*), 'Regionalism and multilateral tariff cooperation,' unpublished manuscript.

Bagwell, K. and Staiger, R. W. (1997), 'Multilateral tariff cooperation during the formation of free trade areas.' *International Economic Review*, vol. 38 (2), pp. 291–320.

Baldwin, R. E. and Flam, H. (1994), 'Enlargement of the European Union: the economic consequences for the Scandinavian countries.' CEPR Occasional Paper No. 16.

Bhagwati, J. and Panagariya, A. (1996), 'Preferential trading areas and multilateralism: strangers, friends or foes?' University of Maryland Center for International Economics Working Paper no. 22.

Bond, E. and Syropoulos, C. (1996), 'Trading blocs and the sustainability of inter-regional cooperation.' In (M. Canzoneri, W. J. Ethier and V. Grilli, eds.), *The New Transatlantic Economy*, Cambridge: Cambridge University Press, pp. 118–41.

Deardorff, A. V. (1995), 'Determinants of bilateral trade: does gravity work in a neoclassical world?' Discussion Paper No. 382, Research Forum on International Economics, University of Michigan.

Ethier, W. J. (1996), 'Regionalism in a multilateral world.' Working paper, Department of Economics, University of Pennsylvania. Forthcoming: *Journal of Political Economy*.

Ethier, W. J. (1997), 'Regional regionalism.' Working paper, Department of Economics, University of Pennsylvania.

Ethier, W. J. and Horn, H. (1984), 'A new look at economic integration.' In (H. Kierzkowski, ed.), *Monopolistic Competition and International Trade*, Oxford: Oxford University Press, pp. 207–29. Reprinted in (A. Jacquemin and A. Sapir, eds.) (1989), *The European Internal Market: Trade and Competition*, Oxford: Oxford University Press.

Garriga, M. and Sanguinetti, P. (1995). '¿Es el Mercosur un bloque natural? Efectos de la política comercial y la geografía sobre el intercambio regional.' *Estudios*, vol. 18 (73), pp. 59–68.

Garriga, M. and Sanguinetti, P. (1997). 'The determinants of regional trade in Mercosur: geography and commercial liberalisation.' Unpublished manuscript, Departamento de Economía, Universidad Torcuato Di Tella, Buenos Aires, Argentina.

Krugman, P. (1991), 'Is bilateralism bad?' In (E. Helpman and A. Razin, eds.), *International Trade and Trade Policy*, Cambridge MA: MIT Press.

Lipsey, R. G. (1960), 'The theory of customs unions: a general survey.' ECONOMIC JOURNAL vol. 70 (279), pp. 496–513. Reprinted in (R. E. Caves and H. G. Johnson) (1968), *Readings in International Economics*, Homewood: Richard D. Irwin.

Panagariya, A. (1996), 'The Meade model of preferential trading: history, analytics and policy implications.' University of Maryland Center for International Economics Working Paper No. 21.

Viner, J. (1950), *The Customs Union Issue*, New York: Carnegie Endowment for International Peace.

Wonnacott, R. J. (1996), 'Free-trade agreements: for better or worse?' *American Economic Review*, vol. 86 (2), pp. 62–6.

PART V:
The Political Economy of Trade Policy

The Political Economy of Trade Policy: *Commentary*

My main concern over the most recent decade or so has been the political economy of trade policy. Arye Hillman, my first grad student, who has himself made central contributions to the area, had long urged me to take it up. Eventually I did so.

The reason was that my work on regionalism, by its nature, had caused me to begin thinking about the overall functioning of the world commercial system. This was addressed in "Unilateralism in A Multilateral World," which concluded that a critical role could be played by policy administrators not concerned with maximizing national welfare, as discussed in the previous section. But this could not be a matter of policy delegation by trade-agreement negotiators, as they would never choose to so delegate (This is another of the papers that I regard as among my best).

A second reason for my concern with the political economy of trade policy is that it seemed to me that the dominant academic literature had it all wrong (Hillman, etc. excepted). This literature gives the central role to governmental concern about the terms of trade and about trade-tax revenue, a concern that I could not see was present at all in reality (as regards the industrial countries).

This found expression in "Political Externalities, Nondiscrimination, and A Multilateral World." I regard this as another of my badly-written papers, though in this case I have been unable to think of anyone else I could possibly blame for that (But I continue to work on it).

Another aspect of my concern with the dominant academic literature was its empirical component. I thought that this component was of great quality in itself, but that it related in a highly suspect way to both the theory and reality. This motivated the papers, "Selling 'Protection for Sale' and The Political-Support Approach to Protection." It also played a big role in the survey piece, "The Political Economy of Protection."

The theoretical literature on trade agreements emphasized the role of trigger strategies in sustaining repeated-game equilibria. This may or may not explain a desire by major countries to adhere to the international order in a general way. But it clearly had nothing to do with the WTO punishment mechanism in its dispute-settlement process. Thus my paper, "Punishments and Dispute Settlement in Trade Agreements: The Equivalent Withdrawal of Concessions." This attempted a theoretical analysis of the actual WTO dispute-settlement mechanism.

The Economic Journal, **112** (*April*), 266–292. Published by Blackwell Publishers, 108 Cowley Road, Oxford OX4 1JF, UK and 350 Main Street, Malden, MA 02148, USA.

UNILATERALISM IN A MULTILATERAL WORLD*

Wilfred J. Ethier

This paper addresses the interplay between unilateralism and multilateralism. I describe their stylised facts and present a simple, multi-country model with high initial tariffs and features that have always been of paramount concern to policy makers, and allow governments to negotiate multilateral agreements. I then find a role for a system with features remarkably similar to contemporary unilateralism. The relationships between multilateralism and unilateralism are subtle: Unilateralism has the properties it has because the world is multilateral (the *insurance triangle*); useful unilateralism requires a *multilateral component* resulting from a *compatibility problem* between those who negotiate multilaterally and those who establish unilateralism.

International trade policy has a split personality. As the nations of the world have gradually and collectively adopted historically low levels of protection for more than half a century, they have gradually and individually initiated protectionist actions at an increasing pace. What's going on here?

1. Introduction

Contemporary international trade policy is built upon two pillars: *multilateralism* (the rounds of multilateral trade negotiations sponsored by the General Agreement on Tariffs and Trade (GATT) and the multilateral World Trade Organisation (WTO)); *unilateralism* (rules – explicit and implicit – for national governments to respond to political pressures for protection).[1] This paper concerns the relationship between these two components and the nature of the system they jointly determine. I shall argue that neither can be properly understood in isolation, and that familiar tools of trade policy appear in a dramatically different light when the two are treated together.

My analysis will be positive, but conclusions will have normative applications. In particular, I shall address the following basic questions: How do the two components, and their interactions, determine the pace of trade liberalisation? Why does unilateralism take the very special form that it does?

In what follows, I first describe the stylised facts of multilateralism and unilateralism. I next present a multi-country model with high initial tariff barriers. These initial barriers would not have been chosen by the policy makers in the model

* I gratefully acknowledge useful comments from Arye Hillman, Henrik Horn, and Rodney Ludema, from referees of this JOURNAL, and from helpful discussions during presentations of this research at EPRU in Copenhagen, the Institute of World Economics in Kiel, the ISER at Osaka University; the RIEB at Kobe University; Doshisha, Keio, Konstanz, Southern Methodist, Texas A&M, Tohoku and Tokyo Universities; the Universities of Helsinki, Maryland, New Orleans, Paris I, Texas and Wisconsin; the 1999 North American Summer Meetings of the Econometric Society.

[1] A third pillar – regionalism – has been resurrected during the past decade, but I shall ignore this below because I have discussed it at length elsewhere (Ethier, 1998*a*, *c*). See Ethier (1998*b*) for a discussion of why multilateralism is what it is, Ethier (2001) for an overview of multilateralism and unilateralism, and Ethier (1998*d*) for an overview of the relation between unilateralism, multilateralism and regionalism.

subsequently presented. Rather, the barriers are assumed to be a legacy of an earlier, different, regime (just as, in the decades since World War II, the world has had to deal with the protection resulting from the radically different inter-war years), but the existence of these barriers produces special interests that resist their removal. Governments negotiate successive tariff reductions in a sequence of periods – a caricature of the GATT negotiating rounds of the last 5–6 decades.

My model is very special but not arbitrary: I attempt to find the simplest structure consistent with the two concerns that have dominated tariff negotiations for centuries:

(i) Dealing with special interests that desire protection
(ii) Negotiators' concerns that the *ex post* environment may turn out significantly different from what they expected when they made the agreements.

This is achieved by the assumed sequence of moves within each period.

First, forward-looking labour allocates itself between the export and import-competing sectors, remaining for the rest of the period specific to the sector it has chosen. Next, governments negotiate tariff reductions. After this, a technology shock occurs. Then trade takes place, with the new technology and constrained by the negotiated tariffs. Because negotiations occur when labour is sector specific, there are special interests; because the negotiations occur before the technology draw, the governments do not then know to what environment the results of those negotiations will apply.

I describe a process of multilateral negotiation resulting in steady liberalisation at a moderate rate. I next investigate the possible role of a system of rules allowing countries, whose import-competing sectors face competition from exports from countries with a favourable technology draw, to impose temporary protection. If such protection also benefits those countries whose exporters must compete with the countries with a favourable technology draw, while being acceptable to the latter (the 'insurance triangle'), it can accelerate the rate of liberalisation and increase the allocation of resources to comparative-advantage sectors. But a time-consistency problem compounded by an externality ensures that negotiators would never themselves adopt such rules for their respective countries: The 'split personality' of trade policy is essential. In short, features remarkably similar to contemporary unilateralism turn out to be crucial, with subtle and essential relationships to multilateralism, that cannot be understood in a two-country context.

2. The Background

This section briefly describes the essential features of multilateralism and of unilateralism motivating the subsequent model.

2.1. *The Stylised Facts of Multilateralism*

I mean the entire GATT–WTO structure, but shall distil it into six stylised facts.

1 *Tariffs* are the instruments of protection.
2 The countries of the world *multilaterally* negotiate tariff reductions.

3 The negotiated liberalisation is *gradual.*
4 Negotiated agreements feature *reciprocity*: the mutual exchange of concessions.
5 *Nondiscrimination* characterises trading relations: each country is a most favoured nation (MFN) of every other country.[2]
6 Punishments for alleged violations of past agreements have consistently been *commensurate with the violation*, that is, tit-for-tat.

Reducing multilateralism to these stylised facts is deficient in one way. Multilateral liberalisation has increasingly shifted from the further reduction of already reduced tariffs to *broadening* liberalisation into additional areas, notably agriculture, services and intellectual property. Attention has necessarily shifted to government policies other than tariffs. Consideration of these would not alter the following argument, so I abstract from them and pretend that continued multilateral liberalisation is only the continued reduction of tariffs.

In an earlier paper (Ethier, 1998*b*), I used a model like that which follows to show how, with initial high protection consisting only of tariffs, most of the other stylised facts — multilateral negotiations, gradual liberalisation, reciprocity and MFN — will develop endogenously, if government behaviour is dictated by a political support function consistent with how governments claim to behave, and if reasonable substitutes for each country's exports are produced elsewhere. Therefore, in this paper, I shall simply take the stylised facts of multilateralism as given. Other authors have also discussed why multilateralism has the properties it has; see Staiger (1995) for a discussion of earlier contributions. The recent papers that come closest to addressing these same properties are Bagwell and Staiger (1999*a*, *b*).

2.2. *The Stylised Facts of Unilateralism*

Unilateralism consists of *rules for intervention* rather than *tariff rates*, and both the nature of the rules and the way they are used have been changing over time. The more important rules, and the changing use, are described in Appendix I. Here I identify five stylised facts that characterise – more or less – a common denominator for the rules of unilateralism.[3]

2.2.1. *Exporters are compensated, at least in part* Rents generated by voluntary export restraints (VERs) accrue to the exporters, who administer the quotas. Usually, the exporting firms themselves capture the rents. Safeguards explicitly require that exporters be compensated, but the compensation is to the exporting *country* rather than the exporting *firms.*

Antidumping and countervailing duties are ostensibly tariffs, but a closer look at how these instruments are actually used reveals that they also confer significant compensation.

[2] One country extends MFN status to another if the former agrees that goods from the latter will never face a duty higher than the duty applied to similar goods from any other country. In practice, this raises the issue of defining 'similar goods', but I shall abstract from such problems.
[3] See also Hillman (1982, 1990).

Roughly one third of US antidumping petitions result in duties, about one third are rejected, and the others are withdrawn. Of these, many are withdrawn after a settlement between domestic and foreign firms. Typically, the foreign firms collectively undertake to raise prices or restrict exports. Prusa (1992) reports that withdrawn petitions restrict trade almost as much, on average, as petitions resulting in duties, implying that negotiated settlements are, on average, more restrictive than antidumping duties.

If, instead, a petition does produce an antidumping duty, the result is usually higher export prices, not tariff revenue. Tariffs collected are often rebated when authorities determine, *ex post*, that the goods were not, in fact, dumped.[4] The exporter, realising that the price in the importing country is going to rise by the dumping margin no matter what he or she does, raises the export price by that amount. The purpose of an antidumping law is *not* to impose temporarily a conventional tariff; it is to force exporters to raise prices. Just as with VERs, the exporters usually get the rents.[5]

I do not claim that unilateralism benefits foreign firms, or that it leaves them more or less indifferent. This is possible. But the first stylised fact of unilateralism is just that *countries denied market access receive significant – if only partial – compensation.*

It is curious that governments should want, in effect, to hand over tariff revenue to foreigners. But this is exactly what they do, routinely, in the conduct of unilateralism. Why? I shall argue that unilateralism is what it is because of successful multilateralism.

2.2.2. *The instruments provide temporary (at least in original intent) protection* Temporary measures are not necessarily short-lived: they can be renewed. Renewals allow for adjustments and so add *flexibility* (relative to measures that require congressional action and/or multilateral negotiation).

2.2.3. *The restrictions are discriminatory* Some industries have displayed a comprehensive web of voluntary export restraints (e.g. textiles and apparel), but individual VERs are bilateral and thus inherently discriminatory.

Antidumping and countervailing duty laws are WTO-consistent, but discriminatory, since they apply to the products of specific countries. Safeguards alone are nondiscriminatory. So it is significant that their use has greatly declined relative to that of the other three instruments and that, in the future, it will sometimes be permissible to employ them in a discriminatory manner.

[4] But, in the USA at least, the importer will incur additional liability if it is determined that the goods were, in fact, dumped by more than the duty. This implies that it is riskier to buy goods from a country against which there is an outstanding dumping determination than from some other source at the same price.

[5] Usually, but not always. Sometimes the duty is large enough to reduce imports drastically, or to eliminate them altogether, so that the higher price is little consolation to exporters. Sometimes, (particularly in Europe) administration hinders the ability of the exporter to capture the price rise. And countries not in the WTO may apply the label 'antidumping law' to any sort of protectionist measure.

2.2.4. *Tariff-quota equivalence is high* The proposition of tariff-quota equivalence asserts that any equilibrium that can be supported by a tariff policy can also be supported by an appropriate quota policy, and *vice versa.* However, tariffs and quotas are seldom equivalent in fact. If an equilibrium is disturbed, the response depends on whether a tariff or a quota is in place, so if a policy must be implemented before all circumstances are known, it matters what tool is used. Unilateralism is one theatre where tariff-quota equivalence is really relevant: each instrument seeks to attain a particular outcome with a restriction that can be readjusted frequently. So it matters little whether the restriction is quantitative.

2.2.5. *The restrictions are designed by officials distinct from those who negotiate international trade agreements* This applies to some degree to most industrial countries, but most dramatically to the USA. For over 60 years, the Congress has repeatedly ceded to the executive considerable authority to set actual tariff levels via reciprocal trade negotiations and, throughout this period, the executive has consistently been less protectionist than Congress. Yet, at the same time, Congress has repeatedly revised the laws governing administered protection to limit executive discretion and to make protection a more likely response to petitions for relief.

3. The Model

I now describe a simple formal model of successive multilateralism. I will then inquire into the possibility of a role for unilateralism. I construct the model to reflect those features of the world that, in fact, have been of the most concern to policy makers. Since this is necessarily subjective to at least some degree, I shall, from time to time, pause to defend a modelling choice.

3.1. *The Constituents*

Assume two goods, A and B, one factor of production, labour (L), and $2N$ identical (almost) countries. Normalise $L = 1$ for each country. Everyone spends equally on the two goods. N countries have a comparative advantage in A and N in B. Labour productivity is αa in the comparative-advantage good and a in the other good, with $\alpha > 1$. I will examine symmetric equilibria in which each country makes the same allocation, ℓ, to the comparative advantage sector.

Assume a succession of periods. Labour is mobile between sectors across periods, but immobile within each period. Initially, each country starts with a common, historically given, tariff t on all imports and an initial state, a, of technology. The state of the world each period is indicated by (t, a), since t and a will remain common to all countries across the symmetric equilibria I consider. At the start of each period, countries differ from each other *only* in regard to which sector possesses a comparative advantage.

Technology is improving across periods. Since my topic is trade policy rather than growth, I am content to assume that this occurs at an exogenously determined rate, that is, $\Delta a/a = \beta - 1 > 0$. Technical progress, regardless of where it originates, spills over – subject to a qualification introduced below – to all countries: It constitutes an international externality.

3.2. *Negotiators' Objectives*

Governments may negotiate tariff reductions. I want an objective function accurately reflecting how government negotiators behave; I build on Corden's (1997, pp. 74–6) description of a *conservative* social welfare function: governments avoid policies that would seriously harm any interest group. In particular, I assume that, in each period, each government's negotiators want to maximise

$$\phi(\tau) = \Delta r_x(\tau) - [-\Delta r_m(\tau)]^{1+\gamma} \tag{1}$$

where τ denotes the rate of tariff reduction

$$\left(\frac{-\dot{t}}{1+t}\right)$$

Δr_x the negotiators' perception of the increase in the real reward of the factor specific to exports, and Δr_m the negotiators' perception of the increase in the real reward of the factor specific to imports.[6]

Appendix II shows that liberalisation will cause $\Delta r_x > 0$ and $\Delta r_m < 0$, with a positive gain overall. So, liberalisation will be desirable if either γ or the degree of liberalisation is modest enough. The parameter γ measures the negotiators' averseness to allowing anyone to suffer a large loss: the *Corden sensitivity*.

3.3. *Sequence of Moves Within Each Period*

At the start of each period, the common tariff and technology, (t, a), is inherited from the close of the previous period. The following sequence then takes place.

- First, L allocates itself among A and B. The allocations become specific for the rest of the period, so each worker decides which sector to enter based on his/her rational forecast of the real rewards that will be offered in the respective sectors during the current period.
- Second, the governments negotiate tariff reductions. These negotiations will be multilateral and feature nondiscrimination. I assume that each government, like the owners of L, does not look beyond the current period, but is forward-looking within that period.
- Third, some countries succeed in anticipating the technological improvement that will be generally realised at the end of the period: $n < N$ of the exporters of one of the goods will now have the large technology gain, $\Delta a/a = \beta - 1$, for their exportables. The identities of the good and of the specific exporters of that good that will succeed in anticipating the technological improvement is determined by a random draw (so, if $\pi \equiv n/N$, then $\pi/2 =$ the probability of

[6] The results that follow would not be qualitatively affected if the objective function were over real incomes instead of over real rewards.

early technical progress for each country). NB: the identity of the gainers (both which good and which countries) is determined *after* the negotiations.

- Fourth, tariff reductions are implemented and trade is realised. The latter will be described subsequently. In each country, tariff revenue is distributed to the populace in lump-sum fashion.
- Finally, the period ends, Δa is realised by all countries and both sectors for the next period, and the negotiated t becomes the initial t for the next period, when new governments will again determine policy.

I intend a period to correspond, in some rough fashion, to the time between the start of one GATT round and the start of the next. I have tried to build the simplest model I can that captures the two features that have always been paramount to those undertaking trade negotiations:

(i) The existence of divergent special interests
(ii) Concern that any agreement might have unforeseen and unfavourable future consequences

This is achieved by my description of within-period timing, which will be crucial to what follows. The assumption that factors are specific when negotiations take place produces the divergent interests.

The assumption that negotiations are conducted before the economic environment to which their results will apply is fully known serves to introduce the second paramount feature.[7] This point has, in fact, always been (since long before the GATT) of acute concern to policy makers. Trade agreements routinely included safeguards (then known as *escape clauses*) enabling participants to readjust their concessions should events not turn out as they had hoped. When the USA first established safeguards as a matter of law, material injury had to be due to increased imports *and* the latter had to be due to a prior trade concession. The GATT itself provided, in Article XXVIII, opportunities for the modification or withdrawal of concessions.

Introducing additional instruments could neutralise both features. Lump-sum transfers would deal with the first, and the ability to implement fully state-contingent trade agreements would do it for the latter. The absence of both instruments from my model does no violence to its realism.

4. Multilateralism

Labour allocates itself across sectors on the basis of a rational forecast of the rate of liberalisation that governments will subsequently negotiate, and when those negotiations take place the allocation of labour is given. I first investigate what rate of liberalisation will be negotiated for a given allocation ℓ, and then go backwards to investigate what labour, armed with an understanding of this relation between ℓ and liberalisation, will actually do.

[7] For example, participants in prior GATT rounds had not known that Japanese automobile firms would become the most efficient producers in the late 1970s.

4.1. *Multilateral Negotiations*

What rate of tariff reduction will be negotiated? At the negotiations, governments know the allocation of resources, but they do not know which countries will be the leaders, the followers (whose exporters compete with the leaders), and the laggards (who import from the leaders) when the tariff reductions are implemented. I assume no external commitment mechanism: a government will actually implement the reduction it has agreed to only if, *ex post*, that government believes its interests will be served by doing so, taking into account credible threats of retaliation.

I assume the retaliation is tit-for-tat. That is, if Country 1 lowers its tariff 5% less than promised, its trading partners follow suit. Why tit-for-tat? The sixth stylised fact of multilateralism (*punishments for alleged violations of past agreements have consistently been commensurate with the violation, that is, tit-for-tat*) gives me little choice. When countries retaliate or threaten to retaliate against some alleged transgression by a trading partner, they consistently emphasise that the threatened retaliation is commensurate with the transgression (i.e. tit-for-tat). The WTO and the GATT before it have consistently operated on the premise that punishment should match violation. Countries have often squabbled over which tit matches what tat, or whether there was a tat in the first place, but as far as I know no country has ever challenged the principle. Given my goal of modelling countries as they actually behave, this makes the tit-for-tat assumption compelling.[8]

Note also that tit-for-tat punishment fits neatly into the present model. With the symmetric equilibria that I consider, such a threat will be well-defined.

Furthermore, the use of tit-for-tat in my model implies government behaviour very much in the spirit of the Corden political support function I use. To see this, note that such a threat can support any negotiated tariff reduction which, *ex post*, every country wants to have generally adopted. However, it can support no reduction in excess of what any country regards, *ex post*, as optimal. Thus the outcome of the multilateral negotiation will be: the smallest of the various tariff reductions which, if generally adopted, would maximise *ex post* the objective functions of the respective negotiating governments. That is, no government negotiator will be taking the risk that its import competing sector might have to take a bigger hit than that negotiator would have been willing to allow.

4.2. *Negotiated Multilateral Liberalisation*

Let P_i and Q_i respectively denote international and domestic relative prices of B in terms of A, when the technical advance occurs first in good i, $i = A, B$. An asterisk distinguishes the country with a comparative advantage in B. Then, with t common to all countries,

$$Q_i = P_i(1+t) \qquad \frac{1}{Q_i^*} = \frac{1+t}{P_i}$$

[8] Adding a lag between deviation and retaliation would complicate the following algebra without affecting the essentials of the argument.

We have, recalling that ℓ denotes the labour allocated to the comparative-advantage sector, (see Appendix 2 for details)

$$P_A(\ell, t) = \pi(\beta - 1)\frac{\alpha\ell}{\alpha\ell + (1+t)(1-\ell)} + 1$$

if A is the leader, and $P_i = P_B = 1/P_A$ if B is the leader. Then $P_A > 1 > P_B$.

The hypothesised spending pattern is consistent with the following indirect utility function:

$$v = Q^{-1/2} I \tag{2}$$

where I denotes income in terms of good A. Factors are paid the values of their marginal products, so that their real rewards, using the utility function (2), are as follows, for a country with a comparative advantage in A:

$$r_x^L = \frac{\beta\alpha a}{Q_A^{1/2}} \qquad r_x^F = \frac{\alpha a}{Q_A^{1/2}} \qquad r_x^G = \frac{\alpha a}{Q_B^{1/2}} \tag{3}$$

$$r_m^L = aQ_A^{1/2} \qquad r_m^F = aQ_A^{1/2} \qquad r_m^G = aQ_B^{1/2} \tag{4}$$

Let

$$\tau^i = \left(\frac{-\dot{t}_i}{1+t}\right)$$

denote the rate of tariff reduction optimal *ex post* for a country that ends up in state i = L (leader), F (follower) or G (laggard). For simplicity, I consider a continuous-time approximation to the negotiated rate of tariff reduction. Then, the *ex post* value of each country's objective function reduces to

$$\phi(\tau) = -\frac{\mathrm{d}r_x^i}{\mathrm{d}t}(\tau) - \left[\frac{\mathrm{d}r_m^i}{\mathrm{d}t}(\tau)\right]^{1+\gamma}$$

where i denotes the state the country finds itself in *ex post*. If $\gamma = 0$, ϕ can be made arbitrarily large by making τ arbitrarily large: The government will want free trade at once. I will accordingly refer to the Corden sensitivity γ, which reflects the government's reluctance to let any sector experience a large hit, as the *willingness to protect*. Now

$$\frac{\mathrm{d}r_x^{\mathrm{L}}}{\mathrm{d}t} = -\frac{\beta\alpha a}{2P_A^{1/2}}(1+t)^{-3/2} = -\frac{r_x^{\mathrm{L}}}{2(1+t)}$$

and

$$\frac{\mathrm{d}r_m^{\mathrm{L}}}{\mathrm{d}t} = \frac{a}{2}(1+t)^{-1/2}P_A^{1/2} = \frac{r_m^{\mathrm{L}}}{2(1+t)}$$

etc. The first-order condition that τ maximise the objective function, given the value of P_i, reduces to

$$(\tau^i)^\gamma = \frac{-\left(\frac{\mathrm{d}r_x^i}{\mathrm{d}t}\right)}{(1+\gamma)\left(\frac{\mathrm{d}r_m^i}{\mathrm{d}t}\right)^{1+\gamma}(1+t)^\gamma}$$

where $i = $ L, F, or G. Substituting yields

$$(\tau^{\mathrm{L}})^{\gamma} = \frac{\beta\alpha}{\left(\frac{a}{2}\right)^{\gamma}} \frac{Q_A^{-1-\frac{\gamma}{2}}}{1+\gamma} \qquad (\tau^{\mathrm{F}})^{\gamma} = \frac{\alpha}{\left(\frac{a}{2}\right)^{\gamma}} \frac{Q_A^{-1-\frac{\gamma}{2}}}{1+\gamma} \qquad (\tau^{\mathrm{G}})^{\gamma} = \frac{\alpha}{\left(\frac{a}{2}\right)^{\gamma}} \frac{Q_B^{-1-\frac{\gamma}{2}}}{1+\gamma}$$

Since $\beta > 1$, $\tau^{\mathrm{L}} > \tau^{\mathrm{F}}$ and $Q_A > Q_B$ implies that $\tau^{\mathrm{G}} > \tau^{\mathrm{F}}$. Intuitively, leaders prefer a relatively liberal regime because of their technological advantage. Laggards take a hit in their import-competing sector, but this is ameliorated by a more favourable terms of trade. Followers, competing with the advantaged leaders in export markets, take the hit in their export sectors, with no terms of trade improvement.

PROPOSITION 1. *The multilaterally negotiated rate of tariff reduction, τ^{M}, equals the rate most preferred, ex post, by those countries that turn out to be the followers:*

$$\tau^{\mathrm{M}} = \left[\frac{\alpha}{\left(\frac{a}{2}\right)^{\gamma}} \frac{1}{1+\gamma}\right]^{\frac{1}{\gamma}} \left[\frac{1}{P_A(1+t)}\right]^{\frac{1}{\gamma}+\frac{1}{2}} \tag{5}$$

Proposition 1 in turn implies $\partial\tau^{\mathrm{M}}/\partial\gamma < 0$, $\partial\tau^{\mathrm{M}}/\partial l > 0$ and $\partial\tau^{\mathrm{M}}/\partial t < 0$. Thus,

PROPOSITION 2. *A greater willingness to protect implies a smaller rate of tariff reduction, and the rate of tariff reduction accelerates over successive rounds.*

4.3. *The Allocation of Resources*

Consider next where labour, understanding the above negotiating process, will have chosen to locate. Let r_i, $i = x, m$, denote the expected quasi-rent of labour specific to sector i, where x refers to the sector in which a country has a comparative advantage. Then

$$r_i = \frac{\pi}{2} r_i^{\mathrm{L}} + \frac{1-\pi}{2} r_i^{\mathrm{F}} + \frac{1}{2} r_i^{\mathrm{G}} \tag{6}$$

where r_i^{L}, r_i^{F}, and r_i^{G} respectively denote the rent when the country is a technological leader, has a comparative advantage in the leading good but is not itself a leader (i.e. is a follower), and has a comparative advantage in the laggard good.[9]

The *ex post* real quasi-rents (3) and (4) imply the expected returns to the quasi-specific factors, *net* of tariff revenue:

$$r_x(P_A, t) = \frac{\alpha a}{2(1+t)^{1/2}} \left[\frac{\pi(\beta-1)+1}{P_A^{1/2}} + P_A^{1/2}\right]$$

$$r_m(P_A, t) = \frac{a}{2}(1+t)^{1/2}\left(\frac{1}{P_A^{1/2}} + P_A^{1/2}\right)$$

[9] For example, in the early 1980s, the Japanese automobile firms, having developed 'lean' production methods, were the leaders, the high-cost European and fledgling Korean firms the followers, and the import-competing US firms the laggards.

Here, t has the value that labour expects to pertain after the subsequent negotiations: $t = t_1 - \tau^M(1 + t_1)$, where t_1 denotes the tariff inherited from the previous period. Assume that labour allocates itself between sectors according to the relative expected quasi-rents. Note that $r_x(P_A,0) > r_m(P_A,0)$: If free trade were expected *ex ante*, no labour would allocate itself to the import competing sector. If in fact $r_m = r_x$,

$$\alpha\frac{\pi(\beta - 1) + P_A(\ell, t) + 1}{P_A(\ell, t) + 1} = 1 + t \tag{7}$$

Let t° solve this equation for $\ell = 1$. Then, when the forecast value of t falls at least to t°, labour will allocate itself fully to the comparative advantage sector. I assume that, at this point, Δr_m receives zero weight in the government's objective function: Multilateral negotiations will deliver free trade.

Next, consider the responsiveness of the quasi-rents to the allocation of labour:

$$\frac{\ell}{r_x}\frac{\partial r_x}{\partial \ell} = \frac{1}{2}\frac{P_A - 1 - \pi(\beta - 1)}{P_A + 1 + \pi(\beta - 1)}\left(\frac{\ell}{P_A}\frac{\mathrm{d}P_A}{\mathrm{d}\ell}\right)$$

$$\frac{\ell}{r_m}\frac{\partial r_m}{\partial \ell} = \frac{1}{2}\frac{P_A - 1}{P_A + 1}\left(\frac{\ell}{P_A}\frac{\mathrm{d}P_A}{\mathrm{d}\ell}\right)$$

Now,

$$\frac{\mathrm{d}P_A}{\mathrm{d}\ell} = \frac{\partial P_A}{\partial \ell} + \left(\frac{\partial P_A}{\partial t}\right)\left(\frac{\partial t}{\partial \ell}\right) = \frac{\partial P_A}{\partial \ell} + \left(\frac{\partial P_A}{\partial t}\right)t_1\left(-\frac{\partial \tau^M}{\partial \ell}\right)$$

This expression is positive, by the definition of $P_A(\ell, t)$ and by Proposition 2. Thus r_m and r_x will be positively related to ℓ and r_x will increase proportionally less in response to a rise in ℓ than will r_m, so, in a neighbourhood of $r_m = r_x$

$$\frac{\partial r_x}{\partial \ell} < \frac{\partial r_m}{\partial \ell}$$

This ensures stability of the process whereby labour allocates itself between sectors, in response to the rational forecast of t, to equilibrate the quasi-rents (see Fig. 1).

PROPOSITION 3. *Suppose that t, the common tariff expected to prevail after this period's negotiations are complete, is greater than* t°. *Then the equilibrium allocation of labour is determined by* (7).

Next, I investigate the implications for resource allocation of a common rate of tariff reduction. Implicit differentiation of (7) yields

$$\frac{\mathrm{d}\ell}{\mathrm{d}t} = \frac{\dfrac{[P_A(\ell, t) + 1]^2}{\alpha\pi(\beta - 1)} - \dfrac{\partial P_A}{\partial t}}{\dfrac{\partial P_A}{\partial \ell}} < 0$$

by definition of $P_A(\ell, t)$.

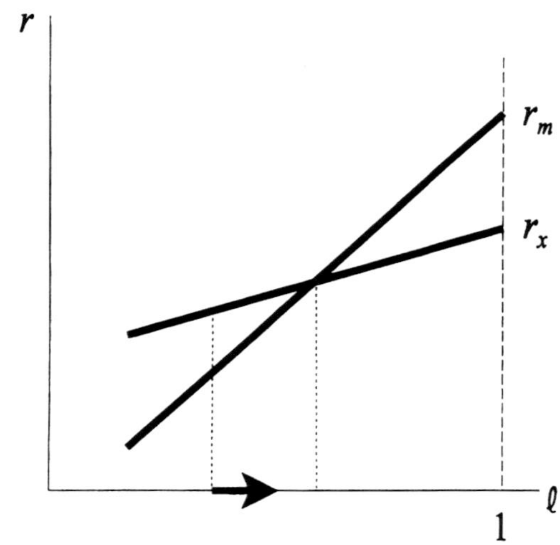

Fig. 1.

Geometrically, the expectation of liberalisation in the negotiations to come shifts the *ex ante* r_m schedule down and the *ex ante* r_x schedule up, implying that the equilibrium ℓ rises. When the expected tariff falls as low as t°, it instantaneously falls to zero. All labour allocates itself to the comparative advantage sector.

The theory of gradual multilateral liberalisation developed in this section can be interpreted as based on time inconsistency. Labour allocates itself to the comparative-disadvantage sector because it knows that, once it is allocated there, the government will not negotiate protection away. Could the government credibly commit to free trade, no labour would enter the comparative-disadvantage sector. Thus there would exist no interest opposed to free trade. Staiger and Tabellini (1987) provide a related analysis.

5. Unilateralism

The rate of multilateral tariff reduction is limited to the lowest reduction any country would prefer *ex post.* Perhaps, as Bagwell and Staiger (1990) argued in another context, a system of unilateralism can improve on this. Would such a system be developed and used? What would it look like? The following subsection argues intuitively what properties such a system should have to produce affirmative answers, and this is followed by a formal analysis.

5.1. *The Potential for Unilateralism*

Suppose countries establish, before some negotiating round, a rule stipulating circumstances under which, *after* the completion of negotiations and *after* the revelation of which goods and countries are the technological leaders, protection might be granted to beleaguered import-competing interests. Since the purpose is to preserve, at least partly, an outcome for special interests in the face of unanticipated developments, they should be either quantitative or sufficiently nimble in execution that it does not matter whether they are quantitative (i.e. tariff-quota equivalence).

The countries that turn out to be laggards could *ex post* apply such a rule. Would they wish to do so? Clearly they would not if they were confident that this would prompt retaliation: This would be a roll-back of the negotiated tariff reductions which are already less than what the laggards want *ex post*. So, would the leaders retaliate? Such a roll-back would move the common tariff reduction even further from what the leaders would want. Still, if the laggards unilaterally increase protection, the leaders are likely to retaliate. Unilateral protection would be *concession reneging*: Since the leaders do not receive all the market access they had bargained for, they will not want to grant all the access they have promised. If everyone realises the leaders will retaliate, such a rule would be of no value. It would be neither instituted nor used, *unless* the rule eliminates the motive to retaliate.

To make concession reneging acceptable, the rule could *compensate* the leaders. They need not be fully compensated, just enough so that they do not forsake the compensation by retaliating instead. Allowing them the trade rents generated by the unilateral measures would contribute to this. There may be a second source of compensation as well: a greater common tariff reduction, if unilateralism allows that to be negotiated.

To see when that might happen, consider the followers. They end up competing, at a disadvantage, with the leaders in the import markets of the laggards. The rents associated with unilateral protection would be worth much less to the followers, with no cost reductions, than to the leaders. Also, they would not gain from any increase in tariff reduction. So, prospects are dim that these countries would be compensated enough to forestall retaliation. More important, since the followers' preferences determine the rate of common tariff reduction, no increase would in fact take place; indeed, that rate may well decrease. Thus the whole case for unilateralism will unravel unless the interests of the followers are addressed. For this reason, the unilateral measures should be *discriminatory*. If they apply to the leaders but not to the followers, the latter would have nothing to retaliate against. The unilateral measures would, instead, enhance the ability of the followers to compete in the markets of the laggards. Consequently, they would now prefer a greater common rate of tariff reduction: the negotiated tariff reduction should increase.

The above argument assigns leaders, followers and laggards distinct roles in the exercise of unilateralism, but the identification of these countries is fixed only for the current period. Thus the unilateral measures should be *temporary* – for the rest of the current period only.

HYPOTHESIS *Multilateralism may induce the introduction of tools of temporary unilateral protection that are quantitative, discriminatory and give compensation to restrained exporters. Such an introduction might accelerate the rate of multilateral tariff reduction.*

Note that four of the five stylised facts of unilateralism have been utilised. I now turn to a formal analysis.

5.2. *A Model of Unilateralism*

I now model unilateralism as a rule allowing laggard countries, after the realisation of the technology draw, to apply temporary (i.e., for the rest of the current period only) quantitative restraints on imports from the leaders, allowing the latter the resulting trade rents. Let ρ denote the (randomly selected) fraction of the leaders whose imports will be restrained by all laggards. I treat ρ as exogenous and use it to index *breadth* of unilateralism. Restrained leaders can export only $X_{RL} = \delta X_F + (1 - \delta) X_{UL}$, where X_F denotes the volume exported by followers and X_{UL} that exported by unrestrained leaders. The parameter δ $(0 \leq \delta \leq 1)$, also exogenous, will index the *intensity* of unilateralism. This model reflects the properties both argued for in the previous subsection and described in Section 2.

Suppose the leaders have a comparative advantage in A. Then, with the assumed tastes, *followers* be in equilibrium when

$$Q_A\left(B + \frac{X_F}{P_A}\right) = A - X_F. \tag{8}$$

Equilibrium for the *unrestrained leaders* requires

$$Q_A\left(B + \frac{X_{UL}}{P_A}\right) = A_L - X_{UL} \tag{9}$$

where X_{UL} denotes exports of the unrestrained leaders and A_L production by the leaders of good A. For the *restrained leaders*:

$$Q_A^{RL}\left(B + \frac{X_{RL}}{P_A}\right) = A_L - X_{RL} \tag{10}$$

where Q_A^{RL} denotes the relative domestic price of imports for the restrained leaders. From (9) and (10), $X_{UL} > X_{RL}$, which implies that $Q_A^{RL} > Q_A$. X denotes the average level of A exports:

$$X = (1 - \pi)X_F + \rho\pi X_{RL} + (1 - \rho)\pi X_{UL} = [1 - \pi(1 - \rho\delta)]X_F + \pi(1 - \rho\delta)X_{UL}$$

Finally, for the *laggards*,

$$Q_A^*\left(B^* - \frac{X}{P_A}\right) = A^* + X$$

Now, (8) and (9) imply

$$Q_A\left(B + \frac{X}{P_A}\right) = \tilde{A} - X$$

where $\tilde{A} = [1 - \pi(1 - \rho\delta)]A + \pi(1 - \rho\delta)A_L$. From this and the above,

$$P_A(\ell, t; \rho, \delta) = \frac{\tilde{A} + (1 + t)A^*}{B^* + (1 + t)B}$$

so that $\partial P_A/\partial\rho,\ \partial Q_A/\partial\rho,\ \partial P_A/\partial\delta, \partial Q_A/\partial\delta < 0$

Also,

$$X = \frac{\tilde{A}B^* + (1+t)^2 A^* B}{(2+t)[B^* + (1+t)B]}$$

Furthermore, (8) and (9) imply

$$X_{UL} - X_F = \frac{A_L - A}{2+t}$$

while (8) and (10) give

$$Q_A^{RL} = Q_A \frac{A_L - X_{RL}}{\hat{A} - X_{RL}} \tag{11}$$

where $\hat{A} = \delta A + (1-\delta)A_L$.

5.3. *The Followers*

Suppose that the breadth ρ of unilateralism is raised above zero, with δ fixed at some positive level. I now investigate whether, as expected, this will improve the fate of the countries that turn out to be followers by reducing competition in their export markets from the leaders. For a given common tariff t and rate of tariff reduction τ, the value of the objective function of each follower government will be

$$\phi(\tau) = \frac{\alpha a}{2} Q_A^{-1/2}\tau - \left(\frac{a}{2} Q_A^{1/2}\tau\right)^{1+\gamma}$$

Each government, realising its country is small, takes P_A as independent of its own actions, but this common value will be affected by the increase in ρ. Consider the marginal effect on the ϕ of each follower government of increasing ρ *after* τ has been implemented.

$$\left.\frac{\partial \phi^F}{\partial \rho}\right|_\tau = -\frac{\dfrac{\rho}{Q_A}\dfrac{\partial Q_A}{\partial \rho}}{2\rho}\left[\frac{\alpha a}{2}\frac{1}{Q_A^{1/2}} + (1+\gamma)\left(\frac{a}{2}Q_A^{1/2}\right)^{1+\gamma}\frac{1}{\tau}\right] \tag{12}$$

Then, since $\partial Q_A/\partial \rho < 0$, an increase in ρ will always raise the ϕ of each follower government, at any τ. So these governments would welcome the exercise of unilateralism, and they would prefer its breadth to be comprehensive ($\rho = 1$) and its intensity complete ($\delta = 1$). Furthermore, it follows from (5) that $\partial\tau^M/\partial\rho > 0$, $\partial\tau^M/\partial\delta > 0$, implying that a system of unilateralism will cause the negotiated liberalisation rate to increase and that the increase will be greater the greater the breadth and intensity of unilateralism.

PROPOSITION 4. *If unilateralism without retaliation is introduced, the negotiated rate of liberalisation will increase, the governments of the countries that turn out to be followers will be better off, and these governments would wish unilateralism to be comprehensive and complete (which would also maximise the rate of liberalisation).*

5.4. *The Unrestrained Leaders*

I next investigate whether, as expected, the increase in ρ would benefit unrestrained leaders. Again, there are no surprises. For a given common t and rate of tariff reduction τ, the value of the objective function of each unrestrained leader government will be

$$\phi^{\mathrm{UL}} = \frac{\beta\alpha a}{2} Q_A^{-1/2}\tau - \left(\frac{a}{2} Q_A^{1/2}\tau\right)^{1+\gamma}$$

So,

$$\frac{\mathrm{d}\phi^{\mathrm{UL}}}{\mathrm{d}\rho} = -\frac{\frac{\rho}{Q_A}\frac{\partial Q_A}{\partial \rho}}{2\rho}\left[\frac{\beta\alpha a}{2}\frac{1}{Q_A^{1/2}} + (1+\gamma)\left(\frac{a}{2}Q_A^{1/2}\tau^{\mathrm{M}}\right)^{1+\gamma}\frac{1}{\tau^{\mathrm{M}}}\right] + \frac{\partial \phi^{\mathrm{UL}}}{\partial \tau}\frac{\partial \tau^{\mathrm{M}}}{\partial \rho} \tag{13}$$

The first term on the right-hand side of (13), which I call the *protective effect*, measures the gain to each unrestrained leader from decreased competition in export markets; this is similar to the right-hand side of (12) but larger, since $\beta > 1$. The second term, the *liberalising effect*, measures the effect on unrestrained leaders of the change in the negotiated tariff reduction implied by the increase in ρ. Since the negotiated rate of tariff reduction is always less than what the unrestrained leaders wish *ex post*, $\partial\phi^{\mathrm{UL}}/\partial\tau > 0$, and the previous subsection showed that $\partial\tau^{\mathrm{M}}/\rho > 0$. Thus an increase in ρ will raise the ϕ of each unrestrained leader government via *both* effects. It would welcome unilateralism, and also prefers to be the only unrestrained leader (that is, that $\rho = (n-1)/n$), and to have the intensity of unilateralism complete.

PROPOSITION 5. *If unilateralism without retaliation is introduced, the governments of the unrestrained leaders will be better off, and these governments will wish complete intensity and as few other unrestrained leaders as possible.*

5.5. *The Restrained Leaders*

The national income of restrained leaders, at domestic prices, equals

$$Q_A^{\mathrm{RL}}\left(B + \frac{X_{\mathrm{F}}}{P_A}\right) + A_{\mathrm{L}} - X_{\mathrm{F}} = (A_{\mathrm{L}} + Q_A^{\mathrm{RL}}B) + (tX_{\mathrm{F}}) + \left(\frac{Q_A^{\mathrm{RL}} - Q_A}{P_A}X_{\mathrm{F}}\right)$$

The first term on the right is the value of production, paid to the workers as wages. The second term equals total tariff revenue, distributed in lump-sum fashion. The third term, which I denote below by R^{RL}, is the rent generated by the restraints, and I assume that this accrues to the export sector. Then the *ex-post* reward of labour employed in the export sector of the restrained leaders is

$$r_x^{\mathrm{RL}} = (Q_A^{\mathrm{RL}})^{-1/2}\left(\frac{A_{\mathrm{L}}}{\ell} + \frac{R^{\mathrm{RL}}}{\ell}\right) \tag{14}$$

and labour in the import-competing sector will earn

$$r_m^{\mathrm{RL}} = a(Q_A^{\mathrm{RL}})^{1/2} \tag{15}$$

After some manipulation, (14) and (15) yield

$$\frac{1+t}{r_x^{\mathrm{RL}}}\frac{\mathrm{d}r_x^{\mathrm{RL}}}{\mathrm{d}t} = -\frac{1}{2}\left(\frac{1+t}{Q_A^{\mathrm{RL}}}\frac{\mathrm{d}Q_A^{\mathrm{RL}}}{\mathrm{d}t}\right) + \frac{R^{\mathrm{RL}}}{A_{\mathrm{L}} + R^{\mathrm{RL}}}\left(\frac{1+t}{R^{\mathrm{RL}}}\frac{\mathrm{d}R^{\mathrm{RL}}}{\mathrm{d}t}\right) < 0$$

and

$$\frac{1+t}{r_m^{\mathrm{RL}}}\frac{\mathrm{d}r_m^{\mathrm{RL}}}{\mathrm{d}t} = -\frac{1}{2}\left(\frac{1+t}{Q_A^{\mathrm{RL}}}\frac{\mathrm{d}Q_A^{\mathrm{RL}}}{\mathrm{d}t}\right) > 0$$

Suppose that initially $\delta = 0$, with ρ set at some arbitrary positive value: unilateralism has no intensity. So the objective function of restrained leaders initially equals that of unrestrained leaders: $\phi^{\mathrm{RL}} = \phi^{\mathrm{UL}}$. Then consider the effect of $\mathrm{d}\delta > 0$ on the restrained leaders; denote this increment, in the absence of retaliation, by $\partial\phi^{\mathrm{RL}}/\partial\delta$. I assume that, should these (now effectively) restrained leaders retaliate, the laggards convert their unilateral measures into conventional (nondiscriminatory) tariffs, allowing themselves to appropriate R^{RL}, that is, unilateralism plus retaliation is equivalent[10] to a reduction in the rate of liberalisation τ. The incremental effect is accordingly

$$-\left.\frac{\partial\phi^{\mathrm{RL}}}{\partial\tau}\right|_{\delta=0,\tau=\tau^{\mathrm{M}}} = -\left.\frac{\partial\phi^{\mathrm{UL}}}{\partial\tau}\right|_{\tau=\tau^{\mathrm{M}}}$$

Thus the restrained leaders will find retaliation tempting only if

$$\left.\frac{\partial\phi^{\mathrm{RL}}}{\partial\delta}\right|_{\delta=0} < -\left.\frac{\partial\phi^{\mathrm{UL}}}{\partial\tau}\right|_{\tau=\tau^{\mathrm{M}}} \tag{16}$$

Now

$$\left.\frac{\partial\phi^{\mathrm{RL}}}{\partial\delta}\right|_{\delta=0} = \frac{\mathrm{d}r_x^{\mathrm{RL}}}{\mathrm{d}\delta} + (1+\gamma)\left(\frac{a}{2}Q_A^{1/2}\tau^{\mathrm{M}}\right)^{\gamma}\frac{\mathrm{d}r_m^{\mathrm{RL}}}{\mathrm{d}\delta} + \frac{\partial\phi^{\mathrm{RL}}}{\partial\tau}\frac{\partial\tau}{\partial\delta}$$

The effect of a marginal restraint on the return to labour in the export sector is

$$\left.\frac{\mathrm{d}r_x^{\mathrm{RL}}}{\mathrm{d}\delta}\right|_{\delta=0} = -\frac{1}{2}\frac{r_x^{\mathrm{RL}}}{Q_A}\left.\frac{\partial Q_A^{\mathrm{RL}}}{\partial\delta}\right|_{\delta=0} + Q_A^{-1/2}\frac{1}{\ell}\left.\frac{\partial R^{\mathrm{RL}}}{\partial\delta}\right|_{\delta=0}$$

The first term on the right is the direct effect of the export restriction and the second term is the compensating emergence of trade rent. From (11),

$$\left.\frac{\partial Q_A^{\mathrm{RL}}}{\partial\delta}\right|_{\delta=0} = Q_A\frac{A_{\mathrm{L}} - A}{A_{\mathrm{L}} - X_{\mathrm{UL}}} + \frac{\partial Q_A}{\partial\delta}$$

and from the definition of R^{RL},

$$\left.\frac{\partial R_A^{\mathrm{RL}}}{\partial\delta}\right|_{\delta=0} = \left(\left.\frac{\partial Q_A^{\mathrm{RL}}}{\partial\delta}\right|_{\delta=0} - \frac{\partial Q_A}{\partial\delta}\right)\frac{X_{\mathrm{UL}}}{P} = (1+t)X_{\mathrm{UL}}\frac{A_{\mathrm{L}} - A}{A_{\mathrm{L}} - X_{\mathrm{UL}}} > 0$$

Then the net effect on the real reward of labour in the export sector reduces to

$$\left.\frac{\partial r_x^{\mathrm{RL}}}{\partial\delta}\right|_{\delta=0} = \frac{A_{\mathrm{L}} - A}{A_{\mathrm{L}} - X_{\mathrm{UL}}}\frac{Q_A^{-1/2}}{\ell}[(1+t)X_{\mathrm{UL}} - \tfrac{1}{2}A_{\mathrm{L}}]$$

[10] Alternatively, the laggards might convert their unilateral measures into conventional tariffs that apply only to the products of the restrained leaders, ie, that discriminate. But I will not consider this possibility as it would presumably make retaliation even more likely.

This will be positive if the term in brackets is positive: a large enough initial export position will generate enough rent to compensate fully for the restrictions. Next, the effect on labour in the import-competing sector reduces to

$$\left.\frac{\partial r_m^{\mathrm{RL}}}{\partial \delta}\right|_{\delta=0} = \frac{1}{2} r_m^{\mathrm{RL}} \frac{A_{\mathrm{L}} - A}{A_{\mathrm{L}} - X_{\mathrm{UL}}} \left[\frac{(1-\pi)A + \pi(1-\rho)A_{\mathrm{L}} + (1+t)A^* + \pi\rho X_{\mathrm{UL}}}{(1-\pi)A + \pi A_{\mathrm{L}} + (1+t)A^*}\right]$$

So, labour in the import-competing sector benefits from unilateralism at a sufficiently small intensity. The overall effect on the objective function of the negotiators of restrained leaders is then

$$\begin{aligned}\frac{A_{\mathrm{L}} - X_{\mathrm{UL}}}{A_{\mathrm{L}} - A}\left.\frac{\partial \phi^{\mathrm{RL}}}{\partial \delta}\right|_{\delta=0} &= Q_A^{-1/2}(1+t)\frac{X_{\mathrm{UL}}}{\rho} + \left.\frac{\partial \phi^{\mathrm{UL}}}{\partial \tau}\right|_{\tau=\tau^M}\left(\frac{A_{\mathrm{L}} - X_{\mathrm{UL}}}{A_{\mathrm{L}} - A}\frac{\partial \tau}{\partial \delta} + 1\right) \\ &\quad + (2+\gamma)\left(\frac{a}{2}Q_A^{1/2}\tau^{\mathrm{M}}\right)^{1+\gamma} \\ &\quad \times \frac{1}{\tau^{\mathrm{M}}}\frac{(1-\pi)A + \pi(1-\rho)A_{\mathrm{L}} + (1+t)A^* + \pi\rho X_{\mathrm{UL}}}{(1-\pi)A + \pi A_{\mathrm{L}} + (1+t)A^*} \\ &> 0\end{aligned}$$

Each of the three terms on the right is positive. Thus, as long as δ is sufficiently small, leaders will not only not be tempted to retaliate, they will also perceive the exercise of unilateralism as beneficial, according to the government negotiators' objective function.

PROPOSITION 6. *Unilateralism, at any breadth, will necessarily be perceived as beneficial by the governments of restrained leaders, if the intensity is small enough.*

5.6. *The Laggards*

The value of the laggards' negotiators' objective function is

$$\phi^{\mathrm{G}} = \frac{1}{2} r_x^{\mathrm{G}} \tau^{\mathrm{M}} - \left(\frac{1}{2} r_m^{\mathrm{G}} \tau^{\mathrm{M}}\right)^{1+\gamma}$$

But, since the laggards would potentially implement unilateralism, I now need to specify the objective function of the bureaucrats who would administer it. The fifth stylised fact of unilateralism (*The restrictions are designed by officials distinct from those who negotiate international trade agreements*) now becomes relevant. I accordingly allow administrators an objective function that, although of the same form as the negotiators' (1), has its own willingness to protect, μ. Thus the value of the laggards' administrators' objective function is now

$$\phi_A^{\mathrm{G}} = \frac{1}{2} r_x^{\mathrm{G}} \tau^{\mathrm{M}} - \left(\frac{1}{2} r_m^{\mathrm{G}} \tau^{\mathrm{M}}\right)^{1+\mu}$$

Perhaps the easiest way to assess the importance of allowing administrators a distinct objective function of their own is to suppose initially that they do not have one and deduce the implications. So I initially suppose that $\mu = \gamma$ and, therefore, $\phi_A^G = \phi^G$.

The total marginal effect on ϕ^G of raising above zero, assuming no retaliation, is

$$\frac{d\phi^G}{d\rho} = \frac{\partial\phi^G}{\partial\rho} + \frac{\partial\phi^G}{\partial\tau}\frac{d\tau^M}{d\rho}$$

where the first term on the right indicates the direct protective effect and the second the indirect liberalising effect. Now,

$$\begin{aligned}\frac{\partial\phi^G}{\partial\rho} &= \frac{\partial r_x^G}{\partial\rho} + (1+\mu)\left[\frac{\partial r_m^G}{\partial t}\tau^M(1+t)\right]^\mu \frac{\partial r_m^G}{\partial\rho} \\ &= \left\{\frac{\partial r_x^G}{\partial t}(1+t) + (1+\mu)\left[\frac{\partial r_m^G}{\partial t}\tau^M(1+t)\right]^\mu \frac{\partial r_m^G}{\partial t}(1+t)\right\}\frac{1}{Q_A}\frac{\partial Q_A}{\partial\rho} \qquad (17) \\ &= \frac{\partial\phi^G}{\partial\tau}\frac{1}{Q_A}\frac{\partial Q_A}{\partial\rho}\end{aligned}$$

The negotiated liberalisation rate τ^M is less than what the laggards' negotiators most prefer *ex post,* if $\mu = \gamma$. Thus $\partial\phi^G/\partial\tau > 0$, which implies that $\partial\phi^G/\partial\rho < 0$. Since a higher rate of liberalisation is perceived as beneficial, a change in the welfare of exporters must, on the margin, dominate the accompanying change in the welfare of import-competitors.

But the indirect liberalising effect will be beneficial, again with $\mu = \gamma$. Thus unilateralism will, on balance, benefit the governments of laggards when the latter effect dominates, which will be so when

$$\frac{d\phi^G}{d\rho} = \left(\frac{\partial\tau^M}{\partial\rho} + \frac{1}{Q_A}\frac{\partial Q_A}{\partial\rho}\right)\frac{\partial\phi^G}{\partial\tau} > 0$$

which, in turn, will hold if and only if

$$\tau^M > \frac{1}{1/\mu + 1/2}$$

The right-hand side is strictly increasing in μ and τ^M decreases in γ, ranging from infinity to zero. Thus, with μ constrained equal to γ, there exists a unique γ° with the property that unilateralism confers a net benefit on the laggards if and only if $\gamma < \gamma^\circ$.

But this is not all. Suppose that $\gamma > \gamma^\circ$ and that governments commit themselves to practice unilateralism should they become laggards. Whenever a country is a laggard, it then shoots itself in the foot, but this benefits all non-laggard countries, raising the rate of liberalisation. If γ is sufficiently close to γ°, the loss when a laggard will be dominated by the gain when not a laggard, so that, *ex ante*, every country is better off.

PROPOSITION 7. *If $\mu = \gamma$ is not sufficiently greater than γ°, all countries can benefit ex ante, according to the objective function* (1), *if each country adopts unilateralism at some intensity. This will raise the rate of liberalisation.*

6. Implications of Unilateralism

The section examines the consequences for the international economy of a system of unilateralism.

6.1. *The Effect of Unilateralism on Resource Allocation*

The previous section examined the effect of unilateralism for a given pattern of resource allocation ℓ. However, if unilateralism exists, forward-looking labour will take that into account when deciding where to locate. With a system of unilateralism in place, the real *ex-post* quasi-rents become as follows, for a country with a comparative advantage in A:

$$r_x^{\text{URL}} = \frac{\beta\alpha a}{Q_A^{1/2}} \qquad r_x^{\text{RL}} = \frac{\beta\alpha a}{(Q_A^{\text{RL}})^{1/2}} \qquad r_x^{\text{F}} = \frac{\alpha a}{Q_A^{1/2}} \qquad r_x^{\text{G}} = \frac{\alpha a}{Q_B^{1/2}} \tag{18}$$

$$r_m^{\text{URL}} = a\,Q_A^{1/2} \qquad r_m^{\text{RL}} = a(Q_A^{\text{RL}})^{1/2} \qquad r_m^{\text{F}} = a\,Q_A^{1/2} \qquad r_m^{\text{G}} = a\,Q_B^{1/2} \tag{19}$$

and the expected returns accordingly become

$$r_i(\ell; t, \rho, \delta) = \frac{(1-\rho)\pi}{2} r_i^{\text{URL}} + \frac{\rho\pi}{2} r_i^{\text{RL}} + \frac{1-\pi}{2} r_i^{\text{F}} + \frac{1}{2} r_i^{\text{G}} \tag{20}$$

for $i = x, m$. Here t denotes the common tariff rate expected (correctly) to prevail after the current round of negotiations – that is, $t = t_1 - \tau^{\text{M}}(1 + t_1)$, where t_1 denotes the tariff inherited from the previous period – and ρ and δ denote the parameters of the system of unilateralism that is in place or expected (correctly) to be put in place. Given the values of these policy variables, the allocation of resources is determined by

$$r_x(\ell; t, \rho, \delta) = r_m(\ell; t, \rho, \delta)$$

Differentiate this expression implicitly to determine the effect of an increase in the intensity of unilateralism on the *ex-ante* allocation of resources.

$$\frac{\mathrm{d}\ell}{\mathrm{d}\delta} = \frac{\left(\dfrac{\partial r_x}{\partial \delta} - \dfrac{\partial r_m}{\partial \delta}\right)}{\dfrac{\partial r_m}{\partial \ell} - \dfrac{\partial r_x}{\partial \ell}} + \frac{\left(\dfrac{\partial r_x}{\partial t} - \dfrac{\partial r_m}{\partial t}\right)}{\dfrac{\partial r_m}{\partial \ell} - \dfrac{\partial r_x}{\partial \ell}} t_1 \frac{\partial \tau}{\partial \delta}$$

The first term on the right is the direct effect of unilateralism on resource allocation, and the second term is the indirect effect due to the fact that the existence of unilateralism will alter the liberalisation expected (correctly) to be negotiated. Consider a differential increase of δ above zero, i.e. the introduction of unilateralism at an arbitrarily low intensity. Then, the discussion in Section 4 establishes that the denominators and the first bracketed term in the numerator of the second term on the right are each positive, and Proposition 7 establishes that $\partial\tau/\partial\delta > 0$. Thus the indirect effect is positive. So, consider the numerator of the first term on the right, the direct effect.

$$\frac{\partial r_x}{\partial\delta} - \frac{\partial r_m}{\partial\delta} = \frac{\rho\pi}{2}\left(\frac{\partial r_x^{\mathrm{RL}}}{\partial\delta} - \frac{\partial r_m^{\mathrm{RL}}}{\partial\delta}\right)$$
$$+\left(-\frac{\partial Q_A}{\partial\delta}\right)\frac{a}{4}Q_A^{-1/2}\left\{\alpha[(\beta-1)\pi(1-\rho)+(1-\rho\pi)]Q_A - \frac{\alpha}{1+t} + (1-\rho) - \frac{1+t}{Q_A}\right\}$$

Since $Q_A > 1$ and $\partial Q_A/\partial\delta < 0$, a sufficiently small value of ρ will guarantee that this term is positive: the direct effect of unilateralism, as well as the indirect effect, will be to reallocate resources toward the comparative advantage sector.

PROPOSITION 8. *The introduction of unilateralism at a sufficiently small intensity and breadth will induce an increased allocation of labour to the comparative advantage sectors.*

6.2. *The Insurance Triangle*

Note two curious features of how unilateralism functions. First, unilateralism is appealing to governments if their willingness to protect (γ) is *low,* not high. This is because a lower willingness to protect produces a greater beneficial liberalising effect.

Second, unilateralism functions as a form of insurance. Unlike the literature on tariffs-as-insurance (Eaton and Grossman, 1985; Dixit, 1987; 1989) though, the role for insurance is itself a product of a positive willingness to protect, and its value is not that a laggard government *itself* have something to fall back on (*ex post* such a government would prefer not to implement it – see below) but rather that its effect on *others* allows all to negotiate a greater rate of liberalisation.[11] Countries know that, should they turn out to be followers (the most reluctant liberalisers), their interests will be safeguarded by the efforts of the laggards to protect their own import-competing interests, and that these efforts will be acceptable to the leaders.[12] This cannot be appreciated in a two-country model. The insurance functions through a subtle interplay between all three groups: the *insurance triangle.*

If this is how unilateralism works, could it not take the form of export subsidies by followers, either instead of or along with, import protection by laggards? An answer will emerge below.

6.3. *The Split Personality*

The analysis thus far in this section, culminating in Propositions 7 and 8, has focused on the possibility that multilateralism might imply a role for unilateralism: causation has been from the former to the latter. But unilateralism, to be effective,

[11] There is a (very rough) analogy here with the role for trade adjustment assistance advanced by Fung and Staiger (1996).

[12] Thus, in the early 1980s, the US automobile industry (laggards) acquired protection acceptable to the Japanese industry (leaders) and beneficial to the Europeans and Koreans (followers).

also requires a multilateral component. This is because Proposition 7, by itself, does not get us far enough. The reason, in part, is time consistency.

Unilateralism will be effective only if countries choose to implement it when they become laggards. They benefit only when the beneficial indirect liberalising effect dominates the harmful protective effect. However, the former will be past history when the laggards decide whether to implement unilateralism. Thus the laggard governments, according to the negotiators' objective function, will decline to implement unilateralism *ex post.*

This time-consistency problem is compounded – and this is absolutely essential – by an *externality*. Governments with the objective function (1) would like, if $\gamma < \gamma^{\circ}$, to convince each other that they will practise unilateralism when they turn out to be laggards, because this would produce a higher rate of tariff reduction, to the *ex ante* benefit of all. However, all know that, *ex post*, the government of a laggard with the objective function (1) would not implement unilateralism. What if governments can precommit to implement unilateralism should they become laggards? Because the time consistency problem is compounded by an externality, no government would undertake such a pre-commitment *unilaterally*: The beneficial liberalising effect depends on a *general* adoption of unilateralism.

PROPOSITION 9. *The introduction of unilateralism (raising ρ above zero) will have no effect, if implemented by authorities who have discretion and who set $\mu = \gamma$, because they will always decline ex post to implement it. Furthermore, no government negotiator with $\mu = \gamma$ would be willing unilaterally to delegate authority to implement unilateralism ex post to some other agent.*

Potentially, there are two ways around this problem, and both require a multilateral component to unilateralism. The first is simply to internalise the externality by having the countries *jointly* adopt binding unilateralism. That is, the latter could itself be the product of multilateral negotiation. (Or they might jointly bind themselves to subsidise exports whenever they turn out to be followers.)

This does not correspond to reality, though: The fifth stylised fact of unilateralism (*The restrictions are designed by officials distinct from those who negotiate international trade agreements*) is at variance with this possibility. So consider instead the consequences of countries individually adopting unilateralism systems with $\mu \neq \gamma$. Let $\tau_A^G(\mu)$ denote the rate of liberalisation that is optimal, *ex post*, for administrators with a willingness to protect of μ, in a country that turns out to be a laggard.

Define $\mu(\gamma)$ to be the solution to

$$\tau_A^G[\mu(\gamma)] = \tau^M(\gamma)$$

Propositions 1 and 2 imply that $\mu(\gamma) > \gamma$. Further, Proposition 2 implies that, if $\mu \geq \mu(\gamma)$, the negotiated rate of liberalisation will be no less than what the laggard administrators most prefer *ex post.* Thus, from (17) $\partial\phi_A^G/\partial\tau < 0$, whence $\partial\phi_A^G/\partial\rho > 0$. Therefore, the administrators will indeed implement unilateralism when their countries turn out to be laggards: the time consistency problem disappears.

PROPOSITION 10. *If $\mu \geq \mu(\gamma) > \gamma$, laggards will implement unilateralism and, at some intensity, this will benefit all other countries; if μ is sufficiently small, this will also benefit the laggards, according to the objective function* (1).

Four comments are in order.

- For unilateralism to work, the willingness to protect of the administrators must not merely marginally exceed that of the negotiators, it must *significantly* exceed the latter.
- This is *not* an example of individual countries strengthening the bargaining positions of their negotiators by pre-committing to *ex post* action. The benefit of unilateralism to an individual country comes from the assurance that all *other* countries will practice it when they are laggards. Regardless of how forward-looking they may be, the negotiators of *no* country will wish their own country to adopt such a system of unilateralism. The fifth stylised fact of unilateralism (*The restrictions are designed by officials distinct from those who negotiate international trade agreements*) is absolutely critical here.
- The higher rate of liberalisation will be perceived as undesirable by the administrators, and, if μ is significantly great, this undesirable indirect effect from introducing a small ρ will necessarily overwhelm the direct protective effect: Unilateralism will be on the whole undesirable from the administrators' point of view. However, this has no effect on feasibility, because the liberalising effect will be past history when the administrators are called on to act. That is, such unilateralism will be time consistent.
- With unilateralism in place, there is no longer a possibility of subsidising the exports of followers, since any such subsidies would be neutralised by the laggards.[13]

6.4. *The Compatibility Problem*

If the restrictions must be designed by officials distinct from those who negotiate international trade agreements, can we be assured that the systems of unilateralism they adopt will possess the desired properties (i.e. the other stylised facts)? Since these officials would prefer unilateralism without complete retaliation rather than with it, and since Propositions 4, 5 and 6 continue to apply, the logic of this section, offering an explanation for those stylised facts, also continues to apply: the desired properties should be there. However, there is no reason to think that either the breadth, ρ, or the intensity, δ, of the unilateralism the officials provide will be desirable from the negotiators' point of view.

This is the *compatibility problem*: if unilateralism is not a deliberate multilateral creation (and, in fact, it is not) then it can be useful to the negotiators only if imposed by officials whose objectives are significantly at odds with those of the negotiators.

Once systems become common, they could be perceived as of potential benefit by government negotiators meeting together, even though no negotiator would

[13] Countervailing duties, of course, do just that.

have been willing to adopt such a system individually. An immediate implication of the compatibility problem (also in accord with actual experience) is that these negotiators have an incentive to expand multilateral negotiations to address the conduct of unilateralism.

PROPOSITION 11. *Government negotiators will, together, have an incentive to accept unilateralism but also to include codes of conduct for it in their multilateral negotiations.*

7. Concluding Remarks

I have argued that unilateralism and multilateralism comprise a coherent international commercial system.

I have reduced each of these to a few basic principles, and discussed how they relate to each other. The essential argument follows.

- Multilaterally negotiated tariff reduction is limited by the smallest reduction any country will want *ex post*: that most advantageous to those countries who compete with the exports of the technological leaders.
- This pace can be accelerated, and the allocation of resources to the comparative advantage sectors can be increased, if those countries that import the exports of the technological leaders make universal use of temporary, quantitative, discriminatory protection compensating restricted exporters.
- Such unilateralism works by conferring a form of social insurance resulting from a subtle interplay between three distinct sets of countries: the *insurance triangle*.
- The use of such a system is constrained by a time – consistency problem *compounded by an externality*.
- With unilateralism adopted by countries individually rather than collectively, to be useful, it must be designed by officials significantly more willing to protect than are the negotiators themselves, who would be unwilling to delegate such authority: trade policy needs its 'split personality'.
- This *compatibility problem* implies an incentive to address the conduct of unilateralism multilaterally.

This theory of unilateralism depends critically on the existence of a multilateral world. The key concepts – the insurance triangle, time-consistency compounded by an externality, the necessity of a split personality, the compatibility problem – cannot be understood at all in a two-country environment.

The process of multilateral trade liberalisation generates a potential motive for protectionist policy tools with exactly those properties that I have argued do in fact constitute contemporary unilateralism. This in turn requires – again in accord with actual experience – a multilateral component. It all fits together.

University of Pennsylvania

Date of receipt of first typescript: February 2000
Date of receipt of final typescript: May 2001

Appendix I: Instruments of Unilateralism

Unilateralism consists of rules, or instruments, that may be explicit or implicit. This appendix describes several of the most important the instruments, and then describes how their nature and their application has been changing over time.

The Instruments

I describe four prominent instruments.

1 *Voluntary export restraints* (VERs)[14] fall outside both national laws and international agreements. The Uruguay Round made them more extralegal than ever. The following instruments, 'administered protection', are provided for in many national laws and sanctioned by the WTO.
2 *Antidumping duties* Dumping[15] is pricing for export below either the cost of production or the price for comparable domestic sales. Antidumping laws provide a two-pronged investigation: determination of the dumping margin, if any; determination of material injury to domestic import-competing firms. If both determinations are positive, a temporary duty equal to the dumping margin is imposed on the good from the country whose firms have dumped. The national interest plays no role, and (in the USA) the President cannot decline to impose the duty. These laws define certain behaviour as objectionable and force import prices up when it occurs. Whether the behaviour *should* be objectionable is beside the point: arbitrary circumstances determine which import-competing interests may obtain temporary protection.
3 *Countervailing duties* apply to imports subsidised for export. Administration is similar to that of antidumping laws.
4 *Safeguards* provide[16] temporary protection for domestic industries harmed by increased imports. Again, a material injury test is applied. But, in the USA, the President may decline to impose a duty. More generally, duties imposed should be nondiscriminatory and should not increase protection overall: duties should be reduced (in a nondiscriminatory way) on goods that are important exports of the exporting countries most affected by the safeguard measures.

This list of four instruments excludes other tools, notably those for aggressive export expansion (e.g. Super 301 in the USA). These are more characteristic of the USA than of other countries. Also, I have analysed these before (Ethier and Horn, 1996), and this paper concerns unilateralism as protection.

Changing Instrument Use

Use of these instruments has changed dramatically. First, usage has greatly increased since the 1960s. With the freedom to conduct traditional tariff policy progressively constrained by multilateral agreements, protectionist pressures have increasingly found outlets in the new protectionism.

Second, multilateral negotiation is broadening to encompass unilateral actions. The Tokyo Round established voluntary codes for the conduct of administered protection, and these were made mandatory for WTO members by the Uruguay Round. Curiously, though, the code for safeguards has been loosened. Countries are now allowed, sometimes, to use them much as VERs have been used. The final outcome is far from clear.

[14] See Harris (1985), Kostecki (1987), Krishna (1989) and Ethier (1991*a*,*b*).

[15] See Ethier (1991*b*, 1993, 1994), Prusa (1992), Baldwin and Steagall (1994) and Tharakan and Waelbroeck (1994).

[16] See Ethier (1994).

Third, individual countries have continually changed their laws. These changes have generally reduced administrative discretion and made protection more likely.

Fourth, the mix among the instruments has changed dramatically, with the number of safeguard cases declining absolutely as well as relatively and the number of countervailing-duty and (especially) antidumping cases exploding.

Appendix II: Prices

Relative Commodity Prices

Recall that everyone spends half of his/her income on each good. Then, if A, B, A^* and B^* denote national production levels and M each nation's trade in B,

$$Q_i(B+M) = A - P_iM \qquad \text{and} \qquad Q_i^*(B^* - M) = A^* + P_iM$$

These expressions can be rewritten as

$$P_i(1+t+1)M = A - P_i(1+t)B \qquad \text{and} \qquad \frac{P_i(1+t)}{(1+t)}M = \frac{B^*P_i}{1+t} - A^*$$

Thus

$$\frac{A}{P_i(2+t)} - \frac{(1+t)B}{2+t} = M = \frac{B^*}{2+t} - \frac{(1+t)A^*}{(2+t)P_i}$$

These, in turn, imply:

$$P_i = \frac{A + (1+t)A^*}{B^* + (1+t)B}$$

and

$$M = \frac{AB^* - (1+t)^2A^*B}{(2+t)[A + (1+t)A^*]}$$

P_i will assume one of two alternative values, depending on which good is the technological leader. Since $A = [\pi\beta + (1-\pi)]\ell\alpha a$, $B = (1-\ell)a$, $A^* = (1-\ell)a$ and $B^* = \ell\alpha a$,

$$P_i = P_A(\ell, t) = \pi(\beta - 1)\frac{\alpha\ell}{\alpha\ell + (1+t)(1-\ell)} + 1$$

if A is the leader, and $P_i = P_B = 1/P_A$ if B is the leader. Then $P_A > 1 > P_B$.

Real Rewards

The responsiveness of rents to the common tariff vector t is

$$\frac{1+t}{r_x}\frac{\partial r_x}{\partial t} = -\frac{1}{2}\left[1 - \frac{1}{1 + \dfrac{\alpha}{1+t}\dfrac{\ell}{1-\ell}}\frac{(P_A - 1)}{P_A}\frac{\pi(\beta-1) - (P_A - 1)}{P_A + 1 + \pi(\beta - 1)}\right] < 0$$

$$\frac{1+t}{r_m}\frac{\partial r_m}{\partial t} = -\frac{1}{2}\left[1 - \frac{1}{1 + \dfrac{\alpha}{1+t}\dfrac{\ell}{1-\ell}}\frac{(P_A - 1)^2}{P_A(P_A - 1)}\right] > 0$$

These imply, when $r_m = r_x$, $\partial r_x/\partial t + \partial r_m/\partial t < 0$.

References

Bagwell, K. and Staiger, R. W. (1990), 'A theory of managed trade', *American Economic Review*, vol. 80, pp. 779–95.

Bagwell, K. and Staiger, R. W. (1999*a*), 'An economic theory of GATT', *American Economic Review*, vol. 89 (1), March, pp. 215–48.

Bagwell, K. and Staiger, R. W. (1999*b*), 'Multilateral trade negotiations, bilateral opportunism and the rules of GATT', Working Paper, Department of Economics, University of Wisconsin.

Baldwin, R. E. and Steagall, J. W. (1994), 'An analysis of US International Trade Commission decisions in antidumping, countervailing duty and safeguard cases', CEPR Discussion Paper No. 990.

Corden, W. M. (1997). *Trade Policy and Economic Welfare*, 2nd edn, Oxford: Oxford University Press.

Dixit, A. (1987), 'Trade and insurance with moral hazard', *Journal of International Economics*, vol. 23 (3/4), November, pp. 201–20.

Dixit, A. (1989), 'Trade and insurance with adverse selection', *Review of Economic Studies*, vol. 56 (2), April, pp. 235–47.

Eaton, J. and Grossman, G. M. (1985), 'Tariffs as insurance: optimal commercial policy when domestic markets are incomplete', *Canadian Journal of Economics*, vol. 18 (2), May, pp. 258–72.

Ethier, W. J. (1991*a*), 'The economics and political economy of managed trade', in (A. L. Hillman, ed.), *Markets and Politicians*, Boston: Kluwer Academic Publishers, pp. 283–306.

Ethier, W. J. (1991*b*), 'Voluntary export restraints', in (A. Takayama, M. Ohyama and H. Ohta, eds), *Trade, Policy, and International Adjustments*, San Diego: Academic Press, pp. 3–18.

Ethier, W. J. (1993), 'An antidumping law with a distorted home market'. Chapter 17 in (H. Herberg and N. V. Long, eds) *Trade, Welfare, and Economic Policies*, Ann Arbor: University of Michigan Press, pp. 279–97.

Ethier, W. J. (1994), 'Protección discrecional en la economa mundial contemporánea, (Discretionary protection and the contemporary world economy)', *Cuadernos Economicos de ICE*, vol. 57 (2), pp. 231–42.

Ethier, W. J. (1998*a*), 'The new regionalism', Economic Journal, vol. 108 (449), July, pp. 1149–61.

Ethier, W. J. (1998*b*), 'Reciprocity, nondiscrimination, and a multilateral world', Working Paper, Department of Economics, University of Pennsylvania, October.

Ethier, W. J. (1998*c*), 'Regionalism in a multilateral world', *Journal of Political Economy*, vol. 6 (106), December, pp. 1214–45.

Ethier, W. J. (1998*d*), 'The international commercial system', *Essays in International Finance* No. 210, September, Princeton: International Finance Section.

Ethier, W. J. (2001), 'Theoretical problems in negotiating trade liberalization', *European Journal of Political Economy*, forthcoming.

Ethier, W. J. and Horn, H. (1996) 'Results-oriented trade policy', *Review of International Economics*, vol. 4 (1), pp. 17–39.

Fung, K. C. and Staiger, R. W. (1996), 'Trade liberalization and trade adjustment assistance', in (M. Canzoneri, W. J. Ethier, and V. Grilli, eds), *The New Transatlantic Economy*, Cambridge: Cambridge University Press, pp. 265–86.

Harris, R. (1985), 'Why voluntary export restraints are "voluntary"', *Canadian Journal of Economics*, vol. 18, pp. 799–809.

Hillman, A. L. (1982), 'Declining industries and political-support protectionist motives', *American Economic Review*, vol. 72, pp. 1180–90.

Hillman, A. L. (1990), 'Protectionist policies as the regulation of international industry', *Public Choice*, vol. 67, pp. 101–10.

Kostecki, M. (1987), 'Export restraint arrangements and trade liberalization', *The World Economy*, vol. 10, pp. 442–50.

Krishna, K. (1989), 'Trade restrictions as facilitating practices', *Journal of International Economics*, vol. 26, pp. 251–70.

Prusa, T. J. (1992), 'Why are antidumping petitions withdrawn?', *Journal of International Economics*, vol. 33, pp. 1–20.

Staiger, R. (1995), 'International rules and institutions for cooperative trade policy', in (G. M. Grossman, and K. Rogoff, eds) *Handbook of International Economics*, volume 3, Amsterdam: Elsevier, pp. 1495–551

Staiger, R. and Tabellini, G. (1987), 'Discretionary trade policy and excessive protection', *American Economic Review*, vol. 77, pp. 823–8.

Tharakan, P. K. M. and Waelbroeck, J. (1994), 'Antidumping and countervailing duty decisions in the E.C. and in the U.S.: an experiment in comparative political economy', *European Economic Review*, vol. 38, pp. 171–93.

Review of International Economics, 12(3), 303–320, 2004

Political Externalities, Nondiscrimination, and a Multilateral World

*Wilfred J. Ethier**

Abstract

During the past half century, multilateral trade liberalization has reduced tariffs to historically low levels. The "Received Theory" of multilateral trade agreements, based solely on terms-of-trade externalities between national governments, offers an explanation that has become the conventional wisdom. But it is dramatically inconsistent with actual trade agreements. This paper offers an alternative explanation, based on intergovernmental political externalities, consistent with what we actually observe. With remarkably little necessary formal structure—in particular, no formal bargaining model—this framework (chosen to parallel actual experience) gives an immediate and transparent role to the basic characteristics of contemporary trade agreements: gradual liberalization, reciprocity, nondiscrimination, and multilateralism.

1. Introduction

Perhaps the most prominent accomplishment of international trade theory in the twentieth century was its theory of international trade agreements. Following Harry Johnson's classic paper[1] (1953/54), literally scores of contributions developed and elaborated this theory. The deservedly influential work of Bagwell and Staiger (1999, 2002) can justly be seen as triumphantly completing the research agenda implied by Johnson nearly half a century earlier.

The central premise of this extensive literature (which, for lack of a better term, I label the "Received Theory") is that trade agreements arise *solely* because countries with market power are concerned, to at least *some* degree, with the fact that trade barriers, imposed for *whatever* reason, can move the terms of trade in their favor, shifting real income there from the rest of the world.

The Received Theory is an imposing accomplishment. It offers a rationale for the multilateral trade liberalization that is easily the most important economic policy accomplishment of our era. It offers an explanation of the very special characteristics of that liberalization. It has furnished the basis for innumerable analyses of a host of other significant international economic policy issues.

There is just one problem. The Received Theory is irrelevant to actual multilateral trade agreements.

2. Multilateral Trade Agreements and the Received Theory

History's greatest act of deliberate economic policymaking is almost certainly the trade liberalization produced by the multilateral negotiating rounds sponsored by the

---

* Ethier: Department of Economics, University of Pennsylvania. E-mail: ethierwj@msn.com. This paper was the Presidential Address to the International Economics and Finance Society, presented in Washington, DC, on 3 January 2003. I gratefully acknowledge very helpful conversations and quarrels with: Gene Grossman, Arye Hillman, Henrik Horn, John Kennan, Petros Mavroidis, Pascalis Raimondos-Möller, Don Regan, Koji Shimomura, and Bob Staiger. I have also benefited from credulous responses to seminar presentations in many quarters of our multilateral world.

General Agreement on Tariffs and Trade (GATT) and establishing the World Trade Organization (WTO). This is widely appreciated.

Much less appreciated, by economists, is the fact that a crucial characteristic of this liberalization is that the resulting trade agreements do *not* prevent countries from trying to influence their terms of trade. Let me repeat this point, since it is crucial and trade theorists[2] have proven rigidly impervious to it: ACTUAL MULTILATERAL TRADE AGREEMENTS DO *NOT* PREVENT COUNTRIES FROM TRYING TO INFLUENCE THEIR TERMS OF TRADE.

To explain, a country with market power, as we all know, can influence its terms of trade by taxing either imports or exports. Now, those parts of the GATT that specify how countries should treat each other, notably Article I (General Most-Favoured-Nation Treatment), Article XI (General Elimination of Quantitative Restrictions), and Article XXVIIIbis (Tariff Negotiations), do generally refer explicitly to barriers to *both* imports and exports. By contrast, those parts addressing actual liberalization, notably Article II (Schedules of Concessions) and Article III (National Treatment on Internal Taxation and Regulation) address *only* import barriers.

Article XI (General Elimination of Quantitative Restrictions), which rules out "quotas, import or export licenses or other measures," on both imports and exports, *explicitly* exempts from this prohibition "duties, taxes or other charges" and, therefore, export taxes.

Nothing in the GATT prevents a country from implementing export taxes.[3] That's a simple fact.

However, Article XXVIIIbis (Tariff Negotiations) does refer to *both* import barriers and export barriers, so it is also true that nothing in the GATT prevents countries from negotiating schedules of concessions that apply to potential export taxes as well as to tariffs, should they so choose. But they have in fact *not* so chosen. In their schedules of concessions, countries have bound their import taxes; they have *not* bound export taxes.

If the US, for example, were to decide, for whatever reason, to impose aggressively a set of export taxes that could improve its terms of trade, its outstanding multilateral trade obligations would not prevent it from doing so.[4]

Thus, while the Received Theory interprets trade agreements as dealing with terms-of-trade manipulation, actual multilateral trade agreements just do *not* do this. A major embarrassment, to be sure. But it's even worse than that.

The more sophisticated and realistic contributions to the Received Theory—such as Bagwell and Staiger (1999, 2002)—allow governments to be concerned primarily with any number of internal or political-economy objectives that relate to the domestic relative price of imports in terms of exports. This price can be manipulated unilaterally with trade policy, but, if a country has market power, such manipulation will impact the terms of trade, creating an international externality. Dealing with this terms-of-trade externality is the *sole* reason for trade agreements in these models.

Two implications are immediate. (i) Small countries will *never* sign on to trade agreements. If they did, they would surrender the use of trade policy for domestic objectives while receiving *absolutely nothing* in return. (ii) Large countries will negotiate *only* trade agreements that constrain terms-of-trade manipulation. Trade agreements that do not do this would, *for no reason*, surrender the use of trade policy for domestic objectives.

In reality we observe exactly the opposite. Small countries eagerly sign on to multilateral trade agreements. Large countries negotiate trade agreements that do not prevent terms-of-trade manipulation, and do not negotiate multilateral agreements that would prevent it.

The Received Theory predicts what we do not see and cannot explain what we do see.[5] An immediate implication is that the Received Theory's explanations of the very special characteristics of the historic post-World War II multilateral liberalization (e.g., reciprocity, nondiscrimination) are vacuous.

So, how to deal with this serious problem? I suggest that we just take seriously what policymakers have *always* said that they are doing (terms-of-trade externalities are notably absent here!). This involves what I term *political externalities*.

This paper proceeds as follows. The next section develops the idea of political externalities and introduces a governmental objective function reflecting these externalities. I then briefly digress to examine a very special case in which the predictions of the Received Theory will be consistent with some of the predictions of my alternative approach based on political externalities. I then show that my alternative delivers what the Received Theory cannot: reciprocal trade agreements, involving even small countries, that do not necessarily constrain export taxes. I then add more structure to the objective function to allow an extended discussion of gradual liberalization, nondiscrimination, and multilateralism.

3. Political Externalities

"Political externalities," by my definition, arise when policymakers in one country believe that their political status (whatever that might be specified to mean) is directly sensitive, to some degree, to actions by policymakers in another country.

My notion of political externalities is derived from two hypotheses about the economic environment which I believe are uncontroversial.

(a) Policymakers try to maximize some objective function. This might reflect political support in some sense, net bribes or contributions *à la* Grossman and Helpman (2002), or simply the probability that their decisions will be ratified by some subsequent legislative process. But, just for convenience, I refer to the maximand as "political support."
(b) Special interests are subject to "bounded rationality" in determining how responsible policymakers are for changes in their welfare. They observe the actions of policymakers, but they also know that many other economic events, plus their own actions, conspire in some complicated way to determine actual outcomes.

Several comments. First, I will not explicitly analyze microeconomic interactions between policymakers and special interests, as in Grossman and Helpman (2002). This is a very worthwhile task for another day. My objective today is the prior one of establishing the central role of political externalities for trade agreements.

Second, asymmetric information will play no role in what follows. *Imperfect* information is critical for (b), but it will not matter whether or not all agents share a common (limited) information set.

Third, irrationality will also play no role in what follows. In particular, I suppose that both policymakers and special interests realize that, given my assumption of no international borrowing or lending, the value of imports must end up equal to the value of exports, so that any policy action impacting one must induce repercussions restoring the equality.

Basic Axioms

Given this (unobjectionable, I hope) environment, I argue the relevance of the following two axioms.

AXIOM 1. *"Political support" is more sensitive to the* direct *effects of government actions than to the* indirect *consequences, because, given bounded rationality, as in (b), a larger fraction of the public is likely to hold the government more responsible for the former than for the latter.*

Suppose, for example, that the US reduces textile import barriers and that textile imports subsequently rise. Those in the textile industry, and others, realize that the former is responsible, at least in part, for the latter. Suppose that foreign textile-exporting countries spend their increased proceeds on US wheat and machine tools, restoring trade balance. Some of those in these latter industries, knowing that trade must balance overall, may well credit at least some of their good fortune to the reduction in textile barriers, but they, and others, will also credit their own business acumen, general economic conditions, random events, etc. Even *if an economically sophisticated individual exporter of machine tools realizes (as I explicitly allow) that an increase in textile imports must generate an equal-valued increase in exports of* something, *he/she has little reason to credit that for his/her* own *additional sales of machine tools.*

If, on the other hand, the US government has negotiated reductions in *foreign* trade barriers on wheat and machine tools, it will most surely get credit for at least part of the rise in exports of these goods. This axiom is in the spirit of Hillman's classic use (1982) of a political support function to analyze protection for declining industries, which argued that such a function should be more sensitive to changes clearly due to government action.[6]

Evidence for the practical relevance of this axiom is truly abundant and should be obvious. Governments consistently attempt to "sell" trade agreements to the public on the basis of the increased exports *directly* implied (in my sense) by the agreements (or the jobs devoted to producing those exports), while opponents point to the increased imports *directly* implied (again in my sense). When a trade dispute arises, the aggrieved government invariably measures the harm it has suffered by the value of the exports it has *directly* lost as a result of the "unfair" trade measures employed by its partners. The same principle has also consistently been employed in trade disputes and in renegotiations under the GATT and the WTO (though the calculations have of course sometimes differed). Furthermore, when the WTO authorizes punishments, it specifies those punishments in terms of the *direct* imports from the punished country that can be curtailed by the punishing countries. See Ethier (2001).

AXIOM 2. *Government officials believe that trade volumes influence political support independently, to some degree, from their implications for factor rewards.*

The consequences of policies for factor incomes obviously matter politically, but the above examples—all involving trade volumes—also amply motivate and illustrate this second axiom. Analogously to the distinction between direct and indirect effects, changes in trade volumes help people to determine how much blame (or credit) for income changes should be attached to government negotiators (as opposed to the Fed, individual merit, nasty employers, unknown shocks, etc.). The evidence supplied in the previous paragraph is completely relevant here as well.

Governmental Objectives

Consider a single economy whose government might conclude international trade agreements with trading partners. Suppose that this home economy produces two goods, exporting A and importing B. (This is an obvious abstraction, for simplicity, from the fact that Axioms 1 and 2 reflect, in no small part, that any modern economy has many sectors.) Consider, also for simplicity, a time horizon in which all factors are specific to either the A sector or the B sector: this establishes a divergence of interests regarding trade liberalization.

This paper concerns tariffs, so the direct effects in Axiom 1 include increases in imports directly due, at the initial terms of trade, to the tariff reduction (the tariff reduction times the price elasticity of import demand times the initial level of imports), denoted ΔM_D. If the reductions are not unilateral but instead part of an international agreement, there will also be a direct effect ΔX_D on exports, equal to the direct increases by trading partners of imports of home goods. Indirect effects consist of changes, ΔM_I and ΔX_I, in imports and exports necessary to restore equilibrium and to maintain balanced trade (which I assume throughout) together with the induced changes, ΔR_x and ΔR_m, in the real rewards of factors specific to exportables and to importables, respectively.

I represent the effect, at the *initial* terms of trade, of a change in trade policy on a linear approximation to the government's objective function S as follows:

$$\Delta S = a\Delta R_x + a\Delta R_m + b\Delta X_D + c\Delta X_I - b\Delta M_D - c\Delta M_I. \tag{1}$$

The parameters a, b, and c are assumed nonnegative. Axiom 2 is accommodated by including changes in both factor rewards and trade volumes. With trade liberalizations, $\Delta R_x > 0$, $\Delta R_m < 0$, and in (1) I assume for simplicity that the government cares simply for the excess of what gainers gain over what losers lose (this will be modified subsequently).

Choose units so that the international price of B in terms of A is unity. The requirement that trade should balance is therefore $\Delta X_D + \Delta X_I - \Delta M_D - \Delta M_I - M\Delta P = 0$. Substituting this requirement into (1) and rearranging terms gives

$$\phi = \Delta y + \mu\Delta MA, \tag{2}$$

where $\phi \equiv \Delta S/a - (c/a)M\Delta P$, $\Delta y = \Delta R_x + \Delta R_m$, $\mu = [(b - c)/c](c/a)$, and $\Delta MA = \Delta X_D - \Delta M_D$. In this expression, $(b - c)/c$, which Axiom 1 requires to be nonnegative, is a measure of the extra sensitivity of political support to direct effects, and c/a measures the sensitivity of political support to trade volumes independently of their effects on factor rewards. I call the term ΔMA the *net* exchange[7] of market access: the excess of the direct amount by which the tariff reductions would raise foreign demand for home exports, at initial world prices, over the direct amount they would raise home demand for imports (in terms of exportables), again at initial world prices. Since ϕ is defined relative to the initial terms of trade, it excludes any effects that might be caused by consequent terms-of-trade movements. I do not assume that governments don't care about such effects: ϕ is simply defined to be net of such concerns.

This net exchange of market access can therefore be written as follows:

$$\Delta MA = \sum_i M_i \varepsilon_i \tau_i - M\varepsilon\tau. \tag{3}$$

Here i indexes over the trading partners of the home country, M_i indicates country i's initial imports from the home country, ε_i country i's relevant elasticity of demand for imports from the home economy, and τ_i the degree of trade liberalization by country i called for by the policy change under consideration. M, ε, and τ denote the analogous terms for the home economy.

The parameter μ, the *market access sensitivity*, reflects the importance the government attaches to market access. μ is positively related to the extra sensitivity of political support to direct effects and to trade volumes independently of their effects on factor rewards; if either of these is zero, ΔMA drops out in (2). Introducing political externalities consists of assuming $\mu > 0$. These externalities amount to the following: by entering into a trade agreement, each government enables its partners to capture a larger share of the credit for the benefits of that agreement by furnishing signals (in the form of "concessions") that the agreement has indeed generated those benefits.

This formulation of the government's objective function accords very well with what people who actually negotiate trade agreements claim to be trying to do. They have been quite consistent about this: they have always said they seek to "exchange market access." Krugman (1991, p. 25) gives a concise description:

> "To make sense of international trade negotiations, one needs to remember three simple rules about the objectives of the negotiating countries:
>
> (1) *Exports are good.*
> (2) *Imports are bad.*
> (3) *Other things equal, an equal increase in imports and exports is good.*"

This sounds like economic illiteracy. But if so, it has been a very persistent illiteracy by the very people who make policy. It is natural to suspect, as Krugman (1991) argues and as I have just done, that this is a reflection of a political-economy concern for special interests. The political-economy approach has become pervasive in the last 15 years in the positive theory of trade policy.[8] My notion of political externalities is exactly consistent with Krugman's description, and gives it a behavioral basis.

4. A (Limited) Rehabilitation of the Received Theory

Before examining the implications of political externalities for trade negotiations, I briefly consider their relation to the Received Theory in a very special case: that of just two countries. Then (3) becomes

$$\Delta MA = M(\varepsilon^*\tau^* - \varepsilon\tau),$$

where an asterisk refers to the foreign country. Thus, since the budget constraint requires an increase in home imports to equal in value an increase in home exports, the exchange of market access just equals the excess demand on world markets for home exports implied, at the initial terms of trade, by the policy changes. This immediately implies that the change in P, the relative world price of home imports in terms of exports (assumed initially unity), necessary to reestablish equilibrium in world markets, is the following:

$$\Delta P = -\frac{\Delta MA}{\varepsilon + \varepsilon^* - 1}.$$

The denominator on the right-hand side of this expression will be recognized as the familiar Marshall–Lerner term. It is also well known that, at the initial terms of trade, the change in real income implied by a trade-policy change equals the implied change in imports multiplied by the wedge between home and world relative prices: $\Delta y = t\Delta M$, where t is the home *ad valorem* tariff.

Now, set $\mu = 1/(\varepsilon + \varepsilon^* - 1)$ and perform the above indicated substitutions into (2) to obtain

$$\phi = t\Delta M - M\Delta P. \tag{4}$$

Equation (4) will be recognized as the standard expression for the effect of a change in trade policy on real national income.[9] Thus (4) is a special case of (2). This implies the following.

PROPOSITION 1. *Any results implied by two-country, two-commodity models of the Received Theory, regarding trade agreements, necessarily apply if those models instead use an objective function based on (my concept of) political externalities.*

A large fraction of the papers concerned with the Received Theory have indeed utilized 2×2 models.[10] But, before heaving a collective sigh of relief, note the following. First, we utilize 2×2 models not because we think the world is 2×2, but because these models display in sharp relief features that we believe are of general significance. So a 2×2 model that is basically misspecified (as is the Received Theory with regard to multilateral trade agreements) is suspect from the very beginning.

Second, the above argument depends critically on the exchange of market access being identical to the world excess demand for home exportables. This identification is valid in a world of two countries, but collapses with more than two, unless reciprocity is universal. Since multilateral trade agreements, by their very nature, involve more than two countries, this objection is fatal.

So, my rehabilitation of the Received Theory does not in the end amount to all that much. But it's the best I can do.

5. Trade Agreements Motivated by Political Externalities

I now describe more fully a simple formal model in which to embed the above objective function. To make it absolutely clear that terms-of-trade effects are not surreptitiously driving my results, I want a model in which individual countries lack market power.

The Background

Assume two goods, A and B, two factors of production, and $2N$ countries. N countries have a comparative advantage in A and N in B; otherwise they are all identical. Technology is neoclassical. N is large enough so that each country perceives itself as too small to manipulate world prices to its own advantage. Assume a succession of periods. Factors are both mobile between sectors across periods, but both are immobile within each period. All consumers spend positively on both goods.

Initially, each country has an historically given tariff t on all imports. Tariff revenue is redistributed to the populace in a lump-sum fashion not altering relative income distribution. I assume away export subsidies.[11] For simplicity I take the initial tariff as nondiscriminatory and common to all countries. Governments determine changes in initial tariffs, either unilaterally or with bilateral or multilateral negotiation. I shall not explicitly model negotiations. The intersectoral immobility of factors for the duration of the period ensures that in each country one interest group prefers more protection and one prefers less protection.

At the close of any negotiations, governments implement tariff changes and trade takes place. Once the period ends, factors become free to move between sectors, and, once they have done so, history repeats itself, with the initial tariffs for the new period equal to the final tariffs from the preceding period and with a new generation of policymakers ready to consider tariff changes.

Note that, if instead of the objective function (2), I were to adopt the perspective of the Received Theory, no trade agreements of any kind would arise in this model. A government that cared only about national welfare would unilaterally adopt free trade. A government that also had some domestic objective that could be influenced only by trade policy would unilaterally adopt the level of protection that optimally trades off national welfare for that objective. In either case, policymakers would unilaterally be doing the best they can and there would be no potential role for trade agreements.

Unilateralism and Reciprocity

For illustration, consider some of the implications in this model of the objective function (2). These implications will be useful for what follows and will also show how the objective function, and the axioms about political support that produced it, cause governments to behave as they do.

Suppose a unilateral reduction $\tau_i = (-\dot{t}/(1+t)) > 0$ in all its tariffs by a single country i. At unchanged world prices, the home relative price of imports falls by the amount of the tariff decrease, so that $\Delta MA = -\varepsilon\tau_i M_i < 0$ and $\Delta y > 0$, with the latter bounded above by the increase in real income that would follow from the adoption of free trade. This immediately implies the following.

PROPOSITION 2. *A government with objective function* (2) *will never liberalize unilaterally, with a large enough market access sensitivity* μ.

Consider instead a unilateral adoption of an export tax $\sigma_i > 0$ by a single country i. At unchanged world prices, the home relative price of exportables falls by the amount of the tax, so that $\Delta MA = \Delta X_D = -\varepsilon\sigma_i X_i < 0$ and $\Delta y < 0$. This immediately implies the following.

PROPOSITION 3. *A government with objective function* (2) *will never implement an export tax.*

Note that Propositions 2 and 3 are *not* simple reflections of the idea that a policymaker, having chosen a best response to the existing environment, would have no reason to change that response without a change in that environment. These propositions are independent of the initial situation, and, therefore, consistent with the possibility that today's policymakers start off with systems of protection, inherited from the past, quite at odds with what they would themselves choose.

This is a property absolutely essential for any theory purporting to be relevant to post-World War II liberalization. The original GATT negotiators had to work with a structure of protection bequeathed to them by policymakers from the 1930s, with a radically different view of the virtues of protection. This heritage, and the reactions to it, has been the starting point for trade negotiations ever since.

Note also that Proposition 3 reflects the small-country assumption: an export tax levied by a country with market power would generate a countervailing terms-of-trade improvement. Proposition 3 would then continue to hold if and only if the political externality outweighed the terms-of-trade externality. Assuming away the latter trivially ensures this.

Define a liberalization as *reciprocal* if accompanied by foreign liberalizations that imply $\Delta MA = 0$. Thus the second term of the governmental objective function vanishes, so that, since $\Delta y > 0$, the following is immediate.

PROPOSITION 4. *A government with objective function (2) will always accept a reciprocal liberalization, and it would prefer a reciprocal move to free trade.*

Reciprocity neutralizes concern about market access, rendering the magnitude of μ irrelevant. Governments will not unilaterally liberalize, but they wish to negotiate reciprocal liberalizations that achieve free trade (there is, however, no assurance that reciprocal liberalizations can in fact produce free trade). All bargaining, whether bilateral or multilateral, will involve reciprocal liberalization. Furthermore, Proposition 3 implies there is no need for a reciprocal trade agreement to rule out export taxes. Recall that I have assumed that trade cannot be subsidized: Tariffs are constrained to be nonnegative.

Recall, however, that the objective function (2) is based on a linear approximation to S. Thus Proposition 4, regarding a reciprocal move to free trade, could become irrelevant if such a move required a sufficiently large amount of liberalization.

Thus political externalities immediately deliver what the Received Theory has dramatically failed to do. To proceed further, I next take a closer look at actual multilateral trade agreements.

6. Stylized Facts of Multilateral Trade Liberalization

The GATT–WTO liberalization has taken a very special form, to wit:

1. *Actual multilateral trade agreements do* not *prevent countries from trying to influence the terms of trade.* This was argued above.
2. *Negotiated agreements feature* reciprocity*: the mutual exchange of concessions.* That is, one country reduces tariffs in exchange for tariff reductions by its trading partners.
3. *Liberalization has been* gradual. By this I do not mean the phased implementation of a negotiated reduction, but rather a succession of negotiated reductions building on each other. Customs unions and free trade areas are typically implemented in phases, but the initial agreement to form one claims to commit (as the GATT requires) the participants to substantially free internal trade by some definite date.
4. Nondiscrimination *is central: Each country should be a most favored nation (MFN) of every other country.*[12] Especially notable here is that Article I of the GATT establishes nondiscrimination as a *basic* principle, instead of defining it as a subject for negotiation, as Article XXVIIIbis does with tariffs.
5. *Trade agreements are* multilateral. Actual negotiations on specific issues need not involve all countries, but the final agreement is signed on to by all.

These features are not inevitable. The Received Theory imagines the exact opposite of the first point. Reciprocity has hardly been universal outside the GATT framework—there have been many unilateral liberalizations, by developing countries and others, in recent years. Nor is there any inherent need for liberalization to be gradual: customs unions and free trade areas purport to do it all at once. Requiring nondiscrimination eliminates at the outset many potential agreements. Before the current half century, trade agreements were seldom multilateral.

So the most important positive accomplishment of trade policy in history has taken a very special form. Why reciprocity? Why gradual liberalization? Why MFN? Why multilateralism? What are their implications?

One would think that explaining this very special form would be a central task of international trade theory. Astonishingly, this has not been so. While the descriptive literature is vast, the analytical literature remains sparse.

For example, MFN has long interested economists, with a slow but steady appearance of papers addressing the theoretical relation of MFN and multilateral liberalization; see Viner (1951), Caplin and Krishna (1988), Ludema (1991), Choi (1995), McCalman (1997), Schwartz and Sykes (1997), and Bagwell and Staiger (1999). In recent years this literature has usually taken a game-theoretic perspective. Analysis has been complicated and has often left the reader uncertain whether real-world essentials were even addressed. An MFN clause was included in the early nineteenth-century trade agreement between England and Portugal that motivated Ricardo's choice of example for his explanation of comparative advantage—the most famous passage in trade theory. Understanding the relation between MFN and trade liberalization has been one of the major unsolved problems in our field from its very beginning.

The theory in the previous section, built on political externalities, has delivered characteristics 1 and 2 above, but is thus far silent on points 3, 4, and 5. To proceed further, I add more structure to the governmental objective function. In particular, consider the following additional axiom regarding the political-economy environment.

AXIOM 3. *Government officials wish to avoid policy actions that would cause a serious reduction in the income of any interest group.*

Subject people to a big hit and they will hate you—and act accordingly. Small damages, though, will be submerged by larger concerns. This is the idea behind the familiar conservative social welfare function advocated by Corden (1997, pp. 74–6) as a useful aid to understanding trade policy. Hillman (1982) shows how similar conclusions can be derived from a political support function. Deardorff (1987) and Brander and Spencer (1994) provide further applications of Corden's conservative social welfare function to trade policy. Finally, prospect theory's treatment of consumer behavior emphasizes an analogous asymmetric valuation of gains and losses by individuals.[13]

To incorporate the concerns of this axiom, I replace the objective function (2) with the following:

$$\phi = \left[\Delta R_x - (-\Delta R_m)^{1+\gamma}\right] + \mu \Delta MA. \tag{5}$$

The parameter $\gamma > 0$ reflects Axiom 3: political support is increasingly sensitive to reductions in the income of any group.[14] I accordingly refer to γ as the *Corden sensitivity*.

Since $\Delta y = \Delta R_x + \Delta R_m > 0$, the following is immediate.

PROPOSITION 5. *A government with objective function (5) will always accept a sufficiently small reciprocal liberalization. It will never accept a move to free trade, provided that the Corden sensitivity γ is sufficiently large.*

So gradualism is a simple consequence of the assumed environment. But nondiscrimination and multilateralism are more involved; they are examined at length in the following section.

7. Characteristics of Negotiated Trade Liberalization

Suppose that, given high initial tariffs, countries may commence negotiations. Because of Proposition 2 no government will liberalize unilaterally, but Proposition 5 implies that each government would concede some market access, harming import-competing interests, for reciprocal foreign market access beneficial to exporters. Governments may negotiate bilaterally or multilaterally. I will not explicitly model the negotiations; instead I ask what might characterize *any* reasonable bargaining process, given the objective function (5).

First, I need to introduce some symbols and some jargon. Let τ_{ij} denote a hypothetical rate of reduction in the tariff country i applies to imports from country j. Let $\mathbf{T} = \{\tau_{ij}\}$. No country attempts to tax the good in which it has a comparative advantage (Proposition 3), so $\mathbf{T}$ is a nonnegative vector with $2N^2$ elements. Because of the common initial tariff, the effective rate of liberalization for country i, τ_i^M, would simply be the largest rate of reduction it would *M*ake: $\tau_i^M = \max_j \tau_{ij}$. Let n_i^M denote the number of countries j for which $\tau_{ij} = \tau_i^M$. Likewise, let τ_i^R denote the largest effective concession country i would *R*eceive: $\tau_i^R = \max_j\{\tau_j^M | \tau_j^M = \tau_{ij}\}$; and let n_i^R denote the number of countries j for which $\tau_{ji} = \tau_i^R$. Finally, let τ^* denote the value of τ that maximizes $\Delta R_x(\tau) - (-\Delta R_m(\tau))^{1+\gamma}$.

Definition 1. *A hypothetical* $\mathbf{T}$ *is an* optimal reciprocal liberalization *if, for every country i,* $\tau_i^M = \tau_i^R = \tau^*$ *and* $n_i^M = n_i^R$.

One optimal reciprocal liberalization is the *symmetric* $\mathbf{T} = \{\tau^*\}$, which can be viewed as multilateral and nondiscriminatory. But there are many others. For example, with *bilateral discriminatory* liberalization the A exporters and B exporters pair off, with each country liberalizing by τ^* with respect to its partner, leaving all other tariffs unchanged; *chained discriminatory* liberalization involves, for example, A exporter i liberalizing only with respect to B exporter j who liberalizes only with respect to A exporter k who liberalizes only with respect to B exporter l who liberalizes only with respect to i; *regional* liberalization has the countries dividing into subgroups, each of which practices bilateral, chained, or nondiscriminatory multilateral liberalization. I've deliberately set up the model so that there are many potential ways to go: *I want it crystal-clear to every reader that the following results are not simple reflections of my objective function or of the assumed axioms that produced it.*

Concession Diversion

Suppose that Carolina, with a comparative advantage in A, has received an offer from Domina, who has a comparative advantage in B, for a reciprocal reduction of 20% in their tariffs on each other's goods. It matters not whether this is in bilateral negotiations between these two countries or part of a broader multilateral effort: it would be part of the overall $\mathbf{T}$, however reached. The government of Carolina believes the implied exchange of market access would be a net benefit. But Carolina would fear that Domina might subsequently offer a reciprocal concession of, say, 21%, to some other country, Euboea, with a comparative advantage in A. This would enable Domina to obtain access to the Euboean market simply by diverting to that country the access it had previously granted to Carolina, leaving the latter with nothing to show for its concession. I call this *concession diversion*: It can be thought of as the logical extension of the possibility of "concession erosion" described by Schwartz and Sykes (1997, p. 62). Concession diversion motivates the following test for whether a proposed negotiated equilibrium **T** might actually be adopted.

DEFINITION 2. *A proposed vector* **T** *of tariff reductions is potentially implementable if there exists no pair of countries, i and j, that can make themselves better off by increasing* τ_{ij} *and* τ_{ji}, *holding all other components of* **T** *fixed.*

To see how serious concession diversion might be, suppose that **T** is an optimal reciprocal liberalization, and consider any B exporter Domina and A exporter Euboea such that neither country is a unique maximal liberalizer to the other.[15] Suppose Domina and Euboea now agree to increase τ_{DE} and τ_{ED} a small amount δ above the levels $\tau_D^M = \tau^*$ and $\tau_E^M = \tau^*$ called for by **T**, holding all other reductions unchanged. Consider the implications for the objective functions of the governments of Domina and Euboea. Domina will experience a small increase in ΔR_x, a small decrease in ΔR_m, a small increase in the demand for importables, and, because of concession diversion from the n_E^M (other) country(s) to which Euboea was the maximal liberalizer, a large *direct* increase $[(\tau^* + \delta)\varepsilon M]$ in foreign demand for its exportables. Thus ΔMA must be significantly positive and must dominate the effect on the government's objective function. Euboea is influenced similarly, so the two countries will find the maneuver tempting. The only effect on the objective function of the government of the other countries to which Domina and Euboea were maximal liberalizers, on the other hand, are direct decreases in the demands for their exports. With enough concession diversion, those other countries' liberalizations would become in effect unilateral, which by Proposition 2 those governments do not want. Of course, they can play the same game, but that only emphasizes further the fragility of the proposed **T**.

PROPOSITION 6. *No optimal reciprocal liberalization is potentially implementable.*

Liberalizing all the way to universal free trade is potentially implementable, but no country wants to do that. Doing nothing, **T** = {0}, though not optimal, is not potentially implementable either, because it is susceptible also to concession diversion. Quite a bind!

Nondiscrimination as an Externality

The basic problem is that governments do not care, *per se*, for the *tariffs* that they levy on each other's goods, but for their *expected effects*. The latter is determined by the tariffs they each levy on the goods of *all* countries, not just on each other. Meaningful negotiations cannot be limited to the tariffs countries levy on each other's goods; the partners must also be constrained in some way with respect to future agreements. But the constraints should not be too tight, or they will prevent future negotiations entirely.

The MFN clause is a natural candidate for such a constraint because it is very simple and offers direct assurance against concession diversion, the heart of the problem. But the assurance is only partial. Including MFN in a trade agreement assures a country that the market access it has bargained for will not be turned over entirely to some other country, but it offers no assurance that this access will not have to be shared. So one might expect inclusion of MFN status to be insufficient to deal with the problem. Surprisingly, it can be sufficient, if its use is sufficiently widespread. The reason is that MFN clauses confer *indirect* assurance in addition to the above direct assurance.

To see this, suppose that the use of MFN is universal and consider the optimal symmetric negotiation $\mathbf{T} = \{\tau^*\}$. Suppose again that **T** implies that Carolina, with a comparative advantage in *A*, and Domina, with a comparative advantage in *B*, will make a reciprocal reduction of τ^* in their tariffs on each other's goods. Suppose Domina were to then consider a reciprocal $\tau^* + \delta$ tariff reduction with *A* exporter Euboea. If Euboea is bound by MFN status with all *B* exporters, this would simply amount, from Domina's point of view, to a further reciprocal liberalization. Since τ^* was optimal, this would not be welcome. Carolina, understanding this, knows that concession diversion by Domina is not a threat, and will therefore agree to **T**.

Proposition 7. *The symmetric reciprocal optimal liberalization* $\mathbf{T} = \{\tau^*\}$ *is potentially implementable with universal MFN.*

Crucial to this result is not the partial *direct* assurance that Carolina, by virtue of its MFN status with Domina, receives of some access to the latter's market. Rather it is the *indirect* assurance that, because of the MFN relation of *each* of Carolina's trade partners (such as Domina) with *all* of its competitors (such as Euboea), none of the former will be tempted to try concession diversion.

MFN and Multilateralism

Since I do not model the bargaining process itself, I must define multilateralism as a property of a potential outcome of such bargaining.

Definition 3. *The result of trade negotiations will be described as multilateral if each country's agreement to that result is contingent upon every other country's agreement.*

The symmetric optimal reciprocal liberalization is the expected multilateral, nondiscriminatory result. But Proposition 7 doesn't require multilateralism: Simultaneous bilateral agreements could achieve the same result. But there are two compelling reasons why, if MFN status is what makes trade agreements possible, those agreements will, sooner or later, be multilateral.

First, in the above argument, MFN is important to Carolina *not* because it receives such status, but because each of its competitors has conceded such status to each of its potential trade partners. This is a classic externality. Bilateral negotiations cannot be expected to acknowledge it; multilateral negotiations can.

Proposition 8. *Multilateralism can internalize the crucial externality that allows MFN status to make international trade negotiations possible.*

Perhaps this explains why, in Article I, the GATT imposes MFN as a general operating principle, instead of allowing countries to negotiate about it, as Article XXVIIIbis does with tariffs.

The second reason is that outstanding agreements featuring MFN constrain the ability to find further beneficial bilateral reciprocal tariff reductions, and the more agreements there are, the more limiting the constraint. So MFN renders bilateralism impractical.

Suppose that some A exporter has reached trade agreements with several exporters of B, calling for a common tariff, and that the agreements all feature MFN status. Consider the implications of another agreement with one of these partners, calling for a further reciprocal tariff reduction of τ. Because of the MFN status provided by the earlier agreements, this reduction would extend to all the countries from which the A exporter actually imports B.

Starting from an initial $\tau = 0$, the effect on the home government's objective function of introducing such a marginal bilateral agreement with some partner, who has m MFN agreements in effect, is

$$\left.\frac{d\phi}{d\tau}\right|_{\tau=0} = \left\{\frac{dR_x}{d\tau} - \left(-\frac{dR_m}{d\tau}\right)^{1+\gamma}\right\} + \mu\varepsilon T\left(\frac{1}{m} - 1\right). \tag{6}$$

Thus, given the Corden and market access sensitivities, $d\phi/d\tau < 0$ for m sufficiently large. The world economy will be in a *saturation state*; if all countries have at least m MFN agreements, there will not exist any pair of countries for which a mutually beneficial reciprocal tariff reduction is possible.

PROPOSITION 9. *For sufficiently large Corden and market access sensitivities, mutually beneficial bilateral negotiations will eventually become impossible, if outstanding agreements all embody MFN.*

Note that I have defined multilateralism as a property of a trade agreement itself, not of the negotiations that produce that agreement. Because I introduce no bargaining model, I cannot rule out the possibility that a multilateral agreement might result from a process that involves a lot of bilateral negotiation. (Since this does in fact happen, it's a good thing that I can't rule it out.)

Odds and Ends

I have assumed relentless symmetry between all countries and perfect substitutability between all A goods and between all B goods. These assumptions put my arguments into sharp relief. What happens if they are relaxed?

1. Note first that my logic depends only on the assumed objective function and on significant—not necessarily perfect—substitutability between the goods of different countries; the higher the elasticity of substitution between competing products, the more debilitating the threat of concession diversion. My assumptions are a matter of degree, not of kind.
2. But degree also matters. I will not try here to generalize to broader circumstances, but I instead describe how I think my assumptions matter. First, if all goods are imperfect substitutes, the direct assurance aspect of MFN should offer relatively more significant protection against the relatively less debilitating concession diversion. This would be even more true if countries differ in size and if countries that trade a lot with each other first commence negotiations. (This is sometimes called the *principal-supplier* approach to trade negotiations.) Both of these considerations suggest that multilateralism might be a delayed consequence of incorporating MFN into trade agreements.
3. Perhaps the analysis of this paper demonstrates: why MFN was common in bilateral European agreements before World War I; why, when the US followed a policy of high protection and had little interest in negotiated tariff reductions, it was

content to use a "conditional" MFN offering partners little real assurance of freedom from concession diversion; why the dozens of bilateral agreements the US reached, before GATT even existed, under the authority of the reciprocal Trade Agreements Act, all featured MFN; why the multilateral approach was adopted soon after these bilateral agreements had been reached.

8. Concluding Remarks

The Received Theory of multilateral trade agreements, based on the idea that terms-of-trade externalities between governments are the *sole* reason for negotiating such agreements, has produced an enormous literature but is inconsistent with actual multilateral liberalization. The reason, I have argued, is that, by focusing *only* on terms-of-trade externalities, the Received Theory has arbitrarily excluded other, far more relevant, intergovernmental linkages, notably what I call political externalitities. It's as though a classical physicist, arrogantly assuming away gravity, were to assert that the planetary orbits must be determined by Brownian motion because that's the *sole* available candidate.

How could the Received Theory, so at odds with the facts, be so dominant for so long? I suppose part of the reason is that we trade theorists shy away from looking at the dirty details of trade agreements, assuming this appropriate for lesser mortals, such as lawyers. Also, arrogance has perhaps led us to dismiss out of hand statements by "ignorant" policymakers about what they are doing in favor of alternative hypotheses that, though absent from the real world, we at least understand. Finally, I suspect that we have tended to reject, as "politically incorrect," arguments critical of, or just distinct from, the Received Theory.[16]

This paper has presented a multicountry model with high initial tariff barriers—a caricature of the world of half a century ago. Government officials with an objective function reflecting political externalities but with no individual ability to influence world prices negotiate with each other in a succession of periods. The analysis presented no formal bargaining model but instead asked what should characterize *any* reasonable model, given the objective function. This gives immediate and transparent explanations[17] of gradual liberalization, reciprocity, MFN, and multilateralism. It allows us, in effect, to take seriously what policymakers have for over sixty years been saying that they are doing.

The picture painted by Propositions 2–9 corresponds nicely to actual historical experience. My point of departure has been a set of axioms about political-economy concerns producing the objective function (5), characterized by political externalities and consistent with how government negotiators actually seem to behave. The essential argument is summarized as follows.

1. If governments, sensitive to political externalities, conduct trade policy as they claim to be conducting it, they will not liberalize unilaterally but will find reciprocal liberalization that does not go all the way to free trade desirable.
2. Reciprocal liberalization is valuable to a government because negotiated foreign liberalization allows that government credibly to claim credit, in an environment where many things change at once, for the good fortune experienced by exporters.
3. If reasonably close substitutes for each country's products exist elsewhere, reciprocal trade negotiations of any sort, that do not intend to go all the way to free trade, require that negotiating governments' subsequent behavior toward third countries be constrained in some way.

4. MFN status is a useful way, and the simplest way, to constrain negotiating governments' subsequent behavior toward third countries. And, if used enough, it works, *not* because of the direct assurance it offers individual countries, but because it functions as an externality.
5. Multilateralism can internalize this crucial externality. Thus it is appropriate that Article I of the GATT establishes nondiscrimination as a *basic* principle, instead of defining it as a subject for negotiation.
6. If trade agreements do feature MFN, negotiations must, sooner or later, be multilateral in any event.

My bottom line The dominant Received Theory of multilateral trade agreements, developed over a half century and based squarely on terms-of-trade externalities, is irrelevant to actual multilateral trade agreements, which do not constrain terms-of-trade manipulation. An alternative approach, based on political externalities, is consistent with such agreements, mirrors what policymakers have always claimed to be doing, and can explain the salient features of the multilateral trade order. The explanation of gradual liberalization, reciprocity, MFN, and multilateralism immediately becomes transparent, elementary, and compelling. Concession diversion is the key.

References

Bagwell, K. and R. W. Staiger, "An Economic Theory of GATT," *American Economic Review* 89 (1999):215–48.

———, *The Economics of the World Trading System*, Cambridge, MA: MIT Press (2002).

Brainard, S. L. and T. Verdier, "Lobbying and Adjustment in Declining Industries," *European Economic Review* 38 (1994):586–95.

Brander, J. and B. Spencer, "Trade Adjustment Assistance: Welfare and Incentive Effects of Payments to Displaced Workers," *Journal of International Economics* 37 (1994):239–61.

Choi, J. P., "Optimal Tariffs and the Choice of Technology: Discriminatory Tariffs vs the 'Most Favored Nation' Clause," *Journal of International Economics* 38 (1995):143–60.

Corden, W. M., *Trade Policy and Economic Welfare*, 2nd edn, Oxford: Oxford University Press (1997).

Caplin, A. and K. Krishna, "Tariffs and the Most-Favored-Nation Clause: a Game Theoretic Approach," *Seoul Journal of Economics* 1 (1988):267–89.

Deardorff, A., "Safeguards Policy and the Conservative Social Welfare Function," in H. K. Kierzkowski (ed.), *Protection and Competition in International Trade*, Oxford: Blackwell (1987).

Ethier, W. J., *Modern International Economics*, 3rd edn, New York: W. W. Norton & Co. (1995).

———, "The International Commercial System," *Essays in International Finance* no. 210, International Finance Section, Department of Economics, Princeton University (1998a).

———, "Regionalism in a Multilateral World," *Journal of Political Economy* 6 (1998b):1214–45.

———, "Punishments and Dispute Settlement in Trade Agreements: the Equivalent Withdrawal of Concessions," PIER working paper 01-021, Department of Economics, University of Pennsylvania (2001).

———, "Unilateralism in a Multilateral World," *Economic Journal* 112 (2002):266–92.

Grossman, G. and E. Helpman, *Interest Groups and Trade Policy*, Princeton: Princeton University Press (2002).

Hillman, A. L., "Declining Industries and Political-Support Protectionist Motives," *American Economic Review* 72 (1982):1180–90.

———, *The Political Economy of Protection*, Chur: Harwood Academic Publishers (1989).

———, "Protectionist Policies as the Regulation of International Industry," *Public Choice* 67 (1990):101–10.

Hillman, A. L. and P. Moser, "Trade Liberalization as Politically Optimal Exchange of Market Access," in M. Canzoneri, W. J. Ethier, and V. Grilli (eds.), *The New Transatlantic Economy*, Cambridge: Cambridge University Press (1996):295–312.
Hillman, A. L., N. V. Long, and P. Moser, "Modeling Reciprocal Trade Liberalization: the Political-economy and National-welfare Perspectives," *Swiss Journal of Economics and Statistics* 131 (1995):503–15.
Johnson, H. G., "Optimum Tariffs and Retaliation," *Review of Economic Studies* 21 (1953/54):142–53.
Krugman, P., "The Move toward Free Trade Zones," in Federal Reserve Bank of Kansas City, *Policy Implications of Trade and Currency Zones*, Symposium Series (1991):7–42.
Long, N. V. and N. Vousden, "Protectionist Responses and Declining Industries," *Journal of International Economics* 30 (1991):87–103.
Ludema, R., "International Trade Bargaining and the Most-Favored-Nation Clause," *Economics & Politics* 3 (1991):1–20.
Nelson, D., "Endogenous Tariff Theory: a Critical Survey," *American Journal of Political Science* 32 (1988):796–837.
McCalman, P., "Multi-lateral Trade Negotiations and the Most Favored Nation Clause," unpublished manuscript, Department of Economics, University of Wisconsin (1997).
Rodrik, D., "Political Economy of Trade Policy," in G. Grossman and K. Rogoff (eds.), *Handbook of International Economics*, Amsterdam: North-Holland (1995):1457–95.
Schwartz, W. F. and A. O. Sykes, "The Economics of the Most Favored Nation Clause," in J. S. Bhandani and A. O. Sykes (eds.), *Economic Dimensions in International Law: Comparative and Empirical Perspectives*, Cambridge: Cambridge University Press (1997):43–79.
Shafir, E., I. Simonson, and A. Tversky, "Reason-based Choice," in W. M. Goldstein and R. M. Hogarth (eds.), *Research on Judgment and Decision Making: Currents, Connections, and Controversies*, New York: Cambridge University Press (1997):69–94.
Viner, J., *International Economics*, Glencoe, IL: Free Press (1951).

Notes

1. Harry Johnson dominated trade theory during his lifetime, but is now remembered mainly for this single paper.
2. By contrast, those policymakers and trade lawyers who know what the terms of trade are (apparently a small minority, I grant) seem to regard this point as quite obvious.
3. Don't take my word for it: read the GATT. This is admittedly not a pleasant experience, but the main text is only 40-odd pages, and the addenda do not address this issue.
4. The US Constitution, however, prohibits export taxes. Thus, by signing on to actual multilateral trade agreements, the US has surrendered the ability to influence its terms of trade while allowing its trade partners to retain theirs. This is inexplicable from the viewpoint of the Received Theory.
5. This critique need not apply to papers that consider intergovernmental externalities that operate independently of the terms of trade. Examples include Hillman et al. (1995), Hillman and Moser (1996), and Ethier (1998a, 2001). But such contributions constitute only a tiny fraction of the theoretical literature on trade agreements.
6. Extensions of Hillman's model may be found in Long and Vousden (1991) and Brainard and Verdier (1994).
7. See Hillman and Moser (1996), and also Hillman (1990).
8. See Nelson (1988), Hillman (1989), and Rodrik (1995) for surveys.
9. See, for example, Ethier (1995, p. A-41).
10. I have myself utilized the argument behind Proposition 1 in Ethier (2001). Bagwell and Staiger (1999, footnote 16) advance, more generally, a closely related point regarding *reciprocal* trade agreements.
11. Unlike export taxes, export subsidies have been of substantial concern to the GATT and to several of the GATT rounds of negotiations. Such subsidies are presumably inhibited by coun-

tervailing-duty laws (in existence *prior* to postwar liberalization and explicitly allowed by the GATT in Article VI).

12. One nation extends MFN status to another if it pledges it will never levy a higher duty on products from that country than on similar products from any other country. The GATT imposes this in Article I, but it also allows, in Article XXIV, exceptions for customs unions and free trade areas.

13. See, for example, Shafir et al. (1997).

14. Note that $\gamma > 0$ appropriately reflects a conservative social welfare function once policy changes are significant enough (or units are chosen so) that $-\Delta R_m > 1$. This observation was prompted by a comment by Rob Feenstra.

15. There will always be many such possible pairs.

16. This suspicion reflects years of experience on both sides of the journal editorial process.

17. This paper has thus attempted to endogenize the basic features of multilateralism. Ethier (1998b, 2002) respectively endogenize regionalism and unilateralism in such a context, and Ethier (1998a) provides a nontechnical overview.

KEIO ECONOMIC STUDIES **42**(1-2), 1–23 (2005)

PUNISHMENTS AND DISPUTE SETTLEMENT IN TRADE AGREEMENTS: The Equivalent Withdrawal of Concessions

Wilfred J. ETHIER

Department of Economics, University of Pennsylvania, Philadelphia, USA

First version received October 2005; final version accepted November 2005

Abstract: I interpret dispute settlement procedures and the principle of equivalent withdrawal ofconcessions as responses to the fact that trade agreements are incomplete contracts. With no adjudication phase and the degree of trade relatedness known with certainty, an agreement will feature commensurate punishments, will induce violation of the dispute settlement ruling, and will deliver optimal liberalization and optimal unilateral trade-related action. With an adjudication phase, the agreement will feature less liberalization, but still presumably approximate commensurate punishment. The agreement will likely induce abiding by the ruling when negotiators attach more importance to the adjudication phase, and violating it when they attach less.

Key words: Incomplete Contracts, Reciprocal Conflict, Substantially Equivalent Withdrawal Of Concessions, Commensurate Punishment, Abidement Property.
JEL Classification Codes: F02, F13.

OVER THIRTY YEARS AGO, Michihiro Ohyama, my Rochester classmate, published in this journal a classic contribution [Ohyama (1972)] to the normative theory of international trade. More recently, he has been investigating issues relevant to the World Trade Organization (WTO). Indeed, negotiated trade liberalization under the auspices of the General Agreement on Tariffs and Trade (GATT) and the WTO has been the big international economic story of the last sixty years. The GATT contained a dispute settlement procedure (DSP) which proved to be of only spasmodic significance. The Uruguay Round of multilateral trade negotiations, which established the WTO, significantly changed this procedure in the hopes of increasing its use. These hopes, at least, have not been frustrated.

Acknowledgements. I thank Catherine Yuhe Chang, Arye Hillman, Henrik Horn, and Peter Rosendorff for many useful exchanges, seminar participants at Columbia, Kiel, Munich, New Orleans, and Southern Methodist Universities for helpful comments, and EPRU in Copenhagen for a congenial environment in which to pursue this research.
E-mail: ethier@econ.sas.upenn.edu

But the recent vociferous (and sometimes violent) protests of environmentalists and social activists have been motivated to a significant (and perhaps dominant) degree by the decisions of the WTO DSP. This paper addresses, in such a context, the *economic* role of a system of punishments and dispute settlement.

1. INTRODUCTION

The GATT/WTO trade liberalization has had to deal with numerous trade disputes between individual countries, and the need to address these has produced a multilateral response.

These disputes within the GATT DSP, outside of it, or within the WTO DSP and the response, can be summarized by the following stylized facts.

1. Trade disputes are inherently *bilateral*, not multilateral.

The direct participants to trade disputes (whether two or several), and only they, initiate the disputes, force their timing, undertake negotiations to settle, and inflict punishments. This is true even if the dispute is conducted within a multilaterally-established DSP.[1] Indeed, a major function of such a system is to keep disputes bilateral by inducing aggrieved nations to go before a panel of experts rather than to seek allies among third countries. This is not necessarily a good thing: An insightful contribution by Maggi (1999) has shown that, in the presence of strategic complementarities across governments imposing tariffs on the same good, a multilateral DSP could enlarge aggregate punishment beyond that obtainable as a sum of bilateral punishments, allowing the negotiation of more multilateral liberalization.

2. A formal DSP was created and continues to evolve.

The procedure was created years ago by the GATT, but the most important steps in its evolution were the Uruguay Round changes mentioned above, embodied in the Dispute Settlement Undertaking of that agreement.

3. The DSP of the WTO has almost always decided in favor of the complainant (C) and, therefore, against the defendant (D).

Defendants clearly won only 2 of the first 44 decisions under the WTO system. Countries file complaints only when confident (usually rightly) that their complaints are justified, and not to acquire a "tough" reputation or to extract a nuisance value. This, too, has basically been the case when a DSP has not been utilized: Countries have provoked confrontations only when confident that concessions would result.

4. Punishments for alleged violations of past agreements have been *delayed*.

A decision to utilize a DSP is in practice a decision to delay punishment until that procedure has run its course. But, even when a DSP is not utilized, countries convinced that partners have violated trade agreements have consistently chosen to negotiate first, and to threaten punishments should the negotiations fail, rather than immediately to punish, and then to cease the punishments should the negotiations succeed.

[1] Third countries with a vital interest in a matter under dispute between major countries sometimes sign on as participants (the banana war between the US and the EU being a notable example). This can be the easiest way for small countries to participate in the system.

5. Defendants have (much more often than not, at least since the institution of the WTO procedure) abided by the decisions of the DSP. But a number of important, highly visible, cases, involving major countries, have resulted in prolonged violations of DSP decisions.

The decisions to abide have been widely viewed as evidence of the "success" of the WTO DSP (unwelcome success, in the opinion of many environmentalists and social activists), whereas the violations (notably the US–EU disputes on hormone-fed beef and bananas) have been viewed as "failures" that threaten the viability of a "rules-based" system.

6. Punishments for alleged violations of past agreements have consistently been *commensurate with the violations* (*i.e.*, tit-for-tat).

This has been true regardless of whether the punishments, or threatened punishments, have been unilateral or products of a DSP. Indeed, this can be regarded as just one facet of the principle of *substantially equivalent withdrawal of concessions*, pervasive throughout the GATT: See Articles XIX, XXIII, and XIV of the GATT. If a country "fails" an obligation to provide some trade liberalization, its trading partners can also withdraw from their obligations to liberalize to a substantially equivalent degree.

These are very special properties. What is the role of such a system? This paper develops a model to propose answers to these questions and to investigate both the general principle of substantially equivalent withdrawal of concessions and also the role of a DSP. Specifically, I shall depend on stylized facts **1–3** (especially **1** and **3**) to motivate my model, which I then use to analyze **5** and **6**.

1.1. Incomplete contracts

Trade agreements are necessarily incomplete contracts; the DSP, weak punishments, and the principle of substantially equivalent withdrawal of concessions deal with that situation in a context in which individual countries sometimes will be tempted to implement a trade related policy and sometimes will have their trade influenced by a partner's implementation of such a policy.

Incomplete-contract problems arise because the subsequent state of the world is not known when negotiations take place. Any agreement must reflect this. The most straightforward way to deal with it is to negotiate *state-contingent* agreements. But these have severe limitations: The negotiation of even state-invariant changes in recognized policy instruments has become enormously complicated and time consuming. So, negotiated trade agreements necessarily remain, by their very nature, incomplete contracts. This is implicitly acknowledged in the GATT itself, where Articles XXII and XXIII allow response to a "nullification or impairment" of concessions not necessarily the result of an explicit repudiation of a trade agreement.

Trade agreements address a limited number of policy instruments that pertain directly to trade, but governments care about economic outcomes, not about the instruments that can be negotiated. And trade is one aspect of the general equilibrium that depends upon *all* economic instruments. So, *ex post*, governments will be doing things that influence trade and that have not been explicitly addressed by trade agreements: a recipe for disagreement about the constraints implied by those agreements.

Each country is aware, *ex ante*, that it may find itself, *ex post*, harmed by a policy that some trading partner wishes to make. So the former will want a recognized punishment procedure as a deterrent. But that country will also be aware, *ex ante*, that it might find, *ex post*, itself in a position where it would be costly not to take some policy action that would harm a partner. This is the *reciprocal–conflict problem*: Each country knows that it might turn out to be either the accuser or the accused. Thus it is in no country's interest, *ex ante*, to agree that, *ex post*, either the accuser should be unconstrained in its ability to punish or the accused should be unconstrained in its ability to proceed without punishment. This generates a role for a dispute settlement mechanism.

The above argument can motivate the use of either an explicit dispute-settlement mechanism (as under the WTO) or an implicit agreement by countries not to punish without first attempting to negotiate a solution and also spelling out in advance what punishments will be used (as with the U.S. Section 301, and as when trade disputes under the GATT were not submitted to GATT procedures). Furthermore, the theory that follows can also be interpreted as an explanation of the practice of "withdrawal of equivalent concessions," basic to the GATT from its very beginning. In what follows there is no need to distinguish among these alternatives; for concreteness I simply consider a formal dispute settlement mechanism.

Much of the theoretical literature on DSPs[2] assumes that trade policies of partners are imperfectly observable and that the procedures serve to transmit information between agents. But actual trade disputes generally proceed *from* the observation and address what to do about these clearly observed policies.[3] Nor does a central purpose of such procedures seem to be to resolve basic uncertainty about whether specific policies are or are not in fact consistent with trade agreements. As pointed out above, WTO DSP decisions normally go against the defendant. Indeed, in the more visible cases, the financial press routinely and correctly predicts in advance which way decisions will go. So, to focus sharply on the fact that trade agreements are incomplete contracts, I shall oversimplify a bit and assume away both informational asymmetries and uncertainty about whether a policy under dispute does in fact violate trade agreements. The purpose of a DSP instead will be (**i**) to supply a formal international statement that such a policy is in fact a violation, (**ii**) to specify explicitly how it is in violation, and (**iii**) to provide, if necessary, a neutral assessment of the "damage" caused by that policy.

[2] This literature includes Hungerford (1991), Ludema (2001), Kovenock and Thursby (1992), Maggi (1999), Furusawa (1999), Bütler and Hauser (2000), and Rosendorff (2000). Staiger (1995) contains an insightful survey. Related issues arise in Bagwell and Staiger (2001).

[3] Recall the most prominent trade disputes over the last 40 years: the "chicken war" between the US and the EC, the US-EC dispute over EC policy toward oilseed production, US-EU disputes about U.S. hormone-fed beef and genetically modified foods, the "banana war" between the US and the EU, complaints about US policies toward Venezuelan oil and toward tuna caught in "dolphin-unfriendly" ways. In all these cases the policies of the accused were common knowledge: It was their acceptability that was under dispute.

Thus I focus on disputes about policy actions that, though not explicitly mentioned in trade agreements, are nonetheless widely perceived to be in violation of those agreements. These correspond to what are called *violation complaints* to the WTO DSP. The relevance of my approach to *non-violation complaints* is less clear. But this is of little consequence: Nonviolation complaints are not of large practical significance.

1.2. Why countries delay punishment

The use of such a mechanism cannot be costless. It implies that punishments *must* be delayed, because the implementation of a controversial policy by some country cannot be required to wait until the dispute settlement mechanism renders its verdict. The reason the mechanism exists in the first place is that no one knows in advance what will come into dispute: Trade agreements are incomplete contracts. So the only way to delay implementation is to require that this be automatically required for any policy action that is disputed, and this would in effect give each country a temporary veto over every economic policy action of every other country, hardly acceptable to anyone.

This is my explanation for why countries choose to delay punishment when they don't have to: THEY ATTACH IMPORTANCE TO THE FACT THAT TRADE AGREEMENTS ARE INCOMPLETE CONTRACTS.

The paper proceeds as follows. Sections 2 and 3 set out the basic model. Section 4 discusses a special case which can be interpreted as an explanation of the principle of the substantially equivalent withdrawal of concessions, and Sections 5 and 6 then discuss the negotiation of a trade agreement featuring a DSP in more general circumstances. The analysis implies a strong presumption that countries will choose to employ tit-for-tat punishments (or the substantially equivalent withdrawal of concessions), and provides an analysis of the circumstances under which countries are likely to negotiate trade agreements that will induce violations of DSP rulings.

2. AN ABSTRACT FRAMEWORK

I first provide a simple framework for the analysis that follows.

2.1. The background

Assume two goods, A and B, and two factors of production. In light of the stylized fact that trade disputes are not inherently multilateral, I also assume 2 countries. One has a comparative advantage in A and the other in B; otherwise they are identical. Technology is neoclassical. Assume a succession of periods. Both factors are mobile between sectors across periods, but immobile within each period. All consumers spend equally on both goods.

Initially, each country has an historically given tariff t on all imports. This comes from a highly protectionist past: I shall not investigate why the present is less protectionist. For simplicity I suppose that this initial tariff is common to both countries. Also, factors in each country are initially allocated between the two sectors. Governments negotiate changes in initial tariffs; I shall not model the negotiations. The inter-sectoral immobility of factors during the period ensures that one interest group prefers more protection and one prefers less. When the governments negotiate changes in their tariffs they do not know the exact state of the world that will pertain when those changes subsequently come into effect.

These two features—the tug of divergent special interests and the fact that agreements must be reached before the environment to which they will apply is fully known—have always been of paramount concern to trade negotiators. They must be addressed in any useful model of negotiated liberalization.

At the close of any negotiations, the state of the world is revealed, governments implement tariff changes, and trade takes place. Once the period ends, factors become free to move between sectors, and, once they have done so, history repeats itself, with the initial tariffs for the new period equal to the final tariffs from the preceding period and with a new generation of policymakers, taking history as given, ready to consider further tariff changes.

2.2. Government objectives

Following Bagwell and Staiger (1999, 2001), I assume a government objective function sensitive both to domestic relative prices and to the terms of trade. But I further specify the functional form in several ways. For one, I suppose that domestic relative prices matter because they influence the distribution of income between factors specific to the export sector and those specific to the import sector, given the terms of trade, and I specify this distributional concern. Also, I allow the possibility that a government may be confronted with the need to decide upon a trade related policy: a policy that directly impacts its objective function but that also influences trade.

Specifically, I use the following objective function.

$$\tilde{\phi}(s,a) = \left[\beta\frac{\Delta R_x(s,a)}{R_x} - \frac{1}{100}\left(-\frac{100\Delta R_m(s,a)}{R_m}\right)^{1+\gamma}\right] + \tilde{\mu}\Delta MA(s,a) + \tilde{\lambda}(s,a)\,,$$

where the three terms on the right reflect the implications, respectively, of distributional concerns, the terms of trade, and a possible trade-related policy action. R_x and R_m denote the real returns earned by factors specific to the export sector and to the import-competing sector respectively. With trade liberalizations, $\Delta R_x > 0$, $\Delta R_m < 0$. The parameter β denotes the weight the government attaches to R_x relative to R_m (presumably greater than unity if the export sector is larger than the import-competing sector, as it will be here). The parameter $\gamma > 0$ captures the idea behind Corden's (1997, pp. 74–76) description of a *conservative* social welfare function: Governments avoid policies that would cause a serious reduction in the income of any interest group.[4] I accordingly refer to γ as the *Corden sensitivity*. Here $\Delta MA = (\Delta X_D - \Delta M_D)/X$, the excess, at initial world prices, of the direct amount by which the tariff reduction would raise foreign demand for home exports over the direct amount it would raise home demand for imports (in terms of exportables), as a proportion of the initial trade

[4] Hillman (1982) shows how Corden's concerns can be generated by a plausible political support function, and applications of Corden's ideas to trade policy are found in Deardorff (1987), Brander and Spencer (1994), and Ethier (2002, 2004).

volume. This can be called the net exchange of market access. The parameter $\tilde{\mu}$, called the *terms-of-trade sensitivity*, reflects the impact ΔMA will produce on the terms of trade (the inverse of the familiar Marshall-Lerner term) multiplied by the importance the government attaches to this. The parameter s indexes the (currently unknown) state of the world that will exist when the new tariff levels are in effect, and a denotes a policy variable determined after s is revealed (more on this later).

As Bagwell and Staiger (1999, 2001) aptly note, the first term on the right in my objective function, corresponding to internal distributional concerns, can be controlled unilaterally whereas manipulating the second term involves international spillovers: Our terms of trade is also our partner's terms of trade. Thus it is only the second consideration—a terms of trade externality—that can motivate trade agreements. I have two comments. First, the third term of my objective function also corresponds to an international externality, but the point of departure of this paper is that it is not possible to negotiate directly about it. Second, an earlier paper, Ethier (2004), used an objective function that incorporated the second term on the right above but that based it on *political* externalities between countries rather than on *terms of trade* externalities. Unlike the earlier paper, for the issues addressed in the two country model of this paper, it doesn't matter at all whether the negotiable externality between the two governments is political or terms-of-trade in origin: The reader is invited to take whichever interpretation he or she finds more congenial.[5]

2.3. Unilateralism and reciprocity

Ignore the trade-related action for the moment, and consider a unilateral reduction $\tau_j = (-\hat{t}/(1+t))$ in its tariff by a single country i. At unchanged world prices, the home relative price of imports falls by the amount of the tariff decrease, so that $\Delta R_x > 0$, $\Delta R_m < 0$, and $\Delta MA = -\varepsilon\tau_i M_i < 0$, where ε denotes the home price elasticity of import demand and M_i the initial volume of imports. Define a liberalization as *reciprocal* if accompanied by foreign liberalizations that imply $\Delta MA = 0$. Thus the second term of the governmental objective function vanishes. The following is immediate.

PROPOSITION 1. *A government will never liberalize unilaterally, with a large enough Corden sensitivity γ and terms of trade sensitivity $\tilde{\mu}$. However, it will always accept a sufficiently small reciprocal liberalization that implies $\beta\Delta R_x/R_x + \Delta R_m/R_m > 0$. It will never accept a move to free trade, provided that the Corden sensitivity γ is sufficiently large.*

Reciprocity neutralizes concern about market access, rendering the magnitude of $\tilde{\mu}$ irrelevant. In what follows I assume that the above conditions are fulfilled: Governments will not unilaterally liberalize, but they wish to negotiate reciprocal liberalizations that do not go all the way to free trade. It is easy to specify bargaining rules that imply equal gains and difficult to specify plausible rules that imply unequal gains: I assume

[5] The political externality appears far more relevant to reality but the terms-of-trade externality is clearly more "politically correct" among trade theorists. So take your choice.

all agreements feature reciprocal liberalization. I also assume that, because of pre-existing countervailing-duty laws, trade cannot be subsidized: Tariffs are constrained to be nonnegative.

2.4. The optimal reciprocal rate of liberalization

Cconsider next the rate of reciprocal liberalization that both governments would, in the absence of trade related actions, regard as optimal: the optimal reciprocal rate of liberalization. To this end, rewrite the objective function as follows.

$$\tilde{\phi} = \left[\beta \frac{\Delta R_x}{R_x} - \frac{1}{100}\left(-\frac{100\Delta R_m}{R_m}\right)^{1+\gamma}\right] + \tilde{\mu}\Delta MA\,.$$

Under present assumptions, a liberalization at the rate τ implies the following.

$$\frac{\Delta R_x}{R_x} = \frac{\tau^*}{2} \quad \frac{\Delta R_m}{R_m} = -\frac{\tau}{2} \quad \Delta MA = \frac{\varepsilon X\tau^* - \varepsilon M\tau}{X}$$

where τ^* denotes the partner country's liberalization. Substituting into the political support function and defining the transformation $\phi = 2\tilde{\phi}/(50)^{\gamma}$, $\mu = 2\tilde{\mu}/(50)^{\gamma}$ gives the following.

$$\phi = [r^{\gamma}\tau^* - \tau^{1+\gamma}] + \mu\Delta MA \tag{1}$$

where $r = (2\beta)^{1/\gamma}/50$. The value of $\tau = \tau^*$ that maximizes ϕ, the optimal reciprocal rate of liberalization, is therefore:

$$\tau_{ORL} = r\left(\frac{1}{1+\gamma}\right)^{\frac{1}{\gamma}}. \tag{2}$$

The optimal rate of liberalization can be interpreted as that rate which would be optimal for all governments were trade agreements complete contracts.

3. A MODEL OF A DISPUTE SETTLEMENT PROCEDURE

I now present a model of a DSP motivated by the earlier considerations. First, I must modify the sequence of events within each period to reflect the incomplete-contract nature of trade agreements and to include the operation of a DSP.

3.1. Trade related actions

Suppose that, *ex post*, some country may determine an action, a, which directly influences that government's level of political support and also affects that country's willingness to import. I am especially concerned with three types of uncertainty to which such an action would be subject *ex ante*. **1** Uncertainty (or complete ignorance) about what actual policy situation (environmental issues, health or safety concerns, etc., etc.) might give rise to such a potential action. **2** Uncertainty about the identity of the country in which the situation might emerge. **3** Uncertainty about the extent to which the potential action might be trade-related. To focus sharply on these concerns, I shall assume away all other sources of uncertainty.

The first aspect is incorporated in the requirement that the trade agreement be an incomplete contract. Next, I suppose that exactly one issue will arise and that it will confer an opportunity for a trade related action on one country or the other, with an equal probability (1/2) of either outcome.

In general, a trade-related action by some country may or may not be welcomed by its partners. But this paper concerns trade *disputes*. Consequently, I assume that such actions are always unwelcome: They cause the country undertaking the action to display more protection rather than less.

Specifically, I assume that implementing an action at the level a (≥ 0) affects the country's demand for imports in the same way as would an increase in its tariff in the proportion αa. Thus the trade-related action in effect reduces the country's liberalization from the negotiated rate τ to the rate $\tau - \alpha a$. The parameter α is a measure of how trade-related the action is: *higher* values of α correspond to more trade-relatedness. Furthermore, independently of its effect on the country's trade, the action has a net direct effect on the government's political support in the amount $\lambda(a)$. When a trade agreement is being negotiated, the value of α is not yet known but has an expected value of unity.

I assume, for simplicity, that the form of the function λ is known at the time of negotiations. In particular, $\lambda(0) = 0$ and λ is strictly convex, increasing at a decreasing rate with $\lambda''' \geq 0$, reaching a maximum at $a = a_{OUA}$. Interpret a_{OUA} as the *optimal unilateral action*: the action the government would take in the absence of trade consequences.

3.2. *The sequence of events*

The model features the following sequence of events.

1. Countries negotiate and then implement a reciprocal rate of liberalization τ, and they also determine a DSP.
2. One country is then presented with the opportunity to make a trade related action a not explicitly covered by the trade agreement, and this country (the potential *defendant*) determines a.
3. The trading partner (the potential *complainant*) then utilizes the DSP.
4. A fixed adjudication time is required for the DSP to reach a determination. During this time, the defendant continues with its action and no punishment is implemented.
5. The DSP renders a decision for the complainant, and the defendant must then decide whether to abide by the decision or to defy it. If it decides to abide, it sets $a = 0$, and the sequence comes to an end.
6. If the defendant decides to violate the DSP decision, the complainant retaliates with trade restrictions proportional to the trade effects of the action a. The degree of proportionality is fixed by the trade agreement. The sequence now comes to an end.

3.3. *Possible outcomes*

The objective functions of the governments of the potential defendant (D) and the potential complainant (C) are as follows.

$$\begin{aligned}\phi^D &= [r^\gamma(\tau - \alpha a) - (\tau - \alpha a)^{1+\gamma}] + \lambda(a) + \mu\varepsilon\alpha a \\ \phi^C &= [r^\gamma \tau - \tau^{1+\gamma}] - \mu\varepsilon\alpha a\,.\end{aligned} \tag{3}$$

Here, τ is negotiated before it is known which country will be D and which will be C, and before the magnitude of α is known. After these are revealed, D chooses a. These expressions are valid before the DSP decision is reached.

If D complies with the DSP decision, a becomes equal to zero in the above expressions. If D refuses to comply and C punishes, the expressions become:

$$\begin{aligned}\phi^D &= [r^\gamma(\tau - \alpha a)(\tau - \alpha a)^{1+\gamma}] - \mu\varepsilon(\rho - 1)\alpha a + \lambda(a) \\ \phi^C &= [r^\gamma(\tau - \rho\alpha a) - (\tau - \rho\alpha a)^{1+\gamma}] + \mu\varepsilon(\rho - 1)\alpha a\end{aligned} \tag{4}$$

where ρ denotes the degree of proportionality for punishment allowed by the DSP.

For the period as a whole, the total value of each government's objective function is a weighted average of its value when the DSP is proceeding and its value after that procedure has run its course. Let δ $(1 \geq \delta \geq 0)$ denote the weight given to the former and $1 - \delta$ that given to the latter. δ is determined by the discount factor (which I assume exogenous and fixed) and by the amount of time allowed the DSP to do its business.

I can now describe the values of the objective functions of the two governments over the period as a whole. **i** If the DSP is not invoked or finds in favor of D they are given by (3) above. **ii** If the DSP finds for C and D abides they are as follows.

$$\begin{aligned}\phi^D &= \delta\{[r^\gamma(\tau - \alpha a_J) - (\tau - \alpha a_J)^{1+\gamma}] + \mu\varepsilon\alpha a_J + \lambda(a_J)\} \\ &\quad + (1 - \delta)[r^\gamma \tau - (\tau)^{1+\gamma}] \\ \phi^C &= \delta\{[r^\gamma \tau - \tau^{1+\gamma}] - \mu\varepsilon\alpha a_J\} + (1 - \delta)[r^\gamma \tau - (\tau)^{1+\gamma}]\,.\end{aligned} \tag{5}$$

Here a_J denotes the action D takes during the adjudication phase.

iii If the DSP finds for C, D refuses to comply and continues to violate, and C implements a punishment strategy, we have:

$$\begin{aligned}\phi^D &= \delta\{[r^\gamma(\tau - \alpha a_J) - (\tau - \alpha a_J)^{1+\gamma}] + \mu\varepsilon\alpha a_J + \lambda(a_J)\} \\ &\quad + (1 - \delta)\{[r^\gamma(\tau - \alpha a) - (\tau - \alpha a)^{1+\gamma}] - \mu\varepsilon(\rho - 1)\alpha a + \lambda(a)\} \\ \phi^C &= \delta\{[r^\gamma \tau - \tau^{1+\gamma}] - \mu\varepsilon\alpha a_J\} \\ &\quad + (1 - \delta)\{[r^\gamma(\tau - \rho\alpha a) - (\tau - \rho\alpha a)^{1+\gamma}] + \mu\varepsilon(\rho - 1)\alpha a\}\,.\end{aligned} \tag{6}$$

In light of one of the stylized facts ("The DSP of the WTO has almost always decided in favor of the complainant and, therefore, against the defendant"), I shall assume away case **i**, that is, the DSP will always find for C. As argued earlier, use of the DSP implies that punishments will be delayed. Goals of the subsequent analysis include delineating when D will abide by or violate the DSP ruling and explaining why punishments are tit-for-tat.

4. THE SUBSTANTIALLY EQUIVALENT WITHDRAWAL OF CONCESSIONS: A BASE CASE

The basic ideas of this paper are best illustrated by a special base case, which arises with two further assumptions, to be subsequently relaxed. **i** The DSP is fast enough so that governments give little weight to what happens before a decision is reached: $\delta = 0$. **ii** The degree of trade-relatedness is known beforehand: $\alpha = 1$.

Since $\delta = 0$, this section can be interpreted as applying to situations in which the post-agreement decision of D results not in a trade dispute but in an acceptable settlement with C before the implementation of a. The parameter ρ can be interpreted as stipulating in advance the principle (*e.g.*, the equivalent withdrawal of concessions if $\rho = 1$) to be applied to such settlements, and a purpose of this section is to endogenize the choice of ρ more generally than just in a DSP. But as the balance of this paper will specifically deal with a DSP, I shall continue to employ the language of the latter.

If D refuses to abide by a DSP ruling, or if a settlement is made, the government objective functions reduce to:

$$\phi^D(a, \tau, \rho) = [r^\gamma(\tau - a) - (\tau - a)^{1+\gamma}] - \mu\varepsilon(\rho - 1)a + \lambda(a)$$
$$\phi^C(a, \tau, \rho) = [r^\gamma(\tau - \rho a) - (\tau - \rho a)^{1+\gamma}] + \mu\varepsilon(\rho - 1)a\,.$$

Consider first D's choice of a, given τ and ρ. This is determined by the first-order condition $\partial\phi^D/\partial a = 0$, which reduces to

$$\tau - a = \left[\frac{r^\gamma + \mu\varepsilon(\rho - 1)\lambda'}{1 + \gamma}\right]^{\frac{1}{\gamma}} \tag{7}$$

(I assume the second-order condition to be satisfied). If λ' does not exceed a critical positive value, this expression can be solved for $a(\tau, \rho)$ possessing the following properties.

$$\tau > a \quad 1 > \frac{\partial a}{\partial \tau} > 0 \quad \frac{\partial a}{\partial \rho} < 0\,.$$

Now turn to the negotiation stage. Assume each government wants to maximize the expected value of its objective function. Since each government has equal probability of turning out to be D or C, both governments share a common *ex ante* objective equivalent to maximizing the sum $\phi^D + \phi^C$. The first order conditions are:

$$\begin{aligned} \frac{d\phi^D}{d\tau} + \frac{d\phi\, c}{d\tau} &= \phi_\tau^D + \phi_a^D\frac{\partial a}{\partial \tau} + \phi_\tau^C + \phi_a^C\frac{\partial a}{\partial \tau} = 0 \\ \frac{d\phi^D}{d\rho} + \frac{d\phi^C}{d\rho} &= \phi_p^D + \phi_a^D\frac{\partial a}{\partial \rho} + \phi_p^C + \phi_a^C\frac{\partial a}{\partial \rho} = 0\,. \end{aligned} \tag{8}$$

Substituting, and setting $\phi_a^D = 0$ because D will subsequently choose a optimally,

$$(1+\gamma)[(\tau-\rho a)^\gamma-(\tau-a)^\gamma] \\ +\left(2-\rho\frac{\partial a}{\partial \tau}\right)[r^\gamma-(1+\gamma)(\tau-a)^\gamma]+\frac{\partial a}{\partial \tau}\mu\varepsilon(\rho-1)=0$$

$$\frac{\partial a}{\partial \rho}\mu\varepsilon(\rho-1)-\left(a+\rho\frac{\partial a}{\partial \rho}\right)[r^\gamma-(1+\gamma)(\tau-\rho a)^\gamma]=0\,.$$

These are solved by $\rho = 1$ and $\tau = a_{OUA} + \left[\frac{1}{1+\gamma}\right]^{\frac{1}{\gamma}} r$, for which the optimal subsequent choice of a requires that $\gamma'(a) = 0$, that is, that $a = a_{OUA}$. Thus the solution of the negotiation phase plus D's choice of a is given by the following.

$$\tau = a_{OUA} + \left[\frac{1}{1+\gamma}\right]^{\frac{1}{\gamma}} r\,, \quad \rho = 1\,, \quad a = a_{OUA}\,.$$

So, commensurate punishment ($\rho = 1$) emerges endogenously. This can be regarded as a response to the reciprocal-conflict problem, as suggested above. But it does more than that. It ensures that the ultimate implications of D's actions on protection are reciprocal, which in turn allows the governments to negotiate an agreement that will allow the country that turns out to be D to implement the optimal unilateral action and both governments to experience the optimal reciprocal liberalization.

Note, also, that this trade agreement ensures that D will in fact take the action a_{OUA} rather than no action at all: the latter would cause D to experience more liberalization than desired in addition to forgoing the direct net benefit of acting. In other words, the two countries will reach a trade agreement that guarantees that the country that turns out to be D will in fact defy a negative ruling by the DSP.

PROPOSITION 2 (substantially equivalent withdrawal of concessions). *If no weight is given to the adjudication phase and if the degree of trade relatedness is known with certainty, the negotiated trade agreement will feature commensurate punishment, will induce D to violate the DSP, and will deliver, ex post, both the optimal degree of liberalization and the optimal unilateral action for D.*

Consider in this light the hormone-fed beef case, widely regarded as a "failure" of the WTO system and as a threat to a "rules-based" international order for trade policy. An alternative interpretation might go as follows. "If governments thought that trade agreements would prevent them from responding to unforeseen deep political pressures of this sort (from the EU viewpoint), they would never sign on to those agreements in the first place. If they thought that such pressures would allow their trade partners to depart from reciprocity, they also would never sign on to such agreements in the first place. Under these circumstances, the experience of the hormone-fed beef case is probably the best feasible outcome, from the viewpoint of long term trade liberalization." Rosendorff (2000) offers a related analysis in which a DSP allows a country to "purchase" a release from its trade commitments, inducing it to agree to more liberalization than it would do in the absence of such a release. Perdikis, Kerr and Hobbs (2001) observe (p. 381), "It has always been recognized that for the WTO to be politically acceptable there have to be provisions which allow governments to ignore their WTO commitments when domestic pressure for protection becomes politically unmanageable." In other words, violation of DSP decisions can be thought of as an *extra-legal* counterpart, applying to a residual of unforeseen circumstances, to various GATT provisions (*e.g.*, Articles XXII and XXIII) allowing the *legal* withdrawal of concessions.

Proposition 2 is, of course, consistent with this interpretation. But it also goes much further, suggesting the possibility of *optimality* properties of current arrangements.

Though the base case solution involves commensurate punishment, one can enquire how much added deterrence stronger punishments would provide. Define the *elasticity of deterrence* as

$$\sigma \equiv -\frac{\rho}{a}\frac{\partial a}{\partial \rho},$$

where D chooses a optimally, that is, to satisfy (7). Deterrence can be said to be strong, uniform, or weak according as σ exceeds, equals, or falls short of unity. Strong deterrence means that a higher *ex ante* punishment proportionality ρ will result, at unchanged τ, in less *ex post* punishment ρa, and so forth.

At the base case solution, (7) implies that

$$\sigma = -\frac{\mu\varepsilon / a_{OUA}}{\lambda'' - \gamma r^{\gamma}/\tau_{ORL}}. \tag{9}$$

Thus deterrence elasticity is enhanced by a high terms of trade sensitivity ($\mu\varepsilon$) or optimal rate of reciprocal liberalization (τ_{ORL}) and by a low willingness to protect (γ), optimal unilateral action (a_{OUA}), or low curvature ($-\lambda''$) of the payoff from unilateral action.

5. THE ADJUDICATION PHASE

The base case gives strong results, but at the cost of suppressing essential aspects of the problem: the adjudication phase and the possibility of different degrees of trade relatedness α. I now consider the implications of these features, proceeding one step at a time. I start by allowing a significant adjudication phase: $\delta > 0$.

5.1. *The adjudication phase*

During the adjudication phase, C cannot punish D, so the respective objective functions, during that period, are as follows.

$$\begin{aligned} \phi_J^D &= [r^{\gamma}(\tau - a_J) - (\tau - a_J)^{1+\gamma}] + \mu\varepsilon a_J + \lambda(a_J) \\ \phi_J^C &= [r^{\gamma}\tau - \tau^{1+\gamma}] - \mu\varepsilon a_J\,. \end{aligned} \tag{10}$$

During the adjudication phase, the optimal action $a_j(\tau)$ corresponding to each negotiated liberalization is implicitly defined by D's first order condition

$$(1+\gamma)(\tau - a_J)^{\gamma} - r^{\gamma} + \mu\varepsilon + \lambda'(a_J) = 0\,. \tag{11}$$

This in turn implies that

$$1 > \frac{da_J}{d\tau} > 0 \qquad \frac{\partial a_J}{\partial \mu} > 0.$$

Consider, initially, the trade agreement of the base case: $\tau = \tau_{ORL} + a_{OUA}$ and $\rho = 1$. Then, with $\mu\varepsilon > 0$, the first order condition requires that $a_J > a_{OUA}$. This reveals three influences of the adjudication phase on the objective functions of the two governments.

First, by taking the trade related action without punishment, D's objective function increases by $\mu\varepsilon a_J$ while C's falls a like amount. This departure from reciprocity might well induce *ex post* apoplectic outrage from C, but it has no direct *ex ante* effect since it does not change the joint welfare of the two governments. It has an indirect effect, however, because it induces D to set a_J higher than it otherwise would: $a_J > a_{OUA}$ implies that $\tau - a_J < \tau_{ORL}$ and $\lambda(a_J) < \lambda(a_{OUA})$. Thus D experiences less effective liberalization than it would otherwise like, and an excessive level of the action a, and this does reduce the joint welfare of the two governments. This is also true of the third effect: because C cannot retaliate during the adjudication phase, it experiences "excessive" liberalization at the negotiated rate. (Another way of saying this is that the DSP causes the C government to behave during the adjudication phase as though it had a lower willingness to protect (γ) than it actually does—aggregate national welfare rises with the actual rate of liberalization).

5.2. The trade agreement

Next, take a step back to enquire whether setting $\delta > 0$ would induce the two governments to reach a trade agreement different from that of the base case. The effect of a change in τ on the joint objective function during the adjudication phase, taking into account D's response in taking its optimal action $a_J(\tau)$, is as follows.

$$\frac{d\phi_J^D}{d\tau} + \frac{d\phi_J^C}{d\tau} = [r^\gamma - (1+\gamma)(\tau - a_J)^\gamma] + [r^\gamma - (1+\gamma)\tau^\gamma] - \mu\varepsilon\frac{da_J}{d\tau}. \qquad (12)$$

With τ close to $\tau_{ORL} + a_{OUA}$, the first term on the right-hand side will be positive and the remaining two terms negative. For small values of $\mu\varepsilon$, a_J will not be much greater than a_{OUA}, so that the first term on the right will be dominated by the second, and the entire expression is thus negative. An increase in $\mu\varepsilon$ will produce an increase in a_J, but it will magnify the third term more than the first (see the Appendix), so the entire expression will remain negative.

With the right-hand side negative, a small decrease in τ below $\tau_{ORL} + a_{OUA}$ will increase the joint welfare of the two governments during the adjudication phase. This will have no first-order effect on their joint welfare during the post-adjudication phase, where $\tau_{ORL} + a_{OUA}$ is first-best. Thus it generates a net overall benefit.

PROPOSITION 3. *If the adjudication phase becomes of concern to the two governments (i.e., if δ becomes positive) they will negotiate a trade agreement with less liberalization than that of the base case.*

Intuitively, if τ is reduced, D will lower a_J. This affects D in two ways: a_J falls back toward a_{OUA}, increasing the non-trade benefits of the action; a_j falls less than the reduction in τ itself so that $\tau - a_j$ falls, further worsening the deficient realized liberalization experienced by D. Thus, the reduction in the negotiated rate of liberalization induces D to give *more* weight to the non-trade implications of the action, and less weight to the trade aspects, during the adjudication phase. Finally, the reduction in τ directly reduces the "excessive" liberalization experienced by C during the adjudication phase, a clear benefit to the C government at least.

Next turn to the implications of $\delta > 0$ for the negotiated punishment factor ρ. The size of ρ is irrelevant to the adjudication phase, but the fact that $\delta > 0$ causes τ to deviate from its post-adjudication first-best value suggests that ρ may also deviate from its post-adjudication first-best value (unity). The second equation in (8) above is the condition that ρ be set optimally, from the *ex ante* point of view of each government. Using this expression to find the implicit derivative of ρ with respect to τ, assuming that D sets a optimally *ex post*, and evaluating the result at the base case trade agreement ($\tau = \tau_{ORL} + a_{OUA}$, $\rho = 1$) gives the following:

$$a\frac{d\rho}{d\tau} = \frac{(\sigma - 1)}{(\sigma - 1) - \sigma \dfrac{\mu\varepsilon / a_{OUA}}{\gamma r^{\gamma} / \tau_{ORL}}}.$$

Thus uniform deterrence ($\sigma = 1$) implies that $d\rho/d\tau = 0$: Commensurate punishment will still be negotiated. Weak deterrence ($\sigma < 1$) implies $1 > ad\rho/d\tau > 0$. The reduction in τ reduces punishment, but in a dampened way: $a\rho$ falls by less than τ. From (9), $\frac{\mu\varepsilon/a_{OUA}}{\gamma r^{\gamma}/\tau_{ORL}} > \sigma$. This in turn implies that strong deterrence gives $-1 < ad\rho/d\tau < 0$, punishment increases, but, again, in a dampened way.

The introduction of an adjudication phase results, during the post adjudication phase, in deficient *ex post* liberalization $\tau - a$ and in an excessive action a. Raising ρ above unity worsens the former problem, since it causes C to liberalize less *ex post*, but lessens the latter problem. Weak deterrence implies that the first effect will be predominant, so that ρ should be reduced; strong deterrence implies the reverse.

The result, though, is an emphasis on commensurate punishment. This is preserved with uniform deterrence. Strong or weak deterrence produces deviations in the punishment factor ρ, but they are dampened in the sense that punishments $a\rho$ change less than τ itself.

The argument thus far in this section assumes that D will violate the DSP ruling and that C will punish. This is necessarily so in the base case, where the two countries will negotiate a trade agreement that guarantees violation. If the adjudication phase is not too important to the two governments relative to the post-adjudication phase (*i.e.*, if δ is small enough), the trade agreement will be close enough to that of the base case still to guarantee violation. But large values of δ require that the possibility of D abiding by the DSP ruling be considered. I turn to this next. To summarize results thus far,

PROPOSITION 4. *For sufficiently small positive δ, the two governments will negotiate a trade agreement in which $\tau < \tau_{ORL} + a_{OUA}$ and ρ approximates unity. This will induce D to violate the DSP ruling.*

Raising δ above zero causes D to set $a_J > a_{OUA} > a$, and it also causes C to experience "excessive" liberalization during the adjudication phase and deficient liberalization during the post-adjudication phase. The trade agreement induces D to adjust its action closer to a_{OUA} in each phase, enhancing the non-trade effects of the action, and it smooths out the variation of liberalization experienced by C.

5.3. The pure adjudication case

Consider now what the negotiated trade agreement would be if the negotiators gave no weight at all to the post-adjudication phase, that is, if $\delta = 1$. This can be thought of as the polar opposite to the base case, where $\delta = 0$. With $\delta = 1$, the magnitude of the punishment coefficient ρ is immaterial, so nothing is lost by setting it equal to unity.

The joint welfare of C and D equals

$$W_J = [r^\gamma(\tau - a_J) - (\tau - a_J)^{1+\gamma}] + [r^\gamma \tau - \tau^{1+\gamma}] + \lambda(a_J). \tag{13}$$

The first-order *ex ante* optimality condition that τ be chosen to maximize W_J, taking into account that D will subsequently choose a_J optimally, reduces to

$$\frac{dW_J}{d\tau} = (1+\gamma)\{[\tau_{ORL}^\gamma - (\tau - a_J)^\gamma] + [\tau_{ORL}^\gamma - \tau^\gamma]\} - \mu\varepsilon\frac{da_J}{d\tau} = 0.$$

If $\mu\varepsilon$ is sufficiently small, this condition implies that $\tau > \tau_{ORL} > \tau - a_J$. This in turn implies that $(1+\gamma)(\tau - a_J)^\gamma < r^\gamma$ which, for sufficiently small $\mu\varepsilon$, requires $\lambda'(a_J) > 0$, so that $a_J < a_{OUA}$. Conversely, if $\mu\varepsilon$ is sufficiently large, the first-order condition implies that $\tau_{ORL} > \tau > \tau - a_J$, whence $a_J > a_{OUA}$ for $\mu\varepsilon$ sufficiently large.

PROPOSITION 5. *If terms of trade effects are sufficiently unimportant to the negotiators, a pure-adjudication-case trade agreement will result in D experiencing deficient liberalization and C excessive liberalization and in D choosing a level of the trade related action below the optimal unilateral level. Sufficiently important terms of trade effects result in both countries experiencing deficient liberalization and in D choosing a level of the trade related action above the optimal unilateral level.*

5.4. Abide or violate?

Consider now the choice that D must make at the end of the adjudication phase: whether to abide (A) by the finding and set $a = 0$ or to violate (V) the finding and set a equal to some positive value, knowing that this will induce punishment by C. The choice between the A and V strategies is independent of what D did during the adjudication process, now past history.

Define $V(\tau, \rho)$ as follows.

$$V(\tau,\rho) = [r^\gamma(\tau - a) - (\tau - a)^{1+\gamma}] + \mu\varepsilon(1-\rho)a + \lambda(a) - [r^\gamma\tau - \tau^{1+\gamma}] \tag{14}$$

where

$$(1+\gamma)(\tau - a)^\gamma - r^\gamma + \mu\varepsilon(1-\rho) + \lambda'(a) = 0.$$

D will violate or abide by the ruling according as V is positive or negative, and $V(\tau_{ORL} + a_{OUA}, 1) > 0$. Define $W(\tau, \rho)$ as:

$$W(\tau,\rho) = \frac{1}{2}[r^{\gamma}(\tau - a) - (\tau - a)^{1+\gamma}] + \frac{1}{2}[r^{\gamma}(\tau - \rho a) - (\tau - \rho a)^{1+\gamma}] + \frac{1}{2}\lambda(a)[r^{\gamma}\tau - \tau^{1+\gamma}]. \tag{15}$$

It will be optimal *ex ante* that whichever country turns out to be D violate or abide by the ruling according as W is positive or negative. Also, $W(\tau_{ORL} + a_{OUA}, 1) > 0$ and $V(\tau, 1) = W(\tau, 1) + 1/2\lambda(a)$.

The above discussion of the pure adjudication case implied that, unless $\mu\varepsilon$ is small enough to prevent it, $\tau_J - a_J$ will be further enough from τ_{ORL} than will τ_J to ensure that

$$[r^{\gamma}(\tau_J - a_J) - (\tau_J - a_J)^{1+\gamma}] < [r^{\gamma}\tau_J - \tau_J^{1+\gamma}].$$

This in turn implies that $V(\tau_J, 1) < 0$ unless $\lambda(a_J)$ is large enough to prevent it. That is, unless trade related action is important enough to governments relative to trade concerns—as measured by $\mu\varepsilon$—governments would prefer to abide by a negative determination, when the degree of liberalization is that of the pure adjudication case, rather than to violate it and experience the rollback of liberalization implied by violation *cum* commensurate punishment. I refer to this circumstance as the *abidement property*.

ABIDEMENT PROPERTY. *$\mu\varepsilon$ is large enough relative to $\lambda(a_J)$ so that $V(\tau_J, 1) <$ 0.*

The definition of $V(\tau,\rho)$ implies that, when $\rho = 1$, $V_\tau = (1+\gamma)[\tau^{\gamma} - (\tau - a)^{\gamma}] > 0$ and $V_p = -\mu\varepsilon a < 0$ so that

$$\left.\frac{d\rho}{d\tau}\right|_{V=0,\rho=1} = \frac{(1+\gamma)[\tau^{\gamma} - (\tau - a)^{\gamma}]}{\mu\varepsilon a} > 0.$$

Also, at $\rho = 1$, $W_\tau = V_\tau + \lambda'\frac{da}{d\tau}$, which is positive with $\lambda' \geq 0$, and $W_p = -\frac{a}{2}[r^{\gamma} - (1+\gamma)(\tau - a)^{\gamma}]$, which is negative with $\lambda' > 0$. Accordingly,

$$\left.\frac{d\rho}{d\tau}\right|_{W=0,\rho=1} = \frac{V_\tau + \lambda'\dfrac{da}{d\tau}}{\dfrac{a}{2}[\gamma^{\gamma} - (1+\gamma)(\tau - a)^{\gamma}]} > 0.$$

Figure 1 depicts the plane of possible trade agreements (τ, ρ). The locus $V = 0$ bisects the plane between those agreements that will induce the country that turns out to be D to abide by or to violate the DSP ruling. The $W = 0$ locus does the same on the basis of whether it is *ex ante* optimal that D abide or violate. Point **B** denotes the base case agreement and must be in the violate zone. Point **J** denotes the pure adjudication agreement with $\rho = 1$, and, if the abidement property holds, will be in the abide zone as depicted in the figure.

The *ex ante* optimal trade agreement is **B** if $\delta = 0$ and **J** if $\delta = 1$. Intermediate values of δ imply other agreements, possibilities illustrated by the bold line in Figure 1. Small values of δ yield agreements that will induce D to violate the DSP ruling. As discussed above, these agreements will feature commensurate punishment if deterrence

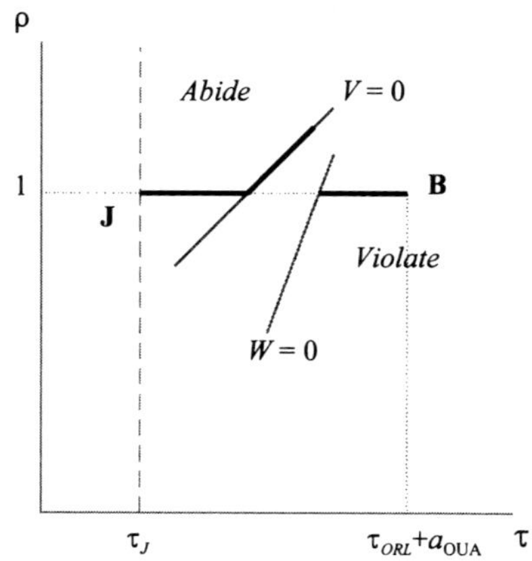

Figure 1. The Trade Agreement Plane.

is uniform, or dampened departures from commensurate punishment otherwise. If the abidement property holds, large values of δ yield agreements that will induce D to abide by the ruling, and commensurate punishment suffices to ensure this.

Yet another possibility is for some range of intermediate values of δ to imply agreements between the $V = 0$ and $W = 0$ schedules. In such cases, an optimal agreement requires D to abide by the DSP ruling, but commensurate punishment would induce D to violate. See Figure 1. Thus punishment must be more severe than this, with ρ at least large enough to correspond to points on the $V = 0$ schedule.

The abidement property, however, tends to minimize the importance of such deviations from commensurate punishment. First, low values of $\lambda(a)$ reduce the distance between the two schedules when $\rho = 1$, limiting the scope for such outcomes. Second, high values of $\mu\varepsilon$ flatten the $V = 0$ schedule, limiting the required deviation above $\rho = 1$.

PROPOSITION 6 (commensurate punishment). *If the abidement property holds, there is a presumption that the optimal trade agreement will feature commensurate punishment, or approximately commensurate punishment.*

With low values of δ the abidement property is irrelevant for commensurate punishment, or a dampened departure from it, as we saw above. High values of δ render the property important. Commensurate punishment is one of the two key results of this section. The second is the delineation of the circumstances under which D will abide by or violate the DSP ruling.

PROPOSITION 7 (abide or violate). *If the abidement property holds, the optimal trade agreement will induce D to abide by the DSP ruling when the negotiators attach more importance to the adjudication phase (large δ), and to violate it when they attach less importance (low δ).*

Why low values of δ induce violation is clear from the earlier discussion of the base case. When δ is large, so the adjudication phase is important, the negotiators, knowing that they have no way of preventing D from implementing a during that phase, will negotiate less liberalization to reduce the incentive for D to set a large a. But when the post adjudication phase commences, this lower negotiated liberalization will increase the damage of further backsliding with violation *cum* commensurate punishment. Thus the agreement should induce D to abide.

Thus abiding by the DSP during the post adjudication phase is associated with *more* (not less) emphasis on the adjudication phase, during which D is free to violate without punishment. This should not be interpreted to mean that high values of δ are desirable because they limit international conflict. Indeed, since the base case is first-best, there is a presumption that the negotiators would prefer lower values of δ and therefore would try to design the adjudication process so that δ is as small as is consistent with the integrity and credibility of that process. Attempting to do just this was a main objective of the revision of the GATT DSP undertaken during the Uruguay Round.

6. THE DEGREE OF TRADE RELATEDNESS

Thus far I have assumed that the negotiators know beforehand what the degree of trade relatedness will be, that is, that α assumes its expected value (unity) with certainty. Now this will be relaxed. It will be convenient to assume that the negotiators are risk neutral with respect to such uncertainty, and proceed on the basis of the expected value of α, reaching the agreement described above. The first problem, then, is to determine how, given this agreement, *ex post* behavior will depend upon the realization of α.

The timing is as follows. First, the governments negotiate a trade agreement (τ, ρ). Next, the identity of D and the magnitude of α are revealed. Then, as above, D chooses a_J, the DSP rules against D, and D decides whether to abide by or to violate the ruling. The interesting question is how this decision is influenced by the realization of the degree of trade relatedness.

6.1. *Abide or violate redux*

When α can deviate from unity, the terms critical for the decision whether to abide or to violate, and for whether either decision is desirable, become

$$V(\tau, \rho) = [r^{\gamma}(\tau - \alpha a) - (\tau - \alpha a)^{1+\gamma}] + \mu\varepsilon(1 - \rho)\alpha a + \lambda(a) - [r^{\gamma}\tau - \tau^{1+\gamma}] \tag{16}$$

where

$$\alpha(1 + \gamma)(\tau - \alpha a)^{\gamma} - \alpha r^{\gamma} + \mu\varepsilon\alpha(1 - \rho) + \lambda'(a) = 0,$$

and

$$W(\tau, \rho) = \frac{1}{2}[r^{\gamma}(\tau - \alpha a) - (\tau - \alpha a)^{1+\gamma}] + \frac{1}{2}[r^{\gamma}(\tau - \rho\alpha a)^{1+\gamma} + \frac{1}{2}\lambda(a) - [r^{\gamma}\tau - \tau^{1+\gamma}]. \tag{17}$$

These expressions imply, if $\rho = 1$ and $\alpha = 1$ initially,

$$\frac{dV}{d\alpha} = -a\lambda'(a) < 0$$

and

$$\frac{\partial a}{\partial \alpha} = \frac{\lambda' + \gamma(1+\gamma)a(\tau - a)^{\gamma-1}}{\lambda'' - \gamma(1+\gamma)(\tau - a)^{\gamma-1}} < 0$$

and

$$\frac{dW}{d\alpha} = a[(1+\gamma)(\tau - a) - r^{\gamma}] + \frac{1}{2}\lambda'(a)\frac{\partial a}{\partial a} < 0\,.$$

When $\rho = 1$, $V_\tau > 0$ and $W_\tau > 0$, as shown above. Thus:

$$\left.\frac{d\tau}{d\alpha}\right|_{V=0,\rho=1} > 0\,, \quad \left.\frac{d\tau}{d\alpha}\right|_{W=0,\rho=1} > 0\,.$$

An increase in α above unity will shift the $V = 0$ and $W = 0$ schedules to the right, causing some trade agreements that would have caused D to violate the DSP ruling (with $\alpha = 1$) to instead cause D to abide by the ruling. A reduction of α below unity does the reverse.

PROPOSITION 8. *A realization of high trade relatedness* ($\alpha > 1$) *increases the set of trade agreements inducing the country that turns out to be D to abide by the DSP ruling. A realization of low trade relatedness* ($\alpha < 1$) *reduces the size of that set.*

When D decides whether to abide or violate, it weighs the favorable direct effect of violation against the unfavorable reduction in liberalization implied by violation *cum* punishment. A high degree of trade relatedness enhances the second, negative, consideration. This can be enough to transform a decision to violate into one to abide for agreements close to $V = 0$, where the two effects balance out.

6.2. Commensurate punishment redux

Negotiators, aware of the possible effects consequent upon the *ex post* realization of α, might possibly negotiate a different punishment proportion ρ as a result. Suppose, for example, that the negotiators settle on an agreement to the left of the $V = 0$ schedule, which will therefore induce D to abide by the DSP ruling if α attains its expected value of unity. Consider the effect of altering this agreement by raising ρ above unity.

This alteration will be of no consequence whenever the degree of trade relatedness is equal to or above its expected value, because D will still abide. If the degree of trade relatedness turns out below its expected value it could cause the agreement, with $\rho = 1$, to lie between the $V = 0$ and $W = 0$ schedules, so that D would choose to violate the DSP ruling even though that would lower the joint welfare of the two governments. If, instead, ρ had been set above unity by enough, that could induce D to abide by the ruling, a social benefit. Even if D still violates, the higher ρ would induce a lower a. A final possibility is that the realized degree of trade relatedness is enough below average so that the trade agreement, with its higher value of ρ, ends up below the $W = 0$ schedule. In this case, having raised ρ above unity causes it to be even further from its optimal *ex post* value if deterrence is uniform or weak, and this must lower joint welfare. With strong deterrence, the increase in ρ might have moved it either towards or away from its optimal value.

Now suppose instead that the negotiators settle on an agreement to the right of the $W = 0$ schedule, which will therefore induce D to violate the DSP ruling if α attains its expected value of unity. In this case, altering the agreement by raising ρ above the level that is optimal when $\alpha = 1$ must lower joint welfare *ex post* whenever the realized degree of trade relatedness is equal to or below its expected value. If α ends up above unity by enough to leave the agreement between the $V = 0$ and $W = 0$ schedules an increase in the negotiated ρ could either raise or lower *ex post* joint welfare, and it would have no effect should the realized degree of trade relatedness be sufficient to put the agreement to the left of $V = 0$.

Note that the abidement property tends to work against the possibility that uncertainty about α could induce the negotiators to increase ρ when the optimal *ex ante* agreement lies above the $V = 0$ schedule. By reducing the difference between the $V = 0$ and $W = 0$ schedules it lowers, other things equal, the chances that the realization of α will leave the trade agreement between those two schedules. By flattening the $V = 0$ schedule it lowers the amount by which increasing ρ could conceivably be beneficial.

All in all, it seems quite unlikely that uncertainty about the degree of trade relatedness would induce negotiators to increase ρ significantly. But it is possible to construct examples where this would happen—for example, a magnitude of δ implying (when $\alpha = 1$) a trade agreement somewhat to the left of the $V = 0$ schedule combined with a subjective probability distribution over α giving no likelihood to the realization of low enough degrees of trade relatedness to leave the negotiated agreement to the right of the $W = 0$ schedule.

7. CONCLUDING REMARKS

This paper explores the idea that observed dispute settlement procedures and punishments are responses to the fact that trade agreements are necessarily incomplete contracts. I argue that this perspective can explain prominent features of these procedures and punishments and also has implications for the trade agreements themselves. The argument can be summarized as follows.

- Trade agreements are of necessity incomplete contracts because trade can be affected by all sorts of potential policies that countries can either not foresee or not be willing to negotiate about.
- If no weight is given to the adjudication phase and if the degree of trade relatedness is known with certainty, the negotiated trade agreement will induce the defendant to violate the DSP and will deliver, *ex post*, both the optimal degree of liberalization and the optimal unilateral action for the defendant.
- This suggests a central role, in the process of multilateral trade liberalization, for an *implicit* agreement to allow countries to violate agreed commitments if the violation implies no retreat from reciprocity. It also provides an argument for the

principle of *the equivalent withdrawal of concessions*, which has permeated the GATT from its very begining.

- If the adjudication phase of a DSP is of concern to the two governments they will negotiate a trade agreement with less liberalization.
- The *abidement* property—that trade matters sufficiently to governments relative to trade related action—implies a presumption that the optimal trade agreement will feature commensurate punishment, or approximately commensurate punishment. That is, the principle of the equivalent withdrawal of concessions, or something close to it, should apply to dispute settlement also.
- If the *abidement* property holds, the optimal trade agreement will induce the defendant to abide by the DSP ruling when the negotiators attach more importance to the adjudication phase, and to violate it when they attach less importance.
- A realization of high trade relatedness increases the set of trade agreements inducing the country that turns out to be D to abide by the DSP ruling. A realization of low trade relatedness reduces the size of that set.

The principle of the equivalent withdrawal of concessions—or of commensurate punishment—has a vital implication for negotiated trade liberalization. A trade agreement can, in the end, deliver liberalization no greater than that desired, *ex post*, by the more reluctant liberalizer.[6]

A question for future research suggested by the above is: What are the implications of uncertainty about the direct magnitude on governments' objective functions of the trade related actions? The important role of the abidement property (essentially that the trade consequences of such actions be sufficiently important relative to the direct consequences) suggests that this is an important question.

This paper also raises another question for future research. With the WTO, essential stylized facts of the DSP are enshrined in trade agreements. Before that they were still present but apparently as elements of an "implicit" contract. Does such "implicitness" matter? Or, put another way, does it matter that such stylized facts are now enshrined in the WTO?

REFERENCES

Bagwell, K. and R. W. Staiger (1999), "An Economic Theory of GATT," American Economic Review 89 (1), March, 215–248.

Bagwell, K. and R. W. Staiger (2001), "Domestic Policies, National Sovereignty, and International Economic Institutions," Quarterly Journal of Economics 116 (2), May, 519–562.

Brainard, S. L. and T. Verdier (1994), "Lobbying and Adjustment in Declining Industries," European Economic Review 38, 586–595.

Brander, J. and B. Spencer (1994), "Trade Adjustment Assistance: Welfare and Incentive Effects of Payments to Displaced Workers," Journal of International Economics, 239–261.

Bütler, M. and H. Hauser (2000), "The WTO Dispute Settlement System: A First Assessment from An Economic Perspective," The Journal of Law, Economics, and Organization 16 (2), 503–533.

Corden, W. M. (1997). Trade Policy and Economic Welfare, 2nd ed. (Oxford: Oxford University Press).

[6] I have exploited this implication in Ethier (2002).

Deardorff, A. (1987), "Safeguards Policy and the Conservative Social Welfare Function." In: Kierzkowski, H. K. [ed.], Protection and Competition in International Trade (Oxford: Blackwell).
Ethier, W. J. (2004), "Political Externalities, Nondiscrimination, and A Multilateral World," Review of International Economics 12 (3), pp 303–320.
Ethier, W. J. (2002), "Unilateralism in A Multilateral World," The Economic Journal 112 (479), 266–292.
Furusawa, T. (1999), "The Role of the WTO Dispute Settlement Procedure on International Cooperation," unpublished manuscript.
Hillman, A. L. (1982), "Declining Industries and Political-Support Protectionist Motives," American Economic Review 72, 1180–1190.
Hungerford, T. L. (1991), "GATT: A Cooperative Equilibrium in A Noncooperative Trading Regime?" Journal of International Economics 31, 357–369.
Kovenock, D. and M. Thursby (1992), "GATT, Dispute Settlement and Cooperation," Economics & Politics 4, 151–170.
Long, N. V. and N. Vousden (1991), "Protectionist Responses and Declining Industries," Journal of International Economics 30, 87–103.
Ludema, R. (2001), "Optimal International Trade Agreements and Dispute Settlement Procedures," European Journal of Political Economy 17 (2), 355–376.
Maggi, G. (1999), "The Role of Multilateral Institutions in International Trade Cooperation," American Economic Review 89 (1), 190–214.
Ohyama, M. (1972), "Trade and Welfare in General Equilibrium," Keio Economic Studies IX (2), 37–73.
Perdikis, N., W. A. Kerr, and J. E. Hobbs (2001), "Reforming the WTO to Defuse Potential Trade Conflicts in Genetically Modified Goods," The World Economy 24 (3), 379–398.
Rosendorff, B. P. (2000), "Stability and Rigidity: The Dispute Settlement Procedure of the WTO," unpublished manuscript, School of International Relations, University of Southern California.
Staiger, R. (1995), "International Rules and Institutions for Cooperative Trade Policy." Chapter 29 in Grossman, G. M. and K. Rogoff [eds.], Handbook of International Economics, Volume 3 (Amsterdam: Elsevier), 1495–1551.

Appendix: Implications of the Adjudication Phase for the Trade Agreement

The rate of liberalization

The condition (11) that a_j be optimally chosen implies that

$$1 > \frac{\partial a_J}{\partial \tau} > 0 \quad \text{and} \quad \frac{\partial a_J}{\partial \tau} = \gamma(1+\gamma)(\tau - a_J)^{\gamma-1}\frac{\partial a_J}{\partial(\mu\varepsilon)} > 0 .$$

Now for small values of $\mu\varepsilon$, the right-hand side of (12) is necessarily negative. The response of this right-hand side to a change in $\mu\varepsilon$, in light of (17), is just

$$-\mu\varepsilon\frac{\partial^2 a_J}{\partial\tau\partial(\mu\varepsilon)} = -\left(\frac{\partial a_J}{\partial(\mu\varepsilon)}\right)^2 \times\left\{-\gamma(1-\gamma)(1+\gamma)(\tau - a_J)^{\gamma-2}\left[1-\frac{\partial a_J}{\partial\tau}\right] - \lambda'''\frac{\partial a_J}{\partial\tau}\right\} > 0 .$$

Thus the right-hand side of (12) is necessarily negative for all values of $\mu\varepsilon$.

Selling "Protection For Sale"

Wilfred J. Ethier[a*]

[a]*Department of Economics, University of Pennsylvania*

Abstract

The Received Theory of trade policy, based solely on terms-of-trade externalities between national governments, has become the conventional wisdom among international trade theorists. But it displays two puzzles that render that theory inconsistent with reality. Significant empirical work, however, supports aspects of the Grossman-Helpman Protection-For-Sale model, a subset of the Received Theory. This paper shows that a simple formulation of the political economy of protection, that dispenses with terms-of-trade externalities, predicts the properties that the empirical work has confirmed, and is free of the counterfactual implications of the Received Theory. The implication is that, despite its claims to the contrary, the empirical literature offers no real support for the Protection-For-Sale model or, therefore, for the Received Theory.

JEL Classification: F02, F13

Keywords: The Protection-For-Sale model, the Received Theory, the Terms-of-Trade Puzzle, the Export-Subsidy-Transfer Puzzle

The Received Theory of trade policy and trade agreements, which thoroughly dominates trade theorists' approach to these problems, assigns a central role to the terms of trade and to trade-tax revenue. The deservedly influential work of Bagwell and Staiger (1999, 2002) excellently elucidates the implications of this approach for trade agreements.

A subset[1] of the Received Theory emphasizes political economy. Grossman and Helpman (1994, 1995, 2002) expound its most widely used component: the "Protection-For-Sale" model. The current state of the Received Theory is therefore conveniently described in two recent books by Bagwell and Staiger (2002) and Grossman and Helpman (2002).

---

* This paper has been prepared for the 2006 APJAE Symposium on International Trade in Honor of Ronald W. Jones. Department of Economics, University of Pennsylvania, Philadelphia, PA 19104–6297, USA. Tel: 215–898–5105, Fax: 215–573–2072. Email: ethier@econ.sas.upenn.edu.

[1] See Hillman (1982, 1990), Hillman, Long and Moser (1995), and Hillman and Moser (1996). Surveys of the literature on the political economy of trade policy may be found in Hillman (1989), Magee (1994), Nelson (1988) and Rodrik (1995).

However, the relevance of the Received Theory should be very much up in the air. While theory suggests that it is dramatically inconsistent with reality,[2] a significant empirical literature claims to have found support for the Grossman-Helpman Protection-For-Sale subset of the Received Theory. In this paper I attempt to resolve this conundrum.

1. Introduction

The central premise of the Received Theory is that trade agreements arise *solely* because countries with market power are concerned, to at least *some* degree, with the fact that trade barriers, imposed for *whatever* reason, can move the terms of trade in their favor. As pointed out in Ethier (2004), this is inconsistent with actual multilateral trade agreements, which do *not* prevent countries from trying to influence their terms of trade. I refer to this discrepancy as the *Terms-of-Trade Puzzle.*

Nothing in the GATT prevents a country from implementing export taxes. In their schedules of negotiated concessions, countries have bound their import taxes: They have not, with very rare exception, bound export taxes. For over four decades, successive GATT rounds have produced trade agreements that do not prevent terms-of-trade manipulation while trade theorists have produced theories of trade agreements in which such prevention is the sole object.[3] To summarize:

> *(i) Actual trade agreements do not prevent countries from manipulating their terms of trade with export taxes;*
> *(ii) industrial countries nevertheless do not, by and large, implement such taxes.*

If the interests of owners of factors specific to export sectors are sufficiently important, governments will not wish to tax exports, so the Terms-of-Trade Puzzle disappears. But this just introduces a new problem (Ethier, 2002), the Export-Subsidy-Transfer Puzzle:

> *In equilibrium, exporting nations will (i) offer large export subsidies, which will (ii) be incompletely countervailed by importing nations, who (iii) would not implement actual countervailing-duty laws (complete countervailing).*

Thus the Received Theory necessarily implies dramatically counterfactual equilibria. Furthermore, the source of these counterfactual predictions is exactly the distinguishing feature of the Received Theory: the central role played by the terms of trade and / or by trade tax revenue (Ethier, 2002).

---

[2] See Ethier (2002).

[3] Although the Received Theory assigns the central role to terms-of-trade considerations, they are ignored virtually without exception by trade lawyers and policymakers. See Regan (2004) for an argument that neither the public rhetoric of trade, nor the specific provisions of trade agreements, nor the full range of policy behavior of countries, is well explained by terms-of-trade considerations.

At the same time, the Grossman-Helpman variant (2002) of the Received Theory has received considerable empirical attention [Goldberg and Maggi (1999), Gawande and Bandyopadhyay (2000), Mitra, Thomakos, and Ulubaşoğlu (2002), and McCallum (2004)]. These papers have been uniformly supportive of the Protection-For-Sale model, but in a highly selective way. They have not investigated the predictions that reflect the central presumptions of the Received Theory (import subsidies for all politically unorganized import-competing sectors and export taxes for all politically unorganized export sectors). But they have given powerful evidence that, in politically organized import-competing sectors, protection is negatively related to the import-penetration ratio, presumably reflecting the tug between sectoral special interests and consumer surplus central to most political-economy approaches to trade policy. Also in such sectors, protection appears to be negatively related to the domestic elasticity of import demand. Furthermore, this literature argues persuasively that distinguishing between politically organized and unorganized sectors is crucial to understanding this dependence.

This paper offers a simple model of trade policy as a tug between sectoral interests and consumer surplus. The model contains no explicit microeconomic analysis, to make it consistent with alternative political-economy approaches. But it is NOT consistent with the Received Theory or, therefore, with the Protection-For-Sale model. The model is free of the counterfactual predictions of the Received Theory while generating the predictions that have been supported by the empirical literature. Thus it suggests the following resolution of the conundrum: Despite claims to the contrary, the empirical literature offers no real support for the Protection-For-Sale model in particular, or for the Received Theory more generally.

2. The Model: Economics

Assume two countries (*H*ome and *F*oreign), two factors (*K*apital and *L*abor), and $N + 1$ traded goods ($0, 1, \ldots N$). Good 0 is a numeráire good, produced by labor alone. Goods 1 to N are produced by capital and labor, with capital specific to each of these sectors. H imports goods 1 to n and exports goods $n + 1$ to N.

Ownership of each specific factor is distributed uniformly over a fraction of the set of capitalists, with each capitalist owning some of only one of the specific factors. Choose units so that a unit of good 0 is produced by a unit of labor. Thus, assuming good 0 is actually produced, the wage $w = 1$.

Preferences in each country can be summarized by the utility function, where c_i denotes consumption of good i, $U = c_0 + u_1(c_1) + \ldots + u_N(c_N)$. This implies demand functions $d_i = d_i(Q_i)$, $i = 1, \ldots, N$, where Q_i denotes the relative price of good i in terms of good 0. Residual income is all spent on the numeráire good 0. I assume that endowments in both countries are such that each both produces and consumes good 0.

Each country may tax or subsidize either imports or exports. For H, let Q_i and P_i denote, respectively, the domestic and international relative price (in terms of the numeráire) of good i, and τ_i one plus the *ad-valorem* trade tax t_i. Thus $Q_i = \tau_i P_i$ for $i = 1, \ldots, n$, and $Q_j = P_j / \tau_j$ for $j = n + 1, \ldots, N$. Analogous F variables will be distinguished by asterisks.

International trade

Equilibrium in the world market for good i, $i = 1 \ldots n$, is represented by $M_i(\tau_i P_i) = X_i^*(P_i/\tau_i^*)$, where M_i and X_i^* respectively denote H import demand and F export supply. H's import tax and F's export tax thus determine P_i, independently of other sectors. This in turn implies the following.

$$\frac{\tau_i}{P_i}\frac{dP_i}{dt_i} = -\frac{e_i}{e_i + f_i^*}$$

and

$$\frac{\tau_i}{Q_i}\frac{dQ_i}{dt_i} = \frac{\tau_i}{P_i}\frac{dP_i}{dt_i} + 1 = \frac{f_i^*}{e_i + f_i^*}$$

$$\text{where } e_i \equiv -\frac{\tau_i P_i M_i'}{M_i} > 0 \text{ and } f_i^* \equiv \frac{P_i X_i^{*\prime}}{\tau_i^* X_i^*} > 0.$$

Similarly, equilibrium in the world market for goods $n + 1$ to N can be represented by $M_j^*(\tau_j^* P_j) = X_j(P_j/\tau_j)$. Thus,

$$\frac{\tau_j}{P_j}\frac{dP_j}{dt_j} = \frac{f_j}{f_j^* + e_j^*}$$

and

$$\frac{\tau_j}{Q_j}\frac{dQ_j}{dt_j} = \frac{\tau_j}{P_j}\frac{dP_j}{dt_j} - 1 = -\frac{e_j^*}{f_j + e_j^*}.$$

H imports of goods $1 \ldots n$ need not equal in value H exports of goods $n + 1 \ldots N$: Trade balance is reached with a net exchange of good *0*.

3. The Model: Policy Formation

I now introduce the political-economy side of the model. My intent is to present a reduced-form model of policy formation consistent with alternative political-economy approaches.

Lobbies

I assume that the owners of each specific factor i potentially organize a lobby to bargain with the government over t_i. Nobody lobbies for policy regarding the numeráire good. The sectors differ in the abilities of the associated factor owners to organize as well as in the abilities of those that do organize to bring pressure to bear on the government (Olson, 1965).

If a sector does not organize, and so does not lobby, the government leaves trade policy unchanged at its existing level, which, for convenience, I assume to be free trade. Organized sectors elicit a government response. In this response, the government wishes to increase the specific-factor income $\pi_i(Q_i)$ of the associated lobby, but is also reluctant to reduce the consumer surplus $S_i(Q_i) \equiv u_i(c_i(Q_i)) - Q_i d_i(Q_i)$.

W_i denotes the objective function of the government if sector i is organized, and, thus, does lobby.

$$W_i(t_i) = (\delta_i + 1)\,\pi_i(Q_i) + s_i(Q_i). \tag{1}$$

Here, $\delta_i \geq 0$ denotes the importance the government attaches to the welfare of the lobby. The government wishes to drive W_i as high as possible, but is constrained in this by a desire not to drive consumer surplus too low:

$$S_i(Q_i) \geq \frac{1}{\varepsilon_i} \tag{2}$$

The parameters δ_i and ε_i both reflect the political influence of the i lobby: Higher values imply more influence. For simplicity I assume that they are always consistent in the sense that,

$$\delta_i > \delta_j \text{ if and only if } \varepsilon_i > \varepsilon_j. \tag{A1}$$

Number each country's imports in decreasing order of political influence, and likewise for each country's exports.

Policy choice

Differentiating (1) yields, for each import-competing sector (the sector subscript i is omitted):

$$\frac{t}{Q}\frac{dW}{dt} = \left[\delta\frac{x}{M} - 1\right] M \frac{f^*}{e + f^*} \tag{3}$$

where x denotes domestic production. If the term in brackets on the right-hand side is positive, a tariff is called for. This will be more likely the greater the degree δ of political influence possessed by that sector's lobby. For a given degree of influence, this will be more likely the smaller the import penetration ratio M/x. If the term in brackets is negative, the sector's organized interest group lacks the power to influence policy: Thus it will not lobby and the government will not depart from free trade.

If dW/dt is indeed positive, the government will impose a tariff. Doing so will both increase x and reduce M: dW/dt will remain positive. Thus the government will raise t until (2) binds. Thus, other things equal, the greater the degree ε of political influence, the greater the tariff t and the lower the import penetration ratio M/x.

Next, from (2),

$$\frac{\varepsilon}{t}\frac{dt}{d\varepsilon} = \frac{d}{S}\frac{f^*}{e+f^*}.$$

More political influence ε implies a higher tariff t, but how much higher is negatively related to the import elasticity e.

Proposition 1 *A sectoral import-competing interest group is more likely to lobby the lower the import penetration ratio. For those that do lobby, the tariff will be positively related to the degree of political influence, and negatively correlated to the import penetration ratio and to the elasticity of import demand.*

Remark 1 *This simple model predicts just those properties that empirical investigations of the Grossman-Helpman model have supported.*

Turning to export sectors, we have

$$\frac{t}{Q}\frac{dW}{dt} = \left[-\delta\frac{x}{X} - 1\right] X \frac{e^*}{e^*+f} < 0. \tag{4}$$

Thus the government will wish to subsidize the exports of all politically-organized sectors. If it does so, the resulting increase in the domestic relative price will reduce domestic demand, so that X/x will rise with the subsidy. From (2),

$$\frac{\varepsilon}{t}\frac{dt}{d\varepsilon} = -\frac{d}{S}\frac{e^*}{e^*+f}.$$

Thus an increase in sectoral influence will increase the subsidy the government is willing to offer, and it will increase it more the smaller is the domestic export elasticity f.

Proposition 2 *The government will be willing to subsidize the exports of all organized export sectors. The government's desired subsidy will be positively related to the degree of political influence, and negatively related to the export-production ratio and to the elasticity of export demand.*

4. The Non-Cooperative Equilibrium

Next, consider the non-cooperative, trade-policy, equilibrium between H and F. Because of the partial-equilibrium structure of the model, the various sectors can be analyzed independently. So look at good 1, which H imports and F exports, and whose respective specific factor owners are organized and sufficiently potent to influence policy in each country. Then by Propositions 1 and 2, the H government wishes to tax imports of good 1, and the F government wishes to subsidize its export. Figure 1 below shows the relevant policy plane.

Figure 1

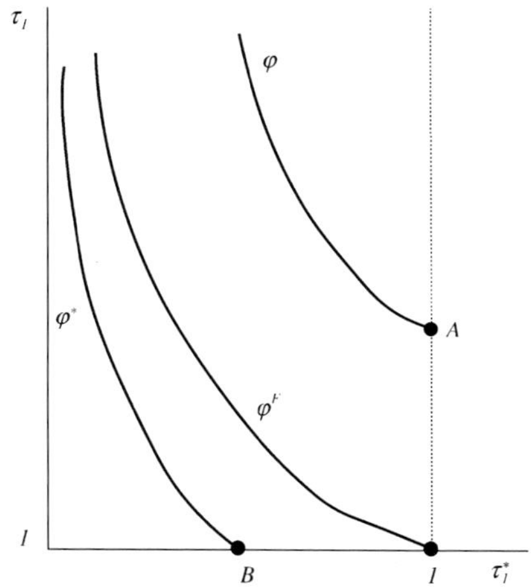

Best responses

Let Q_1^A solve $S_1\ (Q_1^A) = 1\ /\ \varepsilon_1$. In Figure 1, A shows the value of τ_1 that will cause $Q_1 = Q_1^A$ when $\tau_1^* = 1$, that is, it denotes H's best response to $\tau_1^* = 1$. In like manner, B denotes F's best response to $\tau_1 = 1$.

The φ locus depicts all those combinations of τ_1 and τ_1^* implying the same value of Q_1 as at A. Thus φ is the locus of solutions to

$$M_1(Q_1^A) = X_1^*(Q_1^A / \tau_1\ \tau_1^*),$$

so that φ is a rectangular hyperbola. Since $Q_1{}^*$ is uniquely related to Q_1 via the market-clearing condition for good *1*, it too is constant along φ.

Now, suppose F were to depart from A by imposing an export subsidy $dt_1^* < 0$. Then an increase in the H tariff of $dt_1 = -\tau_1\ dt_1^*$ will hold Q_1 and Q_1^* unchanged: We move upwards and to the left along φ. This will maintain the initial situation except that F pays an export subsidy which H taxes away with an equivalent increase in its tariff. This countervailing increase in its tariff constitutes a beneficial H response to F's adoption of an export subsidy.

Equilibrium

In like manner, φ^F depicts the iso-domestic-price locus corresponding to free trade ($\tau_1\ \tau_1^* = 1$) and φ^*, which is F's best-response curve, that corresponding to B. Since these three loci (all rectangular hyperbolae) correspond to different values of the domestic prices, they cannot intersect. Moving northwest along any one of these loci leaves all demands and supplies unchanged: The only effect is to shift trade-tax revenue from F to H.

As φ and φ^* are distinct rectangular hyperbolae, they do not intersect. There is no Nash equilibrium in t_1 and t_1^* alone!

An equilibrium can be obtained if we slightly enlarge each country's set of policy instruments. Suppose that, in addition to setting its trade taxes or subsidies, each country can decide whether to implement, or not to implement, a countervailing-duty law. Such a law would mandate that imports of goods receiving a foreign export subsidy would be subject to a matching tariff, in addition to whatever trade tax or subsidy the importing country might otherwise wish to implement.

If H, for example, were to implement such a law and also to set τ equal to the value that would cause $Q_1 = Q_1^A$ when $\tau_1^* = 1$, those actions would credibly commit H to be on φ. Then F's best response, assuming it doesn't want simply to give government revenue to H, would be A.

Proposition 3 *There is a non-cooperative equilibrium in trade policy. Each country adopts a countervailing-duty law, and employs neither export taxes nor export subsidies. Import-competing sectors with sufficient political influence receive protection and those without do not. Such tariffs will be higher the higher the degree of political influence, and the lower the import penetration ratio and the elasticity of import demand.*

Remark 2 *Countervailing-duty laws emerge here as the result of non-cooperative choices by the two governments,* **not** *as a result of a trade agreement.*

The GATT attempts to curtail the use of export subsidies and also provides a code of conduct regarding countervailing-duty laws. But such laws were in existence *long* before the GATT.

Remark 3 *Proposition 3 displays those predictions of the Protection-For-Sale approach that have found empirical support, and does not display those predictions that appear to be counterfactual.*

Politically organized import-competing products are just one class of traded goods for which the Protection-For-Sale model makes predictions. Imports are predicted to be subsidized whenever the import-competing sector is not politically organized. The empirical literature has shown that, in such sectors, protection is negatively related to the inverse import-penetration ratio, a result important for relating this work to earlier reduced-form studies. But the literature is silent regarding the much more fundamental question of whether imports of such goods are in fact systematically subsidized.

The Protection-For-Sale model also predicts that all exports from unorganized sectors will be taxed. If one wished to look at the practical relevance of the role of terms-of-trade and trade-tax-revenue considerations – central to both the Received Theory and to its Protection-For-Sale special case – this is exactly where one should first look. For three reasons: (i) this prediction is a direct consequence of the assumed concern for the terms-of-trade and for trade-tax revenue; (ii) export taxes are not constrained by trade agreements; and (iii) this sign prediction does not depend upon the validity of estimates of trade elasticities. But, in spite of all this, the empirical literature is silent about the practical success of this most basic implication of the Protection-For-Sale model.

Exports from politically-organized sectors are predicted by the model to be either taxed or subsidized, depending on the relative strength of political considerations. But, again, the empirical literature does not report on this prediction.

5. Concluding Remarks

The Received Theory of international trade agreements, the result of half a century of research by international trade theorists, suffers from fundamental puzzles that call into question its very relevance to reality. These puzzles characterize the Protection-For-Sale model in particular.

- If terms-of-trade motives dominate, each government will (counter-factually) employ both import tariffs and export taxes in Nash equilibrium. Any trade agreement would presumably wish to address export taxes (the Terms-of-Trade Puzzle). If political-support effects dominate, each government will tax imports but not exports, but, again counter-factually, neither country will implement a countervailing-duty law, and each will, with an export subsidy only partly countervailed by its partner, "bribe" the other government into allowing more imports than it otherwise would (the Export-Subsidy-Transfer Puzzle).
- But a number of empirical papers have given powerful evidence that, in politically organized import-competing sectors, protection is negatively related to the import-penetration ratio and appears to be negatively related to the domestic elasticity of import demand, and that distinguishing between politically organized and unorganised sectors is crucial to understanding this dependence.
- This paper has utilized a simple formulation of the political economy of protection based directly on a trade-off between the income of special interests and consumer surplus. The model delivers the predictions that appear to be supported by the empirical evidence, but is free of the puzzles exhibited by the Received Theory.

The empirical literature investigating the Protection-For-Sale model offers no real support for that model or for the Received Theory more generally.

References

Bagwell, K. and R.W. Staiger, 1999, "An Economic Theory of GATT," *American Economic Review* 89 (1), 215–248.

Bagwell, K. and R. W. Staiger, 2002, *The Economics Of The World Trading System* (Cambridge, MA: The MIT Press).

Ethier, W.J., 2002, "The Theory of Trade Policy and Trade Agreements: A Critique," working paper, Department of Economics, University of Pennsylvania.

Ethier, W. J., 2004, "Political Externalities, Nondiscrimination, and A Multilateral World," *Review Of International Economics* 12 (3), 303–320.

Gawande, K. and U. Bandyopadhyay, 2000, "Is Protection for Sale? Evidence on the Grossman-Helpman Theory of Endogenous Protection," *Review Of Economics And Statistics* 82 (1), 139–152.

Goldberg, P.K. and G. Maggi, 1999, "Protection for Sale: An Empirical Investigation," *American Economic Review* 84 (4), 1135–1155.

Grossman, G. and E. Helpman, 1994, "Protection for Sale," *American Economic Review* 89 (5), 833–850.

Grossman, G. and E. Helpman, 1995, "Trade Wars and Trade Talks," *Journal Of Political Economy* 85 (4), 667–690.

Grossman, G. and Helpman, E., 2002, *Interest Groups And Trade Policy* (Princeton: Princeton University Press).

Hillman, A.L., 1982, "Declining Industries and Political-Support Protectionist Motives," *American Economic Review* 72, 1180–1190.

Hillman, A.L., 1989, *The Political Economy Of Protection* (Chur: Harwood Academic Publishers).

Hillman, A.L., 1990, "Protectionist Policies as the Regulation of International Industry," *Public Choice* 67, 101–110.

Hillman, A.L., Long, N.V., and Moser, P., 1995, "Modeling Reciprocal Trade Liberalization: the Political-economy and National-welfare Perspectives," *Swiss Journal Of Economics And Statistics* 131, 503–515.

Hillman, A.L. and P. Moser, 1996, "Trade Liberalization as Politically Optimal Exchange of Market Access", in M. Canzoneri, W. J. Ethier, and V. Grilli (eds.), *The New Transatlantic Economy* (Cambridge: Cambridge University Press), 295–312.

Magee, S.P., 1994, "Endogenous Protection: A Survey", in D.C. Mueller (ed.), *Handbook Of Public Choice* (Cambridge, MA: Basil Blackwell).

McCallum, P., 2004, "Protection for Sale and Trade Liberalization: an Empirical Investigation," *Review Of International Economics* 12(1), 81–94.

Mitra, D., D.D. Thomakos, and M.A. Ulubaşoğlu, 2002, "'Protection For Sale' In A Developing Country: Democracy vs. Dictatorship," *Review Of Economics And Statistics* 84 (3), 497–508.

Nelson, D., 1988, "Endogenous Tariff Theory: A Critical Survey," *American Journal Of Political Science* 32, 796–837.

Olson, M., 1965, *The Logic Of Collective Action* (Cambridge, MA: Harvard University Press).

Regan, D.H., 2004, "Why Do We Have Trade Agreements? And Why Does It Matter? – A Lawyer's View of Some Economic Theory," unpublished manuscript, University of Michigan.

Rodrik, D., 1995, "Political Economy of Trade Policy", in G. Grossman and K. Rogoff (eds.), *Handbook Of International Economics* (Amsterdam: North-Holland), 1457–1495.

10

The Political Economy of Protection

*Wilfred J. Ethier**

1 Introduction

International trade theory has traditionally examined protection from a *normative* perspective: What are its consequences and when is it justified from the point of view of national welfare? Beginning in the 1980s increasing attention has been paid to analyzing protection from a *positive* perspective: What actually determines it? These two approaches are obviously complementary – both are necessary. This chapter addresses the latter. Other surveys are provided by Nelson (1988), Magee (1994) and Rodrik (1995).

I address the ability of our theory adequately to explain trade policy and trade agreements. My bottom line will be tentative: We have made much progress, but we have a good way to go. It is important that we make the effort.

2 An analytical framework

To facilitate comparison across contributions it helps enormously to have a common theoretical framework in which to view them. I shall use the following.

Assume two countries (*H*ome and *F*oreign), two factors (*K*apital and *L*abor), and $N+1$ traded goods $(0, 1, \ldots, N)$. Good 0 is a *numeráire* good, produced by labour alone. Goods 1 to *N*are produced by capital and labour, with capital specific to each of these sectors. *H* imports goods 1 to *n* and exports goods $n+1$ to *N*.

I follow the preponderant part of the political-economy literature in assuming a sector-specific factor. There are two reasons for this. *First*, much of the literature suggests that specific factors are much more likely to be able to organize and so exert political influence. See Olson (1965), Pincus (1975), and Caves (1976). *Second*, specific factors, together with the demand separability discussed below, allows the analysis to employ simple partial-equilibrium techniques.

Ownership of each specific factor i is distributed uniformly over a fraction α_i of the population (labour force), with each individual owning some of at most one of the specific factors. Let $\alpha = \alpha_1 + \cdots + \alpha_N$ denote the fraction of the population owning some of a specific factor. Choose units so that a unit of good 0 is produced by a unit of labour. Thus, assuming good 0 is actually produced, the wage $w = 1$.

In each country individual preferences are summarized by the utility function

$$U = c_0 + u_1(c_1) + \cdots + u_N(c_N),$$

where c_i denotes consumption of good i. This implies individual demand functions $d_i = d_i(Q_i)$, $i = 1, \ldots, N$, where Q_i denotes the domestic relative price of good i in terms of good 0. Residual income is all spent on the numeráire good 0. I assume that endowments in both countries are such that each both produces and consumes good 0. Then an individual's utility can be expressed in the indirect form

$$v(Q_1, \ldots, Q_N; y) = \sum S_i(Q_i) + y, \tag{1}$$

where $S_i(Q_i) = u_i(d_i(Q_i)) - Q_i d_i(Q_i)$, the consumer surplus derived from good i, and y denotes the individual's income.

3 Unilateral trade policy

I briefly describe the principal alternative explanations of tariff determination, before focusing in more detail on the one that has most been used.

3.1 Voting models

Wolfgang Mayer (1984) introduced voting models to endogenize tariff formation.

The median voter approach. To see how this might work in a simple framework, suppose that $n = N = 1$, so that good 1 is imported in exchange for the *numeráire* good, and that H is small, so that the world relative price $P_1 \equiv P$ is given. Thus $Q = P(1+t)$, where t denotes the tariff on good 1. If ϕ denotes some individual's share of national income Y.

$$y = \phi Y = \phi[L + \pi(Q) + tPM]. \tag{2}$$

The three terms in brackets respectively denote labour income, specific-factor income and tariff revenue. Substitute (2) into (1) and differentiate to see the effect of a change in t on the individual.

$$\frac{\partial v}{\partial t} = t\phi P\frac{\partial M}{\partial t} + LPd\left[\phi - \frac{1}{L}\right] + Y\frac{\partial \phi}{\partial t}. \tag{3}$$

(Use has been made of the facts that the derivative of consumer surplus is commodity demand and that that of specific-factor income is commodity supply.) Setting $\partial v/\partial t = 0$ yields the individual's most preferred tariff:

$$t' = \frac{Pd\left[\phi - \frac{1}{L}\right] + Y\frac{\partial \phi}{\partial t}}{-\phi P\frac{\partial M}{\partial t}}. \tag{4}$$

The denominator of the right-hand side of (4) is positive, since an increase in t lowers M. Assume that tariff revenue is distributed to the population in a manner neutral in the sense of Ethier (1984): proportional to each individual's share in factor income. Thus ϕ equals the individual's factor income share.

Individuals in the $1-\alpha$ share of the population that owns no capital have a share of national income ϕ below their share of labour income $(1/L)$, and a tariff will lower their share of national income. Thus $t' < 0$ for such workers: They prefer a particular import subsidy. Since the ownership of capital is distributed uniformly over the share α of the population, this situation is the reverse for them: They all prefer a particular tariff.

Suppose trade policy is decided by a direct popular vote. A majority (and so the median voter) will support the tariff if and only if $\alpha > 1/2$; otherwise the subsidy wins (ignoring the minute possibility of a tie). Mayer investigates such voting in the Heckscher–Ohlin–Samuelson model and in a specific-factors model, but the above simple framework suffices to illustrate several key points.

3.1.1 *Key points about the median-voter approach*

First, the great advantage is that this approach grounds trade policy in a fully specified political-economy model. The political component is not reduced to a black box.

Second, a disadvantage is that trade policy is almost never voted on directly by the public: It is implemented by governments. Elections in which the parties or candidates compete solely on trade policy may proxy for direct voting. Perhaps that did occur sometimes in the nineteenth century, but it is very rare now.

Third, by focusing only on direct voting, this approach excludes lobbying and political campaigning. In particular, it gives no scope to the factors determining the potential for special interests to organize, as emphasized by Olson (1965).

Fourth, the interior solution for t' in (4) is critically due to the fact that individual voters care about their share of trade-tax revenue. If such revenue is ignored, capitalists, if they do want a tariff (which they must do if the import-competing sector is initially large enough), wish it to be prohibitive, and laborers want a very large import subsidy, that is, one large enough that the effect on trade-tax revenue cannot be ignored. But we observe neither this result nor, in the case of industrial countries, any real interest in trade tax revenue (Regan, 2006). Still, trade-tax revenue exists, so it should logically be included in our models, but the critical role it then assumes in the theory seems totally at odds with its apparent negligible practical importance. I refer to this as the Cognitive-Dissonance (CD) issue. I assign it a label because, as will become apparent, it is pervasive in the literature on the political economy of trade policy.

3.1.2 Partisan politics

Brock and Magee (1978) did focus explicitly on the roles of lobbies and parties in the electoral process. See also Magee, Brock and Young (1979) and Austen-Smith (1991). Suppose, in the above context, that capital and labour organize lobbies to influence the outcome of an election between two political parties. This outcome is inherently uncertain, with the probability of success of a particular party dependent on the contributions received by the two parties from the two lobbies plus the platforms announced by the parties. Those platforms consist of proposed tariffs. Each party, eyeing its rival and aware of how lobbies determine their contributions, sets its platform to maximize its chance of success. Each lobby, eyeing the other, reacts to the platforms by making the contribution that will maximize its expected welfare.

This approach accommodates partisan politics and lobbying at the expense of relegating the electoral process itself to a black box (the BB issue). The substitution is, on the whole, a step toward greater realism. But, because of its cumbersome analysis, the approach has been little used.

3.2 Political support

The portion of the literature discussed thus far has focused on the electoral process, but another, larger, portion has addressed the behaviour of an incumbent government in office.

3.2.1 The basic political-support approach

Hillman (1982) introduced the concept of a political-support function to analyze the behaviour of an incumbent government confronted by a special-interest group. See also Hillman (1989, 1990), Long and Vousden (1991) Hillman, Long and Moser (1995), and Hillman and Moser (1996).

Suppose, in the model of section 2, that the owners of capital specific to an import sector i constitute an interest group desiring tariff protection. The incumbent government wishes to set a tariff that will maximize its political support:

$$W^i = f^i(\psi(Q_i) - \psi(P_i),\ Q_i - P_i). \tag{5}$$

Here ψ measures the concerns of the interest group. The first argument of f^i accounts for the influence of the interest group on political support and the second argument that of the population at large. In both arguments, political support depends not only on the outcome (Q_i) but on how that outcome differs from what it would be were the government to take no action. The idea is that the government would be held politically accountable only for what it has done. This is an important distinction. But it is relevant only in cases where the economy is subject to an external shock that influences the free-trade equilibrium – Hillman (1982) for example. So subsume for now the free-trade situation into the functional form. Assuming that f^i is increasing in its first argument and decreasing in its second, the government will maximize its political support W^i in (5) by trading off the general welfare for that of the interest group.

To be more specific, assume that the measure of interest-group benefit is the income of the corresponding specific factor $\pi_i(Q_i)$ and that the measure of the effect of policy on the general welfare is the effect on the per-capita consumer surplus derived from the corresponding good: $S_i(Q_i)$. Then, suppressing for convenience the index i, (5) can be expressed as follows:

$$W = W(\pi(Q[t]),\ S(Q[t])), \tag{6}$$

where W is increasing in both arguments. Differentiating (6) with respect to t and rearranging terms yields

$$\frac{1}{PW_2}\frac{dW}{dt} = I(Q)x - M, \tag{7}$$

where x denotes the output of the sector, and $I(Q) \equiv (W_1 - W_2)/W_2$ can be interpreted as an index of the political influence of the special-interest group. Call the interest group *influential* if the right-hand side of (7) is positive when $t = 0$; that is, an influential interest group is able to obtain protection.

A tariff will increase x in (7) and lower M, so, *unless* I also falls sufficiently rapidly, the government will impose a prohibitive tariff whenever confronted by an influential interest group.

There are two ways to alter the model to avoid this extreme result. One is to add trade-tax revenue appropriately to the arguments of (6), as was done in the voting model discussed above. But of course this will also introduce the CD issue: The chosen tariff or subsidy will depend *crucially* upon its effect on trade-tax revenue.

The second way to alter the model is to suppose that the influence of an influential special-interest group is limited, that is, that I declines as t (and so Q) increases. If I declines rapidly enough, (7) will have an interior solution corresponding to a non-prohibitive tariff. Consider this possibility in more detail.

The influence of a special-interest group can be measured by the value of I when $t = 0$, that is, $I(P)$, and also by the rate of its decline: $I' < 0$. Assume for simplicity that these measures are in accord: $I(P)$ is larger when the absolute value of I' is smaller.

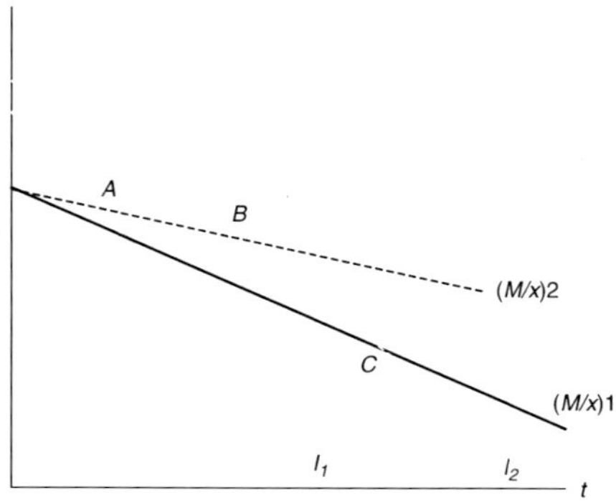

Figure 10.1 The tariff with an influential interest group.

Figure 10.1 shows the case of an influential interest group (the right-hand side of (7) is positive when $t = 0$) where I falls rapidly enough to give an interior solution (at point A). I_2 (where point B indicates the equilibrium) shows more influence than I_1. Other things equal, a greater influence implies a larger t and a lower import-penetration ratio M/x.

The elasticity e of import demand plays an important role in many tariff issues,[1] so it is of interest to examine its effect. This is more complex. In figure 10.1 $(M/x)_2$ reflects a lower elasticity than $(M/x)_1$. Along a given I_1 the reduction in e lowers t and raises M/x. But a lower e also implies a lower deadweight loss to increasing t, so the lobby should become more influential, which is reflected in I_2 replacing I_1. This raises t and lowers M/x, so the net effect is ambiguous. For a given reduction in e, as reflected in given $(M/x)_1$ and $(M/x)_2$, this net effect depends upon the sensitivity of lobby influence to e. With low sensitivity, t falls and M/x increases; with intermediate sensitivity, t and M/x both increase; with high sensitivity, t increases and M/x falls. In other words, at a given level of import penetration, t is negatively related to e.

An influential interest group will of course be concerned that any protection it receives not be undone by the government of a trading partner subsidizing its exports. That the home government shares this concern is implied by (5), which says that the home government is rewarded on the basis of the net effects of its actions. Thus we should expect the government to implement a countervailing duty law, providing that any foreign subsidy be countervailed by an increase in the home tariff. To my knowledge, the political-support literature has not actually made this point, but it seems a clear inference from its approach.

The above discussion applies to an influential interest group. But what happens when it is not influential? There seem to be two alternatives.

(a) An interest group for which the right-hand side of (7) is negative when $t = 0$ will induce the government to subsidize imports without bound (or as much as the treasury will bear) unless I rises sufficiently rapidly as the subsidy is increased.

(b) This literature seems based on the observation that import-competing interests are individually much more affected by trade policy regarding their goods than are the more numerous but more diffused consumers. Then such interests, even if not politically organized at all, are much more likely than consumers to vote on the basis of such policy. This suggests assuming that the right-hand side of (7) is never negative when $t = 0$: It is positive for an influential group and zero for a non-influential group. Thus the latter will result in $t = 0$.

Of these alternatives, (b) seems to me more in accord with the spirit of the general support-function approach, so I shall take it as characterizing that approach. But, to my knowledge, that literature again has not addressed these alternatives at all, much less providing a formal framework to indicate when one or the other might be more appropriate.

Suppose, finally, that the interest group corresponds to an export sector. Analogously to the above, an influential group would be able to induce the government to provide an export subsidy. However, if, as discussed above, foreign governments have adopted countervailing-duty laws, such a subsidy would amount to a cost that conferred no benefit on the interest group and so would not be adopted. The government is powerless to aid such a group with trade policy. Non-influential groups can be treated analogously to such groups in import-competing sectors. That is, $t = 0$ in export sectors with non-influential interest groups. Again, this seems to be a reasonable inference from the nature of the political-support approach, though it is not discussed in that literature.

3.2.2 *Key points about the political-support approach*

First, political support depends upon the effect of the government's actions on agents' well-being, not just the latter itself.

Second, the approach exhibits the BB issue: the political-support function is not derived from microeconomic fundamentals.

Third, for influential import-competing sectors the degree of influence is positively correlated with the tariff rate.

Fourth, for influential import-competing sectors the tariff is negatively correlated with the import-penetration ratio.

Fifth, for influential import-competing sectors the tariff is negatively correlated with the elasticity of import demand, at a given import-penetration ratio.

*Sixth**, if the country has at least one influential import-competing sector it will adopt a countervailing-duty law.

*Seventh**, non-influential import-competing sectors are likely to be characterized by an absence of trade-policy intervention.

Eighth, the government is unable to do anything for, and therefore to extract political support from, influential export sectors.

*Ninth**, non-influential export sectors are likely to be characterized by an absence of trade-policy intervention.

(An asterisk indicates a point that reasonably characterizes the political-support approach but that, to my knowledge, has not been discussed explicitly in its literature.)

3.2.3 The campaign-contributions variant of the political-support approach

This variant of the political-support approach, due to Grossman and Helpman (1994, 2002), identifies such support as financial contributions (or bribes). Following the authors, we can denote this approach as Protection For Sale, or PFS. This has become the most widely used political-economy model of protection, not because it is realistic – or even plausible – but because it delivers a tariff formula based squarely on a complete micro political-economy description of behavior.

The distinguishing assumptions of this version of the political-support approach are as follows: (a) The N specific factors are exogenously divided into N^1 that are politically organized and N^0 that are not (so $N = N^0 + N^1$). (b) Political support consists of campaign contributions (or bribes). (c) Each lobby, with an eye on the other lobbies, offers the government a *contribution schedule* detailing the contribution it will make as a function of the vector of all N trade policies. The lobby wishes to maximize the excess of its specific-factor income over its actual contribution. (d) The government wishes to maximize a weighted average of national income and total contributions,

$$W = \beta Y + (1 - \beta) \sum_{N^1} C^i, \tag{8}$$

where C^i denotes the actual contribution of lobby i and $\beta \leq 1$ the weight the government attaches to national income. (e) The outcome is modeled as a menu-auction equilibrium in the sense of B. Douglas Bernheim and Michael Whinston (1986).

The PFS model yields equilibrium contributions and tariffs. The former are of little interest, given the contrived nature of the model. But the latter, as pointed out by Goldberg and Maggi (1999), follow directly as necessary conditions for maximizing the joint surplus of the government and the lobbies, regardless otherwise of the actual bargaining model. The equilibrium tariffs are given by

$$\frac{t_i}{1+t_i} = \frac{\xi_i - \alpha}{\beta/(1-\beta)+\alpha} \cdot \frac{1}{(M_i/x_i)\cdot e_i} \tag{9}$$

where $\xi_i = 1$ if the industry is politically organized and 0 if it is not.

Note that if the government cares only about social welfare ($\beta = 1$) it adopts a policy of free trade. This is also the result if everyone belongs to some organized lobby ($\alpha = 1$), but this latter result is of little interest as it just reflects the extreme assumptions that all organized sectors are equally potent politically and that they all lobby equally about all trade policies.

Equation (9) implies the following. *Organized import-competing sectors* ($\xi_i = 1$) will receive positive protection that is positively related to the degree of influence ξ_i (though of course that is here constrained to be only zero or unity), and negatively related to the import-penetration ratio and to the elasticity of import demand. This is exactly what the general political-support function approach predicts, of which the PFS model is a special case.

Unorganized import-competing sectors ($\xi_i = 0$) will be confronted with subsidized imports. This contrasts with my interpretation of the spirit of the political-support approach ($t = 0$), though, as pointed out above, that literature has not been explicit about this.

Organized export sectors ($\xi_i = 1$) will find their exports subsidized. This also contrasts with the predictions of the general political-support approach.

Unorganized export sectors ($\xi_i = 0$) will find their exports taxed. This again contrasts with my interpretation of the spirit of the political-support approach ($t = 0$), though, again, that literature has not been explicit about this.

3.2.4 Empirical investigations of the PFS variant

The PFS model has received considerable empirical attention; see Goldberg and Maggi (1999), Gawande and Bandyopadhyay (2000), Mitra, Thomakos, and Ulubasoglu (2002), and McCallum (2004). These papers uniformly claim support for the PFS model, but in a highly selective way. They have confined themselves to import-competing sectors. An important claim in this literature is that they are estimating (9), an equation that comes directly from a detailed microeconomic model (i.e., no BB issue).

These papers do not employ actual tariffs[2] because they are constrained by international trade agreements, not part of the basic PFS model. So data on administered protection is used instead. It is not clear how much this helps, since administered protection very often involves a good deal of bilateral negotiation; for example, Goldberg and Maggi, 1999, 159). But there are more serious concerns.

Administered protection using tariffs involves primarily antidumping and countervailing duties. These are imposed as a result of a well-defined legal procedure that, in sharp contrast to the PFS model, gives no weight to either national welfare or tariff revenue. So if such data does fit (9), even though we *know* it was not generated by what the PFS approach models, one must wonder what such a fit means. (Political organization also plays no role in the administrative procedure, but one might conjecture that politically organized sectors are also better able to file petitions.)

Administered protection using non-tariff barriers involves, in data from the 1980s, primarily voluntary export restraints (VERs). A key property of VERs is that the rents from the barriers are captured by exporters, whereas the assumption in the PFS model that the importing country captures those rents is crucial to the derivation of (9). If the PFS model is altered to constrain the importing country from capturing the rents, necessary if VER data is used, the model predicts nothing like (9). So a good fit to (9) is not a confirmation of the PFS model: Indeed it is a rejection if (9) fits better than what the PFS model would imply for VER data.

The empirical studies have also not investigated the predictions of the PFS model that most closely reflect its central assumptions: import subsidies for all politically unorganized import-competing sectors and export taxes for all politically unorganized export sectors. These predictions involve instruments that are *not* constrained by international trade agreements and are therefore free of the issues that prevented the use of conventional tariffs. But it appears obvious that these predictions are not borne out by the facts.

Thus the empirical work has not provided support for the PFS model itself (apparently the CD issue dominates). But it has given powerful evidence that, in politically organized import-competing sectors, protection is negatively related to the import-penetration ratio, presumably reflecting the tug between sectoral special interests and consumer surplus central to most political-economy approaches to trade policy (see Ethier 2006). Also in such sectors, protection appears to be negatively related to the domestic elasticity of import demand. Furthermore, this literature argues persuasively that distinguishing between politically organized and unorganized sectors is crucial to understanding this dependence.

So we have support not for the PFS model in particular, but for 'something else'. What else? The general political-support approach makes just those predictions that have been verified and is free of the issues attending the PFS model, mentioned above. Thus the empirical literature can be interpreted as providing strong evidence for the general political-support approach, but not for its PFS variant.

This is a notable accomplishment. In my mind it is the most valuable contribution to date in the large empirical literature addressing the political economy of trade policy. And the PFS model, by supplying (9) in explicit form, was critical in stimulating this contribution. However, the more general approach does not derive the political-support function from microeconomic fundamentals, so the BB issue remains. Thus, the empirical literature, intriguing as it is, cannot be interpreted as successfully confirming a structural model derived directly from a theory based on microeconomic fundamentals. More work is called for.

The empirical literature on the PFS model uses its parameter estimates to infer the size of the structural parameter β, the weight the government attaches to social welfare. Typically this weight turns out to be quite high: The government is seen as valuing social welfare much more than contributions. But since that literature has not succeeded in confirming the structure specific to the PFS model, it is not clear what significance, if any, can be attached to this seemingly optimistic inference.

3.2.5 Key points about the PFS variant

First, political support is identified with contributions (bribes).

Second, the approach is free from the BB issue: both the contributions and the trade policies are derived from microeconomic fundamentals.

Third, the PFS variant is subject to the CD issue.

Fourth, for politically organized import-competing sectors the degree of influence is positively correlated with the tariff rate.

Fifth, for organized import-competing sectors the tariff is negatively correlated with the import-penetration ratio.

Sixth, for organized import-competing sectors the tariff is negatively correlated with the elasticity of import demand, at a given import-penetration ratio.

Seventh, unorganized import-competing sectors are characterized by import subsidies.

Eighth, unorganized export sectors are characterized by export taxes.

Ninth, the empirical literature supports those predictions of the PFS model that overlap with the general support-function approach, but fails to support those that distinguish the PFS model from the general approach.

4 An analytical framework for trade agreements

I next turn to the political economy of international trade agreements. For this it is convenient first to extend the analytical framework presented in section 2 to an international equilibrium with two countries.

Each country may tax or subsidize either imports or exports. For H, let Q_i and P_i denote, respectively, the domestic and international relative price (in terms of the *numeráire*) of good i, and τ_i one plus the *ad-valorem* trade tax t_i. Thus

$$Q_i = \tau_i P_i \quad \text{for } i = 1, \ldots, n,$$

and

$$Q_j = P_j/\tau_j \quad \text{for } j = n+1, \ldots, N.$$

Analogous F variables will be distinguished by asterisks.

Equilibrium in the world market for good i, $i = 1, \ldots, n$, is represented by

$$M_i(\tau_i P_i) = X^*(P_i/\tau_i^*), \tag{10}$$

where M_i and X_i^* respectively denote H import demand and F export supply. H's import tax and F's export tax thus determine P_i, independently of other sectors. This in turn implies the following:

$$\frac{\tau_i}{P_i}\frac{dP_i}{dt_i} = -\frac{e_i}{e + f_i^*} \tag{11}$$

and

$$\frac{\tau_i}{Q_i}\frac{dQ_i}{dt_i} = \frac{\tau_i}{P_i}\frac{dP_i}{dt_i} + 1 = \frac{f_i^*}{e_i + f_i^*},$$

where $e_i \equiv -\tau_i P_i M_i'/M_i > 0$ and $f_i^* \equiv P_i X_i^{*\prime}/\tau_i^* X_i^* > 0$.

Similarly, equilibrium in the world market for goods $n+1$ to N can be represented by $M_j^*\left(\tau_j^* P_j\right) = X_j\left(P_j/\tau_j\right)$.

Thus,

$$\frac{\tau_j}{P_j}\frac{dP_j}{dt_j} = \frac{f_j}{f_j + e_j^*}$$

and

$$\frac{\tau_j}{Q_j}\frac{dQ_j}{dt_j} = \frac{\tau_j}{P_j}\frac{dP_j}{dt_j} - 1 = -\frac{e_j^*}{f_j + e_j^*}.$$

H imports of goods $1, \ldots, n$ need not equal in value H exports of goods $n+1, \ldots, N$: Trade balance is reached with a net exchange of good 0.

5 International trade agreements

The political economy of trade agreements must be derivative from the political economy of protection. As there are variants of the latter, there are variants of the former.

There are two basic approaches to trade agreements. The *terms-of-trade externality approach* sees the sole basis for a trade agreement as the possibility that national governments, conducting national policies, ignore the effects of those policies on trading partners through the terms of trade. Thus, all can gain by expanding trade at unchanged terms of trade.

The *exchange-of-market-access approach* sees the attraction of a trade agreement for a national government as due to the fact that such an agreement enables the government to do something for export interests that it cannot do unilaterally. As this applies to all governments, it can serve as a basis for negotiation.

The terms-of-trade externality approach has by far received the most formal attention by trade theorists. But this has not at all been echoed by trade policy makers, who virtually without exception speak in terms of the exchange of market access. Furthermore, some of the formal papers claiming to espouse the exchange-of-market-access approach actually use an analytical framework equivalent to that of the terms-of-trade externality approach, so that, in essence, they offer only an alternative rhetoric.

5.1 The terms-of-trade externality approach

A prominent twentieth-century accomplishment of international trade theory was its theory of international trade policy and trade agreements. Building on Harry Johnson's classic paper (1953–54), scores of contributions developed and elaborated what is now often called the terms-of-trade externality approach. The deservedly influential work of Bagwell and Staiger (1999, 2002) may justly be seen as triumphantly completing the research agenda implied by Johnson nearly half a century earlier. See also Grossman and Helpman (1995).

Suppose initially that $N = 1$, so that H imports good 1 from F in exchange for the *numeráire* good. The H government wishes to maximize the objective function $W(Q, P)$; the subscript 1 is omitted for simplicity. W is assumed to have the following properties:

$$W_1(P,P) > 0, \qquad W_2(Q,P) < 0. \tag{12}$$

W can be thought of as an example of a political-support function. The first assumed property, that W can be increased by departing from trade to protect the import-competing sector, allows the political dimension; the second property simply says that a terms-of-trade deterioration lowers W, presumably because of its negative effect on social welfare. This formulation is consistent with many political-economy models, including much of the political-support approach literature such as the PFS campaign-contributions variant.

The F government analogously wishes to maximize the objective function $W^*(1/Q^*, 1/P)$, where $Q^* = P/\tau^*$, and τ^* denotes one plus the F tariff on the *numeráire* good. $W*$ is assumed to have the properties:

$$W_1^*(1/P, 1/P) > 0, \qquad W_2^*(1/Q^*, 1/P) < 0. \tag{13}$$

Here the political dimension reflects a benefit to the F government from aiding labour via protection, since the import-competing sector in F uses only labour.

5.1.1 *The role of trade agreements*

If neither government cares about the terms of trade ($W_2 \equiv 0 \equiv W_2^*$), each government's objective depends only upon the respective relative domestic price. This can be controlled unilaterally by each government with trade policy, so there is no scope for international cooperation about such policies. In this context concern for the terms of trade is necessary to motivate a trade agreement.

Suppose, by contrast, that both governments care only about social welfare. Then global efficiency requires that agents in both countries face the same prices, $Q = Q^*$, indicating that opportunities for gainful trade are being fully exploited. This will be true when $\tau\,\tau^* = 1$ (Mayer 1981). This *social efficiency locus* includes free trade plus cases where one country taxes imports and the other subsidizes exports, in effect using trade policy to add an international side payment to the free-trade outcome.

However, W and W^* include political influences, so there is no reason to believe that social efficiency will coincide with political efficiency. The set of politically efficient policy pairs can be determined by solving the problem:

$$\text{maximize } W(Q,P) \text{ subject to } W^*(Q^*,P) = W_0^*$$

for all feasible values of W_0^*. This problem has the following first-order conditions, for each feasible value of W_0^*:

$$\frac{\partial W}{\partial \tau} + \lambda \frac{\partial W^*}{\partial \tau} = 0,$$

$$\frac{\partial W}{\partial \tau^*} + \lambda \frac{\partial W^*}{\partial \tau^*} = 0,$$

where λ denotes the Lagrange multiplier. Solving to eliminate λ gives an implicit relation in τ and τ^*: the *political efficiency locus.*

The multiplier λ represents the shadow cost to each government in being constrained in its policy choice by the size of the negative externality it can impose on the other government. In the Nash equilibrium (where each government is implementing the tariff that maximizes its own objective function given the tariff chosen by the other government) λ is in effect set at zero, whereas it is positive along the political efficiency locus. Thus, there is something to be gained by cooperation. So, in the present framework: *A desire to deal with a terms-of-trade externality can motivate a trade agreement, and it is the ONLY thing that can motivate a trade agreement.*

5.1.2 *Reciprocity*

Such a trade agreement is necessarily reciprocal in the sense that each country is departing from its Nash tariff in exchange for its partner doing the same. But the central role of the terms of trade in the present framework suggests a natural precise definition of reciprocity. Let P_0 denote the value of P that obtains in the

Nash equilibrium. Then a *price-reciprocity schedule* can be defined as the set of all $\tau - \tau^*$ pairs that satisfy:

$$M(\tau P_0) = X^*(P_0/\tau^*).$$

Along this schedule,

$$\frac{\tau}{\tau^*}\frac{d\tau}{d\tau^*} = \frac{f^*}{e}.$$

A trade agreement implemented on the price-reciprocity schedule involves the two countries altering their trade policies in such a way as to keep the terms of trade unchanged.

Figure 10.2 illustrates the terms-of-trade externality approach. The SEL, PEL, and PRS curves respectively depict the social efficiency locus, the political efficiency locus and the price-reciprocity schedule. *N* and TA illustrate the Nash equilibrium and an efficient trade agreement. As the two governments move from *N* towards TA along PRS they are reciprocally reducing their tariffs so as to leave the terms of trade unchanged. The tariff reductions generate beneficial reductions in the consumption costs and production costs caused by the tariffs, but they also generate political costs. Initially the efficiency benefits outweigh the political costs because of the terms-of-trade externalities in place at *N*. Beyond TA further political costs begin to outweigh further efficiency benefits.

TA is an efficient reciprocal trade agreement in the sense that any other agreement on PRS could be renegotiated to the mutual benefit of both countries. If governments cared only about social welfare, *TA* would coincide with *S*; if governments were unconcerned with the terms of trade, *N* would be at TA.

5.1.3 Key points about the terms-of-trade externality approach

First, this approach takes the government objective functions W and W^* as given. But this is *not* an example of the BB issue. Rather, it is a source of generality since many models featuring government behavior based on microeconomic fundamentals are special cases of these objective functions.

Second, the approach does display the CD issue. Indeed, it does so in an extreme form, as it posits that government concern for the terms of trade, and so for trade-tax revenue, is the *sole* reason for a trade agreement.

Third, the approach sits uncomfortably with actual trade agreements. While WTO members have bound their tariffs on literally thousands of imports, only a few have bound only a few taxes on exports. The WTO explicitly allows the taxation of unbound exports. Thus actual trade agreements do not prevent countries from manipulating their terms-of-trade. At a trade agreement such as TA in figure 10.2, each country has an incentive to use trade policy to turn the terms of trade in its favour. With the existing GATT/WTO framework of trade agreements, it is fully entitled to do so with export taxes.

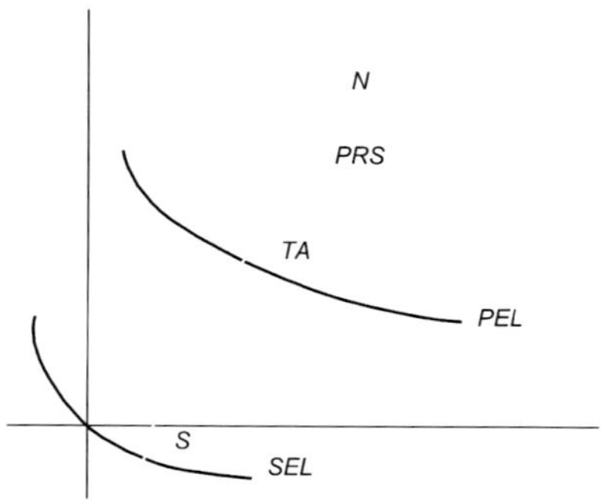

Figure 10.2 The terms-of-trade externality approach.

In the simple model described above, a trade agreement that bound each country's tariff but left export taxes unbound would be completely meaningless, regardless of its purpose. But that extreme result is an artifact of the two-good assumption. If a country binds tariffs on many imports it does constrain its ability to use trade policy to influence the relative prices of those imports in terms of each other. Thus actual trade agreements do have real effects, but constraining terms-of-trade manipulation is not one of them.

There is one exception to this. The U.S. Constitution prohibits the U.S. government from taxing exports. So, from the terms-of-trade externality perspective this raises the following question: Why does the United States sign on to trade agreements that prevent it from influencing the terms of trade in its favor while imposing no such constraint on its trading partners?

While the GATT/WTO allows countries to tax their exports, it significantly constrains their ability to subsidize exports. That is, it explicitly seeks to deny countries the option of conferring a positive terms-of-trade externality upon their trading partners.

Fourth, although this approach is consistent with much of the political-support literature, it does differ from it in a potentially significant way. That literature emphasizes that political support depends on the perceived *actions* of a government, not on *outcomes*. The approach just described, however, makes political support depend entirely on outcomes: Q and P. In some cases this distinction may not matter – if there is a transparent one-to-one relation between actions and outcomes, for example – but in other cases it may. To see this, consider the following simple example.[3] Suppose the H government cares nothing about the terms of trade. Now suppose there is an exogenous, from the H point of view, increase in τ^*. The H government then alters τ to keep Q unchanged.

The political support it receives will not change if that support depends only upon outcomes, which have not changed, but it will increase if that support depends upon *H* government actions, which have changed in response to an event beyond its control.[4] There is a real issue here, which the terms-of-trade externality approach assumes away.

5.2 The exchange-of-market-access approach

A large literature insists that trade agreements seek to *exchange market access*: I will grant your exporters increased access to my market in exchange for increased access to your market for my exporters. For an institutional approach, see Hauser (1986), Finger (1988, 1991), and Moser (1990); for a more formal approach, see Hillman, Long and Moser (1995), Hillman and Moser (1996) and Ethier (2008). Bagwell and Staiger use similar terminology to describe their approach. For example, they state (2002, 28–29), 'we may interpret "cost shifting", "terms-of-trade gain", and "market-access restriction" as three phrases that describe ... [a] single economic experience'. The earlier literature, it seems clear, had 'something else' in mind. But drawing an analytical distinction has proved elusive, largely because the earlier literature, when it expressed its ideas in formal terms (e.g., Hillman and Moser, 1996), did so in models that, as Bagwell and Staiger (2002, 20) correctly observe, were very often special cases of their own. In such cases the distinction from the terms-of-trade externality argument is entirely one of rhetoric, not substance.

The description in Section 3 of the basic political-support approach can provide a formal basis to define trade agreements based on the exchange of market access and to distinguish them from those that are not. The essential idea behind the exchange of market access seems to be that each country, for whatever reason, agrees to allow increased imports of a particular good in exchange for increased exports of another particular good. That is, such trade agreements are necessarily *inter-sectoral*.

The analytical framework of Sections 2 and 4 features extensive separability: equilibrium policies in each sector are determined independently of those in the other sectors. With policies in each sector determined independently, there could be an incentive for independent sector-by-sector international negotiations not involving inter-sectoral trade-offs, such as the 1965 United States – Canada automobile agreement. In such an *intra-sectoral* negotiation the governments would bargain over t_1 and t_1^*, with any implied change in $M_1 = X_1^*$ settled by a change in the trade volume of the *numeráire* good.

Consider the following question. With policy determination in each sector independent of that in the other sector, is it *necessary*, for trade negotiations to serve a useful purpose, that they address inter-sectoral trade-offs? If so, we may regard the negotiations as motivated by a desire to exchange market access:

trade agreements can be said to be based on the exchange of market access if and only if there is no reason for sector-by-sector negotiations.

Note that this definition requires the necessity of inter-sectoral negotiations. Since in this analytical framework agents ignore cross-sectional effects, negotiations addressing those effects could well be useful, as would national policymaking addressing those effects. So defining the exchange of market access on the *sufficiency* of inter-sectoral negotiations would not be a useful discriminatory device.

Our analytical framework and discussion of the basic political-support approach in Section 2 offers no opportunity for an intra-sectoral trade agreement. In sector 1, for example, F is implementing no policy and so can offer H nothing in return for a lower tariff. Thus any trade agreement must be based on the exchange of market access.

To focus on such an exchange in the sharpest possible way, consider a simple trade agreement involving only goods 1 and $n+1$. Suppose for simplicity that the two implemented tariffs are both prohibitive.

The motive for a trade agreement based on the exchange of market access would be to enable each government to offer its export sector something while taking something less from its import-competing sector. It is true that, with a non-cooperative equilibrium featuring countervailing-duty laws, each government is powerless to offer its export sector something in any other way. But it is not clear that it will be tempted to use this way. The reason is that, since retreating from the imposed t_1 would impose a first-order cost on H, doing so would be tempting to H only if the implied negotiated benefit for good $n+1$ is large enough. It is not clear that a trade agreement can be found that would do this for both countries simultaneously.

Now consider a hypothetical trade agreement stipulating $dt_1 < 0$ and $dt^*_{n+1} = \gamma\, dt_1$ for some parameter γ. Such an agreement will raise the joint surplus in each country, and so be perceived as beneficial by each government, if and only if the following holds:

$$\frac{\partial W_1}{\partial t_1} + \gamma \frac{\partial W_2}{\partial t^*_{n+1}} > 0,$$

$$\frac{\partial W^*_1}{\partial t_1} + \gamma \frac{\partial W^*_2}{\partial t^*_{n+1}} > 0.$$

This will in turn be possible for some choice of $\gamma > 0$ if and only if the following condition is met:

$$\left(\frac{\partial W^*_1}{\partial t_1}\right)\left(\frac{\partial W_{n+1}}{\partial t^*_{n+1}}\right) > \left(\frac{\partial W^*_{n+1}}{\partial t^*_{n+1}}\right)\left(\frac{\partial W_1}{\partial t_1}\right) \tag{14}$$

Figure 10.3 illustrates how satisfaction of (14) is equivalent to the existence of a mutually beneficial trade agreement. The vectors labeled t_1 and t^*_{n+1} depict the

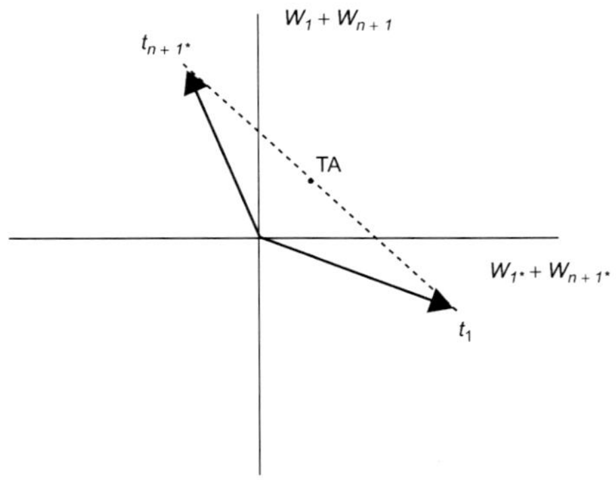

Figure 10.3 A mutually beneficial trade agreement.

effects of reductions in the respective tariffs on the two joint surpluses. When these vectors have the relative slopes illustrated, reflecting (14), an appropriate linear combination, such as at point TA, will be mutually beneficial.[5]

Condition (14) in effect requires that, at the margin, tariffs have relatively greater impact on export lobbies than on import lobbies. This is intuitively understandable, and, since in Nash equilibrium the tariffs were set with exclusive reliance on the effects on the latter lobbies, unlikely to be demanding. So we have the following result: *With* (14) *a mutually-beneficial trade agreement is feasible. This agreement is based on the exchange of market access, and it need not constrain export taxes.*

Condition (14) may appear problematical. But recall that we have chosen this pair of goods arbitrarily. The existence of a trade agreement based on the exchange of market access requires only that the analog of (14) hold for *some* set of goods from both countries. So, this argument can deliver trade agreements resembling those that actually exist.

5.2.1 Key points about the exchange-of-market-access approach

First, the terms of trade play no necessary role in this approach, so it is free of the CD issue.

Second, the exchange of market access is potentially attractive because it enables governments to confer on exporters benefits that they cannot deliver unilaterally. This is due to the countervailing duty laws suggested by the general support-function approach.

Third, the exchange of market access is inherently an exercise in reciprocity.

Fourth, because it is a consequence of the general support-function view, the exchange-of-market-access approach potentially suffers from the BB issue.

5.3 Does it matter?

The terms-of-trade externality and the exchange-of-market-access approach offer very different explanations of why trade agreements exist. But they both imply trade agreements with features broadly like what we see. So does it really matter which explanation is more relevant?

My answer is *yes*, because the actual explanation of the reason for a trade agreement can reveal its points of fragility. In a trade agreement as described by the terms-of-trade externality approach a country is tempted to deviate with measures that will improve its terms of trade; in a trade agreement as described by the exchange-of-market-access approach the temptation is to limit foreign access for the benefit of domestic import-competing firms.

These objectives need not be at odds. If a country were brazenly to violate a trade agreement by simply raising tariffs above their bound levels both objectives would be met. Where the difference matters is with the 'escape valves' that countries use to adjust how they fulfill their obligations without actually repudiating them. Basically, these exist because there is no international policeman to enforce trade agreements between sovereign states, so, in the end, such agreements must be self-enforcing. This involves providing escape valves and/or tolerating those not explicitly provided for. Understanding the true explanation for trade agreements is essential for understanding these escape valves and for recommending policy about them. There are several classes of such escape valves.

5.3.1 Administered protection

This involves measures that are both sanctioned by the GATT/WTO and embedded into national law: primarily antidumping law, countervailing-duty law, and safeguards, with antidumping the most important in practice. See Finger, Hall and Nelson (1982) and Ethier (2002). Antidumping and countervailing-duty laws do indeed provide for tariffs to be levied, but the basic purpose of such laws is simply to force foreign exporters to raise their prices: if they do so the duties are not levied. In other words, the intent is to limit home market access to foreign firms at the expense of a terms-of-trade deterioration. Safeguards are more complex because of the variety of ways in which they might be implemented, but it seems clear that in practice they are used to retreat from obligations to grant market access.

5.3.2 Voluntary export restraints

Before the Uruguay Round these were the most pervasive forms of escape valves. They were in violation of the GATT but tolerated because no one complained.

The Uruguay Round attacked them, partly because they had clearly become a major drag on trade and partly as a component of an implicit bargain between rich countries and poorer countries to eliminate the Multi-fiber Arrangement in exchange for adopting measures to protect intellectual property. But they are still indicative of how escape valves are used. Basically, a country pushing for a trading partner to adopt a VER was offering to accept a terms-of-trade deterioration in return for a denial of market access.

5.3.3 Unresolved trade disputes

If one country complains that another has violated its WTO obligations, if the WTO Dispute Settlement Mechanism rules against the defendant, and if the latter refuses to comply, the complainant is ultimately authorized to retaliate. This authorization is explicitly intended to maintain reciprocity in an exchange-of-market-access sense: the complainant may reduce imports from the defendant in the same amount that the defendant's actions have reduced the complainant's exports. It is possible that this test serves as a rough and ready attempt to maintain price reciprocity and that the agents involved just do not appreciate their own true motives. But actual retaliatory acts seem intended either to maximize the political damage to the defendant government or to limit market access to politically sensitive sectors.

5.3.4 Renegotiation

The GATT/WTO does provide a procedure for the renegotiation of concessions. The principle is the same as with unresolved trade disputes: the maintenance of reciprocity in an exchange-of-market-access sense. Similar comments apply.

5.3.5 So

The escape valves clearly involve a concern for the exchange-of-market-access with virtually no terms-of-trade concern. But this should not be interpreted as evidence against the terms-of-trade externality approach. That approach explicitly allows for political considerations. Countries may wish to deviate from trade agreements to get a step up on their partners. But they also may just be reacting to unexpected political developments. In the latter case, a reaction that addresses market access may well be consistent with a trade agreement that was negotiated to deal with a terms-of-trade externality.

Still, the basic fact is that the escape valves address exchange-of-market-access concerns. If the latter is the reason for trade agreements, this is appropriate. But if trade agreements exist to deal with terms-of-trade externalities the escape valves are likely to be seriously, perhaps fatally, deficient. So it matters.

5.4 Nondiscrimination

The GATT and the WTO impose nondiscrimination as a basic principle. The tariff that each WTO member imposes on a specific good must be the same for all other WTO members. Thus, there is a sharp distinction between liberalization and discrimination: Liberalization is an issue for negotiation; discrimination is not.

Of course 'discrimination' is a negatively loaded word, so that 'non-discrimination' sounds good. But imposing non-discrimination at the outset simply means that we are ruling out discriminatory trade agreements that might potentially dominate those allowed. Furthermore, we are introducing a free-rider issue: If non-discrimination is a basic rule, countries have an incentive to refrain from making concessions, knowing that they will benefit from concessions negotiated by other countries.

So why non-discrimination? The facile explanation is that, historically, countries who were serious about negotiating meaningful trade agreements with other countries did include Most Favored Nation clauses in those agreements. But, more substantively, what does such a requirement do? There are two explanations, and they are not mutually inconsistent. The answers are associated with the terms-of-trade externality approach and the exchange-of-market-access approach respectively, but the logic of each answer applies to the other approach as well.

5.4.1 Relative-price externality

This answer relates naturally to the terms-of-trade externality approach. Suppose some country has tariffs that discriminate between trading partners. Another country changes its policies in response to its own internal goals in ways that result in this country importing more from countries on which it levies low tariffs and less from countries for which high tariffs apply. This makes the country worse off. This could happen even if this country's terms of trade overall are unchanged. Thus this externality is distinct from the terms-of-trade externality.

Non-discrimination will prevent this relative-price externality. But it is not clear why non-discrimination should be imposed at the outset as a basic principle rather than being the object of negotiation, as is the case for amelioration of the effects of the terms-of-trade externality.

5.4.2 Concession diversion

This answer is more fundamental, as it involves whether trade agreements are possible at all. Suppose that H offers F^1 a reduction of 20 percent on its tariff on imports of good 1 from F^1 in exchange for a reciprocal reduction of 20 percent on its tariff on imports of good $n+1$ from H. (It does not matter whether this is part of a broader multilateral agreement or not.) Both governments view the implied exchange of market access as beneficial. But F^1 would reasonably fear that H might subsequently negotiate a reciprocal tariff reduction of 21 percent with another exporter of good $n+1$, say F^2. This would divert the market access in H that F^1 thought it had obtained to another country instead. Of course H would reasonably entertain a reciprocal suspicion about F^1. See Schwartz and Sykes (1996), Horn and Mavroidis (2001), and Ethier (2004). How serious such 'concession diversion' would be depends upon how substitutable exports from different countries are for each other. It could well render impossible the negotiation of any trade agreements.

To deal with this issue the trade agreement between H and F^1 could include a Most Favored Nation clause: Each country would guarantee the other that its goods will receive the lowest tariff applied to similar goods from other countries. Thus, in the above example, F^1 would have assurance that the 21 percent reduction that H might subsequently negotiate with F^2 would apply to its own exports as well. This would ameliorate the issue of concession diversion, but it would not eliminate it. F^1 would still fear that the access to H's market it had negotiated for might subsequently have to be shared with F^2.

The issue can be eliminated if non-discrimination is made a basic principle, rather than something to be negotiated on a deal-by-deal basis. In this case concession diversion becomes impossible, and the bargain between H and F^1 will reflect each country's desired trade policy with the rest of the world. The key feature from the point of view of F^1 is not that it has most favored nation status with H, but that all other countries are bound by non-discrimination as well.

With non-discrimination a general principle, the scope for bilateral deals will become exhausted since, to obtain market access from its partner, each country must grant it to all other countries. Such 'concession saturation' is akin to the free-rider issue. See Caplin and Krishna (1988), Ludema (1991) and Ethier (2004). Dealing with this requires that bargaining become more truly multilateral. This has indeed been the case: while the earlier GATT rounds consisted basically of collections of bilateral deals (or deals negotiated by a few countries), more recent rounds have involved more substantively multilateral issues, such as bargaining over general tariff-cutting formulas, GATT-wide standards on intellectual property, investment and so on.

6 Conclusion

In recent decades the political economy of trade policy has made significant progress. While before it was basically a footnote to the literature on international trade, it is now a major component.

I have argued that much of the literature is characterized either by the DC issue (a dramatic contrast between what policymakers say they are doing and what trade theorists model them as doing) or by the BB issue (a lack of microeconomic fundamentals). When one issue is absent, usually the other is there.

But this should not be viewed with dismay. It just means that, though we have come quite a way, we still have much more work to do.

Notes

I thank Arye Hillman, Donald Regan and Robert Staiger for useful discussions.

* Department of Economics University of Pennsylvania International School of Economics at TSU Tbilisi, Georgia.

1. For contrasting recent examples, see Broda, Limão and Weinstein (2008) and Magee and Magee (2008).
2. McCallum (2004) is an exception.
3. In this example, I have benefitted from discussions with Don Regan and Bob Staiger.
4. This conclusion is sensitive to what the *H* government's 'action' actually is. If that government had earlier acted by committing to allow no change in Q, come hell or high water, then its support will not increase as a result of abiding by that commitment. Such an action corresponds to a variable levy, which the WTO now prohibits.
5. The attentive reader will recognize this logic as that behind the familiar Hawkins-Simon (1949) condition for the feasibility of an input–output system.

References

Austen-Smith, D. (1991) 'Rational consumers and irrational voters', *Economics and Politics* 3: 73–93.

Bagwell, K., and R. Staiger (1999) 'An economic theory of GATT', *American Economic Review* 89: 215–48.

Bagwell, K., and R.W. Staiger (2002) *The Economics of the World Trading System.* (Cambridge, MA: The MIT Press).

Bernheim, B.D., and M. Whinston (1986) 'Menu auctions, resource allocation, and economic influence', *Quarterly Journal of Economics* 101(1): 1–31.

Broda, C., N. Limão and D.E. Weinstein (2008) 'Optimal tariffs and market power: the evidence', *American Economic Review* 98(5): 2032–65.

Brock, W.A., and S.P. Magee (1978) 'The economics of special interest politics', *American Economic Review* 68: 246–50.

Caplin, A., and K. Krishna (1988) 'Tariffs and the most favored-nation clause,' *Seoul Journal of Economics* 1: 267–89.

Caves, R.A. 1976, 'Economic models of political choice: Canada's tariff structure', *Canadian Journal of Economics* 9: 278–300.

Ethier, W.J. (1984) 'Protection and real incomes once again,' *Quarterly Journal of Economics* 99(1): 193–200.

——(2002) 'Unilateralism in a multilateral world', *Economic Journal* 112: 266–92.

——2004, 'Political Externalities, Nondiscrimination, and a Multilateral World,' Review of International Economics 12: 303–320.

——(2006) 'Selling "Protection for Sale"', *Asia-Pacific Journal of Accounting and Economics* 13: 153–62.

——(2007) 'The theory of trade policy and trade agreements: a critique', *European Journal of Political Economy* 23(3): 605–23.

——(2008) 'International trade agreements', in Margit, S. and E. Yu, *Contemporary and Emerging Issues in Trade Theory and Policy* Howard House, UK: Emerald: 381–95.

Finger, J.M. (1988) 'Protectionist rules and internationalist discretion in the making of national trade policy', in H.-J. Vosgerau (ed.), *New Institutional Arrangements for the World Economy.* Heidelberg: Springer-Verlag: 310–23.

——(1991) 'The GATT as an international discipline over trade restrictions', in Vaubel, R., and T.D. Willett (eds), *The Political Economy of International Organizations*. Boulder: Westview Press: 125–41.

Finger, J.M., Hall, H.K. and Nelson, D.R. (1982) 'The political economy of administered protection', *American Economic Review* 72: 452–66.

Gawande, K., and U. Bandyopadhyay (2000) 'Is protection for sale? Evidence on the Grossman-Helpman theory of endogenous protection', *Review of Economics and Statistics* 82: 139–52.

Goldberg, P.K., and G. Maggi (1999) 'Protection for sale: an empirical investigation,' *American Economic Review* 89: 1135–55.

Grossman, G., and E. Helpman (1994) 'Protection for sale', *American Economic Review* 84: 833–50.

Grossman G.M., and E. Helpman (1995) 'Trade wars and trade talks,' *Journal of Political Economy* 103: 675–708.

Grossman, G., and E. Helpman (2002) *Interest Groups and Trade Policy*. Princeton: Princeton University Press.

Hauser, H. (1986) 'Domestic policy foundation and domestic policy function of international trade rules', *Aussenwirtschaft* 41: 171–84.

Hawkins, D., and H. Simon (1949) 'Some conditions of macroeconomic stability', *Econometrica* 17: 245–48.

Hillman, A.L. (1982) 'Declining industries and political-support protectionist motives', *American Economic Review* 72: 1180–87.

——(1989) *The Political Economy of Protection*. Chur, London and New York: Harwood Academic Publishers; reprinted 2001: London: Routledge.

——(1990) 'Protectionist policies as the regulation of international industry', *Public Choice* 67: 101–10.

Hillman, A.L., Long, N.V. and Moser, P. (1995) 'Modeling reciprocal trade liberalization: the political-economy and national-welfare Perspectives', *Swiss Journal of Economics and Statistics* 131: 503–15.

Hillman, A.L., and P. Moser (1996) 'Trade liberalization as politically optimal exchange of market access', in Canzoneri, M., W.J. Ethier, and V. Grilli (eds), *The New Transatlantic Economy*. New York: Cambridge University Press: 295–312.

Horn, H., and P.C. Mavroidis (2001) 'Economic and legal aspects of the most-favored nation clause', *European Journal of Political Economy* 17: 233–79.

Johnson, H.G. (1953–54) 'Optimum tariffs and retaliation', *Review of Economic Studies* 21: 142–53.

Long, N.V., and N. Vousden (1991) 'Protectionist responses and declining industries', *Journal of International Economics* 30: 87–103.

Ludema, R. (1991) 'International trade bargaining and the most favored nation clause', *Economics and Politics* 3.

Magee, C., and S.P. Magee (2008) 'The United States is a small country in world trade', *Review of International Economics* 16(5): 990–1004.

Magee, S.P. (1994) 'Endogenous protection: a survey', in Mueller, D.C. (ed.), *Handbook of Public Choice*. Cambridge, MA: Basil Blackwell.

Magee, S., W.A. Brock and L. Young (1989) *Black Hole Tariffs and Endogenous Policy Theory: Political Economy in General Equilibrium*. Cambridge: Cambridge University Press.

Mayer, W. (1981) 'Theoretical considerations on negotiated tariff adjustments', *Oxford Economic Papers*, New Series 33: 135–53.

——(1984) 'Endogenous tariff formation', *American Economic Review* 74: 970–85.

McCallum, P. (2004) 'Protection for sale and trade liberalization: an empirical investigation', *Review of International Economics* 12: 81–94.

Mitra, D., D.D. Thomakos and M.A. Ulubasoglu (2002) "'Protection for sale" in a developing country: democracy vs. dictatorship', *Review of Economics and Statistics* 84: 497–508.

Moser, P. (1990) *The Political Economy of the GATT*. Grüsch: Verlag Ruegger.

Nelson, D. (1988) 'Endogenous tariff theory: a critical survey', *American Journal of Political Science* 32: 796–837.

Olson, M. (1965) *The Logic of Collective Action*. Cambridge, MA: Harvard University Press.

Pincus, J.J. (1975) 'Pressure groups and the pattern of tariffs', *Journal of Political Economy* 83(4): 757–78.

Regan, D.H. (2006) 'What are trade agreements for? – two conflicting stories told by economists, with a lesson for lawyers', *Journal of International Economic Law* 9(4): 951–88.

Rodrik, D. (1995) 'Political economy of trade policy', in Grossman, G., and K. Rogoff (eds), *Handbook of International Economics*. Amsterdam: North Holland: 1457–95.

Schwartz, W., and A. Sykes 1996 'Towards a positive theory of the most-favored nation obligation and its exceptions in the WTO/GATT System', *International Review of Law and Economics* 16: 27–51.

Global Journal of Economics
Vol. 1, No. 1 (June 2012) 1250001 (14 pages)

DOI: 10.1142/S2251361212500012

THE POLITICAL-SUPPORT APPROACH TO PROTECTION

WILFRED J. ETHIER*
Department of Economics
University of Pennsylvania
Philadelphia, PA 19104–6297
ethier@sas.upenn.edu

This paper offers a selective interpretation of the literature on the political-support component of the political economy of international trade policy. Much of this literature is characterized either by a discrepancy between what policymakers say they are doing and how the theory models their actions (the Cognitive Dissonance problem) or by a lack of a detailed microeconomic foundation (the Black Box problem).

Keywords: Political support function; protection for sale; cognitive dissonance problem; black box problem.

JEL Classifications: F02, F13

1. Introduction

International trade theory has traditionally taken a *normative* perspective: What are the consequences of trade policy for national welfare and when is it justified from that point of view? Beginning in the 1980s increasing attention has been paid to a *positive* perspective: What actually determines trade policy? These two approaches are complementary — both are necessary. This paper addresses the major component of the latter. Other, more comprehensive, surveys are provided by Nelson (1988), Magee (1994), Rodrik (1995) and Ethier (2011).

I address the ability of the political-support approach adequately to explain trade policy. My bottom line will be tentative: There has been much progress, but the nature of that progress is widely misunderstood, and we have a good way to go. We should make the effort.

*I thank Arye Hillman, Donald Regan and Robert Staiger for useful discussions, and participants in the 2011 Asia Pacific Economic Association meetings in Busan for helpful comments.

2. An Analytical Framework

A common theoretical framework helps enormously to facilitate comparison across contributions. I use the following.

There are two countries (*H*ome and *F*oreign), two factors (*K*apital and *L*abor), and $N+1$ traded goods $(0, 1, \ldots, N)$. Good 0 is a numeráire good, produced by labor alone. Goods 1 to N are produced by capital and labor, with capital specific to each sector. H imports goods 1 to n and exports goods $n+1$ to N.

I follow the preponderant part of the political-economy literature in assuming a sector-specific factor. Specific factors, together with the demand separability discussed below, allows the analysis to employ simple partial-equilibrium techniques.

Ownership of each specific factor i is distributed uniformly over a fraction α_i of the population (labor force), with each individual owning some of at most one of the specific factors. Let $\alpha = \alpha_1 + \cdots + \alpha_N$ denote the fraction of the population owning the specific factors. Choose units so that a unit of good 0 is produced by a unit of labor. Thus, assuming good 0 is actually produced, the wage $w = 1$.

In each country individual preferences are summarized by the utility function

$$U = c_0 + u_1(c_1) + \cdots + u_N(c_N)$$

where c_i denotes consumption of good i. This implies individual demand functions $d_i = d_i(Q_i)$, $i = 1, \ldots, N$, where Q_i denotes the domestic relative price of good i in terms of good 0. Residual income is all spent on the numeráire good 0. I assume that endowments in both countries are such that each both produces and consumes good 0. Then an individual's utility can be expressed in the indirect form

$$v(Q_1, \ldots, Q_N; y) = \sum s_i(Q_i) + y \tag{1}$$

where $S_i(Q_i) = u_i(d_i(Q_i)) - Q_i d_i(Q_i)$, the consumer surplus derived from good i, and y denotes the individual's income.

Each country may tax or subsidize either imports or exports. For H, let Q_i and P_i denote, respectively, the domestic and international relative price (in terms of the numeráire) of good i, and τ_i one plus the *ad-valorem* trade tax t_i. Thus

$$Q_i = \tau_i P_i$$

for $i = 1, \ldots, n$, and

$$Q_j = P_j/\tau_j$$

for $j = n+1, \ldots, N$. Analogous F variables will be distinguished by asterisks.

Equilibrium in the world market for good i, $i = 1, \ldots, n$, is represented by

$$M_i(\tau_i P_i) = X_i^*(P_i/\tau_i^*) \tag{2}$$

where M_i and X_i^* respectively denote H import demand and F export supply. H's import tax and F's export tax thus determine P_i, independently of other sectors. This in turn implies the following.

$$(\tau_i/P_i)(dP_i/dt_i) = -e_i/(e_i + f_i^*) \tag{3}$$

and

$$(\tau_i/Q_i)(dQ_i/dt_i) = (\tau_i/P_i)(dP_i/dt_i) + 1 = -f_i^*/(e_i + f_i^*) \tag{4}$$

where $e_i \equiv -(\tau_i P_i M_i')/M_i > 0$ and $f_i^* \equiv (P_i X_i')/(\tau_i^* X_i^*) > 0$.

The equilibria in the world markets for goods $n+1$ to N can be represented analogously. H imports of goods $1, \ldots, n$ need not equal in value H exports of goods $n+1, \ldots, N$: Trade balance is reached with a net exchange of good 0.

3. Unilateral Trade Policy

The subject of this paper, the political-support portion of the literature on the political economy of protection, focuses on the behavior of an incumbent government in office rather than on the electoral process.

3.1. *The general political-support approach*

Hillman (1982) introduced the political-support function to analyze the behavior of an incumbent government confronted by a special-interest group. See also Hillman (1989, 1990), Long and Vousden (1991), Hillman *et al.* (1995), and Hillman and Moser (1996).

Suppose, in the model of Sec. 2, that the owners of capital specific to an import sector i constitute an interest group desiring tariff protection. The incumbent government wishes to set a tariff that will maximize its political support. Assume that the separability of our model allows the government to do this sector by sector, so that, for each i, it wishes to maximize:

$$W^i = f^i(\psi_i(Q_i) - \psi_i(P_i), Q_i - P_i). \tag{5}$$

Here ψ_i measures the concerns of the interest group. The first argument of f^i accounts for the influence of the interest group on political support and the second argument that of the population at large. In both arguments, political support depends not only on the outcome (Q_i) but on how that outcome differs from what it would be were the government to take no action. The government is held politically accountable only for what it has done. This is a potentially important distinction. But it is relevant only when the economy is subject to an external shock that influences the free-trade equilibrium (Hillman, 1982, for example).

So subsume for now the free-trade situation into the functional form. Assuming that f^i is increasing in its first argument and decreasing in its second, the government will maximize its political support W^i in (5) by trading off the general welfare for that of the interest group.

Assume, more specifically, that the measure of interest-group benefit is the income of the corresponding specific factor $\pi_i(Q_i)$ and that the measure of the effect of policy on the general welfare is the effect on the per-capita consumer surplus derived from the corresponding good: $S_i(Q_i)$. Trade tax revenue is, for now, not included in either term. Then, suppressing for convenience the index i, (5) can be expressed as follows

$$W = W\{\pi(Q[t]), S(Q[t])\} \tag{6}$$

with W increasing in both arguments.

Note that the political-support function is not derived from economic fundamentals: It is assumed directly. I refer to this feature, often regarded as undesirable, as the *Black-Box Problem* (BB).

Differentiating (6) with respect to t and rearranging terms yields

$$(1/PW_2)(dW/dt) = I(Q)x - M \tag{7}$$

where x denotes the output of the sector, and $I(Q) \equiv (W_1 - W_2)/W_2$ can be interpreted as an index of the political influence of the special-interest group. Call the interest group *influential* if the right-hand side of (7) is positive when $t = 0$; that is, an influential interest group is able to obtain protection.

A tariff will increase x in (7) and lower M, so, unless I also falls sufficiently rapidly, the government will impose a prohibitive tariff whenever confronted by an influential interest group.

There are two ways to alter the model to avoid this extreme result. One is to add trade-tax revenue to the arguments of (6). In this case, lowering the tariff below its prohibitive level, which will generate trade-tax revenue, would increase the government's political support if trade-tax revenue is given significant weight. The chosen tariff or subsidy will depend *crucially* upon its effect on trade-tax revenue. But we observe, with industrial countries, no real interest in trade tax revenue (Regan, 2006). Still, such revenue exists, so it could logically be included in our models, but the critical role it then assumes in the theory seems totally at odds with its apparent negligible practical importance. I refer to this as the Cognitive-Dissonance (CD) problem. I assign it a label because, as will become apparent, it is pervasive in the literature on the political economy of trade policy, including the political-support component.

The second way to alter the model is to suppose that the influence of an influential special-interest group is limited, that is, that I declines as t (and so Q)

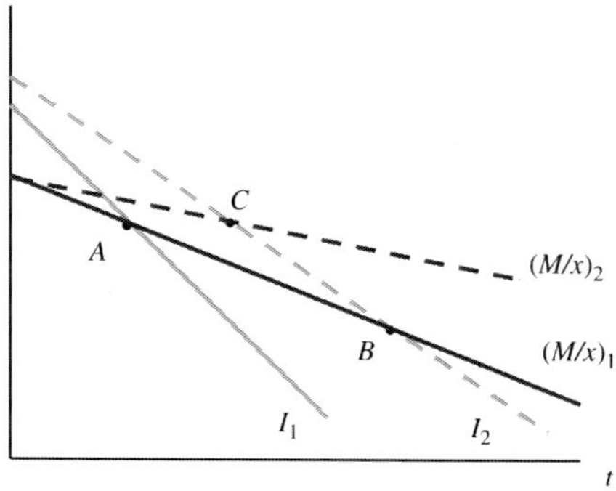

Figure 1. The Equilibrium Tariff.

increases. In other words, as an interest group gets more of what it wants, its influence declines at the margin (diminishing returns to lobbying). If I declines rapidly enough, (7) will have an interior solution corresponding to a non-prohibitive tariff. Consider this possibility in more detail.

The influence of a special-interest group can be measured by the value of I when $t = 0$, that is, $I(P)$, and also by the rate of its decline: $I' < 0$. Assume for simplicity that these measures are in accord: $I(P)$ is larger when the absolute value of I' is smaller.

Figure 1 shows the case of an influential interest group [the right-hand side of (7) is positive when $t = 0$] where I falls rapidly enough to give an interior solution (at point A). I_2 (where point B indicates the equilibrium) shows more influence than I_1. Other things equal, a greater influence implies a larger t and a lower import-penetration ratio M/x.

The elasticity e of import demand plays an important role in many tariff issues,[1] so it is of interest to examine its effect. This is more complex. In Fig. 1 $(M/x)_2$ reflects a lower elasticity than $(M/x)_1$. Along a given I_1 the reduction in e lowers t and raises M/x. But a lower e also implies a lower deadweight loss to increasing t, so the lobby should become more influential, which is reflected in I_2 replacing I_1. This raises t and lowers M/x, so the net effect is ambiguous. For a given reduction in e, as reflected in given $(M/x)_1$ and $(M/x)_2$, this net effect depends upon the sensitivity of lobby influence to e. With low sensitivity, t falls and M/x increases; with intermediate sensitivity, t and M/x both increase; with high sensitivity,

[1] For contrasting recent examples from the trading partner's point of view, see Broda *et al.* (2008) and Magee and Magee (2008).

t increases and M/x falls. In other words, at a given level of import penetration, t is negatively related to e.

An influential interest group will of course be concerned that any protection it receives not be undone by the government of a trading partner subsidizing its exports. That the home government shares this concern is implied by (5), which says that the home government is rewarded on the basis of the net effects of its actions. Thus we should expect the government to implement a countervailing duty law, providing that any foreign subsidy be countervailed by an increase in the home tariff. To my knowledge, the political-support literature has not actually made this point, but it seems a clear inference from its approach.

The above discussion applies to an influential interest group. But what happens when it is not influential? There are again two alternatives.

(i) An interest group for which the right-hand side of (7) is negative when $t = 0$ will induce the government to subsidize imports without bound (or as much as the treasury will bear) unless I rises sufficiently rapidly as the subsidy is increased.

(ii) This literature seems based on the observation that import-competing interests are individually much more affected by trade policy regarding their goods then are the more numerous but more diffused consumers. Then such interests, even if not politically organized at all, are much more likely than consumers to vote on the basis of such policy. This suggests assuming that the right-hand side of (7) is never negative when $t = 0$: It is positive for an influential group and zero for a non-influential group. Thus the latter will result in $t = 0$.

Of these alternatives, (ii) seems to me more in accord with the spirit of the general support-function approach, so I shall take it as characterizing that approach. But, to my knowledge, that literature again has not addressed these alternatives at all, much less provided a formal framework to indicate when one or the other might be more appropriate.

Suppose, finally, that the interest group corresponds to an export sector. Analogously to the above, an influential group would be able to induce the government to provide an export subsidy. However, if, as discussed above, foreign governments have adopted countervailing-duty laws, such a subsidy would amount to a cost that conferred no benefit on the interest group and so would not be adopted. Both the government and the interest group know this. The government is powerless to aid such a group with trade policy. Non-influential groups can be treated analogously to such groups in import-competing sectors. That is, $t = 0$ in export sectors with non-influential interest groups. Again, this seems to be a reasonable inference from the nature of the political-support approach, though it is not discussed in that literature.

3.2. *Key points about the political-support approach*

First, political support depends upon the effect of the government's actions on agents' well-being, not just the latter itself.

Second, the approach exhibits the BB problem: The political-support function is not derived from microeconomic fundamentals.

Third, for influential import-competing sectors the degree of influence is positively correlated with the tariff rate.

Fourth, for influential import-competing sectors the tariff is negatively correlated with the import-penetration ratio.

Fifth, for influential import-competing sectors the tariff is negatively correlated with the elasticity of import demand, at a given import-penetration ratio.

*Sixth**, if the country has at least one influential import-competing sector it will adopt a countervailing-duty law.

*Seventh**, non-influential import-competing sectors are likely to be characterized by an absence of trade-policy intervention.

Eighth, the government is unable to do anything for, and therefore to extract political support from, influential export sectors.

*Ninth**, non-influential export sectors are likely to be characterized by an absence of trade-policy intervention.

(An asterisk indicates a point that reasonably characterizes the political-support approach but that, to my knowledge, has not been discussed explicitly in its literature).

3.3. *The campaign-contributions variant of the political-support approach*

This variant of the political-support approach, due to Grossman and Helpman (1994, 2002), identifies such support as financial contributions (or bribes). Following the authors, we can denote this approach as Protection for Sale, or PFS. This has become the most widely used political-economy model of protection, not because it is realistic — or even literally plausible — but because it delivers an explicit tariff formula based squarely on a complete micro political-economy description of behavior.

The distinguishing assumptions of this version of the political-support approach are as follows

(i) The N specific factors are exogenously divided into N^1 that are politically organized and N^0 that are not (so $N = N^0 + N^1$).

(ii) Political support consists of campaign contributions (or bribes).

(iii) Each lobby, with an eye on the other lobbies, offers the government a *contribution schedule* detailing the contribution it will make as a function of the vector of all N trade policies. The lobby wishes to maximize the excess of its specific-factor income over its actual contribution.

(iv) The government wishes to maximize a weighted average of national income and total contributions,

$$W = \beta Y + (1 - \beta) \sum_i C^i \tag{8}$$

where C^i denotes the actual contribution of lobby i and $\beta \leq 1$ the weight the government attaches to national income Y. The latter importantly includes trade-tax revenue.

(v) The outcome is modeled as a menu-auction equilibrium in the sense of Bernheim and Whinston (1986).

The PFS model yields equilibrium contributions and tariffs. The former are of little interest, given the contrived nature of the model. But the latter, as pointed out by Goldberg and Maggi (1999), follow directly as necessary conditions for maximizing the joint surplus of the government and the lobbies, regardless otherwise of the actual bargaining model. The equilibrium tariffs are given by

$$t_i/(1 + t_i) = ([\xi_i - \alpha]/[\beta/(1 - \beta) + \alpha]) \cdot (1/[M_i/x_i] \cdot e_i) \tag{9}$$

where $\xi_i = 1$ if the industry is politically organized and 0 if it is not. This explicit formula is regarded as the major contribution of the PFS approach. Derivation of the formula depends *crucially* on the inclusion of trade-tax revenue in the objective function (the CD problem).

Note that if the government cares only about social welfare ($\beta = 1$) it adopts a policy of free trade. This is also the result if everyone belongs to some organized lobby ($\alpha = 1$), but this latter result is of little interest as it just reflects the extreme assumptions that all organized sectors are equally potent politically and that they all lobby equally about all trade policies.

Equation (9) implies the following. *Organized import-competing sectors* ($\xi_i = 1$) will receive positive protection that is positively related to the degree of influence ξ_i (though of course that is here constrained to be only either zero or unity), and negatively related to the import-penetration ratio and to the elasticity of import demand. This is exactly what the general political-support function approach predicts, of which the PFS model is a special case.

Unorganized import-competing sectors ($\xi_i = 0$) will be confronted with subsidized imports. This contrasts with my interpretation of the spirit of the political-support approach ($t = 0$), though, as pointed out above, that literature has not been explicit about this.

Organized export sectors ($\xi_i = 1$) will find their exports subsidized. This also contrasts with the predictions of the general political-support approach.

Unorganized export sectors ($\xi_i = 0$) will find their exports taxed. This again contrasts with my interpretation of the spirit of the political-support approach ($t = 0$), though, again, that literature has not been explicit about this.

3.4. *Key points about the PFS variant*

First, political support is identified with contributions (bribes).

Second, the approach is free of the BB problem: Both the contributions and the trade policies are derived from microeconomic and micro-political fundamentals.

Third, the PFS variant is subject to the CD problem.

Fourth, for politically organized import-competing sectors the degree of influence is positively correlated with the tariff rate.

Fifth, for organized import-competing sectors the tariff is negatively correlated with the import-penetration ratio.

Sixth, for organized import-competing sectors the tariff is negatively correlated with the elasticity of import demand, at a given import-penetration ratio.

Seventh, unorganized import-competing sectors are characterized by import subsidies.

Eighth, organized export sectors are characterized by export subsidies.

Ninth, unorganized export sectors are characterized by export taxes.

4. Empirical Investigations

4.1. *Empirical investigations of the PFS variant*

The PFS model has received considerable empirical attention (most notably: Goldberg and Maggi, 1999; Gawande and Bandyopadhyay, 2000; Mitra *et al.*, 2002, and McCallum, 2004). These papers uniformly claim support for the PFS model, but in a highly selective way. They have arbitrarily confined themselves to import-competing sectors. An important claim in this literature is that they are estimating (9), an equation that comes directly from a detailed microeconomic and micro-political model (i.e., no BB problem).

These papers do not employ actual tariffs[2] because they are constrained by international trade agreements, not part of the basic PFS model. So data on administered protection is used instead. It's not clear how much this helps, since administered protection very often involves a good deal of bilateral negotiation (as noted, e.g., by Goldberg and Maggi, 1999: 159). But there are more fundamental concerns.

Administered protection using tariffs involves primarily antidumping and countervailing duties. These are imposed as a result of a well-defined legal procedure that, in sharp contrast to the PFS model, gives *no* weight to either national welfare or tariff revenue. So, if such data does fit (9), even though we *know* it was

[2] McCallum (2004) is an exception.

not generated by what the PFS approach models, one must wonder what such a fit means.[3] Certainly this limitation is far more serious than the fact that bound tariff rates involve international negotiation.

Administered protection using non-tariff barriers involves, in data from the 1980s and before, primarily voluntary export restraints (VERs). The empirical literature calculates tariff equivalents. A key property of VERs is that the rents from the barriers are captured by exporters, whereas the assumption in the PFS model that the importing country captures those rents is crucial to the derivation of (9). If the PFS model is altered to constrain the importing country from capturing the rents, necessary if VER data is used, the model predicts nothing like (9). So a good fit to (9) with VER data is not at all a confirmation of the PFS model. Quite the contrary.

The empirical studies have also not investigated the predictions of the PFS model that most closely reflect its central assumptions: (i) import subsidies for all politically unorganized import-competing sectors, (ii) export subsidies for politically organized export sectors and (iii) export taxes for all politically unorganized export sectors. Perhaps because it is obvious that these predictions are not borne out by the facts.

Neglect of prediction (ii) can be defended on the grounds that, like import tariffs, export subsidies are seriously constrained by trade agreements.[4] But predictions (i) and (iii) involve instruments that are *not* constrained by international trade agreements. They are therefore free of the issues that prevented the use of conventional bound tariffs. These are the predictions of the PFS approach that are the *most* consistent with the available data, and so they should be the last to be neglected.[5]

The empirical literature on the PFS model uses its parameter estimates to infer the size of the structural parameter β, the weight the government attaches to social welfare. Typically this weight turns out to be quite high: The government is seen as valuing social welfare much more than contributions. But since that literature has not succeeded in confirming the structure specific to the PFS model, it is not clear what, if any, significance can be attached to this seemingly optimistic inference.

In summary, the empirical work has not provided support for the PFS model itself; apparently the CD issue dominates. See Ethier (2006, 2007). But this work

[3] Political organization also plays no role in the administrative procedure, but one might conjecture that politically organized sectors are also better able to file petitions.

[4] They might also be ruled out by the existence of countervailing duty laws. But it is not at all clear that such laws are themselves consistent with the PFS model, and, to my knowledge, no one has argued that they are.

[5] Of course one might dispose of (i) and (iii) with arguments like those I have used above to characterize the implications of the general political-support approach. But to do this would be to defeat the basic purpose of the PFS variant, which is precisely to derive policy implications directly from a detailed microeconomic and micro-political model.

has given powerful evidence that, in politically organized import-competing sectors, protection is negatively related to the import-penetration ratio, presumably reflecting the tug between sectoral special interests and consumer surplus central to most political-economy approaches to trade policy. Also in such sectors, protection appears to be negatively related to the domestic elasticity of import demand. Furthermore, and probably most significantly, this literature argues persuasively that distinguishing between politically organized and unorganized sectors is crucial to understanding the determinants of protection.

So we have support not for the PFS model in particular, but for "something else." What else? The general political-support approach makes just those predictions that have been verified and is free of the issues, attending the PFS model, mentioned above. Thus the empirical literature can be interpreted as providing strong evidence for the general political-support approach, but *not* for its PFS variant.

This is a notable accomplishment. In my mind it is the single most valuable contribution to date in the large empirical literature addressing the political economy of trade policy. And the PFS model, by supplying (9) in explicit form, was critical in stimulating this contribution. However, the more general approach does not derive the political-support function from microeconomic and micro-political fundamentals, so the BB problem has not in fact been dealt with. Thus the empirical literature, intriguing and valuable as it is, cannot be interpreted as successfully confirming a structural model derived directly from a theory based on microeconomic and micro-political fundamentals. More work is called for.

4.2. *Empirical investigations of tariffs and trade elasticities*

Recently, Broda *et al.* (2008) investigated the empirical relation between tariffs and trade-partners' export elasticities for a set of non-WTO members (so that their tariffs were not constrained by GATT multilateral agreements). They concluded that actual tariffs are indeed explained by the classic optimum-tariff argument. This would imply that the entire literature on the political-support view of protection is, at best, of little practical significance.

Suppose that the home government wishes only to maximize home welfare. Because of the separability of our model, this will require that all imports be taxed according to the classical optimum-tariff formula:

$$t_i = 1/f_i^* \tag{10}$$

So the tariff is negatively related to t sector-by-sector in the current approach. Broda *et al.* (2008) presented evidence that tariffs and foreign export-supply elasticities are indeed negatively related and based their assertion on this.

But they ignore the possibility that the relation they have established might equally well be explained by something else entirely different from straightforward national welfare maximization. That is, they address necessity, not sufficiency.

Suppose instead, that the government cares not at all for national welfare, but wants to maximize tax revenue and regards a trade tax as the only available instrument.[6] Then, utilizing (3) and again exploiting the model's separability, the first-order condition for choosing t to maximize $t_iP_iM_i$ reduces to

$$t_i/\tau_i = ([f_i^* + e_i]/[f_i^* + 1])(1/e_i) \tag{11}$$

Note that the left-hand side of (11) is positively related to t_i and the right-hand side negatively related to f_i*, if $e_i > 1$. Thus, again, the tariff is negatively correlated with the foreign export-supply elasticity (as long as $e_i > 1$). Of course (11) could be consistent with a positive relationship, *if* t_i is not conditioned on e_i and if e_i is sufficiently negatively correlated with f_i*. But this seems highly unlikely as the two elasticities measure the price sensitivity of the same good in the respective countries. So one might argue that Broda *et al.* (2008) offer support for the position that countries levy tariffs to maximize government revenue.

But there is no reason to stop here. Suppose, next, that the government instead has a target, for whatever reason, for changing Q_i. Then the relative tariff change dt_i/τ_i required to achieve dQ_i/Q_i is immediately given by (4)

$$dQ_i/Q_i = (f_i^*/[f_i^* + e_i])(dt_i/\tau_i). \tag{12}$$

So, if domestic price-change targets are determined exogenously by political concerns or what-not, tariff implementations will, once again, be negatively correlated with f*.

A negative correlation between tariffs and foreign export elasticities seems to be consistent with a large variety of policy objectives. So it is useful to have such a correlation confirmed empirically. But it says nothing really about the objectives of policy makers. Note that (10) says that tariffs depend directly *only* on foreign export elasticities, whereas (11) and (12) also assign a direct role to home import elasticities. This might be a distinction worth exploring.

4.3. *Key points about the empirical work*

First, the empirical literature succeeds in supporting those predictions of the PFS model that overlap with the general political-support function approach. This is a valuable contribution.

[6] While the governments of the industrial countries seem to care little about trade-tax revenue, that is not true for at least some of the countries in the sample used by Broda *et al.* (2008)

Second, that literature fails to support those predictions that distinguish the PFS model from the general support-function approach.

Third, that literature fails to offer support for a theory of protection based on microeconomic or micro-political fundamentals. The BB problem remains.

Fourth, the empirical literature gives support to a negative relation between tariffs and foreign export elasticities, consistent with various policy objectives.

Fifth, since this relation is consistent with many policy objectives, it does little to suggest what the actual policy objectives might be.

5. Concluding Remarks

In recent decades the political economy of trade policy has made significant progress. While before it was basically a footnote to the literature on international trade, it is now a major component. The lion's share of this progress has involved the political-support approach to protection.

I have argued that much of the literature is characterized either by the DC problem (a dramatic contrast between what policymakers say they are doing and what trade theorists model them as doing) or by the BB problem (a lack of microeconomic fundamentals). The significant empirical literature has been widely and fundamentally misinterpreted. That part of the political-support theory that has found valid empirical support remains quite confounded by the BB problem.

But this should not be viewed with dismay. It just means that, though we have come quite a way, we still have much more work to do.

References

Bagwell, K and R Staiger (1999). An economic theory of GATT. *American Economic Review*, 89, 215–248.

Bagwell, K and RW Staiger (2002). *The Economics of the World Trading System*. Cambridge, MA: The MIT Press.

Bernheim, BD and M Whinston (1986). Menu auctions, resource allocation, and economic influence. *Quarterly Journal of Economics*, 101(1), 1–31.

Broda, C, N Limão and DE Weinstein (2008). Optimal tariffs and market power: The evidence. *American Economic Review*, 98(5), 2032–2065.

Ethier, WJ (2002). Unilateralism in a multilateral world. *Economic Journal*, 112, 266–292.

Ethier, WJ (2004). Political externalities, nondiscrimination, and a multilateral world. *Review of International Economics*, 12, 303–320.

Ethier, WJ (2006). Selling protection for sale. *Asia-Pacific Journal of Accounting and Economics*, 13, 153–162.

Ethier, WJ (2007). The theory of trade policy and trade agreements: A critique. *European Journal of Political Economy*, 23(3), 605–623.

Ethier, WJ (2011). The political economy of protection. In D Bernhofen, R Falvey, D Greenaway and U Kreickemeier (Eds.), *Palgrave Handbook of International Trade*. Hampshire: Palgrave Macmillan, pp. 295–320.

Gawande, K and U Bandyopadhyay (2000). Is protection for sale? Evidence on the Grossman–Helpman theory of endogenous protection. *Review of Economics and Statistics*, 82, 139–152.

Goldberg, PK and G Maggi (1999). Protection for sale: An empirical investigation. *American Economic Review*, 89, 1135–1155.

Grossman, G and E Helpman (1994). Protection for sale. *American Economic Review*, 84, 833–850.

Grossman, GM and E Helpman (1995). Trade wars and trade talks. *Journal of Political Economy*, 103, 675–708.

Grossman, G and E Helpman (2002). *Interest Groups and Trade Policy*. Princeton: Princeton University Press.

Hauser, H (1986). Domestic policy foundation and domestic policy function of international trade rules. *Aussenwirtschaft*, 41, 171–184.

Hillman, AL (1982). Declining industries and political-support protectionist motives. *American Economic Review*, 72, 1180–1187.

Hillman, AL (1989). *The Political Economy of Protection*. Chur, London and New York: Harwood Academic Publishers.

Hillman, AL (1990). Protectionist policies as the regulation of international industry. *Public Choice*, 67, 101–110.

Hillman, AL, NV Long and P Moser (1995). Modeling reciprocal trade liberalization: The political-economy and national-welfare perspectives. *Swiss Journal of Economics and Statistics*, 131, 503–515.

Hillman, AL and P Moser (1996). Trade liberalization as politically optimal exchange of market access. In M Canzoneri, WJ Ethier and V Grilli (Eds.), *The New Transatlantic Economy*. New York: Cambridge University Press, pp. 295–312.

Johnson, HG (1953–54). Optimum tariffs and retaliation. *Review of Economic Studies*, 21, 142–153.

Long, NV and N Vousden (1991). Protectionist responses and declining industries. *Journal of International Economics*, 30, 87–103.

Magee, C and SP Magee (2008). The United States is a small country in world trade. *Review of International Economics*, 16(5), 990–1004.

Magee, SP (1994). Endogenous protection: A survey. In DC Mueller (Ed.), *Handbook of Public Choice*. Cambridge, MA: Basil Blackwell.

McCallum, P (2004). Protection for sale and trade liberalization: An empirical investigation. *Review of International Economics*, 12, 81–94.

Mitra, D, DD Thomakos and MA UlubaÕolu (2002). Protection for sale' in a developing country: Democracy vs. Dictatorship. *Review of Economics and Statistics*, 84, 497–508.

Moser, P (1990). *The Political Economy of the GATT*. Grüsch: Verlag Ruegger.

Nelson, D (1988). Endogenous tariff theory: A critical survey. *American Journal of Political Science*, 32, 796–837.

Regan, DH (2006). What are trade agreements for? — Two conflicting stories told by economists, with a lesson for lawyers. *Journal of International Economic Law*, 9(4), 951–988.

Rodrik, D (1995). Political economy of trade policy. In G Grossman and K Rogoff (Eds.), *Handbook of International Economics*. Amsterdam: North-Holland, pp. 1457–1495.

PART VI:
Administered Protection

Administered Protection: *Commentary*

During much of the late 1980s and 1990s I concentrated on issues involving administered protection. I now regard that as a fallow period. Or, more candidly, as time I wish I had spent otherwise — like sipping sake in Kyoto.

Still, there are some contributions I do not wish to repudiate. The early paper, "Dumping," combined the theoretical contractual literature of the time with a hard look at actual anti-dumping policy to give a theory of how I thought antidumping actually worked. I think it is still centrally relevant, though the increased reliance since then on antidumping has made other concerns more prominent than they had been. Still, this paper did not attempt to set antidumping into a more general context of the international commercial system.

I attempted the latter in the (less formal) paper, "The Economics and Political Economy of Managed Trade." This analyzed an international equilibrium, and national welfare, in a context of trade governed by voluntary export restraints. I rather like this paper. But one must ask how relevant it now is in view of the Uruguay Round decision to limit severely such measures. Very relevant, I think. Also, thanks to the Uruguay Round, safeguards can now be used in ways much like voluntary export restraints. The explicit bilateral aspect is not there, but perhaps concerns about diplomacy produce much the same effect.

I also looked at administered protection in an imperfectly-competitive environment. In papers ([1] and [2]), forgotten by everyone except, sometimes, myself. What impressed me was that, the more closely I looked at antidumping law, the more likely it seemed (in the imperfectly-competitive environment) to be beneficial to national welfare, even though the law itself excludes all consideration of such welfare. This possibility — of trade policies ignoring national welfare considerations nonetheless enhancing it precisely because of that — was to figure later in my analysis of the political economy of trade policy.

The Other Articles

[1] Ethier, WJ (1993). An Antidumping Law with a Distorted Home Market. In: H Herberg and NV Long (eds.), *Trade, Welfare, and Economic Policies*, pp. 279–97. Ann Arbor: University of Michigan Press.

[2] Ethier, WJ (1991). Voluntary Export Restraints. In: A Takayama, M Ohyama and H Ohta (eds.), *Trade, Policy and International Adjustments,* pp. 3–18. San Diego: Academic Press.

THE ECONOMICS AND POLITICAL ECONOMY OF MANAGED TRADE

Wilfred J. Ethier*

Even as the virtues of the free market are extolled daily, trade between national markets becomes increasingly managed. Such management has long been commonplace in international primary-product markets and in the trade of the now-unfashionable centrally-planned economies. But recent decades have seen the proliferation of management of the trade of manufactures between industrial (and newly industrializing) economies.

The instrument of such management is the voluntary export restraint. This is an arrangement whereby a government (or firms) protects an industry by persuading the authorities (or firms) in a trading partner to restrict exports. Such protection allows the country to avoid violating existing international agreements (such as the General Agreement on Tariffs and Trade)[1], and sometimes its own trade laws as well, and also to avoid the danger of retaliation posed by unilateral action, all at the cost of forfeiting the revenues that would be raised were tariffs, say, employed instead.

---

* The research for this paper was supported by a grant from the Bank of Sweden Tercentenary Foundation. I am grateful for comments received during the Conference on Markets and Politicians at Bar-Ilan University and during seminars at the Institute for Advanced Studies in Jerusalem, at Tel-Aviv University and at the University of Western Ontario.

[1] More accurately, it is unclear whether such restraints do in fact violate the GATT or not, especially when governments play no official formal role in the restraint agreement itself. But there is no interested party to object: the importing and exporting governments accept the agreement and other interested governments, who compete with the restrained exporters, see themselves as beneficiaries.

During the most recent two decades these arrangements have become the most prominent means by which protectionist initiatives have been implemented in the industrial world. Over one hundred agreements now manage upwards of ten percent of world trade, and in some sectors such arrangements are far more prominent than this summary statistic would indicate. The lion's share of world trade in textiles and apparel is now covered, as is over one third of Japan's export of manufactures to other industrial countries.

These arrangements are invariably sector-specific, though within various frameworks that can vary sector by sector. The arrangement usually limits (or otherwise influences) trade in one direction between two countries, but sometimes two-way trade is addressed (semiconductor trade between the United States and Japan). The framework might be multilateral (the Multifiber Arrangement in textiles) or isolated and bilateral (Canadian lumber exports to the United States). There might be a series of independent arrangements linking a single exporter to diverse importers (Japanese automobile exports), a single importer to several exporters (United States imports of machine tools), or several exporters to several importers (steel). But regardless of the framework, the key negotiations and agreements are bilateral. Thus the evolution of the trade policies of industrial countries toward manufactures has displayed a basic tension, between the spread of bilateral, sector-specific restrictions and the continuing multilateral effort to fashion a liberal trade order (the GATT and its negotiating rounds).

Managed trade is restricted trade. Thus the basic conclusions of the traditional theory of protection remain relevant, indeed they remain centrally relevant. But contemporary efforts to manage trade also share characteristics quite distinct from those addressed by the traditional theory, as, for example, in the archetypal analysis of the effects of a tariff. This paper attempts to identify these characteristics and to address their implications.

I. DISTINCTIVE FEATURES OF MANAGED TRADE

Trade in manufactures among the industrial countries is managed, when it is, through a series of bilateral, sector-specific, voluntary export restraints (VERs).[2] The following features distinguish such arrangements from standard tariffs.

(a) The restrictions are quantitative. That is, the trade is subject to quota rather than tax, though taxes may be present as well.

---

[2] See Kostecki (1987) for a description of actual VERs and Pomfret (1989) for a survey of their theory.

(b) The restrictions are voluntary on both sides of the market. This is essential, because a primary reason to resort to such measures is to circumvent the spirit of the GATT in specific areas, without bringing down the entire GATT structure, by ensuring that no nation involved has a motive to complain. This need not require industry interests in both countries to welcome the arrangement: it will be negotiated, at least to a significant degree, by government officials who may be willing to sacrifice something in one sector for a *quid pro quo* elsewhere, or even without a *quid pro quo*, in order to preserve a relationship that is in the national interest overall.[3] This should be kept in mind. Nevertheless, there must be a strong presumption that industry interests are not hurt, or at least not hurt too much: these agreements are typically negotiated in a politically-charged atmosphere that draws the attention of the interests concerned and that induces them to exert themselves to the utmost politically.[4] And of course the negotiations are sector-specific.

(c) The restrictions are temporary (at least in original intent) responses to established import positions that have harmed import-competing interests. It is true that management arrangements often seem to linger for quite a while, and in textiles and apparel, at least, they have acquired the status of a permanent fixture. But actual agreements are invariably for quite short periods and usually the original intent is not to renew them many times. The original agreement itself is almost always the response to a large, established import presence (usually a recently established or recently enlarged one), not to the prospect that such a presence may come about.[5] No doubt this is partly a matter of political economy: being able to point to a recently large volume of imports makes it easier to enlist the sympathy of fellow citizens for restrictions. But it is also a reflection of the voluntary element in these arrangements: for us to offer importers significant rents from their share of our market they must have a significant share of that market. Finally, there must be a significant import-competing interest adversely affected by the imports. This interest is, of course, the source of the political pressure to manage trade.

---

[3] This is clearly a possibility in the case of orderly marketing arrangements, which involve explicit agreements between the two governments involved. But governments also usually play a central role in the formation of other restraints in which they take no formal part.

[4] It is also sometimes the case, though, that one purpose of the negotiations is to prevent the atmosphere from becoming even more politically charged.

[5] Of course there may well be the prospect that the import presence might become much larger yet in the absence of an agreement to prevent that.

All this indicates the presence of an implicit social commitment to grant import-competing sectors the possibility of temporary relief from trade-related difficulties. In a deeper sense it is this implicit commitment itself that is the true instrument of protection, analogous to the permanent tariff addressed by traditional theory. Actual temporary trade arrangements are merely incidents in the operation of the permanent protection afforded by the commitment. Thus the implicit commitment may affect industries with significant import potential that are not currently managed.

(d) The restrictions are discriminatory. This is a major way in which managed trade violates the spirit of the GATT. It implies that an analysis of such trade should consider the roles played by at least three distinct groups of firms: import-competitors, restrained exporters and unrestrained exporters. As noted above, unrestrained exporters can usually be expected to benefit from a VER and so do not pressure their government to protest its formation. The activities of such firms have been central to how many such agreements have in fact functioned, and in some industries they have played a dominant role in the evolution of trade management (e.g., textiles, steel). Discrimination is thus a vital property of managed trade.

Discrimination also implies a fourth potential group of firms: import-competitors that are not part of the arrangement. In reasonably competitive markets characterized by constant costs these firms are unlikely to be affected very much by trade management in which they do not participate. But significant economies of scale raise the possibility that restrained exporters may divert production from the newly restricted markets to compete in countries not within the arrangement. For example, the negotiation of the VER on Japanese automobiles sold in the United States aroused fears in some countries that the Japanese would be induced by the agreement to compete more fiercely in those countries in order to maintain production levels. Thus there is a part of the global industry that is threatened by such arrangements, and this holds the potential for defeat of the basic goal of bypassing the GATT by ensuring that no one will file a protest. But this does not happen. Perhaps unprotected import-competitors require significant diversion, and not just the threat of such diversion, to be roused to effective action. Probably more important is a desire on their part to acquire managed trade of their own, regardless of whether diversion takes place or not. They would then not be likely to agitate for legal challenges to a VER, as that would make it more difficult for them to acquire a VER of their own. The response by other importers of Japanese cars to the VER on Japanese exports to the United States was not to challenge that agreement formally; it was to negotiate VERs of their own with Japan.

The situation is more complex if trade management involves two-way trade, that is, the exporting country that restrains (in some way) its exporters also establishes a floor for (or otherwise encourages) imports from its partner. In this case third-country firms are threatened both with diversion and with the loss of an established or potential export market. It is interesting that the U.S.-Japanese semiconductor agreement, involving two-way trade management, did induce the formation of a GATT dispute panel.

The rest of this paper is concerned with an analysis of the circumstances under which trade management might arise and the implications thereof. To limit the scope of the paper, I ignore two potentially interesting features mentioned above. First, I will not consider cases where one party to an arrangement is induced to participate by a concession in some other industry or by some other aspect of its international position. Thus I consider only cases where the agreement is detrimental to none of the interests involved in its implementation. As argued above, this is likely in practice to be at least approximately correct, and, in any event, I have elsewhere analyzed to some extent the case of trade-offs.[6] Second, I shall not enquire into implications of the apparent implicit social commitment to import-competing interests. Again, I have discussed this elsewhere.[7]

II. MANAGEMENT IN COMPETITIVE MARKETS

Consider first the possibility of managed trade emerging when markets are competitive. Figure 1 shows a free-trade equilibrium at E, the intersection of the home (H) and foreign (F) offer curves. The home economy imports the quantity OC of good A in exchange for the quantity CE of good B, implying an international price of A in terms of B of CE/OC. Consider the possibility of a VER on foreign exports of A.

The negotiation and implementation of such an agreement almost always involves the two governments and the two national A industries. We are interested in arrangements that are truly voluntary, that is, that all four of these agents are willing to accept. The two A industries are presumably concerned with the incomes accruing to them,[8] but the interests of the governments depend upon the political economy. The interesting polar cases are where the government is simply an agent of the industry,

---

[6] See Ethier (1989).

[7] See Ethier and Fischer (1987) and Ethier (1989). Also relevant are Dean and Gangopadhyay (1989) and Yano (1989).

[8] The industry pressure groups presumably include factors specific to the industry. In a Heckscher-Ohlin-Samuelson context, where there are no specific factors, it presumably includes the factor employed intensively in the A sector.

Figure 1

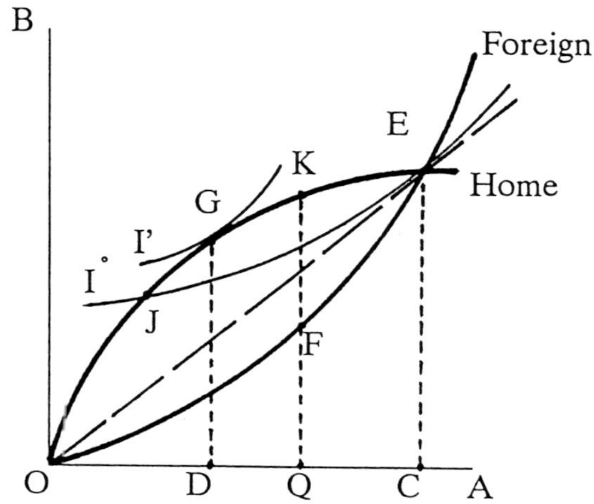

and so not an additional agent in its own right, and where the government is concerned with national welfare, represented , say, by a system of trade indifference curves. In general, the government can be thought of as wishing to maximize some weighted average of A-industry welfare and national welfare, with the weights depending upon the underlying political economy.

To see what this implies, consider how the four agents would be affected by a VER of OQ in Figure 1. Home residents import OQ and pay KQ for it, of which KF constitutes rent accruing to holders of the quota rights. I° denotes the foreign trade-indifference curve corresponding to free trade. Exclusive of the quota rents, the foreign economy trades at F and so experiences a decline in welfare as a result of the restraint. Also at F the foreign relative price of A is lower than at E, so the foreign A industry is also worse off. This illustrates the key role of the quota rents: without them neither foreign agent would accept the restraint, regardless of the foreign political economy.

So assume that the rents are given to the foreign A industry, as is in fact nearly always the case. Then the foreign economy will trade at K and experience higher welfare than at free trade, provided the quota is not large enough to place K at or to the left of J. The foreign government would desire such an arrangement as long as it attaches sufficient weight to national welfare. If it is concerned only with national welfare, the government would prefer a quota of OD, which corresponds to the optimum export tax, but it would be willing to accept any quota leading to trade between E and J.

The effect of the restraint on the foreign A industry is ambiguous: the industry loses because of the lower foreign price of A, but it gains the rent. Whether the industry gains over all depends on the size of the rent, and that depends upon the home offer curve not being too elastic.[9] At J the foreign economy has the same welfare as in free trade, but its B sector is better off. Thus the foreign A sector must be worse off, even with the full quota rent; the range of restrained trades that the sector will accept is some proper subset of the range from E to J. At G, a small increase in a quota will leave foreign welfare unchanged but make the B sector better off. Thus the A sector is made worse off, that is, it is beyond its most desired point, which therefore must lie to the right of G (and could simply be E). Suppose that this is K. Then between E and K both the foreign industry and the foreign government would favor a more restrictive restraint. Between K and G the industry would want a less restrictive restraint while a government seeking to maximize foreign welfare would want a more restrictive one. Between G and J both would want the restraint to be less restrictive. A welfare maximizing government would accept no restraint more restrictive than J, and the industry would wish to cast its veto before getting that far.

The situation is simpler at home. Any restraint moves the home economy to a lower trade-indifference curve (not shown) and so would be unacceptable to a welfare maximizing government. The home A industry, on the other hand, wants as restrictive an arrangement as possible. Thus the key is the home political economy, the extent to which the home government wishes to maximize the welfare of its A industry. Since the point is easily understood, we may as well assume that the government is simply the agent of the industry. Then there are three independent agents: the home A industry, the foreign A industry and the foreign government. A VER will be negotiated if it is in the interest of each of these agents.

In the present case this means that there will be a VER leading to trade in a proper subset of the interval from K to J, at a particular point depending on details of the bargaining process between the three agents. All three desire a restraint more binding than any that would produce trade between E and K. Between K and G the key bargaining is within the

[9] If the home offer curve is perfectly elastic, so that E, G and J coincide, a small quota will have a negative second-order effect on foreign welfare and a positive first-order effect on the welfare of the foreign B industry. Thus it must have a negative first-order effect on the A industry.

foreign economy, as the foreign A-sector wants a less restrictive agreement and a welfare-maximizing government a more restrictive one. Between G and J the key bargaining is international: the home agents want a more restrictive agreement and the foreign agents a less restrictive one.

In sum, two conditions are necessary for a VER in a competitive context. The home political economy must be such that the home government attaches sufficient weight to the interests of the home industry, and the home offer curve must be sufficiently inelastic to generate rents sufficient to allow a restraint to benefit the foreign industry.[10]

The competitive model has been the traditional framework for the study of trade restraints, and has also been the basis (implicit or explicit) for most empirical work. But in the remainder of this paper I consider imperfectly competitive markets. There are several reasons for this. First, the competitive analysis is large and well-known, while the imperfectly competitive work is more recent and still being developed. Second, imperfect competition is in fact prevalent in many industries where trade has been managed. Finally, several of the features discussed in Section I become interesting or significant only in an imperfectly competitive context.

III. THE BASIC IMPERFECTLY COMPETITIVE MODEL

Consider an imperfectly competitive domestic market in which n home firms and n* foreign firms sell a homogeneous product. Furthermore, I assume that n and n* are each at least as large as two, so that each firm faces competition from firms in both countries.

Assume the following profit functions for the representative foreign and home firms:

$$\pi^*(x;y) = p(z)x - F^* - c^*x$$

$$\pi(y;x) = p(z)y - F - cy$$

where y denotes sales by each home firm and x the sales of each foreign firm, $z = ny + n^*x$ and p(z) is the inverse demand function. F and c denote the constant fixed and marginal costs faced by each home firm and F* and c* those faced by each foreign firm.

[10] An alternative to the second condition would be for the foreign government to compensate the foreign industry even beyond the quota rents, or simply to coerce it into acceptance. Note that this implies an international asymmetry in political economy: in one country the industry controls the government while in the other it is the reverse.

I shall focus exclusively on Cournot-Nash equilibria. The first-order condition for foreign-firm profit maximization is:

$$\text{(FFE)} \qquad p = \frac{c^*}{1 - (1-\theta)/n^*\epsilon}$$

where $\epsilon = -zp'/p$ and $\theta = ny/z$, the share of the home market supplied by home firms. Note that, while ϵ is the *market* elasticity of demand, the Cournot-Nash equilibrium description implies that the elasticity relevant to the foreign *firm* is $n^*\epsilon/(1-\theta)$. Assuming for simplicity that the elasticity ϵ is constant and exceeds unity, *FFE* gives a negative relation between p and θ, and this is shown in Figure 2 below.

Also, profit maximization by home firms requires:

$$\text{(HFE)} \qquad p = \frac{c}{1 - \theta/n\epsilon}$$

HFE gives a positive relation between p and θ that is also shown in Figure 2. The intersection of *FFE* and *HFE* determines the equilibrium price and home-firm share of the home market. Figure 2 shows an equilibrium with domestic production ($\theta > 0$). The case where domestic firms are driven out of business by foreign competition may also arise if *HFE* lies entirely above *FFE*, and, of course, *HFE* may alternatively lie entirely below *FFE*, so that no trade takes place.

This model differs from the previous competitive one in that there are three -- not four -- relevant groups of agents: foreign firms, who care about foreign profits; home firms, who care about their own profits; the home government, who cares about either home welfare or home profit, or some combination of the two. Of course the foreign government is still also relevant, but the foreign economy is affected only by the profits earned by foreign firms. Thus the interest of the foreign government is identical to that of the foreign firms.

It will prove convenient to see how contours corresponding to particular values of the variables of concern to each of the agents appear in the p-θ plane. I start with home welfare.

(a) Home welfare contours. A change in domestic welfare u can result from an income effect of an alteration in the cost of the country's import bundle, or from a change in production acting on the wedge p-c between the country's valuation of production and its cost. Thus the welfare change can be expressed as follows.

Figure 2

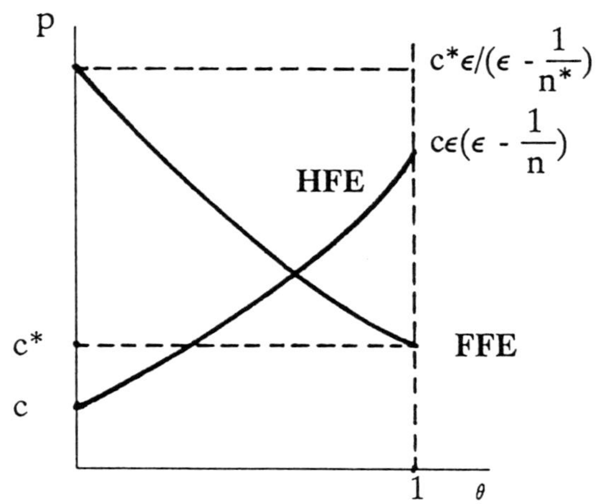

$$du = -Mdp + n(p\text{-}c)dy = -z\,dp + n\,d\pi.$$

Here M denotes total imports. Substitution produces the second equality. Under this interpretation, an increase in p lowers welfare because it decreases consumer surplus in the distorted z market. An increase in π, at given p, increases welfare because it means that the source of supply of z is shifted from foreign firms to domestic firms, saving p-c in resources. Home welfare contours are depicted in Figure 3(a). Note that the indifference contours have "reverse curvature", giving preference to autarky and to extensive dependence on imports rather than to moderate dependence. This will be important for what follows. It arises because an increase in p lowers welfare by reducing consumers' surplus, while an increase in θ substitutes domestic production for imports, thereby saving p - c per unit, and this saving becomes more and more pronounced as p becomes larger.

When $\theta = 0$, *HFE* is steeper than the welfare contour passing through it. But a tedious calculation reveals that some welfare contour has the same slope as *HFE* at some critical value $\theta°$. Furthermore, this contour lies entirely above *HFE*, and another critical market share $\theta' < \theta°$ yields the same welfare as does autarky ($\theta = 1$). Thus international trade is necessarily *beneficial* if *FFE* intersects *HFE* below the critical level θ'. But above the critical level international trade is *harmful*. In general, trade allows the economy to increase its consumer surplus at the cost of buying the goods at a greater price (p) than the social cost (c) of producing them

Figure 3

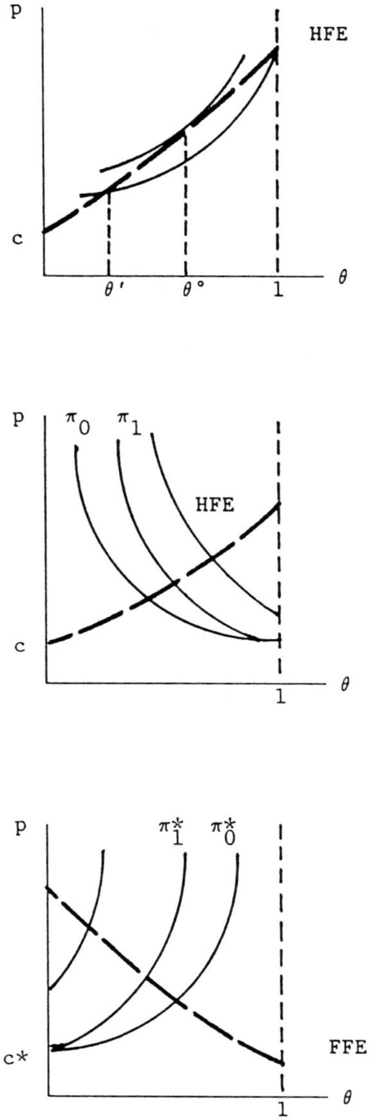

(a) Home welfare contours

(b) Home profit contours

(c) Foreign profit contours

at home. The latter effect dominates if p - c becomes too large.

(b) Home profit contours. Now consider how the profits of home firms relate to the equilibrium values of p and θ. Along the p axis, and when p = c, π = -F and du = -z dp. In the interior of the p-θ plane:

$$\pi = (p-c)y - F = (p-c)(\theta z/n) - F$$

implies[11]

$$d\pi = (\theta z/n)[(p-c)\hat{\theta} + (c\epsilon - p[\epsilon-1])\hat{p}].$$

Therefore π contours are negatively sloped and convex to the origin as long as p lies between c and $c\epsilon/(\epsilon-1)$, which include all points of interest. Profit contours are shown in Figure 3(b). Movements up and to the right along *HFE* always result in successively higher home profit contours.

(c) Foreign profit contours. The properties of foreign-firm profit contours can be derived in an exactly analogous fashion, so I omit the details. Figure 3(c) shows the results. Movements upward and to the left along *FFE* bring successively higher foreign profit levels.

IV. A VER IN THE BASIC MODEL

Now consider a voluntary export restraint. First I describe how this would alter the above equilibrium, and then I enquire into when such a VER can be expected to emerge.[12]

(a) Equilibrium effects of a VER. I suppose that a VER establishes an exogenous upper bound on the exports of *each* foreign firm. If in equilibrium x was less than or equal to this constraint it obviously has no effect, as long as we continue to look at Cournot-Nash equilibria. If the constraint is binding, foreign firms will find themselves off *FFE*, exporting the constrained amount, and each would be able to raise its own profit if it could export more, given the sales of all n + n* - 1 rivals. Home firms, however, will still be on *HFE*, because here each home firm maximizes profit given the sales of its rivals, *regardless* of what determines those sales. Thus in this model a binding VER can be described as simply a movement up and to the right along *HFE*.

(b) A profit-seeking home government.[13] Suppose first that the home government acts as the agent of the home industry, whose profit it wishes

---

[11] A circumflex denotes logarithmic differentiation.

[12] This section borrows heavily from Ethier (1989).

[13] This subsection may be thought of as offering a formal analysis of one of the possibilities raised in Hillman (1990).

to maximize. Since these profits are always increased by an upward movement along *HFE*, the home government will always wish to negotiate as stringent a restraint as possible. But if the agreement is truly voluntary, the foreign government will accept it only if foreign profit is not affected adversely. To see when this will be the case, we must superimpose foreign profit contours onto *HFE*. This is done in Figure 4.

Panel (a) shows the case where all foreign profit contours cut *HFE* from below. Straightforward algebraic manipulation reveals that this will happen if $c > c^* > c[1 - 1/\epsilon(n+1)]$ or if $c[1 - 1/\epsilon] > c^*$. In this situation upward movements along *HFE* necessarily lower foreign profit. Thus a VER cannot emerge in this case.[14]

In panel (b) $c^* > c$. Here -- or if $c[1 - 1/\epsilon(n+1)] > c^* > c[1 - 1/\epsilon]$ --there must exist a critical market share θ_v where foreign profit is maximized. If the free trade θ exceeds this critical value, the foreign government will again refuse to accept any binding VER. But when $\theta < \theta_v$ it will find a trade restriction to be in its own interest. I will refer to the situation of $c^* > c$, or of $c[1 - 1/\epsilon(n+1)] > c^* > c[1 - 1/\epsilon]$, and $\theta < \theta_v$ as the *HK* or Harris-Krishna case (not to be confused with *Hare-Krishna*) since it corresponds to the possibilities uncovered by Harris (1985) and Krishna (1989). Of course these particular conditions are determined by this model structure.[15] But the circumstances have intuitive appeal: if the foreign firms have a cost advantage they may want to be free to compete with home firms; if they are at a disadvantage, they may be willing to strike a deal. In the latter case they are more likely to want to deal the smaller is the market share they have been able to establish[16].

Suppose, then, that we are in the *HK* case. Then there must exist a market share $\theta^*(\theta)$ that exceeds θ_v and that yields foreign firms the same profit as does θ. Both governments desire an agreement at least restrictive enough to leave θ no less than θ_v. The home government wants as restrictive an agreement as possible. The foreign government would prefer θ_v, but will not lose with any agreement implying a home share in the interval $[\theta_v, \theta^*(\theta)]$. The latter is thus the core, and the two governments

[14] This is also trivially true if $c^* > c/(1 - 1/n\epsilon)$, since then **HFE** will lie entirely below all contours corresponding to nonnegative foreign profit, so there will be no active foreign firms.

[15] Harris and Krishna use different models than I and so obtain different conditions, but they were concerned with the same basic phenomena. See also Eichenberger and Harper (1987) and Hillman and Ursprung (1988).

[16] If $c = c^*$, the ***HK*** case cannot emerge in this model unless there are more foreign firms than domestic ones, if $n = n^*$, the ***HK*** case cannot emerge unless foreign firms are at a cost disadvantage.

Figure 4

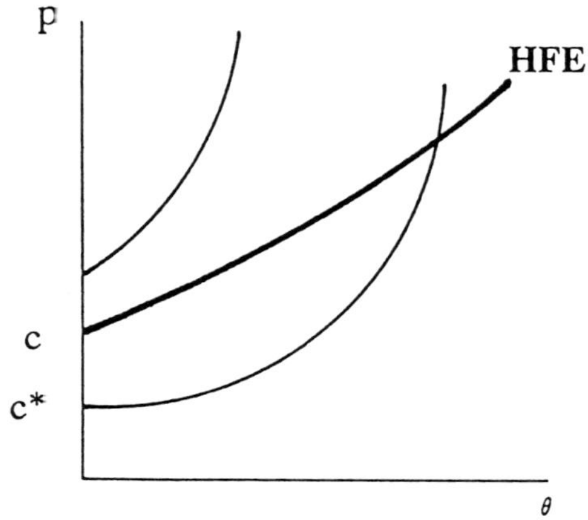

(a) No Agreement

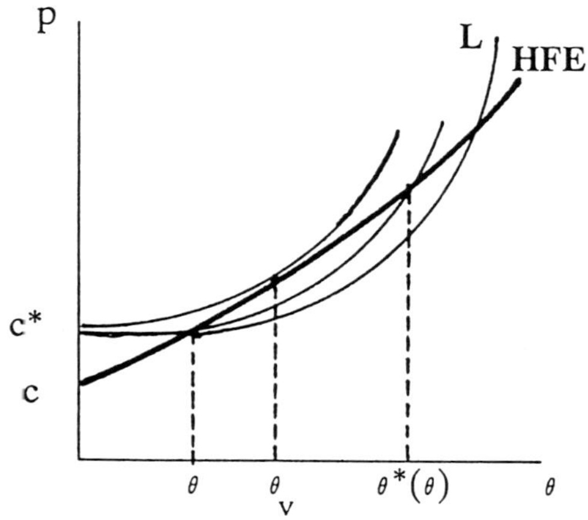

(b) *HK* Case

will agree to establish a VER that results in being in the interval, at a position determined by the actual bargaining process.

That it may be possible to establish a VER that benefits both home and foreign firms is the basic Harris-Krishna conclusion. A little thought reveals that it might be possible to raise both countries' welfare as well. To investigate this, alter the home government's assumed objective.

(c) A welfare-seeking home government. Suppose now that the home government wishes to maximize national welfare. There are now three distinct agents, and I suppose again that a VER can be established only if all three agree. As before, home firms always want a restraint and the foreign government will accept one only in the *HK* case. So consider the latter and ask whether the home government will want a restraint. This requires an examination of home welfare contours. This is provided in Figure 5.

Clearly, if the free trade θ is less than θ' no binding constraint will be in the home interest. Thus both sides will desire a VER only if $\theta' < \theta_v$ and if the free trade θ lies between the two. It also matters whether θ exceeds θ° or not.

Suppose first that it does. Then, just as when profit was its only concern, the home government wants as restrictive an agreement as it can get. Again, the foreign government will not accept anything outside of $[\theta_v, \theta^*(\theta)]$. Thus they will agree on a VER that puts θ somewhere in this interval. This is shown in Figure 5(a).

Suppose next that θ is less than θ°, as in Figure 5(b) and 5(c). Let $\theta^{+}(\theta)$ denote that home market share that exceeds θ° and yields the same level of home welfare as does θ. The home government will accept no VER that does not increase the home share to at least $\theta^{+}(\theta)$, and the foreign government will not allow it to increase to more than $\theta^*(\theta)$. Thus no VER will emerge if $\theta^*(\theta) < \theta^{+}(\theta)$, as in Figure 5(b). But if $\theta^*(\theta) > \theta^{+}(\theta)$, the core will be $[\theta^{+}(\theta), \theta^*(\theta)]$ or $[\theta_v, \theta^*(\theta)]$, whichever is smaller, and a VER will be negotiated leading to a home market share somewhere in the relevant interval. Figure 5(c) depicts this possibility.

Thus a VER may be useful even when both governments conscientiously try to raise national welfare. But the conditions for this are restrictive. They include: (i) the *HK* case; (ii) $\theta \geq \theta'$; (iii) either $\theta \geq \theta^{\circ}$ or $\theta^*(\theta) > \theta^{+}(\theta)$. How are such Pareto-improving restraints on trade possible? One of the consequences of trade management is *production shifting*. If production is shifted from a location where marginal costs are high to one where marginal costs are low, the benefit could be large enough to generate a welfare improvement overall. The condition $c \leq c^*$ is not necessary for the *HK* case, but it is necessary for a Pareto-improvement.

Figure 5

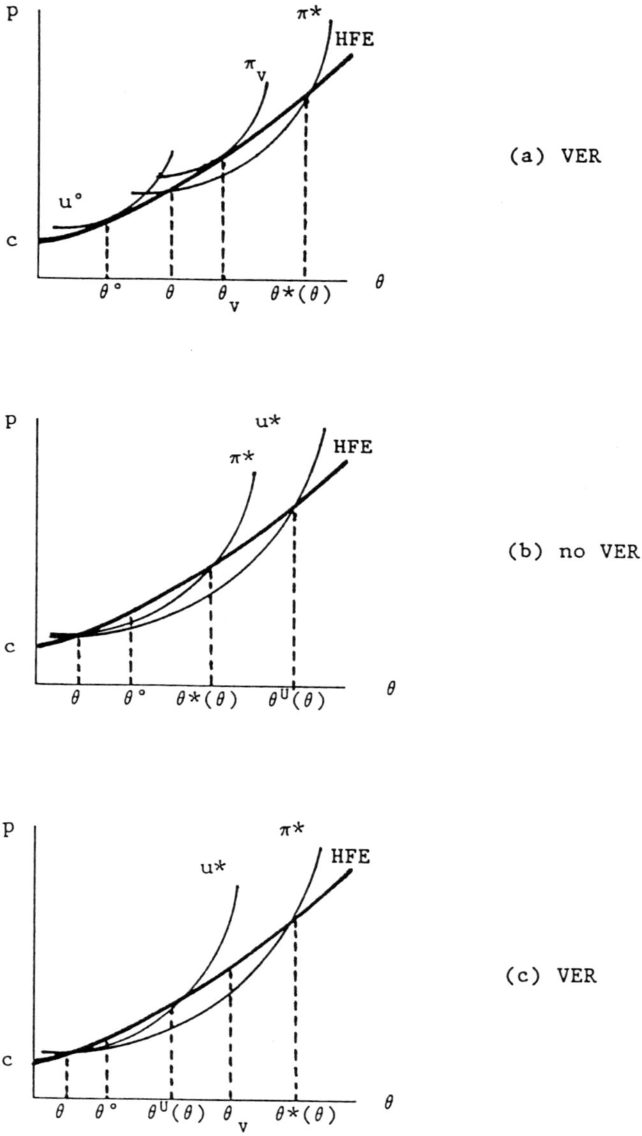
p
π*
HFE
π_v
u°
c
θ°
θ
θ_v
θ*(θ)
θ
(a) VER
p
u*
HFE
π*
c
θ
θ°
θ*(θ)
θ^U(θ)
θ
(b) no VER
p
π*
HFE
u*
c
θ
θ°
θ^U(θ)
θ_v
θ*(θ)
θ
(c) VER

At this point probably most of us would respond by suggesting that VERs do not in fact often emerge when the import-competing firms are the low-cost producers. This apparently implies that actual arrangements are not Pareto-improving, and that government policy is motivated by some sacrifice of national welfare for sectoral interests. I think there is considerable merit to such a view. But I also think that it is easy to accord it too much emphasis. This is because central features of managed trade, not included in the basic model of this section, cast different light on that view. This will become clear below.

V. ENTRY IN THE IMPERFECTLY COMPETITIVE MODEL

Thus far we have taken n and n* as given. But a central feature of trade management in an imperfectly competitive context is its relation to entry and exit. Suppose now that foreign firms can be expected to enter the market until the profit of the typical foreign firm falls to some long run level. The contour labeled L in Figure 4(b) corresponds to that level of profit, presumably lower than what foreign firms are earning now. This is not the long-run profit contour, where n* is endogenous; that would be a horizontal line at the height corresponding to long-run average revenue. Rather it is the contour, *given the present configuration of firms*, that corresponds to the long run-profit level. As foreign firms enter and n* increases, profit contours shift.

Note first that entry of foreign firms cannot transform a situation like Figure 4(a) into one like Figure 4(b), since n* plays no role in the conditions that distinguish the two. Thus if marginal costs and the number of home firms preclude the *HK* case, foreign entry will not alter this fact.

Suppose, then, that foreign profit contours do cut *HFE* from above, for a while, so that the *HK* case is conceivable. Then, if foreign firms focus only on the long run, they would welcome any VER that precluded entry (by giving all quota allowances to existing firms), provided that the resulting θ left them on a profit contour above L. Thus any point on *HFE* lying above L is acceptable. Clearly this must enlarge the range of acceptable agreements (relative to those that are preferable to the existing short run value of θ), and it could introduce the *HK* case into a situation from which it would otherwise be absent because the present θ exceeds θ_V.

Of course, foreign firms care about present profit as well as future profit. Thus only a subset of that part of *HFE* above L would presumably be acceptable, the size of that subset depending upon the speed of industry adjustment that would occur without an arrangement and the existing firms' rate of time preference. But it is clear that the entry of foreign firms increases the likelihood of the *HK* case and increases the range of acceptable quotas. This is the first basic implication of entry.

Existing foreign firms presumably care only about their own future profit and not that of potential rivals. But a foreign government that values foreign national welfare would be concerned about total profit extracted from the domestic market by foreign firms, and not about the distribution of that profit among older foreign firms and newer entrants. Thus the prospect of entry might make the foreign government either more willing or less willing to enter into a VER, depending upon the likely effect of such entry on total profit. Also a foreign government that values foreign welfare may be less willing than existing foreign firms would like to use the quota mechanism to restrict entry. But the basic point is that the prospect of entry means that the profit of existing foreign firms no longer coincides with the effect on foreign welfare, so the foreign government once again becomes a separate agent from foreign firms.

These considerations seem to be quite important in practice in at least some industries. A major implication of the restraints on Japanese automobile exports to the United States, where quotas were allotted in proportion to past sales, was that firms with established positions, such as Toyota and Nissan, were shielded from increased competition by firms, such as Toyo Kogyo and Isuzu, that had not yet built up market share.

We have considered entry of foreign firms. The potential entry of domestic firms is less interesting. First, entry of import-competing firms does not in practice appear to be relevant in industries where trade management does occur, although the possible role of such management in retarding exit might be. Second, existing firms want as restrictive an agreement as they can get in any case, and the prospect of entry or exit does not change this, even if it does change the value an existing firm would attach to such an agreement.[17]

A third possible type of entry would be that of foreign firms who can bring their technology into the domestic market and produce there. If these firms are also subject to management, no new element is added, because our earlier discussion is not sensitive to where production actually takes place. The United States automobile industry, for example, has in the past argued that American production of Japanese firms should be included in the quotas, and the issue has arisen in a third country context with the European proposal to include American production in future European

---

[17] Exit of domestic firms might have some influence on the willingness of ***foreign*** firms to deal, however. As we have seen, one of the conditions allowing for the emergence of the ***HK*** case is $c[1 - 1/\epsilon(n+1)] > c^* > c[1 - 1/\epsilon]$. If exit takes place it will reduce n, thereby lowering the left-most term and so reducing the range of possible values of c^*. In this sense exit can reduce the probability of the ***HK*** case emerging.

restraints on imports of Japanese automobiles. Nevertheless, common practice has been not to include such production in the arrangement. Foreign firms producing in the home market are not part of the domestic industry interest group, and their profits are not part of domestic welfare.[18] In effect, these firms play the same role as unrestrained exporters: the fact that their production takes place in the domestic economy does not matter. Thus the basic issue raised is that of discrimination. The next section addresses that explicitly.

VI. THE DISCRIMINATORY EFFECT OF MANAGED TRADE

The fact that managed trade is essentially discriminatory can have a profound effect on the implications of such management for economic welfare, especially for that of importing countries.[19] A frequent situation where discrimination arises is when a VER is established with a group of exporters who have large established positions in the domestic market, but not with another group of exporters, newer producers, who do not yet have established positions but who have lower costs. This is consistent with our earlier discussion: with lower costs they are unlikely to be in an *HK* situation; without an established base it would be difficult for home interests to rouse resentment against them.

Suppose, then, that in addition to the home (H) and foreign (F) firms as above, there is also a low-cost group L of foreign firms with marginal cost $c_L < c, c^*$. They have their own Cournot-Nash equilibrium condition:

$$(LFE) \qquad p = \frac{c_L}{1 - \mu/n_L\epsilon}$$

where n_L is the number of L firms and their market share is $\mu = n_Lx_L/z$. Here x_L denotes the sales of the typical L firm and now $z = ny + n^*x + n_Lx_L$. The equilibrium condition for H firms continues to be *HFE*, but that for F firms must be rewritten:

[18] Both statements need to be qualified to the extent that these firms increase the rents of domestically-owned specific factors that they employ.

[19] But this aspect has not received much attention in the literature. Indeed Pomfret (1989, p 204) states, "The most surprising feature of economists' analysis of VERs is the lack of attention given to their discriminatory nature." But the issue is addressed empirically in Dinopoulos and Kreinen (1988) and theoretically in Dean and Gangopadhyay (1989).

$$(FFE^\circ) \qquad p = \frac{c^*}{1 - (1-\theta^\circ)/n^*\epsilon}$$

where $\theta^\circ = \theta + \mu$. *HFE*, *FFE°* and *LFE* jointly determine equilibrium p, θ and μ.

Point E in Figure 6(a) depicts an equilibrium between H and F firms, before the L firms enter the market. In the case shown, $c^* < c$ and all F profit contours cut *HFE* from below. Thus the *HK* case is not possible and trade management cannot be negotiated, even though H firms desire a VER and it may also be possible to enhance H welfare in this way (H welfare contours are not shown).

Now allow the L firms to enter. Since *FFE* has the same functional form as *FFE°*, the latter can be depicted by the same curve in Figure 6(a), if the horizontal axis is also used to measure θ°. F profit contours are also drawn the same as before. Substitute *LFE* into *HFE* to obtain, after some manipulation:

$$(HFE^\circ) \qquad p = \frac{c^\circ}{1 - \theta^\circ/n^\circ\epsilon}$$

where $n^\circ = n + n_L$ and $c^\circ = (n/n^\circ)c + (n_L/n^\circ)c_L$. Clearly $n^\circ > n$, $c^\circ < c$ and $n^\circ c^\circ > nc$. Thus *HFE°* lies below *HFE*, and, at each value of p, has a smaller slope $dp/d\theta$.

Equilibrium is determined by the intersection of *HFE°* and *FFE°* at E′ in Figure 6(a). This point shows equilibrium p and θ°; θ is determined by the corresponding point H′ on *HFE*, and therefore μ equals the distance H′E′. Entry of the L firms lowers the market price and reduces the shares of both H and F firms.

There are also additional possibilities for trade management. We must consider a possible restraint on only F exports, a restraint on only L exports, and a restraint on both F and L exports. H firms, of course, want as binding a restraint as possible on as many firms as possible. Our earlier discussion suggests that the L firms, as the least-cost producers, would be the least likely to wish to have their exports restrained, so assume that they would not in fact agree to a VER on themselves alone.

A VER that restrains only F firms can be depicted as a movement upwards and to the right along *HFE°*. In the situation depicted in Figure 6(a) F firms are willing to negotiate a VER involving themselves alone. At first blush it would seem paradoxical that F firms, originally unwilling to restrain their exports, should be made willing to do so by the advent of lower-cost competitors who would remain unrestrained. The reason is that

Figure 6

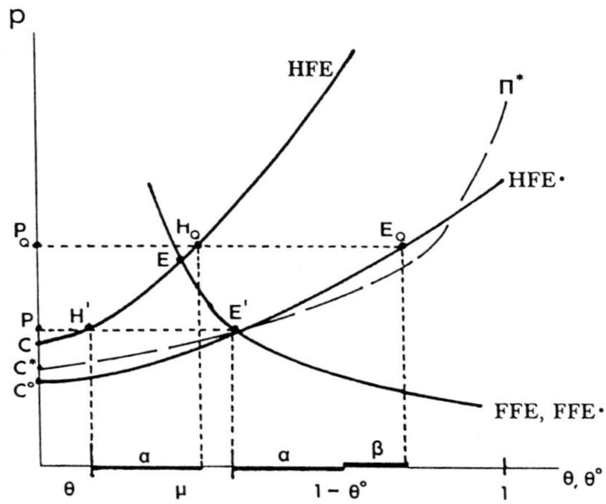

(a) Porous Management

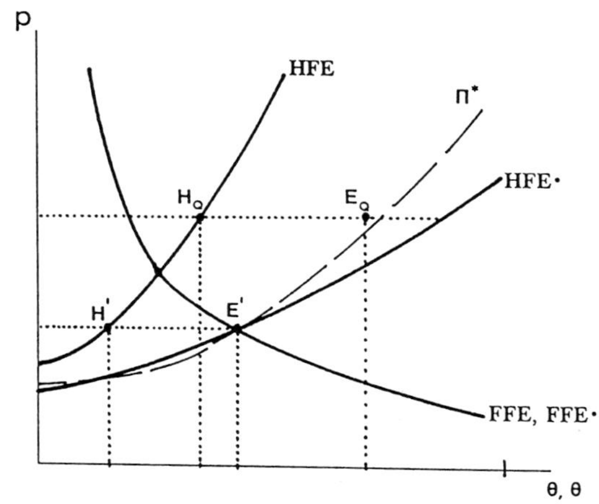

(b) Comprehensive Management

the loss of the status of least-cost producers reduces the attraction of unrestrained competition to the F firms relative to that of implicit collusion, even if only among themselves.

Consider a VER that moves equilibrium from E′ to E_Q. H firm equilibrium moves from H′ to H_Q. Both H firms and L firms experience increased market shares with a higher price, so their profits rise a result of the management. F firms experience the price rise while losing market share, but since they move to a higher profit contour they also benefit. Depending on circumstances, H welfare might even rise. The possibility of a Pareto improvement arises because of the production switching brought about by the arrangement. In the figure, α represents a switch of market share from F firms to H firms; with c > c*, as in this case, this switch reduces global production efficiency. But β represents a switch from F firms to L firms, and this is globally beneficial.

Figure 6(b) shows another possibility. Here the F iso-profit contour at E′ cuts $HFE°$ from below. Thus a movement up along the latter reduces profit for the F firms, and they will not agree to a VER limited to themselves alone. But if the profit contour possesses a sufficiently gentle slope, a VER restraining both F and L firms can be negotiated that benefits all firms. Consider a restriction that moves H firms from H′ to H_Q in Figure 6(b). Suppose quotas are set so that E_Q determines the division between μ and $\theta°$. If the profit contour at E′ is less steep than *HFE* at H′, as in the figure, it is possible to find an E_Q that both raises μ and is on a higher F profit contour than that through E′. Thus the arrangement brings all firms an increase in profits. Again, both harmful and beneficial production switching occurs, and this may or may not increase global production efficiency. Note that in Figure 6(b) all firms are included in the arrangement, but it is still discriminatory in the sense that it reallocates production among the restrained firms. Note also that in this case all restrained firms have lower marginal costs than H firms, but a Pareto improvement is still possible because of this internal reallocation.

The critical importance of the discrimination inherent to managed trade should now be apparent. That the deflection of output to low-cost outsiders could add a welfare-enhancing aspect to such arrangements should come as no surprise. More surprising is the possibility that the existence of such firms might facilitate the commencement of such management, even if they themselves decline to participate. The "porous" nature of VERs, where outsiders replace restrained imports at least in part, is often observed in practice. Import-competing firms would like to minimize this by including as many foreign sources in the arrangement as possible. As we have seen, under some circumstances a VER must indeed be comprehensive to be feasible, but under other circumstances just the reverse is true.

Section IV implied that relatively high foreign marginal costs were important in inducing voluntary foreign participation and, especially, in allowing for welfare-enhancing trade management. The observation that import-competing firms are in practice least anxious to press for management when they have a cost advantage therefore causes the theory to generate scepticism about the voluntary nature of participation and about the possibility of welfare-enhancing (or, at least, cushioned welfare-reducing) management. But consideration of discrimination changes this outlook radically because it shifts attention to the role of relative cost differences *between* foreign firms.

Time and time again we have in practice witnessed trade management implemented by restraints on the exports of foreign firms with established positions while leaving unrestrained the exports of newer, lower-cost producers. Presumably this is because their lower costs make them less likely to agree to participate and because their lack of established market share makes it difficult both for import-competing firms to marshall domestic political support for their inclusion and for the importing country to offer them rents as compensation. Typically these firms increase their exports as a result of the management. Sometimes this results in the successive expansion of management to include most of the world's producers (e.g., textiles and apparel), sometimes it causes the management to collapse (e.g., shoes), and sometimes it results in the continued restraint of only some firms (e.g., automobiles). But the concerns emphasized in this section seem to be of central importance in any case.

VII. CONCLUDING REMARKS

This paper has sorted out the circumstances under which managed trade might be expected to emerge and has investigated the implications of a policy environment in which it is an endogenous possibility. Two features that appear to be crucial are the allocation of rents and the discrimination inherent in such management.

A major result is the conclusion that trade management might in fact prove useful even if policy is directed toward enhancing national welfare. A countervailing implication is the complex sensitivity of welfare consequences upon exogenous parameters. In addition, the models I have considered are very special. I have used an informal and geometric exposition to avoid investing specific conditions with excessive dignity. More important are the possibilities (or "parables") that the analysis suggests and explains.

References

Arad, R. and A. L. Hillman, 1979. "Embargo threat, learning and departure from comparative advantage," *Journal of International Economics*, 9, 265-276.

Dean, J. and S. Gangopadhyay, 1989. "Strategic trade practices in the presence of a VER," unpublished manuscript.

Dinopoulos, E. and M. E. Kreinen, 1988. "Effects of the U.S.-Japan auto VER on European prices and on U.S. welfare," *Review of Economics and Statistics*, 70, 484-491.

Eichenberger, J. and I. Harper, 1987. "Price and quantity controls as facilitating devices," *Economics Letters*, 23, 223-228.

Ethier, W. J., 1988. "Antidumping," unpublished manuscript, International Economics Research Center, University of Pennsylvania.

Ethier, W. J., 1989. "Voluntary export restraints," unpublished manuscript, International Economics Research Center, University of Pennsylvania. Forthcoming in: Takayama, A., H. Ohta and M. Ohyama, editors, *Trade, Policy, and International Adjustments*, Academic Press.

Ethier, W. J. and R. Fischer, 1987. "The new protectionism," *Journal of International Economic Integration*, 2, 1-11.

Fischer, R., 1986. *Essays in Game Theory and International Economics*, Ph. D. dissertation, University of Pennsylvania.

Harris, R., 1985. "Why voluntary export restraints are 'voluntary'," *Canadian Journal of Economics*, 18, 799-809.

Hillman, A. L., 1990. "Protectionist policies as the regulation of international industry," *Public Choice*, forthcoming.

Hillman, A. L. and H. Ursprung, 1988. "Domestic politics, foreign interests, and international trade policy," *American Economic Review*, 78, 729-745.

Kostecki, M., 1987. "Export-restraint arrangements and trade liberalization," *The World Economy*, 10, 442-450.

Krishna, K., 1989. "Trade restrictions as facilitating practices," *Journal of International Economics*, 26, 251-270.

Pomfret, R., 1989. "The economics of voluntary export restraint agreements," *Journal of Economic Surveys*, 3, 199-211.

Yano, M., 1989. "Voluntary export restraints and expectations: An analysis of export quotas in oligopolistic markets," *International Economic Review*, 30, 707-723.

Dumping

Wilfred J. Ethier

University of Pennsylvania

Traditional dumping theory consists of an analysis of monopolistic price discrimination between national markets. The present paper develops an alternative theory motivated by contemporary experience. This theory views dumping as an integral part of the relationship between domestic factor markets and international commodity markets in a world of uncertainty and sluggish adjustment. Key determinants identified by the theory include the pattern of demand uncertainty, alternatives available to the unemployment of factors, and relative endowments of factors with distinct contractual arrangements. The balance of the paper isolates the role of each determinant.

Numerous instances of alleged dumping have characterized recent tariff debates within and among the industrial countries. In the United States the issue has been joined on Mexican tomatoes, European steel, Italian shoes, Japanese televisions, European automobiles, Philippine ceramic tile, Canadian and Australian lead, Polish golf carts, Japanese and Italian rail cars, and many others. If dumping is interpreted broadly enough to include low export prices due to subsidies, add automobile tires from Canada, textile apparel from many LDCs, shoes from Spain and Brazil, Spanish olives, Taiwanese zoris, and, for the European Economic Community (EEC), synthetic fibers from the United States. And of course the dumping of agricultural surpluses remains a central issue. In the United States, outstanding findings of dumping increased from about 40 early in 1975 to over 80 by 1980, and in 1979 there were 37 countervailing-duty actions, in

I have benefited from the useful comments of Assaf Razin and of seminar participants at the University of Pennsylvania and Princeton.

[*Journal of Political Economy*, 1982, vol. 90, no. 3]

contrast to three in 1973. The steel reference-price system now covers a basic industry with no need for any formal actions at all. More generally, Lloyd (1977, p. 42) has pointed to an increased concern with dumping problems since 1974.

Recent changes in the administration of U.S. antidumping and countervailing-duty statutes will likely further increase their use. More generally, the marked postwar reduction of tariffs on manufactured goods within the General Agreement on Tariffs and Trade (GATT) framework of international responsibility, together with a secular convergence of cost structures in the industrial economies, prompt the conjecture that antidumping and antisubsidy statutes will be the principal battleground for the "new protectionism" as concerns trade in manufactures among the developed economies.[1] If so, the theory of dumping must become a major part of the positive theory of protection relevant to such trade.

What, then, is the contemporary state of dumping theory? My search of *The Journal of Economic Abstracts* and the *Journal of Economic Literature* from 1963 to March 1980 turned up a total of six English-language articles on the subject, of which a mere three (Kudrle 1974; Löfgren 1977; Tarr 1979) were relevant to trade in manufactures among developed countries.[2] But while the contemporary literature is sparse, we have an enormous stock of pre–World War II publications on the subject.

This early literature generally defines dumping as price discrimination between national markets. This is the definition adhered to by Viner (1923) in his classic treatment and followed by most major authors. Aside from sporadic instances, dumping is thus treated either as profit maximization by a discriminating monopolist or as an oligopolistic tactic to eliminate competition or to enforce a cartel (predatory dumping). Although the second of these two instances received extensive comment, it was generally judged to be of secondary practical importance. Haberler (1937, p. 300), for example, states that "this aggressive form of dumping is the spectre often used to frighten public opinion into imposing tariffs. Nevertheless this form of dumping very seldom occurs." Viner (1931, p. 275) concurs:

[1] One is not tempted toward the same conjecture about the second major sore spot currently festering protectionism in the DCs: the expansion of imports of manufactures from transitional LDCs. But the two are related: The alleged dumping of European steel in the United States is said to be due in part to the European industry's exposure to LDC competition.

[2] Among other recent contributions, Wares (1977) contains a detailed statement and development of the conventional theory, Bryan (1980) discusses at length U.S. antidumping and countervailing-duty law, and Brander and Krugman (1980) supply the most interesting contribution in some years to conventional theory. For a good discussion along traditional lines, see Corden (1974, pp. 235–47).

"German cartels have also been charged with predatory dumping intended to crush competitors, but of this there have not been many well authenticated instances." More recently, Lloyd (1977, p. 8) concludes, "it is doubtful that a monopolist would use such a method to extend his monopoly and very few cases of predatory dumping have ever been proven." In any event, the formal theory of dumping essentially consists only of the theory of monopolistic price discrimination between two markets.[3] As emphasized by Haberler (1937), the basic conditions for dumping as identified by the traditional theory are monopoly and protection (the latter providing the international segmentation of markets).

It is evident that such a theory is quite inadequate to deal with contemporary problems. The theory is by no means irrelevant: Kravis and Lipsey (1971, 1977) establish the existence of extensive international price discrimination, to which Gilbert (1941) had called attention years ago, and some of the examples cited at the beginning of this paper involve allegations of such discrimination. But the requirement of monopoly is unduly and quaintly extreme, protection is now the objective rather than the cause of contemporary allegations, and the traditional theory completely excludes those considerations fundamental to most contemporary problems: imperfectly adjusting factor markets in the presence of changing conditions of product demand. The earlier literature did consider the related problem of dumping to stabilize production over the business cycle. Haberler (1937, p. 310) dismisses the phenomenon, which he calls "trade cycle dumping," as a special case of the price-discrimination theory, and Viner (1923, p. 28), although conjecturing that "it is probable that this is the most prevalent form of dumping," basically treated it as only a distinct motive. Completely absent is any notion of an interdependence between such dumping and factor-market equilibrium within the relevant industries of the two countries.

This absence is perhaps due in part to the insistence of the traditional literature on defining "dumping" as price discrimination. Popular usage of the term has always been much more extensive, and an alternative definition has in fact long been professionally recognized: export sales at a price below the cost of production. Early antidumping laws were often defined on the basis of price discrimination, and administration on these terms has generally been easier. But later statutes have largely been in terms of "fair market price," allowing at least some scope for production costs, and contemporary practice in most countries gives a role to both concepts. In U.S. law,

[3] The basic references are Yntema (1928) and Robinson (1933, bk. 5). See also Haberler (1937, pp. 302–13).

"constructed values" are essentially backups that may be used when transaction prices in the exporting country are ruled out. But transaction prices may no longer be used when they are less than costs of production. Furthermore, the American reference-price system for steel is based on cost-of-production calculations. Narrowing the scope of dumping to price discrimination, as done by the traditional literature, excludes essentials of contemporary experience. If European steel firms, because of either increased LDC competition or a developing world recession, experience contracting demand for their products, in the face of binding contracts for inputs and the industry specificity of many factors, the temptation to unload steel at prices below long-run average cost will extend to all markets. If price discrimination was tempting before, it will probably still be so. A change in the optimal degree of discrimination resulting from the altered demand conditions is surely a secondary aspect of the problem. Yet, by insisting on the narrow price-discrimination definition of dumping, the traditional theory restricts itself to this minor facet while completely ignoring the fundamental relation between factor-market equilibrium in the European steel industry and the opportunity to sometimes sell below cost on world markets. Tarr (1979), after briefly arguing that the traditional theory supplies, in general, no justification for cyclical dumping on the price-discrimination definition,[4] presents evidence that fails to show price discrimination varying with the business cycle.

I do not claim that the traditional theory is irrelevant. Not only is international price discrimination pervasive, suggesting widespread relevance to at least some degree, but there are important contemporary problems to which the concerns of the traditional theory appear central. For example, the rapid LDC expansion of certain manufactures involves low export prices (for market penetration) together with high domestic prices (because of protection). My contention is that the traditional theory is tangential to much that is central to intra-DC trade. The lack of a modern theory of dumping does significantly neutralize the contemporary relevance of the international economics of protection.

I. Essentials of a Modern Theory of Dumping

An efficient modern theory of dumping should, first of all, dispense with price discrimination and monopoly. Of course, a general treatment of dumping would encompass both the modern theory and a

[4] It should be noted, however, that Tarr does not address Haberler's basic argument (1937, p. 310).

general-equilibrium version of the traditional theory. But first we must have a modern theory. More generally, I mean to ignore changes in the relative prices of traded goods. Thus the search for a modern theory of dumping may commence with the following assumption.

> ASSUMPTION 1: A (single composite) traded good—call it steel—is produced by competitive firms and sold at a single world price (in the absence of tariffs, etc.).

There are many goods, both traded and nontraded, in addition to steel, but they will not be a focus of attention in what follows. Assumption 1 ensures that my theory, whatever its intrinsic worth, must diverge fundamentally from the traditional theory of dumping. This is the sole purpose of the assumption: Price discrimination could be added in several natural ways to what follows, and an analysis of the interaction between such discrimination and the features I elucidate could be of great interest, but is beyond the scope of the present paper.

Thus far I have specified what should be dispensed with in an efficient modern theory, but what must be included? Obviously, a nexus of changeable product-market conditions and inflexible factor markets is essential. There are three components of this nexus. The first is firm uncertainty about future demand for traded goods; as the firms are competitive this means price uncertainty. I shall incorporate this as simply as possible.

> ASSUMPTION 2: There are two states of the world, A and B, each with probability one-half of occurrence, distinguished, from the firm's point of view, solely by distinct steel prices, $P_A \leqslant P_B$.

Assumption 2 describes the world from the viewpoint of the competitive firm; later, P_A and P_B will be determined endogenously. All prices are expressed in terms of a cost-of-living index. To simplify the analysis, I assume that the cost of living at home bears a fixed relation to the cost of living abroad. Thus domestic and foreign steel prices are commensurate.

A second crucial component to be stylized is the difficulty of reallocating factors of production between the steel sector and the rest of the economy.

> ASSUMPTION 3: Steel is produced by means of two factors under constant returns to scale. Both factors are specific to the steel sector.

More generally, other sectors of the economy will be treated exogenously.

The final component is the observation that wages are "sticky" and that firms adjust instead through layoffs. But the ability to utilize layoffs varies greatly across inputs and between countries. I stylize all this as follows.

> ASSUMPTION 4: Each factor's returns (call them wages and salaries) are independent of the realized state of the world. Firms hire factors before this state is known. Hired quantities of one factor, called managers (M), must be employed in all states, but firms may lay off the other factor, laborers (L), once the state becomes known.

Laid-off workers receive (not from the firm) an exogenous income equivalent, known initially. If some state involves layoffs, the identities of the laid-off workers are not determined until the state of nature is realized. Steel is but one good, so I assume for simplicity that its price makes only a negligible contribution to the cost of living in each country. Then variations in the price of steel do not directly affect the real values of wages and salaries.

The distinction between M and L is intended to capture the distinct arrangements customarily found in industry. Factor M is representative of such factors as "key" employees who are not laid off in recessions and of capital financed by bonds or bank loans, whereas L corresponds more closely to blue-collar workers, equity capital, and energy. The relative sizes of L and M depend not only on endowments of various inputs but also on social and legal arrangements. For example, a certain American worker might be likely to lose his job in a recession, whereas his Japanese counterpart has an implicit guarantee of lifetime employment and his European counterpart might be sheltered by government regulations or a trade-union agreement.

Wares (1977, p. 12) observes that much dumping occurs in the cement, steel, and chemical industries and, more generally, involves raw materials and semifinished goods that "are likely to be produced in continuous-run plants where the costs of changeover are great and the continuous use of capacity required." Lloyd (1977, p. 7) also notes that dumping is "particularly likely in industries in which there is surplus capacity in large plants, either because of cyclical reduction in demand or because of the irregular pattern of investments in large plants," and he also points to the prominence of DC chemical producers in actual antidumping actions. One would therefore expect a country's relative endowment of what I call managers and laborers to help determine the propensity of its firms to dump in unfavorable states. At the same time, the possibility of dumping should influence the behavior of the firm in domestic factor markets. Elucidation of this interdependence should be a major goal of a modern theory of dumping.

Assumptions 1–4 express in stylized form the essential constituents of such a modern theory. The greater generality that would follow from less stylization would be welcome, but my objective in this paper is to focus as clearly as possible on what I regard as central. Also, the starting point of my analysis will be this collection of stylized facts and not a microeconomic theory explaining, say, wage stickiness. Such theories do exist and could be used to derive some of my assumptions from more fundamental hypotheses about individual behavior and the completeness of markets. The implicit-contracts theory of Azariadis (1975) is a notable candidate. But the profession is far from a consensus on such a microeconomic foundation, and it is therefore more convenient and more general to avoid imposing any particular explanation of assumptions 1–4 and to simply commence from them as stylized facts. However, this does imply that I will be unable to give any complete discussion of the welfare consequences of government policies toward dumping.

II. Factor-Market Equilibrium

Individual steel firms are competitive and so hire managers at a market-determined salary s, with the cost-of-living index as numeraire. The attractiveness of a firm's job offers to laborers depends on the wage w and the security of employment, which is positively related to e, the fraction of hired laborers retained in the unfavorable state A. The $\bar{u}$ curve in figure 1 depicts a set of w–e combinations regarded as equivalent by laborers. The individual steel firm can hire as many laborers as it wishes at any w–e combination on the market-determined $\bar{u}$ curve. Each firm chooses its employment of laborers and managers and its w–e combination so as to maximize expected profit, given s and the $\bar{u}$ curve. Because of as-

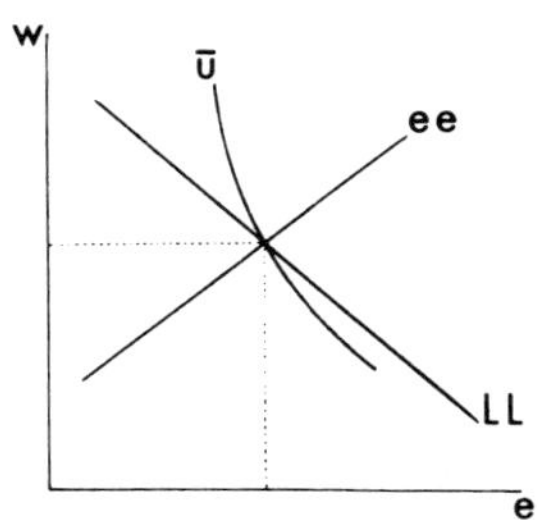

FIG. 1

sumption 3, each firm's scale of operations is indeterminate. In market equilibrium s and $\bar{u}$ adjust so that the total profit-maximizing employment offers of all steel firms equal M and L, and expected profits are zero.

The maximization problem generating this equilibrium is set out in the Appendix. Here I turn to the conditions which characterize factor-market equilibrium. To maximize expected profits, firms hire M until the expected value of its marginal product equals its salary:

$$s = \tfrac{1}{2}P_A[f(em) - emf'(em)] + \tfrac{1}{2}P_B[f(m) - mf'(m)]. \qquad (1)$$

Here f denotes a standard neoclassical production function (so $f' > 0$ and $f'' < 0$), and m denotes the laborer-manager ratio hired by the firm. The firm would never hire more laborers than it planned to employ in the favorable state B because that would simply require paying a higher wage to compensate laborers for the risk of unemployment; then, since factor prices adjust to clear factor markets ex ante, $m = L/M$, the exogenous endowment ratio.

Similarly, firms hire laborers up to the point where the expected value of the marginal product of each hiree equals the wage the firm expects to pay him:

$$w(1 + e)/2 = \tfrac{1}{2}P_Af'(em)e + \tfrac{1}{2}P_Bf'(m). \qquad (2)$$

Note that, because of constant returns to scale, (1) and (2) together imply that in equilibrium expected profits are driven to zero. This means that firms will sell traded goods below cost in state A and above cost in state B.

Suppose the firm is in equilibrium and hires one more laborer. Since workers would be laid off in state A in any event, the additional hiree would contribute revenue only in state B; thus expected marginal revenue would be $\tfrac{1}{2}P_Bf'(m)$. The hiree would also need to be paid only in state B, so his expected wages equal $w/2$. But an increase in the number of hirees increases the chances that any particular hiree will be laid off in state A and thereby reduces the attractiveness to workers of being hired by this firm at the original wage. To remain competitive with other firms, this firm must therefore increase the wage paid to all workers. Let V denote the amount by which the firm must increase its wage in order to leave employment at that firm no less attractive after a marginal fall in e. Then the expected increase in the wage bill paid to L hirees is $VL[\tfrac{1}{2} + (e/2)](-de/dL)$. Noting that $de/dL = -e/L$, the expected revenue from one more hiree will equal the expected increase in cost when

$$w = P_Bf'(m) - Ve(1 + e). \qquad (3)$$

The quantity V is presumably increasing in w and decreasing in e; also, V would be reduced by an increase in the (exogenous) income equivalent of unemployment.

Analogous reasoning applied to the possibility of increasing e (or, equivalently, the substitution of [3] into [2]) yields the final characteristic of expected-profit maximization:

$$w = P_A f'(em) + V(1 + e). \tag{4}$$

Note that in state A each employed factor is paid more than the value of its marginal product, and in state B it is paid less.

Given the exogenous supplies of both factors and the price of traded goods in each state, equations (3) and (4) jointly determine w and e, as depicted in figure 1, where the graph of (3) is labeled LL and that of (4) ee. Implicit differentiation of (3) and (4) yields the slopes of these curves:

$$\left.\frac{dw}{de}\right|_{LL} = -\frac{-V(1+e) - Ve - e(1+e)V_e}{-e(1+e)V_w - 1},$$

$$\left.\frac{dw}{de}\right|_{ee} = -\frac{P_A m f''(em) + V + (1+e)V_e}{(1+e)V_w - 1},$$

where V_e and V_w denote the partial derivatives of V with respect to e and w, respectively. I impose the following restriction on these terms.

Assumption 5: $-(1 + e)V_e/V = 1$ and $(1 + e)V_w > 1$.

This assumption divides the analysis into its alternative cases. Treatment of those which violate the assumption is straightforward and left to the reader. Also, the assumption will imply reasonable properties, and it can be justified directly by an appeal to implicit contract theory. This is deferred to an Appendix. The assumption implies:

$$\left.\frac{dw}{de}\right|_{LL} = -\frac{(1+e)V}{e(1+e)V_w + 1} < 0, \tag{5}$$

$$\left.\frac{dw}{de}\right|_{ee} = \frac{-P_A m f''(em)}{(1+e)V_w - 1} > 0. \tag{6}$$

Thus the curves are sloped as illustrated in figure 1, and equilibrium is unique. An exogenous rise in P_B shifts LL up, raising equilibrium w and e. The increase in e raises the marginal productivity of managers in state A so that, from (1), s also increases by more than the increase in the expected value of managerial marginal product at initial employment levels. An increase in P_A, by shifting ee down, will *reduce* w but increase e. The latter again implies that s rises by more than the expected value, at initial employments, of managerial marginal product. Assumption 5 implies that, from (5), the slope of LL is greater than $-V$. Thus a downward movement along this line yields a more favorable employment situation for workers: The rise in e (and therefore in job security) more than compensates for the fall in w.

III. International Equilibrium

Consider next the international equilibrium of two trading countries. The home country—call it America—is as described in the preceding section. The foreign country—Japan—has an analogous structure. Asterisks will distinguish variables pertaining exclusively to Japan.

In either country, an increase in P_A shifts down the respective ee schedule, so that e and P_A are positively related: $e = \phi(P_A)$ in America and $e^* = \phi^*(P_A)$ in Japan. The American curve is illustrated in figure 2a. Note that the position of this curve depends on the exogenous endowments M and L and also on the assumed value of P_B. Movements along the curve away from the origin correspond to lower wages w but more favorable job opportunities for laborers.

I assume that uncertainty about the future is ultimately due to uncertainty about demand conditions for steel. Expectations are rational in that P_A equals the price that would actually clear the international steel market should state A materialize, and similarly for P_B in state B. Equilibrium in each state can be described as follows:

$$\lambda_A D(P_A) + \lambda_A^* D^*(P_A) = f(em)M + f^*(e^*m^*)M^*, \qquad (7)$$

$$\lambda_B D(P_B) + \lambda_B^* D^*(P_B) = f(m)M + f^*(m^*)M^*, \qquad (8)$$

where D and D^* denote state-independent components of demand in America and Japan, respectively, and λ_i and λ_i^* are state-dependent shift parameters; D and D^* are decreasing in P. The event (λ_A, λ_A^*) has probability one-half of occurrence, as does the event (λ_B, λ_B^*), and, in

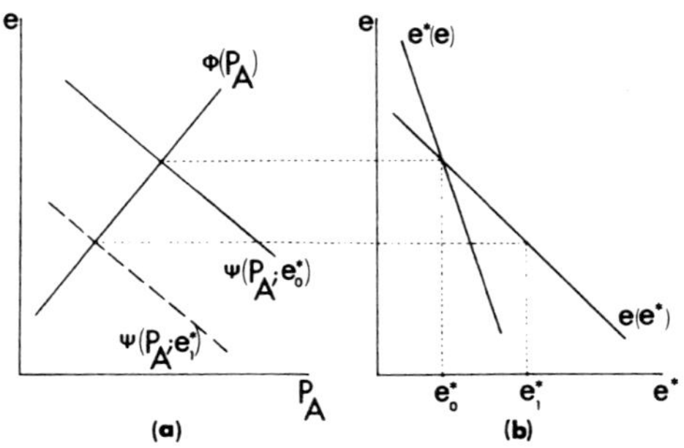

FIG. 2

order that state B unambiguously be the high-demand state, I assume that for all P, $\lambda_A D(P) + \lambda_A^* D^*(P) \leq \lambda_B D(P) + \lambda_B^* D^*(P)$. The randomness of demand might reflect uncertainty about private aggregate demands, future government policies, supply terms of competing steel from third countries or of substitutable goods, and so forth.

Equation (8) directly determines P_B, given the exogenous factor endowments. Equation (7), on the other hand, furnishes an implicit relation between P_A, e, and e^*. The ψ curves in figure 2*a* depict the relation between P_A and e for distinct values of e^*; each curve must have a negative slope and is steeper the greater the price elasticity of demand in both countries and the smaller the marginal product of American laborers. An increase in e^* shifts ψ down, from (7), so the curve $e(e^*)$ in figure 2*b*, generated by varying e^*, has a negative slope ($\phi[P_A]$ is drawn on the assumption that P_B equals the solution to [8]). This curve shows, for each e^*, that value of e that will simultaneously clear the international steel market in state A and also equilibrate American factor markets, given that P_B clears the international market in state B.

A similar analysis applied to Japan yields the curve $e^*(e)$ in figure 2*b*. Full international equilibrium is given by the intersection of the two schedules. The Appendix shows that $e^*(e)$ must cut $e(e^*)$ from above, as shown.

In state A steel is sold below cost, so whichever country exports steel in that state is a dumper. In state B steel is sold above cost so that no dumping takes place. Dumping thereby emerges as an integral part of international equilibrium.

I must stress that this dumping really looks like dumping: Steel is being sold below cost not only because firms are stuck with "too many" managers which they must pay in any event, but also because they restrain themselves in laying off laborers. The latter's wage exceeds the value of its marginal product. This restraint is, of course, in the perceived long-run interest of the firms, but it does make their behavior appear more aggressive than a strategy of minimizing losses in the face of fixed costs. The evolution of American antidumping law in recent years has been precisely in a direction to make that law especially sensitive to this sort of dumping: In testing for the presence of dumping the foreign transaction price cannot be used for comparison with the American sales price if the former is less than the cost of production, and when constructed values are instead used they must include general expenses equal to at least 10 percent of manufacturing cost plus a profit margin of at least 8 percent.

The present theory identifies three key determinants of dumping: international differences in laborer-manager endowments, the wage equivalents of unemployment in both countries, and the pattern of demand uncertainty. The remainder of this paper attempts to elucidate the role of each of these determinants.

IV. The Comparative Statics of Dumping: Japan and America in Phase

In order to isolate the influences of the major determinants, I shall assume that America and Japan are otherwise identical:[5] $D \equiv D^*$ and $f \equiv f^*$. A detailed analysis naturally depends on the stochastic process responsible for world demand for traded goods. Suppose first that the Japanese and American economies are in phase. A simple way to model this is to assume that $\lambda_B = \lambda^*_B = 1$ and $\lambda_A = \lambda^*_A = \lambda < 1$.

To establish a point of reference, suppose for a moment that Japan and America are completely identical, so that $m = m^*$ and $M = M^*$. Then $\phi \equiv \phi^*$ and ψ is symmetric in e and e^*. Thus $e(e^*)$ and $e^*(e)$ will be symmetric about the 45 degree line, so that in equilibrium $e = e^*$; equilibrium will be at point E in figure 3. Trade balances will equal zero in both states. Japan and America will be identical parallel economies.

I investigate first the influence of different factor endowments. The most direct way of doing this is to suppose that, from an initial "parallel" equilibrium, m is arbitrarily increased and m^* decreased an equal small amount. At the same time, reduce M and increase M^* so as to hold constant $f(m)M$ and $f(m^*)M^*$ (the purpose of this is to avoid confusing the effects of relative endowment differences with changes in relative sizes).

From equation (8), P_B will not be affected by such an endowment

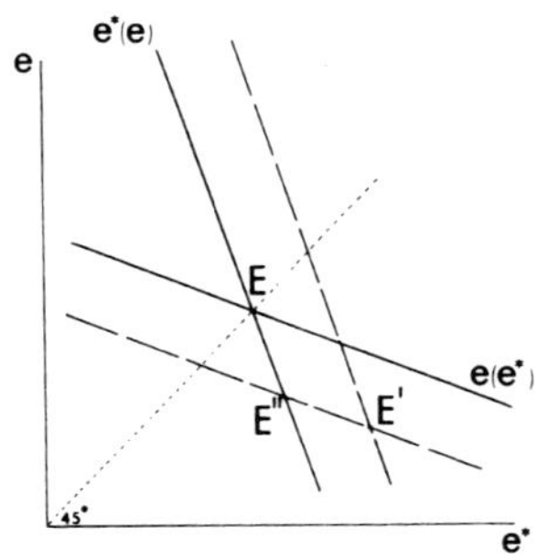

FIG. 3

[5] Because the distinction between M and L is social and legal as well as technological, the assumption of identical production functions does not have quite the same meaning here as in the Heckscher-Ohlin model.

change. Also, small changes will not shift ψ in a neighborhood of the original $e_0 = e_0^*$. It is clear from the previous analysis that ϕ will shift down, while ϕ^* shifts up by a like amount. The analysis of the previous section implies that this produces a downward shift of $e(e^*)$ and an equal rightward shift of $e^*(e)$, as depicted in figure 3. Equilibrium moves from E to E'.

Note first that the fall in e just equals the rise in e^* under the present assumptions. Thus from (7) and the initial assumed symmetry, P_A has the same value in the new equilibrium as in the old. Thus the demand for traded goods in each country, in each state, is unchanged.

If the American production of traded goods in state A is denoted $X_A = f(em)M$, then

$$\frac{dX_A}{dm} = Mf'(em)\left[e - \frac{f'(m)}{f'(em)}\frac{f(em)}{f(m)} + m\frac{de}{dm}\right].$$

For e close to unity, this term has the sign of de/dm (negative), but it becomes ambiguous for lower values of e. To economize on exposition I shall assume that dX_A/dm is negative and shall leave the symmetric analysis of the alternative, apparently perverse, case to the reader.

Assumption 6:

$$-\frac{m}{e}\frac{de}{dm} > 1 - \frac{mf'(m)/f(m)}{emf'(em)/f(em)}.$$

Under this assumption,[6] state A production of steel falls in America and rises in Japan. Steel production in state B is unchanged in both countries. Thus America has a trade deficit in state A and trade is balanced in state B: Japan dumps steel in America whenever the unfavorable state materializes, but America never dumps.

One might suggest that repercussions in other sectors of both economies would move trade toward balance, especially if steel represents all traded goods. This suggestion could be accommodated in extreme form by replacing $D(P_i)$ in (7) and (8) by $\mu D(P_i)$ for America and $\mu^* D(P_i)$ for Japan; μ and μ^* are shift parameters summarizing the effect of repercussions from the rest of each economy on its demand for steel. Initially $\mu = 1 = \mu^*$, and assume that, after the endowment change, $\mu + \mu^* = 2$ and $P_B[\mu D(P_B) - f(m)M] + P_A[\mu\lambda D(P_A) - f(em)M] = 0$. That is, the expected trade balance in steel must be zero. This modification would not change the earlier

[6] The term on the right-hand side of the inequality in assumption 6 is negative if and only if the elasticity of substitution of managers for laborers in f exceeds unity. Thus this is a sufficient but not necessary condition for the validity of the assumption, which can accordingly be interpreted as requiring that substitution possibilities between the factors not be "too limited."

analysis at all; the sole effect is that America would now have a trade deficit in state A and an equal-valued trade surplus in state B. In the latter case steel is sold above cost, so that America does not dump. Japan is still unambiguously identified as the dumper.

With P_A and P_B unchanged, equations (3) and (4) imply that the endowment change can be illustrated as a simultaneous upward movement of ee in figure 1 and downward movement of LL, and the reverse in Japan. The American wage may either rise or fall. But, since the slope of LL is gentler than $-V$, the ex ante employment opportunity facing American laborers deteriorates, even if those laborers that remain employed do in fact receive a higher wage. The indeterminacy of the wage results from the fact that the greater laborer-manager ratio reduces labor's marginal product at constant employment rates, but the lower employment rate, which is not applied also to managers, tends to raise that marginal productivity. For similar reasons the effect on salaries is ambiguous. The overall effect is deleterious: Prices are constant and output and employment fall in state A while not changing in state B. Opposite conclusions apply to Japan.

Additional perspective can be gained by investigating what would be the effects of the endowment change if international markets were not affected. Suppose again that Japan and America are initially identical in every way and that American antidumping legislation prevents Japanese dumping in state A and in effect forces balanced trade in both states. Then, for America, (7) and (8) are replaced by

$$\lambda D(P_A) = f(em)M, \tag{9}$$

$$D(P_B) = f(m)M. \tag{10}$$

The price P_B has the same value as before and, again, is uninfluenced by the hypothesized endowment change. Equation (9) can be solved, given the endowment, for a demand curve $e = d(P_A)$, depicted in figure 4. If m increases and M falls as hypothesized above, $\phi(P_A)$ shifts down as before. Then, as shown in figure 4, the resultant downward movement along the demand curve indicates that P_A rises, thereby stimulating the supply of steel in state A and cushioning the fall in e that would otherwise result from the increased relative supply of laborers. This is reinforced by a rightward shift of the demand curve implied by (9). The new (autarkic) equilibrium is point A in figure 4. Thus a closed economy with a greater laborer/manager ratio has less price variability across states and may also have less variability of the employment rate, depending on the shapes of the production and demand functions (it must have a higher absolute volume of unemployed labor in state A), than would a similar economy with a lower laborer/manager ratio.

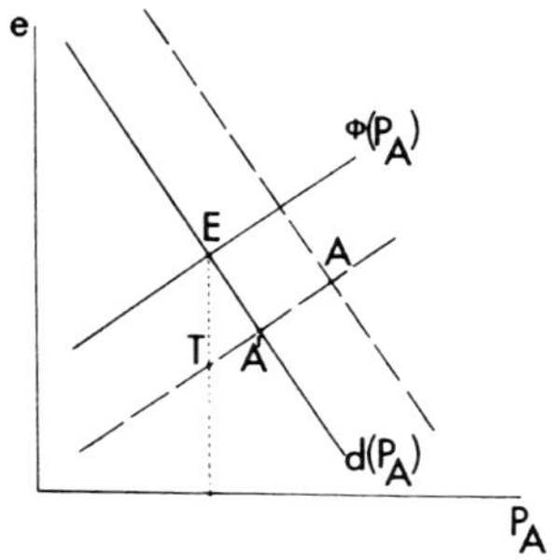

FIG. 4

But all this is changed if America and Japan are free to trade with each other. Since, as shown earlier, P_A will now not be influenced by the endowment change, American equilibrium moves from E to T rather than from E to A, and the opposite in Japan. Employment variations are accentuated in the relatively laborer-abundant country by Japanese imports which keep prices down in the low demand state. The opportunity to dump allows that country which is relatively more reliant on state-independent employment arrangements to limit fluctuations in the employment of those factors not subject to such arrangements by in effect exporting the fluctuations to countries with more flexible arrangements.

If America wishes to limit employment variations she clearly has an incentive to adopt protectionist measures to limit dumping. Just as clearly, if the Japanese have a preference for state-invariant employment conventions, the opportunity to dump could induce a more extensive use of such contracts.

Hasty conclusions about the desirability of protection must, however, be avoided. Since the present model essentially abstracts away the classical gains from trade, it also abstracts away the corresponding costs of protection. First-best policy presumably would involve measures to deal with the root causes of incomplete markets and/or demand variations; a normative evaluation of protection is impossible without a detailed analysis of the microeconomic foundations of the market conditions simply hypothesized in this paper. Since the profession certainly lacks a consensus on such an analysis, we must do without normative conclusions with any claim to generality. The role of protection at this stage is a form of the use of tariffs to deal with domestic distortions. Thus one is tempted to conjecture by analogy that, in the absence of direct measures, a small tariff would improve matters while the overall effects of a large tariff are ambiguous. The adoption of measures, such as an antidumping law, to focus protection more narrowly on the phenomenon at issue is certainly understandable. But note one important distinction between the present theory and the standard domestic-distortions argument. A higher laborer/manager ratio in a sense reflects a lower degree of domestic distortions, because managers differ from laborers only in that they are subject to an additional constraint on employment arrangements; thus the American difficulties stem not only from American distortions but also from a relative Japanese "abundance" of distortions.

Thus far I have examined the effects of one type of international variation in factor-market arrangements. A second possible variation involves the wage equivalent, denoted W, available to unemployed laborers in state A. Suppose, again, that America and Japan are initially identical in every way, so that equilibrium is at E in figure 3, and consider the effect of an increase in the American W. Such an increase would render unemployment less onerous and thereby reduce V, for given w and e. Differentiation of (3) and (4) reveals that this produces an upward shift in both the ee and LL curves in figure 1 but that ee shifts by more than does LL. Thus, at the initial steel prices, w rises and e falls, so that $\phi(P_A)$ in figure 2a shifts down, producing a downward shift in $e(e^*)$ in figure 2b. If W^* is maintained at its initial value, $e^*(e)$ is not affected. The effect of the rise in W is therefore a movement from E to E'' in figure 3.

An American attempt to increase the wage equivalent of unemployment induces the dumping of Japanese goods and increases the variability of American unemployment (although such unemployment is presumably less onerous). The increased opportunity to dump in America during unfavorable states reduces the variability of employment in Japan.

The international economy thereby exposes to foreign dumping countries which attempt to ameliorate unemployment by relatively high W's, and such attempts would accordingly be likely to induce demands for protection. Alternatively, the opportunity to dump abroad provides countries with an incentive to deal with employment variations by reducing W and/or increasing the proportion of factors categorizable as M rather than as L.

In this analysis W can include Trade Adjustment Assistance (TAA) if two conditions are met. First, equilibrium must be such that the country is a net importer of steel whenever W is in fact paid; this is true in the exercise just performed after the shift to point E''. Second, TAA must be reliable in the sense that the steel industry is confident in advance that it will be available should state A materialize. This has been reasonably so for American TAA for some multiyear periods but not for others. If W is interpreted as including TAA, the present analysis suggests surprising conclusions. The mere provision of TAA induces Japanese dumping and increases American employment variations! Furthermore, if the presence of dumping has the political effect of generating protectionist sentiment, the addition of *TAA* will increase such sentiment—just the opposite of its political intent and contrary to general belief. Lloyd (1977, p. 52), for example, states that "pressure for antidumping action following trade negotiations will only be reduced if adjustment assistance is provided in a form which is acceptable to producers (and their employees)."

V. Japan and America Symmetrically Out of Phase

Thus far I have assumed that the American and Japanese economies were in phase. The next step is to see how the modern theory works when they are out of phase. The simplest approach is to suppose that the economies are identical in every respect save demand for steel, wherein they are mirror images of each other. Thus, in (7) and (8), assume that: $\lambda_B = \lambda_A^* = 1$ and $\lambda_A = \lambda_B^* = \lambda < 1$. Under the assumption that $D(P_i)$ and $D^*(P_i)$ are identical, world demand will equal $(1 + \lambda)D(P_i)$ in both states; that is, the two states are essentially indistinguishable. The equilibrium will feature $P_A = P_B$ and $e = e^* = 1$.

America will have a trade surplus in state A and Japan an equal surplus in state B. In both cases steel will be sold at cost, so dumping never occurs. The effects of symmetric demand variability are completely neutralized by the ability of the two countries to run trade deficits and surpluses.

International differences in m would in this case have no effect, because the employment opportunities offered laborers in equilibrium are as certain as those offered managers. And because the employment of laborers is certain, the magnitudes of W and W^* also do not now matter, as long as they are not high enough to cause laborers to prefer unemployment.

VI. Japanese and American Asymmetry

The next step is to relax the assumption that demands in the two countries are perfectly symmetric. Suppose now that Japan and America are still out of phase but that demand fluctuations are more pronounced in Japan. In all other respects the two economies remain identical. Assume, then, that in (7) and (8) $\lambda_A = \lambda_B^* = 1$; $\lambda_B = \lambda < 1$; $\lambda_A^* = \alpha\lambda$, $\alpha < 1$. World demand now fluctuates across states with state B (American recession) the high-demand state. Then (7) and (8) become

$$D(P_A) + \alpha\lambda D(P_A) = f(em)M + f(e^*m)M, \tag{11}$$

$$\lambda D(P_B) + D(P_B) = f(m)M + f(m)M. \tag{12}$$

Equilibrium will now feature $e = e^* < 1$. In state A Japanese steel is dumped in America and in state B America has a trade surplus, with the steel sold above cost.[7] Were America to actually find herself in state A, the temptation of antidumping measures would be high: Laborers are unemployed in spite of high domestic demand, whereas Japan, the source of the deficiency of world demand, is maintaining an unemployment rate no lower than America's by dumping in the American market. But in state B America can achieve full employment while selling steel to Japan at a high price, so the overall attractiveness of the arrangement to America is ambiguous and depends on the actual values of α and λ. If α is nearly unity, the present case will not differ much from that of Section V, and the dominant consideration to America is the smoothing of fluctuations resulting from the opportunity to trade with an out-of-phase partner. But if λ were nearly unity and α small, America would find autarky attractive.

VII. Concluding Remarks

This paper has attempted to develop a modern theory of dumping to complement the traditional view of the phenomenon as an exercise in international price discrimination. The present theory, by contrast, views dumping as an integral part of the relationship between domestic factor markets and international commodity markets in a world of uncertainty and sluggish adjustment. In order to focus on essential points, the analysis has been based on certain stylized facts. The basic conclusions are therefore broadly consistent with alternative microeconomic theories explaining what this paper assumes. (However, the algebra of this paper need not be robust in detail. For example, one would want to abandon the simplification of risk-neutral firms were the foundation of this analysis specified as a form of "second generation" implicit contract theory stressing asymmetric information.) But further work should include a detailed welfare analysis and the consideration of commercial policy, and this requires that a specific microeconomic foundation be employed.

Two other extensions seem called for. I have already mentioned the incorporation of price discrimination to link the present theory to the traditional one. In addition, the present theory has interpreted uncertainty as demand uncertainty, whereas many contemporary problems seem related to changes in technological conditions.

Appendix

Factor-market equilibrium: The problem of the representative steel firm is to choose values of M, m, e, and w to maximize expected profit,

$$\tfrac{1}{2}M[P_A f(em) - s - wem] + \tfrac{1}{2}M[P_B f(m) - s - wm]$$

[7] This assumes that the expected trade balance in steel is zero. Description of alternative possibilities is straightforward.

subject to the condition that the $w-e$ combination be competitive:

$$U(w, e) = \bar{u}, \tag{A1}$$

where $U(w, e)$ is the implicit formula for laborers' indifference curves of w and e combinations.

The first-order conditions for this problem, which cannot of course specify the scale variable M, reduce to equations (1)–(4) in the text, with V defined as $-U_e/U_w$. In market equilibrium, m and M equal their exogenous supplies, and equations (1)–(4), of which only three are independent, together with (A1), determine equilibrium values of e, w, s, and $\bar{u}$.

Properties of V: Suppose that laborers are risk averse and that their preferences can be represented by a (strictly concave) utility function u. Then, for a given w, e, and W, the expected utility of a laborer is

$$½u(w) + ½\{u(w)F(e) + u(W)[1 - F(e)]\} \equiv U(w, e),$$

where $F(e)$ is the probability of being employed in state A, and $F'(e) > 0$. Define V to be $-(\partial w/\partial e)$, where expected utility is held constant. Thus

$$V = \frac{F'(e)}{1 + F(e)} \frac{u(w) - u(W)}{u'(w)}.$$

Assumption 5 then follows directly from the assumption $F(e) = e$, which would be true if the identity of unemployed workers in state A were determined by a random drawing from all hirees once the state of nature becomes known.

Figure 2*b*: The curve $e(e^*)$ in figure 2*b* is the solution of

$$e = \phi(P_A),$$
$$e = \psi(P_A; e^*),$$

from which

$$\frac{de}{de^*} = \frac{\phi' \psi_{e^*}}{\phi' - \psi_{P_A}}, \tag{A2}$$

where ϕ' is the derivative of ϕ and ψ_i the partial derivative of ψ with respect to i. We have $\phi' > 0$, and, from differentiation of (7), $\psi^*_e < 0$ and $\psi_{P_A} < 0$. Thus $e(e^*)$ has a negative slope. The Japanese curve $e^*(e)$ is the solution to

$$e^* = \phi^*(P_A),$$
$$e = \psi(P_A; e^*),$$

from which

$$\frac{de^*}{de} = \frac{\phi^{*\prime}}{\phi^{*\prime} \psi_{e^*} + \psi_{P_A}}. \tag{A3}$$

That $e^*(e)$ cuts $e(e^*)$ from above now follows directly from (A2) and (A3).

References

Azariadis, Costas. "Implicit Contracts and Underemployment Equilibria." *J.P.E.* 83, no. 6 (December 1975): 1183–1202.

Brander, James, and Krugman, Paul. "A 'Reciprocal Dumping' Model of International Trade." Mimeographed. Cambridge: Massachusetts Inst. Tech., 1980.

Bryan, Greyson. *Taxing Unfair International Trade Practices: A Study of U.S. Antidumping and Countervailing Duty Laws.* Lexington, Mass.: Heath, 1980.

Corden, W. M. *Trade Policy and Economic Welfare.* Oxford: Clarendon, 1974.

Gilbert, Milton. "A Sample Study of Differences between Domestic and Export Pricing Policies of United States Corporations." In *Investigations of Concentration of Economic Power,* U.S. Senate Temporary National Economic Committee. Washington: Government Printing Office, 1941.

Haberler, Gottfried von. *The Theory of International Trade with Its Applications to Commercial Policy.* Translated by Alfred Stonier and Frederic Benham. New York: Macmillan, 1937.

Kravis, Irving B., and Lipsey, Robert E. *Price Competitiveness in World Trade.* New York: Columbia Univ. Press (for Nat. Bur. Econ. Res.), 1971.

———. "Export Prices and the Transmission of Inflation." *A.E.R. Papers and Proc.* 67 (February 1977): 155–63.

Kudrle, Robert T. "A 'Reverse Dumping Duty' for Canada?" *Canadian J. Econ.* 7 (February 1974): 75–81.

Lloyd, Peter J. *Anti-dumping Actions and the GATT System.* Thames Essay no. 9. London: Trade Policy Res. Centre, 1977.

Löfgren, K. G. "Dumping, Devaluation and Monopoly Prices: A Generalization of Yntema's Results." *Rivista Internazionale Sci. Econ. Commerciali* 24 (August 1977): 658–67.

Robinson, Joan. *The Economics of Imperfect Competition.* London: Macmillan, 1933.

Tarr, David G. "Cyclical Dumping: The Case of Steel Products." *J. Internat. Econ.* 9 (February 1979): 57–63.

Viner, Jacob. *Dumping: A Problem in International Trade.* Chicago: Univ. Chicago Press, 1923.

———. "Dumping." In *Encyclopedia of the Social Sciences.* Vol. 5. New York: Macmillan, 1931.

Wares, William A. *The Theory of Dumping and American Commercial Policy.* Lexington, Mass.: Heath, 1977.

Yntema, Theodore O. "The Influence of Dumping on Monopoly Price." *J.P.E.* 36, no. 6 (December 1928): 686–98.

PART VII:
Some Topics in Trade Theory

Some Topics in Trade Theory: *Commentary*

This section includes some papers that I like but that do not fit naturally into the above categories.

(i) The theory of effective protection was a very active topic of inquiry in the 1970s, but it then quickly disappeared as a subject for theoretical research. I've been told that my paper, "The Theory of Effective Protection in General Equilibrium: Effective-Rate Analogues of Nominal Rates," was part of the reason. I doubt that. But in any case that was not my intent.

In August 1973, the *Journal of International Economics (JIE)* published a symposium on the theory of effective protection in general equilibrium. This included a paper by Jagdish Bhagwati and TN Srinivasan which dealt with ideas I had been in contact with Bhagwati about. I felt that justice had not been done to these ideas, so I prepared the paper reprinted here and submitted it to the *JIE*. The editor, none other than Bhagwati, said he would not accept it, but also said that he was sure that Harry Johnson would want it for the *Journal of Political Economy (JPE)*.

Young and naive, I followed Bhagwati's advice, and Johnson promptly rejected the paper. (In fairness to Johnson, I point out that he had previously accepted for the *JPE* another paper of mine—now completely forgotten—on the same topic of effective protection).

I then submitted the paper to the *Canadian Journal of Economics (JIE)*, which accepted it and published it. By then, Harry Johnson had died, at an unfairly young age. A Harry Johnson Prize was established to honor the best paper published in the *CJE* each year. My paper, which Harry himself had rejected, shared the prize in its first year. Sometimes things just turn out that way.

(ii) The formal academic discussion of globalization was largely concerned with explaining its apparent positive effect on the skilled-wage premium. The basic empirical conclusion was that trade liberalization (or globalization) was much less important an explanatory variable than the emergence of skill-biased technical change. This was reinforced by the fact that a Stolper-Samuelson explanation seemed confounded by the fact that the skill premium rose in both sides of the international market.

The paper, "Globalization, Globalisation: Trade, Technology and Wages," was motivated by the suspicion that changes in intra-sectoral substitution due to globalization were much more important than the traditional trade-theory, inter-sectoral substitutions. This led to my central argument that the skill-biased technical change did not come from god but was itself at least partly an endogenous effect of globalization.

(iii) As mentioned in the comments to (ii) above, there was in the 1980s a dominant erroneous view that comparative-advantage could not explain the large volume of trade in similar goods between similar countries. The logical error was just that the statement, "trade is due to differences between countries," does not imply that "the greater the differences, the greater the trade." But the theory of comparative advantage did seem to suggest that more differences meant more gains.

So I was motivated to address this in the paper, "The Greater the Differences, the Greater the Gains?" It's not for me to judge how successful I may have been, but this does seem to me one of the very fundamental issues in the theory of international trade that should have been addressed long ago.

I suspect that one of the reasons that I have a fondness for these three papers is that none was judged worthy of publication in a major journal. But if I had included all the papers that satisfied that criterion the present publication would look more like a library than a volume.

***

Well, this is what I have done with my life. Perhaps I should have done something more useful, like inventing a new flavor of ice cream. But anyway it is all transient. The Floating World.

Trade and Development Review
Vol. 2, Issue 2, 2009, 70-78
http://www.tdrju.net

The Greater the Differences, the Greater the Gains?♣

Wilfred J. Ethier♦

This paper addresses the fundamental question of whether, in a comparative-advantage context, the gains from trade will be greater when the differences between trading countries are greater. Such a presumption is established. The paper then discusses circumstances that could cause the presumption to fail.

JEL Classification: D60, F13, H20

Keywords: Trade gains, International differences

1. Introduction

In the late 1970s and early 1980s trade theorists devoted much effort to developing non-comparative-advantage models featuring economies of scale and imperfect competition. This development was explicitly motivated by accumulating empirical evidence emphasizing that the larger part of world trade consisted of the exchange of (relatively similar) manufactures between (relatively similar) industrial countries. One often heard statements like, "Comparative-advantage trade is trade to exploit differences, so this can't be comparative-advantage trade." Such statements were nonsense. It is true that, in a comparative-advantage world, if autarky relative prices do not differ much across countries, trade can produce only modest relative-price changes in each country. But such modest changes can induce large trade volumes if import price-elasticities are high enough, and it is exactly with trade between similar countries in similar goods that we would expect elasticities of substitution (and so import elasticities) to be the highest. This is illustrated in Figure 1, where highly elastic home import-demand (M) and foreign export-supply (X^*) relations produce a large volume of trade despite only modest differences in autarky relative prices.

♣ This paper was presented at the international seminar on "Gobalization, Agglomeration, and Inclusive Growth," May 21-22, 2009 at Jadavpur University, Kolkata, India. This paper exists because of the stimulation provided by Kemp and Tran-Nam (2007). Roy Ruffin contributed valuable comments.

♦ Department of Economics, University of Pennsylvania, Philadelphia, PA 19104-6297, USA. Email: ethier@econ.sas.upenn.edu

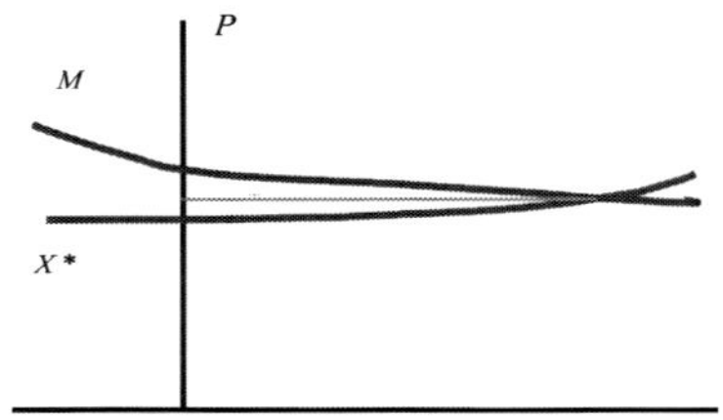

Figure 1: Volume of Trade

Figure 2 makes a similar point in the context of a Ricardian model, where the high elasticities come from substitution in production. Here, *A* and *A** denote autarky equilibrium in a situation where the two countries are pretty similar, and *B* and *B** autarky equilibrium in an alternative situation of very dissimilar countries. If tastes are the same in both cases, the free-trade equilibria, denoted *T* and *T** will be identical. Clearly, the volume of trade is the same when international differences are small as when they are huge, but the two situations differ dramatically regarding the *gains* from trade.

So, to our students we may say something like: "But it still matters whether this trade is due to comparative advantage rather than to something else. While comparative advantage need not imply 'the greater the differences, the greater the **trade**,' it does suggest '*the greater the differences, the greater the* ***gains***.' This suggests that the more important consequences of trade policies are those impacting trade between dissimilar countries, even though that may be a smaller part of world trade. But if this trade is due to something other than comparative advantage, all bets are off."

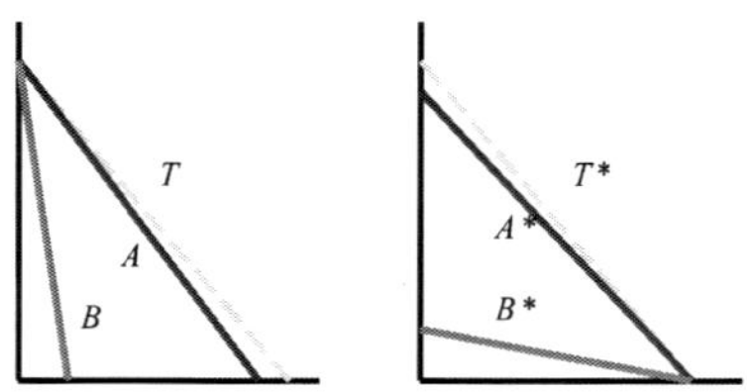

Figure 2: Volume of Trade in a Ricardian Model

But we can point our students to no formal proposition addressing the statement in italics! Instead we may present a few (well-chosen, we hope) examples. Such a proposition should be a fundamental part of comparative-advantage trade theory, comparable in importance to the comparative-advantage theorem itself. This paper investigates whether, in a comparative-advantage world, greater differences do imply greater gains. When greater differences imply greater trade, or when greater trade can be expected to be correlated with greater gains, is **not** addressed here.

2. The Framework

I wish to address the issue of *the greater the differences, the greater the gains* (**GD–GG**) in a framework of general differences, confined of course to a comparative-advantage context. Suppose a two-country, two-good, comparative-advantage world (perfect competition, no externalities) with a free-trade equilibrium described by:

$$M(P, \alpha) = X^*(P, \alpha), \qquad \textbf{(1)}$$

where M is home excess demand for good B, X^* foreign excess supply, and P the free-trade relative price of B in terms of A. Designate the country with the comparative advantage in A as the home country (so that M and X^* are positive). The vector α encompasses all parameters determining the degree of comparative advantage of the two countries: endowments, technology parameters, taste parameters, relevant government policies.

With so many parameters, it's desirable to restrict parameter changes in some way to ensure that comparisons are meaningful. A natural point of reference is a given free-trade equilibrium **(1)**. Consider the set of all possible changes $d\alpha$ that satisfy:

$$M_\alpha \bullet d\alpha = X^*_\alpha \bullet d\alpha \qquad \textbf{(r1)}$$

$$de + de^* = 0 \qquad \textbf{(r2)}$$

and,

$$P(\partial b_0/\partial\alpha + \partial b_0^*/\partial\alpha) + (\partial a_0/\partial\alpha + \partial a_0^*/\partial\alpha) \leq 0. \qquad \textbf{(r3)}$$

Here e and e^* denote home and foreign expenditure in the free-trade equilibrium, and (b_0, a_0) and (b_0^*, a_0^*) respectively denote home and foreign autarky production (= consumption) of the two goods. So **r1** and **r2** restrict attention to parameter changes that leave the world relative price and the world income (but not the international distribution of that income) unchanged in the free-trade equilibrium. The reason for **(r2)** is that a change in the size of the world economy would itself change the gains from trade, independently of whether the countries had become less alike or not, and the purpose of **(r3)** is to prevent the parameter change from eroding trade gains simply by enhancing the value of autarky. The roles of these constraints will be discussed later. The basic idea is to start with a given free-trade equilibrium and then ask whether the gains that that equilibrium generates are greater the greater the differences in the countries that are trading.

Consider **only** $d\alpha$ that satisfy **r1**, **r2** and **r3**. **(R)**

With the point of reference thus set, the next step is to specify what is meant by "greater differences" **(GD)**. I think that, in a comparative-advantage setting, the compelling candidate is simply autarky price differences. Autarky prices are given by

$$M(P_0, \alpha) = 0 = X^*(P_0^*, \alpha). \qquad \textbf{(2)}$$

Since the home country has the comparative advantage in A, $P_0 > P_0^*$. So a parameter change can be said to produce greater differences between the two countries if:

$d\alpha$ implies that $dP_0 > dP_0^*$. **(GD)**

Finally I must specify what I mean by "greater gains" **(GG)**. Measure the global gains from trade in the following conventional way.

$$G = e + e^* - (Pb_0 + a_0) - (Pb_0^* + a_0^*). \qquad \textbf{(3)}$$

If G is positive, world income with free trade is more than sufficient, at free trade prices, to purchase the world autarky consumption bundle. By "greater gains" I mean simply that G increases.

$d\alpha$ implies that $dG > 0$. **(GG)**

So, my criterion is that, globally, gainers gain more than losers lose. This is analogous to the basic gains-from-trade proposition of comparative advantage that, in each country, gainers gain more (strictly: not less) from trade than losers lose. Of course the literature has gone beyond that to investigate the existence of a lump-sum transfer scheme that would produce a Pareto improvement [see Kemp (1962), Samuelson (1962), Grandmont and McFadden (1972), and Kemp and Wan (1972)]. Also, Dixit and Norman (1980, pp 79, 80) have demonstrated the use of commodity and factor taxes and subsidies to generate a Pareto improvement. Analogously, I could now also ask what further restrictions on **R** might guarantee that all individuals gain, not just the world as a whole (while ruling out *international* lump-sum transfers). But I instead investigate only the more basic issue.

3. Analysis

So, now the stage is set to pose the basic question: When must a $d\alpha$ consistent with **R** and implying **GD** necessarily also imply **GG**? An answer comes fairly easily.

From **(2)**,

$$dP_0 = -\frac{M_\alpha^0 \bullet d\alpha}{M_{P^0}^0}, \qquad dP_0^* = -\frac{X_\alpha^{*0} \bullet d\alpha}{X_{P^{*0}}^{*0}}$$

Now, $X_{P^0}^{*0} > 0 > M_{P^0}^0$, since these expressions are evaluated at autarky where income effects wash out. Impose the following.

> **Assumption 1** Given $d\alpha$, $M_\alpha \bullet d\alpha$ has the same sign over all P for which $M \geq 0$, and $X_\alpha^* \bullet d\alpha$ has the same sign over all P for which $X^* \geq 0$.

Now, **r1** requires $M_\alpha \bullet d\alpha$ to have the same sign as $X_\alpha^* \bullet d\alpha$, in the initial free-trade equilibrium, and Assumption 1 ensures that this will be the same sign as that of $M_\alpha^0 \bullet d\alpha$ and $X_\alpha^{*0} \bullet d\alpha$. Because of the assumed pattern of comparative advantage, $P_0 > P_0^*$. If the signs of $M_\alpha^0 \bullet d\alpha$ and $X_\alpha^{*0} \bullet d\alpha$ are both positive, $dP_0 > 0$ and $dP_0^* < 0$, by **(4)**, whereas both signs being negative gives the opposite result. Thus, a $d\alpha$, consistent with **R**, causes **GD** with $dP_0 > 0$ and $dP_0^* < 0$, given Assumption 1, if it causes both terms to be negative.

So, given **GD**, differentiate **(3)**:

$$dG = de + de^* - P\left[\frac{\partial b_0}{\partial \alpha} + \frac{\partial b_0^*}{\partial \alpha}\right] - \left[\frac{\partial a_0}{\partial \alpha} + \frac{\partial a_0^*}{\partial \alpha}\right] - \left[P\frac{\partial b_0}{\partial P_0} + \frac{\partial \alpha_0}{\partial P_0}\right]dP_0 - \left[P\frac{\partial b_0^*}{\partial P_0^*} + \frac{\partial \alpha_0^*}{\partial P_0^*}\right]dP_0^*$$

$$\geq -\left[P\frac{\partial b_0}{\partial P_0} + \frac{\partial \alpha_0}{\partial P_0}\right]dP_0 - \left[P\frac{\partial b_0^*}{\partial P_0^*} + \frac{\partial \alpha_0^*}{\partial P_0^*}\right]dP_0^*$$

$$= \left[(P_0 - P)\frac{\partial b_0}{\partial P_0} \right] dP_0 - \left[(P - P_0^*)\frac{\partial b_0^*}{\partial P_0^*} \right] dP_0^*$$

The inequality in **(5)** follows from **r2** and **r3** and the second equality from the production envelope theorem valid in comparative-advantage models.

The terms $(P_0 - P)$ and $(P - P_0^*)$ are both non-negative, with at least one strictly positive, since the home economy has a comparative advantage in A. Production substitution in a comparative-advantage world implies that db_0/dP_0 and db_0^*/dP_0^* are both positive (assuming we are not confined to an endowment model). Finally, **r1** and Assumption 1 give **GD** with $dP_0 > 0$ and $dP_0^* < 0$. Thus $dG > 0$.

Proposition 1 Given Assumption 1, any da consistent with **R** that implies **GD** also implies **GG**.

Proposition 1 establishes a "presumption" that, indeed, the greater the differences, the greater the gains.

4. Discussion

Proposition 1 gives only a presumption because it depends upon Assumption 1 and, also, on how the problem is defined by **R**. In particular, the requirements **r2** and **r3** restrict the domain of relevance of Proposition 1. This section addresses circumstances that could cause the presumption to fail, that is, circumstances under which greater differences do *not* cause greater gains.

Inferiority

We have an opportunity for counterexamples to **GD–GG** if we dispense with Assumption 1. Assumption 1 says that the parameter change should shift the import-demand (export-supply) curve unambiguously in one direction or another. This is true in most of the standard exercises. But sufficient inferiority in consumption could produce violations. Suppose, for example, that imports are very inferior. Then a parameter change that caused an economy to want to import more near autarky, where income effects basically wash out, might cause it to want to consume less in free trade, with significant income effects.

Figure 3 illustrates how a failure of Assumption 1 might vitiate the presumption. The initial equilibrium is at E with free-trade relative price P'. The parameter change $d\alpha$ shifts the initial M and X^* schedules to M' and $X^{*\prime}$, respectively, with the equilibrium moving to E'. The free-trade price remains at P', as required by **(R)**. Both autarky prices rise, but P_0 rises more than P_0^*, so **(GD)** is satisfied. This is possible because X^* shifts to the left near autarky but to the right with a higher volume of trade, that is, X^* "twists" as a result of the parameter change. Foreign inferiority in the consumption of B could cause this: Near autarky the income gain from trading more could raise foreign consumption of B, leaving less for export, whereas at the higher income levels produced by larger trade gains foreign consumers purchase less of the inferior B, leaving more for export. The last two terms on the right-hand side of **(5)** now work to cross purposes, and the last term will dominate if $P - P_0^*$ is large enough relative to $P_0 - P$, that is, if trade is sufficiently more valuable to the foreign economy than to the home economy. (The figure shows $P - P_0^*$ larger than $P_0 - P$).[1]

Assumption 1 is only a sufficient condition, not a necessary one. So the suggestion is that while counterexamples are unlikely to be important, they do exist, and they would likely (but not necessarily) involve significant inferiority in consumption. This is consistent with the message delivered by Kemp and Tran-Nam (2009).

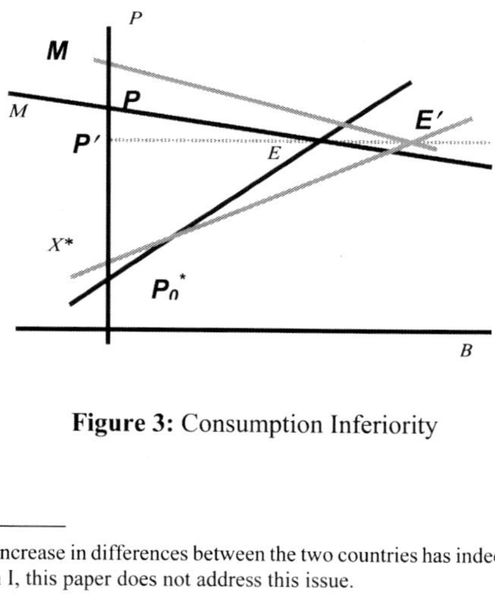

Figure 3: Consumption Inferiority

1. Note that, in Figure 3, the increase in differences between the two countries has indeed increased the volume of trade. But, as mentioned in Section I, this paper does not address this issue.

The Heckscher-Ohlin-Samuelson model

Perhaps more interesting, though, is the role played by **R**, especially by **r2**. Note that, if $de + de^* > 0$, the above logic is not affected (indeed, reinforced), so that Proposition 1 still holds. Thus **r2** can be generalized to $de + de^* \geq 0$.

So, suppose that a $d\alpha$, consistent with **r1** and implying **GD**, also implies that $de + de^* < 0$. In this case, the above logic still implies that, with **GD**, the world does gain relative to the *initial* free-trade world income, but that the actual free-trade world income falls, leaving the net gain from trade indeterminate.

For a concrete example, consider the textbook Heckscher-Ohlin-Samuelson world with two countries that, except for endowments, are identical, including identical homothetic tastes. Let Assumption 1 hold, and consider the role of **R**.

Suppose that with free trade both countries are in a common free-trade diversification cone. Then a transfer of capital from one country to the other, provided it leaves both in the diversification cone, clearly satisfies **r1** and **r2**. Consecutive transfers of capital from the labor-abundant country to the capital-abundant one make the two countries more dissimilar. Also, such transfers move capital from the country where, in autarky, its marginal productivity is higher to where it is lower, so that **r3** is also satisfied. Thus such transfers satisfy Proposition 1 and consecutively increase the gains from trade, as long as both countries remain in the diversification cone.[2]

But when at least one country leaves that cone, the free-trade equilibrium will feature specialization by at least one country. Then a further transfer of capital from the labor-abundant country to the capital-abundant one, which would increase even more the international disparity in relative factor endowments, would now also shift capital from where, with free trade, its marginal product is now relatively high to where it is now relatively low, thus lowering world income with free trade at the initial P. Thus **r2** fails while **r3** still holds. On balance, the net gain from trade could either rise or fall.

The moral seems to be that, if free trade features specialization, trade has not been sufficient to counteract completely the effect of national borders. Thus making countries even more dissimilar accentuates the negative effect of those borders in the trading equilibrium. This is a significant

2. Note that, in this case also, such transfers do increase the volume of trade.

qualification to the **GD-GG** presumption, perhaps more important than counter-examples involving departures from Assumption 1. And **r2** is very useful in exposing the argument.
In principle, a failure of **r3** could also vitiate the prediction of Proposition 1. But I have been unable to find any significant counter-examples. The HOS model discussed in this section satisfies **r3**, as does the Ricardian example illustrated in Figure 2.

Understanding the qualifications to the presumption facilitates a judgment about when it is most likely to be pertinent. For example, trade between rich countries tends to feature substitution effects that are strong relative to income effects and much diversification in national production. So the presumption established by Proposition 1 can be expected to be high in this context.

5. Concluding Remarks

I have addressed the fundamental question of whether, in a comparative-advantage context, the gains from trade will be greater when the differences between trading countries are greater. When the question is formalized in what I regard as the natural way, such a presumption does indeed hold, but it is not a certainty. Two sets of plausible circumstances could cause the presumption to fail: large income effects relative to substitution effects combined with significant inferiority in consumption, and specialization in production under free trade.

References

1. Dixit, A. K. and V. Norman (1980). Theory of International Trade, Cambridge, UK: Cambridge University Press.
2. Grandmont, J. M. and D. McFadden (1972). A Technical Note on Classical Gains from Trade. Journal of International Economics, 2, 109–125.
3. Kemp, M. C. (1962). The Gain from International Trade. Economic Journal, 72, 803–819.
4. Kemp, M. C. and H. Y. Wan (1972). The Gains from Free Trade. International Economic Review. 13, 509–522.
5. Kemp, M. C. and B. Tran-Nam (2009). On Trade Gains and International Disparities in Factor Proportions? In: Kamihigashi, T. And L. Zhao, eds., International Trade and Economic Dynamics: Essays in Memory of Koji Shimomura, Springer: NY.
6. Samuelson, P. A. (1962). The Gains from International Trade Once Again. Economic Journal, 72, 820–829.

Trade and Development Review, Vol. 2, Issue 2, 2009

ELSEVIER International Review of Economics and Finance 14 (2005) 237–258

International Review of Economics & Finance

www.elsevier.com/locate/econbase

Globalization, globalisation: Trade, technology, and wages

Wilfred J. Ethier*

Department of Economics, University of Pennsylvania, United States

Accepted 15 December 2004
Available online 19 January 2005

Abstract

I address a complex of globalization issues: the effect of globalization on the skill premium; on unemployment; on the ability of national governments to conduct independent social policies; the relative importance of globalization and exogenous technical change. A large empirical literature concludes that trade has played a relatively minor role, relative to skill-biased technical change, in the rise of the skill premium. This paper replaces the Stolper–Samuelson theorem's focus on inter-sectoral with attention to intra-sectoral relations between inputs. Specifically, I assume out-sourcing and unskilled labor are highly substitutable, equipment and skilled labor are complementary, production methods are flexible, and that the country undertaking out-sourcing has a significantly different structure from that providing it. Globalization then offers a simple and immediate possible explanation for prominent stylized facts regarding the skill premium *and* the presence of skill-biased technical change.

JEL classification: F02
Keywords: Fragmentation; Equipment utilization; Out-sourcing; Input substitution; Input complementarity

GLOBALIZATION-TALK makes me puke. You just can't get away from it. So I've decided to stop trying and to investigate, in this paper, four basic issues central to globalization.

* Tel.: +1 215 898 5105; fax: +1 215 573 4217.
E-mail address: ethier@econ.upenn.edu.

1059-0560/$ - see front matter
doi:10.1016/j.iref.2004.12.001

1. Introduction

What is globalization? Presumably a reduction in the barriers – whether technological or legislative – to economic exchanges between nations. But the consequences of this have been the central focus of trade theory from its very beginning. So what's new here? I perceive three new foci of concern.

- i The reduction in barriers has proceeded to the point where the increasingly widespread practice of international out-sourcing (also known as "slicing up the value-added chain," "fragmentation," or "production sharing") has become of fundamental practical significance, especially with respect to the wages of less skilled workers.
- ii It has become possible quickly to adjust production methods globally in response to changes in the economic environment.
- iii The historic GATT–WTO multilateral trade liberalization has, since World War II, focused mainly on the exchange of industrial goods between (relatively similar) advanced economies. But in the last 10–15 years less advanced and formerly communist nations have attempted fundamental economic reform and are struggling to become part of the multilateral system. This raises the prospect of a reallocation of global production more fundamental than that experienced thus far in the post World War II period.

I endorse all these concerns. But, from the standpoint of abstract trade theory (and I am an unabashedly abstract trade theorist), they are matters of degree rather than of kind. Therefore, in what follows, I also approach globalization from the viewpoint of the concerns[1] and issues associated with it. I will address in particular four of these.

1 *Globalization and the skill premium.* In recent decades wages of skilled workers have risen relative to those of the less skilled both substantially and globally.[2] The supposed link of this phenomenon to globalization has generated wide public comment, and investigation by academics of such a link constitutes probably the single largest part of the formal globalization literature.
2 *Unemployment.* Continental European countries have also experienced significant increases in rates of persistent unemployment of unskilled workers. This is widely thought to be a manifestation, in countries with distinct labor-market institutions and government social policies, of the phenomenon underlying the rise in the skill premium. Thus, its relation to globalization is a natural question to pursue.[3]
3 *Technology.* Much empirical work has investigated skill-biased technical change as a possible explanation for the rise in the skill premium and in unemployment. Usually such technical change and globalization have been treated as exogenous alternatives, but it is natural to want to investigate possible relations between the two.[4]

[1] See Rodrik (1997) for a good expression of globalization concerns.
[2] For the U.S., see Katz and Autor (1999).
[3] Davidson and Matusz (2001) address employment consequences of globalization. For the contrast between the U.S. and continental Europe, see Davis (1998) and Sapir (2000).
[4] For this see Falvey and Reed (2000), Feenstra and Hanson (1996), Jones (1997), and Neary (2001a).

4 *Independent national social policies.* One of the most prominent public concerns about globalization is its possible erosion or destruction of the ability of individual national governments to pursue distinct social objectives. Suppose that (unspecified) policies exist that allow a government to trade off increased unskilled unemployment for greater wage equality between the skilled and the unskilled. I address two questions. What effect does increased globalization have on the terms of this trade-off? How does globalization affect the ability of different countries to achieve distinct trade-offs?

The next section argues that an appropriate model to address these issues should emphasize certain features. I then present a model doing just that. Following sections analyze globalization, modeled to reflect the first two of the above foci, from the perspective of an economy able to transact on fixed terms with the rest of the world. The next two sections then provide a two-country international analysis, reflecting the last of the three above foci. The concluding section concludes.

2. Globalization building blocks

A simple trade-based hypothesis explaining the rise in the skill premium employs the standard two-factor, two-sector, Heckscher–Ohlin–Samuelson (HOS) model with the factors identified as skilled and unskilled labor. An increased export of unskilled-labor intensive goods from the unskilled-labor abundant country could then induce, via the familiar Stolper–Samuelson mechanism, an increase in the real wage of skilled workers and a decrease in that of unskilled workers in the skilled-labor abundant country. An alternative hypothesis posits, in the same 2×2 model, *exogenous* skill-biased technical change in both sectors, inducing firms to substitute skilled for unskilled labor.

A large empirical literature has addressed the trade vs. technology debate[5] and, for the most part, has found the trade explanation lacking.[6] This has largely been the result of three empirical regularities that have emerged from the literature. **i** There has not been a significant increase in the relative price of skilled-labor intensive goods. **ii** The ratio of the employment of skilled labor to that of unskilled labor has *risen* in all sectors rather than fallen, and there is little evidence of the inter-sectoral movements of both that are central to the Stolper–Samuelson explanation. **iii** The rise in the skill premium is not confined to countries that are net importers of unskilled-labor intensive goods, but appears to be a global phenomenon.

These regularities do not square with the Stolper–Samuelson story. Neary (2001a, 2001b) argues that they also do not sit well with exogenous skill-biased technical change in the 2×2 model, and he responds by introducing oligopolistic competition. Epifani and Gancia (2002) introduce inter-sectoral differences in economies of scale and high consumption substitution. An equally reasonable response is to hypothesize that inter-sectoral differences in technology – the very heart of the HOS model – have in practice little importance for the relation between trade and wages (or technology and wages). This paper follows the latter route.

---

[5] See Bound and Johnson (1992), Desjonqueres, Machin, and van Reenan (1999), Feenstra and Hanson (2001), Francois and Nelson (1998), Johnson and Stafford (1999), Lawrence and Slaughter (1993), and Slaughter (1998).

[6] But see Dasgupta and Osang (2002), Feenstra and Hanson (1996), Leamer (1998), and Wood (1994) for accounts giving trade more significance.

More precisely, I wish to minimize the role of *inter-sectoral* technology differences and concentrate instead on the *intra-sectoral* ease of substitution (or lack thereof) between inputs. To this end, I adopt a model in which all firms can use the same techniques. As I also assume constant returns to scale, this amounts to adopting an aggregate production function. The purpose of international trade in this model is to allow an international fragmentation of the production process. Thus, the model is consistent with the approach forcefully (and, in my view, convincingly) advocated by Feenstra and Hanson (1996, 2001). Although empirical work in trade has tended to take the HOS model as its point of departure, trade theory has for decades given much attention to the international, intra-sectoral, allocation of the production process.[7] Recent examples include Arndt and Kierzkowski (2001), Burda and Dluhosch (2001), Glass and Saggi (2001), and Jones (2000).

The suppression of inter-sectoral distinctions is one of the building blocks of this paper. Another is its treatment of the intra-sectoral relation between inputs. There are three aspects to this. First, focus **i** of concern about globalization (fragmentation) will be addressed by assuming a high degree of substitution in production between unskilled labor and out-sourcing. Second, the idea that skilled labor and equipment are complements, prominent since Griliches (1969), will be stressed here.[8] Third, to keep these first two aspects in clear relief, I also assume intermediate substitutability of equipment and skilled labor for unskilled labor and outsourcing.

Equipment must be provided for from output. As another building block of this paper, I incorporate the second focus of concern (quick global adjustment of production methods) by allowing firms to choose freely, in equilibrium, their degree of equipment utilization. I also allow the possibility of neutral, exogenous, technical change. However, assuming that equipment utilization is a choice variable, together with the assumption that equipment is complementary to skilled labor but substitutable for unskilled labor, allows the possibility of *endogenous* skill-biased technical change. A decision to utilize more equipment is a decision to switch to a more skill-biased technology.

The final building block accommodates the third focus of concern (the fuller entry into the multilateral system of countries with different economies) by considering trade between countries that differ significantly. In particular, I consider a two-country model in which one country, that can out-source part of the production process and can also supply equipment, trades with another country, that can provide out-sourcing but not equipment.

3. The home economy: small-country version

I use the following aggregate production function.

$$AF(U,V,E,S) = A[U^{\gamma} + V^{\gamma}]^{\frac{\alpha}{\gamma}}[E^{\sigma} + S^{\sigma}]^{\frac{1-\alpha}{\sigma}} \tag{1}$$

Here A indexes total factor productivity (TFP), U denotes the employment of unskilled labor, and V is a measure of the quantity of tasks out-sourced abroad. The economy possesses a stock U_0 of unskilled

[7] For a personal example, Ethier (1979, 1982, 1986, 1998) all assigned a central role to international production sharing. More generally, the theoretical literature on trade in intermediate goods, middle products, etc. is very large, and has been so for decades.

[8] See also Bergstrom and Panas (1992), Fallon and Layard (1975) and Krusell, Ohanian, Rios-Rull, and Violante (2000). The present paper draws especially on the latter reference.

labor: $U_0 - U$ equals unemployment. E denotes the stock of equipment and S that of skilled labor. This functional form has been chosen to focus directly on the degree of substitutability between inputs.

The central maintained hypothesis of this paper is the following.

$$1 > \gamma > 0 > \sigma \tag{H1}$$

The assumption $\sigma < 0$ is that E and S are complements;[9] $\gamma > 0$ means that U and V are substitutes; $1 > \gamma$ means that there are diminishing returns to out-sourcing: Some tasks can be more easily out-sourced than others. The Cobb–Douglas relation between the $U - V$ and $E - S$ sub-aggregates implies that U and V are more substitutable for each other than for E or S.

The services of V must be paid for with exports.

$$X = \frac{v^*}{g} V \tag{2}$$

The foreign price for effective units of V is v^*, and g is the "globalization index." It indexes the extra cost of foreign out-sourcing (because of legal restrictions, cultural differences, trade barriers, communication cost, etc.). I assume $1 \geq g \geq 0$. A higher value of g reflects more globalization. Thus, nationally owned output (income) equals

$$y = AF - \frac{w^*}{g} V. \tag{3}$$

For simplicity, I assume that incomplete globalization, $(1-g)/g$, reflects only real costs such as those of transport, communication, administration, and so on, and therefore generates no tax revenue to be accounted for.

Equipment services E require that a portion of output be devoted to investment I:

$$I = \frac{E}{Q}, \tag{4}$$

where Q measures the technology for providing equipment services. Consumption c accordingly equals output minus investment minus exports.

$$c = AF(U, V, E, S) - \frac{E}{Q} - \frac{v^*}{g} V \tag{5}$$

Next, I define two critical endogenous variables. First the "fragmentation index" f:

$$f \equiv \frac{V^\gamma}{U^\gamma + V^\gamma}.$$

Here $1 > f \geq 0$; f measures the relative importance of out-sourcing to the $U - V$ sub-aggregate. The second is the "equipment utilization index" e.

$$e \equiv \frac{S^\sigma}{E^\sigma + S^\sigma}$$

9 Alternative definitions of complementarity are in the literature. In this paper I *define* complementarity between E and S to mean $\sigma < 0$.

Here $1>e>0$; e measures the relative importance of equipment in the $E-S$ sub-aggregate. Differentiating these definitions yields the following.

$$\frac{V}{f}\frac{\mathrm{d}f}{\mathrm{d}V} = \gamma(1-f)$$

$$\frac{U}{f}\frac{\mathrm{d}f}{\mathrm{d}U} = -\gamma(1-f)$$

$$\frac{E}{e}\frac{\mathrm{d}e}{\mathrm{d}E} = -\sigma(1-e)$$

Thus, an increase in V or a decrease in U raises f if and only if $\gamma>0$. V measures out-sourcing and f indexes the extent that this *displaces* U, given that the two are substitutes. Were $\gamma<0$, the relevant fragmentation index would be $1-f$.

Similarly, e responds positively to an increase in E if and only if $\sigma<0$. Were $\sigma>0$, the relevant equipment utilization index would be $1-e$.

3.1. *Input prices*

Assuming competitive markets in which inputs receive the values of their marginal products, the following input pricing relations apply.

$$w = AF_U = \alpha\frac{AF}{U}(1-f) \tag{6}$$

$$\frac{v^*}{g} = AF_V = \alpha\frac{AF}{V}f \tag{7}$$

$$\frac{1}{Q} = AF_E = (1-\alpha)\frac{AF}{E}(1-e) \tag{8}$$

$$s = AF_S = (1-\alpha)\frac{AF}{S}e \tag{9}$$

Here w denotes the wage paid to unskilled labor U and s that of skilled labor. Thus, the *skill premium* $\pi=s/w$.

This model contains three pairs of exogenous variables.

Endowments: U_0 and S
Trade parameters: v^*, g
Technology parameters: A, Q.

The endogenous variables are y, V, E, s, π (or w), and U. Given the exogenous variables, the equilibrium conditions determine y, V, E, s, and a relation between π (or w), and U. The government pursues an active social policy which causes it to choose a particular $\pi-U$ combination from those available.

4. Globalization, out-sourcing, and fragmentation

Before getting into more detail, I first look at what can be said thus far about the skill premium π.

4.1. A preliminary look at the skill premium

From the input pricing relations,

$$\pi = \frac{1-\alpha}{\alpha}\frac{U}{S}\frac{e}{1-f}. \tag{10}$$

As expected, the skill premium responds positively to an increase in the employment U of unskilled labor and negatively to an increase in the stock S of skilled labor. It also responds positively to an increase in e or in f. Recall that e is an appropriate index of equipment utilization if and only if $\sigma<0$ and that f is an appropriate index of fragmentation if and only if $\gamma>0$.

Proposition 1. *An increase in equipment utilization will raise the skill premium if and only if skilled labor and equipment are complements ($\sigma<0$). An increase in fragmentation will raise the skill premium if and only if unskilled labor and out-sourcing are substitutes ($\gamma>0$).*

The following corollary is immediate.

Proposition 2. *An increase in the stock S of skilled labor can coincide with an increase in the skill premium if also accompanied by a sufficient increase in the index of equipment utilization or in the index of fragmentation, provided that $\sigma<0$ and/or $\gamma>0$.*

These results are preliminary in the sense that e and f are endogenous variables, and they are jointly determined in equilibrium. I turn to this next, but first note the elementary bottom-line implication of (10).

Proposition 3. *Given α, U, and S, changes in technology or in trade will influence the skill premium solely through their effect on equipment utilization and on fragmentation.*

4.2. Equilibrium out-sourcing

Differentiation of the equilibrium pricing condition for out-sourcing implies the following.

$$\varepsilon_{VV}\hat{V} - \varepsilon_{VU}\hat{U} - \varepsilon_{VE}\hat{E} = \hat{A} + \hat{g} - \hat{v}^* \tag{11}$$

Here $\varepsilon_{VV} \equiv -\frac{VF_{VV}}{F_V} = 1 - [\alpha f + \gamma(1-f)] > 0$, $\varepsilon_{VE} \equiv \frac{EF_{VE}}{F_V} = (1-\alpha)(1-e) > 0$, and $\varepsilon_{VU} = \frac{UF_{VU}}{F_V} = (\alpha-\gamma)(1-f)$.

Thus, given the exogenous parameters (the right-hand side equals zero), an increase in equipment utilization ($\hat{E}>0$) implies more out-sourcing ($\hat{V}>0$), given the volume of employment ($\hat{U}=0$). More E increases the productivity of V, so the volume of the latter must also increase to hold constant the value of its marginal product.

But employment U plays a more complex role. An increase in U increases F, and, therefore, the share, αF, that goes to U and V together, but it also reduces the portion f of this that goes to V. The latter effect dominates if and only if $\gamma>\alpha$; in this case an increase in U must be accompanied by a reduction in V to maintain the value of the latter's marginal product.

Proposition 4. *Given the cost of out-sourcing and TFP, an increase in equipment utilization implies more out-sourcing; an increase in employment implies less or more out-sourcing according as γ exceeds or falls short of α.*

4.3. Equilibrium equipment utilization

Differentiation of the equilibrium pricing condition for equipment utilization implies the following.

$$\varepsilon_{EE}\hat{E} - \varepsilon_{EV}\hat{V} - \varepsilon_{EU}\hat{U} = \hat{A} + \hat{Q} \tag{12}$$

Here $\varepsilon_{EE} \equiv -\frac{EF_{EE}}{F_E} = \alpha(1-e) + e(1-\sigma) > 0$, $\varepsilon_{EV} \equiv \frac{VF_{EV}}{F_E} = \alpha f > 0$, and $\varepsilon_{EU} \equiv \frac{UF_{EU}}{F_E} = \alpha(1-f) > 0$. Thus, given the level of technology, an increase of either employment or out-sourcing requires an increased use of equipment to maintain the value of the latter's marginal product.

Proposition 5. *Given the price of equipment and the level of technology, an increase in either out-sourcing or employment implies an increase in equipment utilization.*

4.4. The elasticity of demand for unskilled labor

From (6) the elasticity of the demand for unskilled labor is

$$-\frac{w}{U}\frac{\partial U}{\partial w} = \frac{1}{(1-\gamma) + (\gamma - \alpha)(1-f)} \equiv \frac{1}{\varepsilon_{EE}}.$$

Thus, the following is immediate.

Proposition 6. *A higher level of fragmentation is associated with a more elastic demand for unskilled labor if and only if $\gamma > \alpha$.*

The possibility and consequences of globalization making the demand for unskilled labor more elastic is discussed in Rodrik (1997); Slaughter (2001) provides interesting empirical support.

4.5. The relation of the skill premium to globalization and to technical change

Eqs. (11) and (12) imply, after some algebra, the following.

$$\varepsilon\hat{V} = (\varepsilon_{VE} + \varepsilon_{EE})\hat{A} + \varepsilon_{VE}\hat{Q} + \varepsilon_{EE}(\hat{g} - \hat{v}^*) + \eta_V\hat{U}$$

$$\varepsilon\hat{E} = (\varepsilon_{EV} + \varepsilon_{VV})\hat{A} + \varepsilon_{VV}\hat{Q} + \varepsilon_{EV}(\hat{g} - \hat{v}^*) + \eta_E\hat{U} \tag{13}$$

Here,

$$\eta_V \equiv \varepsilon_{VE}\varepsilon_{EU} + \varepsilon_{EE}\varepsilon_{VU}$$

$$\eta_E \equiv \varepsilon_{VV}\varepsilon_{EU} + \varepsilon_{EV}\varepsilon_{VU}$$

$$\varepsilon \equiv \varepsilon_{EE}\varepsilon_{VV} - \varepsilon_{EV}\varepsilon_{VE} = \alpha(1-e)(1-\gamma)(1-f) + e(1-\sigma)[f(1-\alpha) + (1-\gamma)(1-f)]$$

Thus, $\varepsilon > 0$. Any sort of technological progress or any reduction in the cost of out-sourcing will increase both equipment utilization and out-sourcing. Then, Propositions 1 and 3 imply the following.

Proposition 7. *Given the level of employment, either an increase in globalization or any sort of technology improvement will increase the skill premium, provided that skilled labor and equipment are complements and that unskilled labor and out-sourcing are substitutes.*

Globalization increases out-sourcing, which is substitutable for unskilled labor and therefore exerts downward pressure on the latter's wage. Since out-sourcing implies trade, trade will appear to be the cause. But globalization also increases equipment utilization; since equipment is complementary to skilled labor, this will put upward pressure on the latter's wage. This second effect will *appear* as skill-biased technical change: It shifts the production relation between U and S in such a way as to induce firms, at initial wages, to substitute skilled for unskilled labor. But this shift is itself the result of globalization. Hypothesis (H1) is obviously central to this result. Similar comments apply to the effects of an increase in TFP (unbiased technical change).

4.6. The relation of equipment utilization and out-sourcing to employment

The influence of employment is more complex. Looking first at the effect of employment on out-sourcing,

$$\eta_V = (1 - f)\{e[(1 - \sigma)(\alpha - \gamma)] + (1 - e)\alpha(1 - \gamma)\}. \tag{14}$$

The expression on the right is necessarily negative if γ is sufficiently close to 1 and necessarily positive if γ is sufficiently close to 0 (or negative).

Proposition 8. *Given the technology and the external variables, an increase in employment will reduce out-sourcing if U and V are highly substitutable but will increase out-sourcing if they are not.*

Look next at the effect on equipment utilization.

$$\eta_E = \alpha(1 - f)(1 - \gamma) > 0 \tag{15}$$

Proposition 9. *Given the technology and the external variables, an increase in employment will increase equipment utilization.*

5. Social policy

Assume that social policy is driven by an egalitarian need to limit the skill premium π plus a need to maximize employment U. The government's preferences are convex: Successive increases in the skill premium must be accompanied by successively larger increases in employment to leave the government indifferent. I also assume that the government is aware of the relation between the two and possesses policy instruments that enable it to choose whatever $\pi - U$ combination it most prefers. Thus, the key question is the effect of globalization on the trade-off between these two goals.

5.1. The skill premium again

The expression (10) for the skill premium implies that accepting unemployment will *directly* lower the skill premium: $\hat{U}<0$ implies $\pi<0$ other things equal. But there will also be *indirect* effects, since a change in U will influence e and f. Differentiating (10),

$$\hat{\pi}(1-\gamma f)\hat{U} - \sigma(1-e)\hat{E} + (\gamma f)\hat{V}. \tag{16}$$

Thus, if equipment utilization (e) and fragmentation (f) are low, a change in employment will influence the skill premium both directly and through its effect on equipment utilization, but only slightly through its effect on out-sourcing. If equipment and skilled labor are complements ($\sigma<0$), the indirect effect through equipment utilization is positive but becomes less significant as equipment utilization increases; if unskilled labor and out-sourcing are substitutes ($\gamma>0$), an increase in fragmentation reduces the direct effect while increasing the indirect effect through out-sourcing. These conclusions reflect diminishing returns in production.

5.2. The policy trade-off

To see the net effect of changes in employment on the skill premium, substitute (13) into (16) and rearrange terms.

$$\hat{\pi} = \left[(1-\gamma f) + \gamma f\frac{\eta_V}{\varepsilon} - \sigma(1-e)\frac{\eta_E}{\varepsilon}\right]\hat{U} + \frac{1}{\varepsilon}[\gamma f(\varepsilon_{VE}+\varepsilon_{EE}) - \sigma(1-e)(\varepsilon_{EV}+\varepsilon_{VV})]$$
$$\hat{A} + \frac{1}{\varepsilon}[\gamma f\varepsilon_{VE} - \sigma(1-e)\varepsilon_{VV}]\hat{Q} + \frac{1}{\varepsilon}[\gamma f\varepsilon_{EE} - \sigma(1-e)\varepsilon_{EV}](\hat{g} - \hat{v}^*) \tag{17}$$

To establish a benchmark frame of reference, consider the special case $\gamma=\sigma=0$. Here (17) reduces to just $\hat{\pi}=\hat{U}$. The skill premium can always be reduced by 1% by accepting a 1% fall in employment, and changes in the exogenous variables have no effect on the policy trade-off. The explanation is straightforward: $\gamma=\sigma=0$ implies that the production function is Cobb–Douglas in its four arguments, which in turn implies that income shares are constant and that $e+f=1$ (recall that e and f are meaningful indices of equipment utilization and of fragmentation only if $\gamma>0>\sigma$). Thus, from (10), π is strictly proportional to U.

Next, note that $\gamma>0>\sigma$ implies that the coefficients of $\hat{A}$, $\hat{Q}$, and $\hat{g}-\hat{v}$ in (17) are all positive. Thus, a favorable technology shock or a favorable trade shock will make the government's task harder: To keep employment unchanged it must accept a rise in the skill premium.

Proposition 10. *If unskilled labor and out-sourcing are substitutes and skilled labor and equipment are complements, an increase in TFP, the relative cost of providing equipment services, or the degree of globalization, or a fall in the foreign price for out-sourcing, will require the government to accept a rise in the skill premium to keep employment unchanged.*

The coefficient of $\hat{U}$ in (17) has no clear relation to the value of f, even as γ approaches unity. An increase in fragmentation might make the policy trade-off more favorable or less favorable, depending on circumstances.

To put the role of substitutability of U and V into sharp relief, look at the limiting case of perfect substitution: $\gamma=1$. Then (17) reduces to

$$\hat{\pi} = \frac{1}{e(1-\alpha)}\hat{A} + \frac{1-e}{e}\hat{Q} + \frac{e(1-\alpha)+\alpha}{e(1-\alpha)}(\hat{g} - \hat{v}^*). \tag{18}$$

The policy trade-off ceases to exist. If unskilled labor and out-sourcing are perfect substitutes and if the latter is available at a constant cost, variations in the employment of unskilled labor will be offset exactly by variations in out-sourcing and will therefore have no effect on the skill premium.

Proposition 11. *Given the degree of complementarity between skilled labor and equipment, if unskilled labor and out-sourcing are sufficiently substitutable the government will be unable to influence significantly the skill premium with policies involving variations in employment.*

Note also that each of the coefficients of exogenous shocks in (18) is decreasing in e and independent of f.

Proposition 12. *Given the degree of complementarity between skilled labor and equipment, if unskilled labor and out-sourcing are sufficiently substitutable, an increase in equipment utilization will worsen the policy trade-off and reduce the impact of changes in the exogenous variables on either the skill premium or the volume of employment; an increase in fragmentation will also worsen the policy trade-off, but will have a negligible effect on the impact of changes in exogenous variables.*

Finally, for a perspective on the role of complementarity between skilled labor and equipment, look at what happens when $-\sigma$ is allowed to become arbitrarily large. In this case (17) converges to the following.

$$\hat{\pi} = \frac{(1-\alpha)(1-\gamma)}{(1-\gamma)+(\gamma-\alpha)f}\hat{U} + \frac{1-e}{e}\frac{\left(\gamma\frac{f}{1-e}\right)f + (1-\gamma)}{(\gamma-\alpha)f+(1-\gamma)}\hat{A} + \frac{1-e}{e}\hat{Q} + \frac{(\gamma-\alpha)+\frac{\alpha}{e}}{(\gamma-\alpha)+\frac{1-\gamma}{f}}(\hat{g} - \hat{v}^*). \tag{19}$$

The coefficient of $\hat{U}$ in (19) is necessarily less than unity: The policy trade-off is less favorable than in the Cobb–Douglas case. Also, this coefficient decreases in f if $\gamma>\alpha$ and increases in f if $\gamma<\alpha$. Thus, more fragmentation implies a worsened policy trade-off if unskilled labor is sufficiently substitutable for out-sourcing *and* skilled labor is sufficiently complementary to equipment.

Proposition 13. *If the complementarity between skilled labor and equipment is sufficiently strong, an increase in fragmentation will worsen the policy trade-off if $\gamma>\alpha$ and improve it if $\gamma<\alpha$. An increase in equipment utilization will have a negligible effect on the trade-off.*

Finally, the coefficients of the changes in the exogenous variables in (19) immediately imply the following.

Proposition 14. *Given the degree of substitutability between unskilled labor and out-sourcing, if skilled labor and equipment are sufficiently complementary, an increase in equipment utilization will reduce the impact of changes in the exogenous variables on either the skill premium or the volume of employment; an increase in fragmentation will have a negligible effect on the impact of changes in the technology for providing equipment services, but will increase the impact of changes in the other exogenous variables.*

6. The Southern economy

Thus far, the Home economy has been supposed able to out-source at a constant price. I now explicitly introduce a trading partner, the South, with a distinct structure.

6.1. A model of the South

The South possesses following aggregate production function.

$$A^*F^*(U^*, E^*, S^*) = A^*[U^*]^{\alpha}[(E^*)^{\sigma} + (S^*)^{\sigma}]^{\frac{1-\alpha}{\sigma}} \tag{20}$$

Here A^* indexes South TFP, U^* Southern employment of unskilled labor, S^* skilled labor, and E^* the quantity of equipment in the South. This production function is analogous to that of Home, and I assume it has the same parameters α and σ, so that, in the South also, equipment and skilled labor are substitutes. The Southern index of equipment utilization is also defined analogously:

$$e^* = \frac{(S^*)^{\sigma}}{(E^*)^{\sigma} + (S^*)^{\sigma}}$$

Thus, the South differs from Home in not producing equipment, in not out-sourcing, and in providing out-sourcing for Home. As a final distinction, I suppose that South utilizes equipment at a low level, in particular, that

$$e^* < \frac{(1-\alpha)}{(1-\alpha)-\sigma}. \tag{H2}$$

Southern output may be used to provide either consumption or out-sourcing.

$$c^* + V = A^*F^*(U^*, E^*, S^*)$$

The South does not produce equipment and so must import it from Home, paying for it by performing out-sourcing:

$$E^* = v^*QV. \tag{21}$$

Thus, $v^*Q \equiv P$, the relative price of out-sourcing in terms of equipment, is also the terms of trade.

Assuming competitive markets in which inputs receive the values of their marginal products, the following input pricing relations apply.

$$\frac{w^*}{v^*} = A^*F^*_U = \alpha\frac{A^*F^*}{U^*} \tag{22}$$

$$\frac{1}{Q_v^*} = A^*F^*_E = (1-\alpha)\frac{A^*F^*}{E^*}(1-e^*) \tag{23}$$

$$s^* = A^*F^*_S = (1-\alpha)\frac{A^*F^*}{S^*}e^* \tag{24}$$

Here w^* denotes the wage paid to unskilled labor and s^* that of skilled labor. Thus, the South skill premium equals:

$$\pi^* = \frac{1-\alpha}{\alpha}\frac{U^*}{S^*}e^*. \tag{25}$$

Since e^* is an appropriate index of South equipment utilization if and only if $\sigma<0$, the following is immediate.

Proposition 15. *An increase in equipment utilization will raise the South skill premium if and only if skilled labor and equipment are complements ($\sigma<0$).*

6.2. Equilibrium equipment utilization

Differentiation of the equilibrium pricing condition for equipment utilization implies the following.

$$\varepsilon^*_{EE}\hat{E}^* - \alpha\hat{U}^* = \hat{A}^* + \hat{v}^* + \hat{Q} \tag{26}$$

Here $\varepsilon^*_{EE} \equiv -(E^* F^*_{EE}/F^*_E) = \alpha(1-e^*) + e^*(1-\sigma) > 0$. Note that $\varepsilon^*_{EE} > \alpha$. Also, (H1) implies that ε^*_{EE} is decreasing in e^*.

Proposition 16. *Given the terms of trade and Southern TFP, an increase in employment implies a less than proportionate increase in equipment utilization.*

In light of the pattern of trade, (26) can also be interpreted as showing the response of the demand for imports to changes in the terms of trade, employment, and TFP. The elasticity of South import demand with response to the terms of trade is thus $1/\varepsilon^*_{EE}$ Thus, this elasticity decreases as South's index of equipment utilization rises. (H2) implies that $\varepsilon^*_{EE} < 1$ and therefore amounts to assuming that equipment utilization in the South is sufficiently low to render South import demand elastic. Likewise, the first equation of (13) shows the response of Home import demand to changes in its determinants.

6.3. South social policy

South policy makers are also concerned about both wage inequality and unemployment. Differentiating (25) and substituting into (26) yields the following.

$$\hat{\pi}^* = \left[1 - \alpha\frac{\sigma(1-e^*)}{\varepsilon^*_{EE}}\right]\hat{U}^* - \frac{\sigma(1-e^*)}{\varepsilon^*_{EE}}\{\hat{v}^* + \hat{Q} + \hat{A}^*\} \tag{27}$$

The following is immediate.

Proposition 17. *If and only if South skilled labor and equipment are complements:* ***i*** *A decrease in employment will produce a more than proportional fall in the skill premium;* ***ii*** *An improvement in the terms of trade or in TFP will oblige the South government to accept an increase in the skill premium to keep employment unchanged, or a reduction in employment to leave the skill premium unchanged;* ***iii*** *An increase in complementarity implies an improvement in the policy trade-off and increased sensitivity to the terms of trade and to TFP;* ***iv*** *An increase in equipment utilization implies a deterioration in the policy trade-off and decreased sensitivity to the terms of trade and to TFP.*

7. The global economy

Turn now to the comparative statics of international equilibrium.

7.1. Trade

These comparative statics are described by the first equation of (13), by differentiation of (21), and by (26). After some algebra, these yield the following.

$$\hat{P} = \frac{1}{\varepsilon^*}\left\{\varepsilon\hat{A}^* - \varepsilon^*_{EE}(\varepsilon_{VE} + \varepsilon_{EE})(\hat{A} + \hat{Q}) - \varepsilon^*_{EE}\varepsilon_{EE}\hat{g} + \alpha\varepsilon\hat{U}^* - \varepsilon^*_{EE}\eta_V\hat{U}\right\} \tag{28}$$

$$\hat{E}^* = \frac{1}{\varepsilon^*}\left\{(\varepsilon - \varepsilon_{EE})\hat{A}^* - (\varepsilon_{VE} + \varepsilon_{EE})(\hat{A} + \hat{Q}) - \varepsilon_{EE}\hat{g} + \alpha(\varepsilon - \varepsilon_{EE})\hat{U}^* - \eta_V\hat{U}\right\} \tag{29}$$

$$\begin{aligned}\hat{V} = \frac{1}{\varepsilon\varepsilon^*}\{&-[(\varepsilon_{VE} + \varepsilon_{EE})\varepsilon(1 - \varepsilon^*_{EE})](\hat{A} + \hat{Q}) - \varepsilon\varepsilon_{EE}(1 - \varepsilon^*_{EE})\hat{g} - \varepsilon\varepsilon_{EE}\hat{A}^* - \alpha\varepsilon\varepsilon_{EE}\hat{U}^* \\ &+ \varepsilon_{EE}\varepsilon^*_{EE}\eta_V\hat{U}\}\end{aligned} \tag{30}$$

where $\varepsilon^* = \varepsilon^*_{EE}\varepsilon - \varepsilon - \varepsilon^*_{EE}\varepsilon_{EE} = -\varepsilon^*_{EE}\varepsilon_{EE}(1 - \varepsilon_{VV}) - \varepsilon^*_{EE}\varepsilon_{EV}\varepsilon_{VE} - \varepsilon < 0$. Thus,

Proposition 18 (Globalization). *If (H1) holds, an increase in globalization turns the terms of trade in favor of South, increases South equipment utilization, and increases Home out-sourcing.*

Proposition 19 (Home Technological Progress). *If (H1) holds, an increase in either Home employment or Home TFP, or a decrease in the relative cost of equipment, turns the terms of trade in favor of South, increases South equipment utilization, and increases Home out-sourcing.*

Note also that

$$\varepsilon - \varepsilon_{EE} = -\alpha(1 - e)[f + \gamma(1 - f)] - e(1 - \sigma)(1 - [(1 - e)(1 - \gamma)\alpha + f(1 - \alpha)]) < 0.$$

Thus,

Proposition 20 (South Technological Progress). *If (H1) holds, an increase in either South employment or South TFP turns the terms of trade in favor of Home, increases Southern equipment utilization, and increases Home out-sourcing.*

7.2. Globalization and skill premia

Rewrite the second equation of (13) as follows.

$$\varepsilon\hat{E} = (\varepsilon_{EV} + \varepsilon_{VV})(\hat{A} + \hat{Q}) + \varepsilon_{EV}(\hat{g} - \hat{P}) + [\varepsilon_{VV}\varepsilon_{EU} + \varepsilon_{EV}\varepsilon_{VU}]\hat{U} \tag{31}$$

Thus, globalization will have a direct positive effect on Home equipment utilization, and Proposition 18 indicates that it will also increase Home out-sourcing. This is just as in the small-country case. But

Proposition 18 also indicates that it will turn the terms of trade against Home, and (31) then indicates that this will have a countervailing influence on equipment utilization. To see the net effect, note that (28) implies, if technology and employments do not change,

$$\hat{P} = -\frac{\varepsilon^{*}_{EE}\varepsilon_{EE}}{\varepsilon^{*}}\hat{g}<\hat{g}$$

since $-(\varepsilon^{*}_{EE}\varepsilon_{EE}/\varepsilon^{*})= -(\varepsilon^{*}_{EE}\varepsilon_{EE}/(-\varepsilon^{*}_{EE}\varepsilon_{EE}-\varepsilon(1-\varepsilon^{*}_{EE})))<1$ because (H2) implies that $\varepsilon^{*}_{EE}<1$.

Thus, in (31) the direct effect of globalization on Home equipment utilization dominates the countervailing influence through the terms of trade. So globalization increases the Home skill premium and it increases equipment utilization in both countries. Finally, (27) implies that an improvement in South's terms of trade $\hat{Q}+\hat{v}>0$, will also raise the skill premium in South, provided that equipment and skilled labor are complements. Thus, we have the following basic result.

Proposition 21 (Globalization and Skill Premia). *If (H1) and (H2) hold, an increase in globalization will increase the skill premium in both countries. It will also increase equipment utilization in both countries, implying common skill-biased technical change in the sense that, at unchanged wages, firms world-wide will wish to substitute skilled labor for unskilled labor.*

The story is as follows. An increase in globalization causes Home to increase out-sourcing. Since out-sourcing substitutes for Home unskilled labor, it depresses the wage of the latter. It also increases the marginal product of equipment, which will tend to induce Home to increase equipment utilization. But in addition it turns the terms of trade against Home, producing a countervailing effect. If equipment utilization in South is sufficiently small, South import demand will be elastic and the deterioration in the terms of trade will not be large enough to reverse the direct positive effect on Home equipment utilization. Since skilled labor is complementary to equipment, this increases the wage of the latter. Finally, the improvement in its terms of trade will induce South to utilize more equipment, and this will increase the wage of skilled labor there, again because of the complementarity of the latter with equipment.

7.3. Technology and skill premia

In Proposition 21, the skill-biased change in production technique is endogenous, a consequence of globalization. But this does not imply that such a change reflects the presence of globalization: It could be caused by something else. In particular, consider the effects of changes in Home TFP, South TFP, or the relative cost of equipment.

From (31), $\hat{A}+\hat{Q}>0$ implies a direct positive effect on Home equipment utilization, and Proposition 19 indicates that it will also increase Home out-sourcing, but that, in addition, it will turn the terms of trade against Home, and (31) then indicates that this will again have a countervailing influence on equipment utilization. To see the net effect, note that (28) and (31) imply, if foreign technology, globalization, and employments do not change,

$$\begin{aligned}\hat{E} &= \frac{1}{\varepsilon\varepsilon^{*}}\left(\varepsilon^{*}[\varepsilon_{EV}+\varepsilon_{VV}]+\varepsilon_{EV}\varepsilon^{*}_{EE}[\varepsilon_{VE}+\varepsilon_{EE}]\right)(\hat{A}+\hat{Q})\\ &= \frac{1}{\varepsilon\varepsilon^{*}}\left(\varepsilon_{EV}\left[\varepsilon^{*}+\varepsilon_{EE}\varepsilon^{*}_{EE}\right]-\varepsilon\varepsilon_{VV}-\varepsilon\varepsilon^{*}_{E}[1-\varepsilon_{VV}]\right)(\hat{A}+\hat{Q})\end{aligned}$$

(H2) implies that the coefficient of $\hat{A}+\hat{Q}$ in the bottom line is positive. Thus, the direct effect of $\hat{A}+\hat{Q}$ on Home equipment utilization dominates the countervailing influence through the terms of trade, and therefore it increases the Home skill premium and equipment utilization in both countries. Again, (27) implies that an improvement in South's terms of trade will also raise the skill premium in South, provided that equipment and skilled labor are complements. Thus, the following result.

Proposition 22 (Home Technology and Skill Premia). *If (H1) and (H2) hold, an improvement in Home TFP or in the technology for providing equipment will increase the skill premium in both countries. It will also increase equipment utilization in both countries generating common skill-biased technical change.*

Globalization and improvements in Home technology produce qualitatively identical effects on the skill premia in the two countries, and both induce a skill-biased change in production techniques in both countries. This paper therefore strongly endorses the argument of Feenstra and Hanson (2001, p 2) that "distinguishing whether the change in wages is due to international trade, or technological change, is fundamentally an empirical rather than a theoretical question." Furthermore, the presence of skill-biased changes in observed technology does *not* contribute to making this distinction.

Next, consider an improvement in South TFP. Eq. (31) reveals that an increase in A^* has no direct effect on Home equipment utilization, but will increase it indirectly if it causes an improvement in the Home terms of trade. This plus Proposition 20 therefore imply:

Proposition 23 (South Technology and Skill Premia). *If (H1) holds, an increase in South TFP will increase the skill premium in both countries. It will also increase equipment utilization in both countries, generating common skill-biased technical change.*

Thus, an improvement in South technology produces the same qualitative effects as an improvement in Home technology on fragmentation, equipment utilization, and the skill premia. The only difference is in the effect on the terms of trade.

7.4. Globalization and social policy

Next, examine the interrelation between Home social policy and South social policy, and how this interrelation is sensitive to the degrees of: substitution between inputs (as reflected in γ and σ), fragmentation (f), and equipment utilization (e). To this end, substitute (28) into (17) and (27), note that $P=Qv^*$, and rearrange terms to obtain, for given g, A, Q, and A^*,

$$\hat{\pi} = \mu_U \hat{U} + \mu_{U^*} \hat{U}^*$$

$$\hat{\pi}^* = \mu^*_U \hat{U} + \mu^*_{U^*} \hat{U}^* \tag{32}$$

where

$$\mu_U = \frac{1}{\varepsilon}\left\{\varepsilon(1-\gamma f) + \gamma f \eta_V - \sigma(1-e)\eta_E + [\gamma f \varepsilon_{EE} - \sigma(1-e)\varepsilon_{EV}]\frac{\varepsilon^*_{EE}}{\varepsilon^*}\eta_V\right\}$$

$$\mu_{U^*} = -\frac{\alpha}{\varepsilon^*}[\gamma f \varepsilon_{EE} - \sigma(1-e)\varepsilon_{EV}]$$

$$\mu^*_U = \frac{1}{\varepsilon^*}[\sigma(1-e^*)\eta_V]$$

$$\mu^*_{U^*} = \frac{1}{\varepsilon^*}[\varepsilon^* - \alpha\sigma(1-e^*)(\varepsilon - \varepsilon_{EE})] \tag{33}$$

Note, first, if $\gamma=\sigma=0$ (the Cobb–Douglas case), $\mu_U=\mu^*_{U^*}=1$, $\mu^*_U=\mu_{U^*}=0$. Thus, there is no policy interdependence between Home and South, and neither country's policy trade-off is influenced by fragmentation or by equipment utilization.

Further, (H1) implies that $\mu^*_{U^*},\mu_{U^*}>0$, so that a reduction in South employment will reduce the skill premium in both countries if Home employment is unchanged. Next, look at the consequences of the following additional assumption.

$$\mu_U>0, \qquad \mu_U\mu^*_{U^*}>\mu_{U^*}\mu^*_U \tag{H3}$$

This is not a strong assumption, as it is satisfied for many values of the underlying parameters, but it is not innocuous: Cases do exist where it is not met. (H3) implies that, given the skill premium in the partner country, policies that lower employment in a country will also reduce the skill premium there, both directly and after international repercussions are accounted for.

Note that, if γ is sufficiently large, $\mu^*_U>0$ Then both of the cross terms in (33) will be positive: Policies intended to reduce the skill premium in one country, by accepting a reduction in employment, will also reduce the skill premium in the other country. Thus, the actions of policymakers in one country will facilitate policymaking in the other if both are trying to move in the same direction, but will frustrate policy if they are not. That is, the international environment will reduce national policy autonomy.

Proposition 24 (Erosion of National Autonomy). *If (H3) holds and γ is sufficiently large, the actions of policymakers in each country will tend to frustrate the actions of policymakers in the other, whenever they attempt to pursue divergent objectives.*

Proposition 24 is consistent with the concerns of many globalization critics. But there is more to it than that. To put the concerns of this paper into sharp relief, let $-\sigma$ become indefinitely large. Then the terms in (33) converge to the following.

$$\mu_U = 1-\gamma f+\frac{1-e}{e}\frac{\alpha f}{G}(1-\gamma)-\left[\frac{\gamma f(1-f)}{G-1}+\frac{1-e}{e}\frac{\alpha f(1-f)}{G(G-1)}\right](\gamma-\alpha)$$

$$\mu_{U^*}=0$$

$$\mu^*_U=\frac{1-e^*}{e^*}\frac{1-f}{1-\gamma+f(\gamma-\alpha)}(\gamma-\alpha)$$

$$\mu^*_{U^*}=1+\alpha\frac{1-e^*}{e^*} \tag{34}$$

where $G\equiv1-\gamma f(\gamma-\alpha)>0$. Note that, if γ is sufficiently large, $\mu_U>0$, which in turn implies $\mu_U\mu_{U^*}{}^*>\mu_U{}^*\mu_{U^*}$. This establishes the relevance of Proposition 24 when the maintained hypothesis of this paper is pronounced.

Proposition 25. *If γ and $-\sigma$ are sufficiently large, (H3) necessarily holds.*

Note next that, if complementarity between skilled labor and equipment is complete, fluctuations in employment in South will have no spillover effects on the Home skill premium. An increase in South unskilled employment will not increase South demand for equipment if the latter is strictly complementary to the unchanged stock of skilled labor. Thus, South demand for imports will not change nor, at the initial terms of trade, will its supply of out-sourcing. An increase in South employment will therefore raise the skill premium in South with no effects on either the volume or the terms of trade and, therefore, on the Home skill premium.

But this no-spillover conclusion is not symmetric. When $\gamma > \alpha$ an increase in Home employment raises the skill premium in the South. This is because it raises Home demand for out-sourcing which turns the terms of trade in favor of the South, inducing the latter to increase equipment utilization, which in turn raises the skill premium.

Proposition 26 (Asymmetric Spillovers). *If skilled labor and equipment are highly complementary, employment fluctuations in South will have negligible effects on the Home skill premium, but Home employment fluctuations will significantly influence the South skill premium.*

Finally, note that the spillover effect of Home employment fluctuations on South's skill premium become negligible once the degree of fragmentation becomes large, and so do the effects on Home's skill premium if γ is also large. If V is large and substitutable for U, changes in the latter have little effect on the $U-V$ sub-aggregate.

Proposition 27. *If γ and $-\sigma$ are sufficiently large, fluctuations in Home employment will have little effect on Home and South skill premia when fragmentation is extensive.*

8. Concluding remarks

Popular concern about globalization embraces a large (and amorphous) number of concerns. This paper addresses a complex of issues that have been of concern to economists: the effect of globalization on the skill premium; the effect of globalization on unemployment; the relative importance of globalization and exogenous technical change; the effect of globalization on the ability of national governments to conduct independent social policies. Thinking about these topics has been dominated by a large empirical literature concluding, for the most part, that trade has played a relatively minor role in the rise of the skill premium, while exogenous skill-biased technical change has played a major role.

Most of this work has utilized, at least implicitly, the standard 2×2 HOS model as a theoretical framework. This paper investigates the consequences of replacing the focus on inter-sectoral substitution that is at the heart of the Stolper–Samuelson theorem with more attention to the intra-sectoral relations between inputs. Specifically, I assume that out-sourcing and unskilled labor are highly substitutable and that equipment and skilled labor are complementary, that production methods are flexible, and that the country undertaking out-sourcing (Home) has a significantly different structure from that providing it (South). The more important results include the following.

- An increase in fragmentation or in equipment utilization will raise the skill premium. Thus, an increase in the stock of skilled labor can coincide with an increase in the skill premium if also accompanied by a sufficient increase in equipment utilization or fragmentation.
- More fragmentation is associated with a more elastic demand for unskilled labor if and only if out-sourcing and unskilled labor are sufficiently substitutable.

- Given the complementarity between skilled labor and equipment, if unskilled labor and out-sourcing are sufficiently substitutable the government will be unable to influence significantly the skill premium with policies involving variations in employment.
- If the complementarity between skilled labor and equipment is sufficiently strong, an increase in fragmentation will worsen the policy trade-off if out-sourcing and unskilled labor are highly substitutable and improve it if they are less highly substitutable.
- An increase in globalization turns the terms of trade in favor of South, increases Southern equipment utilization, and increases Home out-sourcing.
- An increase in globalization will increase the skill premium in *both* countries. It will also increase equipment utilization in both countries, generating common skill-biased technical change.
- An increase in Home TFP or fall in the relative cost of providing equipment will increase the skill premium in *both* countries. It will also increase equipment utilization in both countries, generating common skill-biased technical change.
- If unskilled labor and out-sourcing are sufficiently substitutable, the actions of policymakers in each country will tend to frustrate the actions of policymakers in the other, whenever they attempt to pursue divergent objectives.
- If skilled labor and equipment are highly complementary, employment fluctuations in South will have negligible effects on the Home skill premium, but Home employment fluctuations will significantly influence the South skill premium.
- If skilled labor and equipment are highly complementary and unskilled labor and outsourcing highly substitutable, fluctuations in Home employment will have little effect on Home and South skill premia when fragmentation is extensive.

In summary, when detail about intra-sectoral relations between inputs replaces focus on inter-sectoral substitution, globalization offers a simple and immediate possible explanation for the prominent stylized facts regarding the emergence of the skill premium *and* for the presence of skill-biased technical change. Trade vs. technology remains as an empirical issue, though, because exogenous neutral technological change offers an alternative simple and immediate possible explanation. But globalization-talk still makes me puke.

Appendix A. Elasticities

For convenience, definitions of elasticities used in the text are collected here.

A.1. Home elasticities

$$\varepsilon_{VV} \equiv -\frac{VF_{VV}}{F_V} = 1 - [\alpha f + \gamma(1-f)] = (1-\gamma) - (\alpha - \gamma)f$$

$$\varepsilon_{VU} \equiv \frac{UF_{VU}}{F_V} = (\alpha - \gamma)(1-f)$$

$$\varepsilon_{VE} \equiv \frac{EF_{VE}}{F_V} = (1-\alpha)(1-e)$$

$$\varepsilon_{EE} \equiv -\frac{EF_{EE}}{F_E} = \alpha(1-e) + e(1-\sigma)$$

$$\varepsilon_{EV} \equiv \frac{VF_{EV}}{F_E} = \alpha f$$

$$\varepsilon_{EU} \equiv \frac{UF_{EU}}{F_E} = \alpha(1-f)$$

$$\varepsilon_{UU} \equiv -\frac{UF_{UU}}{F_U} = 1 - [\alpha(1-f) + \gamma f] = (1-\gamma) - (\alpha-\gamma)(1-f)$$

$$\varepsilon_{UV} \equiv \frac{VF_{UV}}{F_U} = (\alpha-\gamma)f$$

$$\varepsilon_{UE} \equiv \frac{EF_{UE}}{F_U} = (1-\alpha)(1-e) = \varepsilon_{VE}$$

$$\varepsilon \equiv \varepsilon_{EE}\varepsilon_{VV} - \varepsilon_{EV}\varepsilon_{VE} = \alpha(1-e)(1-\gamma)(1-f) + e(1-\sigma)[f(1-\alpha) + (1-\gamma)(1-f)])$$

$$\eta_V \equiv \varepsilon_{VE}\varepsilon_{EU} + \varepsilon_{EE}\varepsilon_{VU} = (1-f)\{e[(1-\sigma)(\alpha-\gamma)] + (1-e)[\alpha(1-\gamma)]\}$$

$$\eta_E \equiv \varepsilon_{EU}\varepsilon_{VV} + \varepsilon_{EV}\varepsilon_{VU} = \alpha(1-f)(1-\gamma)$$

A.2. South elasticities

$$\varepsilon^*_{EE} \equiv -\frac{E^*F^*_{EE}}{F^*_E} = \alpha(1-e^*) + e^*(1-\sigma) > 0.$$

$$\varepsilon^* \equiv \varepsilon^*_{EE}\varepsilon - \varepsilon - \varepsilon^*_{EE}\varepsilon_{EE}$$

A.3. International elasticities

$$\mu_U \equiv \frac{U}{\pi}\frac{\mathrm{d}\pi}{\mathrm{d}U} = \frac{1}{\varepsilon}\left\{\varepsilon(1-\gamma f) + \gamma f\eta_V - \sigma(1-e)\eta_E + [\gamma f\varepsilon_{EE} - \sigma(1-e)\varepsilon_{EV}]\frac{\varepsilon^*_{EE}}{\varepsilon^*}\eta_V\right\}$$

$$\mu_{U^*} \equiv \frac{U^*}{\pi}\frac{\mathrm{d}\pi}{\mathrm{d}U^*} = -\frac{\alpha}{\varepsilon^*}[\gamma f\varepsilon_{EE} - \sigma(1-e)\varepsilon_{EV}]$$

$$\mu^*_U \equiv \frac{U}{\pi^*}\frac{\mathrm{d}\pi^*}{\mathrm{d}U} = \frac{1}{\varepsilon^*}[\sigma(1-e^*)\eta_V]$$

$$\mu^*_{U^*} \equiv \frac{U^*}{\pi^*}\frac{\mathrm{d}\pi^*}{\mathrm{d}U^*} = \frac{1}{\varepsilon^*}[\varepsilon^* - \alpha\sigma(1-e^*)(\varepsilon - \varepsilon_{EE})]$$

References

Arndt, S., & Kierzkowski, H. (Eds.) (2001). *Fragmentation: New production and trade patterns in the world economy*. Oxford: Oxford University Press.

Bergstrom, V., & Panas, E. E. (1992). How robust is the capital–skill complementarity hypothesis? *Review of Economics and Statistics*, *74*, 540–552.

Bound, J., & Johnson, G. (1992). Changes in the structure of wages in the 1980s: An evaluation of alternative explanations. *American Economic Review*, *82*, 371–392.

Burda, M., & Dluhosch, B. (2001). *Fragmentation, globalization and labor markets*. Research Paper 2001/05, Leverhulme Centre, University of Nottingham.

Dasgupta, I., & Osang, T. (2002). Globalization and relative wages: Further evidence from U.S. manufacturing industries. *International Review of Economics and Finance*, *11*(1), 1–16.

Davidson, C., & Matusz, S. (2001). *Globalization, employment, and income: Analyzing the adjustment process*. Research Paper 2001/04, Leverhulme Centre, University of Nottingham.

Davis, D. R. (1998). Does European unemployment prop up American wages? National labor markets and global trade. *American Economic Review*, *88*, 478–494.

Desjonqueres, T., Machin, S., & van Reenan, J. (1999). Another nail in the coffin? Or can the trade based explanation of changing skill structures be resurrected? *Scandinavian Journal of Economics*, *101*, 533–554.

Epifani, P., & Gancia, G. A. (2002). *The skill bias of world trade*. Working paper.

Ethier, W. J. (1979). Internationally decreasing costs and world trade. *Journal of International Economics*, (1), 1–24.

Ethier, W. J. (1982). National and international returns to scale in the modern theory of international trade. *American Economic Review*, *72*(3), 389–405.

Ethier, W. J. (1986). The multinational firm. *Quarterly Journal of Economics*, *101*(4), 805–833.

Ethier, W. J. (1998). Regionalism in a multilateral world. *Journal of Political Economy*, *6*(106), 1214–1245.

Fallon, P. R., & Layard, P. R. G. (1975). Capital–skill complementarity, income distribution, and output accounting. *Journal of Political Economy*, *83*, 279–301.

Falvey, R., & Reed, G. (2000). *Trade liberalisation and technology choice*. Research Paper 2000/1, Centre for Research on Globalisation and Labour Markets, University of Nottingham.

Feenstra, R. C., & Hanson, G. H. (1996). Globalization, outsourcing, and wage inequality. *American Economic Review Papers and Proceedings*, *86*, 240–245.

Feenstra, R. C., & Hanson, G. H. (2001). *Global production sharing and rising inequality: A survey of trade and wages*. NBER Working Paper 8372. Cambridge: National Bureau of Economic Research.

Francois, J., & Nelson, D. (1998). Trade, technology, and wages: General equilibrium mechanics. *Economic Journal*, *108*, 1483–1499.

Glass, A. J., & Saggi, K. (2001). Innovation and wage effects of international outsourcing. *European Economic Review*, *45*, 67–86.

Griliches, Z. (1969). Capital–skill complementarity. *Review of Economics and Statistics*, *51*, 465–468.

Jones, R. W. (1997). Trade, technology, and income distribution. *Indian Economic Review*, *32*, 129–140.

Jones, R. W. (2000). *Globalization and the theory of input trade*. Cambridge: MIT Press.

Johnson, G., & Stafford, F. (1999). The labor market implications of international trade. In O. Ashenfelter, & D. Card (Eds.), *Handbook of Labor Economics*, *vol. 3b* (pp. 2215–2228). Amsterdam: North Holland.

Katz, L. F., & Autor, D. (1999). Changes in the wage structure and earnings inequality. In O. Ashenfelter, & D. Card (Eds.), *Handbook of Labor Economics*, *vol. 3a* (pp. 1463–1555). Amsterdam: North Holland.

Krusell, P., Ohanian, L. E., Rios-Rull, J. -V., & Violante, G. L. (2000). Capital–skill complementarity and inequality: A macroeconomic analysis. *Econometrica*, *68*(5), 1029–1053.

Lawrence, R., & Slaughter, M. (1993). International trade and American wages in the 1980s: Giant sucking sound or small hiccup? *Brookings Papers on Economic Activity*, 161–226.

Leamer, E. E. (1998). In search of Stolper–Samuelson linkages between international trade and lower wages. In S. Collins (Ed.), *Imports, exports and the American worker*. Washington: Brookings Institution.

Neary, J. P. (2001a). *Competition, trade and wages*. Research Paper 2001/03, Leverhulme Centre, University of Nottingham.

Neary, J. P. (2001b). *Foreign competition and wage inequality*. Discussion Paper University College Dublin and CEPR.

Rodrik, D. (1997). *Has gobalization gone too far?* Washington: Institute for International Economics.

Sapir, A. (2000). Who is afraid of globalization? The challenge of domestic adjustment in Europe and America. *CEPR Discussion Papers*, 2595.

Slaughter, M. J. (1998). International trade and labour-market outcomes: Results, questions, and policy options. *Economic Journal*, *108*, 1452–1462.

Slaughter, M. J. (2001). International Trade and labor-demand elasticities. *Journal of International Economics*, *54*, 27–56.

Wood, A. (1994). *North–South trade, employment and inequality*. Oxford: Oxford University Press.

The theory of effective protection in general equilibrium: effective-rate analogues of nominal rates

WILFRED ETHIER / University of Pennsylvania

The theory of effective protection in general equilibrium: effective-rate analogues of nominal rates. This paper provides explicit conditions for the existence of measurable indices of effective protection that yield information about certain quantities comparable to the information obtainable from nominal rates in the absence of intermediate goods. These conditions enable one to address the basic issues in the multi-commodity theory of effective protection without the usual reliance on extensive, tedious mathematical manipulations.

The specific results that emerge tend to emphasize both the extremely severe nature of the technological restrictions necessary for a simple measure to be correct and also the great sensitivity of such a measure to the specification of exactly what the object of interest is.

La théorie de la protection effective en contexte d'équilibre général: la construction d'indices de protection effective analogues aux indices de protection nominale. Ce mémoire définit les conditions explicites pour l'existence d'indices mesurables de protection effective qui puissent servir les mêmes fonctions que les taux nominaux de protection dans des modèles où il n'y a pas de biens intermédiaires. Ces conditions permettent d'étudier certains problèmes de la théorie de la protection effective dans un univers à plusieurs biens sans avoir à s'en remettre à des manipulations mathématiques extensives.

L'auteur tire de ses analyses un certain nombre de conclusions spécifiques: *a/* il n'y pas de relation entre d'une part la validité du changement proportionnel dans la valeur ajoutée par unité comme mesure de la protection effective pertinente pour les produits bruts et d'autre part la séparabilité des fonctions de production; *b/* les changements proportionnels dans les produits en valeur ajoutée (pour les fonctions de production séparables) ne sont pas en général égaux aux changements proportionnels dans les produits bruts; donc des mesures distinctes de protection effective sont nécessaires; si les deux valeurs coincident, la mesure appropriée et le changement dans la valeur ajoutée par unité; *c/* contrairement à ce qu'on trouve colporté dans la littérature scientifique, le produit en valeur ajoutée et la valeur ajoutée dégonflée par le prix du produit sont des concepts différents qui appellent des mesures distinctes de protection effective, même si la fonction de production est séparable; dans le cas très spécial où les changements proportionnels dans les deux mesures sont égaux, le taux de protection effective est mesuré par le taux nominal; *d/* le rationale pour l'utilisation d'un ensemble de taux effectifs plutôt que les taux nominaux (ou quelqu'autre mesure de protection effective) comme mesures des

Canadian Journal of Economics/Revue canadienne d'Economique, X, no. 2
May/mai 1977. Printed in Canada/Imprimé au Canada.

effets d'allocation des ressources ne repose pas sur des assises bien solides; e/ si l'objectif fondamental est l'efficacité économique ou le bien-être économique, il faut s'attacher aux produits nets plutôt qu'aux produits bruts ou aux valeurs ajoutées dégonflées; dans ce cas-là, les mesures pertinentes de protection sont clairement les taux nominaux; ainsi les arguments à l'appui des bénéfices potentiels de tarifs préférentiels accordés par les pays développés doivent être considérés comme suspects quand ils sont simplement fondés sur la magnitude calculée des taux de protection effective.

When is there a measurable index of effective protection that yields information comparable to that obtainable from nominal rates in the absence of intermediate goods? This general question has, implicitly or explicitly, been central to many recent theoretical studies of effective protection in general equilibrium.[1] A large number of specific results have been obtained. While some of these are, to be sure, repetitive, the relationship between others has been obscured by the use of different models or the pursuit of different specific objectives, and some seem to lead to differing conclusions. Furthermore, a direct, reasonably general, answer to this question has yet to be given.

The present paper attempts to provide a concise answer in a fairly general context. The answer will then be used to derive new results and to obtain a perspective on the existing literature. One of the less appealing characteristics of that literature is the use of tedious, largely manipulative, mathematics[2] to obtain very few positive conclusions relevant to a world of many goods. One objective is to demonstrate that, by directly addressing the opening question, the basic issues involved can be attacked without such lengthy mathematical arguments.

PRELIMINARIES

First some notation. I write

$$Y = (I - A)X, \tag{1}$$

$$K \geqslant BX. \tag{2}$$

X denotes the (column) vector of actual gross outputs of the various industries and A the matrix of intermediate input requirements for the techniques of production actually being used. Thus Y denotes the vector of net outputs: the quantities of goods available for final consumption or export. B is the matrix of primary factor input requirements for the techniques of production in use, and K the vector of available supplies of the various primary factors.

1 This question was posed in Ethier (1971, 1972) and also addressed in Bhagwati and Srinivasan (1973) and Bruno (1973). Closely related problems were investigated in Corden (1969, 1971), Ruffin (1969), Jones (1971), Ramaswami and Srinivasan (1971), and Khang (1973), among others.

2 I do not mean to claim innocence for myself in this regard.

With constant returns to scale the spectrum of available techniques for each good i can be summarized by the unit isoquant

$$f^i(b_i', a_i') = 1, \tag{3}$$

where b_i and a_i denote the ith columns of B and A respectively. The isoquants need not be smooth. Economy-wide factor supplies K will be taken as fixed, and it is supposed that they, together with the spectrum of available techniques, determine a concave frontier of possible net outputs Y. I shall simplify by assuming, first, that some of each good is always produced domestically and, second, that the collection of gross outputs (and of any other quantities subsequently under investigation) corresponding to the frontier of possible net outputs is itself a concave surface. These are by no means innocent assumptions; their violation is at the heart of many problems in the literature. But I have treated them at length elsewhere[3] and so shall not do so here.

One of the secondary objectives of this paper is to clarify the role of production-function separability. The latter holds if there exists a production function $g^i = g^i\ (b_i')$ such that (3) can be written in the form

$$f^i(g^i, a_i') = 1. \tag{3'}$$

That is, the production process for each good can be visualized as consisting of two stages in which primary factors are first combined to produce g^i, called the 'value-added-product of industry i,' which is then combined with intermediate inputs to produce gross output. While separability at some level must be assumed for empirical work, there is no a priori reason either to accept it at all or to think that it is especially relevant to the particular classification of inputs as primary factors or intermediate goods.

In a competitive economy the vector P of actual domestic prices supports the actual vector Y of net outputs:

$$PdY \leqslant 0, \tag{4}$$

for any feasible vector dY of changes in net outputs. Also, for any goods i and j the appropriate relative price P_i/P_j equals the corresponding marginal rate of transformation $\partial Y_j/\partial Y_i$, provided that the latter is well defined. Thus the scale of nominal tariff rates (including the tariff equivalents of all price distortions) indicates the proportional changes in the marginal rates of transformation between the Y_i brought about by the tariff structure. In the absence of intermediate goods ($A = 0$), Y_i can be variously interpreted as the net output of good i, as the gross output of good i, or as the value in terms of good i of the primary factors being used in industry i.

A theory of effective protection must be precise both about the quantities of ultimate interest and about the desirable properties of effective-protection

3 See Ethier (1971, 1972). Special cases of some of the results contained therein are also derived in Bhagwati and Srinivasan (1973).

measures appropriate to the chosen quantities. As regards the first, taxonomy is necessary because the literature has been divided among different objectives, each of which can be defended on its own grounds. With respect to the second I shall follow the methodology of my earlier papers:

> the scale of effective rates for any quantity concept will be taken to be the array of proportional changes induced by the tariff structure in the 'prices' supporting the actual levels of those quantities. (*M*)

Of course any choice of methodology must at bottom be arbitrary, but a number of considerations recommend this particular choice for present purposes. For each quantity concept it gives a precise and logical formulation of the effective rate; this choice preserves the analogy with nominal rates and no intermediate goods; it is broad enough to imply most reasonable properties of effective rates yet not so broad as to preclude definite results; it enables one to say quite a bit without the complicated but tedious analysis typical of this literature; and it minimizes the danger of inadvertently focusing on properties that are the consequences of special assumptions (such as a specific number of goods).

Under my assumptions about technology, 'prices' that support the actual levels of most interesting quantity concepts will always exist (see Ethier, 1971). But these prices will be useful only if they can be calculated without a great deal of information about the economy. For, in a multicommodity world without intermediate goods, the array of nominal tariff rates does not really tell us a great deal about net outputs. Thus if a structure of effective rates furnishing comparable information about, say, gross outputs, could be calculated only by knowing elasticities of substitution, changes in these elasticities, and so on, then surely these effective rates would be superfluous whenever they could in fact be computed. In this paper I will therefore be concerned only with 'price' systems that can be expressed directly in terms of nominal prices and input coefficients. This in effect means that I will be concerned with nominal prices P, values added per unit $v = P(I - A)$, and, in the special case of separable production functions, value-added-product prices $q_i = v_i/g^i$. The proportional changes in these three candidates give nominal tariff rates and the two definitions of effective protection that have been the focus of nearly all papers in this area.

The quantity concepts investigated by most authors (when they have been precise) are gross outputs and resource flows in some sense. I proceed to each in turn.

GROSS OUTPUTS

I denote by v the vector of values added per unit in nominal terms; thus $v = P(I - A)$ and $vX = PY$, the value of national output. Let dY denote some feasible differential change in net outputs and dX a corresponding differential change in gross outputs. Then, from (1),

$$PdY = vdX - P(dA)X. \tag{5}$$

Since P is a price system supporting Y, it follows at once from (4) and (5) that

> The values added per unit v will be a price system supporting the levels of gross output X if, for *all* feasible differential changes in net outputs,

$$P(dA)X \leqslant 0. \tag{6}$$

That is, the basic condition is simply that no efficient differential change in technique should increase, at constant prices, the total cost of the intermediate inputs required per unit of output.[4]

Consider a change in nominal tariffs. If (6) holds for all feasible differential changes in outputs from the initial situation and also for all feasible differential changes in outputs from the terminal situation, then the change in the structure of effective protection relevant (as formulated in criterion (M) above) to gross outputs is just the array of proportional differences in values added per unit between the two situations.

A few aspects of this result deserve special emphasis, and a number of results follow directly from it:

1/ It is not necessary that the basic condition hold either globally or between the two situations (pre and post tariff change), but only for differential departures from each situation.

2/ Three special cases which satisfy condition (6) are immediately apparent. First if the intermediate input requirements are fixed, then $dA = 0$ and (6) is met. This case has often been discussed in the literature. Second, if instead the primary factor input requirements are fixed and intermediate inputs can be smoothly substituted for each other, then cost minimization by firms will imply that $Pda_i = 0$, so that (6) is again met. Third, if the production functions are separable, if the value-added product input coefficients g^i are fixed, if primary factors can be smoothly substituted for each other, and if intermediate inputs can be smoothly substituted for each other, then cost minimization by firms will again imply that $Pda_i = 0$.

3/ There is no relationship whatever between the validity of the proportional change in value added per unit as the measure of effective protection relevant to gross outputs and separability of the production functions.
Of course if condition (6) is met because A is fixed (the most interesting special case), then the production function will in fact be separable, but separability itself is not at all relevant.

Special cases (of little inherent interest in themselves) can easily be con-

4 Strictly speaking, the condition need not hold for any industry individually, but only for the economy as a whole, with individual industries weighted by gross output levels.

structed that satisfy (6) but do not display separability.[5] Ethier (1972) provides an explicit model with separable production functions where condition (6) need not hold, so that the appropriate effective rate of protection is a complex term involving changes in elasticities of substitution, and so on. Condition (6) is a strong restriction on input substitution, which, in the 'well-behaved' technologies usually considered in the literature, is unlikely to be met without at least some constant input coefficients. Separability gets us nowhere without constant value-added-product input coefficients g^i.

4/ If A does vary as a result of the tariff change, but the basic condition is nonetheless met (or its failure ignored), then the change in effective protection for an industry is the *actual* proportional change in value added per unit, and not the change computed on the basis of a constant A. The latter has been employed by a number of authors, following Corden (1966).[6]

5/ The scale of effective rates is subject to the same qualitative limitations as is a scale of nominal rates in the absence of intermediate goods. For example, when the number of commodities exceeds two, a ranking of effective rates need not coincide with a ranking of proportional induced gross output changes.

OWN-VALUE-ADDED

Much of the literature has concerned total allocations of primary factors in some sense. This gives rise to a serious preliminary problem not present in the previous section. For while the gross output of a good possesses a natural specific unit of meaurement (the good itself), the natural units of measurement for primary resources attach to the various factors allocated among sectors. If different factors shift between industries in different proportions, and perhaps in different directions as well, what is meant by the resource pull? If a change in tariffs causes some industry to employ 10 per cent more capital, 5 per cent more labour, and 10 per cent less land, for example, in what direction and at what rate have resources in general flowed? Thus in order to develop measures of effective protection relevant to the flow of primary factors in general between industries, it is necessary first to determine commodity-specific indices of primary factors. An index suggested by the no-intermediate-good case is own-value-added: nominal value added deflated by the nominal price of the indus-

5 Suppose for example that good i requires goods 1 and 2 and factors 1 and 2 as inputs and that the available independent techniques of production are those that simultaneously satisfy both $(a_{1i}b_{1i})^{1/2} + (a_{2i}b_{2i})^{1/2} = 1/2$ and $(a_{1i}a_{2i})^{1/2} + 2(b_{1i}b_{2i})^{1/2} = 3/4$. The production function is not separable. If $P_i = P_1 = P_2 = w_1 = w_2 = 1$ (where w_j denotes the rental of a unit of factor j) then the technique $a_{1i} = a_{2i} = b_{1i} = b_{2i} = 1/4$ will be chosen to minimize cost. Any differential change in technique can be represented as a weighted average of terms that satisfy both $1/2(da_{1i} + da_{2i}) + 1/2(db_{1i} + db_{2i}) = 0$ and $1/2(da_{1i} + da_{2i}) + (db_{1i} + db_{2i}) = 0$, which imply that $da_{1i} + da_{2i} = 0$.

6 But it should be remembered that gross output was often not their object of interest; moreover, their attention was sometimes confined to differential changes.

try's output.[7] With no intermediate goods ($A = 0$), own-value-added coincides with net output and gross output, so that nominal tariff rates are relevant.

Thus in general consider total own-value-added of industry i: $V_i = v_i X_i / P_i$. V_i denotes the number of units of good i equivalent, at current prices, to the total resources used in industry i. Consider again any differential change dY and an associated change dV in own-values-added. Then, since $PV = vX = PY$,

$$PdV = PdY + (dP)(Y - V), \tag{7}$$

where dP denotes the changes in P that accompany dY. Now, since P is a price system supporting Y it follows at once from (4) and (7) that

> the nominal prices P will be a price system supporting the levels of own-values-added V if, for *all* feasible differential changes in net outputs,

$$(dP)V \geqslant (dP)Y = [P(dA) + dv]X. \tag{8}$$

That is, the basic condition is that the change in nominal prices associated with any efficient change in techniques should increase the value of the intial net outputs by no more than the value of the initial own-value-added.

Consider a change in the structure of nominal tariffs. If condition (8) holds for all feasible differential changes in outputs from the initial situation and also for all feasible differential changes in outputs from the terminal situation, then the change in the structure of effective protection relevant (as formulated in condition M above) to own-values-added is just the array of proportional changes in nominal tariffs.

A number of further conclusions follow directly from this simple formulation of the problem.

6/ As in the previous section, the basic condition in effect imposes a severe restriction on input substitution. For example the condition will be satisfied if, first, for small enough changes in outputs, the primary factors are all perfect substitutes for each other (for then differential output changes can be accommodated without price changes); or, second, if all input coefficients are fixed. It will also be met if, third, for *any differential* price change

$$\frac{dP_j - \sum_i a_{ij} dP_i}{v_j} = \frac{dP_j}{P_j}, \quad \text{for all } j,$$

that is, if the Corden (1966) measure of a change in effective protection coincides at the margin with the nominal measure for all goods.

7 The concept of own-value-added was developed and applied to effective protection in Ethier (1971, 1972). It was independently developed by Khang (1971) and applied to effective protection in Khang (1973), and has also been referred to in Bhagwati and Srinivasan (1973) and elsewhere.

7/ The comments made in the second section are all relevant, in analogous form, here as well. For example separability is not relevant. See Ethier (1972) again. This is perhaps surprising in view of the prominence given to separability in the literature on effective protection and resource flows. Condition (8) is a very strong restriction on input substitution that is quite unlikely to be met in the usual 'well-behaved' technologies, regardless of whether they are separable or not.

8/ An important difference from the previous section is the perhaps surprising result that when own-value-added displaces gross output from the centre of attention the nominal rate of protection replaces the proportional change in value added per unit. Some authors (see Cohen, 1969; Guisinger and Schydlowsky, 1971) have noted that calculated effective and nominal rates of protection tend to be highly correlated, at least at certain levels of aggregation, thus prompting concern whether it is worthwhile to calculate effective rates. The present result gives an (admittedly limited) further theoretical basis for this concern.

The discussion thus far might suggest that an appropriate strategy for obtaining an idea of the effective protection generated by a tariff structure would be first to examine the scales of proportional changes in values added per unit and of nominal tariffs (with reference to gross output and resource allocation effects respectively) and then to ask how serious the departures from the above strict conditions are likely to be. To the extent that the conditions are not met, the actual effective rates, even with separability, depend upon data (involving elasticities of substitution, relative shares, and so on, and their changes) whose possession would render the true effective rates themselves quite superfluous. In any case the present analysis certainly does not imply that applied economists should simply use nominal rates to predict resource flows and ignore available information regarding input-output relations. Rather, it reveals the weak basis for any specific simple formula, and thus implies that available technological information is all the more important in particular cases. A further, and more fundamental, drawback is that, without a natural industry-specific index of resource use, the formulation of any such index, such as own-value-added, is necessarily arbitrary. Different indices give rise to different measures of effective protection. To this problem I shall now briefly turn, and it is here that separability may become important.

OTHER MEASURES OF RESOURCE USE

Several indices suggest themselves, each leading to a different measure. One example is 'own-value-added at world prices' $V_i = \bar{v}_i X_i/\bar{P}_i$, where $\bar{v}_i$ and $\bar{P}_i$ denote what V_i and P_i would be in the absence of all tariffs. V_i' is strictly proportional to X_i, and so the relevant measure of effective protection is the measure relevant to gross outputs, and the discussion in the second section applies exactly. This amounts to observing that gross output is itself a natural index of resource use.

Another natural index arises with separable production functions, for now the value-added-product can be used. The price q_i of a unit of the ith value-added-product is given by its cost of production:

$$q_i = \sum_j w_j \frac{b_{ji}}{g^i} = \frac{v_i}{g^i}. \tag{9}$$

Thus the measure relevant to the value-added-products is the proportional change in v_i/g^i, value added per unit divided by the input requirement of value-added-product.

A few comments are in order:

9/ If the change in the tariff structure is differential, this formula gives

$$\frac{dq_i}{q_i} = \frac{dv_i}{v_i} - \frac{dg^i}{g^i} = \left(\frac{dP_i - \sum_j a_{ji} dP_j}{v_i}\right) - \left(\frac{\sum_j P_j da_{ji} + q_i dg^i}{v_i}\right).$$

Now, if smooth substitution of inputs is possible, cost minimization implies that the last term on the right equals zero, so that the rate of effective protection reduces to the Corden (1966) measure. This often-noticed fact makes separability desirable. But the simplification is strictly true only for differential changes; otherwise the last term on the right will be positive. The structure of effective protection in practice depends upon the various elasticities of substitution.

10/ Separability is used not only to obtain a relatively simple measure, as was the case with the restrictions on input substitution discussed in the previous sections, but also to formulate the index that is the object of inquiry in the first place. For g^i and q_i cannot even be defined unless the production function is separable. If this assumption fails, the measure of effective protection does not merely become more complicated, as was the case above; it ceases to exist.[8]

11/ Since total value-added-product Z_i equals $g^i X_i$, proportional changes in value-added-products will equal proportional changes in gross outputs if and only if, in addition to separability, the value added input coefficients g^i are constant. In this case the basic condition of the second section will be met, and also (9) implies that proportional changes in q_i equal those in v_i. Thus if production functions are separable *and* if the g_i are constant, the effective rates of protection are the proportional changes in values added per unit induced by the tariff structure, regardless of whether one is interested in gross output, own-value-added at world prices, or value-added-product.

12/ Even when production functions are separable, value-added-product and own-value-added are distinct concepts with different measures of effective

8 See Jones (1971) for a very interesting attempt to deal with this problem.

protection. Since $V_i = q_i Z_i / P_i$, proportional changes in own-value-added will equal those in value-added-product if and only if proportional changes in value-added product prices equal those in commodity prices. In this very special case the structure of *nominal* rates will also be the relevant structure of effective protection.

The distinction between these two concepts has never been made explicit in the literature, which has tended either to speak loosely of 'real value added,' without specifying the deflator, or to imply (erroneously) that value-added-product is a special case of own-value-added that obtains if the production functions are separable. Thus Khang (1973) is inaccurate when he claims that Corden's (1969) value-added-product concept is a special case of his own: the two are definitely distinct, regardless of separability. The (Corden) measure of effective protection that Khang uses is appropriate to value-added-product, if separability holds and the price changes are 'small,' but not to own-value-added; the measure 'works' only because of the very special model employed.[9] As another example, the 'quantity index' of value added used by Bhagwati and Srinivasan (1973) in no way represents own-value-added (to which they refer at the start of their paper), even if either of their sets of 'sufficiency conditions for ERP theory' are met.[10]

CONCLUDING REMARKS

I have attempted to demonstrate that an appropriate approach to the question with which this paper opened can yield much on the basis of very simple analysis. The dozen or so specific conclusions need not be repeated in detail. To what general impressions do they seem to lead?

One prominent impression, one that also pervades the recent literature, concerns the extremely severe nature of the technological restrictions necessary for a simple measure to be correct. This severity is further reinforced with respect to resource allocation by the lack of a compelling index of such allocation, with different indices giving different results. On balance the case for using any specific array of effective rates rather than nominal rates or some other definition of effective rates as measures of the resource-allocation effects of a tariff structure is quite weak. With regard to gross outputs the case is stronger: gross output is an unambiguous physical concept, so that value added per unit is unambiguously the proper 'price' if the relevant technological restriction is satisfied, and that restriction appears less severe, though still formidable.

The second impression, not at all prominent in the literature, is that the proper measure of effective protection is extremely sensitive to the specification

9 Of course Khang's objective was in fact the analysis of that specific model and not the general appropriateness of the Corden measure.

10 I do not mean to imply that Bhagwati and Srinivasan claimed otherwise, but only that the distinction between the two concepts is not explicitly made. Nor is it brought out in my work (1971, 1972).

of exactly what the object of interest is. This is brought out most forcefully in the case of real value added, where different specifications of the concept, none inherently preferable to the others, could alternatively make nominal rates, changes in values added per unit, or changes in value-added-product prices the 'correct' effective rates. But it is also true at a more fundamental level. The problems discussed thus far in this paper, and in the literature generally, all presume that, for some reason, gross output or resource allocation are of inherent interest in themselves. The basic objective is *not*, and this point can hardly be emphasized enough, economic welfare or efficiency in general. If it were, then the direct objects of interest would instead be *net* outputs: the total quantities of the various goods available for export or for final use after subtracting intermediate input requirements from gross outputs. In this case the correct prices are in fact the actual commodity prices, as has been known for many years (see for instance Samuelson, 1953), so that the relevant measures of protection are unambiguously the nominal rates.[11] After all, regardless of the structure of intermediate goods, nominal rates measure the distortions in the terms at which the domestic economy can transform available quantities of goods into each other. Thus, arguments regarding, say, the economic efficiency of less developed countries or the potential benefits of tariff preferences by the developed countries should be viewed with suspicion when based simply upon the size of calculated effective rates of protection.

An additional motivation for effective protection, largely ignored by the analytical literature, is of great practical importance nonetheless. This motivation is of inherent interest itself and also leads directly to a measure entirely free of the serious problems discussed above. One might be interested in the immediate impact of a change in tariffs on income distribution. For example such information would have a clear and direct importance in tariff negotiations and other problems with a political dimension. In this case the array of changes in nominal rates could be interpreted, in the absence of intermediate goods, as the array of proportional changes in income accruing, before induced reallocations take place, to the factors actually employed in the various sectors at the time of the change in tariff structure. With $A \neq 0$ the relevant array becomes that of proportional changes in values added per unit.[12] In effect all factors are regarded as industry-specific, rather than, as is more usual, all factors being regarded as perfectly mobile (for an intermediate case, see Jones, 1975). From the point of view of resource allocation, the emphasis is simply on the impact effect of a tariff structure, ignoring induced substitution and reallocation (which would be examined were an elaborate general equilibrium treatment practicable).

This amounts of course to simply being interested in value added per unit for

11 This does not imply, of course, that it is impossible to formulate correct propositions of welfare economics in terms of specific effective rate formulas. See, for example, Ruffin (1971) and Bertrand (1972).

12 It is not clear how to treat induced changes in A. But the problem is no longer one of price theory but rather of the precise specification of the object of interest.

its own sake, in which case the theoretical problems discussed above and in the literature all become quite irrelevant. This simple motivation constitutes, in my opinion, the most significant potential application of the basic idea of effective protection.

I close with a (not unbiased) comment on the scope of the question with which this paper opened. That question essentially views the basic problem of effective protection as an attempt to treat an economy with interindustry flows like one without. But the literature has also attacked a second, quite distinct, problem. Consider an economy in which there are n domestically-produced, final goods (not also used as intermediate inputs), which are produced by means of primary factors and m imported intermediate goods, which are not produced at home and are not used as final goods. Thus the net and gross outputs coincide for the n domestic goods, and the amounts imported of the m intermediate goods can be regarded as (negative) net outputs. The relevant 'prices,' then, are simply the $n + m$ commodity prices (see Samuelson, 1953). This gives rise to the question: when is it possible to devise a measurable index of effective protection so that the n effective rates will yield information about the n gross (equal net) outputs of the domestically produced goods comparable to what the full array of nominal rates implies about net outputs? This question essentially views the basic problem of effective protection as an attempt to treat an $n + m$–good economy like an n-good economy. The models employed by Jones (1971) and Khang (1973) are appropriate for this second question.

The literature has not distinguished between these two quite different problems.[13] Sometimes one of them is talked about while in fact the other is analysed. By assuming that all intermediate goods are also domestically produced I have ensured that this paper focuses unambiguously on the first. The second question I think is of inherently very little interest. Why, in a multicommodity world, should one ever want to go to the trouble of calculating effective rates for this purpose? There seems to be no advantage to looking at n rates rather than at $n + m$ rates. Also, the basic results obtained are in terms of two- or three-commodity models and offer no hope of generalization.[14] A multicommodity point of view is central to the raison d'etre of effective protection, which has to do with the disaggregated effects of a tariff structure.[15] Furthermore, it should be noted that the presence of intermediate goods is something of a red herring in discussing this second question, which can be posed equally well even if imports are all final goods.

13 This time I think that I can claim innocence (1971).

14 This is not to dismiss the literature out of hand; a general negative result can be obtained by a specific example.

15 I do not mean to imply that, in other areas of international economic theory, multicommodity models either deserve such precedence or seem similarly unlikely to reflect properties of simple models. See Ethier (1974) for an opposing argument with regard to some other problems.

REFERENCES

Bertrand, T.J. (1972) 'Welfare indexes with interindustry flows: comment.' *Journal of Political Economy* 80, 796–800

Bhagwati, J.N. and T.N. Srinivasan (1973) 'The general equilibrium theory of effective protection and resource allocation.' *Journal of International Economics* 3, 259–81

Bruno, M. (1973) 'Protection and tariff change under general equilibrium.' *Journal of International Economics* 3, 205–25

Cohen, B.I. (1969) 'The use of effective tariffs.' Discussion Paper No. 62, Economic Growth Center, Yale University

Corden, W.M. (1966) 'The structure of a tariff system and the effective protective rate.' *Journal of Political Economy* 74, 221–37

Corden, W.M. (1969) 'Effective protective rates in the general equilibrium model: a geometric approach.' *Oxford Economic Papers* 21, 135–41

Corden, W.M. (1971) *The Theory of Protection* (Oxford: Clarendon Press)

Ethier, W. (1971) 'General equilibrium theory and the concept of the effective rate of protection.' In H.G. Grubel and H.G. Johnson, eds, *Effective Tariff Protection* (Geneva: GATT and GIIS) 17–44

Ethier, W. (1972) 'Input substitution and the concept of the effective rate of protection.' *Journal of Political Economy* 80, 34–47

Ethier, W. (1974) 'Some of the theorems of international trade with many goods and factors.' *Journal of International Economics* 4, 199–206

Guisinger, S. and D.M. Schydlowsky (1971) 'The empirical relationship between nominal and effective rates of protection.' In H.G. Grubel and H.G. Johnson, eds, *Effective Tariff Protection* (Geneva: GATT and GIIS) 269–86

Jones, R.W. (1971) 'Effective protection and substitution.' *Journal of International Economics* 1, 59–81

Jones, R.W. (1975) 'Income distribution and effective protection in a multi-commodity trade model.' *Journal of Economic Theory* 11, 1–15

Khang, C. (1971) 'An isovalue locus involving intermediate goods and its applications to the pure theory of international trade.' *Journal of International Economics* 1, 315–25

Khang, C. (1973) 'Factor substitution in the theory of effective protection: a general equilibrium analysis.' *Journal of International Economics* 3, 227–43

Ramaswami, V.K. and T.N. Srinivasan (1971) 'Tariff structure and resource allocation in the presence of substitution.' In J.N. Bhagwati et al., eds, *Trade, Balance of Payments, and Growth* (Amsterdam: North-Holland)

Ruffin, R. (1969) 'Tariffs, intermediate goods and domestic protection.' *American Economic Review* 59, 261–9

Ruffin, R. (1971) 'The welfare implications of effective protection.' In H.G. Grubel and H.G. Johnson, eds, *Effective Tariff Protection* (Geneva: GAAT and GIIS) 85–108

Samuelson, P.A. (1953) 'Prices of factors and goods in general equilibrium.' *Review of Economic Studies* 21, 1–20

References

Balassa, B (1967). *Trade Liberalization among Industrial Countries.* New York: McGraw-Hill.

Bhagwati, JN and TN Srinivasan (1973). The General Equilibrium Theory of Effective Protection and Resource Allocation. *Journal of International Economics* 3(3), pp. 259–281.

Deardorff, AV (1980). The General Validity of the Law of Comparative Advantage. *Journal of Political Economy* 88, pp. 941–957.

Dixit, AK and V Norman (1980). *Theory of International Trade.* Cambridge: Cambridge University Press.

Gans, JS and GB Shepherd (1994). How Are the Mighty Fallen: Rejected Classic Articles by Leading Economists. *The Journal of Economic Perspectives* 8(1), pp. 165–179.

Gray, HP (1973). Two-Way International Trade in Manufactures: A Theoretical Underpinning. *Weltwirtschaftliches Archiv* 109, pp. 19–29.

Grossman, SJ and OD Hart (1986). The Costs and Benefits of Ownership: A Theory of Vertical and Lateral Integration. *Journal of Political Economy* 94(4), pp. 691–719.

Grubel, HG and PJ Lloyd (1975). *Intra-Industry Trade: The Theory and Measurement in International Trade in Differentiated Products.* London: Macmillan.

Helpman, E (1981). International Trade in the Presence of Product Differentiation, Economies of Scale and Monopolistic Competition. *Journal of International Economics* 11, pp. 305–340.

Hillman, AL (1982). Declining Industries and Political-Support Protectionist Motives. *American Economics Review* 72, pp. 1180–1187.

Jones, RW (1977). "Two-Ness" in Trade Theory: Costs and Benefits. *Special Papers in International Economics.* International Finance Section, Princeton University.

Krugman, P (1979). Increasing Returns, Monopolistic Competition, and International Trade. *Journal of International Economics* 9, pp. 469–480.

Lancaster, K (1980). Intra-Industry Trade under Perfect Monopolistic Competition. *Journal of International Economics* 10, pp. 152–176.

Leontief, W (1953). Domestic Production and Foreign Trade: The American Capital Position Re-Examined. *Proceedings of the American Philosophical Society* 47, pp. 332–349.

Markusen, JR (1983). Factor Movements and Commodity Trade as Complements. *Journal of International Economics* 14, pp. 341–356.